Export and Import Management

Export and Import Management

Text and Cases

Second Edition

RAM SINGH
Professor
Indian Institute of Foreign Trade
New Delhi, India

WILEY

Export and Import Management

Text and Cases

Second Edition

Ram Singh

Published by Wiley India Pvt. Ltd.,
4436/7, Ansari Road, Daryaganj, New Delhi-110002.

Printed at: Yash Printographic

First Edition: 2021
Second Edition: 2023

ISBN: 978-93-5746-182-5
ISBN: 978-93-5746-178-8 (ebk)

Other Wiley Editorial Offices:
John Wiley & Sons, Inc. 111 River Street, Hoboken, NJ 07030, USA
Wiley-VCH Verlag GmbH, Pappellaee 3, D-69469 Weinheim, Germany
John Wiley & Sons Australia Ltd, 42 McDougall Street, Milton, Queensland 4064, Australia
John Wiley & Sons (Asia) Pte Ltd, 1 Fusionpolis Walk #07-01 Solaris, South Tower Singapore 138628
John Wiley & Sons Canada Ltd, 22 Worcester Road, Etobicoke, Ontario, Canada, M9W ILI

Reprint : 2025

www.wileyindia.com

Dedicated to

His Holiness
108 Sant Sukhdev Singh Ji Maharaj
(Kutia Wale)

who, with all his blessings,

moulded my intellect, thoughts and ideals to become who I am today.

Preface to the Second Edition

Recently, the management of export–import (EXIM) operations has become more complex due to several factors including the COVID-19 pandemic, trade and tech wars, and evolving geopolitical conflicts and geo-economic alignments among countries such as the Russia–Ukraine conflict. The world economy is still recovering from the wrecking consequences of COVID-19. Prevention measures, such as mass lockdowns, transportation restrictions and workforce disruptions, have severely disrupted global supply chains, leading to delays, shortages and logistical challenges for both exporters and importers around the world. Trade tensions and conflicts, such as the ongoing trade and tech wars between major economies, have resulted in the imposition of tariffs, import restrictions and non-tariff barriers. Political tensions, sanctions and territorial disputes can disrupt trade relationships, alter market dynamics and impact the feasibility of certain trade routes. India is not untouched by the emerging challenges and is accordingly focusing on programmes such as Make in India, Assemble in India, Production Linked Incentives, Skill India and Digital India.

While taking these geopolitical and geo-economic developments into account, this second edition keeps giving the readers deep insight into managing the EXIM operations. It covers the latest reforms in foreign trade policy, export–import finance, business environment, operational rules such as INCOTERMS 2020 and Convention on International Sales of Goods (CISG), and other associated issues to enlighten the readers with the required knowledge and skills to manage the business globally. The chapter plan remains the same; however, the content stands enriched with updated information and cases.

I hope that the latest edition of the book will play a significant role in shaping the minds of young professionals and aspiring individuals in the domain of export–import management. It offers in-depth knowledge, insights and practical guidance that will help them understand the complexities, strategies and best practices involved in international trade.

Instructor Resources

Additional valuable supplemental material for instructors can be accessed at the Wiley website (https://www.wileyindia.com/Instructor_Manuals/Register/login.php). These include:

- Instructor's Manual
- PowerPoint Slides
- Test Bank

Preface to the First Edition

Foreign trade plays a very important role in the economic development of any country. There is no country in the world today which produces all the commodities it needs. Every country, therefore, tries to produce those commodities in which it has comparative advantage. The significance of foreign trade for a country like India cannot be underestimated. India aspires to be a $5 trillion economy by 2025; therefore, it is important for our policymakers to leverage economic resources in all areas of economic activity, that is, agriculture, manufacturing and services. Its external engagements so far have not been to the true potential of its capacities and capabilities. It is ranked at number 18 in the list of top exporting countries, and it is ranked among the top 10 as an importer. It leaped among the top 10 countries in services trade but more needs to be achieved in areas other than services trade. Its share in the world trade is merely 1.7 percent, in imports around 2.4 percent and contribution of exports and imports in India's GDP is around 35 percent. It has plenty of natural resources, as well as demographic dividend, and our policymakers need to play the right cards in devising a road map for trade expansion and diversification from India. As a nation, we Indians need to understand that one of the ways, other than domestic reforms, of accelerating the economic growth is exporting where India can produce quality goods at competitive rates, enhance its services' capabilities and create manufacturing competencies to serve global client in an efficient manner.

An efficient and trade-oriented policy framework requires the professionals and industry who are ready to move forward in global markets and tap them in areas of India's economic strengths. It is extremely pertinent to train and skill the stakeholders of the Indian trade supply chain, that is, exporters, importers, freight forwarders, logistics experts, bankers, financial institutions, shipping companies, cargo transporters, air freighters, packers and movers, consolidators and port officials. Exporters need to understand the ways and means for right market and product selection, regulatory formalities, trade terms and negotiations, export incentives, benefits, duty neutralization, support and assistance and so on. In a highly volatile trading environment, a trader needs to understand the risks involved at various stages of trade operations, that is, transport risks and credit and exchange rate fluctuations risks. It is high time for us to impart knowledge and skills in export and import (EXIM) operations aimed at effectively managing the EXIM process, procedural formalities, documentation, custom clearance and ensuring regulatory compliance with various involved authorities and finally realizing payments from abroad safely and systematically.

In this context, an endeavour has been made to impart knowledge and skills on EXIM issues to future business Turks of India's industry, management professionals, commerce graduates, exporters and importers, bankers, logistics professional and policymakers. This book entitled *Export and Import Management: Text and Cases* encapsulates all vital elements of EXIM functions and is conceptualized for meeting the syllabus of all prominent universities of India. To supplement the theoretical foundations, illustrative caselets, exercises, quizzes and critical thinking questions form an integral part of the book.

Jai jawaan, jai kisaan, jai exporter!

About the Author

Dr Ram Singh is Professor and Head (MDPs) at IIFT with over 20 years of teaching experience. His academic qualifications include BCom, MBA, PhD, UGC-NET Qualified, PGDIBO and Certificate in Managing Global Governance from the German Development Institute, Bonn, Germany. He also holds a Master Certificate in SCM and Logistics from Michigan State University, USA. He specializes in both training and research in areas such as EXIM procedure, trade policy and trade logistics. He has authored two textbooks, *International Trade Operations* and *International Trade Logistics*. He has also co-authored a book on 'EXIM finance'. He has authored 38 research publications and has done nine structured content modules for trade courses for universities such as Jamia Millia Islamia, New Delhi; Sikkim Manipal University, Bengaluru; Pondicherry University, Puducherry; Maharshi Dayanand University, Rohtak; and Indira Gandhi National Open University, New Delhi.

Acknowledgements

To start the work on the book *Export and Import Management: Text and Cases* was a puzzle, and I, as an author, could not decide from where to begin. I talked to my inner conscience several times, and it is the will of God that I have been conscientiously hammered until this work has come to light. I express my utmost gratitude to the Almighty for constantly guiding me to complete this work spanning over almost three and a half years. I am at a loss of words to express my gratitude, hence quoting a line from Shri Guru Granth Sahib to thank the invisible force guiding us all.

जह मुसकल होवै अति भारी ॥ हरि को नामु खिन माहि उधारी ॥

I am blessed that I had an opportunity to meet two great saints of the Terai region: first and foremost, I express my profound respect and a sense of deep devotion to 108 Saint Sukhdev Singh Ji who devoted his whole life for the betterment and well-being of humanity. His selfless service to the leprosy patients, *kar seva* (public service) to bridges, *dharamshala*s (community halls) and gurudwaras meant for the common public and his noble idea of integrating *seva* (service) and *simran* (devotion to the supreme being) has enthused in me such a high degree of spiritual quotient that I dare to meet the challenges in every walk of life without fear and awe. Further, 108 Swami Gauri Shankar Ji Maharaj (*Sunasar Ghat wale*) has enthused in me the feeling of self-sacrifice and staying focused on oneself, away from the worldly tantrums of today's hyper-normal lifestyles.

I am thankful to my research guide, Dr Manukant Shastri, who, in the beginning of my career as an academic, evaluated my skill set and guided me to accept the challenges of the ever-evolving, ever-changing and dynamic field of international business. I am blessed that I have worked under the guidance and supervision of Professor Harkirat Singh, who shaped my training skills and guided me at each stage of my professional career. I express my deepest gratitude, profound respect and sincere thanks to him for his encouragement, help and cooperation.

I acknowledge the support and inputs I received from Dr Surendar Singh, Senior Deputy Director EEPC, who always shared his views frankly about the changes we need to bring in the conceptualization of various elements of EXIM operations. I am thankful to my colleagues in Trade Discipline of Indian Institute of Foreign Trade (IIFT), Dr Deepankar Sinha, Dr Areej Aftab Siddiqui and Dr Tamanna Chaturvedi, who have provided me constant support and motivation during the entire project. Interactions with trade academics such as Dr Navneet Gera, Professor M. P. Singh, Professor Vijay Bansal, Professor Ashok Advani, Professor S. L. Ganapati and Professor Sarabjit Butlaia have always been a source of encouragement during the entire work of this book. I express a sense of immense respect and regards to the stalwarts in the trade field such as Mr Ajay Sahai (Federation of Indian Export Organisations), Dr L. B. Singhal (DC-Noida SEZ), Mr Rajesh Rawat (Export Promotion Council for Handicrafts), Mr Prabir De (Research and Information System for Developing Countries) and Mr Suranjan Gupta (Engineering Export Promotion Council).

Words fall short to express my gratitude towards my parents who not only moulded and shaped me but also enthused in me the undaunting courage, will power and inclination to meet challenges in every walk of life. This book I am authoring is nothing but an embodiment of their opulent bliss. I would also like to thank my family who has always cooperated with me during the entire work of this book.

List of Cases

List of Abbreviations

ACU	Asian Clearing Union
AEZs	Agri export zones
AIRs	All industry rates
AOA	Articles of association
APEDA	Agricultural & Processed Food Products Export Development Authority
API	Active pharmaceutical ingredients
ARAI	Automotive Research Association of India
ASEAN	Association of Southeast Asian Nations
ASIDE	Assistance to States for Development of Export Infrastructure and Allied Activities
ASYCUDA	Automated System for Customs Data
AWB	Air waybill
B2B	Business-to-business
B2C	Business-to-consumer
BEP	Buyer exposure policy
BIS	Bureau of Indian Standards
BOA	Board of Approval
BOLERO	Bill of Lading Electronic Registry Organization
BPLR	Benchmark prime lending rate
BRC	Bank realization certificate
BS	Bharat Stage
BSMs	Buyer–seller meets
BSOs	Business support organizations
BTP	Biotechnology park
C2C	Customer-to-customer
C2B	Customer-to-business
CB	Commodity board
CBEC	Central Board of Excise and Customs
CBI	Centre for the Promotion of Imports from Developing Countries
CBIC	Central Board of Indirect Taxes and Customs
CCP	Custom clearance permit
CENVAT	Central value-added tax
CFR	Cost and freight
CFS	Container freight station

CGST	Central Goods and Services Tax
CHA	Customs house agent
CIF	Cost, insurance and freight
CIN	Corporate identification number
CIP	Carriage and insurance paid
CIS	Commonwealth of Independent States
CISG	Convention on International Sales of Goods
CMM	Capability Maturity Model
CPT	Carriage paid to
CST	Central sales tax
D/A	Documents against acceptance
D/P	Documents against payments
DAP	Delivered at place
DAT	Delivered at terminal
DC	Development commissioner
DDP	Delivered duty paid
DDU	Delivered duty unpaid
DEEC	Duty Exemption Entitlement Certificate
DFTP	Duty-free tariff preference
DGCI&S	Director General of Commercial Intelligence and Statistics
DGFT	Directorate General of Foreign Trade
DIN	Director Identification Number
DPU	Delivered at place unloaded
DTA	Domestic tariff area
EBA	Export Bills Abroad
EBPLR	External benchmark prime lending rate
ECGC	Export Credit Guarantee Corporation
ECIE	Export Credit Insurance for the Exporter
ECNOS	Export credit not otherwise specified
EDA	Export development authority
EDF	Export declaration form
EDI	Electronic data interchange
EDPMS	Export Data Processing and Monitoring System
EEFCA	Exchange earners' foreign currency account
EGM	Export General Manifest
EHTP	Electronic Hardware Technology Park
EIA	Export inspection agency
EIC	Export inspection council
EOUs	Export-oriented units

EPCG	Export Promotion Capital Goods
EPCs	Export promotion councils
ERIC	Export Risks Insurance Corporation
EU	European Union
EURIBOR	Euro Interbank Offer Rate
EXIM	Export and import
EXW	Ex works
FAS	Free alongside ship
FCA	Free carrier
FCL	Full container load
FCR	Forwarder certificate of receipt
FDA	Food and Drug Administration
FEDAI	Foreign Exchange Dealers Association of India
FEMA	Foreign Exchange Management Act
FERA	Foreign Exchange Regulation Act
FIEO	Federation of Indian Export Organisations
FOB	Free on board
FPO	Foreign post office
FSSAI	Food Safety and Standards Authority of India
FTA	Free trade agreement
FTDR	Foreign Trade (Development and Regulation)
FTP	Foreign trade policy
GATT	General Agreement on Tariffs and Trade
GCC	Gulf Cooperation Council
GDP	Gross domestic product
GIV	Gross invoice value
GMP	Good manufacturing practice
GNP	Gross national product
GOI	Government of India
GSP	Generalized system of preferences
GST	Goods and Services Tax
GSTP	Generalized System of Trade Preferences
HACCP	Hazard Analysis and Critical Control Points
HS	Harmonized system
HUF	Hindu Undivided Family
IATA	International Air Transport Association
IBAN	International Bank Account Number
ICC	International Chamber of Commerce
ICD	Inland container depot

ICES	Indian Customs EDI System
ICT	Information and communications technology
IEC	Importer Exporter Code
IEM	Industrial Entrepreneur Memorandum
IGM	Import General Manifest
IGST	Integrated Goods and Services Tax
IIFT	Indian Institute of Foreign Trade
IL	Industrial licence
IMF	International Monetary Fund
IMO	International Maritime Organization
INCOTERMS	International commercial terms
IPQC	In-process quality control
ISBP	International Standard Banking Practice
ISC	International sales contract
ISI	Indian Standards Institution
ISP 98	International Standby Practices 98
IT	Information technology
ITC(HS)	Indian Trade Clarification based on Harmonized System
ITC	International Trade Centre
ITPO	Indian Trade Promotion Organization
JNPT	Jawaharlal Nehru Port
L&T	Larsen & Toubro
L/C	Letter of credit
LCL	Less than container load
LDCs	Least developed countries
LEO	Let export order
LIBOR	London Interbank Offered Rate
LLP	Limited liability partnership
LOI	Letter of intent
LOP	Letter of permission
LUT	Letter of undertaking
MAI	Market Access Initiative
MAWB	Master air waybill
MDA	Marketing Development Assistance
MEIS	Merchandise Exports from India Scheme
MENA	Middle East and North Africa
MEP	Micro Exporters Policy
MIGA	Multilateral Investment Guarantee Agency
MNCs	Multinational corporations
MOU	Memorandum of understanding
MPEDA	Marine Products Export Development Authority

MSME	Micro, small and medium enterprise
MTTs	Merchanting trade transactions
NCB	No claim bonus
NCTI	National Centre for Trade Information
NEIA	National Export Insurance Account
NOC	No objection certificate
NSIC	National Small Industries Corporation
NTP	Normal transit period
PAN	Permanent account number
PBE	Postal bill of export
PC	Personal computer
PCFC	Pre-shipment credit in foreign currency
PSUs	Public sector undertakings
PTA	Preferential trade agreement
R&D	Research and development
RBI	Reserve Bank of India
RCMC	Registration-cum-membership certificate
ROC	Registrar of Companies
RoDTEP	Remission of Duties or Taxes on Export Products
SAARC	South Asian Association for Regional Cooperation
SCOMET	Special chemicals, organisms, materials, equipment and technologies
SDF	Statutory declaration form
SEI	Software Engineering Institute
SEP	Small Exporter Policy
SEZ	Special economic zone
SGST	State Goods and Services Tax
SKU	Stock keeping unit
SMEs	Small and medium enterprises
SOLAS	International Convention for the Safety of Life at Sea
SPS	Sanitary and phytosanitary
SSP	Specific Shipment Policy
STPI	Software Technology Parks of India
SWIFT	Society for Worldwide Interbank Financial Telecommunication
TBT	Technical barriers to trade
THC	Terminal handling charges
UAC	Unit Approval Committee
UCPDC 600	Uniform Customs and Practice for Documentary Credits 600
ULD	Unit load device
UN/CEFACT	United Nations Centre for Trade Facilitation and Electronic Business
UN	United Nations
UNCITRAL	United Nations Commission on International Trade Law

UNCTAD	United Nations Conference on Trade and Development
UNDP	United Nations Development Programme
UNSC	United Nations Security Council Resolution
URC 522	Uniform Rules for Collections 522
UTGST	Union Territory Goods and Services Tax
VAT	Value-added Tax
VGM	Verified gross mass
WAN	Wide area network
WANA	West Asia and North Africa
WASME	World Association for Small and Medium Enterprises
WCO	World Customs Organization
WHO	World Health Organization
WTO	World Trade Organization

Contents

Detailed Contents

CHAPTER 1

Understanding Export–Import Operations

CHAPTER OBJECTIVES

- To explain the concept of export and import (EXIM) operations.
- To explain the elements of success in EXIM operations.
- To understand the success elements required in EXIM operations.
- To explain the various risks involved in EXIM trade.
- To discuss the importance of EXIM operations for the nation and international traders.
- To elaborate the competitive international marketplace.

1.1 Introduction

Export and import are important economic activities for each country in today's globalized world. They both are vital to the health and dynamism of developed as well as developing economies. International economic engagements through exports and imports benefit an economy as well as business organizations in several ways; for example, India's gems and jewellery exporters cannot sustain their business operations until they import two vital raw materials, that is, gold and diamonds, from abroad. India as an economy earns more than $43 billion from gems and jewellery exports, thus generating employment for millions of workers involved in diamond cutting, polishing and jewellery making. In today's changed economic scenario, exporting and importing are the most established forms of international involvement for firms across the globe and are recognized as a viable strategy by firms, both merchandised goods and services, for tapping increased global business opportunities, thus enabling their expansion and diversification. There are several levels of global economic engagements in different forms, for example, investing in firms in other countries, forming joint ventures and acquiring firms in international markets, but exporting is the most traditional and well-established form of operating in international markets. Exporting is preferred as the most cost-effective way of international economic engagement and is defined as 'exchange of goods, services and ideas between two or more countries'. Merchandise export is a function of international trade operations wherein goods produced or manufactured in one country are shipped to another country for future sale or trade. Services export means rendering of services to a client or customer based in another country. The sale of such merchandise or rendering of services to a client in the international market adds value to the exporting country's gross domestic output. Import, on the other hand, refers to the process of bringing in the merchandise or services into one country from another country. The terms export and import are derived from the word 'port', as the goods are often shipped via ships to foreign countries or brought into the country. Both are vital for any country; however, higher exports are preferred, as it means, first, a country has favourable balance of trade, and, second, it brings in more dollars from other economic systems, thus helping to create additional economic activity and generate more employment opportunities. The term 'foreign trade' comprises both export and import and is defined as exchange of goods, services and ideas between two countries.

The process of economic liberalization coupled with globalization has opened the Indian economy to global entrepreneurs, multinational enterprises and investors for such exchange of goods, services and ideas. Nations, across the world, foresee great economic opportunities for speeding up the process of economic development, uplifting the quality of the life of citizens, improving per-capita income and generating additional employment opportunities through economic, financial and social integration of their economies with other economies. In order to achieve this economic integration and other forms of economic integration such as custom union, common market and economic union, countries sign preferential and free trade agreements. The process of economic integration has been strengthened with the formation of the World Trade Organization (WTO) in 1995, and transparent and non-discriminatory trade with a rule-based system of dispute resolution is the basis of such globalization. India cannot remain untouched by such global development; Figure 1.1 depicts India's merchandise trade with the global economy.

The process of economic liberalization started in India in 1991. It ensured favourable macroeconomic policies aimed at the promotion of industrialization and foreign trade, as India's export of goods and services as percentage of gross domestic product (GDP) has started increasing constantly. India adopted a five-year stable foreign trade policy (FTP) regime and ensured that imports are also facilitated as they are vital to many sectors of India's economy and exports. In fact, India's top five exportable items have significant import contents, for example, India's largest exportable items are petroleum, oil and lubricants which are manufactured largely from imported crude oil. Similarly, the second-most exported items are gems and jewellery, and both diamonds and gold are largely imported in India.

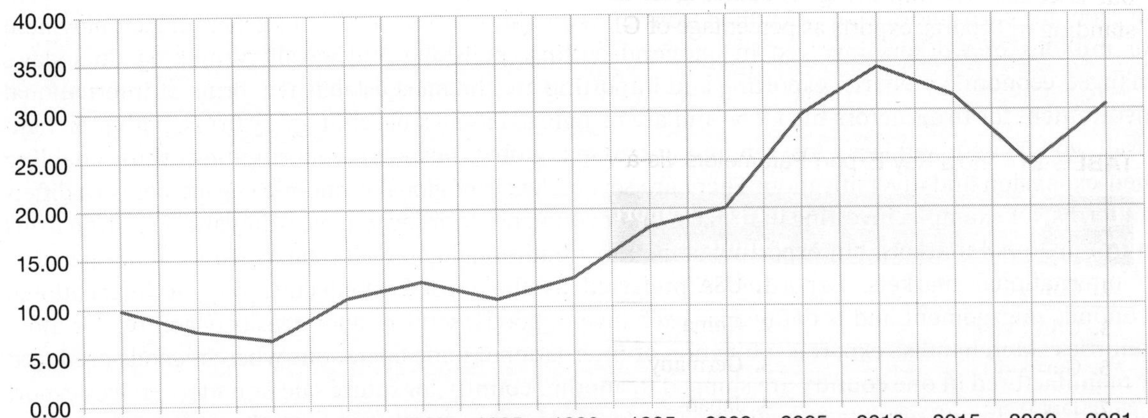

FIGURE 1.1 Merchandise trade (% of GDP).

Source: World Development Indicators. https://data.worldbank.org/indicator/TG.VAL.TOTL.GD.ZS?locations=IN (accessed on 29 March 2023).

India has adopted a policy of systematic economic integration by signing a free trade agreement (FTA) with SAARC (South Asian Association for Regional Cooperation) countries, separate FTAs with Sri Lanka, ASEAN (Association of Southeast Asian Nations) countries, South Korea and Japan and a couple of preferential trade agreements (PTAs) with countries as far as in Latin America (MERCOSUR and Chile) and Afghanistan. A favourable trade regime coupled with liberalized economic policies has changed the psyche of new generations of Indians who firmly believe that this century is going to be the Asian Century and Indians must endeavour hard to get their economic dividend in this global trade tussle with rising and shining China. Recent global economic development of depressed economic growth and low-trade activity in North America and Europe reinforces this in the psyche of new-generation Indian entrepreneurs who largely believe that the future of global economy lies in Asia, particularly in China and India. Indian entrepreneurs and multinational corporations (MNCs) are of firm opinion that the future lies in tapping the global markets, particularly in Latin America, Africa and CIS (Commonwealth of Independent States) countries, and further deepening our relationships with traditional markets such as the Gulf region and ASEAN countries. Large domestic opportunities will certainly provide them an additional dividend in generating economies of scale, hedging risks and tapping Indian demographic dividend in establishing Indian products, services and brands across the globe. They are particularly designing and devising their moves for international forays all around the globe through green-field investment, joint ventures and acquisitions. *All such trading, manufacturing and business activities which are taking place across the national boundaries are referred to as international business.*

Export and import (EXIM) activity is crucial to India's economic health as India can generate additional employment opportunities for the country through the exchange of goods, services and ideas, and it also helps to bring precious foreign exchange to the nation. Greater EXIM operations mean more economic growth as natural and physical resources of the country are effectively exploited, managed, used and traded, resulting in employment generation, foreign exchange accumulations, improved living standard, capacity enhancement in manufacturing and infrastructure and increased status of the country in global economic, political and social issues. The FTP of India is also shaped for making India a global manufacturing, trading and services hub. India is not so great currently in the global ranking of exports and imports but is constantly improving its standing in the international markets. Table 1.1 depicts India's global standing in exports, exports as percentage of GDP, imports, per capita exports and foreign investment.

TABLE 1.1 India Key Export Parameters vis-à-vis Others in 2021

Largest Exporting Countries	Largest Importing Countries	Export of Goods & Services as % of GDP	
1. China	**1.** USA	**2.** China	20.03
3. USA	**2.** China	**4.** USA	10.89
5. Germany	**3.** Germany	**6.** Germany	47.03
7. Japan	**4.** Japan	**8.** Japan	18.42
9. South Korea	**5.** Hong Kong, China	**10.** South Korea	42.03
18. India	**10.** India	**18.** India	21.39

Source: World Development Indicators. https://data.worldbank.org/indicator (accessed on 29 March 2023).

1.2 Understanding the Concept of EXIM Operations

Export of goods refers to the movement of goods beyond the territorial waters of the country, wherein the goods produced or manufactured locally are shipped to another country via land, air or sea (Box 1.1). Service export, on the contrary, refers to rendering of services beyond territorial waters of India. It can be done using data transfers, email, web hosting, installation and so on, and can be used by Internet or telephone or any other medium (e.g., travel services are rendered to visiting travellers, medical services are rendered to patients visiting India for treatment and so on). Two preconditions to qualify as export transaction are as follows: goods must cross territorial waters of India and realization of export proceeds must be from a customer of another country, preferably in a freely convertible foreign currency.

In contrast to exports, imports are goods and services that are brought into a country to fulfil the needs of goods and services which are not available locally. In the changed global economic scenario, imports are also vital as, *first*, they help in managing the demands and supply of vital essential material for domestic consumers; *second*, some of the inputs for the industry may not be available locally, hence, they need to be imported; and, *third*, low-cost imports from the foreign market help a country specialize in areas where it enjoys comparative cost advantages; thus, it can exchange goods and services with a partner country where it has relative cost advantages so both the countries benefit from such trade. The difference in the total value of exports and the total value of imports is referred to as a country's balance of trade and is called favourable when exports are more than imports and unfavourable when imports are more than exports (Figure 1.2). When exports and imports are equal, it is called equilibrium in balance of trade.

The changes in the balance of trade are due to changes in exports and imports as exports of any country mainly depend on many factors. *First*, the export of a country will get affected by the import dynamics of other countries; for example, if import demand is weak like post sub-prime crisis in the world economy, it is going to impact the export pattern of countries. India's exports have witnessed a high growth performance in the first decade of this century; however, India's exports performance has witnessed a declining trend in the second decade, only to recover in the last two–three years. India's exports stood at a mere $442 billion in 2021–2022, which is not an impressive trend as exports are stuck in the bracket of $300 billion this decade. *Second*, there will be changes in exports and imports and resultant changes in balance of payment due to price competitiveness of production of a country, leading to cost advantages of exporters of that country. The key factors leading to the price changes in

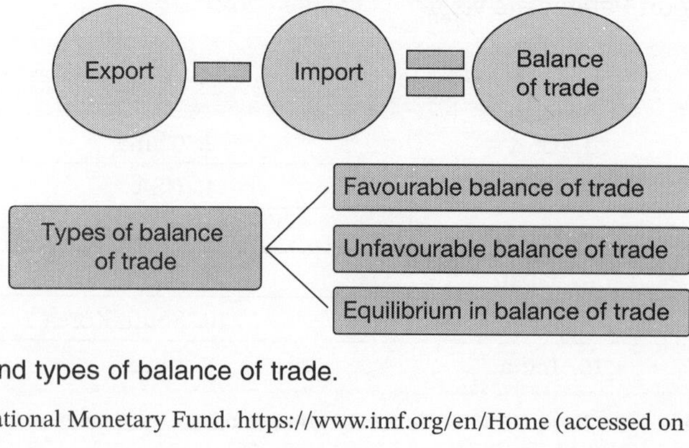

FIGURE 1.2 Concept and types of balance of trade.

Source: Adapted from International Monetary Fund. https://www.imf.org/en/Home (accessed on 24 May 2023).

BOX 1.1 ► Concept of Territorial Waters of India

The law of sea is defined by the United Nations Convention on the Law of the Sea, agreed among nations in 1982, which broadly classifies the maritime zones into four broad areas, wherein the territorial waters are classified as a belt of coastal waters extending at the most 12 nautical miles (around 22.2 km) from the baseline which is usually the mean low-water mark of a coastal state. As per the United Nations (UN) convention, the territorial waters of any country are regarded as the sovereign territory, meaning no foreign vessel can enter these areas without permission, except the cases of the innocent passage of foreign vessel. Every country enjoys sovereign rights over territorial waters, including the airspace over and seabed below. The area beyond territorial waters is known as the contiguous zone and extends up to 12 nautical miles. A maritime extending 200 nautical miles from the baseline of a country is known as exclusive economic zone and any area beyond is known as international waters. The Customs Act, 1962, follows these globally agreed rules and accordingly applies them on incoming carriers whether by sea, air, road or rail, as the term territorial waters under the Customs Act, 1962, refers to any area of water over which a state has jurisdiction, including internal waters, the contiguous zone, the exclusive economic zone and potentially the continental shelf.

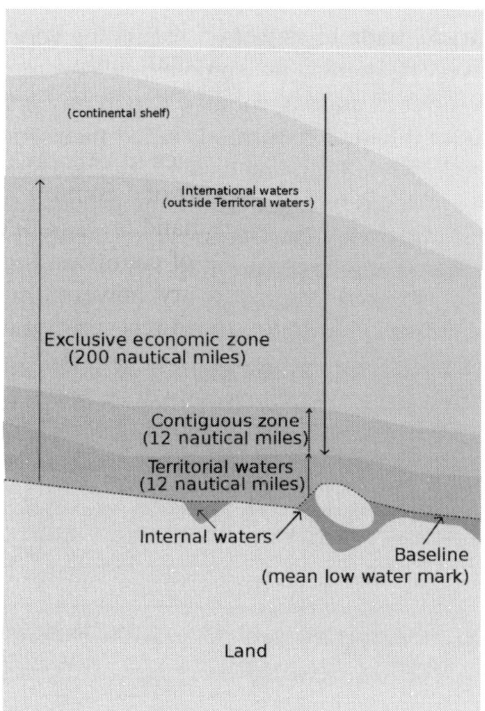

Source: Adapted by the author from Wikipedia (https://en.wikipedia.org/wiki/Territorial_waters#/media/File:Zonmaren.svg, accessed on 10 May 2023).

exportable goods are improved productivity of labour, enhanced state aids to a particular sector by government, favourable exchange rate and higher rate of inflation in countries of imports than countries of exports. *Third*, exports, imports and balance of trade are impacted by non-price competitiveness which is arising from improved branding strategies, greater innovation and use of improved technology, higher product quality and innovative products; it leads to higher exports, thus impacting the imports of partner countries. *Fourth*, exports and imports are also impacted by the hindering factors such as lack of information about import markets, trade barriers (both tariff and non-tariff), changes in modal choice leading to higher or lower transport costs and cultural dissimilarities such as business practices, etiquettes and customer preferences. *Fifth*, the external economic engagements through export and import of goods and services and resultant impact on the balance of payment of a country also arise from the level of services provided by complementary players, such as international banks, guarantee funds, trade fair services and consulting firms. *Sixth*, historical linkage with certain target countries also has its impact on foreign trade; for example, India enjoys better trade linkages with countries which have Indian diaspora or have cultural exchanges with India. Mauritius, UAE, Singapore and Malaysia are examples of this. Seventh, exports and imports are also impacted by policy interventions aimed at achieving economic integration with the partner country; thus, structural changes may come up in patterns, composition and direction of both exports and imports, leading to changes in balance of trade with other countries.

In addition to merchandise trade, trade in services is expanding very fast at the global level. Service export refers to the sale and delivery of an intangible product, called a service, between a service provider from one country and service receiver in another country. Export and import of services (intangible and invisible) between two traders from different countries is called international trade in services. The size, scale and scope of services trade in world economy have witnessed metamorphic changes in the era of globalization. For harmonization of trade rules governing the exports and imports of services, member countries at WTO have negotiated and drafted the General Agreement on Trade in Services, and it defines the trade in services into four modes of supply (Figure 1.3).

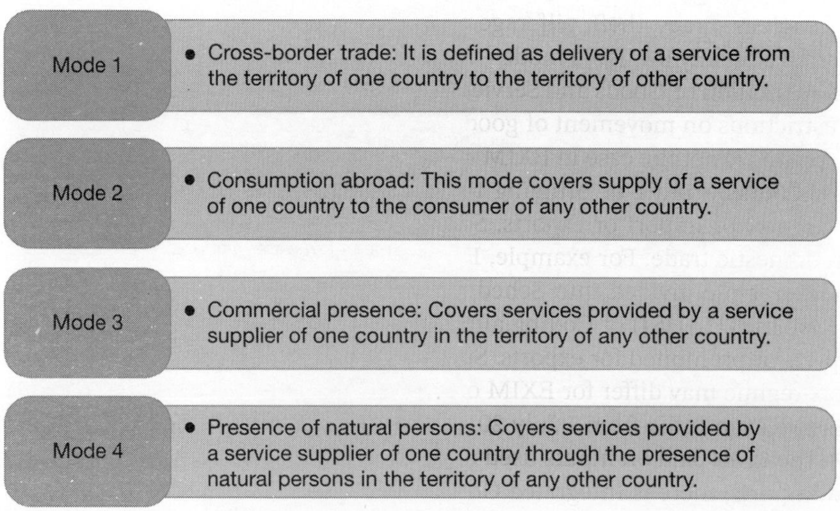

FIGURE 1.3 Kinds of mode of supply of services in foreign trade.

Source: World Trade Organization. wto.org (accessed on 24 May 2023).

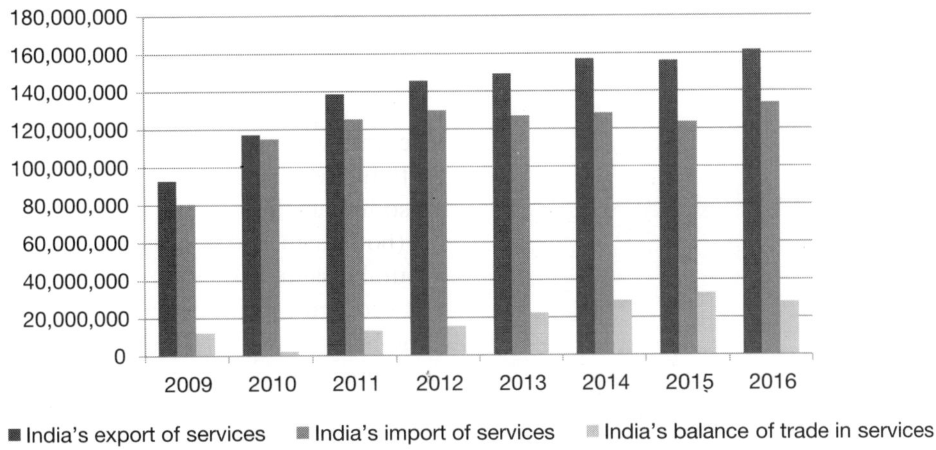

FIGURE 1.4 India's exports, imports and positive balance of trade in services.

Source: World Trade Integrated Atlas (2019).

Trade in services is classified into 12 sectors. Some of the examples of trade in services are banking, medical services, business consultancy services, information technology (IT) and IT-enabled services, and tour and travel services. Status of India's export and import of services in the world market and favourable balance of trade are illustrated in Figure 1.4.

1.3 Differences between Domestic and EXIM Business

EXIM trade is different from domestic trade in many aspects (Figure 1.5). *First*, the distance involved in EXIM operations is higher than in domestic transactions, thus exposing an exporter or importer to transport risks such as piracy, theft, pilferage and stranding of ships. Domestic business is far simpler; the goods can move on any available mode—road, rail, air or multimodal—from one place to another. With the implementation of Goods and Services Tax (GST), the tax regime has become harmonized and there are no restrictions on movement of goods to any place in India for the purpose of trade and commerce. However, this is not the case in EXIM trade as one has to seek the permission of Indian customs for taking goods outside India or bringing them into India and another similar permission may be desired from country of import or exports. *Second*, rules and regulations governing foreign trade are different from domestic trade. For example, Directorate General of Foreign Trade (DGFT) announced the foreign trade regime divided into Schedules 1 and 2 of the Indian Trade Clarification based on Harmonized System (ITC[HS]) of Coding aimed at regulation of foreign trade as free, restricted, state trading enterprise or prohibited for exports. Such rules are not applicable to domestic trade operations. Further, the tax regime may differ for EXIM operations; for example, only GST is applicable for supply of goods and services in India from 1 July 2017, but in case of exports, goods are free from any kind of taxes and even the taxes paid on inputs used to manufacture the exportable goods are refunded as duty drawback. On imports, there is Integrated Goods and Services Tax' (integrated tax/IGST). *Third*, there is dissimilarity in currencies used in domestic and EXIM operations. One can deal in domestic currency while invoicing within the country; however, the same is not the case of foreign trade where the

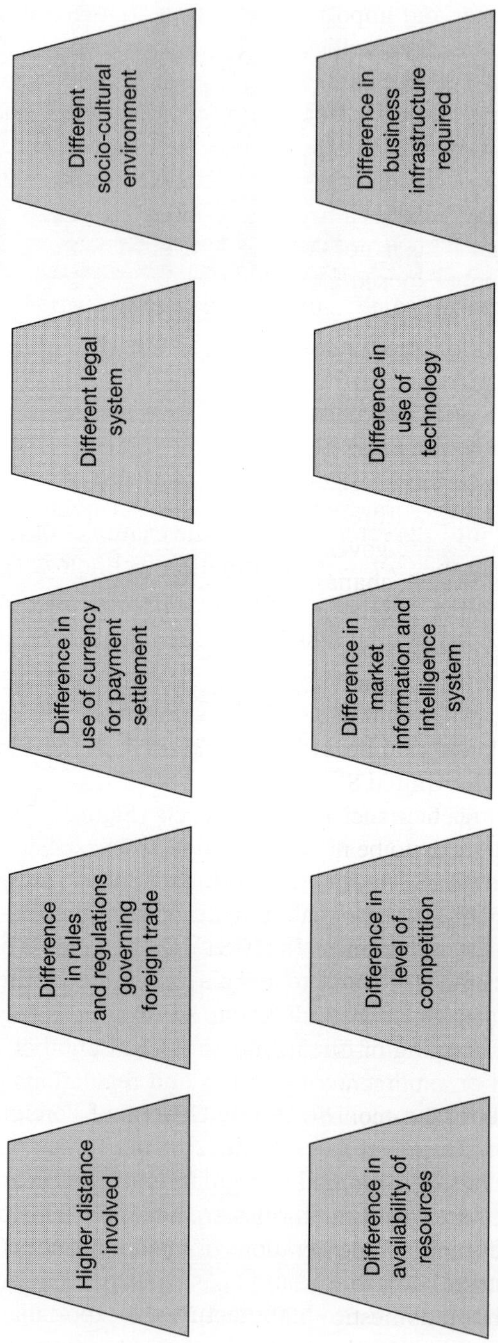

FIGURE 1.5 Key differences in domestic and EXIM operations.

Government of India (GOI), through an Act called Foreign Exchange Management Act (FEMA) and regulations thereunder, mandated for realization of export proceeds only in freely convertible foreign currency. Hence, both the exporter and importer are exposed to the exchange fluctuation risk as their currencies are different from what they use to settle international payments, forcing at least one party to switch its currency into another. Other party will also be exposed to risks as he/she will get payment only in the local currency. *Fourth*, there are differences in legal systems in which they operate internationally unlike in the domestic market. Both exporter and importer are compelled to adjust their trading practices to comply with the law of the counterparty. The compliance of other country's legal systems or even of international law usually act as a barrier and may sometimes be irreconcilable for trading parties to engage with each other. This is not the case for domestic trade where the trader has to deal only with one law which is widely exposed and it is easy to comply because the thinking process of traders is shaped in that environment.

Fifth, domestic trade varies from international business due to differences in cultures. The socio-cultural environment of countries may vary due to different religious backgrounds, ethnicities and socio-economic classes. Accordingly, the exporter may be compelled to bring desired changes in his/her working styles, communication and business practices and in products so as to meet the expectation of others. For example, Chinese firms have forbidden the use of pork for their employees and associates when doing business with Muslim cultures. Foreign firms have issued an advisory to be sensitive towards 'cows' due to the change in the government policy regarding the protection of cows in India. Domestic traders need not adapt to such changes. *Sixth*, there are differences in availability of resources by countries. For example, a country may be rich in natural resources but poor in skilled labour; for example; Saudi Arabia is resourceful in energy resources and the UK is resourceful in services but need to import energy resources, both can exchange their resources for higher public welfare. India has a trained pool of manpower but lacks capital where the United States has advantages. The trade patterns of such trading partners will have manifestation of such factor advantages, for example, labour-extensive exports from India to the United States and capital-intensive imports from the United States to India. A domestic trader does not face such challenges. *Seventh*, the level of competition a trader will experience in foreign markets is likely to be more dynamic and complex than he/she faces in domestic markets. Accordingly, international traders have to do analysis of the competitors by factoring elements such as power of suppliers, buyers, threat of competitor products, substitutes and the threat of new entrants to the market. *Eighth*, domestic and EXIM operations vary on the system of market intelligence. A domestic trader has full access to information pertaining to his/her markets, for example, public records and statistics, newspaper, consultancy services, research reports, and access to chambers and mercantile association at a fraction of cost; however, an international trader has to scramble for business information and market intelligence. Access to reliable information and data for potential markets, particularly for less-developed economies, is tough and costly as their statistical agencies may not be as sophisticated as in the developed market. *Ninth*, the degree of technology one has to use in the foreign market is substantially higher in foreign markets than domestic markets. Use of technologies such as global positioning system and radio frequency identification is common in international logistics so as to track and trace the exact location of merchandise which is not a case in the domestic market. *Finally*, the business infrastructure required for foreign markets will be at different levels of development than required for the domestic market. The size and sophistication of ports, shipping services, stevedoring operations, hinterland logistics, warehousing services, dry port operations and stage of development of logistics services providers are far more important in the case of dealing with foreign markets than in the case of the domestic market.

1.4 Preparing for EXIM Operations

In the rapidly changing global economic environment, getting started with EXIM operations is considered far more complex than domestic business. There are various reasons for it. *First*, the number of parties involved in EXIM operations is more than domestic business. Such parties may include customs officials, DGFT, RBI, GST officials, customs and duty drawback officials, insurance companies, shipping companies, freight forwarders and banks. All of these trade intermediaries help in administering, regulating, facilitating and financing the EXIM business. *Second*, the distance involved in EXIM trade transaction is far higher, exposing the goods to various kinds of transport hazards during the course of transport from one country to another. The layered working capital is also on the higher side as due to long distance and resultant higher time involved in sales turnover, the requirement of working also remains higher in exports and imports than in domestic business. *Third*, there are differences in business etiquettes and practices of different countries. This coupled with varied cultural styles, behaviour patterns, preferences and different language used in business complicates the process of business. Exporters need to have near accurate, comprehensive and complete information to overcome the challenges arising out of these socio-cultural challenges. *Fourth*, there are differences in legal environment under which businesses operate domestically and internationally, exposing both exporters and importers to vagaries of different interpretations of law, thus leading to disputes with the other party. *Fifth*, differences in currencies involved also expose exporters and importers to vagaries of exchange rate fluctuation, and they have to incur higher costs to manage such risks by leveraging the techniques such as forward cover, future contract and option. Additionally, in order to manage the credit risks involved in international transactions, an exporter has to take credit insurance cover so as to manage extra cost and expense. Last but not least, the change in political environment exposes exporters and importers to unseen business situations such as dealing with business in war-torn country, expropriation, strikes and hostile host government. Managing timely information is important for any exporter so as to complete the export- and import-related formalities on time and additionally take appropriate corrective measures so as to manage the differences in unknown international markets. If such information about a country's cultural, economic and social aspects is successfully managed, traders will have advantages in successfully conducting the business (Figure 1.6).

Hence, it is essential for the exporters of both goods and services to have a plan ready for meeting the changed geo-economic realities of international markets. While developing an export plan, exporters as well as importers should use all available information, tools and techniques to prepare a foolproof road for international business entry as well as trade operations. Following are some established and time-tested components of a convincing and dynamic export plan:

1. Dedication, devotion and commitment from the top management of the company to make it a global company.
2. Careful identification and selection of markets through sustained market research, including the identification of cultural differences, buying patterns, national standards, import restrictions, entry and exit barriers, investment limits and other regulatory policy framework for foreign firms.
3. Inculcating a professional approach at each stage within the organization and business, including an effective training programme for trade division staff focusing on sales, marketing, finance, production and HR activities.
4. Deciding and selecting effective trade terms particularly related to export pricing (international commercial terms [INCOTERMS]) that include the additional costs of exporting overseas.

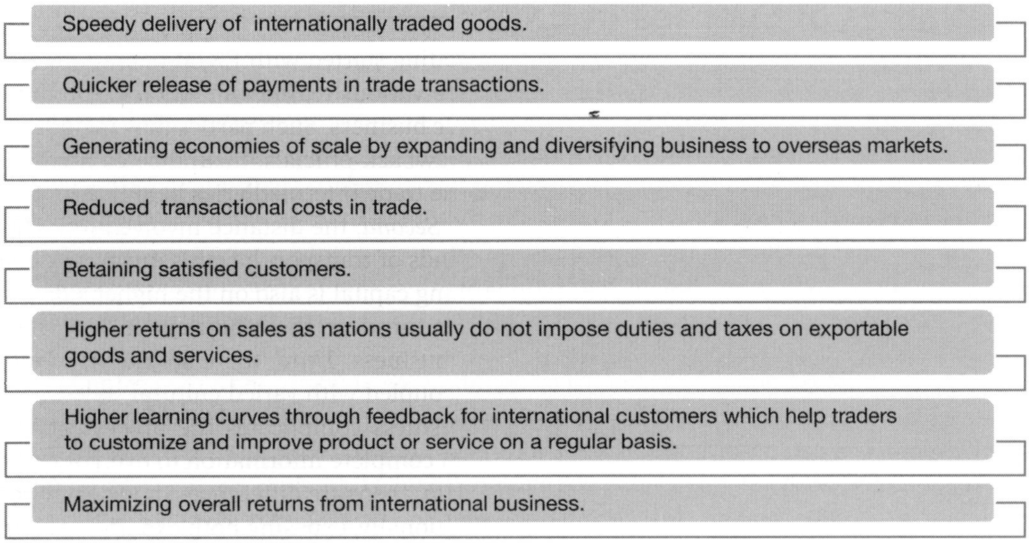

FIGURE 1.6 Planning elements in EXIM operations for success.

5. Explaining precisely and clearly in the plans other trade terms of the company such as mode of payments, delivery terms, and packaging and shipping terms.
6. Elaborating the openness of the company for doing business transactions in the local currency and in the local language, premeditating that such currency and language shall also be suitable and easy to administer by the company in EXIM trade transactions and such currencies shall not be prone to vagaries of exchange rate fluctuations.

After forming a successful export plan, an international trader shall invest considerable time and energy in devising a strategy to achieve the objectives as enshrined in export plans. One such area to look into is the customer choices, preferences and requirements regarding the product or services. An international trader is required to make the right product available to the right costumer at the right time with right price and effective communication. It has been observed locally as well as internationally that one has to be transparent with the customers for trade transactions as it is in the long-term interest of the business enterprise and helps a firm to retain satisfied loyal customers. For developing an effective and efficient international marketing strategy, the following points should be kept in mind by an organization:

1. It offers wide and comprehensive networks of distributors, making products and services available to consumers at their doorsteps.
2. It offers dedicated after-sales services to customers, as good as provided by other local competitors.
3. It offers better products and services at a lower cost as compared to local competitors.
4. It uses local languages for communicating about its products and regards the local values, customs and beliefs.
5. It offers the products and services which are better in quality, have aesthetic appeal and are designed as per choices, preferences and expectations of the local customers.

1.5 Elements of Success in EXIM Operations

While foraying into international markets, one has to start smartly and perfectly from the entry stage and slowly and steadily take the business towards expansion and diversification. As the competition is high in international markets, the customers expect perfect offers for both products and services to which they can place orders. An exporter, accordingly, has to make a right mix of various elements of his marketing offer, that is, product, price, place and promotion. In other words, an international buyer is looking for the 'right product' in the 'right quantity' from the 'right source' in the 'right condition' at the 'right time' at the 'right place' and at the 'right cost'. International customers as well as clients of both goods and services solicit products or services which fulfil their needs, wants, desires and demands perfectly. Accordingly, exporters should be able to deliver orders and make shipments perfectly every single time they get international orders by factoring into special attention to the customers' requests, if any. If an export firm fails to do so, it may lose global customers and clients in today's fierce environment. Any export firm can accordingly have medium- or long-term objectives and goals that sustain their market entrance. Based on the level of competition in the target markets, the exporter or importer has to choose a specific strategy for each target market. One should leverage several elements (as discussed in the sub-sections) in business planning so as to succeed in EXIM trade operations.

1.5.1 Export Planning of Firm

Planning is vital for international business as it helps the marketers to foresee the emerging challenges and problems and helps devise coping strategies. A firm should scan the potential markets for exports and analyse the specific issues related to market entry strategy, exporting, joint ventures, franchising, licensing or investment. It must analyse both tariff and non-tariff issues and customer's choices and preferences for the kinds of products it is going to offer. An export plan should consider any requirement for 'product modification' or 'adaptations'. It should also assess the degree of competition and answer that what types of channels of distribution can be of help for the firm in the prospective markets. An effective market plan is a road map which is used in achieving the strategic results of the firm. The most important factor that the new exporters need to keep in mind is that they have to keep control on high expectations in the beginning as EXIM operations require a degree of patience. High expectations and unachievable goals may result in frustration for a new business team of an export firm. One must keep in mind that each piece of information cannot be assessed in advance and one learns many new aspects about products, price, place and promotion when we enter any market. The firm has to be prepared for any kind of hiccup in the beginning and has to accordingly change its planning and implementing strategy for achieving the desired and realistic goals. Some of the key areas of consideration in export business planning are illustrated in Figure 1.7.

1.5.2 Understanding Foreign Cultures, Business Etiquettes and Practices

An exporter and importer should know and understand the cultural sensitivities, business etiquettes and practices, customers' beliefs and preferences of the target market. Cultural beliefs, values, preferences, customs and taboos have an important bearing on the minds of consumers, and one should factor them while doing business in the international markets. For example, Amazon had to face a lot of resistance from Indian consumers as Amazon Canada was selling shoes with photos of Mahatma Gandhi to which the Indian public expressed clear dissonance and it had to withdraw not only such a product portfolio but delist the vendor as well. Due to varied cultural backgrounds, there can be cultural

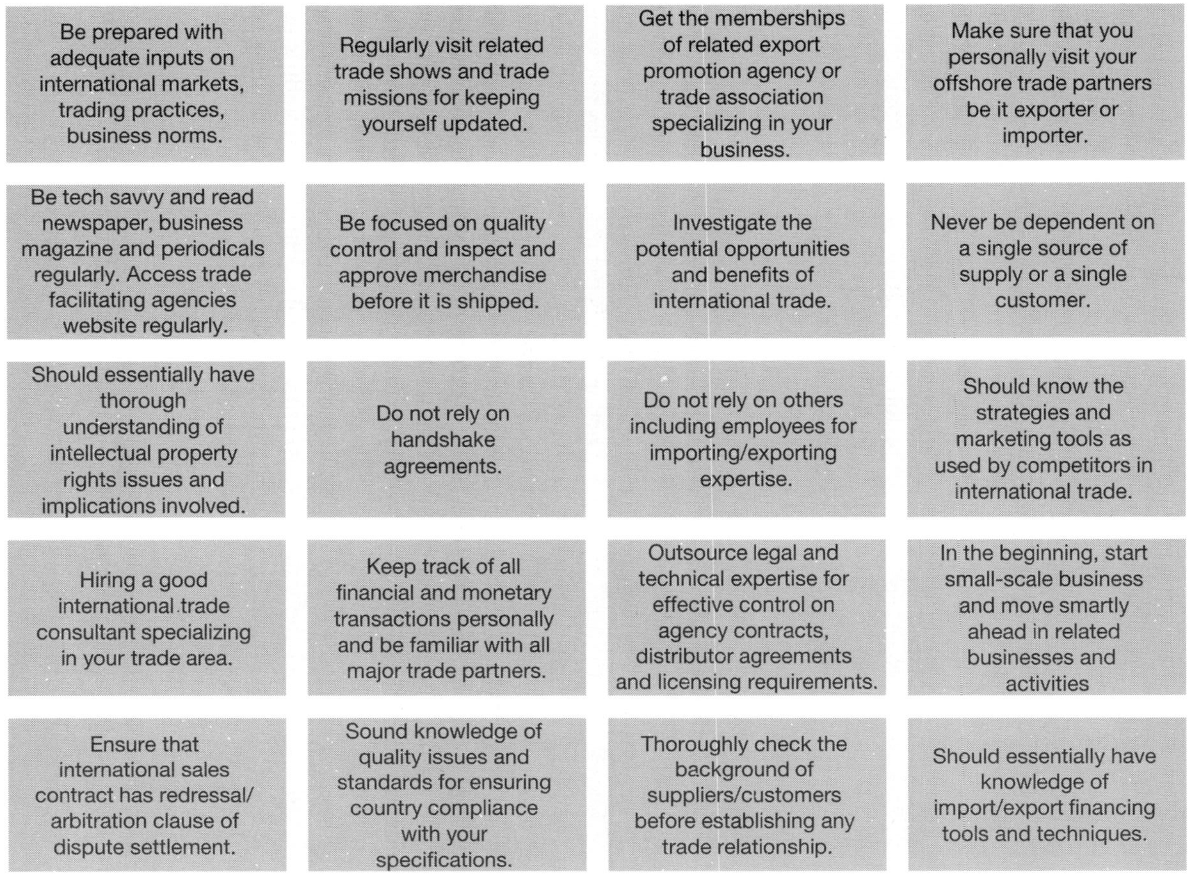

FIGURE 1.7 Areas of precautions in international trade.

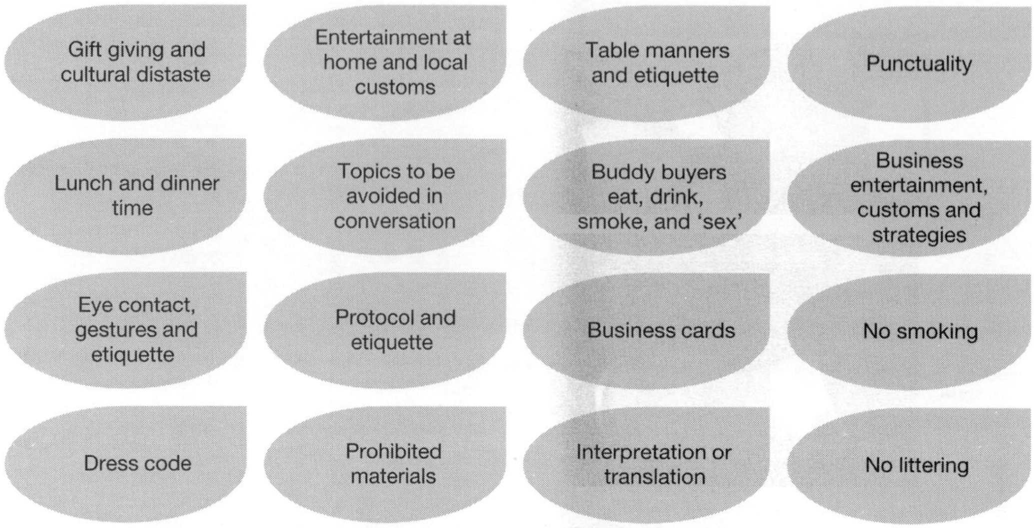

FIGURE 1.8 Understanding foreign cultures: Areas of general precautions.

conflict or misunderstanding; for example, green is the favourite colour of Muslims all around the world except in Malaysia where it is considered a symbol of ill will, poor health and bad mongering, although more than 75 percent of Malaysian population is Muslim. Similarly, white colour is considered bad in China, North Korea, South Korea and Japan; however, it is the colour of joy and celebration among Christians as the brides usually wear white. Some of the important aspects which an exporter and importer should factor while engaging in international markets are illustrated in Figure 1.8.

Business etiquettes and practices are an integral part of any country's business culture and encompass the prescriptive elements of a culture, for example, what is expected to do or not to do and to talk or not to talk. Certain topics may be of interest for people of a certain culture or there could be topics they wish to avoid in their discussions; for example, Germans prefer not to discuss about Adolf Hitler and the Second World War due to their painful historical past. The waves of economic globalization have brought the managers and business people closer to each other; hence, it becomes important that involved managers must be exposed to understand the cultural sensitivities involved in dealing with a particular marketplace. Caselet 1.1 explains the business etiquettes to be followed in China for dealing with customers, suppliers and even the common public.

CASELET 1.1

Business Etiquettes for Dealing with Chinese

Mr Puneet is an MBA (IB) pass out of prestigious Indian Institute of Foreign Trade (IIFT) and got placed with a Chinese company at Shanghai. While leaving for the new job, he consulted one of his professors of export procedure to help him deal with the new business environment in China and to know as to what precautions he could take in order to smoothly land in a new job in a completely different business

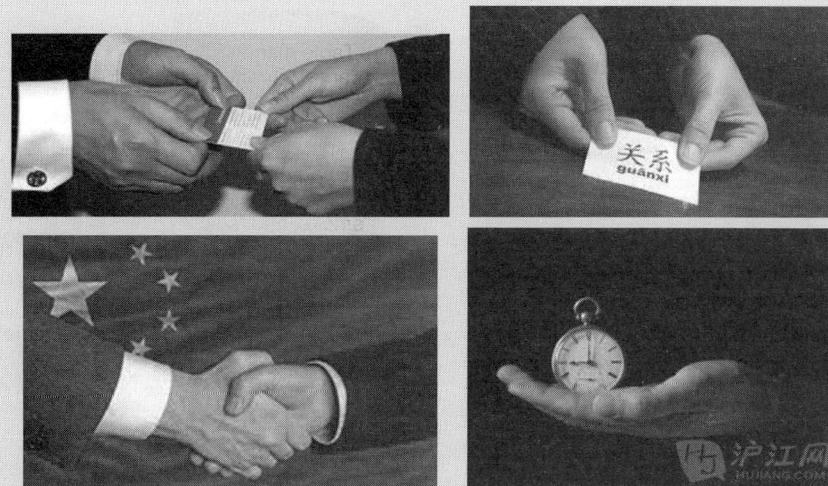

environment. Mr Puneet got the following briefing from his professor. He was advised that 'bowing or nodding' is the common greeting among Chinese; however, if offered, he could shake hands. As Chinese believe in hierarchy and rank, it is advised to 'wait for the Chinese' to offer their hand first. Introductions are formal in a Chinese set-up, and they use formal titles to address their seniors. As Chinese names are tough to pronounce for Westerns, they often use nicknames such as 'James' for 'Jiang' and David for 'Dequan'. They applaud while greeting a crowd and the same is expected in return. They are very particular about time and one must have appointment(s) fixed in advance while visiting them. Further, it is expected to contact the person formally about availability before you depart on a trip to China. The Chinese prefer to involve each level of management in decision-making and, as a result, the decision-making process is slow. It is advised to have several copies of all written documents for your meetings so as to distribute among decision-making members and one should never expect to conclude business meetings swiftly as the Chinese may a leave meeting midway to consult with their 'seniors' or 'stars' or 'wait for a lucky day' before they make a decision. Mr Puneet was further guided by the professor that it is desired to 'present and receive cards' with both hands and one should never write on a business card or put it in their wallet or pocket; it is desired to have a separate cardholder or a small card case. As Chinese believe in rank and hierarchy, it is expected that an important member of the visiting delegation should lead important meetings. Further, one must have a working knowledge of Chinese culture and as matter of importance or regard allow the Chinese to leave a meeting first. Never gift a watch to a Chinese, as they consider it a bad omen.

Business enterprises around the world have their culture shaped by the values, ideas and purpose for which such enterprises are working. When business is global, manpower diverse and multilingual, it becomes extremely important to respect the diversity as values of employees, customers, suppliers and government officials may vary and such stakeholders should be sensitive to the firm's culture and the firm should also be sensitive towards their social aspects. This will help any firm to create a genuine sense of fairness and goodwill among employees and customers. For example, customers in Saudi Arabia feel great when hotels do not cater food in daytime during the month of Ramadan and prepare delicious *Iftaar* for breaking the fast. Figure 1.9 explains the social aspects of people of Saudi Arabia, which can be a ready reckoner for any marketer to leverage appropriate marketing strategies in the Arabian market.

Appearance	• Saudis are very conservative and as a matter of regard to local people, one is expected to never show bare shoulders, stomach, calves and thighs. Hence, wearing sari/skirt/short pant/collar-less shirt is not considered good and one must cover his/her whole body including a head scarf. People of other cultures are expected to abide by local standards of modesty, however, do not adopt native clothing as usage of traditional clothes by outsiders may be considered offensive. During summer, climate is very hot in Saudi Arabia, however, despite the heat, most of the body must always remain covered. Under such circumstances, the ideal dressing for an outsider man is a jacket and tie with long pants and a shirt, preferably long sleeved, buttoned up to the collar at any public appearance in Saudi Arabia. Further, men should also avoid wearing visible jewellery, particularly around the neck. Women should always wear modest clothing in public. High necklines and sleeves at least to the elbows are expected. Hemlines, if not ankle-length should at least be well below the knee. A look of baggy concealment should be the goal, pants or pant suits are not recommended. It is a good idea to keep a scarf handy, especially if entering a Mosque.
Behaviour	• In Saudi Arabia, it is common to remove shoes before entering a building and one should follow the lead of his/her host. In compliance to Islamic traditions, alcohol and pork are illegal and if found, strictly punishable. One should never disturb suppliers/buyers on Friday as it is day of prayers and rest in Muslim world. The styles of greeting may vary even within Saudi Arabia depending on your tribe, status and hygiene. Hence, one should wait for his/her counterpart to initiate the greeting. In common practice, men shake hands with other men. Some men may shake hands with a woman, however, it is strictly advisable for businesswoman to wait for a man to offer his hand. For special relationships, Saudis may greet by grasping each other's right hand, placing the left hand on the other's right shoulder and exchanging kisses on each cheek. Saudis are very particular about hygiene and accordingly the left hand is considered unclean and reserved for hygiene. One should never eat with left hand. One is expected to avoid gestures with the right hand and one should not point at another person. If two men are walking hand in hand, it is a sign of friendship. One should not try to cross his/her legs while sitting and never show the bottom of his/her feet. The 'thumbs up' gesture is offensive in Saudi Arabia. Gifts are not necessary for host, but appreciated if you take one and avoid admiring an item too much as your host may feel obligated to give it to you. If your host offer you a gift, it is impolite to refuse. Women in Saudi Arabia are not permitted to drive vehicles, however, Saudi women in recent years are breaking rules.
Communications	• As Saudis are conservative, one should never discuss the subject of women, not even to enquire about the health of a wife or schooling of daughter. Saudis have a distaste for Israel like anything, hence, the topic of Israel should always be avoided. One should discuss sports which is an appropriate topic for Saudis. Saudi names are often confusing. One should prepare the name list in English language of all probable persons to be met and practise their full name in advance. Saudis are slow, hence, communications occur at a slow pace. One should never feel obligated to speak during periods of silence. 'Yes' usually means 'possibly' in Saudi Arabia. Saudis practise religion by hear and accordingly may interrupt the guests, stop conversation and may leave the room for 15–20 minutes for the purpose of their daily prayers. interestingly, the person who asks most questions during the meeting is likely to be the least important. The decision-maker is likely a silent observer. A customary greeting is *salaam alaykum*. Shaking hands and saying *kaif halak* comes next.

FIGURE 1.9 Social aspects of Saudi people.

1.5.3 Hard Work, Dedication, Devotion and Reliability

For success in EXIM operations, it is important for the marketers to dedicate their whole marketing efforts towards business goals. Export marketing teams of firms should dedicate whole time, mental energy, sweat and tears in achieving their goals. Hard work, dedication, devotion and trust work as inbuilt advertising tools and help the exporters in bringing fruitful sales contracts and orders. Export endeavour is a continuous struggle for the survival of a firm. There may be ups and downs, but dedication and devotion pay at last. The export success of Taiwan, China, Japan, South Korea, Germany and other countries is not a miracle, it is the result of hard work. The success in business will not happen without working hard and smartly. Export marketing teams should also, accordingly, take necessary steps to win the trust and loyalty of the importer through their actions and words. It is well said that the relationship of the exporter and importer is similar to that of the husband and wife. Just as the cycle of life runs effectively because of good relations between the husband and wife similarly, good exporter–importer relation is important for the success of an EXIM trade, as broken or false promises reduce trust and loyalty.

1.5.4 Product Adaptation and Labelling Requirements

Product specifications, standards and requirements vary from country to country due to various technical and regulatory reasons. Export firms must understand what changes are required in the products and investigate the requirement for marking, labelling and packaging that might apply to a product entering a specific foreign market. Some requirements may be mandatory and some other may be voluntary. One must be particular about the mandatory marks and labels which are typically related to public safety, health and environmental concerns. For example, use of plastics in packing of goods destined for Germany is restricted; an exporter must be ready to pay additional fees for 'Green Dot License' before clearance of goods by German customs. Hence, product adaptations and modifications are essential for any company entering foreign markets. Coco-Cola had to sweeten the Thumps Up as Indians take more sugar than their counterparts in the United States or elsewhere. A Hyderabad-based firm had to market its meat by declaring it prominently on the pack that meat packed is halal in the Middle East. Indian pharmaceutical companies had to change their packing of medicine due to Federal Drug Administration rules. Singer company shows a man operating its sewing machine, as showing women in public advertisements is against Islamic traditions in the Middle East.

1.5.5 Identifying Customers' Wants and Needs

Identification of customer needs and wants is a predominant element for success in export operations. An export firm needs to assess what kind of features in planned products the potential customers would like to see. The export marketing team should also list the changes based on how the potential customers currently operate and the way forward for meeting these changes in the firm's proposed product. An export firm should clearly assess both needs and wants, as 'need' refers to what the export firm offers and 'want' refers to what the customer wants. It can make use of the secondary data of the previous years. A systematic analysis of customer data mining can make the life of any exporter far easier as one can scale up research of identified products to the next level, that is, finding the 'emotional connections' of potential customers with the firm's product and how it fits into their personal lifestyle. Feedback so received can help any marketer to improve his product and position in the market. Finally, an export firm must do competitive analysis of identified products, keeping in mind the target customers. An understanding of the competitive landscape of foreign markets from experts, research consultancy, potential customers and users provides a great way to deal with the strengths and weaknesses of the firms and assess the changes that a firm needs to make in order to win customers in the foreign market.

1.5.6 Managing Financial Resources

The large distance between exporting and importing countries coupled with the documentation involved leads to higher sales turnover time for any exporter. The exporter has to be particularly more careful in planning and managing the financial resources as the gestation period of international transactions is more than domestic transactions. Additionally, EXIM trade is prone to various risks such as exchange rate fluctuations, problem of balance of payments, economic crisis leading to the breakdown of the banking system and the failure of the electronic system facilitating fund transfer. These may result in a longer time in the realization of payment or non-receipt of payment. It is rightly said that 'finances are the lifeblood of an organization' and should accordingly be used with utmost planning and care. Planning of working capital, especially financing of export transactions, requires due diligence on the part of the exporter. The Reserve Bank of India (RBI) offers liberal credit to exporters and a special rate of interest for micro, small and medium enterprises (MSMEs) and agricultural exporters, and an exporter must make use of such government schemes in his financial planning. Further, pre-shipment finance in foreign currency is also allowed, which leads to significant cost-cutting of interest rates and protection from exchange rate fluctuation risks, as the exporter will prefer to take foreign currency loans only in the currency of invoice. Effective financial planning and execution can help any exporter to avoid any unforeseen situation during the course of business.

1.5.7 Positive Attitude and Futuristic Thinking

EXIM operations in today's context are extremely competitive, and a trader must be of positive attitude along with futuristic thinking so as to take his organization ahead in competition. Any firm, whether involved in export or import, should not only beat the competition in the markets but also scan the customers' needs for future requirements. For example, Akio Morita of Sony Corporation could think ahead and designed the Walkman by taking cue from his daughter who wished to listen to music during walking. Apple iPhone has become a household name with the dedication and futuristic thinking of Steve Jobs by leapfrogging technologically much ahead of its competitors. Jack Welch wanted General Electric to be among the top 10 organizations in the world; the day he envisioned this along with his future thinking, he achieved his dream in due course. Positive and futuristic thinking is the best way of doing things as it helps in winning the importer's trust and confidence, thereby building long-term relations and loyal customers for the firm.

1.5.8 Effective Coordination and Communication

Due to various stakeholders involved in the foreign trade chain, both exporter and importer must be very smart in timely and effective communication and coordination with various counterparts. An exporter has to deal with several stakeholders to ensure compliance of various commercial and regulatory requirements. An international trader who enjoys working with different people and winning new overseas customers in a systematic manner can take his business to newer heights. Effective communication and coordination with various parties, for both commercial and regulatory purposes, become extremely important in the context of different business environments, as an international trader has to deal with people coming from diverse social, cultural, political, economic and legal backgrounds. An international trader has to be committed in winning such new markets through mutually benefiting relationships and sustained market research. A quiz on exporter readiness is given in Appendix 1.

1.5.9 Documentation Knowledge Is Essential

'Documentation is the soul of EXIM trade', and an international trader must have a sound knowledge of documentation practices for compliance with both Indian authorities and international agencies and organizations, including compliance with regulations of the country of imports. He/she must be well versed in using and understanding the role and importance of both commercial and regulatory documents, as no EXIM trade transactions can be complete without these documents. Payments may be at risk if any discrepancy is found while negotiating these trade documents with the bank. The trader's insurance claim may be in danger if he/she has chosen the wrong policy of marine insurance. Therefore, it is mandatory for international traders to have sound knowledge of EXIM documentation and procedure for being successful in EXIM trade.

1.6 Importance of EXIM Trade to Nation

In a globalized set-up, almost all nations of the world endeavour to develop their export markets, as export has increasingly become an instrument for increased economic growth, development and socio-economic prosperity. The export success of small economies such as Taiwan, Singapore and South Korea is based on the fact that these economies are the centre of global manufacturing, trading and services activities. The importance of EXIM trade to a nation can be understood on the basis of several factors. *First*, when the domestic markets are small, foreign markets provide opportunities to any firm to achieve economies of scale, trade expansion and sustained economic growth. *Second*, countries tend to export the commodities, goods and services, in case the demand for them in the local markets is limited such as export of agricultural products by the European Union, the United States and Australia, and oil export from countries of the Middle East. *Third*, countries are using trade expansion as an important activity in shaping their economic success, for example, China, India and Turkey. *Fourth*, countries are increasingly trading all around the world so as to mitigate the effects of domestic recession. *Fifth*, countries are using exports to accumulate the foreign exchange reserves which help them in meeting their import requirements, debt servicing and improving their status in global markets, for example, China, South Korea and Japan. In an era of rule-based and rule-imposed trade tussle, each country tries to increase its exports to fulfil its developmental requirements, improving the living standard of the people and employment generation. *Finally*, even in the case of developed countries, export operations are the prime fulcrum of domestic economic activity, helping countries deal with international competition, enjoy the scale and scope of advantages and reap benefits of technological breakthroughs. This is evidenced in the success of major export countries such as Germany, the United States, France and Britain.

TABLE 1.2 India's Rank vis-à-vis Major Export Champions in the World in 2019

Rank	Name of the Country	Billion $ of Exports
1.	China	2,498
2.	United States	1,645
3.	Germany	1,486
4.	Netherlands	709
5.	Japan	705
18.	India	334

Source: UN Comtrade (2019).

India still lags behind in reaping benefits arising out of exports as it enjoys only 1.6 percent share in the world export market and is ranked 18th (Table 1.2), whereas China enjoys 13.5 percent share in world exports and is ranked as the largest exporter of the world. For becoming an export champion in the next decade, Indian policymakers should first improve the domestic competitiveness of manufacturing, services and agriculture products, only then can India sustain in global markets. In a globalized set-up, one needs to become domestically competitive first, as the domestic market is also free for investment and entry to foreign players. Increased trade will flow from such enhanced domestic competitiveness, as trade is not an end in itself, but a means to economic growth and national economic and social prosperity and development. The primary purpose of enhanced export operations is not mere earning of foreign exchange but the stimulation of greater economic activity so that all sections of society may be benefited through this exchange of goods, services and ideas, and, more importantly, such development must be inclusive and shall take care of all stakeholders for sustainable economic development and well-being. Percentage increase in export of goods and services and that of India's GDP is given in Table 1.3. Higher growth in exports and imports will translate into higher growth of GDP, as economists now consider exports to be the fourth pillar for contributing to the economic development of a country, in addition to agriculture, manufacturing and services.

Export in India has been resounding in the 21st millennium except for the last two years when exports have contracted largely due to weak international demand. India has been consistently increasing its percentage share in the world trade. Exports are extremely vital for India to leapfrog its journey of economic development. From the point of view of national economy, the importance of export business can be understood in the points elaborated in the following sub-sections.

TABLE 1.3 India's Growth (%) of GDP vis-à-vis Growth of Export of Goods and Services

	2010	2011	2012	2013	2014	2015	2019
India's percentage growth of export of goods and services	19.61	15.57	6.78	7.80	1.71	5.36	6.39
India's percentage growth of GDP	10.26	6.63	5.48	6.54	7.17	7.93	5.2

Source: World Bank. https://www.worldbank.org/en/home (accessed on 24 May 2023).

1.6.1 To Meet Imports of Industrial Needs

In a globalized set-up, no country can chalk out a sustainable development plan for pervasive economic growth and inclusive development. Each country, whether developed or developing, large or small, needs to engage with the outside world in order to fulfil the industrial needs of the country, as each commodity or service cannot be generated within. For example, India has been importing the capital equipment, raw materials of critical nature and technical knowhow from many countries in order to ensure its faster and sustainable industrial and agricultural development. There is always a scope for flow of investment from capital-rich countries to developing countries so as to ensure rapid industrialization and widening of social and economic infrastructure. For programmes like Make in India to succeed, India needs to attract foreign capital, technology and plant and machinery to start the production of value-added products in India. In an era when policymakers are looking for reaping the benefits through participation in the 'global value chain', that is, the process of producing goods, from raw materials to finished products, which is increasingly carried out wherever the necessary skills and materials are available at a competitive cost and quality, it will be vital for India to focus on the areas of cost comparative advantages for enhanced foreign trade. Table 1.4 provides us the rising percentage of import content of India's exports in an era of global value chain, where India is importing cheap raw material for the purpose of value addition and then exports, thus earning precious foreign exchange to service its imports.

1.6.2 Debt Servicing

Exports help a lot in debt servicing of a country, especially if it is underdeveloped or developing and has taken foreign aids from other countries and developmental institutions to speed up its developmental requirements like improving and widening the industrial base, social support such as health, employment guarantees, water supply and sanitation. As a result of such aid, countries have to pay back the principal as well as liberal interest on aid for debt servicing to donor countries and institutions. Debt payment is usually done through the equalized instalments of foreign exchange currency. Figure 1.10 indicates India's ratio of debt services as the percentage of exports of goods and services from 1975 to 2015. Foreign exchange can be earned through export operations; hence, a country should use foreign aid to develop export-oriented industries and can service its debt out of export earnings so generated. Hence, countries can use aid and exports for not only debt servicing but also the larger economic development of the country.

TABLE 1.4 Rising Percentage of Import Contents of India's Exports

Year	% of Import Contents
1995	9.33
2000	11.27
2005	17.45
2010	22.25
2015	24.03
2019	24.73

Source: World Bank. https://data.worldbank.org/indicator/DT.TDS.DECT.EX.ZS?locations=IN (accessed on 21 April 2023).

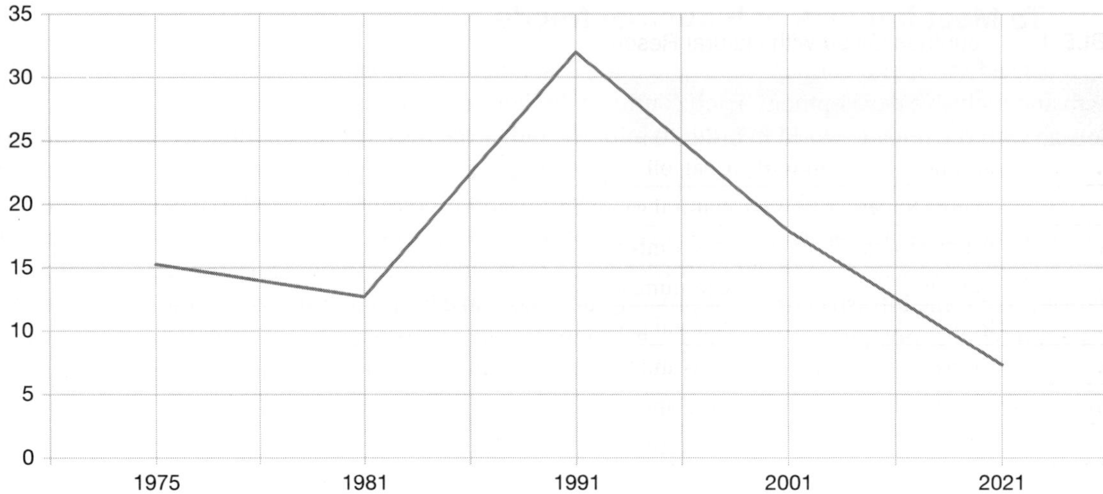

FIGURE 1.10 Total debt service (% of exports of goods and services).

Source: World Bank. https://data.worldbank.org/indicator/DT.TDS.DECT.EX.ZS?locations=IN (accessed on 21 April 2023).

1.6.3 Rapid Economic Growth

Policymakers in the changed economic scenario consider 'exports' as the fourth component of GDP, the other three normally being agriculture, manufacturing and services. The countries which centred their economic planning around foreign trade have achieved rapid economic growth and development. Expansion and diversification in export lead to positive changes in all other components of an economy and add dynamism to its developmental needs, processes and ends. If a country can expand and diversify its exports in the areas where it enjoys surplus production and innovation-based manufacturing and offer unique services, then it will not only effectively utilize domestic resources but will also grow rapidly, thus improving the socio-economic status of its citizens. Further, export promotion aimed at winning the global markets with export in non-traditional, high-value, elastic demand area will help any country to accumulate respectable exchange reserves commensurate with the country's needs and enable it to import necessary plants and machinery which can be effectively used for import substitution and export expansion in surplus areas through value addition in products and services.

1.6.4 Profitable Use of Natural Resources

Any country which ideally has natural resources more than its future requirements can exploit these natural resources for its economic development. Countries rich in natural resources such as oil, gold, coal, iron ore, timber, gases, silver and uranium can make profitable exports and earn precious foreign exchange which can be used for socio-economic development of the country. Table 1.5 lists the top 10 countries embedded with natural resources and total costs of such natural resources in the world economy.

The economic prosperity of people in countries such as Qatar, Oman, Canada, Australia, the United States and China is largely attributed to natural resources these countries possess. Russia has the largest natural resources in the world, and it has survived the crippling economic sanctions of Europe and the United States with the might of its natural resources, mainly exports of gas to European countries.

TABLE 1.5 Countries Gifted with Natural Resources

S. No.	Country Name	Main Natural Resources	Total Cost of Natural Resources (Trillion)
1.	Russia	Coal, oil, gold, gas and timber	$75.7
2.	United States	Natural gas, gold, copper and oil	$45
3.	Saudi Arabia	Gas, timber and oil	$34.4
4.	Canada	Uranium, timber, oil, phosphate and gas	$33.2
5.	Iran	Natural gas and oil	$27.3
6.	China	Coal and timber	$23
7.	Brazil	Gold and uranium	$21.8
8.	Australia	Coal, iron ore, timber and copper	$19.9
9.	Iraq	Oil and natural gas	$15.9
10.	Venezuela	Iron, oil and natural gas	$14.3

Source: http://countrydetail.com/top-10-countries-natural-resources-world/ (accessed on 10 May 2023).

1.6.5 Dealing with Competition Successfully

In a globalized set-up, each nation strives for its exporters to be in a strong position in global markets and each government offers certain benefits to their exporters to deal with the global competition. Exporters, in order to avail these benefits, incentives, export assistance and support, and tax neutralization, concentrate intensively on improving the quality, image and brand value of their products by extensive use of latest technology so that their products can face global competition successfully. Nowadays, government gives benefits to exporters at each stage of production, trading and financing. Such support from government agencies not only helps the exporter, but it also helps in improving the country's image through better quality products in overseas markets and in bringing valuable foreign exchange to the country.

1.6.6 Increase in Employment Opportunities

In recent years, countries have been effectively using exports as a tool for generating employment in the country. DGFT, in its FTP document (2015–2020), has given extra incentives to sectors which generate employment; for example, textiles, leather, handloom, sport goods, agricultural products and handicrafts have higher support from GOI for exports. The Scheme for Integrated Textile Parks is aimed at generating employment in the textiles sector.

1.6.7 Role of Exports in National Income

Increased exports help generate additional inflow of foreign exchange into the country; thus, its ability to service its imports becomes better and foreign exchange reserves grow. Enhanced exports help increase national income, as domestic economic resources are traded in foreign markets resulting in inflow of wealth from other economic systems to the country's economic system. Exports help in foreign exchange accumulation and a country can use such resources for infrastructure funding and

TABLE 1.6 Countries with Highest Foreign Exchange Reserves ($ Billions) in 1960–2021

	1960	1970	1980	1990	2000	2010	2020	2021
China	0.00	0.00	10.09	34.48	171.76	2913.71	3357.24	3427.93
Japan	1.95	4.88	38.92	87.83	361.64	1104.56	1390.81	1405.75
Euro area	0.00	0.00	0.00	0.00	351.98	787.90	1077.85	1196.16
Switzerland	2.36	5.32	64.75	61.28	53.62	270.48	1083.40	1109.82
United States	19.66	15.24	171.41	173.09	128.40	488.93	628.37	716.15
India	0.67	1.02	12.01	5.64	41.06	300.48	590.23	638.48
Russian Federation	0.00	0.00	0.00	0.00	27.66	479.22	596.77	632.24
Hong Kong SAR, China	0.00	0.00	0.00	24.66	107.56	0.00	491.78	496.87
Saudi Arabia	0.19	0.67	26.13	13.44	20.85	459.31	472.85	473.89

Source: World Development Indicators. https://data.worldbank.org/indicator/FI.RES.TOTL.CD?locations=CN (accessed on 29 March, 2023).

nation building. Countries such as China, South Korea, Japan and Singapore have leveraged exports as an instrument for generating additional wealth for the country. The countries with highest foreign exchange reserves are shown in Table 1.6.

1.6.8 Increase in the Standard of Living

A country with increased export engagements will certainly improve the standards of living of its people, as export generates employment and business opportunities for the people. Exports help in improving the quality of life as: *First*, such a country can import some essential goods with ease, for example, with improved foreign exchange reserves, India has liberalized its import regime, thus making available to local public goods such as olive oil, Swiss cheese, green coffee, avocado oil and a variety of pulses. *Second*, exports help in enhancing the employment opportunities with increased economic activity, thus supplementing the income of the common people who can buy more with increased purchasing power. *Third*, exports promote rapid industrialization of the country through trading of manufactured and agricultural goods along with increased trade in services. The process of rapid industrialization helps the exporters and traders to sell some part of their production in the domestic markets which makes quality goods available to the local people.

1.7 Importance of EXIM Trade to Industry

Business in today's world is driven by small, medium and large enterprises, but the government has transformed its role only as a facilitator to foreign trade. All kinds of firms foresee great business opportunities in foreign trade and accordingly participate in international commercial and trade activities so as to reap benefits such as greater economies of scale, coping with recession in the domestic markets, higher profitability on exports, benefits under duty drawback schemes/tax benefits, improved learning and technology curve, utilization of installed capacity, higher productivity and fulfilling the social objectives by employment generation and bringing foreign exchange to the country. Export–import is extremely important for firms of all sizes—small, medium and large—due to the reasons explained in the following sub-sections.

1.7.1 Lack of Domestic Demand

Any export firm shall be interested in exports if there is not adequate demand for the product or services offered by it in the domestic market. An exporter can sell extra production or surplus production in the foreign market to increase sales volumes and overcome the challenges posed by weak demand in the domestic market. Textiles and leather exporters from India are more interested in foreign markets as it helps them synchronize their production by selling in overseas markets and operate sustainably in the foreign market. Indian firms have production surplus in many areas such as mica, magnesium, jute, coffee, tea, natural rubber, fruits and vegetables where they have no option except to engage with foreign markets. Similarly, when an export firm has more installed capacity than the expected demand for any product or service, it can enter into the international market and utilize its unutilized installed capacity for selling the goods and services in the international market.

1.7.2 Legal Restrictions

Engaging in export–import sometimes becomes the legal requirement for a firm, as it is mandated by domestic law to export a certain proportion of its production so as to earn foreign exchange reserves. In 1991, GOI had mandated big industrial houses to export so that the country could earn foreign exchange to service its import requirement and debt payments. Even the present foreign trade policy provides for a liberal import regime for those jewellery manufacturers who engage in exports, thus earning foreign exchange for the country. Government can mandate firms of certain sectors to mandatorily export; MMTC has been mandated for export of iron ore to Japan and South Korea.

1.7.3 Higher Productivity and Profitability

When an export firm produces goods and services on a large scale, it enjoys scale and scope advantages, leading to higher productivity in operations. For increased quality compliance, an export firm also upgrades its scientific and technological processes, leading to higher productivity. Chinese firms have successfully used their mass production and mass consummation strategy to tap the global markets. They enjoy scale, scope and system advantages at each stage of procurement, production, logistics, warehousing and selling, thus making them compete aggressively with domestic firms even after tariff and non-tariff barriers. Higher productivity leads to higher profitability and this in addition to neutralization of all taxes, government incentives, assistance and support makes their overseas business operations far more successful. As a result, firms are usually interested in exports as they avail exports benefits at each stage of production, processing, selling and financing.

1.7.4 Social Responsibility

Sometimes export firms engage in foreign trade in order to fulfil social responsibilities (Caselet 1.2). An export firm in Delhi exports handicrafts, crafted by rural women, wherein the larger objective is not merely earning of foreign exchange but also empowerment of rural women. Similarly, handmade candles and chocolates are exported with the objective of empowering women. Some business firms, especially those which are public enterprises, take the decision to contribute to the national exchequer by exporting their production. In India, many public sector enterprises such as Hindustan Zinc Ltd, Bharat Earth Movers Ltd, Bharat Electronics, Defence Research & Development Organisation and Hindustan Aeronautics contribute to foreign exchange reserves and exchequer through exports.

CASELET 1.2

Exporting for Social Obligations: Barefoot College Training Rural Women for Tapping Solar Energy

Bunker Roy, a social entrepreneur, is convinced that solutions to problems faced by rural people all over the world lie within the community, and they can leverage newer technologies in their traditional set-up to overcome these challenges. To transform this conviction into action, he founded Barefoot College in Tilonia village, Ajmer, Rajasthan, in 1972. Small in infrastructure but big in its dream of transforming the life of millions, Bunker Roy worked on the idea of tapping solar energy by training young people and semi-literate and illiterate rural women to be solar engineers. It attracted the trainees, especially women all over the world, and to overcome the language barrier, they identified the parts by shape and colour, mimicked the instructions so as to impart panel design skills and executed technical tasks by making a prototype and through example. It achieved huge success in India; Bunker Roy shared, 'train a grandmother, who will always be in a village to serve society instead of youth who will leave village in search of better avenues in the city,' highlighting the need and benefits of training women, especially aged ones, to ensure that rural societies gain from their expertise and improve the lifestyles of others.

barefoot college

Barefoot College has tasted success in the Himalayan region of India, where it has done extraordinary work in providing access to solar energy to rural people who otherwise have no electricity connection due to extremely hostile terrain. Bunker Roy decided to go global to achieve the bigger dream and replicate the solar panel development programme for rural women of developing and least developed countries (LDCs). Ethiopia and Afghanistan were the first two countries chosen, and rural women from these countries were provided training in a humble environment in Tilonia, Ajmer. As a first export of solar development skills, solar installation, with all key components exported from India, was completed by a woman in the village of Tukul in Ethiopia in 2004. Expanding wings further, the United Nations Development Programme (UNDP) was roped in and a total of 36 semi-literate and illiterate villagers were trained who completed solar installations in 19 Ethiopian villages, building 250 solar lanterns in 11 rural electronic workshops that they set up themselves in Ethiopia by 2006. Similarly, UNDP funded the training of illiterate Afghan women and helped in installing solar panels in five villages of Afghanistan, providing electricity to around 150 houses, which was further expanded with the help of Norway. Many international organizations have come forward to help women develop solar panel installation skills; for example, Foundation Ensemble (Together Foundation) and the Dutch organization Het Groene Woud (the Green Forest) have so far successfully trained women from remote villages in Benin, Bolivia, Bhutan, Cameroon, the Gambia, Malawi, Mali, Mauritania, Rwanda, Sierra Leone and the United Republic of Tanzania. All have returned home to install photovoltaic systems in their villages and maintain them. Training has also just started for women from Senegal, Djibouti and Sudan. Export of skills and solar components has provided access to electricity to thousands by the noble efforts of Barefoot College.

Source: Adapted from https://www.barefootcollege.org/wp-content/themes/barefoot-college/download/strategic-plan.pdf (accessed on 22 April 2023).

1.7.5 Technological Improvements

EXIM operations are important as firms from developing countries enter into alliances and joint ventures with foreign firms for the sake of technological transfer and improvements, which transform the technical landscape of a country with spillover effects. Indian firms have learned a lot from Russia, Israel, the United States, Germany, France and the United Kingdom in improving the technological landscape of the country. BrahMos Aerospace is a great collaboration of Indian and Russian scientists. Such jointly owned firms have better understanding of local and overseas markets and can effectively utilize their experiences, knowhow and core strengths for penetrating new markets through their technological improvements and face the competition successfully in the overseas markets as such firms can offer better quality products to end users.

1.7.6 Managing Product Life Cycle and Seasonal Ups and Downs

The production cycles, especially of agricultural goods, have mismatch in demand and supply leading to business challenges. An export can manage such ups and downs in any market by engaging with multiple overseas markets and mitigate the risks of sharp fluctuations in the business activity of the firm. Downward trend in one market may be partly or fully counterbalanced in other markets, and the business will not be at stake due to such ups and downs in one or another country. Further, stages of product life cycle make the demand pattern fluctuate and an export firm has an advantage of selling even obsolete products in overseas markets.

1.7.7 Greater Opportunities for International Collaboration

Exports and imports offer greater opportunities for international collaborations for firms, especially between developed countries and developing countries, aimed at transfer of technology, improved management knowhow, capacity building and training, joint research product development and so on. Indian Railways is collaborating with Japanese and Spanish counterparts to execute the bullet train project in India. Similarly, Larsen & Toubro (L&T) of India has signed a deal with Hanwha Techwin of South Korea to jointly manufacture guns urgently required by the Indian Army so as to have a conventional edge over its arch-rival Pakistan. L&T will manufacture 100 ‘K9 VAJRA-T’ howitzers for the

Indian Army in collaboration with its South Korean partner for an order worth ₹45,000 million. International collaboration helps firms gain knowledge and expertise from each other. BrahMos Aerospace is the best example of international collaboration between India and Russia.

1.7.8 Closer Cultural Relations

Exports and imports, especially among firms between two trading countries, bring various countries closer culturally, as better trade relations are established with people's participation. The importance of Indian IT firms in the United States is such that it has brought the two governments closer to each other, opening up various other business avenues between the two countries. Sikhs from Punjab initially migrated to Canada as soldiers, agri-farmers and taxi drivers and now have become an integral part of Canada's composite culture (Caselet 1.3). Punjabi professionals such as doctors, engineers, nurses, chefs and economists have transformed the cultural relations between India and Canada and significantly influenced the political system of Canada to an extent that Canada's prime minster is nicknamed Justin Singh Trudeau.

CASELET 1.3

Export of Punjabi Culture to the Political System of Canada

Caring

Sharing

Daring

The people of Punjab have been entrepreneurial and are considered suitable for the Armed Forces due to historical and cultural reasons which shaped their past, Punjab being the gateway for many attacks on India. The Sikhs of Punjab have represented overwhelmingly the Armed Forces the world over and have fought many battles during the First and Second World Wars. As a result, Sikhs were exposed to many parts of the world, and they started migrating to Western countries, especially to Canada, where their entrepreneurial and risk-taking capacity was appreciated. The present prime minister of Canada, Justin Trudeau, has special liking for Sikhs and is influenced by their culture, especially their art of sharing (langar), caring (donation) and daring (valour). He is occasionally seen dancing to the bhangra beat in the Indian community event in Canada. The family of Justin Trudeau danced at the song 'Dil Bole Hadippa' at an event organized by the India–Canada Association of Montreal. He is popularly known as Justin Singh Trudeau. To the surprise of all, he inducted four Sikhs in his 30-member cabinet in 2015, and the Sikhs' representation became even larger in 2019, with a Sikh deputy prime minister. So much is the cultural influence of the Indian community on the culture of Canada that local broadcasting on radio, TV and other media is done in Punjabi, Gujarati and Hindi. Sikhs constitute a mere 2 percent of India's population and in Canada, they are less than 2 percent of its population of 36 million.

1.8 Managing Risks in EXIM Operations

Factors such as different political, legal and economic environments, different currency of invoicing and language of business, large distance involved and operating in different socio-cultural marketplaces expose exporters and importers to various risks in trade operations. Accordingly, export firms need to develop a professional approach when entering the field of foreign trade operations. The export marketing team must have a clear-cut road of managing such risks and confidence to handle unforeseen situations in foreign markets. Above all, export firms must have financial resources and commitment to start their export campaign. Export and import are certainly more risky than domestic business. Some of the risks that an export firm has to handle are discussed further in the following sub-sections.

1.8.1 Credit Risk

Any export transaction is a gift, unless the payment is realized from an overseas buyer and it is one of the most important worries for any exporter engaged in export operations. Accordingly, an exporter must scan, assess and appraise the credit-worthiness of an importer before engaging in trade operations. Additionally, he/she must also assess the complexity and transparency of rules and regulations of the country of foreign buyers such as the state of balance of payment, levels of foreign exchange, foreign exchange rules, availability of banking channels, international sanctions and convertibility of local currency with freely convertible foreign currency. The Foreign Exchange Management Act, 2000, and regulations thereunder mandate for the realization of export proceeds, first, only through proper banking channels; second, only in freely convertible foreign currency except Nepal and Bhutan; and third, within the period of 270 days from the date of exports unless otherwise permitted by RBI. In order to manage the credit risks, an exporter can take help of credit-rating agencies such as Export Credit Guarantee Corporation (ECGC) and Dun & Bradstreet, which provide useful information about the credit-worthiness of the foreign buyers. If required, it is always recommended to take a suitable insurance cover to manage the credit risks as, first, the period of 'trade cycle' in international trade is longer; second, the degree of risk is also higher; and third, the quantum of working capital is also involved, and even one failed realization of export proceeds can pose grave survival challenges for an export firm.

1.8.2 Foreign Exchange Fluctuation Risk

As the exporter and importer deal in different currencies for the settlement of payment, both parties are exposed to risks of foreign exchange fluctuations. An exporter deals in Indian rupee domestically and accordingly procures key inputs for manufacturing or purchase of exportable goods in the Indian rupee, wherein the export proceeds are to be realized in freely convertible foreign currencies such as US dollar, euro, yen and pound sterling, thus exposing to foreign exchange fluctuation risks due to changes in the internal value of the Indian rupee vis-à-vis foreign currency which always keeps on depreciating and appreciating. An appreciating rupee will reduce the net realization of export proceeds and a depreciating rupee will increase the net realization. Hence, in order to cope with such fluctuation risks, an exporter has to hedge with bank with forward cover, future contracts, options and so on. Accordingly, an exporter can get the risk covered from the authorized dealer's thorough forward exchange cover and options. In addition to managing through derivatives, an exporter can minimize the fluctuation risks by taking pre-shipment finance in a foreign currency; hence, his risks to the level of working capital automatically stand managed. Further, an exporter can manage such risk by invoicing in currencies which are less prone to day-to-day vagaries of ups and downs and are usually stable in their valuations.

1.8.3 Importer's Country Risk

An exporter is exposed to political, legal and economic risks emanating from the importer's country. Weak political, economic and legal framework of the importer's country can expose the exporter to risks such as expropriation, balance of payment, payment restriction, non-conversion of local currency to freely convertible foreign currency, freezing of account in the country of settlement and unavailability of banking channels. Indian exporters suffered heavy losses when the United States attacked Iraq in 1991. Similarly, Indian exporters lost the established markets of Libya, Tunisia and Syria after the Jasmine Revolution in these countries. A mere change in government in Maldives has cost the Indian company GVK scrapping of contract to build the international airport in Male. Indian exporters pay a heavy price for economic sanctions in Iran, as they cannot export to this established and lucrative market to their true potential. Collapse of banking and financial system in Greece in 2012 has cost Indian exporters a heavy price, as their export shipment to Europe decreased drastically due to weak demand. Sometimes natural disasters in the importer country such as tsunami, earthquake, volcano explosion, drought or flood may adversely affect a country's potential to import and pay on time. Challenges on balance of payment front or low level of foreign exchange reserves may prompt the import country to restrict or prohibit certain unessential imports, and the exporters can suffer losses if such orders adversely affect their exports.

1.8.4 Quality Risks

Quality risks are one of the notable risks and are tough to manage as, first, the perception about quality may vary among different exporters and second, the mechanisms of quality control are complex in EXIM trade. Quality control in exports and imports can be done through inspection by the official agency of the exporting country, agency appointed by the importer and finally quality inspection agency of the importing country. If exported goods are not inspected by an independent third-party agency, there can be quality risks for the exporter, as the entire shipment may be rejected by the importer, exposing the exporter to risks such as offering export discounts, complete rejection and resultant loss of payment. Quality control inspection at any stage can protect both the importer and the exporter. Alternatively, the exporter can ship one or two samples of the goods to the importer and on his satisfaction about quality, he/she can produce the goods and export them. Quality control disputes have serious repercussions for any country's exports. For example, the Japanese government has put a ban on agricultural products of China, fearing they are contaminated with pesticides; Spain has put a ban on import of sunflower oil from Ukraine, fearing it is detrimental to people's health; and South Korea after widespread mass protest against the US beef has put a ban on import of the US beef, as consumers feel that the US beef is contaminated with the Mad Cow disease.

1.8.5 Cargo Risks

Cargo risk is also referred to as transport risk, marine risk and logistics risk. Cargo can be subject to several kinds of damages during the course of the journey, for example, physical damages to cargo, theft, pilferage, loss arising out of change in temperature, biological hazards and atmospheric hazards. The risks of piracy are real as maritime lanes are flooded with pirates across the globe. There are increased risks of terrorist attacks today than a decade ago, and fire on ship, collision, jetsam, diversion and ship standing have become common things due to crowded maritime lanes. The increased movement of goods from one continent to another exposes the goods to several cargos, and an exporter must understand all aspects of international logistics, especially the modal choice and contract of carriage. The contract of carriage is drawn up between a shipper and carrier (ship, air, road and rail), and it narrates the legal rights of the cargo owner to claim damages against carriers. An exporter and importer should also have strong knowledge of INCOTERMS, which are globally accepted rules for distribution of costs and risks between an exporter and importer. One of the ways through which either party to trade can minimize their cargo risks is by taking a cargo insurance cover from a general insurance company. The knowledge of Institute Cargo Clauses as framed by the London Institute of Underwriters helps an exporter to choose the right clauses of insurance, keeping in mind the nature of goods.

1.8.6 Cultural and Language Risks

Misunderstandings of culture can be very costly in foreign trade, and an exporter or importer should sincerely consult a cultural guide while dealing with the other party of trade. Our understanding about business practices, tax systems, etiquettes, rules and regulations, eating and dining habits, and greeting gifts manners is shared in the context of the culture we live in. Hence, an exporter can misunderstand or wrongly interpret the gestures of the other party and may assume certain things which are never agreed. Accordingly, an exporter and importer must ensure that they fully understand these differences of the buyer's culture and, if required, are open to go for 'market visit' to the target country of imports or exports.

1.9 Advantages and Disadvantages of EXIM Operations

Export–import is one of the most discussed subjects as it offers advantages to some countries; however, there are some disadvantageous situations. In order to understand why trade is advantageous to some countries and disadvantageous to others, the answer lies with various trade theories. Ricardo's theory of comparative cost advantage proposes that foreign trade can occur between countries if the countries differ in their factors of production of goods and services. The factors of production are land, labour and capital, which translate into outputs either as goods or as services. *First*, a country which can manufacture the goods using a lower labour input cost can be advantageous vis-à-vis one using a higher input of labour to produce the goods of the same standard and quality. Further, resource endowment theorists propose that advantageous trade can occur between countries if the countries differ in their endowments of resources which are skills and abilities of a country's workforce; for example, India has more skilled labour in diamond cutting, hence, it will have more gainful foreign trade of gems and jewellery. *Second*, foreign trade also becomes advantageous with abundance of natural resources available within a country (minerals, farmland and so on); for example, Australia has advantageous trade in both minerals and farm produce, as it has abundant land area which is rich in minerals. *Third*, the sophistication of its capital stock (machinery, infrastructure, communications systems and so on) can also put any country in an advantageous situation vis-à-vis its competitors; for example, the United States has an advantage in trade of defence equipment, armaments and aeroplanes. Factor proportions, that is, differences in endowments of countries, globally allow them to trade the goods as well as services. Advantageous trade can also happen between countries if demands or preferences for goods and services differ between consumers of the countries. Customers may have different preferences or demands for various products in a particular country; for example, Indians have great affection for owning gold and as a result it emerged as the largest importer of gold in the world. Japanese may have a great demand for fish, especially of whale fish, and they would like to import it from anywhere in the world, even at a premium cost. 'Scale advantages' are another basis that provide some countries the advantages in foreign trade and others disadvantages. The Chinese can manufacture iron and steel at a fraction of the cost; thus, they have advantages in exports of iron and steel goods. Indian IT firms can do the monotonous back office work with pooling of large number of employees at a fraction of costs; hence, India has advantages in export of IT and IT-enabled services. Scale advantages refer to a production process in which fixed cost of production falls as the scale of production rises, thus resulting in total product costs. Tax exemption by any government can also make some products attractive in international markets, as tax sops, incentives, subsidy, export assistance and support can significantly alter the prices charged for goods and services, thus making them attractive for foreign markets. In such a scenario, advantageous exports may arise solely due to differences in government policies vis-à-vis tax exemptions, incentives, support and subsidy to certain sectors. India's agricultural exports have increased significantly, as it has a strong institutional mechanism to support Indian agri-farmers to engage with the outside world. A country can have several advantages arising out of its engagement with another country in both exports and imports. The comparative advantage in international production and trade comes when each trading partner has a product that will bring a better price in another economy than it will in the domestic market. If each nation continues to specialize in producing the same kind of goods and services in which it has a comparative advantage, in every likelihood, more goods will be produced, traded and sold among nations, thus creating wealth for societies and economies. Figure 1.11 illustrates the specific advantages and disadvantages of EXIM business.

Some of the key advantages of EXIM operations are: *First*, they result in increase in domestic competitiveness as when any firm do production for global market, it has to be extra cautious of both quality and costs, failing which it cannot compete in foreign markets. This leads to lower cost of production, better products and higher revenue in sales along with globally satisfied customers. *Second*, export–import also helps address the cyclical trends such as dealing with depressed sales and reduces dependence on existing markets. It helps in more efficient and increased global production, thereby allowing nations and firms to consume a larger and more diverse bundle of goods and services. It is particularly more relevant and beneficial to smaller nations possessing limited natural resources, as it enables them to participate in global buying and selling and makes them able to produce and consume more than otherwise could have been possible. *Third*, the establishment of EXIM operations helps the firms and nations to expand into a number of potential markets in which a country can sell its goods and services. The increased global consumption for goods and services results in more production and more extensive use of raw materials and labour, which in turn leads to growth in domestic employment in exporting nations. Better use of corporate technology and technical knowhow which comes from international learning of production and marketing techniques also forces domestic firms to become more efficient through modernization and innovation.

International trade can be disadvantageous for some countries, as they may not be fully prepared to deal with the outside world; for example, the firm has to publish new promotional material in the language of the country of imports, thus increasing the cost of sale. The gains in EXIM operations are only

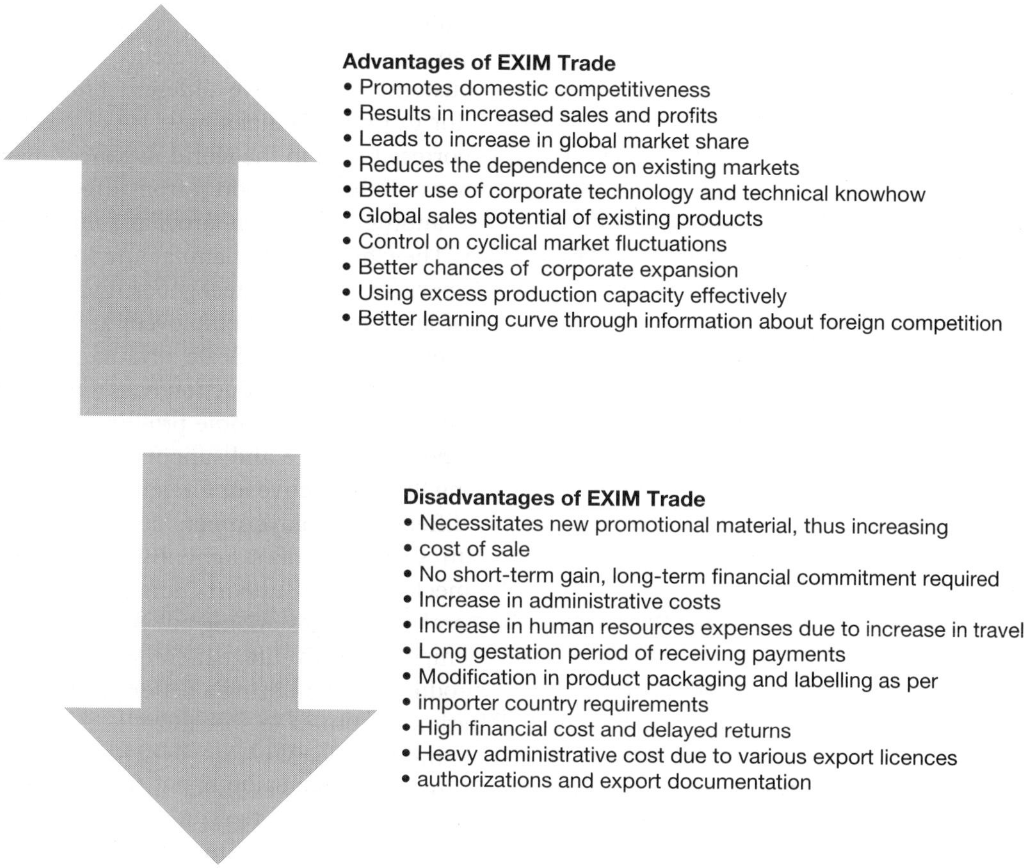

FIGURE 1.11 Advantages and disadvantages of EXIM operations.

in the long run; hence, firms engaged with short-term objectives of maximizing their sales are not likely to gain much even at higher administrative expenses and production costs. Foreign trade leads to increased travel of the firm's manpower, thus leading to increased expenses on trade. One of the major challenges for any firm interested to do business globally is to deal with a long gestation period of payment along with delayed payment or even no payment in some cases. A firm has to adapt its product which leads to higher costs, thus leading to heavy administrative costs. Further, there are huge costs in availing licences, authorization and engaging a consultant who can do EXIM documentation for the firm. Even after several associated disadvantages, nations as well as firms globally use EXIM trade as an instrument to expand their domestic market and to give boost to economically poor and depressed sectors within the national economy. Many nations use trade for supplementing their national income and increasing the goods and services for domestic consumption so that precious foreign exchange can be saved through import substitution. In a globalized trade regime, international trade has largely been viewed as an instrument to promote economic growth in the national economy. Various international organizations/developmental banks and groups and associations working for trade promotion have increasingly emphasized the role of international trade for economic progress.

1.10 Summary

Export and import are important economic activities for each country in today's globalized world. Both are vital to the health and dynamism of developed as well as developing economies. Exporting is preferred as the most cost-effective way of international economic engagement and is defined as 'exchange of goods, services and ideas between two or more countries'. Merchandise export is a function of international trade operations, wherein goods produced or manufactured in one country are shipped to another country for future sale or trade. Services export means rendering of services to a client or customer based in another country. The sale of such merchandise goods or rendering of services to a client in the international market adds value to exporting the country's gross domestic output. Import, on the contrary, refers to the process of bringing in the mechanize goods or services into one country from another country. Factors such as different political, legal and economic environments, different currency of invoicing and language of business, large distance involved and operating in different socio-cultural marketplaces expose exporters and importers to various risks in trade operations. Accordingly, export firms need to develop a professional approach when entering the field of foreign trade operations. The export marketing team must have a clear-cut road of managing such risks and confidence to handle unforeseen situations in foreign markets. Above all, an export firm must have financial resources and commitment to start their export campaign.

Export–import is different from domestic trade in many aspects. *First*, the distance involved in EXIM trade transactions is higher than in domestic transactions, thus exposing an exporter or importer to transport risks such as piracy, theft, pilferage and stranding of ships. *Second*, domestic business is far simpler; the goods can move on any available moderoad, rail, air or multimodal—from one place to another. *Third*, there is dissimilarity in currencies used in domestic and EXIM trade. One can deal in domestic currency while invoicing within the country; however, the same is not the case of foreign trade where GOI, through FEMA and regulations thereunder, mandated realization of export proceeds only in a freely convertible foreign currency. *Fourth*, the level of competition a trader will experience in foreign markets is likely to be more dynamic and complex than he faces in domestic markets. *Fifth*, there are differences in business etiquettes and practices in different countries. This coupled with varied cultural styles, behavioural patterns, preferences and different languages used in business complicates the process of business.

While foraying into international markets, one has to start smartly and perfectly from the entry stage and slowly and steadily take the business towards expansion and diversification. As the competition is high in international markets, the customers expect perfect offers for both products and services to which they can place orders. An exporter accordingly has to make a right mix of various elements of his marketing offer, that is, product, price, place and promotion. In other words, an international buyer is looking for the 'right product' in the 'right quantity' from the 'right source' in the 'right condition' at the 'right time' at the 'right place' and at the 'right cost'.

In a globalized set-up, almost all nations of the world endeavour to develop their export markets, as export has increasingly become an instrument for increased economic growth, development and socio-economic prosperity. The export success of small economies such as Taiwan, Singapore and South Korea is based on the fact that these economies are the centre of global manufacturing, trading and service activities. *First*, when the domestic markets are small, foreign markets provide opportunities to any firm to achieve economies of scale, trade expansion and sustained economic growth. *Second*, countries tend to export the commodities, goods and services in case the demand for them in the local markets is limited such as export of agricultural products by European Union, the United States and

Australia and oil export from the Middle East. *Third*, countries are using trade expansion as an important activity in shaping their economic success, for example, China, India and Turkey. *Fourth*, the countries are increasingly trading all around the world so as to mitigate the effects of domestic recession. *Fifth*, countries are using exports to accumulate the foreign exchange reserves which help the country in meeting its import requirements, debt servicing and improving its status in global markets.

Factors such as different political, legal and economic environments, different currency of invoicing and language of business, large distance involved and operating in different socio-cultural marketplaces expose exporters and importers to various risks in trade operations. Accordingly, export firms need to develop a professional approach when entering the field of foreign trade operations. The export marketing team must have a clear-cut road of managing such risks and confidence to handle unforeseen situations in foreign markets. Above all, export firms must have financial resources and commitment to start their export campaign. Export and import are certainly more risky than domestic business. Some of the risks that an export firm has to handle are: credit risks, foreign exchange fluctuation risks, importer's country risks, quality risks, cargo risks, cultural and language risks. Export–import is one of the most discussed subjects as it offers both advantages and disadvantages (Figure 1.11).

CASE STUDY Do Sectoral Trade Agreements Make Sense for India?

India has signed a series of PTAs and FTAs aimed at expansion and diversification of its exports; on the contrary, the economic gains from these trade agreements have been far more limited. For example, India had bilateral trade deficit of mere $500 million with the ASEAN countries in 2011, which has increased to approximately $10 billion in 2019. India's trade deficit has increased with South Korea as well as with Japan, two comprehensive economic partnerships; India aims at boosting trade and investment ties with its close Asian trade partners. Some of the trade agreements are rather used by its competitors to penetrate into the Indian market through trade deflection; for example, China has invested in Bangladesh and Sri Lankan textiles and clothing industry, which made great inroads into India's domestic markets. India's bicycle industry is also taken over by the Chinese leveraging trade deflection as an instrument. India's vegetable oil industry has shifted base to Sri Lanka, as import duties for edible oil in Sri Lanka are lower than that of India. Palm oil exports to Sri Lanka have increased manifold, wherein value-added products of vegetable oil origin, made in Sri Lanka, are exported to India. There is a debate among policymakers as well as trade community whether FTAs have worked for India or not.

Prior to the visit of President Trump to India, there were hectic negotiations between India and the United States for a trade deal. As no party ceded ground, a comprehensive trade deal could not be negotiated and signed. Policymakers on both sides are now exploring the possibility of starting trade negotiations for sectoral trade agreement, like promoting India's exports of drugs and pharma to the United States, as India is not only a reliable supplier but also very cost-effective, thus providing required medicines at an affordable cost to American citizens. The United States can make a strategic investment in not only research and development (R&D) but also production and distribution rights of the pharma industry in India. It will create a win-win situation for both the countries to start with and get required political mandates to move ahead in the India–US trade deal.

India has a strong drugs and pharma industry, especially for generic drugs, and trade data indicate that India is the third-largest producer of drugs and pharma by volume and is among the leading suppliers as well. As Indian pharma products are priced in lower segments, trade data do not provide the real picture of India's capacities and capabilities as a reliable and cost-effective supplier of drugs to world markets. India is acknowledged globally as the pharmacy of the world, especially in African and Latin American countries. India exported medicines valuing almost \$8.5 billion in 2018, making it the second-most exported product from India to the United States, after gems and jewellery. The United States, on the contrary, explored the potential of exports of medical devices to India and has objected to existing regulatory framework of price cap that is on stents/hardware used in hearts and so on. India's 10th largest imported item is medical devices (HSN-90), and this segment is growing very fast. Both the countries are endeavouring to promote their business interest, India for its low-cost pharma products in the United States and the United States for its medical devices in India. As trade of affordable pharma, medicines and medical devices is far more welfare creating and trust building, it can work as a base for subsequent trade negotiations and take the India–US trade partnership to the next level.

Such a sectoral trade agreement is not free from potential challenges; for example, US-based drug makers lobby group Pharmaceutical Research and Manufacturers of America want greater intellectual property protection and market access opportunities in growing Indian markets along with abolishing of restriction on prices caps, favourable regulatory regime, patent protection, exclusive manufacturing and marketing rights and so on. United States Trade Representative has unfavourable views for such trade to happen and highlighted unpredictable patent environment, regulatory data protection failures, high tariffs and taxes on medicines, discriminatory and non-transparent market access policies and unpredictable environment for clinical research as the key challenges before the US companies that operate or wish to tap the Indian market. The US companies, on the contrary, are eyeing Indian markets and complain about high tariffs faced by them for active ingredients and finished products. What may be operational challenges in negotiating such a trade deal, strategically, it makes sense for both the countries to gain from each other, and trade of medicines and pharma can be a basis of Indo-US trade partnership to go to the next level.

Questions

1. Why cannot India leverage FTAs to its favour?
2. Why is India considering sectoral FTA rather than full-fledged FTA across the merchandised goods?
3. What makes pharma to be an important sector for the India–US sectoral trade deal?
4. What are the key hurdles in the India–US sectoral trade deal in the pharma sector?

Appendix 1: Export Readiness Quiz

Think your business is ready to enter into international and global marketing activities. Take the quiz, check your score and be sure.

1. Is your product or service already available?
   a. Currently marketed nationally
   b. Currently in production or being developed
   c. At the prototype stage
   d. At the idea stage only
   e. None of these
2. Is your product or service selling in the Indian market?
   a. Selling and market share is growing
   b. Selling and market share is stagnant
   c. Selling, but market share is decreasing

   d. Selling in only one city in India
   e. None of these
3. Do you have the surplus production capacity or available specialists to meet increased demand for your product or service?
   a. Surplus production available
   b. Have funds to increase production capacity
   c. Bank support required to enhance production capacity
   d. Can outsource it from outside
   e. None of these
4. Do you have the financing required to adapt your product or service to suit your target market and to promote it?
   a. Financing is in place
   b. Financing is being arranged
   c. No financing available
   d. None of these
5. Are you committed to sustain your export effort?
   a. 100 percent committed.
   b. Is thinking to start export by my own
   c. Is looking for government support
   d. Can start if given a chance
   e. None of these
6. Does your firm have a good track record of meeting deadlines?
   a. We are ahead of deadlines
   b. We can meet demands if required
   c. We can meet demands in 3 months' notice
   d. We are planning
   e. None of these
7. Does your management have experience in export markets?
   a. Yes, we have overseas research department in place
   b. We are occasional exporter
   c. We are deemed exporter
   d. We are planning
   e. None of these
8. Does your product or service have a distinct competitive advantage (quality, price, uniqueness, innovation) over your competition?
   a. We are no 1 nationally
   b. We are no 1 in region
   c. We are domestic trader
   d. We are planning
   e. None of these
9. Have you adapted your packaging (labeling and/or promotional materials) for your target market?
   a. We are promoting/labeling in language of destined country/region
   b. We are promoting/labeling in English
   c. Promotional material/labeling not required
   d. None of these

10. Do you have the capacity and resources to provide after-sales support and service in your target market?
    a. After sales services mechanism in place
    b. We have tie up with other organization for after sales services
    c. We can provide after sales services if requested
    d. Our product is good hence after sales services not required
    e. None of these
11. Do you have a Free on Board (FOB) or Cost, Insurance and Freight (CIF) price list for your product, or a rate list for your service?
    a. We follow Incoterms 2000 practices
    b. We work as per importers wishes
    c. We follow domestic rate list in exports
    d. None of these
12. Have you undertaken any foreign market research?
    a. Completed primary and secondary market research, including a visit to the target market
    b. Completed some primary research
    c. Completed some secondary market research
    d. We can do it if required
    e. No research
13. Is your promotional material available in the language of your target markets? (Business cards, brochures, web sites)
    a. Available in the language of target market
    b. Available in the language of that region
    c. Available in English only
    d. Promotional material not required
14. Have you started marketing your product or service in your target market?
    a. Marketing Department in place
    b. We are selling occasionally
    c. Marketing not required
    d. None of these
15. Have you engaged the services of a sales representative/distributor/agent, or partnered with a local firm?
    a. Have partnered with a local firm which has good distribution network
    b. We have sales agents
    c. We sell by our own
    d. None of these
16. Have you hired a freight forwarder or customs broker?
    a. We have independent freight forwarder
    b. We hire freight forwarder occasionally
    c. We can do documentation work by our own
    d. None of these
17. Do you have knowledge of Export Documentation?
    a. Full knowledge
    b. Good knowledge
    c. Somewhat knowledge

d. A little bit
e. No knowledge

Higher the score, poorer your knowledge in export business.

Your score ....

Review Exercises

Multiple Choice Questions

1. Which of the following countries is the largest exporter in the world?
   a. China
   b. India
   c. The United States
   d. Germany
   e. None of the above
2. What refers to exports?
   a. Moving out of services from one country to another
   b. Moving out of goods and services from one country to another
   c. Moving out of goods services and ideas from one country to another
   d. Moving out of only goods from one country to another
   e. None of the above
3. Which of the following countries is the largest importer in the world?
   a. China
   b. India
   c. The United States
   d. Germany
   e. None of the above
4. Which of the following countries has the largest per capital exports as per information provided?
   a. Liechtenstein
   b. Singapore
   c. Hong Kong
   d. Qatar
   e. None of the above
5. Which of the following is the most solid reason for an exporter to export goods and services?
   a. Lack of domestic demand
   b. Legal restrictions
   c. Higher productivity and profitability
   d. Social responsibility
   c. Nonc of the above
6. Credit risk in export business refers to
   a. Default by an importer on payments
   b. Insolvency of an importer
   c. Breakdown of banking channels, thus non-realization of payment

   d. International sanctions and inconvertibility leading to non-payments
   e. All of the above

7. A restriction by the importer country for halal compliance for food importers will be called
   a. Mandatory labelling requirement of country
   b. Product adaptation
   c. Compliance to cultural norms
   d. Adherence to Islamic law
   e. All of the above

8. Commercial presence of a service exporter in a foreign country will fall under which of the following modes of General Agreement for Trade in Services?
   a. Mode 1
   b. Mode 2
   c. Mode 3
   d. Mode 4
   e. None of the above

9. Transportation risks in export business refer to
   a. Loss of goods due to fire in course of transit
   b. Loss of goods due to climatic changes in course of transit
   c. Terrorist attack leading to loss of goods
   d. Sinking of ship leading to loss of goods
   e. All of the above

10. Expropriation, balance of payment crisis, payment restrictions, non-conversion of local currency to freely convertible foreign currency, freezing of account in country of settlement and unavailability of banking channels refer to which of the following risks?
   a. Importer's country risks
   b. Export risks
   c. Product risks
   d. Cargo risks
   e. Exchange rate fluctuation risk

Critical Thinking Questions

1. What legally constitute the term 'exports'? How is export business different from domestic business?

2. What are the key elements of success that an exporter should keep in mind while foraying in export business?

3. What are the various risks involved in EXIM trade? Explain.

4. Examine any two of the following:
   a. Importance of export–import to a nation
   b. Importance of EXIM trade to an exporter
   c. Advantages of export business
   d. Disadvantages of export business

CHAPTER 2

International Trading Environment

CHAPTER OBJECTIVES

- To assess the global trading environment affecting EXIM operations.
- To appraise the elements of the global trading environment, that is, political, economic, social, technological, legal and so on.
- To analyse the business challenges and precautions therein.
- To appreciate the ways and means to manage such environment and minimize risks.

2.1 Introduction

A firm has no control over the external environment even in a domestic business where it has to deal with issues such as tax rates and policy, changes to the economic structure, threats from competition, political factors, government regulations, industrial licensing and approvals, environmental concerns, legal compliances to different acts and rules as well as the changing technological landscape. This becomes extremely complex when a firm enters international trade, as it must deal with different business environments in countries of imports. International trading environment is regarded as the 'sum of all the external forces working upon the firm as it goes about its affairs in foreign markets'. A firm can plan a course of action to manage uncontrollable external factors in the domestic business as managers are familiar with the business landscape of the country and forces shaping it, including the political economy of the home country. This is not the case for international trade operations where many uncontrollable external forces affect the firm, for example, uncertainty of foreign trade regime, dealing in different political environments, changed economic legislation, confusing tax policies and procedures, misleading cultural interpretations and complex legal compliances which make the functioning of an export firm extremely complex. These challenges have widely differing impacts on a firm when it deals with these in foreign markets with different international trading features, prospects and challenges. Under these circumstances, it is important that the managers of an export firm should take an active interest in scanning the key elements of the international trading environment. The key elements are illustrated in Figure 2.1.

Any firm intending to go global requires trade data to interpret, analyse and make cross-border comparisons using standard criteria to understand the external environment affecting its business. Fortunately, such data is available online and an exporter can easily analyse the nature of the environment on a country-by-country basis. Each economy has national accounts data, indicating estimates of gross national product (GNP) including growth trends, GDP, consumption, investment, government expenditures and price levels. An exporter can also access the demographic data indicating the

FIGURE 2.1 Key elements of international trading environment.

number of people, their distribution by age category and rates of population growth. Any business activity that takes place within the political environment requires understanding of sub-elements such as governmental institutions, political parties and organizations through which a country's people and rulers exercise power. Any export firm must carefully study the government structure in the target country and analyse salient issues arising from the political environment which primarily include the governing party's attitude towards sovereignty, people's attitudes towards foreign firms, political risk, trade wars and resultant retaliations, the threat of equity dilution and expropriation. Understanding of the legal environment is equally important as nations are governed by force of law which includes rules and principles that nation states consider binding upon themselves to administer. An exporter should pay attention to both sets of law: the 'public law' or the law of nations and international commercial law, which is evolving. Laws of nations such as common law, code law and 'Islamic law' provide the base for evolution and framing of international commercial law. An export firm should also acquire knowledge of diverse cultural environments to be successful in international trade operations. It must have internationally trained staff without culturally tinted glasses to independently study the international socio-cultural environment. An international marketer explicitly recognizes the non-economic bases of marketing behaviour and their growing role in today's globalized markets. Barbie doll does not come only in white colour any more, but one can find black, Chinese and Indian style as well, and children can easily correlate when they find someone similar. Consumption, in today's globalized set-up, is a function of many other cultural influences and is not merely a function of income as only non-economic factors can explain the different patterns of consumption of two individuals with identical incomes or by analogy of two different countries with similar per capita incomes. Globally, there is increased awareness about saving the environment, and firms are reducing their carbon footprints to retain such awakened global customers. Finally, an exporter can also not ignore the technological environment of the country and should accordingly adapt his product for such markets.

Knowledge of the various elements of external factors affecting the firm's engagement in international market allows management to allocate resources so that they reap the benefits and operate with high efficiencies in any country. For instance, any shoe manufacturer will be interested in trade data of the demographic profile of the population of a desired country such as gender mix, size of shoe, weather conditions, income levels, disposable income and level of economic development of a country. It also needs to understand the key competing nations and firms, their cost and marketing strategies and unique selling proposition to plan counter strategy for such markets. Hence, export firms intending to go international should carefully consider various elements of international trading environment such as socio-cultural, political, legal, macroeconomic, technological and ecological and other global factors in the context of the host country for correct planning of marketing strategy. Any export firm may face certain constraints in international markets such as inability to face competition, inadequate financial resources, unskilled manpower and challenges in understanding consumer behaviour. As international business is far more complex, ambiguous, volatile and uncertain, the competitive forces operating in the international markets are always difficult to handle and require a planned approach and business strategy. An export firm may have to face the challenges arising out of not only existing competitors but also from substitute products developed with innovative technologies, diversifying product mix, value addition to the existing product, newer price segments and innovative marketing strategies. Waves of globalization coupled with tapping of increased international marketing opportunities have led to creation of global brands and products with specialized production, marketing and distribution networks. The result has been the expansion and diversification of global trade leading to quantum jump in export earnings, on the one hand, and also helping the consumers in getting global products at affordable prices, on the other. With increasing competition among global players, the task of an international marketer has become complex as there is no guarantee of continued marketing opportunities for any product or service in the global markets. There are several factors that make this competition extremely tough to cope with, for example, technological leapfrogging resulting in product obsolescence, faster and prompter diffusion of marketing information, continuously declining product prices and tapping of newer segments with advanced marketing analytics. With waves protectionist measures in the United Stated and Europe, the job of an international marketer or any new exporter becomes extremely tough. Over the years, international institutions have been helping countries to dismantle the trade barriers through institutional and business support which is also not proving to be successful with the new set of protectionist measures as announced by the United Kingdom as a result of Brexit. Tariff and non-tariff barriers are now significantly reduced and there is hope among international traders that new reforms measures such as agreement on trade facilitation, increased cooperation on infrastructure projects and increasing emphasis on plurilateral trade measures will succeed the protectionist measures of the United Kingdom and other countries, and ultimately, it will be 'trade' that will win. In the above context, it is important that future managers must be able to appraise, analyse and assess the global trading environment so as to take proper decisions to manage export operations.

2.2 Appraising International Trading Environment

Waves of liberalization, globalization and privatization have influenced the global trade environment so dramatically that producers, exporters and policymakers in developing countries like India are struggling to respond to emerging changes and challenges, especially with reference to an ever-evolving trade regime which is manifested by both protectionist and reformist measures. For example, WTO's agreements are aimed at reforming the trade regime and ensuring increased foreign trade activity in the world market. On the contrary, protectionist measures by the United States, which is the largest economy and importer of the world, have put a question mark on the future of expansion and diversification by many in the industry. Brexit does not forebode well for the future of European countries which when put together are the largest, reliable and most stable market for tapping export opportunities by a large number of countries. Indian exporters are not untouched from these global developments and must constantly apprise the global business environment so as to tap the international trade opportunities.

On the domestic front, India's external sector largely remains protected and is not exposed to international competition since Independence. The Indian domestic industry remains complacent and cannot build competitive strengths in R&D, value addition and tapping international marketing opportunities. Aspects related to quality compliance and sanitary standards were completely ignored. With changes in international marketing environment under WTO, they are compelled to align themselves with global phytosanitary standards in addition to being price competitive. With the emergence of free trade regime and sub-zero level duties, India's export sector is compelled to change its manufacturing practices, business perspectives and marketing strategies. At the same time, changed environment has provided ample business and trade opportunities to Indian exporters who have been able to respond to these challenges on a real-time basis. The increasing volumes and values of both imports and exports are manifestations of that for India.

For an Indian firm to succeed in international markets, it is important that it must appraise and assess its competitive advantages in the light of prevailing international trading regime and environment. Indian firms, both small and large, should reorient their efforts on how effectively such facets of its competitive advantages can be synchronized with key features of target markets. Appraising of international marketing environment considering its competitive strengths can provide an Indian firm with a sustainable environment for growth, expansion and diversification. It is difficult to analyse and generalize the factors which may be of help for an Indian firm in some international markets, but a reference can essentially be made to the elements shown in Figure 2.2 while arriving at a decision to enter a market for international marketing efforts or not.

A major mistake that Indian firms usually make is that they try to replicate home success in international markets which is a laid-back approach. The market fundamentals and characteristics of the international market are completely different from the Indian market. For example, Indians prefer fresh vegetables, while Europeans prefer chopped, processed and packed vegetables. Indians still prefer to buy fresh milk from their local dairy or sourced directly from an agri-farm, while Americans prefer only pasteurized and packed milk. Indians love to do shopping from nearby pop-and-mom stores on a daily basis, while in Western countries, there is a trend of mega shopping stores where households do shopping for a week or fortnight. Indians have a liking for a fresh catch of shrimp, Japanese prefer shrimp with bold eyes, while the size of the shrimp matters to Americans. Organic foods are just catching up with affluent Indians in metros, while it is an established concept in many developed countries. Indians earn and do shopping; however, a concept of monthly installment through a loan or credit is catching up fast, while in Western countries, people buy and earn later to pay the equated monthly instalments. The takeaway from this discussion is that Indian marketers must remain open to product, price and promotional adaptations when exporting or selling goods and services internationally. It is important for an international marketer to scan and appraise the international marketing environment before getting started or entering any international market. Figure 2.3 illustrates the factors that an international marketer must appraise.

The challenges to Indian producers and exporters in the international marketing environment can be understood from the following sub-sections.

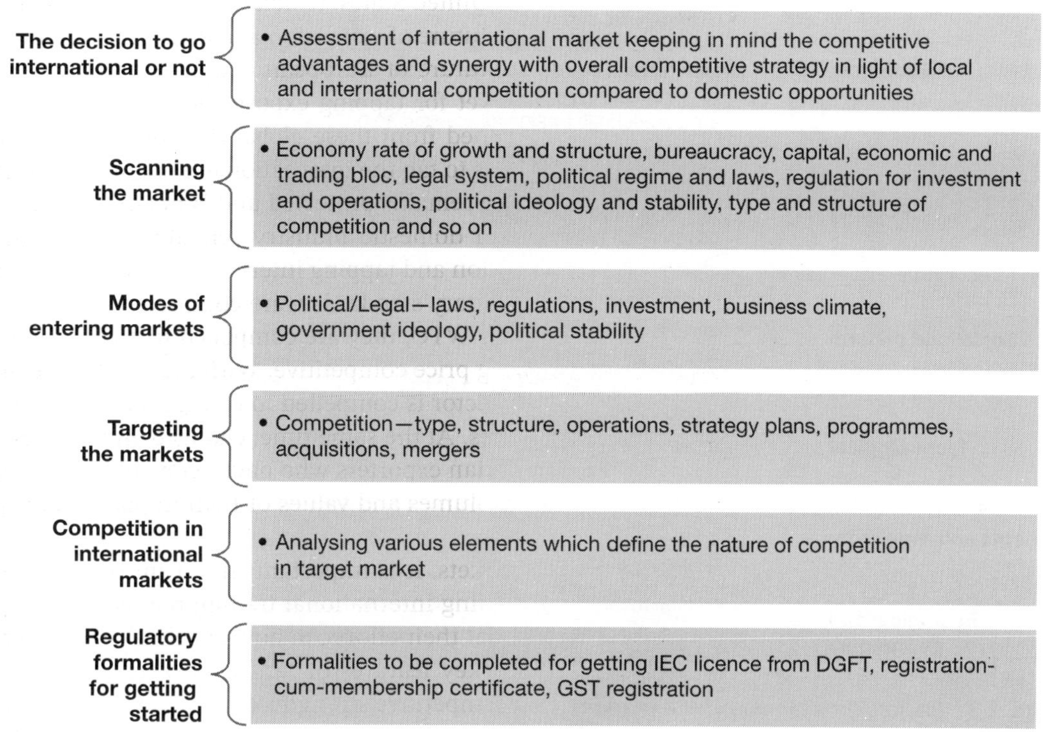

FIGURE 2.2 Factors affecting decision criteria for EXIM opportunities.

Source: Adapted from Lee et al. (2009).

2.2.1 International Economic Environment

Economic environment refers to those economic factors which have impact on the international trade. It includes economic conditions, economic policies, economic system, phases of business cycle, foreign investment, international organizations [the International Monetary Fund (IMF), the World Bank, WTO and so on], international trade agreements and so on. There are various international organizations which issue various guidelines and make different rules and regulations for regulating international trade. Among these important organizations are IMF, the World Bank, WTO and so on. Since the inception of WTO in 1995, the global trade policy has been shaped on the basis of various trade agreements as negotiated, agreed and ratified by member countries; for example, the Agreement on Agriculture is aimed at shaping harmonized and standardized trade policy governing the conduct of agricultural products and, similarly, the Agreement on Trade-Related Aspects of Intellectual Property Rights is for the protection of intellectual property through patents, copyrights, geographical indications and so on. WTO allows the integration of world economy through free and regional trade agreements. There has been a plethora of FTA signed and implemented by member countries, thus allowing member–partners the preferential and duty-free market access for goods as well as services. An exporter cannot underestimate the significance of such FTAs in world economy as such an arrangement can be a game changer either in favour of an exporter or that of his competitor (refer to Caselet 2.1).

Economic	• GDP growth, agri output, growth, size and productivity, level of inflation, per capita income, disposable incomes, taxes, exchange rates, financial architecture, current account deficit, size of the economy, composition of the economy, economic health, economic policies, fiscal inventory and entrepreneurial, foreign capital and so on
Political	• Political system, political installation, political ideologies of parties, political stability, political culture and so on. System of government, distribution of power between national and local government, culture of civil servants, government policy on business and so on. Risk, instability, attitude towards 'foreigners'
Social and cultural	• People, demographics, culture, subculture, pressure groups, interest groups, cultural life of people, rites, rituals, festivals, heritage invasion of alien culture, business culture, roles and so on. Values, beliefs, language, religion, education, literacy, time, orientation
Technological	• Current technological stage, rate of change, available infrastructure for research and innovation, technological orientation, research and development technology, import and absorption technological obsolescence and so on
Legal and regulatory	• Business-related laws governing competition, consumer protection, contractual obligations regulation of foreign participation, respect for judiciary efficiency of the same and so on
Ecological and geographic	• Natural resources and reverses, need for protection of fragile zones, pollution control, the geography of a region such as the terrain, vegetation cover, location, attitude, rainfall and climate

FIGURE 2.3 Factors for scanning EXIM markets.

CASELET 2.1

India–ASEAN FTA Boosts India's Marine Exports to Vietnam

India and ASEAN FTA came into force in 2012 and has brought an enhanced opportunity for export of marine products. ASEAN countries are major importers of marine products exported from India, and India's marine exports have witnessed a high growth trajectory post implementation of India–ASEAN FTA. In absolute terms, imports of the marine products of ASEAN countries have increased from \$3.67 billion to \$10.55 billion, almost three times in a decade. ASEAN countries' share of marine imports from India is constantly increasing from 4.80 percent to 8.35 percent which indicates that ASEAN countries' market for marine products is growing due to factors such as inadequate domestic supply, rising per capita income, higher disposable income and availability of cheap marine products vis-à-vis India's complementary products. Changes in dietary consumption can also be reasons for growth of significant import volumes of marine products for ASEAN countries. The following figure provides insights into major export destinations for India's marine products, that is, the ASEAN countries along with Vietnam, Thailand and Malaysia, and India's exports (million USD) to these countries. Micro-level analysis provides interesting results as Vietnam, which has emerged as the largest importer of marine products from India with a share of 73.69 percent in 2018, used to contribute a mere 20.55 percent in India's total exports to ASEAN countries.

India's Export (Million USD) of Marine Products to ASEAN Countries with Top Three Destinations

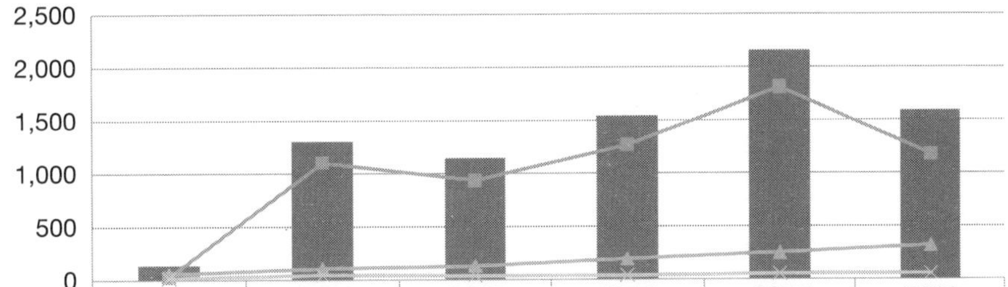

	2009	2014	2015	2016	2017	2018
ASEAN Total	136.904	1,301.796	1,145.066	1,540.801	2,156.041	1,592.862
Vietnam	28.14	1,099.07	933.63	1,264.64	1,809.63	1,173.82
Thailand	55.84	106.09	129.23	193.17	249.99	319.50
Malaysia	16.98	44.80	38.44	38.96	51.48	55.08

Source: UN Comtrade (2019).

Similarly, the export share of Thailand has come down from 40.79 percent to a mere 20.06 percent which is primarily due to the fact that at one point of time, Thailand was a gateway for Indian goods in the ASEAN region as India has FTA with Thailand since 2004. With introduction of ASEAN FTA, there is shift in trade from gateway to the actual buyer country, that is, Vietnam. Same is evident in case of trade with Malaysia which is the third-largest destination for India's marine products export. As India and Malaysia had FTA far prior to ASEAN FTA, Indian exporters used to route their export consignments through Malaysia due to lower tariff regime; however, with introduction of India–ASEAN FTA, exports to Malaysia have also shifted to other actual buying ASEAN countries. Destinations shift is significant as actual trade to each of the partner countries, in absolute terms, is increasing but marine products exports to Vietnam has outpaced the growth rate with each of the other partner countries, resulting in change of export share of each member of ASEAN.

Appraisal of international economic environment helps the exporters and importers understand the pattern and structure of markets and quantifies the size, scale, segments and sales system. An exporter should appraise the GDP size, growth rates, net national income, per capita income and disposable income per family unit, output of key agricultural crops, their growth pattern, cyclical trends and level of productivity. An economy can lead a path of prosperity and sustainable economic development only with improvements in indicators such as GDP growth rates, level of inflation, net national income and disposable income per family unit. India has emerged as a leading business destination for global suppliers as broad economic indicators of Indian economy are very positive on these parameters. Table 2.1 provides a snapshot of some of the leading markets using these indicators.

Per capita GDP, disposable income and size of population are of great significance for an exporter, as one can broadly extrapolate the demand using these three parameters. Level of inflation, demand–supply disequilibrium, taxes and duties rates, exchange rates, economic interlinkages among various sectors of economy are the key factors affecting the economic environment of any economy and should be properly scanned by an exporter while entering any international market. High level of inflation can

TABLE 2.1 Economic Indicators for Scanning EXIM Markets

S. No.	Country	Gross Domestic Product (Real GDP, billion)	GDP Growth (%)	Population	GDP Per Capita	Share of World GDP (%)
1.	United States	$23,315	2.27	325,084,756	$70,248.6	24.08
2.	China	$17,734	6.90	1,421,021,791	$12,556.3	15.12
3.	Japan	$4,940	1.71	127,502,725	$39,312.7	6.02
4.	Germany	$4,259	2.22	82,658,409	$51,203.6	4.56
5.	India	$3,176	6.68	1,338,676,785	$2,256.6	3.28

Source: International Monetary Fund (2021).

be of concern as it eats away the disposable income of potential customers and leads to economic instability in a market. Macroeconomic issues such as financial architecture, current account deficit, foreign exchange reserves, composition of the economy, level of economic development, foreign investment, ease in doing business, macroeconomic health, monetary and fiscal policies, fiscal inventory and entrepreneurial openness have an important bearing on planning of EXIM business with the target country. An exporter should also consider the level of foreign debt and foreign exchange reserve of a country, as it indicates the country's ability to remain solvent. If a country suffers from the problems of balance of payment due to lower exports, higher imports, increasing trade and current account deficit, unfavourable foreign investment flow and so on, then this will lead to lower or depleting foreign exchange reserves, thus putting pressure on the currency of the country. Such a scenario, in any country, may invite policy interventions aimed at restricting imports, promoting exports and attracting foreign investment aimed at local production. Economic sanctions imposed by an international body or a powerful country/economic bloc may also result in unfavourable economic scenarios (Caselet 2.2) of an otherwise very attractive market for an exporter. An exporter should always be careful of such economic scenarios emanating from any potential country of business.

CASELET 2.2

Western Sanctions to Hit Russian Economy Very Hard

Western countries, Japan and Australia have imposed economic sanctions on Republic of Russia for attacking Ukraine and violating its territorial integrity. These economic sanctions have huge cost for Russia particularly in a scenario of low energy prices. Economic sanctions resulted in shrinkage of Russian economy which was already struggling under the weight of low oil prices, high inflation and a battered currency, thus resulting in huge outflow of capital. Sanctions resulted in, among other things, the freeze of assets of Russian companies in Europe to which they have major exposure and prohibition on trade transactions with specific state-owned Russian companies and individuals. Economic sanction also aimed to restrict financial transactions of European firms with Russian firms and ban certain exports that are used in oil and gas exploration or have possible military uses.

One of the most significant effects of the sanctions has been the disruption of financial channels, which has made it difficult for Russian businesses and individuals to access global financial markets. This has resulted in a decline in investment and capital flight, as well as a significant devaluation of the Russian Ruble, leading to inflation and reduced purchasing power for Russian citizens. The sanctions have also affected specific sectors of the economy, with the energy industry being hit particularly hard. Many of Russia's major energy companies have been subject to sanctions, which has reduced their ability to invest in new projects and expand their operations. In addition, the sanctions have made it difficult for Russian companies to access financing for their energy projects, which has further restricted their growth. The defense industry has also been impacted by the sanctions, as many of the country's key defense companies have been subject to restrictions on their ability to access Western technology and financing. This has made it difficult for these companies to maintain their competitiveness and develop new technologies.

An oil price cap as introduced by Western nations would limit the price of oil and prevent it from increasing beyond a certain level. While there is no current oil price cap in place, if one were to be implemented, it could have a significant impact on the Russian economy. Russia is heavily dependent on its oil and gas exports, which account for a significant portion of its GDP and government revenues. If an oil price cap were put in place, it would limit the amount of revenue that Russia could generate from its energy exports. This would have a significant impact on the country's budget and could result in cuts to government spending or an increase in taxes to make up for the loss of revenue. In addition, a lower oil price would lead to a decrease in investment in the Russian energy sector, which could have a negative impact on the country's economy in the long term. Russian oil companies may also struggle to maintain profitability, which could lead to layoffs and a reduction in wages.

Overall, the sanctions have had a significant impact on the Russian economy, and the long-term effects are still uncertain. The Russian government has implemented various measures to try and mitigate the impact of the sanctions, such as promoting import substitution and increasing investment in domestic industries. However, it remains to be seen whether these measures will be enough to offset the economic damage caused by the sanctions.

An exporter essentially needs to understand the nature of economic structure of a country so as to understand the wealth and resources of a country in terms of the production and consumption of goods and services. As size, scale and level of sophistication of economic wealth of various countries differ significantly, an exporter must scan economic environment properly, especially the issues such as economic growth, per capita income, disposable income and nature of economy, that is, formal and informal economy. Formal economies are those which are driven by forces created by the market or are results of planned policy interventions of a government. The level of economic regulations in these economies is mature, structured and wisely planned. Informal economies, on the contrary, exist without formalized policies or regulations and have an element of economic anarchy. As a result, informal economies are usually characterized by lack of structured policy action and effective economic regulation by the government. In a formal economy, policymakers will have better control on monetary and fiscal regimes, wherein in an informal economy, the state can intervene a little without decisive and time-bound action for any corrective action. The formal economic system of any country can be capitalist or socialist or a mixture of both like in India. In a capital economy, market forces determine the economic regime, wherein in a socialist system, policy interventions are introduced by a government aimed at creating welfare for society. Informal economic system, on the other hand, is an underground system which is the diversified set of economic activities, enterprises, jobs and workers that are not regulated or protected by the state.

Exporters should prefer formal economies as they can operate within limits of established and monitored policies and regulations of a government whether they are capitalist, socialist or mixed formal economies. Exporters can accordingly frame their polices for capitalist or socialist economies wherein the major difference between two economic ideologies revolve around the role of the government and equality of economics. The capitalist model is based on pillars of economic freedom, consumer choice and economic growth, whereas the socialist model is an economy which is controlled by the state and planned by a central planning authority and is aimed at creating greater social welfare among public. The model is bereft of business fluctuations, as in the case of the capitalist model, as it is planned and implemented by a central planning authority of a government or a party. The key characteristics of both capitalist and socialist models are briefed in Figure 2.4.

While the capitalist model provides varied choices to consumers and leads to more competition and better products and services, the socialist model believes in mass production and mass consumption of standard products for the welfare of the society. There is no doubt that capitalist system is more efficient, and production of goods and rendering of services are based on demand which create incentives to cut costs and avoid waste, but not in the case of the socialist model. There is faster economic growth and expansion which increases GNP and leads to improved living standards than the socialist model. There are inherent risks in both the models of economic development; for example, the capitalist model as it

Basis of Difference	Capitalist Economy	Socialist Economy
Market structure	Market structure offers choices to both sellers and buyers wherein private sellers or corporate-owned companies sell variety of products to informed consumer	Production in socialist economy is owned by public enterprises or cooperatives owned by state
Profit motive	The goods and services are produced and sold by private players to make a profit which is again reinvested into the economy	Purpose is not to make profit but to create welfare in the society
Government interference	Very limited as it is free market, meaning, the market determines investments, production, distribution	Government makes and investment, does production and distribution planning
Free to operate	Capitalist economy requires continual production and purchase so as to operate efficiently	Socialist economy is based on the concept of central planning, where in it is the government which decides how to produce and sell in the market so as to create welfare
Economic thought on production	Capitalists believe that government does not use economic resources as efficiently as private enterprise	Resources are safe in government's hand and there is focus on large-scale government-owned industries
Basis of payment to worker	Workers are paid wages on market rates, that is, demand and supply along with regulation of welfare of individuals is the criteria for payment	Employees and workers are paid as per the principle of individual contribution

FIGURE 2.4 Differences between capitalist and socialist economies.

operates in the free market can create a monopoly in the market, wherein one supplier can abuse his/her position by charging higher prices which is not the case in the socialist model where prices are governed and regulated by government agencies.

In addition to the above, an exporter should particularly need to appraise the market structure of various segments where import demand exists. The marketing team of an export firm should specially scan the issues such as entry and exit barriers, number of competing firms, market share of each competing firm in that sector and average size of competing firms. Tariff barriers in terms of duty structure on imported goods are of vital significance as lower duty rates can make goods competitive in the target market and vice-versa for higher duty rates. Similarly, non-tariff barriers such as sanitary and phytosanitary (SPS) measures for food products and technical standards for consumer and industrial goods can render a product unfit for import in a target if specific standards of the import countries are not met (Caselet 2.3).

The growth of market is of prime importance and is measured in terms of local currency and adjusted for inflation. If a country is affected by frequent exchange rate fluctuations, its scope for market growth also gets affected badly as exports and imports become prone to frequent price changes mainly due to volatility of domestic currency. GDP and per capita are significant and help assess a firm that what segments of markets should be explored for export opportunities. Trade openness of the economy which is the ratio of a country's imports and exports to its GNP helps an exporter to understand the trends, patterns and vulnerabilities associated due to frequent fluctuations in international trade. Various indicators aimed at understanding a country's attractiveness for business are measured by the World Bank and are referred to as 'ease of doing business'. Some variables of such index are very important like ease in trading across borders. If a country has better rank in ease of doing business and trading across borders, it indicates that it has openness for setting up business and operating it along with the ability to export

CASELET 2.3

Red Chilli Import Banned in Saudi Arabia

India's spices industry suffered a jolt when Saudi Arabia banned the import of chilli pepper from India in 2014 due to high presence of pesticides residue. Saudi Arabia is one of the leading importers of spices from India. Saudi Arabia had decided to ban import of chilli pepper after a sample testing from the Indian shipment showed the presence of high levels of pesticides. The Saudi government issued an advisory to the Indian Agricultural & Processed Food Products Export Development Authority (APEDA), stating that high levels of pesticide residues were detected in some consignments of red chilli including consignment of fresh chilli, and when Saudi officials found high contents in large number of samples, they decided to ban it. According to the Indian Spices Board, chilli peppers are one of India's largest foreign currency earners, and being an agricultural commodity, it generates employment for a large number of people at the bottom of pyramid. India has exports of chillies worth $2.75 million to Gulf Cooperation Council (GCC) countries of which Saudi Arabia is an important market which is almost 28 percent of its global chilli exports. In terms of quantity, India exported 15,778 tons of chillies to GCC countries in the year 2014. GOI took this issue very seriously and ensured that quality compliance of India's chillies exports is maintained. The Spices Board and APEDA have played a pivotal role in this regard and ban on import of chillies was lifted by Saudi Arabia.

more and import more with efficiency and effectiveness. Last but not the least, a potential market must be economically stable as economic volatility in the country of import may affect scope for scouting for international marketing opportunities.

2.2.2 International Political Environment

Political environment is one of the most important and defining factors for appraising the business environment in international business. It refers to the influence of the system of government and judiciary on a country's internal as well as international business. The system of government, especially political thought and ideology of any political party in power, has a considerable impact on its trade and commerce and business relations with partner countries. The type and structure of government in power in any country decides, promotes and implements the suitable policy regime to foster, shelter and control business variables for economic development of that country. An exporter should also scan the political environment and appraise issues such as political system and ideology, political installation and stability and political culture of the country. Business leaders, especially the exporters and importers, look forward to a stable, honest, efficient and dynamic political regime which is based on democratic credentials, fosters people's participation in decision-making and assures personal security to the citizens. The developed countries such as Britain, the United States and Germany owe their success to a large extent to the stable and efficient political system they richly enjoyed. On the other hand, Zimbabwe, a once economically prosperous country, has become extremely volatile and poor mainly due to the ongoing political stalemate in the country (Caselet 2.4).

CASELET 2.4

Political Mismanagement Made Zimbabwe a Basket Case from the Breadbasket of the Region

Zimbabwe used to be the breadbasket for the whole of Southern Africa in the 1980s. After independence, it grew very fast, largely, due to economic reforms aimed at equal distribution of land, participation of the locals in the mainstream economy and foreign investment. In the 21st century, however, political leadership in Zimbabwe practised exclusionary politics which is characterized by fracturing the nation across political divides, wherein politicians are always on each other's throats and preach the message of hate based on colour, ethnic group and race. Due to political instability and mismanagement, the economy of Zimbabwe shrunk significantly from the beginning of the 21st millennium which resulted in an extremely volatile and ambiguous situation for the country. Zimbabwe witnessed hyperinflation and depletion of foreign exchange, thus inviting widespread poverty and a 95 percent unemployment rate in 2012. Hyperinflation in Zimbabwe was a major problem and as a result it suspended its own currency as people had no faith in Zimbabwe's currency. Political mismanagement has invited a complete economic catastrophe for Zimbabwe even after the fact that it has vast reserves of metallurgical-grade chromite, coal, asbestos, copper, nickel, gold, platinum and iron ore which can turn it into a regional economic powerhouse. Many political thinkers have opined that Zimbabwe's land reform programme, recurrent interference and intimidation of the country's judiciary, as well as maintenance of unrealistic price controls and exchange rates have led to a sharp drop in investor confidence, thus ensuring the breakdown of a once-prosperous economy. It is estimated that the Zimbabwean economy has contracted as much as by 40 percent from 2000 to 2007, inflation vaulted to over 56,000 percent in the same period and there were persistent shortages of foreign exchange reserves resulting in problem of balance of payment. Investor confidence dropped and traders refused to supply essential items such as fuel, medicine and food. Zimbabwe was once the breadbasket for the whole region and now it has become a basket case where general masses are suffering from hunger, shortage of medicine, high infant mortality and complete breakdown of law and order, thus prompting looting, snatching and rioting. Zimbabwe is completely cut-off from the world economy largely due to economic sanctions as politicians in Zimbabwe from across all political formations overestimated their capacities to solve the country's economic challenges. Political leaders have practised a game of outsmarting each other in the power game, thus wasting time and energy on trivial things and ignoring important things such as nation building and bringing people together and harnessing their minds and energy for economic development. In recent years, there has been considerable economic hardship in Zimbabwe.

In a globalized set-up, the political (Caselet 2.5) and economic issues are interrelated and broadly shape the international trading environment in which any business operates and flourishes. Economic legislation of any government which is aimed at contract formation, sales terms including legal issues therein, product promotion and advertising and consumer protection is largely shaped by the political thoughts that ruling parties have in a country. The political environment of any country has its direct bearing on EXIM operations, especially issues such as tariff and non-tariff barriers, restrictions on market entry, regulatory framework of licensing, restricting maximum sale price and provisions to repatriate profits to home country.

CASELET 2.5

Political Instability Forced Dabur to Shut Down Nepal Operations

Nepal has witnessed political instability post end of monarchy as the multiparty democratically elected government has failed to fulfil people's rising aspirations for economic development. In the imminent political vacuum in Nepal, dissonance increased among common Nepali citizens against enterprises, especially Indian firms which form the backbone of Nepal's economy. More than 80 percent of Nepal's exports and imports are routed through India and Indian firms enjoy leadership in almost each market segment of Nepali consumer and durables markets. There is greater mistrust and discomfort among Nepali people about the growing presence of Indian enterprises. Indian firms have been scared of doing business in Nepal after Maoists have forced a shutdown in one of the factories of an Indian company, Dabur, located in the Terai region, in the year 2008. Maoists, who are also in power with Prachanda-led government, have forced Dabur to shut Nepal operations, learning that Dabur is sponsoring the Miss Nepal contest. The labour union of Dabur factory which was led by Maoists were demanding a bonus, equivalent to 10 percent of the company's profits, for the workers in the Dabur plant which produced fruit juice. Dabur sells this juice under the brand name Real. The plant was located at Rampur Tokani in Bara district. It is important to mention that Dabur is one among the largest investors in the economy of Nepal, especially nutrition and fruit beverages segment. Indian enterprises, like Dabur, are facing the brunt of political instability which has led to lower economic growth, resultant unemployment and increased economic unrest among common people of Nepal. In the period 2000–2010, the Maoists had shut down several Indian joint ventures and burnt down Dabur's apiary in Nepal, thus evoking strong objection from the Indian government about the safety and security of Indians living in Nepal.

Government, whether legitimate or not, has absolute control over the territory, jurisdictions, economic law and allied rules and regulations as nations enjoy this power through 'sovereignty' which rests the absolute power with the state and enables it to take independent decisions related to regulation and management of trade and commerce, marketing of goods, external relations, domestic governance, economic assistance and defence. Such sovereign power in any country may rest either with the parliament of the country or president of the country or military dictator or council of ministers or prime minister of the country. The legal regime to form a contract and cancel it is governed by economic legislation which is framed by governments. Any exporter or investor must scan the political stability and risks involved including attitudes of the local population towards foreign companies; for example, Dabur had to shut its Nepal business operations as local population was extremely hostile to Indian enterprises operating in Nepal at that point of time. Any exporter or importer would like to avoid the political instability which may arise from the people's revolution against the ruling party, insurgency and terrorism, rebellion within ranks of government, civil disobedience, wars with other countries and a military coup. Political instability leads to frequent changes in government, thus affecting normal business operations in the country and inviting problems such as volatile international trade relations, falling economic growth and resultant economic activity, unemployment, youth unrest, food price inflation, rising foreign debt and increase in public anger. This can further catalyse problems such as physical destruction of a firm's assets, higher tax regime, import controls, nationalization, expropriation and control on outflows of foreign exchange from the country.

2.2.3 International Social and Cultural Environment

An international marketer, operating in an international business environment, needs to understand the importance of society in which he/she lives and operates business. The main factors of appraisal consist of the sum of a society's beliefs, customs, values, languages, rites and rituals, behaviour and business etiquettes and practices. Important elements of study in appraising the socio-cultural environment are discussed further. People of the country is a crucial factor as they become your potential customer. An export firm should also scan variables such as demographics, culture and subculture of a country which have an important bearing on business decisions. Our society is usually divided based on 'social classes'; for example, upper, middle and lower is the classification based on economic wealth. Similarly, in India, society is divided based on caste or ethnic group. The level of perception of each class towards various goods and services vary based on the social class they belong to. For example, the frequency of buying goods and services may be slightly higher in the case of upper and middle class than the lower-class income group. More so, social environment is dynamic, meaning changing with changes in the overall business environment; for example, in countries like India, perception and trends of the consumers towards goods and services are changing owing to the liberalization and the changes in lifestyles. It is important for an international marketer to also understand another important aspect of society, that is, '*group*'. It is a proven fact that the performance of groups differs in individualistic and collectivist societies. The 'family' is an important part of the social environment as some countries have a joint-family system, while others follow the nuclear-family system which affects operating business environments and product offers. The traditional family life cycle has been changing owing to the differing lifestyles; for example, the concept of a family without kids, DINKS (double income no kids) is also getting popular in urbanized society. Social class, group and family influence significantly the consumption and buying behaviour of consumers in a country. Nations vary greatly in customs, beliefs, practices and behaviours; however, there exist similarities as well. A ready-to-eat food export firm based in South India finds it hard to sell its pickles in European countries as it is considered very spicy and uneatable by the Europeans. Indian meat exporters have success in export of bovine meat in the Gulf and South East Asian countries but find it hard to penetrate Nepal mainly due to cultural similarities between India and Nepal. A kesar–badaam drink from Guru Brand finds it easy to export to Gulf countries but not to Africa and Europe as they find it too sweet. Values, beliefs, language, religion, education, literacy, time and orientation are some of the other important variables which no exporter can ignore; for example, association of a red-coloured dress is deep-rooted in the belief system of Africans as black-magic, aimed at putting harm to others, hence one should avoid red colour dressing in business meeting with Africans. Similarly, Kenyans belief that number 7 is unlucky, one should not use such number in pricing and invoicing to respect the feelings of local culture. Religion has an important role in any society and marketers use it in associating with a society through festivals or other occasions to market their products.

Mistakes in cross-cultural communication often go unnoticed by the communicators, but these mistakes have the potential to cause damage to international relationships and negotiations. It is not feasible for an exporter and importer to be an expert on the entire world's cultures; however, it is possible to construct a cross-cultural framework involving important cultural variables which can help the marketer understand the broad characteristics of a market. An exporter can never underestimate the importance of variables such as cultural life of people, rites, rituals, festivals, heritage invasion of alien culture and business culture of a market. For example, many European firms used the 'business model of intercultural analysis' involving variables such as cultural themes, the art of communication, the significance of numbers, ways of greetings, business mentality and group dynamics. 'Cultural themes' are an integral part of any culture and have a substantial impact on ways of doing business in a country; for example, Indian cultural themes are rooted in folk belief and core Hindu values which include practising joint family system, thrift, mutual cohesiveness, endurance and trustworthiness. These values are deeply engrained in the Indian consumer's psyche. Similarly, Chinese consumers are grossly impacted by cultural themes which are rooted in Confucian thought and values. Cultural themes have a profound impact on international business operations. For example, the Chinese negotiators usually practise 'protracted negotiations' aimed at testing the counterpart's endurance. Chinese will usually start negotiations with an inconceivably low-price offer to haggle with their Western counterpart about the price of the product. Western cultural theme preaches for straight eye-to-eye negotiation and as a result, European negotiators exhaust in trade negotiation as they are never prepared for such protracted haggling from their Chinese counterparts and make price concessions way too early. Understanding the 'business mentality' is an important element of the culture of any country; for example, Chinese business people are very punctual for a meeting, hence, it is expected that the counterpart is also available on time for any meeting or visit. Chinese expect that counterparty should have at least 20 copies of their business proposal ready as Chinese take business decisions collectively by involving each member of the negotiating team. The Chinese like only black-and-white drafts of a business presentation or proposal and one should avoid coloured prints. Chinese business culture demands small informal talk between leaders of both teams so as to frame an agenda at the beginning of a meeting. Chinese have a business mentality of establishing a strong relationship before closing a business deal and they prefer to meet several times to establish a strong rapport with the counterparty. Endurance is integral part of China's culture, hence, one should maintain composure during business meetings. Rushing to conclude a meeting or causing embarrassment or showing too much emotion during negotiation may result in loss of business deal with the Chinese. Chinese are very smart negotiators and endurance is a key in business negotiations with Chinese. Chinese negotiators intentionally extend business negotiations far beyond the agreed deadline to exhaust the counterparty's endurance on each specific part of the business deal and ensure that they gain maximum advantages by testing the negotiation strength of the counterparty. Accordingly, it is recommended that one should be prepared for delays in business negotiations as having patience in reaching a final decision can help you seal a business deal with the Chinese at lucrative terms. In business negotiations, one must be aware that hierarchy and rank are vital in China and business teams should enter the meeting room only in hierarchical order for the Chinese team to recognize the key members of the negotiation team. Like Germans, Chinese are also very particular about time as business hours are fixed in China which are from 8:00 AM to 5:00 PM. Like Europe, Chinese weekdays are from Monday to Friday. Chinese prefer to relax on weekends with their family members and they usually never entertain on an off day and after business hours. Some of the key aspects of Chinese socio-cultural aspects are exhibited in Figure 2.5 to provide a basic understanding in dealing with the Chinese in business negotiations.

International marketers are particularly interested in understanding the 'social values and norms' of potential customers so as to implement desired changes in their products and services. Values and norms are evaluative beliefs of individuals that synthesize affective and cognitive elements to orient people to the world in which they live. The international marketing team of any export firm must utilize such social values and norms of the host country and should adapt to the society's social preferences (Caselet 2.6) for specific needs and wants and accordingly offer customer solutions. Customer needs, wants and preferences are greatly influenced by their values, beliefs and practices. If marketers fail to understand social norms, values and preferences of a potential country, then such export venture is doomed to fail. It is the prime reason that business firms partner with societies to find out solutions to their problems and offer implementable solutions yet create a business opportunity for themselves. For example, Indian rice export firms have been successful in shaping the behaviours of European consumers towards basmati rice.

The international marketing team of an export firm has to also align their marketing campaigns to create trends that can be used by consumers, retailers and distributors. In appraising a socio-cultural environment, marketers must take cognizance that they also have to deal with pressure groups, interest groups, varied cultural life of people, rites and rituals and festivals of consumers and associated stakeholders in the target country and have to find a business opportunity for them. Marketers increasingly bank on synching their marketing themes as per local festivals so as to prompt potential customers for purchase decisions which are mostly driven by emotions; for example, LG Group (Caselet 2.7) came out with an extensive advertising campaign synching it with Deepawali festival, thus connecting with Indian customers. Festivities provide any global marketer a very good opportunity to reconnect with their current and prospective clients or customers. One can

Greetings and Conversation

- Handshakes are common but wait for your Chinese counterpart to initiate the gesture.
- Regarding titles of courtesy, most people should be addressed with a title followed by their last name. Careful not to use 'comrade' unless you are a committed communist of course.

The Art of Conversation

- Chinese people will appreciate it if you use a couple of words in Chinese, but make sure you are aware of the meaning and the appropriate occasions.
- In the Chinese culture, the questions 'Have you eaten?' or 'Where have you been?' are pleasantries equivalent to the traditional 'How are you?' in the English-speaking culture. Therefore, do not take it literally and start getting into details in your answer! Simply answer 'yes' if you have eaten, even if you haven't, or simply smile and say 'thank you!'.
- **Popular welcome topics** are themes about China: art, scenery, landmarks, climate and geography. You can mention your travelling experiences in other countries and include your positive impressions as a tourist in China!
- **Try to avoid** political discussions, such as the Cultural Revolution or Chairman Mao, the 'Tibet' and 'Taiwan' questions, human rights, animal treatment.
- Chinese people are very careful about strong negative statements. For instance, negative answers are considered impolite, so find alternatives (I'll think about it/maybe/we'll see) instead of a blunt 'no'.
- Similarly, if your Chinese counterparts say 'not a big issue' or 'the problem is not serious', they usually mean that there still are problems or that the problems are serious.

Body Language

- Body language and movements are things you have to be constantly conscious of when doing business in China. As mentioned above, you have to stay calm, collected and controlled.
- Body posture should always be formal and attentive as it demonstrates self-control and respectfulness.
- Be careful about what you do with your hands as well, putting your hands in your mouth, biting your nails, removing food from your teeth and similar practices are considered rude.

Numbers

- Always pay attention to numbers and their significance or avoid as appropriate.
- 8 is the luckiest number in Chinese culture. If you receive 8 of something, consider it a gesture of good will.
- 6 is considered a blessing for smoothness and progress.
- 4 is a taboo number because it sounds like the word 'death' and is considered unlucky.
- 73 means 'the funeral'.
- 84 means 'having accidents'.

Meal Manners

- If you are invited to a business meal, wait to be seated, as there is a seating protocol based on hierarchy. Do not discuss business during the meal.
- During a meal, 20–30 courses can be served, so try not to eat too much at once! The trick is to try a sample of each dish.
- Scorpions, locusts, snake skin, dog meat and blood may come your way—they are considered premium delicacies.
- It is also important to know how much to eat. Leaving an empty dish signifies that you were not given enough food and not touching your food is offensive as well.
- Do not be startled if everyone starts slurping and belching—these are signs of enjoyment while eating.
- If you are invited for drinks, you have to go, as building a personal relationship (*guanxi*) during your business is very important. Sadly or not, part of this implies participating in the drinking culture existing in the country.
- It might happen that your Chinese counterpart will test your ability to handle alcohol, especially *bai jiu* (common brand names are 'Mao Tai' and 'Er Guo Tou')—a powerful drink that might be compared to airline fuel! If you go for it, make sure to eat something beforehand otherwise find a good excuse—a medical one will be accepted.
- Giving tips is generally considered an insult in China, implying the recipient needs money.

FIGURE 2.5 Socio-cultural aspects of Chinese culture.

Source: https://www.kwintessential.co.uk/resources/guide-to-china-etiquette-customs-culture-business.

CASELET 2.6

Waves of Globalization and Changing Consumption Pattern: Europeans in Love with Indian Basmati Rice

Waves of globalization have resulted in migration of labour and capital from one country to another, thus bringing societies closer to each other. This has resulted in changes in consumption pattern also. Europeans used to primarily eat bread before the 1980s but with the arrival of a lot of South Asians in Europe and opening of food chains by South Asians has resulted in a change in the consumption pattern of the Europeans. The Europeans got in love with aromatic varieties of rice called basmati, mainly at the expense of traditionally baked wheat bread. This is where marketers stepped in delving into the preferences of Europeans so as to identify the right segments for the marketing of different varieties of rice, mainly basmati rice from India. Marketers divided the rice into broadly two segments as per cooking specifications of Europeans, namely as untreated normal cooking rice and the treated fast-cooking instant rice. This brought great fortune to Indian exporters as they focused their attention to treated instant-cooking rice and as a result, sales volumes of instant rice in Europe increased enormously, paying dividends to their understanding of societal preferences of the Europeans. Beyond segmentation, further understanding of social behaviour indicates that southern European countries show higher rice consumption levels than northern European countries, which is mainly because there is production of rice only in southern Europe, Spain and Italy. Furthermore, a difference in preferences is noticeable across Europe as customers in southern Europe traditionally prefer sticky, wet rice for the preparation of risotto dishes (Italy) or paella (Spain and France), wherein customers in northern Europe, generally, prefer dry cooked rice. Understanding of societal preferences further indicates that North European consumers show a growing interest in special rice varieties such as waxy or glutinous rice, jasmine rice, wild rice and coloured rice (red, black).

With increasing concerns for health, consumers prefer natural food and as a result organic rice is also becoming increasingly popular; the share of organic rice is expected to increase at least in the short to medium term as consumers are increasingly demanding health conscious natural products. Increasingly disposable income is also a contributing factor for increased demand of organic rice. As of now, Italy is the largest market for organic rice in absolute size; however, Germany as a market is witnessing the highest growth in demand for organic rice. Exporters from India and Pakistan are further trying to understand the specific niche segments of basmati rice and are looking at the following specific segments for further growth in sales volumes:

- **Rice bran:** Rice bran is high in demand and is produced from the outer layer of the brown rice grain. It is primarily used in cereals, mixes and vitamin concentrates due to its high levels of Vitamin B6, iron and magnesium. It is also very rich in fibre. It is exported from Kerala, India.
- **Rice bran oil:** Marketers are looking at increasing demand for rice bran oil which is extracted from the outer layer of the brown rice kernel. Scientific studies show that it is effective in lowering blood cholesterol levels. China has emerged as one of the largest exporters of rice bran oil. India has limited export capacity primarily due to shortage of edible oil for domestic consumption. Indians also like rice bran oil as it is good for health.
- **Rice flour:** Rice flour is very high in demand in Europe, mainly southern Europe. It is produced from either milled or ground brown rice. It is free from gluten and therefore non-allergenic. It is used to produce rice pasta, crisps, cereals and snacks.
- **Rice hulls:** Rice hull which is inedible outer husk layer of rice also has many uses. There is limited import of rice hull. It is used for animal feed and as fuel in power plants.

- **Rice starch:** Rice starch is required by pharmaceutical industry. It is produced from the endosperm of the rice grain and is used as a thickener in sauces and desserts.
- **Rice syrup:** Rice sweetener is also a value-added product but has limited medical demand in Europe. It is a natural sweetener, less intense than traditional sugar syrups and honey and is required by the pharmaceutical industry.
- **Broken rice:** There is a growing demand for broken rice in southern Europe. Broken rice refers to pieces of rice kernels, which are used in the manufacture of various products including rice flour and pet foods.
- **Brewers rice:** Some aromatic varieties of basmati rice are primarily imported in Europe by breweries as it is used as an ingredient in brewing, especially prized by some beer manufacturers where it is the premium ingredient.

CASELET 2.7

LG Connects with Indian Consumers through Deepawali Festival

South Korean chaebol LG is positioning itself in complete sync with Indian customs and traditions. It is promoting its products with a theme based on Indian festivals like Deepawali which set the mood right for purchasing by Indian families. The promotional campaign signifies the joy and celebration of festivals coupled with shopping of new electronics such as TV, refrigerator and washing machine. Indian culture is testament of great celebratory spirit coupled with shopping and sharing of joy with near and dear ones. The shopping offers of LG are aimed at enhancing the joy of Indian households with newer and smarter technologies so as to strengthen the spirit of the festivity. By these shopping offers with deep discounts, LG celebrates happiness with India and its people on the auspicious occasion of Deepawali and wishes to make every Indian a part of it.

plan out effective marketing strategies during the festivals that can help any export firm in making a better connect with their customers or clients.

2.2.4 International Technological Environment

Trade in today's borderless regime is driven by technology. In fact, technological development has only facilitated such fast expansion and diversification of foreign trade in world economy. An exporter must assess the current stage of technological development as the products must be conforming to the level of the technological stage of a country. Sometimes, countries witness very fast technological transformation due to variety of factors and an exporter should factor it in decision-making; for example, when Romania became the member of European Union, it witnessed very fast technological transformation with the introduction of European products to its market. Any firm with international intentions should also appraise the available infrastructure for research and innovation so as to map the diffusion of any technological advances among its consumers. Finally, a firm should assess the orientation of public policy for research and development as it will determine the future nature of industry in the country and resultant imports of hardware to facilitate such technological upgradation. An exporter must map the technological advances broadly in the six areas mentioned in Figure 2.6 which have shared the dynamics of world trade in the last two decades. First and foremost is the *increasing role of information and communications technology* (*ICT*) in foreign trade. Technological innovations such as e-commerce platforms have provided enormous opportunities for growth and development of foreign trade as the Internet allows both small and big companies to expand their global presence at a lower cost than ever before. Consumers also find it much easier and economical to find newer products and services, compare proposals from various vendors, choose the right price and order the delivery of goods at the desired place of whatever size and quantity. Similarly, *telecommunication technologies such as 3G, 4G and MMS* have a great impact on facilitation and development of global business. Some of the key challenges that exporters can overcome through technology are distance and language barriers in international business. *Logistics-tracking technology* helps exporters and importers to track their shipment any time, thus increasing their confidence to buy or sell internationally. *Logistics disruptions*, for any exporter, can be most troublesome as they result in loss of not only time and money but also important customers. An exporter can track the level of stock using barcoding, movement of goods from one place to another through radio-frequency identification and actual location of cargo through the global positioning system. Such technology-driven tools can help plan trade routes, monitor any trade restrictions or problem areas and track shipments. Exporters and importers are extensively leveraging 'logistics-tracking technology' to rework movement of goods on disrupted routes to get their deliveries back on track to desired destinations.

Similarly, translation and language-learning software and services can help overcome the challenges arising out of different language barriers for both exporters and importers. Software is crucial for both exporters and importers to be able to communicate effectively with customers, leaders and business partners. The key areas where technology has helped international business grow faster and at lower cost are exhibited in Figure 2.6.

Technological advances and international business are interconnected with each other and are highly interdependent as well. Technology transfers are the backbone of globalization of production networks and markets. The waves of economic globalization under harmonized policy regime of WTO have brought free passage of goods and services across the globe. Rise of low-cost production centres has been primarily due to access to technology from advanced economics which in turn has facilitated

FIGURE 2.6 Technology-driven international trade.

large-scale productions at low cost and with greater efficiency. The rise of the IT industry in India is largely attributed to technological transfers whether through contractual arrangement or through reverse brain drain. It is the technological transfers that have significantly made India a global hub for IT which is well reflected in India's services exports (Figure 2.7) where the share of ICT exports is constantly rising.

Globalization of production networks has been possible only through the technological breakthroughs in three broad areas: first being the seamless flow of information between production, transport, distribution and consumers; second being the speed of communication; and last being the efficiency of transportation. Large-scale globalized production at low-cost destinations such as China, Taiwan, South Korea and ASEAN countries has been possible only because of the sophisticated technological advances that these countries have made in these three areas. Technological advances have also facilitated the globalization

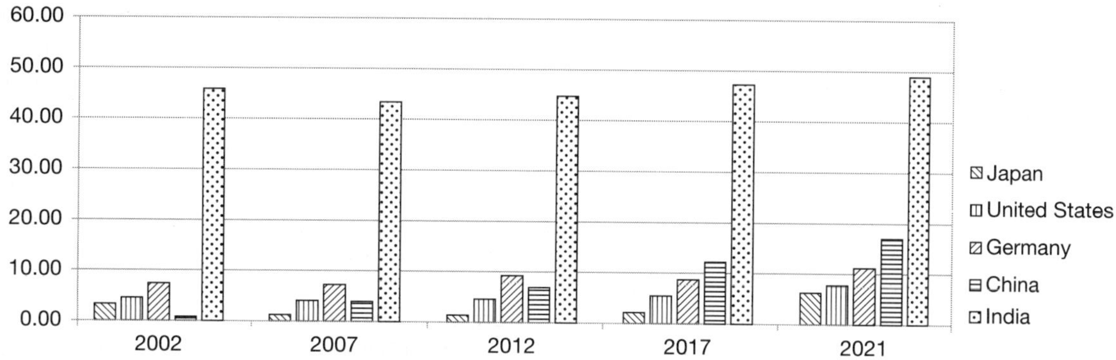

FIGURE 2.7 Percentage share of ICT exports as balance of payment of a country–India is global leader.

Source: World Bank Database. https://data.worldbank.org/indicator/BX.GSR.CCIS.ZS?locations=US-CN-JP-DE-IN&view=chart (accessed on 27 March 2023).

of markets. Globalization of markets means the process of integrating and merging of the distinct world markets into a single market, thus eliminating tariff and non-tariff barriers and also bringing homogeneity in the standards, preferences and prices of goods and services. Exporters leverage technological instruments to identify some common norm, value, taste, preference and convenience and slowly enable the cultural shift towards the use of common product or service among global customers. In fact, technological advances in transportation are one of the most significant contributors to growth and development of international trade. The ever-increasing size of ships has facilitated the movement of goods from low-cost production centres to areas of consumption at fraction of cost of products. Seventh-generation container vessel can transport as much as 22,000 containers (TEU), thus significantly reducing the freight cost due to higher economies of scale. The introduction of dedicated air cargo freighters has ensured that distance will not be a key factor in the sourcing of goods across the globe. Mechanized handling of cargo at technology-driven maritime and airports has enabled that loading and unloading costs are cut significantly and lead time for both exports and imports is reduced, thus paving the way for lower transaction cost in international trade operations. The modernization of both railways and highways with latest technological advances is also facilitating the effective and efficient movement of goods across the globe. The international marketing division of any export must appraise all such factors while venturing into any potential markets for exports or imports.

2.2.5 International Legal Environment

Legal environment refers to regulatory requirements to operate a business in a country. The legal system refers to the rules and laws that regulate the behaviour of individuals and organizations. Failure to comply with the laws means that penalties will be inflicted by the courts depending on the seriousness of the offence. The legal system of a country is of immense importance to international trade. Legal environment of a potential country helps an export firm understand the issues related to laws governing competition, consumer protection, contractual obligations, regulation of foreign participation, respect for judiciary efficiency of the same and so on. A country's laws regulate business practice, define the manner in which business transactions are to be carried out, and set down the rights and obligations of those involved in business deals. An international marketer should also analyse the regulatory environments and may have to confront different sets of laws in various countries of the world. One must consider the fact that international business is more complex than domestic business, as an international marketing firm has to abide by not only the domestic laws of each nation but also by the supranational and transnational laws which impose regulatory obligations beyond those which exist in domestic business. Figure 2.8 lists some of the areas where an exporter or importer can face challenges in an overseas market vis-à-vis compliance with the regulatory and legal system of a country.

Law governing intellectual property	Law governing consumer protection	Law governing environment and climate change	Law governing carriage of goods	Law governing competition among business firms
Law governing foreign exchange and payments	Law governing sales of goods	Law governing contract formation	Law governing corruption and bribes	Law governing food safety and marketing practices

FIGURE 2.8 Areas of compliance for law in EXIM operations.

As the laws of two countries may differ, it exposes exporters and importers to the challenge of deciding which country's law should be incorporated in the contract; in such cases, internationally agreed laws as framed by the member countries of United Nations General Assembly help both the parties to incorporate a neutral law, thus making an agreement consistently enforceable. Both the parties can also mutually agree on jurisdiction where litigation or arbitration proceeding will take place. It is easy for an Indian exporter or importer to bank upon internationally agreed UN conventions and treaties, as they provide transparency and help avoid conflict of law, thus giving confidence to both the parties to trade. The regulatory and legal system of some countries of the world is much better developed than others, especially that of developed countries of Europe, North America and Asia. These countries have an efficient system of administration, justice delivery and enforcement of court rulings. Gulf countries also have very fast and efficient system of law enforcement; however, it ignores certain aspects of human rights and is very rigid. An international marketer must understand the regulatory and legal system while entering international agro-markets. The legal system of most nations in world economy may be based on any one of the following:

1. **Common law:** Common law applies throughout the English-speaking world including most countries of the Commonwealth. These systems rely on precedents, judgments in specific cases and on ad hoc legislation to create and interpret statutes.
2. **Code law:** Countries with code law systems have all their laws written down in criminal, civil and commercial codes which are used to determine all legal matters. Most continental European countries and their former colonies have code law systems. Although they are quite different in principle, common law and code law systems have similarities in practice. A large part of the law in the common law countries is derived from statutes and legally binding regulations, while code law relies heavily on judicial interpretations of the words embodied in legislative codes.
3. **Islamic law:** This is derived directly from the Koran and typically is mixed with the pre-existing common law or civil code provisions of the country concerned. Important practical rules apply to the conduct of business in Islamic countries, such as 'interest payments on financial dealings are forbidden since it is improper to reward those with excess funds while penalising those who need to borrow. Islamic banks do not pay interest on deposit but give investors "profit shares" that are the result of the deployment of the funds deposited'.
4. **Socialist law:** Socialist law is predominantly popular in communist countries of the world and is based on the premise that 'the government is always right'. Such law rests all power with the lawmakers and government-owned enterprises, thus leaving limited scope of people's participation in evolving the law in a democratic manner. Socialist law typically lacks the sophisticated framework of contracts and fails to protect vital areas of free trade, intellectual property, investment and transparency trade regime. It is based on the premise of 'you do what the governments tell you to do' and is practised in few countries of eastern Europe, Russia and China.

An exporter and importer should be careful in apprising the legal environment as there can be legal disputes, disputed regulations, unethical state policies and the powerful domestic lobbies in the partner country which can create serious business challenges. The counterparty may apply such restrictive and unhealthy trade practices to disturb the business operations of an exporter or importer. Counterparty may also resort to unethical practices to import or export goods or services either by mis-declaring their values, quantity or description or by violating the state regulations regarding compliance with quality and other technical standards. For example, GMR Group (Caselet 2.8) had to face a lot of legal tussle against Maldivian government as it scrapped the licence to develop and operate the Male International Airport in 2012.

CASELET 2.8

GMR Group Stopped from Developing Male Airport

Maldives, a tiny island nation in the Indian Ocean, had cancelled its biggest foreign investment project which was for the development of a new international airport at its capital, Male. GMR Group, which has developed Delhi-based international airport, had planned to invest around $511 million for this project. The cancellation resulted in a widespread dissonance among foreign investors as it has exposed them to great business risks associated with this tiny island nation. The change in political regime has been the main reason for the cancellation of this deal as the new political establishment is pro-China and anti-India. The case was contested by GMR Group in arbitration proceedings and the result was not in favour of GMR. It was given seven days to leave the Indian Ocean island chain. The legal battle along with hectic political parleys which were aimed at saving the deal for Indian infrastructure firm had not been fruitful and had exposed it to severe political and legal risks in the Maldives.

Internationally engaged firms are exposed to some of the greatest threats and opportunities in the form of taxes and duties levied by the country of imports on goods and services. Similarly, corporate taxes are big challenges, as firms will always prefer to base their corporate operations in tax-free centres such as Singapore and Hong Kong. Any internationally engaged firm would like to carefully examine whether the foreign country has a tax treaty aimed at tax avoidance, protection of investments and repatriation of returns. Similarly, a firm can be exposed to legal challenges in intellectual property in the form of patents, copyrights, trademarks and other trade secrets. There is internationally agreed intellectual property regime known as 'Trade Related Intellectual Property Rights' as negotiated and framed by WTO, and as a result, exporters and importers have exposure to intellectual property disputes. Some of the common legal problems that exporters and importers have to face are related to licensing, quality disputes, conformity and compliance of standards, variance in quantity, adaptation of specification, especially of weight and measures, packing labelling and marking, difference between invoiced and realized value of cargo, restriction on importability and fulfilment of contractual obligation of negotiated contract. Sometimes, there may arise disputes on issues related to compliance of rules of origin of goods, transfer of profits and dividend and other state polices which often change without prior notice, thus exposing one party to serious disadvantages in negotiated contract (Caselet 2.8). One must remember that securing and enforcing these harmonized rules of WTO can be expensive in an overseas market. Legal provisions regulating the movement of funds/payments also require use of much brainpower for both exporters and importers. There can be exchange control regulations in at least developed countries making any small omission of compliance as criminal offence resulting in penalty or forfeiture of funds. One must understand that movement of money across borders is far more complex than in the domestic markets as, first, there is loss due to conversion; second, the fee for transfer is very high; and third, there is a risk of whether the funds reach to the right person or not. Finally, there are always legal challenges arising out of termination of business relationships. Exporters and importers can be in a messy position if they fail to address such situations early on. It must be noted that it is a lengthy and costly process to wind up a business in an overseas market. There can be interventions from the local government in the winding-up proceeding, and it may also result in significant tax consequences. Legal provisions protecting the rights of creditors, employees and investors, especially small investors, may pose serious challenges upon termination of business relations. In addition to this, there can be problems of limited access to the legal systems to redress grievances against other parties. Litigation is one way of dispute resolution which should be avoided as it is very costly to litigate, especially in a developed country; other ways of dispute resolution are arbitration and mediation.

2.2.6 Ecological and Geographic Environment

An export firm should appraise the presence of vital and required natural resources in the country where it intends to do business. For example, natural resources such as gas, oil, wood, metals and minerals are vitally important for sustainable growth and development of not only an economy but for economically viable business operations of the firm as well. A country deficient in ecological resources such as gas, oil, metals and minerals, water resources, forests, fauna and flora can never become an attractive investment destination as it does not provide environment for orderly and systematic development of human settlement. Environment protection has emerged as an important area of concern as human existence will be possible only in a clean and natural environment. There is increasing concern on pollution that some industries emanate, thus inviting government intervention or public outcry resulting in negative publicity for any internationally engaged firm (Caselet 2.9).

CASELET 2.9

Water Scarcity: Coca-Cola to Close a Bottling Plant in Uttar Pradesh

Due to increasing exploitation of water from a water-starved state, Coca-Cola India had to shut down one of its bottling plant at Mehdiganj, close to Varanasi district of Uttar Pradesh. This area is already under severe water stress and over-exploitation of water resources by Coca-Cola had resulted in widespread dissonance among local farmers who required water for their agriculture, the main livelihood for the local people. State licensing authorities withdrew consent for the Hindustan Coca-Cola Beverages plant in the state of Uttar Pradesh, due to falling water table in the district. Coca-Cola was blamed for over-exploitation of water resulting in water scarcity for other multinational companies which are also facing water shortage for their manufacturing and utilities operations. The step was aimed at addressing growing anger among agri-farmers and to save the other industries which do not over-exploit water resources.

This step has been significant in the context of addressing the demand for industrialization of state and to ensure the balance with over-exploited natural resources. Many parts of India are facing acute water shortages, largely because of wasteful irrigation practices prevalent in agri-farming in India. India has witnessed a similar case in the southern state of Kerala where a similar shutdown of another Coca-Cola bottling plant was to be done due to draining and polluting of local water supplies. The Kerala incident has galvanized awareness about conservation of water resources among multinationals and many of them have taken corrective steps so as to minimize the use of water or return back to mother nature by water harvesting and other similar means aimed at conservation of water resources. Shutdown of this plant in Uttar Pradesh has invoked a sense that there is need for greater concern for preservation of natural resources like water for our future generations and businesses have to learn to create a balance with depleting natural resources in their overall policy and strategy of business across the globe.

Similarly, interest groups are coming forward for protection of fragile zones posing a challenge for export firms. A depleting cover of mangrove in coastal area (Caselet 2.10) has been an area of concern for environmentalists, thus opposing the Adani Ports and Special Economic Zone Limited in Mundra, Gujarat.

An export firm should also appraise the geography of a region where it intends to export or invest in plant and machinery for local production. Geographical topography such as hilly, plain, marshy and sandy has significant bearing on business operations. Transportation cost is bound to be higher in hilly terrain wherein sandy and marshy areas will have problems of transportation. Transportation of goods whether for domestic or international trade is always a challenge in mountainous regions. Roads and railways are expensive and difficult to build in steep mountain valleys as, first, the investments are too high considering possible returns; second, it takes years to build infrastructure such as tunnels and bridges; third, roads and railway networks require huge maintenance cost; and finally, natural calamities such as heavy snowfall, avalanches, landslides and floods may block the roads and railway networks, thus defeating the scope of industrialization of hilly areas. One should also scan the vegetation cover because absence of vegetation cover will result in problems such as dust, poor air quality, climatic disorders and poor rainfall.

CASELET 2.10

Mangrove Case: Allegations of Environmental Mismanagement by Adani Enterprises

Adani Enterprises has set up a port facility cum special economic zone (SEZ) in the state of Gujarat on western fronts of India. The setting up of port required to reclaim the sea areas to achieve the navigable draft for both arriving and departing vessels from the Mundra Port. Adani Enterprise was given conditional clearance for environmental compliance vis-à-vis setting up of port cum SEZ, adjoining to coastal areas in Mundra, Gujarat. A committee, set up by the Ministry of Environment and Forests, had found violation of environmental norms in setting up of Mundra Port and allied infrastructure for SEZ by Adani Enterprises. Various environmental management agencies had alleged that Adani waterfront and power plant project had violated the norms of the high tideline and low tideline that determine the declaration of coastal regulation zones as mandated under regulatory framework. Adani Enterprise faced public ire over alleged environmental destruction and non-compliance with these norms with fishers and peasants staging protests against the group. The committee had used remote sensing technology and found that over 75 hectares of mangroves had been destroyed in Bocha island since the inception of work for Mundra Port and allied industries under SEZ by Adani Enterprise. Satellite imagery of the area as accessed by a group of experts including Sunita Narain found that there is deterioration and loss of creeks near the proposed North Port due to construction activities of Adani Enterprise. Adani Enterprise had also violated the norms for utilization and disposal of fly ash from its power plant. Discharge outlets were also not lined to prevent increase in salinity and contamination of potable water which was already facing severe shortage. It was alleged by the expert committee that there had been instances to circumvent statutory procedures of compliance by using different agencies of both centre and state and clearances were made in an opaque and ambiguous manner. The party that would be worst affected by the loss of mangrove was the fisher community, whose livelihood depended on sea and effective catchment of marine products.

In international trade operations, it is essential to know of physical settings or the geography of the market which is the environment structure of a potential country. Countries vary in terms of their natural features such as climate, soils, vegetation cover, longitude and latitude, weather conditions, topography, humidity levels, rainy seasons and level of rains and temperatures. The prime reason for understanding geographical environment is to explain the differences from home environment and accordingly adapt the product for such markets by taking necessary corrective measures. An exporter can manage such differences and diversity in geographic environment to his advantage only if he knows of differences and diversity of the potential market. Consumers' choice, irrespective of their background, is governed by where they are, what are they doing and choice of their location. This helps an exporter to locate different opportunities of business at different locations in the world market. In short, scanning geographical environment for international trade operations includes:

- Weather condition of the identified country and its impact on agriculture, industry and services such as transport and building design.
- Time zone, length and breadth of the country, distance, distance to travel.
- Topography—mountains, flat land—and availability and suitability of different modes of transport.
- Longitude and latitudes of country, tropical or arctic, number of days and hours of sunshine, seasons and difference in minimum and maximum temperature.

Appraising geographical environment helps an export firm to make better decisions in many areas of international business. Geographic data can be gathered and organized so as to devise appropriate business strategy of any export firm, factoring the vital pieces of information of the potential market. For example, the geography of a market has a big place in e-commerce exports and imports, especially the influence of distance on shipping products which are sold online. It is the prime reason that exporter firms rely on 'geographic information system' so as to gather and disseminate useful information about firm's products and services, thus enabling firms to save hundreds of millions of dollars through increased productivity and efficiency in the international trade supply chain. Understanding of the geography of a market also helps the top management to decide the location of plants or warehouses so as to plan the transportation routes for spatially located markets. The location and time of any international market are of great importance for those engaged in international business as export firms continuously face changes in their operating environment. How export firms respond to these changes can have far-reaching consequences for the geographical organization of their activities. Last but not the least, the study of ecology and geography of a market has corresponding relationship with other business environments—economic, social, cultural, political and technological. No export firm can succeed in international business without knowing about the people they do business with, that is, who they are, what they are like and why, how they interact over space, and what kind of landscapes of human use they erect on natural landscapes they occupy.

2.3 Minimizing Implications of Trading Environment on Business

For appraising the various facets of international trading environments, the efforts of international marketers are aimed at managing or leveraging them to the firm's advantage in the target market. This requires preparation at both ends, sensitizing the workforce about the issues, fundamentals and sensitivities of target markets and turning the table of host country's challenges into strengths for the firms. It is only the local communities who can preserve the local resources more effectively as their livelihood depends on local resources. The foreign firms, especially the exporters and importers from foreign markets, are not that bothered about resource conservation and management. Managing environmental concerns, that is, sustainable management of local resources has been the key area for international marketers. A case in reference as discussed above is shut down of the bottling plant of Coca-Cola in the state of Uttar Pradesh. Environmental concern has been pre-dominating the firms from international opportunities; a case in reference can be 'ban on plastic packing' and 'phasing-out emission' norms to stricter Bharat Stage VIth. Green, organic, farm to port are the established concepts in Western countries, and international marketers must inculcate and nurture this culture within the firm's international marketing plans and implementations. Accordingly, firms planning to tap international marketing opportunities can ensure proper certification and labelling requirements for sustainably produced products and make global customers aware to make informed purchasing decisions. For example, Government of Germany has put in place the system of 'green dot' license for mandatory disposal of 17 recyclable goods as per standard code of conduct for sustainable development. The sign of 'Swachh Bharat, Swastha Bharat' on all government sources, stationery and public buildings is an attractive way of educating the public about the benefits of cleanliness. The Export Promotion Council for Handicrafts has come up with the logo of 'VRISH' so as to promote the export of wooden handicrafts from India, indicating that they abide by the set procedure of EU Timber Regulations. Fairtrade sign for coffee sourcing from Africa is another example of minimizing the trade costs associated with environmental concerns.

An international trader should understand the implications of economic risks and know how to deal effectively and manage the macroeconomic circumstances that may result in significant loss for a business. As discussed, these include inflation, changes in exchange rates, new government regulations and other decisions that may adversely affect profits of an internationally engaged firm. There are many types of economic risks that an export firm may have to face in international markets and accordingly need to identify and manage to best defend against global supply chain risks. For example, changes in interest rates may pose a challenge to the rising cost of business as with any business loan, increasing interest rates can lead to reduced profit margins. Hence, an international marketer must research the interest rate environment of a country along with other macroeconomic fundamentals impacting changes in interest rates. Similarly, if minimum wages are increased, the cost of production may also increase resulting in the increase in product or service prices, thus impacting profits. For example, an increase in wages led to the shifting of some of the key industries from European countries to Balkan countries and from China to Vietnam, Sri Lanka and India. Changes in tax regimes may affect the business' profits. When a government introduces new taxes, it can negatively impact a business' financial performance. For example, Amazon faced the economic effects of the new tax regime as imposed by the US President Donald Trump in June 2017 which is known as 'Internet tax'. Amazon has been the largest victim of this new tax regime and accordingly is diversifying its portfolio so as to spread to newer avenues. The newer tax regime aimed at China has impacted the business plans of many Indian firms to make forays in the US market.

One should minimize the impact of political risks which are taking new and different forms in international trade operations. In the developed economies, respective governments are dealing not only with real and perceived income inequalities but also with high levels of sovereign debt, especially in the Eurozone. The sanction imposed on Iran by Donald Trump has exposed all firms which were dealing with EXIM operations. Indian exporters are badly affected as it exposes them to vulnerability on non-realization of export payments due to freezing of banking channels for Iranian banks. Other types of political risk including state actions to promote state-owned companies like the one implemented by the Venezuelan government to tap into the cash flow of companies operating within national borders to address the ongoing economic crisis can also pose international firms to risks for which they need to form a risk minimization strategy by deciding the time when to exit a market or minimize the losses arising out of nationalism, expropriations and so on. Firms engaged in international business are particularly exposed to tariff and non-tariff barriers which can be imposed by countries to cut their imports from a specific country or from all the countries; for example, the countries in North Africa, especially Algeria, Morocco, Tunisia and Egypt, have imposed homologation norms for imports of automobiles which favour European trade partners and are against the trade interests of Indian automobiles manufactures. Policymakers should have mechanisms in place to address such problems and minimize the political risks associated with such countries as such trade barriers have the potential to pose significant problems to many companies.

Minimizing socio-cultural risks is a major challenge for any internationally engaged firm as differences in socio-cultural environment can pose challenges of 'embedded' behaviours and beliefs that customers in a market have and an export firm has to adapt its product, price, distribution and promotion so as to adhere to policies or procedures. When magnified, socio-cultural risks can become a challenge for a firm's sustainable growth and expansion, and timely assessments of such risks will enable an export firm to distinguish between customers with similar or near-similar attitude and know how to apply practical knowledge from those who just have factual knowledge. By leveraging a socio-cultural risk-mitigation strategy, an export firm will pinpoint exactly where it can mitigate risk, reduce cost and increase operational performance in any area. Export firms can verify, in depth, the cultural challenges such as attitude, values and likely behavioural tendencies of customers as well as of prospective employees in a target country. Such a risk-mitigation approach can help plan, execute and implement the desired cultural and behavioural change initiatives and address the socio-cultural problems in the target country.

The challenges arising out of coping with differences in legal environment may be related to types of laws, for example Islamic, common or code law and allied legal interpretation of such laws. Any export firm involved in EXIM operations should document the business relationship when working with others in an international environment. All contracts including international sales contract (ISC) need to be in writing and signed by the exporter and the customer or client. Written agreements minimize risk by ensuring both the exporter and importer. Each party knows the law, contract formation and expectations from each other vis-à-vis performance of contract; thus, clarity is achieved in the working relationship, including confirming the scope of business performance, allied responsibilities and sharing of costs and risks and any other issue. Legal law related to 'intellectual property' is an important consideration; as business grows, exporters can take steps to protect intellectual property.

2.4 Summary

A firm has no control on external environment even in domestic business where it should deal with issues such as tax rates and policy changes to the economic structure, threats from competition, political factors, government regulations, industrial licensing and approvals, environmental concerns, legal compliances to different acts and rules and dealing with changing technological landscape. This becomes extremely complex when a firm enters international trade as it must deal with different business environments in countries of imports.

International trading environment is regarded as the 'sum of all the external forces working upon the firm as it goes about its affairs in foreign markets'. Knowledge of the various elements of external factors affecting the firm's engagement in the international market allows management to allocate resources so that they reap the benefits and operate with high efficiencies in any country. Hence, export firms intending to go international should carefully consider various elements of international trading environment such as socio-cultural, political, legal, macroeconomic, technological and ecological and other global factors in the context of the host country for correct planning of marketing strategy. Economic environment refers to those economic factors which have an impact on international trade. It includes economic conditions, economic policies, economic system, phases of business cycle, foreign investment, international organizations (IMF, the World Bank, WTO and so on), international trade agreements and so on. Political environment is one of the most important and defining factors for appraising the business environment in international business. It refers to the influence of the system of government and judiciary on a country's internal as well as international business.

An international marketer, operating in international business environment, needs to understand the importance of society in which he lives in and operates business. The main factors of appraisal consist of the sum of a society's beliefs, customs, values, languages, rites and rituals, behaviour and business etiquettes and practices. Important elements of study in appraising the socio-cultural environment are the people of a country as they become your potential customer. Trade in today's borderless regime is driven by technology. In fact, technological development has only facilitated such fast expansion and diversification of foreign trade in world economy. An exporter must assess the current stage of technological development as the products must be conforming to the level of technological stage of a country. Sometimes, countries witness very fast technical transformation due to a variety of other factors; an exporter should factor this in decision-making. Legal environment refers to the legal system obtaining in a country. The legal system then refers to the rules and laws that regulate behaviour of individuals and organizations. Failure to comply with the laws means that penalties will be inflicted by the courts depending on the seriousness of the offence. The legal system of a country is of immense importance to international trade. An export firm should appraise the presence of vital and required natural resources in the country where it intends to do business. For example, natural resources such as gas, oil, wood, metals and minerals are vitally important for sustainable growth and development of not only an economy but for economically viable business operations of the firm as well.

Minimizing the implications of economic risks centres on effectively managing the macroeconomic circumstances which may result in significant loss for a business. Rising inflation, changes in exchange rates, new government regulations and other decisions may adversely affect the profits of an internationally engaged firm. There are many types of economic risks that an export firm may have to face in international markets, and accordingly need to identify and manage to best defend against global supply chain risks.

Review Exercises

Multiple Choice Questions

1. Which of the following countries has the largest GDP in the world?
   a. China
   b. The United States
   c. Japan
   d. India
2. Size of the economy falls under which type of environmental scanning for global business?
   a. Political environment
   b. Socio-cultural environment

c. Economic environment
d. Technological environment

3. Appraising of the geographical region such as the terrain, vegetation cover, location, altitude, rainfall and climate falls under which type of environmental scanning for global business?
   a. Ecological environment
   b. Socio-cultural environment
   c. Economic environment
   d. Technological environment
4. Which of the following countries has the largest exports in the world?
   a. China
   b. The United States
   c. France
   d. Germany
5. Available infrastructure for research and innovation falls under which type of business environment scanning?
   a. Ecological environment
   b. Socio-cultural environment
   c. Economic environment
   d. Technological environment
6. State promotes both public and private enterprises, and such an economy is known as
   a. Capitalist economy
   b. Socialist economy
   c. Mixed economy
   d. Hybrid economy
7. Culturally, which of the following number is considered as unlucky in China?
   a. 4
   b. 8
   c. 9
   d. 10
8. Number 7 is considered unlucky in which of the following countries?
   a. Poland
   b. Japan
   c. Kenya
   d. Peru
9. What does number 84 signify in the Chinese culture?
   a. Having an accident
   b. Having a business hike
   c. Having a great relationship
   d. Having miracles
10. What is the largest exported commodity in India?
    a. Petroleum oil and lubricants
    b. Gems and jewellery
    c. Rice
    d. Tea

Critical Thinking Questions

1. Why is assessing the global trading environment considered vital for success in EXIM operations?
2. What are the key indicators that an exporter should keep in mind for appraising the economic environment of the target country?
3. Scanning socio-cultural environment is vital for successful EXIM operations. What precautions should one take while dealing with the Chinese?
4. What are the various ways and means to manage the global trading environment, and how can one minimize the risks associated with such a trading environment?
5. Write a short note on any two of the following:
   a. International economic environment
   b. International political environment
   c. International social and cultural environment
   d. International technological environment

Further Reading

1. Lee, Kiefer, and Carter, S. *Global Marketing Management.* Second Edition, 565, Oxford University Press: Great Britain and New York, 2009.

CHAPTER 3

Direction and Composition of India's Foreign Trade

CHAPTER OBJECTIVES

- To understand the historical perspective of India's foreign trade.
- To explain the present status of India's foreign trade in goods and services.
- To explain the direction of India's foreign trade.
- To appraise the composition of India's foreign trade.
- To explain the way forward for India's foreign trade expansion and diversification.

3.1 Introduction

Economic engagements vis-à-vis direction and composition of trade of a country are an important barometer to understand the process of economic development of a country. Foreign trade is an important instrument used by countries to transform their economies from traditional to developed, as exports and imports help in effective, efficient and systematic utilization of a country's economic resources in all sectors—agriculture, manufacturing and services. The direction and composition of foreign trade of a country are determined by the 'trade policy' of the country, paving the way for achieving the objectives of rapid economic growth and self-reliance. Economic theories such as absolute advantage, comparative advantage, factor endowments and product life cycle help us understand the static and dynamic gains of trade. Policymakers decide the future course of action on the basis of these economic insights and design a case for trade controls, phases of liberalization of trade and free trade. For example, when a country like India specializes on the basis of its comparative cost or production/service efficiency and designs its areas of export and import thrust, it becomes enable to make optimum use and allocation of its available resources. India gives thrust to export of pharma products as it has comparative cost advantage and to import edible oil as it cannot be economically produced in India at the cost of the import price offered by the existing supplier. In the whole process, output, income and welfare of its people increase as it produces what it can produce at a low cost and import what cannot be produced at the offered import price.

Understanding the direction and composition of foreign trade serves many purposes. First, policymakers can estimate the demand for key products in world markets. Understanding the demand pattern of products or services is an essential component of international trade. For example, the world market has the highest demand for electronic products, contributing an import share of more than 15 percent in 2019–2020, but India lacks both capability and capacity to produce them. India's export share in electronic products is a mere 2.5 percent. It is the prime reason that policymakers are giving increased attention to the production of electronic products such as mobile phones, chips, semiconductor items and computers. 'Assemble in India' programme started by GOI in 2020 is a testimony of the same. Similarly, understanding the import trend of value-added oil products in the world market has made oil products to be the largest exportable product from India. Trade destinations and origins also help a country to plan economic engagements such as whether to sign an FTA or not. Further, policymakers can invite investments in critically important technology where India does not have cost-competitive exportable products and lack capabilities in terms of technology. It serves two purposes, the country's imports become less and exports increase, thus resulting in the inflow of foreign exchange and faster economic development. Hence, for a developing country like India, the integration of the domestic economy through the twin channels of trade and capital flows is vitally important. Hence, capital inflows are also important for India as they lead to faster expansion of a country's foreign trade and may energize an otherwise stagnant economy to faster economic growth and prosperity.

Second, policymakers also need to factor the 'barriers to trade' which affect the balance of exports and imports. Barriers to trade can be of three types. *First*, the imposition of high tariffs can make goods unattractive in an importing market. *Second*, there are non-tariff barriers such as technical standards, sanitary and phyto-sanitray standards, and customs rules, which can add higher costs of compliance, rendering goods uncompetitive in the destination country. *Third*, domestic support such as export subsidies, benefits and incentives given by a country also impacts the direction and composition of foreign trade. For example, India cannot export many of its agricultural products to the United States and the European Union, as domestic subsidies offered by these countries outplace the competitiveness of India agro-products in these markets. Hence, the countries that are insular and have restrictive trade policies such as high tariff/non-tariff barriers and enhanced domestic support may be cut off from the global production network. Such countries may have higher trade deficits than countries which have liberal and open trade policies. It can be said that policymakers of a country need to factor these elements in their decision so as to pave the way for expansion and diversification of trade in the growing markets and product segments.

For a diversified export destination and deepened export basket, diversification of exports is extremely important due to several reasons. *First*, a diversified export basket, that is, having a variety of products in the export composition of the country, provides a hedge towards price variations and shocks in specific product markets. *Second*, diversified export and destination help a country to cope up easily with economic meltdown, which may happen in a country and region, by shifting attention to other countries in the large world market. *Third*, export diversification with more technically advanced products or newer products can open more business opportunities and help deal with competitors through such technological leapfrogging. Sophisticated products so developed shall be beneficial for all resulting in more trade and foreign exchange inflow, finally leading to higher income and improved quality of life, thus achieving the objective of a welfare state. Technology diffusion and innovations also help improve existing products across sectors both in goods and services and help them to compete better in global markets. Diversified export composition and destinations can be achieved in ways as illustrated in Figure 3.1.

Figure 3.1 illustrates that for having a diversified export basket and market destination, policymakers should endeavour to plan export diversification for products having revealed comparative advantage, sectors of strengths based on factor endowment or comparative cost, technologically superior products and variety in trading partners. Export firms as well as industrial units need to shift to a more varied production structure with introduction of newer products having product-length, product-width and

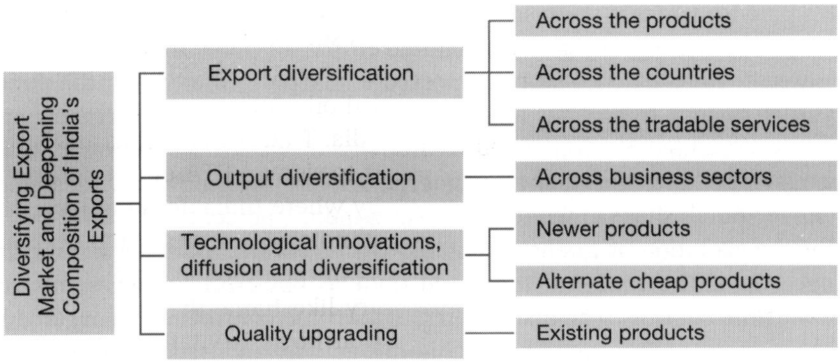

FIGURE 3.1 Diversifying export market and deepening composition of India's exports.

Source: McIntyre et al. (2018).

product-depth. Innovations aimed at upgrading the existing products so as to meet the changing consumer demand in varied markets is also required. For example, Bangladesh has achieved an export expansion in the sector of textiles and apparels. China has diversified its complete export basket as well as destinations. South Korea, a small but technologically advanced country, has decided to achieve export diversification in certain sectors—electronics, engineering, steel products, vehicles, ship building and medical devices—in recent years. India has diversified its export markets through incentivization with Focus Africa, Focus Latin America and Focus CIS countries schemes. Export basket of India has diversified and now India exports products across almost 8,000 tariff lines annually, but there is a long way to go for India as an export champion and economic superpower.

3.2 Evolution of India's Foreign Trade

Although foreign trade has been in vogue for past few centuries, it has been part of our life since the evolution of mankind. All ancient civilizations, be it Mesopotamia, Indus and China, used to trade with other parts of the world. The need for trading existed among civilizations even during ancient time due to the variations in availability of resources, skill set and comparative advantage. Indus Valley Civilization is one of the early urban civilizations (2300 BC) where trade was an integral part of socio-economic life. Trade routes in Indus Civilization were centred around oceans, seas and river basins of Sutlej, Ravi and Indus. Agricultural crops such as barley, wheat, melon seeds and oil crops such as sesame, mustard and dates which were grown on the fertile land were traded with other counterparts of the world. Crafted goods included pots, plates and glasses made of mud and clay and unearthed ornaments such as seashells, pearls and beads were also traded. The Harappan terracotta pots, coloured gemstones such as turquoise and lapis lazuli, metals and tools made up of flint stones and so on were considered to be a prized product in the international markets. With further evolution of large empires, trade flourished in India and merchants of the world used to visit India for trade and commerce. It is documented that India used to contribute around 33 percent of the world trade at the end of the first millennium. In the second millennium, even the invaders patronized the foreign trade although India was divided into small kingdoms and scale of foreign trade with the outside world became lower.

Barter system was practised among these small kingdoms to exchange the produce they had in surplus and what they needed. At the beginning of the colonial empire in India, India's share in the world trade was around 24 percent. India's rich history witnessed a sharp decline during the colonial empire as under the mercantilist system, India's raw materials were exported to Britain, in exchange for supply of manufactured goods. Dadabhai Naoroji called it 'drainage of wealth' as Indians had to pay more for manufactured goods in exchange for their raw material. India's foreign trade witnessed a sharp decline during colonialism as India's share in world trade was a mere 1 percent in 1947.

Internationally, the evolution of foreign trade had witnessed many changes; for example, the First World War changed the entire course of the world trade as powerful countries created walls around themselves with wartime controls. The dismantling of wartime controls was staggered for many years resulting in mistrust among nations and lower economic activity and trade, finally leading to economic recession. Powerful countries again leveraged this economic crisis to their favour and changed the balance of the world trade again. Many countries reaped economic fortunes due to fluctuation of their currencies and the resultant increase in foreign exchange reserves. Even the 'World Economic Conference' organized in May 1927 by 'League of Nations' which had drawn a multilateral trade had failed to revive the world economy and trade.

Many countries around the world witnessed economic meltdown, creating economic pressures on various governments to adopt protective mechanisms by raising the import tariffs. The mistrust among nations finally led to the Second World War. With the end of the Second World War, three economic institutions were created: first, to ensure macroeconomic stabilization among countries (IMF); second, to speed the process of economic development of war-ravaged and developing countries (International Bank for Reconstruction and Development); and third, to frame policies for liberal trade (International Trade Organization).

Under these disturbed socio-economic developments at the global level and with the objective of independence being achieved, India started its journey for economic development. World trade, especially among developed countries, expanded rapidly; however, India remained cut-off from such economic gains as the domestic industry was not ready and the focus of policymakers was also on 'import-substitution'. India's external engagements were largely restrictive, meaning policy regime for expansion and diversification of both exports and imports was largely controlled. It was only from 1969 that India decided to tap the increased export opportunities, supported by large trade institutions, bodies and export promotion councils (EPCs). The period from 1947 to 1969 was largely marked by a persistent shortage of foreign exchange and deficit in trade balance because trade policy had put greater emphasis on import restrictions rather than focusing on exports expansion. Due to shortage of foreign exchange, India engaged in barter system of trade with the Soviet Union and other countries with which India used to enjoy friendly relations. Following are some of the important developments vis-à-vis evolution of India's foreign trade in the initial decades.

- Export, as well as import regime, was largely restrictive. Policymakers paid no attention to external sector engagements.
- Import substitution was the theme, especially for agricultural items. Accordingly, the focus of the First Five-Year Plan was on agriculture.
- Imports expanded manifold mainly to fulfil the needs of economic development of the country.
- The Mudaliar Committee recommended framing of EXIM policy.
- Devaluation of rupee was done for the first time so as to boost exports with the framing of FTP.

Similarly, during the period 1970–1980, the following were the key developments in the evolution of India's foreign trade:

- GOI framed the progressive export policy in India aimed at mobilizing domestic resources for the expansion of exports.
- India passed the Export Policy Bill in 1970 as rising oil prices had hit India's exports and increased import bills.
- The United States offered India the non-reciprocal trade preference through Generalized System of Preferences scheme.
- India witnessed a trade surplus for the first time after Independence in 1972–1973 and again in 1977–1978.
- Gems and jewellery emerged as the focal area of India exports, supported by plantation crops, textiles and engineering goods.
- The share of manufactured goods in India's exports witnessed a sharp increase.

During the period 1980–1990, following were the key developments in India's foreign trade:

- Rising import bills compelled India to approach the IMF for economic stabilization fund in 1981.
- Trade deficit compelled policymakers to curb the policy of easy import licences.
- Policymakers focused on export promotion and import liberalization with the longer objective of speeding up economic activity and reducing the trade deficits. Policy plan for this was recommended by the Tandon Committee.
- Further, the Abid Hussain Committee (1985) recommended an approach of balancing import liberalization with export promotion. Accordingly, GOI continued the policy of import liberalization so as to speed up manufacturing and resultant trade.

During the period 1990–2000, following events shaped the evolution of India's foreign trade:

- Liberalized industrial policy was enacted in 1991, so as to end licence raj and promote industrial manufacturing.
- Gulf war, rising oil prices, domestic challenges on political as well as economic fronts coupled with the rising insurgency in Kashmir vitiated the economic environment of the country. Imports were rising, whereas exports were lagging. In this context, economic reforms were initiated by Rao–Singh duo who steered the economy from crisis to normalcy.
- The process of economic liberalization started in 1991, leading to great transformational phoenix. Tariff and non-tariff barriers were reduced but not eliminated. Licence raj was largely uprooted.
- The period of EXIM policy was increased to five years from the existing three years.
- Devaluation of currency promoted exports from India in a big way.
- Export scrips were introduced which allowed duty-free imports. It resulted in making exports attractive for domestic firms, especially which were import-dependent as duty credit scrips can be used for payment of custom duties which were very high.
- Waves of globalization facilitated the entry of foreign firms into India, thus promoting foreign investment, speeding up economic development and exports.

- India followed a three-tier policy of liberalization, industrial privatization and macroeconomic globalization, catalysing faster economic development of the country.
- Liberalized exchange rate management system was introduced, and currency value was largely determined by market forces with managed peg.
- Growth of exports was much higher than imports, thus bridging the gaps leading to favourable balance of payment in the country.
- Entry into WTO (1995) heralded new environment and challenges, and India's exporters stood to occasion to surpass all barriers and win global markets.
- Services exports from India became the buzz in the global markets as US-returned and globally exposed IT professionals set-up business centres in India at low cost to cater to vast markets of the United States and Europe.

India emerged on the global landscape in the 21st century with new vigour as it is now recognized as the most attractive market in the world. India's trade witnessed huge jump in 2000–2010 due to the following reasons:

- The policy of SEZs was introduced, leading to dedicated export production and assured foreign exchange realization.
- Global economic boom from 2004 to 2008 helped increase both exports and imports at a very fast pace. This was one of the finest decades in terms of evolution of India's foreign trade with quantum jump in exports as well as imports.
- Exports basket became very diversified with exports to almost 182 countries and deep with trade of more than 8,500 tariff lines.
- Foreign exchange earnings from services exports coupled with an increasing value of remittances helped register positive current account deficit for many years in this decade.
- Sub-prime crisis could not wither the confidence of Indian economy, both domestically and internationally.
- FTAs were negotiated; for example, India–Sri Lanka FTA became operational.

The decade 2010–2020 was one of the most challenging decades as India's exports could not register a jump, stuck at the $300 billion bracket, many years even lower. Some of the events shaping the evolution of India's foreign trade are listed as follows:

- India signed several PTAs/FTAs, especially in the period 2010–2013.
- Export could not witness jump as this decade was one of the most turmoiled, coining terms like volatile, uncertain, complex and ambiguous as India's most important market, the United States, was still recovering from shocks of sub-prime crisis.
- The European market also witnessed a recessionary trend due to the Greek economic crisis. The exit of the United Kingdom from the European Union has further vitiated the economic atmosphere of EU countries for enhanced trade and commerce.
- Proliferation of non-tariff barriers increased the cost of compliance and cost of trade.
- India could not reap the commensurate economic gains from rising Asia as Indian products were priced-out in these competitive markets of ASEAN, Far East and China.

- FTAs did not translate into economic gains that India had imagined, and India registered an increasing negative balance of payment with all FTA partners, ASEAN countries, Japan and South Korea.
- Bitten by bitter experience of the existing FTA and realizing the fact that Indian industries still have structural challenges of technology, scale, scope, system and sophistication, policymakers were hesitant to enter Regional Comprehensive Economic Partnership, even after seven years of trade negotiations.
- Import substitutions became the buzz with programmes like 'Make in India' for defence production and 'Assemble in India' for electronics and engineering goods.
- Rising domestic concerns and political ideology of policymakers that 'India has to be developed by the Indians' led to slowing up of the process of economic reforms.
- There is no definitive policy breakthrough for increasing exports. It is more of a hit-and-trial method of increasing export incentives, lowering EXIM finance rates, increasing duty drawbacks and so on. Strategic thinking to break the deadlock is missing in recent policy initiatives.

In these 75 years, the patterns of India's foreign trade have changed from mainly as exporter of agro-products and raw material to exporter of finished goods. Foreign trade has expanded significantly; for example, exports were mere $18 billion in 1991 which has become almost US$447 billion in 2022–2023. Similarly, imports have grown from a mere $24 billion to US$714.24 billion in 2022–2023 (https://www.pib.gov.in/PressReleasePage.aspx?PRID=1916220, accessed on 26 April 2023). In the past three decades, the Indian economy has transformed from a closed economy to an emerging economy, widely recognized at the global level and is factored as the growth engine of global economy. In terms of trade, India must go a long way as India stands at number 10 in the list of largest importing countries and 18 in the list of largest exporting countries. India's export destination has also changed, from the USSR in initial decades to developed markets of Europe and North America and finally moving towards the Asian countries in the last decade.

3.3 Direction of India's Foreign Trade

India's export destinations have diversified since Independence, both country-wise and region-wise, in the world market. Sources of imports have also witnessed metamorphic changes since Independence. India is the third-largest economy of the world in the terms of purchasing power parity, fifth largest in real GDP and seventh largest in terms of geographic area. India stands at first position in terms of population, but unfortunately, 18th largest in terms of exports and 10th largest in terms of imports in the world. Figure 3.2 illustrates the exports, imports and balance of trade of India wherein the India has constantly rising trade deficit.

Such a change in EXIM destinations is expected as: first, India's foreign trade expanded rapidly with the reforms measures introduced by GOI since 1991; second, formerly state-run economy is now a market-driven economy; third, services trade has contributed significantly to India's foreign trade; fourth, Asian countries witnessed rapid trade expansion and India's engagements in the Asian region contributed to growth of both exports and imports; fifth, India's trade basket has become far more deeper; sixth, young professionals are leading India's foreign trade story to newer heights and avenues—largely driven by market dynamics—and finally, global trade institutions like WTO have

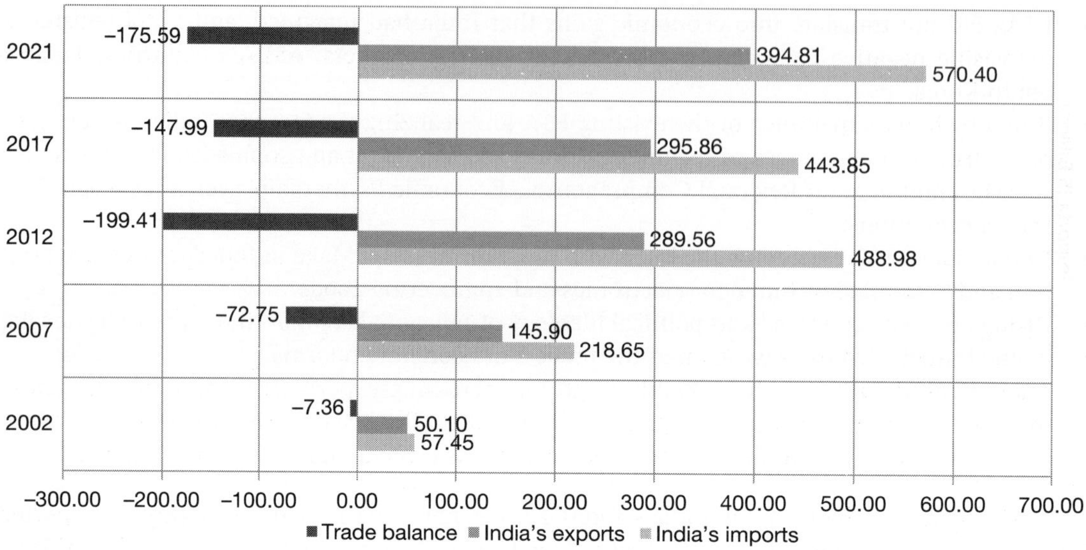

FIGURE 3.2 India's exports, imports and trade balance ($ Billion).

Source: UN Comtrade. https://www.trademap.org/Product_SelProductCountry.aspx?nvpm=1%7c699%7c%7c%7c%7cTOTAL%7c%7c%7c2%7c1%7c1%7c1%7c1%7c1%7c1%7c1%7c1%7c1 (accessed on 28 March 2023).

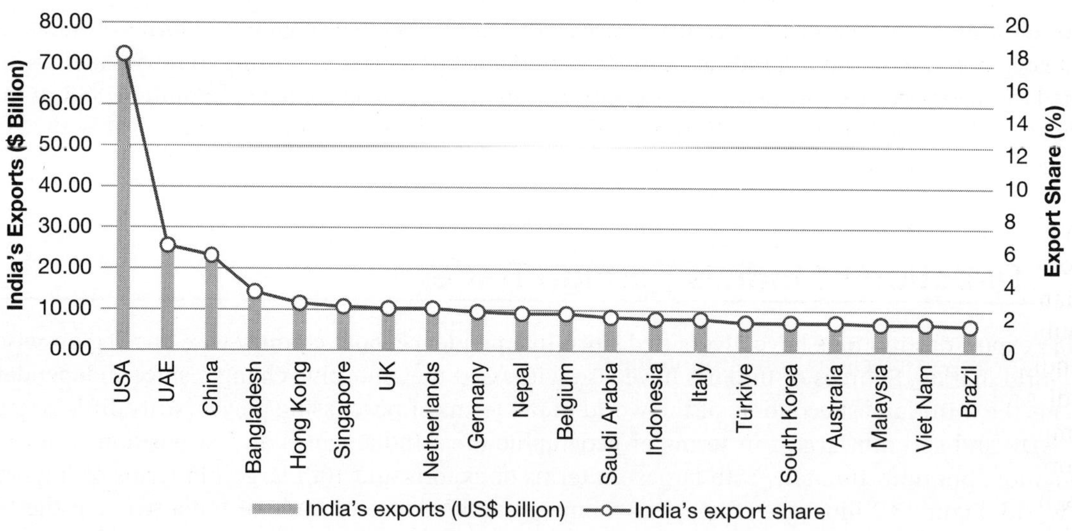

FIGURE 3.3 India's exports in $ billion in 2021 with export share (%).

Source: UN Comtrade. https://www.trademap.org/Country_SelProductCountry_TS.aspx?nvpm=1%7c699%7c%7c%7c%7cTOTAL%7c%7c%7c2%7c1%7c1%7c2%7c2%7c1%7c2%7c4%7c1%7c1 (accessed on 28 March 2023).

provided transparent, non-discriminatory and rule-based trade rules leading to faster expansion of global foreign trade. Country-wise, India's exports with key trade partners along with exports share (%) is exhibited in Figure 3.3.

The key destinations for India's exports are the United States, the United Arab Emirates, China, Hong Kong and Singapore. The United Arab Emirates, Hong Kong and Singapore have emerged as

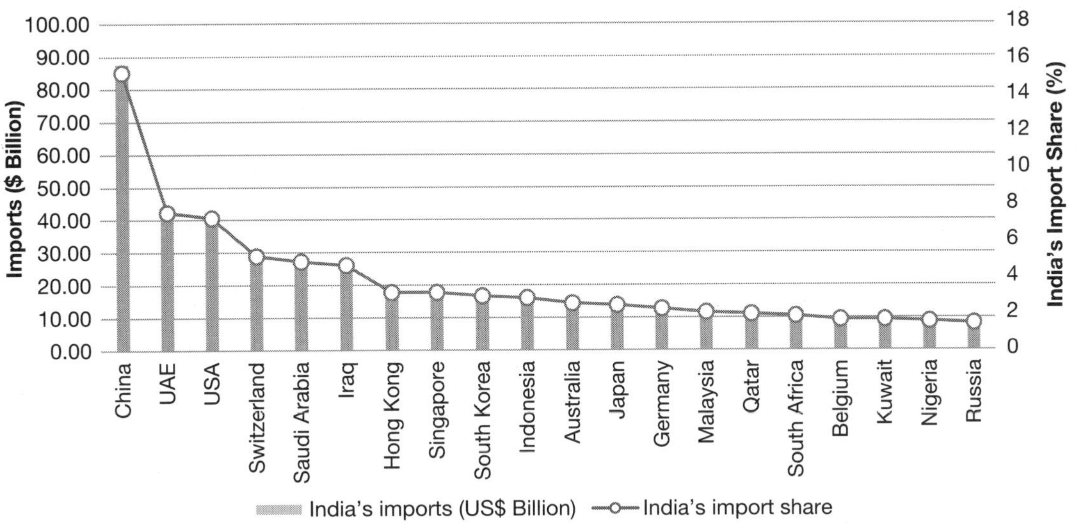

FIGURE 3.4 India's import partners in $ billion & import share (%) in 2021.

Source: UN Comtrade. https://www.trademap.org/Country_SelProductCountry_TS.aspx?nvpm=1%7c699%7c%7c%7c%7cTOTAL%7c%7c%7c2%7c1%7c1%7c2%7c2%7c1%7c2%7c4%7c1%7c1 (accessed on 28 March 2023).

major trading centres from where India's goods are trans-shipped to final markets which are not well connected with India in terms of logistics and banking facilities. For example, a small Gulf country, the United Arab Emirates, is India's second-largest trading partner, as it has Jebel Ali Port, along with free trade and warehousing zone. Indian merchants ship goods to Jebel Ali Port, which is the most efficient and well-connected port of the GCC region, and finally, Indian goods are moved to markets of Saudi Arabia, Oman, Bahrain, Qatar, Kuwait, Iraq and Iran. Due to economic sanctions, a lot of trade with Iran is also routed through the United Arab Emirates. Similarly, Singapore is a gateway for Indian exporters to markets of East Asia region. Hong Kong is one of the most facilitative financial centres and Indian exporters ship their cargo to Hong Kong, from where it ends up in markets of China, the Republic of Korea, Japan and even North America.

India is importing cargo from around the world with major suppliers being China, the United States, Saudi Arabia, the United Arab Emirates and Iraq. Its main exports are largely import-dependent; for example, India imports petroleum crude from Saudi Arabia, Iraq and the United Arab Emirates and exports it to markets of the world after processing and value addition. China, a factory for world markets, is the largest supplier of India and India imports a variety of products from China such as engineering, electronics, pharma inputs and excipients, chemicals and silk. The United States is the second-largest supplier of goods and in recent years, India's imports have increased so as to address the US concerns on rising trade deficit between the two countries. India has started importing a lot of crude oil from the United States in the recent years. Figure 3.4 explains the import partners and import share of top suppliers to India in 2021.

Table 3.1 provides insights into changing direction of India's exports. India's exports have grown 23.24 times in the period 1988–2018. Exports to Latin America have however expanded much faster as India's trade engagements with Latin America and the Caribbean were negligible. With the opening of Indian economy coupled with waves of globalization and rule-based trade under WTO has enabled Indian exporters to expand and diversify their export operations to these far-flung regions of the world.

TABLE 3.1 Region-wise Exports (US$) from India (2016–2017 to 2022–2023 – up to January 2023)

Region/Countries	2016–2017	2017–2018	2018–2019	2019–2020	2020–2021	2021–2022	2022–2023 (P)
Europe	53.33	60.35	64.38	60.56	55.32	86.15	80.02
Africa	23.13	24.90	28.54	28.99	27.73	40.22	42.43
North America	47.68	54.17	59.12	59.58	57.68	84.31	73.28
Latin America	7.23	8.61	9.74	10.06	10.10	14.93	15.05
Asia	137.75	149.64	161.22	146.63	135.82	189.48	154.25
CIS & Baltics	2.79	3.01	3.47	4.19	4.06	4.71	3.78
Unspecified Region	3.94	2.85	3.62	3.35	1.09	2.09	3.25
Total	275.85	303.53	330.08	313.36	291.81	421.89	372.07

Source: Ministry of Commerce and Industry, Government of India. https://www.indiastat.com/table/foreign-trade/region-country-wise-exports-us$-india-2016-2017-20/820400 (accessed on 28 March 2023).

Similarly, there were issues of transport connectivity to Sub-Saharan Africa. India increased its exports engagement with these countries with improved transportation, shipping and communication services. India's exports have grown faster to all regions, except North America, than the national average.

Since Independence, India's trade has witnessed many changes in both direction and composition. India exports to all regions; however, around a quarter of India's exports go to East Asia and Pacific region, followed by Europe and Central Asia (20.92%), Middle East and North Africa (17.32%), North America (16.89%), South Asia (7.65%), Sub-Saharan Africa (6.42%) and Latin America and the Caribbean (4.09%). India's export engagements are getting deeper with variety of products exported from India to world markets. Table 3.2 provides the insights of key products' exports to some of the key markets of India.

TABLE 3.2 Selected Country-wise Export (US$ billion) of Major Commodities from India (2022–2023, up to January 2023)

Commodities	USA	UAE	Netherland	China	Singapore	Bangladesh	UK
Petroleum products	4.79	6.62	8.89	1.61	3.98	0.80	0.77
Pearl, precs, semiprecs stones	7.98	1.93	0.01	0.05	0.59	0.00	0.20
Drug formulations, biologicals	5.53	0.13	0.39	0.04	0.05	0.06	0.42
Iron and steel	0.81	0.92	0.28	0.34	0.02	0.27	0.19
Gold and other precs metal jewellery	2.89	2.57	0.02	0.00	0.56	0.00	0.32
Electric machinery and equipment	2.34	0.31	0.10	0.14	0.44	0.13	0.56
Telecom instruments	1.65	2.25	0.96	0.15	0.05	0.01	0.70
Organic chemicals	1.18	0.26	0.50	0.61	0.29	0.08	0.07
Products of iron and steel	2.62	0.36	0.25	0.07	0.08	0.17	0.29

Commodities	USA	UAE	Netherland	China	Singapore	Bangladesh	UK
Aluminium, products of aluminium	0.92	0.09	0.78	0.22	0.01	0.22	0.08
RMG cotton including accessories	2.65	0.50	0.35	0.03	0.02	0.01	0.71
Indl. machinery for dairy, etc.	1.41	0.23	0.16	0.23	0.34	0.36	0.09
Motor vehicle/cars	0.19	0.39	0.01	0.01	0.00	0.12	0.00
Marine products	2.24	0.12	0.11	1.24	0.03	0.03	0.12
Residual chemical and allied product	0.91	0.28	0.37	0.38	0.11	0.15	0.13
Auto components/parts	1.47	0.14	0.04	0.10	0.02	0.33	0.11
Cotton fabrics, made-ups, etc.	2.06	0.15	0.09	0.02	0.00	0.46	0.18
Rice (other than Basmati)	0.03	0.12	0.01	0.47	0.05	0.26	0.01
Other commodities	1.22	0.66	0.05	0.06	0.24	0.51	0.06
Agro-chemicals	1.29	0.05	0.05	0.07	0.03	0.07	0.05
Man-made yarn, fabrics, made-ups	0.62	0.28	0.07	0.03	0.01	0.24	0.13
Sugar	0.01	0.27	0.00	0.14	0.02	0.30	0.00
Bulk drugs, drug intermediates	0.44	0.12	0.09	0.21	0.03	0.14	0.07
Rice, Basmati	0.20	0.26	0.05	0.00	0.01	0.01	0.10
Other misc. engineering items	1.19	0.14	0.06	0.10	0.04	0.03	0.16
Sub total	46.64	19.15	13.67	6.33	7.04	4.75	5.54
Total export	65.54	25.90	16.36	12.20	9.77	9.66	9.39

Source: Ministry of Commerce and Industry, Government of India. https://www.indiastat.com/table/foreign-trade/selected-country-wise-export-us$-major-commodities/1424856 (accessed on 28 March 2023).

India's imports are also witnessing a directional change by regions. Dramatic and significant increase in imports from Sub-Saharan Africa can be attributed to two reasons. *First*, the base was too small as India's imports from Sub-Sahara were negligible as India was not well connected to the region due to lack of transport connectivity and shipping services. *Second*, Sub-Saharan countries witnessed a rapid rise in exploration, excavation and trade of minerals, raw materials and agro-products which are in high demand in India; for example, India started importing crude oil, forest produce, coffee and minerals from Sub-Saharan Africa. Further, in order to promote imports originating from LDCs, GOI has offered duty-free import scheme, in sync with India's WTO commitments to offer preferential tariff to LDCs. For Latin America and the Caribbean countries, the base of imports was very low, mere $390 million in 1988, and with improved transportation connectivity, overcoming language and cultural barriers, improved business ties and signing of PTAs, imports have expanded faster than the national average. Table 3.3 provides insights into region-wise imports for the period April to January 2022–2023.

TABLE 3.3 Region/Country/Month-wise Total Imports (US$) by India (2022–2023, up to January 2023)

Region/Country	April	May	June	July	August	September	October	November	December	January
Region: EU countries	4229.92	4488.5	5347.65	5293.02	4562.53	4167.18	4178.71	4501.86	5025	5126.7
Region: European Free Trade Association (EFTA)	622.01	2885.72	869.25	1301.98	1430.3	2163.41	1750.98	1663.29	554.83	451.44
Region: Other European countries	703.7	1228.34	1656.67	1463.88	1237.51	1363.27	1200.98	940.72	890.94	824.47
Region: Southern African Customs Union (SACU)	1048.2	1555.87	1101	942.41	929.6	852.22	934.55	650.3	806.3	710.43
Region: Other South African countries	444.44	575.36	566.9	655.04	330.06	362.24	513.12	771.45	656.82	508.54
Region: West Africa	2067.73	2680.24	2118.8	1828.73	1905.06	1446.17	1709.46	672.54	1617.4	436.04
Region: Central Africa	47.9	47.99	59.8	38.72	39.95	81.68	71.51	48.38	54.69	7.79
Region: East Africa	382.01	265.61	250.76	233.51	209.83	220.91	278.26	259.31	326.03	204.15
Region: North Africa	647.54	681.5	536.31	424.11	657.27	653.39	1198.85	606.67	972.37	480.39
Region: North America	5114.08	5030.22	5394.67	4987.18	5703.32	4400.05	4656.63	4993.17	5568.63	4952.57
Region: Latin America	1780.22	1945.02	1954.38	3051.21	1940.44	2077.04	2014.63	2311.92	1327.16	1269
Region: East Asia (Oceania)	2021.87	2219.55	2526.05	1921.83	1633.94	1294.35	1460.16	1525.72	1369.77	1109.47
Region: ASEAN	7274.74	7481.4	8708.76	7485.65	8164.64	7643	7003.47	7038.22	8617.37	5890.55
Region: West Asia, GCC	13012.14	11932.59	11939.8	12514.21	11183.98	13535.38	10513.36	11466.94	10969.39	9315.88
Region: Other West Asia	4726.69	4088.12	4562.87	3745	3520.85	3406.25	3414.44	2550.85	3067.16	2899.35
Region: NE Asia	13136.3	12947.99	14030.7	15644.92	14926.04	14682.46	12748.65	12779.42	13259.7	12442.34
Region: South Asia	407.67	300.95	374.26	414.31	621.75	466.6	503.73	610.19	354.92	389.69
Region: CARs countries	6.32	14.78	37.33	19.2	27.69	34.73	7.13	45.27	6.09	4.23
Region: Other CIS countries	2500.87	2874.18	4274.9	4276.71	4468.46	5134.53	4816.92	4766.2	4728.57	5290.75
Region: Unspecified	12.22	11.39	23.15	12.51	84.05	32.28	15.37	17.44	11.62	14.94

Source: Ministry of Commerce and Industry, Government of India. https://www.indiastat.com/table/foreign-trade/region-country-month-wise-total-imports-us$-india-/1425716 (accessed on 28 March 2023).

TABLE 3.4 Selected Country-wise Import (US$) of Major Commodities by India (2022–2023, up to January 2023)

Commodities	China P RP	United Arab Emirates	United States of America	Russia	Saudi Arab	Iraq	Indonesia
Petroleum: crude	0.00	14.68	9.38	24.70	24.79	28.92	0.03
Coal, Coke, Briquittes, etc.	0.45	0.52	3.32	4.01	0.00	–	13.00
Petroleum products	0.45	8.50	2.73	2.47	3.46	0.58	0.15
Gold	–	2.31	1.62	0.00	0.13	–	–
Pearl, precious, semiprecious stones	0.08	7.98	4.69	0.93	NA	–	0.00
Electronics components	6.70	0.06	0.54	0.01	0.00	0.00	0.02
Vegetable oils	0.00	0.01	0.08	0.83	0.00	–	5.10
Organic chemicals	5.53	0.16	1.44	0.02	1.15	0.00	0.14
Plastic raw materials	2.85	1.36	0.96	0.03	1.11	–	0.10
Computer hardware, peripherals	6.44	0.02	0.50	0.00	0.00	0.00	0.04
Fertilizers manufactured	2.25	0.37	0.33	2.61	2.07	–	0.14
Telecom instruments	6.00	0.01	0.51	0.00	0.00	0.00	0.01
Iron and steel	1.77	0.89	0.90	0.34	0.08	–	1.28
Indl. machinery for dairy, etc.	5.14	0.05	0.57	0.07	0.02	0.00	0.02
Residual chemical and allied products	3.17	0.10	0.72	0.03	0.33	0.00	0.25
Electric machinery and equipment	2.89	0.04	1.39	0.02	0.01	0.00	0.05
Electronic instruments	3.22	0.10	0.71	0.04	0.00	–	0.05
Inorganic chemicals	0.87	0.13	0.25	0.06	0.79	–	0.26
Consumer electronics	2.81	0.26	0.15	0.00	0.00	0.00	0.03
Aircraft, spacecraft and parts	0.01	1.48	0.77	0.00	0.42	0.00	0.00
Copper and products made of copper	0.29	0.40	0.31	0.00	0.22	–	0.01
Aluminium, products of aluminium	1.22	0.43	0.92	0.03	0.35	0.00	0.05
Bulk minerals and ores	0.02	0.64	0.05	0.00	0.01	–	0.79
Auto components/parts	1.31	0.00	0.38	0.00	0.00	0.00	0.08
Ship, boat and floating structures	0.05	0.48	0.06	0.03	0.05	–	0.20
Sub total	53.53	40.98	33.29	36.21	34.99	29.51	21.79
Total import	83.76	44.29	42.90	37.28	35.48	29.58	25.20

Source: Ministry of Commerce and Industry, Government of India. https://www.indiastat.com/table/foreign-trade/selected-country-wise-import-us$-major-commodities/1424895 (accessed on 28 March 2023).
NA: not available.

Similarly, Table 3.4 describes the key imports of India from prime sources of imports which are petroleum and crude oil, coal, coke and briquettes, precious metals, electronics and components, vegetable oils, organic chemicals, plastic raw material, computer hardware and fertilizers. In order to diversify its import sources, India needs to deepen its economic engagements with Latin America and the Caribbean and Sub-Saharan Africa and same can be done by engaging in PFAs and FTAs, improving logistical connectivity, promoting cultural exchanges, students–faculty exchange, buyers–seller meet, trade fair and exhibitions and overcoming linguistics and other business barriers.

With the regulatory permission for services trade in 1994–95, India's services export grew dramatically to almost US$312 billion in mere three decades. Imports of services is also increasing, indicating India's growing economic integration with global economy. Services trade has been a major contributor of foreign exchange, boosting economic activity and generating employment opportunities for an emerging country like India. India enjoys positive balance of payment in services trade with both exports and imports rising steadily; however, the growth rate of services tax has become slower in recent years. Figure 3.5 illustrates that India's services trade as a percentage of GDP has multiplied almost three times in the period 1991–2020 wherein the merchandise trade is just one and half time to that of 1991. It indicates that India's services trade growth is faster than that of merchandise trade growth.

The figure explains several achievements of India in services trade: first, India has become a net exporter of services rather than net importer. The process of economic liberalization, especially of exports of services with facilitative business environment for IT and IT-enabled services has promoted India's services exports exorbitantly. Second, India's services exports have grown exponentially (54 times) than India's services imports (23.12 times) under the period of study. This augurs well for a populous country like India, helping it leverage its demographic dividend and generate employment opportunities for its people.

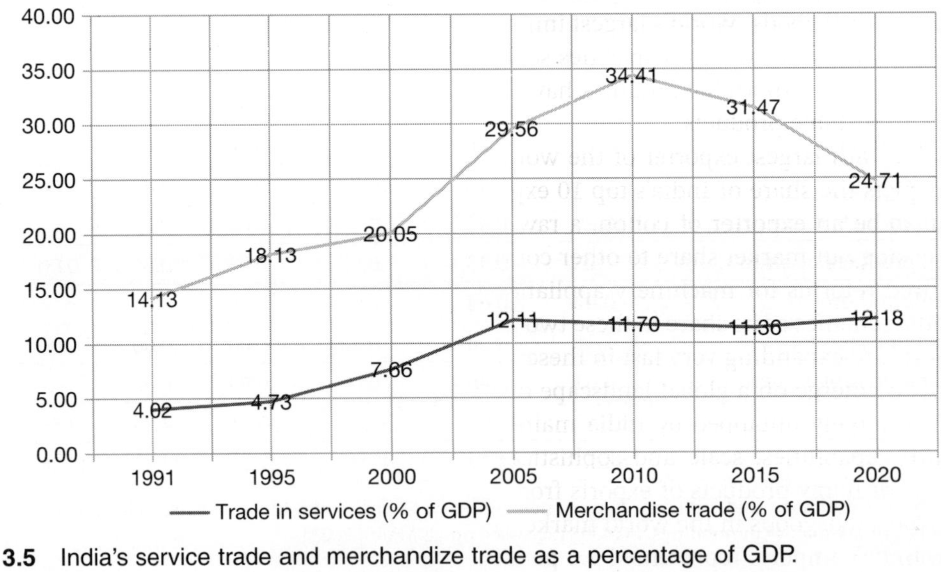

FIGURE 3.5 India's service trade and merchandize trade as a percentage of GDP.

Source: World Integrated Trade Atlas. https://wits.worldbank.org/CountryProfile/en/Country/IND/StartYear/1991/EndYear/2020/Indicator/TG-VAL-TOTL-GD-ZS# (accessed on 28 March 2023).

3.4 Composition of India's Foreign Trade

India's exports have witnessed changes in terms of composition, that is, export basket of India. India's largest exportable products in 2021 were mineral fuels that constituted around 14.29 percent of total exports of India which was mere \$3.62 billion in 2003 with a share of 6.1 percent in India's total exports, meaning the share of mineral fuels in India's export basket has more than doubled in the period 2003–2021. India's export basket of drug and pharma products has expanded faster than precious stones and gems. It is noteworthy that India is improving its competitiveness in products of iron and steel, as well as manufactured products such as machinery and appliances; competitiveness in vehicles has also improved in the period 2003–2021. However, apparels, an employment-intensive industry, has lost share in India's overall exports. It is unfortunate that cotton exports are growing, meaning value realization for export of raw material will be far lower than what it can be in case of apparels and textiles. Export of electrical machinery is constantly growing, and it is an important segment of the world market where future capabilities should be developed to increase India's presence in the world export market.

Out of the top 10 products of India's exports basket, India has negative balance of trade in 6 of them, indicating that these sectors are highly import-dependent, thus exposed to vulnerabilities which emanate from global economic shocks. For example, India's highest exportable products, mineral fuels, are largely import-dependent and are subject to price as well as supply shocks. If prices go up for oil, India's import bill increases significantly and so does the exports values. Hence, imports are far more than exports due to large domestic consumption; the oil trade is always registered negative balance of trade. Precious stones, gems and diamond trade is also subject to economic shocks as buying gems and jewellery is the last priority of an individual, after taking care for physiological and social needs. It is unfortunate that an emerging economy like India has negative trade balance for machinery and appliances, and electrical goods. World's largest import segment is engineering goods; hence, India needs to develop its capabilities as well as capacities so as to cater to growing world demand. Table 3.5 further indicates that India's exportable products have outperformed the annual growth of world imports for many of the exportable products.

India is the 18th largest exporter of the world with a mere 1.7 percent share in the world exports. Table 3.6 depicts the share of India's top 10 exportable products and its ranking in the world. India is moving out to be an exporter of cotton, a raw material for textiles and apparel industry, where it is constantly losing out market share to other counterparts of the world. India has to initiate systematic and structured reforms for machinery appliances and electrical sector under Assemble in India and Make in India schemes as its share in these two products is far below the national average. Interestingly, world imports are expanding very fast in these segments. With strong manufacturing base and ecosystem, India can emerge on a global landscape of vehicles and transport equipment—a segment which has remained largely untapped by India mainly due to higher steel prices. India has to improve its technological capabilities, scale and sophistication for low-cost manufacturing of steel which will become base for many products of exports from India. Further, Table 3.6 illustrates the concentration of India's exportable goods in the world market using the Herfindahl–Hirschman index.

In 2018, India's imports represented 2.6 percent of the world imports and its ranking in the world imports was 10. India should devise a import substitution strategy to replace some of the imports which can be substituted; for example, import of electrical machinery and machinery appliances has witnessed a sharp increase and these products can be produced domestically so as to substitute imports and also scale up production capacity in these areas. Although India has reduced the share of edible

TABLE 3.5 India's Trade Balance in Top 10 Products and Annual Growth in India's Exports and World Imports

	Value Exported in 2021 (USD thousand)	Trade Balance 2021 (USD thousand)	Annual Growth in Value Between 2017–2021 (%, p.a.)	Annual Growth of World Imports Between 2017–2021 (%, p.a.)
All products	394.81	−175.59	4	4
27: Mineral fuels	56.40	−114.00	3	0
71: Natural or cultured pearls	38.16	−50.19	−7	9
84: Machinery, mechanical appliances	24.17	−24.25	6	3
72: Iron and steel	21.20	9.52	13	5
29: Organic chemicals	21.18	−6.06	9	3
30: Pharmaceutical products	19.46	16.16	11	10
87: Vehicles other than railway	18.90	12.49	0	−1
85: Electrical machinery and equipment	18.84	−37.89	18	5
10: Cereals	12.35	12.31	12	10
52: Cotton	10.03	9.32	4	0

Source: UN Comtrade. https://www.trademap.org/Product_SelProductCountry.aspx?nvpm=1%7c699%7c%7c%7c%7cTOTAL%7c%7c%7c2%7c1%7c1%7c2%7c1%7c%7c1%7c1%7c1%7c1 (accessed on 28 March 2023).

TABLE 3.6 India's Export Share, Ranking and Concentration Index of Key Products in 2018

	Share in World Exports (%)	Ranking in World Exports	Concentration of Importing Countries
All products	1.8	18	0.05
27: Mineral fuels	2.4	11	0.05
71: Natural or cultured pearls	4.5	6	0.22
84: Machinery, mechanical appliances	1	23	0.07
72: Iron and steel	3.8	7	0.04
29: Organic chemicals	4.4	9	0.05
30: Pharmaceutical products	2.4	12	0.12
87: Vehicles other than railway	1.3	21	0.04
85: Electrical machinery and equipment	0.6	24	0.07
10: Cereals	8.1	3	0.06
52: Cotton	16	2	0.18

Source: UN Comtrade. https://www.trademap.org/Product_SelProductCountry.aspx?nvpm=1%7c699%7c%7c%7c%7cTOTAL%7c%7c%7c2%7c1%7c1%7c2%7c1%7c%7c1%7c1%7c1%7c1 (accessed on 28 March 2023).

TABLE 3.7 India's Imports, Trade Balance and Import Indicators in 2021

	Value Imported in 2021 (USD thousand)	Trade Balance 2021 (USD thousand)	Annual Growth in Value Between 2017–2021 (%, p.a.)	Annual Growth of World Exports Between 2017–2021 (%, p.a.)
All products	570.40	–175.59	2	4
27: Mineral fuels, mineral oils	170.40	–114.00	2	0
71: Natural or cultured pearls, precious	88.35	–50.19	–1	6
85: Electrical machinery and equipment	56.73	–37.89	2	6
84: Machinery, mechanical appliances	48.41	–24.25	4	3
29: Organic chemicals	27.25	–6.06	6	4
39: Plastics and articles	19.26	–10.70	6	6
15: Animal or vegetable fats and oils	17.46	–15.81	8	9
72: Iron and steel	11.68	9.52	-1	6
90: Optical, photographic, cinematographic	11.32	–7.41	5	3
28: Inorganic chemicals	9.64	–7.23	10	6

Source: UN Comtrade. https://www.trademap.org/Product_SelProductCountry.aspx?nvpm=1%7c699%7c%7c%7c%7cTOTAL%7c%7c%7c2%7c1%7c1%7c1%7c1%7c1%7c1%7c1%7c1%7c1 (accessed on 28 March 2023).

oils in total import but import of edible oils in absolute values has increased manifold, more than $10 billion. Agri-incentives aimed at improving the domestic production of edible crops with high-yield varieties and higher minimum support price can help India save this precious foreign exchange in the long run. Plastics and articles thereof and medical devices are another area to work upon to reduce the import dependence for these sectors.

Table 3.7 depicts India's imports, trade balance and analysis of average growth of India's imports vis-à-vis world imports for top 10 products. The unfavourable trade balance is 36.35 percent of India's total imports; however, for some importable products, it is very high. The unfavourable balance of trade is relatively contributed much higher in case of edible oil (88.97%), mineral fuels (71.35%), electrical machinery (77.50%), medical devices (66.06%) and several other products (Table 3.7). Similarly, the annual growth of imports for top 10 products is much higher than the world import growth. India needs to initiate reforms at all levels, production and manufacturing, skilling of manpower, developing manufacturing ecosystem, technological improvements and so on, so as to not only substitute the growing imports but also make some of these products export-oriented, thus substituting imports and emerging as the net exporter to compensate for essential and non-replaceable imports such as precious gems, gold and mineral fuels.

Further, analysis of India's import basket indicates India's share in world imports, ranking and concentration of supplying markets. India is the largest importer of edible oil with an import share of 10.4 percent as Indians have preference for vegetable oils for cooking as well as industrial usage. Organic chemical is another area where India should reduce its import dependence as it imports

TABLE 3.8 India's Share in Imports, Ranking and Concentration of Key Products in 2021

	Share in World Imports (%)	Ranking in World Imports	Average Distance of Supplying Countries (km)	Concentration of Supplying Countries
All products	2.5	10	5793	0.05
27: Mineral fuels, mineral oils	6.5	3	5743	0.08
71: Natural or cultured pearls, precious	10.1	3	6991	0.15
85: Electrical machinery and equipment	1.6	15	4585	0.25
84: Machinery, mechanical appliances	1.9	16	5384	0.18
29: Organic chemicals	5.1	5	4967	0.21
39: Plastics and articles	2.4	13	4944	0.09
15: Animal or vegetable fats and oils	11.5	1	6449	0.16
72: Iron and steel	2.1	17	5416	0.08
90: Optical, photographic, cinematographic	1.6	16	6460	0.1
28: Inorganic chemicals	6.1	4	5943	0.07

Source: UN Comtrade. https://www.trademap.org/Product_SelProductCountry.aspx?nvpm=1%7c699%7c%7c%7c%7cTOTAL%7c%7c%7c2%7c1%7c1%7c1%7c1%7c1%7c1%7c1%7c1%7c1 (accessed on 28 March 2023).

excipients and active pharmaceutical ingredients (API) for generic drug manufacturing mainly from China. Higher concentration index for electrical machinery and edible oil indicates that India is dependent for supplies of these products on few markets. Make in India should be leveraged properly to reduce the import dependence on some of these products. Table 3.8 illustrates the status of India's import basket in 2021.

3.5 Future of India's Foreign Trade

To be a developed economy and achieve a short-term objective of a five-trillion economy, India needs to execute some of the reforms on an urgent and immediate basis which can be focal areas for increasing exports from India. *First and foremost*, India needs to develop inhouse capabilities, technical know-how to manufacture steel and a variety of 'grades of steel' for meeting the domestic requirements as well as making it available for the export-oriented industry. India is import-dependent for iron and steel even after 75 years of Independence which does not augur well for India. R&D institutions should focus on improving the metallurgy science aimed at low-cost manufacturing by using suitable technology and domestic resources. Metals constitute a sizable percentage of world imports and improving India's innate capabilities and capacities with scale, size, system and sophistication can help India emerge as a global champion of exports in the world markets. *Second*, India has a very strong pharma industry with a proven track record of supplying quality drugs and pharmaceuticals to the world. India should reduce its very high import dependence for excipient and API, especially from China, and create an in-country ecosystem for world-class manufacturing of pharma products. The cost advantages at which India manufactures bulk generic drugs make it one of the most reliable and trusted suppliers of pharma products. India can enter sector-specific trade agreements with top 10 import destinations so as to cut the cost of clinical trials, regulatory compliances, drug registrations and associated red tape in order to further leverage on strong domestic capabilities to increase its pharma and drugs exports. *Third*, textiles, clothing and apparel are the backbone of India's economy. India has been losing out share in finished products of apparel, textiles and clothing and has emerged as a major supplier of raw materials, that is, cotton and yarn which does not augur well for India. This sector can generate millions of employment opportunities, additional economic activity and significant foreign exchange accumulations. *Fourth*, India has vast production of leather, hides and skins as it owns the largest cattle population of the world. India has 58 percent of the world buffalo population, tapping the vast reservoir of leather hides. India and China were at the same level of exports of leather and accessories in 1983; however, in 2018, China's leather and accessories exports is almost five times that of India. India needs to tap this sector aggressively as it will create millions of employment opportunities in the country. *Fifth*, transport equipment and vehicles trade are expanding very fast in the world markets. India has developed a strong ecosystem for vehicles manufacturing both light and high commercial vehicles. Motorcycles made in India are very popular in Africa, Latin America and developing countries of Asia. *Sixth*, India has been already established as an unparalleled exporter of agro-products and it is high time to value add them and get higher dollars realizations for our agro-produce. For example, India's meat, marine, fruits, vegetables, processed food, tobacco, spices, tea, coffee, coir products, honey, shellac, rubber plantation products and so on are already established in the world market. Last but not the least, India should aggressively venture into all service sectors and reap the economic opportunities in the vast and growing markets of the world.

Like the export strategies, India should also devise import strategies and should substitute the imports wherever possible. In some cases, India needs to find alternative products to cut its import bill. Table 3.9 maps out product-wise top 25 products where India need to work upon to cut its import bill and become self-sustainable with favourable balance of trade.

TABLE 3.9 India's Import Strategies for Top 15 Products

<table>
<tr><th>Importable Products</th><th>Import Strategy for India</th></tr>
<tr><td>27: Mineral fuels</td><td>Develop alternatives of energy such as solar, wind, gas and hydro</td></tr>
<tr><td>71: Precious gems and stones</td><td>Import substitution not possible; hence, improve ecosystem for low-cost sourcing through free trade and warehousing zones in India</td></tr>
<tr><td>85: Electrical machinery</td><td rowspan="2">Import substitution possible through improvement in technology, production scale, improved metallurgy and semiconductor and chip industry. Increase peak duties to WTO bound rates and invite foreign technology, promote Assemble in India and Make in India</td></tr>
<tr><td>84: Machinery and appliances</td></tr>
<tr><td>29: Organic chemicals</td><td>Ecosystem for domestic production of excipient and APIs, improve R&D frameworks and regulation, invite investment and scale up production and quality ladder</td></tr>
<tr><td>39: Plastics and articles</td><td>Promote base industries for plastics close to refineries, promote MSMEs</td></tr>
<tr><td>72: Iron and steel</td><td>Iron and steel sector requires maximum attention of GOI and industry players as only low-price and high-quality uninterrupted availability of iron and steel can make India a global export champion. Iron and steel can help develop medical devices, transport and vehicles, defence products, ships, arms and ammunition, machinery, tools and other industries</td></tr>
</table>

(*Continued*)

TABLE 3.9 *(Continued)*

Importable Products	Import Strategy for India
15: Edible oil	Promote high yield varieties and domestic production, enter agro-trade agreements to promote value-added exports of Vanaspati to Indian diaspora
90: Medical devices	Import substitution is possible through policy interventions and availability of metallurgy expertise required for medical devices
28: Inorganic chemicals	Invest in foreign countries and own mines so as to cut costs of imports of inorganic chemicals
87: Transport vehicles	Import substitution in critical areas through domestic production with improved availability of required metals at low cost
38: Miscellaneous chemicals	Import substitution through high-end R&D and development of base material industries
31: Fertilizers	Import substitution with domestic production like for urea, import raw material only at low cost and invest abroad in mines of raw material
26: Ores and slags	Invest in mines for low cost sourcing

3.6 Summary

Although foreign trade has been in vogue for the past few centuries, it has been a part of our life since the evolution of mankind. All ancient civilizations, be it Mesopotamia, Indus and China, used to trade with other parts of the world. In a globalized era, economic engagements vis-à-vis direction and composition of trade of a country are an important barometer to understand the process of economic development of a country. Foreign trade is an important instrument used by countries to transform their economies from traditional to developed as exports and imports help in effective, efficient and systematic utilization of a country's economic resources in all sectors—agriculture, manufacturing and services. The direction and composition of foreign trade of a country is determined by 'trade policy' of a country, paving way for achieving the objectives of rapid economic growth and self-reliance. Diversified export and destination also help a country to easily cope with the economic meltdown which may happen in a country or a region, by shifting attention to other countries in the large world market. Moreover, export diversification with more technically advanced products or newer products can open more business opportunities and help deal with competitors through such technological leapfrogging. Sophisticated products so developed shall be beneficial for all resulting in more trade and foreign exchange inflow, finally leading to higher income and improved quality of life, thus achieving the objective of a welfare state. Technology diffusion and innovations also help improve existing products across sectors both in goods and services and help them to compete better in global markets. India's export destinations have diversified since Independence both country-wise and region-wise in the world market. Sources of imports have also witnessed metamorphic changes since Independence. Such changes in export, as well as import destinations, are expected, as: first, India's foreign trade expanded rapidly with the reforms measures introduced by GOI since 1991; second, formerly state-run economy is now a market-driven economy; third, services trade has contributed significantly to India's foreign trade; fourth, Asian countries witnessed rapid trade expansion and India's engagements in Asian region contributed to the growth of both exports and imports; fifth, India's trade basket has become far more deeper; and sixth, young professionals are leading India's foreign trade story to newer heights and avenues, largely driven by market dynamics. India is 18th largest exporter of the world with a mere 1.7 percent share in world exports. In 2018, India's imports represented 2.6 percent of the world imports and its ranking in world imports is 10. India should develop its future capabilities in sectors such as mineral fuels, precious stones and diamonds, machinery and appliances, vehicles, organic chemicals, pharmaceutical products, electrical machinery, iron and steel, and cotton and apparels and similarly devise a strategy to replace the imports of products where they can be replaced.

Review Exercises

Multiple Choice Questions

1. Which of the following regions was the main source for India's imports in 2018?
   a. East Asia and Pacific
   b. Europe and Central Asia
   c. Middle East and North Africa
   d. North America
2. Which of the following countries is the prime destination for India's exports?
   a. The United States
   b. The United Arab Emirates
   c. China
   d. Germany
3. Which of the following countries is the prime supplier for India's imports?
   a. China
   b. The United States
   c. Saudi Arabia
   d. The United Arab Emirates
4. Which region has the lowest share in India's total exports?
   a. Latin America and the Caribbean
   b. East Asia and Pacific
   c. South Asia
   d. Sub-Saharan Africa
5. Which of the following is the second largest exported product from India?
   a. Gems and jewellery
   b. Oil and lubricant
   c. Engineering products
   d. Tea
6. Which of the following is the third largest most imported product in India?
   a. Electrical machinery
   b. Oil and lubricant
   c. Gems and jewellery
   d. Gold

7. Who among the following propounded the theory of 'drainage of wealth' of India?
   a. Dadabhai Naoroaji
   b. Jamshed Ji Tata
   c. Adam Smith
   d. Ricardo
8. What is the share of India in the world total exports in 2018?
   a. 1.7 percent
   b. 2.6 percent
   c. 1.9 percent
   d. 2.1 percent
9. What is the rank of India as an importer in the world?
   a. 10
   b. 11
   c. 18
   d. 3
10. What is the rank of India in the world in edible oil imports?
   a. 1
   b. 10
   c. 18
   d. 7

Critical Thinking Questions

1. Explain critically the historical viewpoint of India's foreign trade.
2. What is the present status of India's foreign trade? Examine.
3. What are the key regions to which India exports? What are the major products of exports from India?
4. What are the prime sources of India's imports? What commodities are mainly imported in India?
5. Write a short note on any two of the following:
   a. Evolution of foreign trade in India
   b. Direction of India's foreign trade
   c. Composition of India's foreign trade
   d. Future of India's exports
   e. Strategies for India's imports
6. Write an essay on India's trade expansion and diversification since Independence.

Further Reading

1. McIntyre, Arnold, Mike Xin Li, Ke Wang, and Hanlei Yun. 2018. 'Economic Benefits of Export Diversification in Small States'. IMF Working Paper No. WP/18/86, International Monetary Fund, Washington, DC.

CHAPTER 4

E-commerce and Trade Information for Exporters

CHAPTER OBJECTIVES

- To understand the concept of e-commerce and e-business for EXIM operations.
- To elucidate the advantages of e-business and essentials for venturing into e-commerce business.
- To explain the procedure for exports through e-commerce.
- To elaborate the sources of trade information for EXIM business.

4.1 Introduction

Electronic commerce or e-commerce refers to any virtual business or commercial transaction where the transfer of information takes place on the Internet and goods move from the producer to the consumer via express or courier or virtual means. E-commerce essentially entails the transfer of information across the Internet to create a virtual exchange, where buyers and sellers can do trading. In today's globalized era, e-commerce covers different types of businesses, for example, consumer-based retail sites such as Amazon, Flipkart and Snapdeal; auction or music sites such as gaana.com and e-Auction.com; and business exchanges such as trading goods and services between corporations such as Yatra.com, Makemytrip.com and Alibaba.com. E-commerce, in fact, is the most beautiful gift of the Internet to mankind, as it allows consumers to electronically exchange goods and services with no barriers of time or distance. E-commerce, as of today, is the most flourishing industry in world economy and helps connect the buyers and sellers across the world. It, in fact, has become a medium to reap the benefits of the business innovation for an enterprise in real time. E-commerce, even in international operations, has expanded rapidly over the past few years, and it is predicted that it will grow even faster with proliferation of IT in the markets of Africa, Asia and Latin America. Experts of this industry believe that in the near future, the boundaries between 'conventional' and 'electronic' commerce will become increasingly blurred, as more and more business enterprises are moving towards putting a section of their business on e-platform. For example, Aditya Birla Group has introduced an e-tail platform for e-business of their apparel goods.

Companies foresee significant potential business gains by carrying out business transactions electronically as e-commerce and e-business provide vast competitive advantages over traditional methods of doing business. In countries where there has been deep Internet penetration, e-commerce is gaining ground in all potential areas of business. In fact, the sales volumes through e-commerce are growing faster than the overall growth of product segments. It means that more and more customers are using e-commerce for trade and business. If any firm properly implements e-commerce, then customers can

- Lower time to deliver the products and no warehouse required
- Easy and updated information about products or services to global customers
- Greator flexibility and adaptability of online marketing and product promotion
- Benefit of lower import duty in cases goods are cleared by use of de minimis clause of importing countries
- Customer access to different products or services round the clock on every day of the year
- Real-time responses to customers' changing needs
- Ease in product ordering and efficient order processing
- Real-time market intelligence about customers such as demographics, market segments and competitors
- Reduced inventory level as electronic rather than physical delivery of certain products
- Unrestricted access to global exporters and importers, thus more trade opportunities

FIGURE 4.1 Benefits of e-commerce and e-business.

get significantly benefitted as it is faster, cheaper and more convenient than the traditional methods of bartering goods and services in a physical market. Some of the benefits of e-commerce and e-business to customers and associated stakeholders are listed in Figure 4.1.

Electronic transactions in export operations have been around for quite some time in the form of electronic data interchange or EDI in order to bring close various associated stakeholders in a long logistics chain, that is, shipping companies, insurers, cargo inspection companies, custom authorities, transport companies like road and rail carriers, and stevedores. In order to conduct these information exchanges and business transactions between suppliers and customers, there is a need for electronic data interchange through a dedicated data link, which provides a cost-effective method for doing business globally. The success of such electronic platforms has led to the development of electronic marketplaces where suppliers and potential customers are brought together to conduct mutually beneficial trade. One needs to be well versed in principles of IT before setting such e-commerce platform and needs to have an e-business plan so as to create a successful e-business model. One of the two guiding principles for the success of any e-commerce platform is time as in today's commercial markets, time plays an important role in both the business and for consumers. Time is an important factor for any exporter as less time spent during each transaction means he can achieve more transactions daily and lesser will be resultant working capital employed. It means that e-commerce is beneficial to both exporters and importers as the payment and documentations can be completed with greater efficiency. Even for domestic business, e-commerce is much more cost-effective as compared to traditional commerce methods as it eliminates the cost of the middlemen to sell its goods and services. The end result is that the goods and services sold through e-platforms are cost-effective, thus attracting more buyers which helps generate economies of scale in business resulting in higher business.

In addition to getting access to potential customers, e-commerce helps in achieving a better 'customer-to-cost ratio' as advertising commercial products on the Internet is comparably much cheaper than putting up a roadside banner, erecting a signboard, filming a television commercial and paying to various media vendors for advertorial and products promotion. Hence, e-commerce, enabled on a technology platform, offers scope for global trade operations at a larger scale with initial relatively very small investments. For example, an e-commerce firm needs not to have various branches all over the world like in traditional business. Similarly, most of the other costs, for example, cost of staffing, maintenance of business operations, communications and other logistical arrangements are substituted by a single cost, web hosting for the e-commerce business. E-commerce, thus, brings consumers and business firm close which is very important for the success of any export firm. From the importers' point of view, e-commerce is much more convenient for import business operations as they can virtually browse various business directories or catalogues of information without any hassle, compare the prices of various international suppliers and can initiate import decisions in real-time. More so, one can order the best quality and competitive price goods from any location of the world from his/her home or workplace. Above all, e-commerce cuts red tape for both customers and exporters in comparison to traditional methods of commerce. In today's globalized set-up, technology-enabled business through e-commerce has opened up various windows of opportunities for a variety of exporters, such as, start-ups, small, medium, large, new or established exporters. Even established retail companies are endeavouring with their e-commerce forays as more and more investments and resources are being directed towards e-commerce; for example, an Indian apparel company, Mudra Fashion, has opened an online store called 'abof' so as to sell merchandise online to new category of customers and not to lose business to others. Similarly, there are several e-commerce web portals launched by established automobile companies so as to tap various segments of automobile business nationally and globally, for example, carwale and cardekho (for new car and resale of old car), meru (for rental services), and uber and ola (taxi aggregator). In the non-standardized and differentiated market segments for both goods and services, e-commerce is fast emerging as a potent business tool and it is fast becoming an essential business plan for globally engaged business firms to not only survive but stay competitive in the ever-changing market. In order to tap these emerging global business opportunities, even DGFT has allowed e-commerce for Indian exporters who are increasingly looking for an outstanding global customers base at e-commerce sites to explore and promote their products or services.

4.2 Understanding E-commerce and E-business

Marketplace, especially in the developed and emerging markets, is fast changing from physical markets to virtual markets, as consumers are increasingly looking forward to buying online instead of going to the physical marketplace. There is ease in doing so, as goods are cost-effective because many trade intermediaries get eliminated, it is very simple to order, it saves time, comfort of services is provided at home and above all, there is possibility of returns if not found satisfactory. All this has been possible only because of two electronic networks known as 'e-commerce' and 'e-business'. For a layman, it is not easy to differentiate between the two because they are closely interconnected terms. E-commerce refers to buying and selling of goods at the virtual marketplace hosted by the web, whereas e-business is a little different in the sense that it is not limited to commercial transactions only, but it also provides other services. E-commerce and e-business can be understood comparatively through Table 4.1.

E-commerce refers to online buying, selling, dealing, ordering and paying for the goods and services and is done on a virtual platform. For e-commerce transactions to be executed, there must be a website wherein the seller can communicate with the buyer without having a face-to-face interaction, thus offering insights into proposal of sale, product features, product price, reviews and photos displaying the type of product and so on. For example, one can book online ticket, order goods at eBay from anywhere in the world, process payment to any place in the world. Social networking sites such as 'Facebook' and 'Quora' are nothing but e-platforms for 'exchanges of ideas' which is an integral part of foreign trade. In a nutshell, any monetary transaction, involving exchange of goods, services and ideas, which is done with the help of electronic media is called e-commerce. E-commerce can be of various types as exhibited in Figure 4.2.

TABLE 4.1 Basis of Comparison between E-commerce and E-business

Basis for Comparison	E-commerce	E-business
Activity	E-commerce is trading of goods over the Internet	E-business is the execution of business functions by use of the Internet
Structure	It is a subset	It is a superset
Monetary transactions	Monetary transactions happen in e-commerce	No monetary transactions happen in e-business
Nature of transactions	Commercial transactions	Business transactions
Approach	Extroverted	Ambivert
Need of IT infrastructure	Website	Website, customer relationship management, enterprise resource planning and so on
Type of network	Internet	Internet, intranet and extranet

Business-to-business (B2B)	• Electronic website wherein the buying and selling (export–import) of goods and services is conducted between two businesses is called B2B e-commerce, for example, Alibaba, Oracle and Qualcomm
Business-to-customer (B2C)	• Electronic website wherein the goods and services are sold by a business group to customers across the world in a virtual marketplace, for example, Intel and Dell
Customer-to-customer (C2C)	• Electronic website wherein commercial transactions are carried out between customers, for example, OLX and Quikr
Customer-to-business (C2B)	• Electronic website facilitating the commercial transactions between customer and business, for example, Trip Advisor, Travel Triangle and Craigslist

FIGURE 4.2 Types of e-commerce.

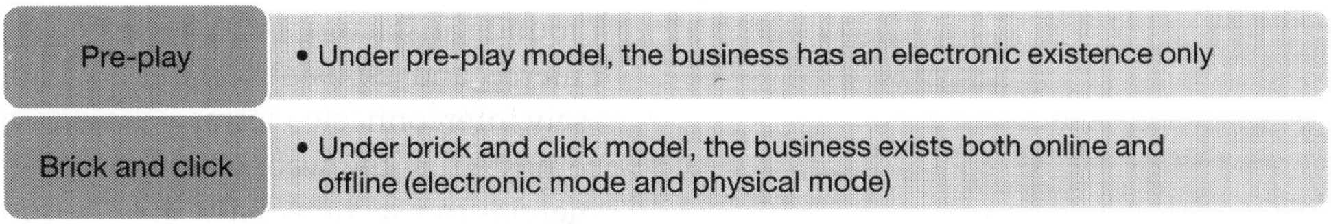

FIGURE 4.3 Types of e-business.

Electronic business, in short 'e-business', refers to the online presence of business, wherein the business is done with the help of the Internet or electronic data interchange. The scope of e-business is greater than e-commerce as it is not limited only to buying and selling of goods and services but includes other activities of business processes such as providing online services to the customers, communicating with employees, online interaction with clients or business partners and any other issues that involve providing services to business partners. In fact, e-commerce is merely an important component of e-business and not an essential part. In e-business, all the basic business operations including that of exports and imports are done by using electronic media. Figure 4.3 explains the two types of e-businesses.

There are many differences between e-commerce and e-business. *First*, e-commerce involves mere buying and selling of goods and services through the Internet, whereas e-business refers to an electronic presence of business for conduct of all the business activities with the use of the Internet. *Second*, e-business is a broader concept of business and e-commerce is mere a major component of e-business. *Third*, transactions conducted through e-commerce are of a monetary nature, whereas e-business includes monetary as well as allied activities of business. *Fourth*, e-commerce is an extroverted approach of doing business and covers stakeholders such as customers, suppliers and distributors, while e-business is an ambivert approach that covers internal as well as external processes of business. *Fifth*, e-commerce requires electronic presence, meaning there must be a website for e-commerce, whereas e-business requires a website and a support mechanism for conduct of business and includes modules on customer relationship management and enterprise resource planning for running the business over the Internet. *Sixth*, the Internet is a must for e-commerce to happen, while e-business needs the Internet, intranet and extranet to conduct business with associated parties. *Finally*, e-commerce is a type of e-business website, but e-business is not necessarily an e-commerce website. In addition to these differences, there are similarities in e-commerce and e-business as both require online presence to conduct virtual commerce.

4.3 Advantages of E-commerce

The introduction of a virtual marketplace through e-commerce has dramatically changed the business landscape, and with increased digitalization in world economy, it will continue to do so in the ways that cannot be predicted. There are plenty of business advantages that e-commerce offers to the marginal and small exporters, especially in certain sectors such as accessories, leather products, handicrafts, handlooms, textiles and apparels, electronics and gifts. Global customers have quick and easy access to a tremendous amount of information that enables them to find, assess, compare, review and select a product of their choice virtually from anywhere in the world. E-commerce websites offer an easy and cost-effective option to avail a significant amount of information in a fraction of time without any

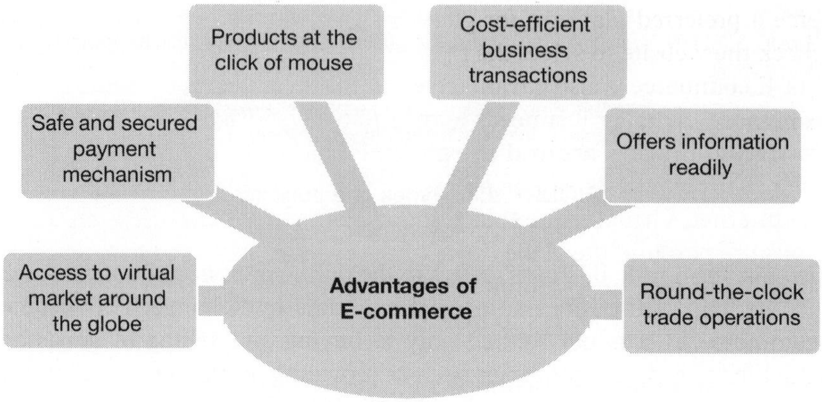

FIGURE 4.4 Advantages of e-commerce.

discrimination and restriction. Interestingly, exporters and importers need not be from the same geographic location. Indian exporters, especially small and new, are increasingly banking upon e-commerce to market their products and explain the uniqueness of their product's features. The advantages of e-commerce for exporters and importers can be understood through Figure 4.4 and explained in depth as follows:

1. **Products at the click of the mouse:** E-commerce is the world's most convenient, easily accessible and cost-effective virtual marketplace which helps exporters to sell their products and services and allow choice of purchase to global customers. A seller can get registered with a virtual marketplace such as Amazon, Flipkart, Snapdeal and eBay which will issue him a stock-keeping unit (SKU), thus displaying the pictures of products, their features, purchase review and prices. Global customers, especially with urbanized landscape, prefer to buy online as it helps them to make the right choice of products and benefits of delivery of products at their home at any time. Global customers save both time and costs, and e-commerce eliminates the middlemen involved in a physical marketplace. E-commerce offers many options for payment, for example, after delivery and before delivery, wherein the transferring of funds is also at the click of the mouse. E-commerce websites offer search engine facility and global consumers can easily locate the products by typing the products they wish to buy online. E-commerce is an online market which is operated with a click of the mouse and busy customers need not go in search of shops.
2. **Round-the-clock trade operations:** Global customers can have access to websites round the clock, as online stores stay open 24/7 every day of the year. Customers from anywhere in the world can order products, thus increasing the possibility of increased international sales through e-commerce. Global customers need not worry about time differences that exist otherwise among various countries and there is no fear of closing of store.
3. **Cost-efficient business transactions:** Any business firm needs some physical infrastructure such as store and sales-generating assets, hence requiring an initial investment to start their business transactions, but e-commerce makes the process more economical as it is a virtual marketplace which can be accessed by anyone across the globe. The initial investment needed for online selling is extremely less than having a physical presence in the marketplace. This makes

e-commerce a preferred platform for global sales. Customers, anywhere across the globe, just have to check the website to select the right product, and the purchase process is far easier with lower costs. E-commerce is also advantageous as it lowers the cost of inventory of varied product portfolios because the seller just needs to maintain a web-based system of inventory.

4. **Access to virtual market around the globe:** E-commerce is advantageous as the products or services of various exporters can be accessed by different customers across the world with the help of the Internet. Virtual marketplace at an e-commerce platform offers a variety of products and any consumer around the globe can find the products or services of his choice within a fraction of seconds. In fact, an e-commerce platform reduces all barriers that exist in this world market and enables the exporters to make their products and services reach the global market without any restrictions.
5. **Offers information readily:** E-commerce website offers the customers with a lot of information about product's features, past purchase history, reviews and so on, which is not possible with the physical store with the same level of ease. E-commerce platform offers different customers with the information needed without waiting for a second in any language anywhere in the world at the time of customer's choice. E-commerce website also provides information readily on offers, coupons, product bundling and marketing discount to the customers in a much more convenient way. Customers across the globe can take benefit of such offers and marketing discounts with ease and enjoy world-class products from sellers located across the globe.
6. **Safe and secure payment mechanism:** Realizing timely payment from customers located in another country is a key concern for any Indian exporter. E-commerce websites allow the exporters to make their customer first pay for the product or product is delivered only against payment at delivery, thus assuring guaranteed payment realization as there is no credit involved in the process. A unique feature of any e-commerce platform is that it combines various business functions such as product marketing, inventory management, logistics and payment realization at one website, thus ensuring ease in business operations in a secure manner.

4.4 Essentials for Venturing into E-commerce Business

E-commerce is a virtual marketplace and in order to export online globally, an exporter has to buy the market space online for publishing the product portfolio and information on the World Wide Web. Hence, one should be well versed in computers, the Internet, email or setting up own website, online banking and other related instruments of sharing information. An exporter must have, at a minimum, an adequate computer system (laptop), telephone system (mobile and landline both) and the ability to send and receive faxes. It is the computer system including the access to the Internet, email and other software that supports the business in e-commerce, hence it is essentially required. The telephone system of an exporter should also support worldwide communications and might include the ability of teleconferencing with several parties at a time. Access to the telephone system which has features of adding one or more parties to a telephone call can be useful in closing a business deal in complex business operations. Although business takes place at an online platform, an exporter needs to constantly be in touch with associated stakeholders, that is, overseas customer, virtual marketplace operator, overseas agent and so on. Following are the essential requirements for an exporter planning to sell goods and services in a virtual marketplace called e-commerce.

1. **Personal computers (PCs) with access to the Internet:** Any export firm, planning to sell online globally, must have access to PC with high-speed Internet access in order to meet most of the business needs for selling online to global customers. A PC system must have the following essential tools which are required to operate effectively in a virtual marketplace to sell goods and services.
   a. Word processor
   b. Spreadsheet software
   c. Database management system
   d. Email software for prompt communications
   e. Contact management software like Electronic Rolodex for maintaining history of communications
   f. Antivirus software for scanning email and files
   g. Firewalls to prevent unauthorized communication
   h. Accounting/billing software (prepackaged, off the shelf)
2. **Digital marketing expertise:** In order to succeed in global e-commerce operations, it is essential that one should have knowledge of digital marketing techniques including how to effectively place the product adverts in the e-commerce websites. A digital marketing expert can attract potential traffic of customers from social networking websites to product adverts in an e-commerce platform. The beauty of digital marketing is that an exporter can market his products and services through the Internet relatively with ease and even with limited financial resources. E-commerce-based export operations are low-cost market-entry techniques, and an exporter can use marketing material from a range of options like simple brochure to a full-blown e-commerce website for the firm's products.
3. **Voicemail:** As time zones differ worldwide, especially with developed markets of North America and emerging markcts of Latin America, it is worth having the voicemail facility so as to deal with intense competition with local players if one intends to export products and services globally. Voicemail provides the opportunity to a foreign customer to contact an exporter based in India to establish a link outside of normal business hours. More so, technological development has ensured that voicemail or a personal answering service can now respond in several languages and guide callers to price quotes or service information even when exporter's business is closed for the day or weekend, thus brightening one's prospects of great e-commerce business. An exporter can retrieve such messages anywhere; for example, he may be travelling but will be in a position to answer important calls of customers around the globe with voicemail facility.
4. **Facsimile (FAX) machines:** E-commerce is a virtual marketplace operated through the Internet, wherein one needs to respond to a global clientele of business customers. In order to quickly deliver important documents to globally scattered foreign buyers, customers and financial institutions, there is no substitute for a FAX machine which reproduces the original contents of messages. It is essential for an exporter to have a FAX machine if he intends to do business globally by selling online. With improved technological developments, simple business communications are no more done with FAX machine as one can scan the document and send it as an attachment through email, thus delivering the same content with a lower cost of operations. The potential disadvantage related to use of computer scanning is that one can manipulate the computer text with software which is not the case with the FAX machine. Hence, it is considered as an essential need for operating in global e-commerce business.

5. **Email:** It is very essential for an exporter to have knowledge of email, bulk emailing and designing contents for emails. Email, in today's global business environment, is the primary and most cost-effective method of communications that any business firm, whether large or small, uses to communicate internally as well as externally. In fact, email is the most inexpensive and expeditious way of staying in touch with various stakeholders of export business, that is, employees, custom broker, logistics company, customers, agents, website operator and so on. Email is an essential means of communication for any exporter if he/she has decided to sell his/her product or service exclusively on the e-commerce website.
6. **Website:** A website is a must if one intends to sell products and services globally as it is an inexpensive and highly effective way to market a product or service globally. One needs to do the groundwork so as to design the right contents about the product and services considering the applicable rules and regulations including technical details that may affect the ability of potential customers to view the firm's website. One also needs to take certain technical precautions while designing the website so as to enable someone to help or hinder others in their attempt to locate the firm's website using search engines. Content material should be designed with precautions, as when translated into another business language, it may have an altogether different interpretation, thus confusing global customers. One should provide the contact information and links in such a manner that foreign customers are at ease to quickly find information about products and services.
7. **Export-related 'online services' and search engine optimization:** An online seller should follow the trade leads that emanate from an e-commerce business and there should be an adequate mechanism for collection, compilation and classification of such trade leads. An e-commerce business also needs to engage the search engine optimization services so as to ensure that firm's website should come in top when someone searches about similar products and services anywhere in the world. Figure 4.5 highlights time-tested mechanisms for tracking down business leads and opportunities in e-commerce operations globally.
8. **Electronic banking:** In order to manage global e-commerce operations, it is essential to have electronic banking as use of computer-based banking can certainly expedite the financial tasks of the firm's export business. An exporter can open, maintain and operate electronic banking facility with any commercial bank in India and access, monitor and manage firm's account balances and statements. Electronic banking also facilitates the email letters of credit, documentary collections and fund's wire transfer acknowledgements. There are accounting packages

Trade lead services	• Buyer–seller meet, exhibitions, trade fairs, Indian embassies
Popular virtual marketplaces	• One can sell at popular virtual marketplaces such as eBay, Amazon, Flipkart and Snapdeal
Search engines	• E-commerce website should be optimized by major international search engines such as Google and Yahoo
B2B exchanges	• An exporter should specialize in market exchanges in the commodity he/she deals in so as to supplement firm's e-commerce operations

FIGURE 4.5 Online search tools for EXIM opportunities.

that can help a firm to manage other associated banking functions such as currency hedging, regulatory compliance and other documentation.

9. **EDI:** EDI is the electronic transfer of globally transacted e-commerce operations of firm wherein the business operation's information can be transferred on real-time basis from one computer to another computer(s) in an agreed-upon standard format. It is designed for very specific use of an e-commerce firm and may help manage critical business operations such as inventory management, logistics management, procurement, working capital management and customer relationship management. An e-commerce business can make the best use of the EDI system for exchanging useful business information integrated with the firm's order entry, delivery and inventory systems.
10. **Electronic tracking of shipments:** The development in the field of IT helps in online tracking of shipment and an e-commerce business can make best use of such IT platforms to track global shipments electronically. An exporter can check the stage of delivery of globally shipped goods with the click of a mouse so as to track the location of the firm's shipments, when they will be delivered and can also see the exact stage, for example, whether shipments are delayed with formalities of importer's country's customs and finally when a buyer receives those shipments. Learning from these experiences, an e-commerce firm can accordingly intimate the tentative delivery time while booking orders from global customers. It can accordingly design the logistics strategy in close coordination with freight forwarders and carrier companies to manage firm's global business operations. Some of the ways and means for profiling potential markets are listed in Figure 4.6.

Market Type	Economic Features	Political Features	Business Information	Cultural Considerations	Support for Market-entry Strategies
• Fast-paced and competitive markets • Relation-ship-based markets • Dependent markets based on foreign/ official develop-ment assistance funding	• Sectoral contribution in domestic economy • Macro-economic trends • General profile of imports and exports • Size of GDP and per capita income	• Type of government • Power centres within government • View of mainstream political parties • Relations with neigh-bouring countries	• Currency types and stability • Language spoken • Business practices and etiquettes • Business regime and regulations • Legal framework • Government procurement • Work relationships and office hours	• Business visa • Work permits • Business support services • Availability of hotels • Telecommuni-cations standards • Electrical voltage • Religious holidays	• Industry and chamber associations • Trade events and exhibitions • Networking options • Trade media and channels • Research facilities • Market research assistance

FIGURE 4.6 Checklist for profiling potential markets for export operations.

Source: Adapted from S. Carter (1997). *Global Agricultural Marketing Management*. (*Marketing and Agribusiness texts-3*), the FAO Regional Office for Africa.

4.5 Procedure for Exports through E-commerce

Realizing the fact that e-commerce has an important role to play in India's export story, DGFT defined e-commerce as 'means of buying and selling of goods and services including digital products, conducted over digital and electronic network' in FTP 2015–2020 and allowed the exports of goods through e-commerce platforms. Export through the use of e-commerce shall be entitled to duty credit scrip as offered under Merchandise Exports from India Scheme (MEIS) to Indian exporters. E-commerce shall mean the export of goods hosted on a website accessible through the Internet to a purchaser. While the dispatch of goods shall be made through courier or postal mode as specified under MEIS, the payment for goods purchased on an e-commerce platform shall be done through international credit/debit cards as per the Reserve Bank of India Circular (RBI/2015-16/185 A. P. [DIR Series] Circular No. 16 dated September 24, 2015) as amended from time to time. The following six commodities have been notified for being eligible for reward under the scheme:

Handicraft items/ products	Handloom products	Books/ periodicals	Leather footwear	Toys	Customized fashion garments: These are garments that are made on specific request/order of customer and accordingly tailored/manufactured.

Source: Director General of Foreign Trade, Ministry of Commerce & Industry, GOI.

For exports of handicrafts and handloom, it is mandatory that these are only genuine handloom and handcrafts products to the satisfaction of Indian custom officials and in case of doubt, an exporter is required to get the certificate from the development commissioner (handcraft) certifying the products as handicraft products. The benefit of duty credit scrip under the MEIS scheme as notified by DGFT will be admissible only to these six categories of products. In addition to the above, following are other general guidelines applicable to the export of goods through courier or foreign post offices (FPOs) using e-commerce:

1. Any exporter holding a valid import–export code shall be permitted to export goods sold through e-commerce through FPOs at Delhi, Mumbai and Chennai.
2. The scheme of export through e-commerce is in the pilot basis meaning that DGFT intends to learn more from exporter's feedback so as to revamp the policy. As a matter of fact, the notified six categories of goods can be exported in manual mode through FPOs at New Delhi, Mumbai and Chennai.
3. Exports of goods for the 'free on board' (FOB) value not exceeding up to ₹25,000 per consignment shall be entitled to rewards under the MEIS scheme. It is important that an exporter must have followed the necessary documentation for proving the export of goods as notified under the Courier Imports and Exports (Clearance) Regulations, 1986.
4. DGFT has made it clear that if the value of exports using e-commerce platform is more than ₹25,000 per consignment, an exporter shall be entitled to MEIS reward only to the extent of ₹25,000 only.
5. Exports through a registered courier service are permitted as per notification issued by the Department of Revenue. However, importability/exportability of such items shall be regulated

in accordance with FTP/ITC(HS) Codes. Goods including free samples may be exported/imported by airfreight or through FPO or through courier, as per customs procedure.

6. Export of such goods under courier regulations shall be allowed manually on pilot basis through airports at Delhi, Mumbai and Chennai as per appropriate amendments in regulations to be made by the Department of Revenue. The Department of Revenue has notified for the detailed procedure by use of the postal bill of export (PBE) and has also fast-tracked the initiatives for the implementation of EDI mode at courier terminals.
7. The declaration for claiming of benefit under MEIS shall be made by the exporter on PBE. Every PBE shall be filed in duplicate and shall cover only 1 consignor and up to 10 consignees. In other words, a maximum of 10 shipments can be affected using a single PBE.
8. Export shipments filed under all categories of the shipping bills would need the following declaration on the shipping bills in order to be eligible for claiming rewards under MEIS: 'We intend to claim rewards under Merchandise Exports From India Scheme (MEIS)'. Such declaration shall be required even for export shipments under any of the schemes of Chapter 4 (including drawback), Chapter 5 or Chapter 6 of FTP. In the case of shipping bills (other than free shipping bills), such declaration of intent shall be mandatory with effect from 1 June 2015.
9. The exporter shall be required to attach the invoice(s) with PBE. He shall also be required to provide specific details of the e-commerce transaction in PBE, namely:
   a. URL of the website through which goods have been sold.
   b. The SKU number as a reference link to the sale through e-commerce on the website.
   c. Payment transaction reference number corresponding to the payment received through international credit card/debit card for the sale made on the website.

   In addition, the exporter shall continue to comply with the requirements under Section 82 of the Customs Act, 1962, namely filing of the label or declaration as prescribed by the postal department (e.g., CN23).
10. PBE along with goods shall be presented to customs at FPO. PBE shall be processed manually. Upon processing of PBE by customs, the goods shall be presented to the postal department, who will acknowledge receipt of the shipment on PBE and affix the tracking number of each shipment on the same. Upon affixation of the tracking number by postal authorities, PBE shall be brought back to the proper officer for grant of 'let export order' (LEO).
11. The original PBE will be retained by customs and the duplicate PBE will be handed over to the exporter. Since e-commerce shipments are time-bound express shipments, principal commissioners/commissioners are advised to ensure speedy clearance of the parcels and use non-intrusive examination techniques like X-ray for facilitating clearance. In the event of any specific intelligence/suspicion regarding the goods contained in the parcel, which necessitates examination, the approval of the deputy commissioner of customs/assistant commissioner of customs shall be obtained by the proper officer for opening and examining the same.
12. Commissionarates are advised to make suitable arrangements for noting and processing of PBEs. All other extant norms for processing of shipping bills, like amendments, shall also apply to PBE.
13. Applications for export of goods through courier or FPOs using e-commerce can be filed online, using digital signature in Ayat Niryat Form (ANF 3D) by the exporter. The applicant shall file a separate application for each port of export and concerned regional authority of DGFT will manually examine the submitted documents before the grant of scrip.

4.6 Trade Information System for Exporters

In order to cater to the growing needs of trade information and trade promotion from India, GOI has set up a dedicated Ministry of Commerce and Industry which is headed by a minister of cabinet rank and there are several promotion and facilitation bodies in order to cater to the varied needs of the export community of India. The mandate of the Department of Commerce under the Ministry of Commerce and Industry is to regulate, develop and promote the foreign trade of India including international commerce through the formulation of appropriate international trade and commercial policy and implementation of the various agreements that India has signed with partner countries at bilateral, regional and multilateral levels. The prime function of the Department of Commerce is to facilitate the creation of an enabling economic and trade environment for expansion and diversification of foreign trade and commerce into and from India including the required infrastructure at all levels such as roads, rail, ports, airports, testing and inspection labs, banks and credit institutions, training institutes and so on for accelerated growth and expansion of international trade and commerce in India. The Director General of Commercial Intelligence and Statistics (DGCI&S) is the nodal agency under the Ministry of Commerce for collection, compilation and dissemination of trade data in India. Similarly, there are many other trade institutions providing vital information on emerging trade opportunities all over the world. These trade information institutions are discussed in the following sub-sections.

4.6.1 Director General of Commercial Intelligence and Statistics

DGCI&S is the prime trade data collection, compilation and dissemination agency in India and is working under the administrative control of DGFT. It provides the vital trade data for decision on issues related to exports and imports to policymakers, exporters, importers and researchers across the country which is a source of guidance and direction for EXIM trade and help these stakeholders to formulate trade policies, roadmaps and strategies. It provides the foreign trade data to trade communities and policymakers in many forms, for example, it brings out computer disc of monthly and quarterly trade statistics of India. It also generates data on the specific request of policymakers, for example, data related to the particular commodity or port or state of India for a particular year as per the user's request. DGCI&S has a priced information system so as to provide data on a commercial basis to exporters, importers, researchers except for purely central and state governments and UN bodies which demand data for framing the new trade policy, analyses and policy correction, if any. DGCI&S has also put in place a data suppression policy so as not to disclose commercially sensitive information of an exporter to another; for example, DGCI&S never provides the trade statistics of at what price a particular exporter has exported to an importer. Hence, data suppression policy allows DGCI&S to maintain confidentiality of importer's and exporter's commercially sensitive business data and no one can have access to transaction-level data of an exporter or importer, thus protecting the privacy of the trader's business information. DGCI&S data can be in any of the following single combinations depending on the customer's specific data requirements:

1. Data for a specific commodity and country
2. Data for a specific port with specific commodity and country
3. Data for a particular commodity only
4. Data for a particular country only
5. Data for a particular port only

4.6.2 World Association for Small and Medium Enterprises

World Association for Small and Medium Enterprises (WASME) is based in Noida, India, and is set up as a global civil society organization with the prime aim of facilitating and spearheading the cause and development of small and medium enterprises (SMEs) in the changing world order where only large enterprises with scale, systems, speed and superior technology are gaining increased market share in the world trade. WASME was set up in 1980 and provides a great forum to micro, small and medium enterprises which are the backbone of many developing economies including India where 40 percent exports in value are contributed by MSMEs. WASME has effectively emerged as one of the most representative, effective and leading international organization, working towards the promotion of SMEs through information dissemination and networking by using appropriate online and offline tools so as to facilitate small and medium exporters to collaborate in production, exports, imports and other business areas.

4.6.3 National Centre for Trade Information

National Centre for Trade Information (NCTI) was set up as a Section 25 company (no profit and no loss) in March 1995, and started functioning from March 1996. NCTI is an important trade information agency as it analyses the trade data of various countries according to the requirements of several ministries, export promotion councils and other associated organizations including foreign missions abroad. NCTI conducts global trade analysis by using different and very useful databases which are of vital significance in the decision-making of exporters, importers and policymakers in India. The depth of trade data analysis is very high, thus NCTI provides vital leads in possible areas of business opportunities to all concerned. These analyses conducted by NCTI on exports, imports and investments at state, national and international levels are very useful for the following stakeholders:

1. NCTI trade analysis guides Indian exporters about the avenues to export their merchandise and services, and also provides them leads on prospective regions and countries with which Indian exporters should engage with.
2. NCTI trade analysis guides Indian importers to know about tariff concessions and duties imposed on them by other countries including the negotiated tariff preference in signed FTAs.
3. NCTI trade analysis provides vital leads to GOI trade negotiation team and other policymakers to engage effectively on India's concerns in various FTAs and PTAs with foreign countries including taking the corrective actions in the existing FTA, if so required.
4. NCTI trade analysis is of vital significance for EPCs/commodity boards (CBs)/export development authorities (EDAs) and so on to analyse their tariff line and share in trade data and plan new policies aimed at expansion and diversification of foreign trade from India.

4.6.4 International Trade Centre

The International Trade Centre (ITC) has emerged as a prime agency for dissemination of trade data and knowledge of international business among exporters and importers. ITC was set up as a subsidiary organization under the joint aegis of WTO and the United Nations Conference on Trade and Development (UNCTAD). ITC provides trade-related technical assistance and information at zero cost to exporters and importers of developing countries and LDCs. It has developed several trade analytical tools like 'Trade Map' which is an interactive online database on international trade statistics. Trade Map offers vital indicators on export performance, international demand and alternative markets in time series data and trade indicators data. It also offers information on the role of competitors from both the product and country perspectives, thus helping exporters to take appropriate international trade decisions. The Trade Map is in fact one of the largest trade databases in the world as it covers trade data information for around 220 countries and territories and 5,300 products defined at the 2-, 4- or 6-digit level of HS. It also offers specific trade data information at 8-digit levels to Indian exporters. An exporter and importer can collect the trade information either with pre-calculated trade indicators (e.g., growth, market shares, average unit values and so on) or in time series (e.g., monthly, quarterly and yearly) from 2001 onwards. Another important database of ITC called 'Market Access Map' also presents comprehensive information on the different types of trade barriers such as tariff and non-tariff barriers. One can understand the tariff structure in different forms such as applied customs tariffs (MFN duty/preferential duty and so on) ad valorem equivalents, tariff rate quotas, trade remedies, rules of origin, certificate of origin, bound tariffs of WTO members and non-tariff measures.

4.6.5 Indian Institute of Foreign Trade

Indian Institute of Foreign Trade (IIFT) was set up in 1963 primarily to train the manpower of the country in the external sector. It has been playing an important role in professionalizing the manpower in the areas of foreign trade management through a regular course offered at the Graduate Studies Division. Moreover, it focuses on primary trade research aimed at increasing exports in both goods and services. IIFT also conducts training programmes for developing human resources of policymakers and industry. It has systems in place for analysing and disseminating trade information and policy inputs and other associated operational research. Centre for WTO studies of IIFT plays an important role in providing policy inputs to Indian negotiators in engaging trade negotiations at WTO. Similarly, Centre for MSME Studies provides training, incubation services and hand-holding support to Indian traders to grow as exporters or importers. Management development division is playing a vital role through Niryat Bandhu programme aimed at skilling new entrepreneurs for international markets.

4.6.6 Indian Trade Promotion Organization

Indian Trade Promotion Organization (ITPO) is one of the premier trade promotion agencies of the Ministry of Commerce and Industry, GOI, and provides a wide array of services aimed at export promotion and expansion in newer markets by linking Indian exporters to international markets. ITPO is the largest nodal agency for organizing various trade fairs, exhibitions and expositions across the country. It organizes, finances and hand-holds various expositions in India so that exporters and importers can expose their merchandise and services without any problems, thus network for future trade opportunities. ITPO prepares the directory of international buyers and sellers, and share it with exporters and importers for trade information, business planning and networking.

4.6.7 Export–Import Bank of India

Export–Import Bank of India (Exim Bank) was set up in 1981 and started functioning from 1982. It provides financial assistance to Indian exporters and importers including trade information on emerging trade opportunities extended through lines of credit. Exim Bank is, in fact, a banker's bank, thus coordinating the working of commercial banks in India engaged in financing export and import of goods and services so as to expand and diversify India's international trade. Exim Bank provides information and support services to Indian exporters and helps improve their prospects for securing business in multilateral agencies funded projects such as the World Bank and the Asian Development Bank. Exim Bank is playing a vital importer role to establish India as a hub of global services and in order to promote Indian consultancy, it has tied up with a number of international organizations such as International Finance Corporation and Eastern and Southern African Trade and Development Bank. It also offers business information as consultant to various developing countries in promoting exports and imports finance. Finally, it helps in knowledge gaining and sharing through the conduct of seminars, workshops and carrying out research studies on projects, sectors, countries and macroeconomic issues. The banks offer vital information through sector-specific studies for identifying the market potential for Indian goods and services and also country-specific reports for emerging markets. Exim Bank gathers and disseminates foreign trade information to Indian exporters, importers and industry through market and country report.

4.6.8 Export Credit Guarantee Corporation

ECGC Limited was set up as a GOI enterprise in 1957, mainly to cover the credit risks and offer guarantees to Indian exporters, thus strengthening India's export promotion efforts. ECGC is the fifth largest credit insurers of the world and has a corresponding relationship with other important credit insurers in the world for sharing of credit rating information, exposure limits, payment history, credit rating of the buyer and the buyer's country, credit rating of the issuing bank in case of L/C and so on, thus offering important business and trade information to Indian exporters. In addition to credit insurance protection to Indian exporters against international payment risks, ECGC provides guidance in export-related activities by making available information on different countries with its own credit ratings. This makes exporters' job easy in availing the export finance from commercial banks and financial institutions and assists Indian exporters in recovering bad debts. ECGC provides complete information on credit-worthiness of overseas buyers including the names and addresses of prospective buyers in the overseas markets.

4.6.9 Centre for the Promotion of Imports from Developing Countries

Centre for the Promotion of Imports from Developing Countries (CBI) was established in 1971 under the aegis of Ministry of Foreign Affairs, the Netherlands. CBI provides the real-time business intelligence related to exports and imports of European countries to exporters and business support organizations (BSOs) in developing countries so as to enable them to effectively engage in European markets. CBI offers trade-related information about relevant government and private agencies and guides exporters from developing countries on the ways and means to engage in international trade in European countries. It has an online facility that links the manufacturers and suppliers based in developing countries to connect with reliable international buyers in the European Union. CBI also provides training to exporters and BSOs from developing countries like India on the export marketing, trade promotion, management of international trade fair participation and developing client-oriented market information systems.

4.6.10 Federation of Indian Export Organisations

Federation of Indian Export Organisations (FIEO) is the apex trade promotion organization in India which was jointly established by the Ministry of Commerce and Industry, GOI, and Indian exporter's community. FIEO conducts a number of training programmes aimed at business networking, knowledge dissemination and has the largest database of Indian exporters. It also conducts trade fairs, leads business delegations, invites exporters' feedback and publishes primary research information aimed at promotion of exports from India. It is directly involved in promotion of all involved in foreign trade, that is, exporting firms, consultancy firms, service exporters, banks, export management training institutes and so on, and brings them under one umbrella for exploring the potential export opportunities and learning from each other's experiences.

4.6.11 National Small Industries Corporation

National Small Industries Corporation (NSIC) is a GOI undertaking, set up under the administrative control of Ministry of Micro, Small & Medium Enterprises of India in 1955. The prime purpose of its establishment was to promote and develop micro and small-scale industries and enterprises in the country and provide them a helping hand in scaling up their business first to domestic markets and then preparing them to engage in global trade operations in the changing world trade scenario. In order to promote industrialization in the country and provide additional employment opportunities, NSIC provides machinery on hire–purchase basis and assists small and micro enterprises in India and also supports them in marketing their products internationally. For those who are intending to start export business afresh, NSIC is a vital link, as it provides assistance in setting up incubation centres in other countries where Indian small enterprises can make footprints for exports. It also organizes IT fairs to provide aspiring entrepreneurs and emerging small enterprises a platform to develop skills, identify appropriate technology, provide hands-on experience on the working projects, manage funds through banks and practical knowledge on how to set up an enterprise. New exporters can get significant business information by exchanging their new business ideas at international trade fairs and showcasing the competencies of their business enterprise and capture international market opportunities. Member exporters of NSIC participate in selected international trade exhibitions every year. NSIC facilitates the participation of small enterprises by providing special discount on stall rental and airfare, thus providing the important international exposure to small business units in the international market and enhancing their business prowess. NSIC, in fact, is a brand name for the development and promotion of Indian small-scale industry internationally, as it provides vital business information and trade links under the NSIC banner and facilitates Indian small-scale units to grow and expand their business in global markets.

4.6.12 Export Promotion Councils

EPCs are set up by GOI in major areas of finished exports with the basic objective of promoting and developing the exports of the country. Each of the EPCs is responsible for the promotion of a particular group of products, projects and services. There were 27 EPCs in India by the end of the year 2022. Their main role is to project the image of Indian goods and services in international markets and encourage their member exporter's to become reliable suppliers of high-quality goods and services. In today's globalized world, it is important for EPCs to encourage and monitor their exporter members for observing the international standards and specifications for both goods and services so that India is recognized as a reliable supplier in world markets. EPCs do a great job in updating their members about emerging imports trends and opportunities in international markets for goods and services, and assist them in taking advantage of such opportunities in order to expand and diversify India's exports. The major functions of the EPCs are listed as follows:

1. They provide commercially useful information to Indian exporters so as to assist them in expansion and diversification of exports from India.
2. They provide professional export advice to their members for improvements in manufacturing technology, quality upgradation, product design improvement, enhanced compliance in established standards and specifications and so on, thus improving the overall products or services offer of Indian exporters in international markets.
3. They are funded by GOI so as to take business delegations of Indian exporters in proven trade fairs, buyers–sellers meet, goodwill visit missions and so on, which helps Indian exporters to explore overseas market opportunities in greater degree and scale.
4. They are mandated to organize trade fairs, exhibitions and expositions in India and abroad, wherein the buyers and sellers network for enhanced business opportunities.
5. They are supposed to promote interaction between the exporting community and the government, wherein bringing exporters' problems at both the central and state levels, thus ensuring redressal of the same through bureaucratic actions.
6. They are also required to build a statistical base of both exporters and importers and make available such data to their members so as to increase networking. They are also required to keep records of sectoral exports—year-wise, quarter-wise and month-wise—so as to understand firsthand the exports and imports of the country, exports and imports of their members, as well as that of key importing countries.

4.6.13 Commodity Boards

In order to promote the trade of agro-commodities, GOI has set up Commodity Boards (CBs) as a separate export promotion organization. CBs play a vital role in the promotion and facilitation of exports and imports of agro-products and do required handholding with Indian agro-exporters from the stage of post-harvest of these identified commodities. There are seven CBs: Tea, Coffee, Coir, Rubber, Tobacco, Spices and Coconut Development Board which are playing a significant role in export-promotion efforts in these areas. CBs are at par with EPCs, in terms of legal mandates for export promotion. EPCs are primarily aimed at export promotion of value-added manufactured products, while CBs look after the export promotion of primary and traditional items of export. In the changing business environment and to strengthen their backward linkages for export surplus and promotion, CBs are also taking up product diversification, expansion and development. The functions and objectives of CBs are as follows:

1. They advise DGFT on policy matters such as fixing quotas for exports and entering into trade agreements with foreign countries in the areas of commodities they handle.
2. They undertake promotional activities for export promotion such as participation in exhibition and trade fairs, opening of foreign offices abroad, conducting marketing surveys, sponsoring trade delegations and organizing buyers–sellers meet.

3. They take required steps so as to increase the consumption of commodities in their jurisdiction by opening branch offices in foreign countries. This may involve planning advertisements and other promotions aimed at changing the consumption pattern of prospective consumers.
4. They are required to resolve all problems of exporters and importers in the areas of their operations.
5. They undertake research activities to develop production and marketing activities within the country. Many of the CBs have expertise and experience for research studies and they occasionally conduct such studies.
6. They are also required to impart training to workers engaged in the production of the commodity concerned. For example, the National Coir Training and Design Centre, Kerala, and Indian Institute of Handloom Technology at Salem and at Varanasi are the training institutes set up by their respective CBs.

4.6.14 Export Development Authorities

In order to strengthen the value chain for export of value-added agricultural items, the GOI has set up two EDAs, namely the Marine Products Export Development Authority (MPEDA) and APEDA. While MPEDA was constituted in 1972 under the Marine Products Export Development Authority Act, 1972, APEDA was set up under the Agricultural & Processed Food Products Export Development Authority Act, 1985. MPEDA replaced the erstwhile Marine Products Export Promotion Council, which was the nodal agency for growth, promotion and development of export of marine products from India. The role envisaged for MPEDA is much wider in scope, scale and significance as it has a comprehensive mandate for export promotion for fisheries of all kinds at all stages of economic activity, namely production, processing, marketing, extension, export standards and training of those involved in India's fisheries sector. MPEDA plays a vital role with the registration of infrastructural facilities for seafood export trade including collection and dissemination of trade information for this sector. MPEDA is directly involved in the promotion of Indian marine products in overseas markets by organizing joint and direct participation in international trade fairs and international seafood fairs. GOI as well as respective state governments implement the development schemes for fisheries and marine products sector including extending financial assistance for the purchase of insulated fish boxes for captive production which can be exported out of India. MPEDA extends vital support through the improvement of peeling sheds, establishment of captive peeling sheds, modernization of seafood industry to upgrade the processing machinery, installation of IQF machinery, generator sets, flake-ice-making machineries, quality control laboratory and so on. The role of MPEDA cannot be underestimated in creating additional economic activity, promoting employment through the export of aquaculture, deep sea fishing, test fishing and in augmenting the marine products infrastructure through joint venture and equity participation.

The efforts of APEDA are aimed at the promotion of value-added agro-products including processed products, thus increasing the farm income by augmenting the capacity of production, processing and export of these products to international markets. The specific functions performed by APEDA include the development of industries relating to the agro-products for exports and this is achieved by extending financial assistance to involved stakeholders. Further, APEDA conducts a large number of agricultural surveys and feasibility studies including studies aimed at improving market access in international markets. APEDA is directly involved in fixing of standards and specifications for the agro- and processed food products in consultation with international bodies. It is involved in carrying out the inspection of meat and meat products in slaughterhouses, including compliance of Halal standards, hygiene and cleanliness of processing plants, storage premises, reefer facilities and conveyances used for transportation of processed agro-products. APEDA advises Indian exporters on improvement of the packaging of the agricultural products from the stage of post-harvest in sync with country-specific packing, labelling and marking standards. Additionally, APEDA trains staff of export companies involved in marketing and exports of agro-products in international markets.

4.7 Summary

E-commerce refers to any virtual business or commercial transaction where the transfer of information takes place on the Internet and goods move from producer to consumer via express or courier or virtual means. It essentially entails the transfer of information across the Internet to create a virtual exchange where buyers and sellers can do trading. Marketplace, especially in the developed and emerging markets, is fast changing from physical markets to virtual markets as consumers are increasingly looking forward to buying online instead of going to the physical marketplace. There is ease in doing so, as goods are cost-effective as many trade intermediaries get eliminated, it is very simple to order, it saves time, the comfort of services is provided at home and, above all, there is possibility of returns if not found satisfactory. All this has been possible only because of two electronic networks known as 'e-commerce' and 'e-business'. The introduction of a virtual marketplace through e-commerce has dramatically changed the business landscape and with increased digitalization in world economy, it will continue to do so in the ways that cannot be predicted. There are plenty of business advantages that e-commerce offers to the marginal and small exporters, especially in certain sectors such as accessories, leather products, handicrafts, handlooms, textiles and apparels, electronics and gifts. Global customers have quick and easy access to a tremendous amount of information that enables them to find, assess, compare, review and select a product of their choice virtually from anywhere in the world. E-commerce is a virtual marketplace, and in order to export online globally, an exporter has to buy the market space online for publishing the product portfolio and information on the World Wide Web. Hence, one should be well versed in computers, the Internet, email or setting up own website, online banking and other related instruments of sharing information. An exporter must have, at a minimum, an adequate computer system (laptop), telephone system (mobile and landline both) and the ability to send and receive faxes. It is the computer system including the access to the Internet, email and other software that support the business in e-commerce, hence are essentially required. Realizing the fact that e-commerce has an important role to play in India's export story, DGFT defined e-commerce as 'means of buying and selling of goods and services including digital products, conducted over digital and electronic network' in FTP 2015–2020 and allowed the exports of goods through e-commerce platforms. Export through e-commerce shall be entitled to duty credit scrip as offered under the MEIS scheme to Indian exporters. E-commerce shall mean the export of goods hosted on a website accessible through the Internet to a purchaser. In order to cater to growing needs of trade information and trade promotion from India, GOI has set up a dedicated Ministry of Commerce and Industry which is headed by a minister of cabinet rank and there are several promotion and facilitation bodies in order to cater to varied needs of the export community of India. The various sources of vital information for promoting both exports and imports in India are DGCI&S, WASME, NCTI, ITC, IIFT, ITPO, Exim Bank, ECGC, CBI, NSIC, EPCs, CBs, EDAs, etc.

Review Exercises

Multiple Choice Questions

1. E-commerce refers to
   a. Virtual exchange of business information
   b. Buying and selling online
   c. A marketplace supported by the Internet services
   d. A platform for transacting virtually
   e. All of the above

2. An electronic website where commercial transactions are carried out between customers is referred to as
   a. B2B
   b. B2C
   c. C2B
   d. None of the above

3. An electronic website which facilitates commercial transactions between customers and businesses is known as
   a. B2B
   b. B2C
   c. C2C
   d. C2B
   e. None of the above

4. Alibaba, Oracle and Qualcomm are which of the following types of e-commerce platforms?
   a. B2B
   b. B2C
   c. C2C
   d. C2B
   e. None of the above

5. Electronic website wherein the goods and services are sold by a business group to customers across a virtual marketplace is known as
   a. B2B
   b. B2C
   c. C2C
   d. C2B
   e. None of the above

6. For export through e-commerce model, DGFT has allowed exports only up to how many thousand rupees per transaction?

a. ₹25,000 per transaction
b. ₹50,000 per transaction
c. $25,000 per transaction
d. $50,000 per transaction
e. None of the above

7. Which of the following is the most important agency for trade data collection, compilation and dissemination in India?

a. DGCI&S
b. IIFT
c. NCTI
d. DGFT
e. None of the above

8. How many EPCs are there in India?

a. 25
b. 37
c. 27
d. 26
e. None of the above

Critical Thinking Questions

1. What is the concept of e-commerce and e-business? How far is e-commerce a reality for EXIM business?

2. Critically elucidate the advantages of e-business and essentials for venturing into e-commerce business.

3. What is the procedure for exports of merchandize through e-commerce? Who frames this policy in India? What are the salient features of the existing e-commerce policy for exports?

4. What are the sources of trade information for EXIM business? Examine.

5. Write a short note on any two of the following:

a. DGCI&S

b. WASME

c. NCTI

d. ITC

6. Write a brief note on any two of the following:

a. ITPO

b. Exim Bank

c. ECGC

d. EPCs

CHAPTER 5

Legal Formalities for Getting Started in Foreign Trade

CHAPTER OBJECTIVES

- To explain the various types of business formation for getting started in EXIM business.
- To appraise the key features of each type of business formation.
- To understand HS of nomenclature for product classification and description.
- To explain the various formalities for getting started in EXIM operations.
- To explain the formalities for reducing and neutralizing the incidence of taxes in the EXIM chain.

5.1 Introduction

For getting started in international business in cultural goods, it is a must that one should have an organization such as sole proprietorship, partnership firm, joint stock company and limited liability partnership (LLP). Law and business practices in India allow different types of business enterprises which are organized in several forms and may vary from one another on the basis of ownership, formation, existence, purpose and so on. Each form of business organization has its own merits and demerits, and the ultimate choice of selecting a particular business model largely depends on the balancing of advantages and disadvantages of the various forms of business. One should be particular while organizing a firm under a particular form of business. The choice of the particular form of business is important, as it determines the sharing of profit and loss, management power and control, and risk and responsibility of the businessman. Since EXIM business requires long-term commitment from a businessman, the choice of a particular form of business should be done after due deliberations, consultation and diligence. The factors explained in Figure 5.1 can guide someone interested to form a new organization for getting started in export business. *First* and foremost is the 'ease in formation and dissolution' of business. Ease in formation of an organization is a prime and important criterion, as exporters are usually SMEs. Sole proprietorship is the easier model of starting a business, and it can be dissolved at the will of the owner any time. Partnership firms are also easy to form, and regulatory formalities in the beginning as well as at the time of dissolution of both sole proprietorship and partnerships are lower. Other forms of business such as joint stock companies, trusts, cooperatives and Hindu Undivided Family (HUF) take time to form and dissolve, as there is a prescribed regulatory procedure for doing so. *Second*, one should understand the 'nature of business', which is one of the most important factors for making choice on formation of a particular type of business organization. There are businesses which require a lot of financial resources and manpower like a big manufacturing firm.

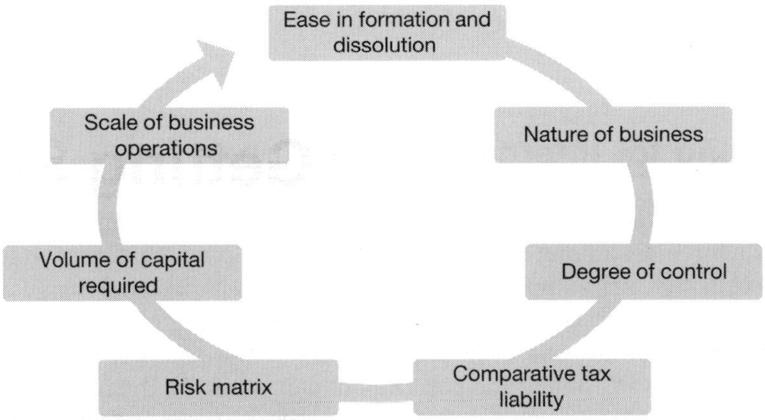

FIGURE 5.1 Factors affecting the choice of business form in EXIM business.

These are suitable with joint stock companies; however, businesses such as restaurants, consultancy and professional services such as doctors, chartered engineers, lawyers and chartered accountants are usually organized as proprietary concerns. Some businesses like product merchandising require pooling of specialized manpower and financial resources and can be successfully anchored upon on the partnership business model that facilitates it. Moreover, some other firms when engaging in the business of welfare, that is, social service, can be best leveraged with a 'trust' or a 'society'.

Third, the 'size and scale of business operations' are important guiding factors. The size of businesses like micro, small, medium or large and scale of business operations such as local, regional, national and international serve as important factors in making a choice of appropriate forms of business organization in export business. Businesses with greater volume and scale of business operations catering to national and international markets are usually organized as public or government companies. Small businesses are usually organized as partnerships, LLPs and proprietorships. *Fourth*, the 'degree of control' is an important criterion while deciding the business form, as the degree of control varies in different forms of business organizations and one should consider how much he/she wants to leverage his/her control on business operations of the firm. One can exercise a higher degree of control in business operations through proprietorship which decreases the degree in partnership, LLP, HUF, private company, public company and government company. *Fifth*, one should factor in the 'volume of capital required' for any business formation as the need of financial resources is an important guiding factor for choice of a suitable form of business organization for export business. Higher capital needs can be suitably met in forms like public sector which can raise capital from public after having completed the required formalities through the Securities and Exchange Board of India. If capital needs are smaller, one can start with proprietorship and can convert it into partnership, LLP, private company and public company with increasing need for volume of capital required. *Sixth*, one should consider and evaluate the 'risk matrix' while selecting a business form for getting into international business. Risk matrix varies in different types of business organizations. One can choose a business form depending upon his/her willingness to bear the volume of risks and liabilities that are involved in particular types of businesses. As company is an artificial person, individual risks are less but there are higher regulatory compliances; similarly, liability is limited in proprietorship and partnership to the extent of contributed capital. *Last but not least*, one should factor the comparative tax liability among different forms of business as certain business forms like HUF offer lower tax liability in comparison to joint stock companies. Trust and societies also attract lower tax rates due to the business objective being creation of welfare in the society.

5.2 Organizing for International Business

There exist different forms of business organizations in India to do business both domestically and internationally. The foremost among them is sole proprietorship which is easy to form and simple to operate. When more capital and manpower is required, individuals can pool their capital and resources and form a partnership firm. For doing business at a larger scale, the preferred form is joint stock company which is created under law and is an artificial person and has perpetual succession. The joint stock companies can be private, public and government depending on the needs and purpose of incorporation. For promoting the Indian value system of a joint-family system and ensuring employment to such family members, GOI offers simple and incentivizing form of business called 'Hindu Undivided Family'. Limited Liability Partnership (LLP) is a clone of partnership firm and a joint stock company and Indian legislation allowed such business forms with the enactment of the Limited Liability Partnership Act, 2008. Trusts and cooperatives are other business forms which are mainly formed for creating welfare in the society with no-profit no-loss objectives. The choice of formation of any business form for international business may vary on the basis of the factors given in Figure 5.2.

Based on the factors highlighted in Figure 5.2, any form of the business organization (Figure 5.3) can be chosen to incorporate a business organization for starting international business in India.

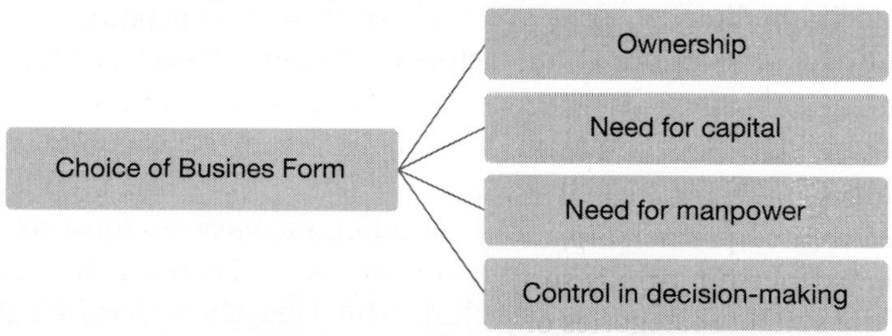

FIGURE 5.2 Factors affecting choice of business form.

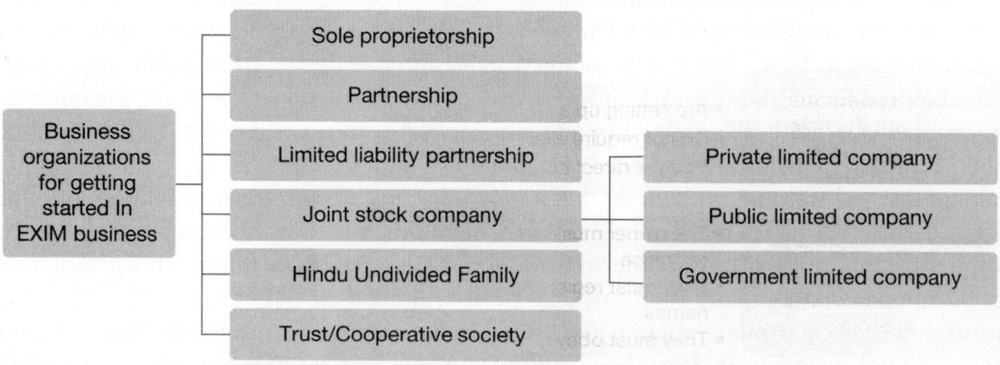

FIGURE 5.3 Various forms of business organizations for getting started in EXIM business.

5.2.1 Sole Proprietorship

A sole proprietorship is the simplest and easiest form of doing business as any business activity under this model is owned, operated and managed by only one person. It is also the least costly among all forms of business model to get started. Under this business form, sole proprietor faces the unlimited liability and even the personal assets of the owner are under stake in case of losses and creditors of the business may go after owner's personal assets if he/she fails to pay his/her creditors. It is suitable for use by small business entities as one does not need to fulfil the long list of legal formalities, which is usually the case in other forms of doing business. For example, starting a chemist shop, provision store, a consultancy firm, tour and travel operator or a restaurant. Figure 5.4 depicts the suitable as well as mandatory formalities for starting sole proprietorship in India.

One has to take a 'trade licence' in the desired area of sole proprietorship from the competent authority. The size and scale of business operations can be to any limit but since only one person manages it, he/she has limitations such as capital, labour and risk exposure. Sole traders are the most common form of business in case of domestic trade in India; however, there are few sole traders venturing into international business. This business form is very popular for domestic business. The business under this form is owned and operated by one person only, but he/she is free to employ any number of persons to assist him/her to do business. The key advantages and disadvantages of sole proprietorship are depicted in Figure 5.5.

5.2.2 Partnership

The partnership firm is formed to overcome the disadvantages associated with sole proprietorship. Under the partnership form of business organization, the business is owned and operated by two or more persons who contribute financial resources in the agreed proportion into the entity. The persons who create such business forms are called partners and divide the profits or losses among themselves in the proportion of their contributed capital. Under partnership, the partners have unlimited liability, meaning creditors can claim their personal assets as well in case of losses. However, there exists a business formation called limited partnership, under which creditors cannot claim the personal assets of limited partners. The partnership firm is suitable for the people venturing into international business (refer Figure 5.6 for the suitable categories of people).

Partnership is defined as 'an association of two or more than two persons who contribute jointly their financial and managerial resources and agree to carry on a business and share its profit and losses

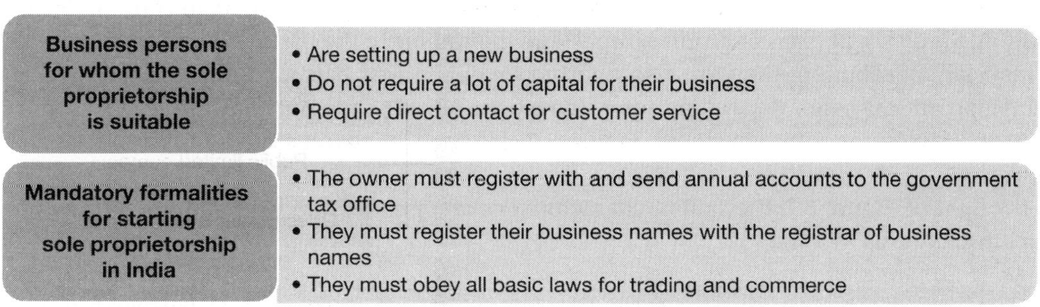

FIGURE 5.4 Mandatory formalities or starting sole proprietorship in India.

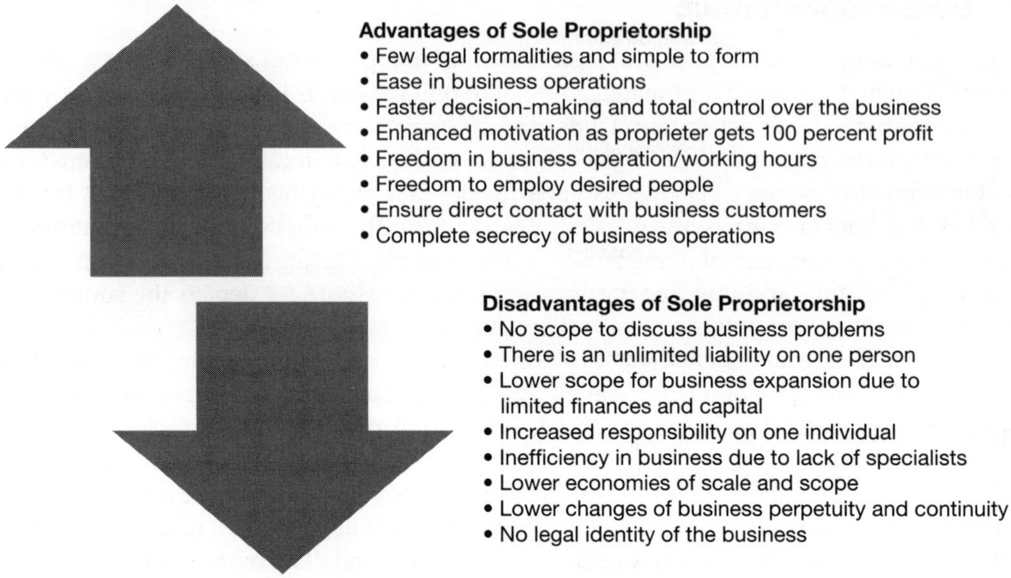

FIGURE 5.5 Advantages and disadvantages of sole proprietorship.

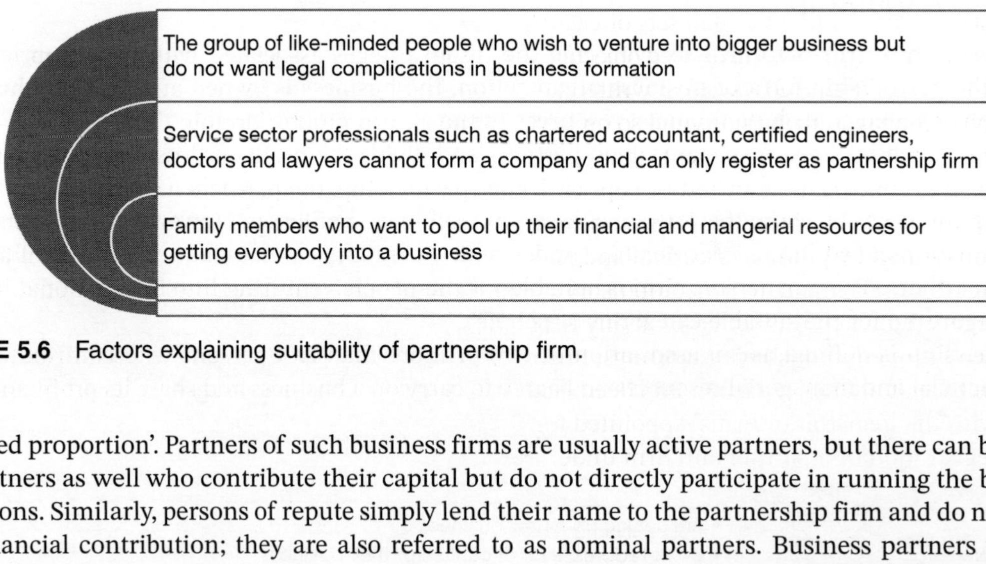

FIGURE 5.6 Factors explaining suitability of partnership firm.

in agreed proportion'. Partners of such business firms are usually active partners, but there can be sleeping partners as well who contribute their capital but do not directly participate in running the business operations. Similarly, persons of repute simply lend their name to the partnership firm and do not make any financial contribution; they are also referred to as nominal partners. Business partners under a partnership firm may vary depending upon the extent of participation, sharing of profits and losses, liability and involvement into business. Figure 5.7 classifies the various types of partners in a partnership firm.

In the light of Figure 5.7, the salient characteristics of a partnership firm and the process of formation are discussed as follows:

1. The legalisation governing the formation, execution and dissolution of partnership in India is called the Partnership Act, 1932.

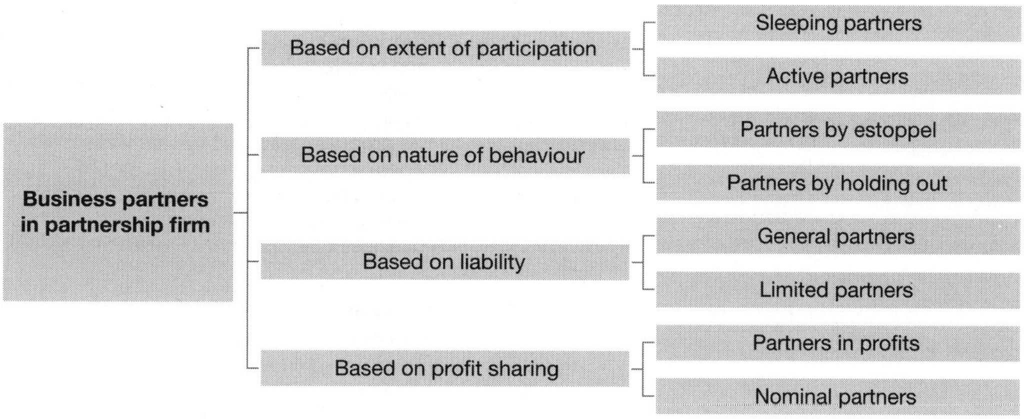

FIGURE 5.7 Classification of business partners in partnership firm.

Source: Adapted from Partnership Act, 1932.

2. The Act mandates that there has to be minimum two members to form a partnership. It further mandates the maximum limit of 10 members in case of banking firm and 20 in other kinds of businesses.
3. The formation of partnership is rooted in the fact that there should be like-minded persons, specialists complementing the skill sets of each other and the ones who intend to undertake the business as their own to fulfil the desired objectives for which they have come under partnership business.
4. It is ideally preferred to have a written agreement stating the objectives, share of capital, power to make managerial decisions and so on among partners. Such agreement must be duly signed by all the partners. Such agreement, that is, the partnership deed must contain the certain aspects of business information for smooth operations in future among partners as illustrated in Figure 5.8.
5. There can be a partnership firm without a written partnership deed, and it is construed to be constituted by pooling of capital and joint business operations among partners. The Partnership Act does not mandate for compulsory registration; however, it is highly recommended to get it registered when it is set up or at any time during its existence. Partnership firm without written deed is open to misunderstandings, mistrust and litigation among partners.
6. In case of a written partnership deed, such partners should get their partnership firm registered with the 'registrar of firms' appointed for this purpose by the concerned state. The procedure for registration of a partnership firm under the Partnership Act is given in Figure 5.9.

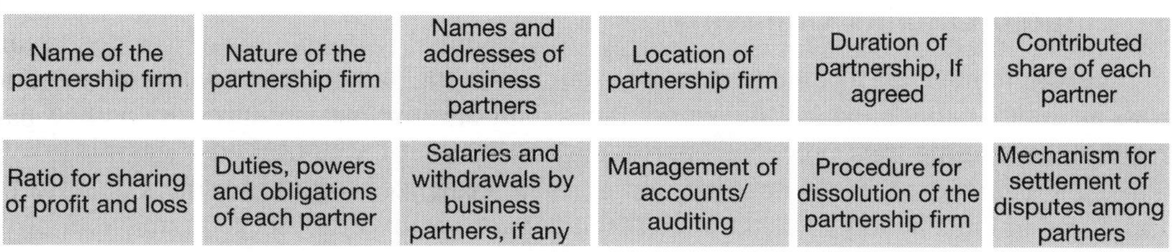

FIGURE 5.8 Information that should be integral part of partnership deed.

Source: Adapted from Partnership Act, 1932.

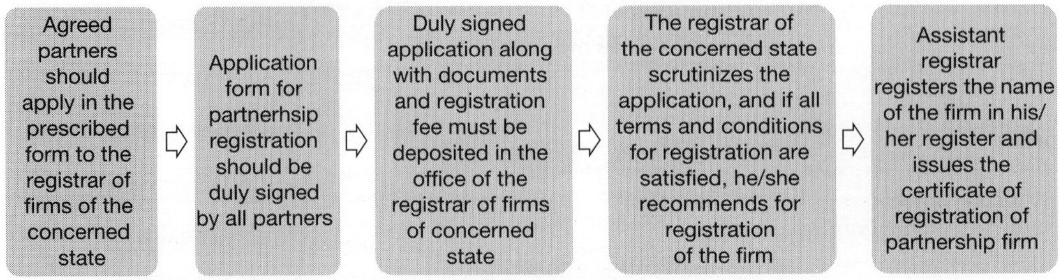

FIGURE 5.9 Step-by-step procedure for registration of partnership firm in India.

Source: Adapted from Partnership Act, 1932.

FIGURE 5.10 Advantages and disadvantages of partnership business form.

Partnership firm is a contractual relationship between one or more than two persons (maximum 20) whereby they agree to start an international business unit for the attainment of commonly agreed goals and the sharing of profits and losses is usually proportionate to contributed capital. It has lawful existence whereby the relationship of each partner with a partnership firm is that of principal as well as that of its agent. It overcomes many disadvantages associated with sole proprietorship; however, it has several disadvantages when compared with other types of business formation. Figure 5.10 depicts the advantages and disadvantages of a partnership firm.

5.2.3 Limited Liability Company

Cost and unease in business formation was the prime factor for India's poor ranking in ease of doing business, an index maintained by the World Bank. Foreign investors usually complained about a lengthy, time-consuming legal process to start a new business in India. LLP is an answer to all such questions. LLP is preferred, easy-to-operate and globally recognized form of business organization. It was introduced in India by way of the Limited Liability Partnership (LLP) Act 2008, and became operational from 1 April 2009. A limited liability partnership, popularly known as LLP, uniquely combines the best features of both a joint stock company and partnership. Under LLP, one partner is not responsible or liable for misconduct or negligence of another, thus, protecting each business partner from

Advantages of LLP

- Globally accepted form of business, easy to form and easy to manage and operate
- Lower cost in forming LLP and easy to dissolve or wind up the business operations
- No restrictions on number of partners and professionals to form multidisciplinary LLP
- No restrictions on pooling of minimum capital and limited liability of partners except in case of fraud
- LLP partners have exclusively distinct relationship and are not liable for acts and omissions of associated partners
- Minimum regulatory compliance and lower need for maintenance of statutory records
- Lower government intervention and audit of accounts only above contributions exceeding ₹2.5 million or turnover exceeding ₹4 million

Disadvantages of LLP

- Any fraud or omission or commission of associated partner may bind the honest partner to liability to the extent of his/her contribution in LLP
- If wilful misconduct is proved, then the liabilities of partners may even extend upto their personal assets
- Under LLP, partners cannot raise the capital from public

FIGURE 5.11 Advantages and disadvantages of LLP business form.

unlimited partnership. Further, the partner liability is limited to the extent of contributed capital in LLP and no claim arises to personal assets of partners in case of losses except in case of proven fraud or international misconduct. Hence, all partners under LLP have limited liability. It is unique as it provides freedom to work and decision-making as partners have the right to manage business directly unlike in case of a joint stock company. The key advantages and disadvantages of LLP are explained in Figure 5.11.

The legislation in India prescribes that the conduct of a LLP firm should be governed and managed as per the LLP agreement of the partners and in case a written agreement does not exist among partners, it would be governed by the framework and procedure as laid down and prescribed under the Schedule 1 of the LLP Act, 2008. LLP is a separate legal entity whereby the liability of partners is limited to the full extent of its assets but limited to their agreed contribution in LLP. It further provides that no partner in LLP shall be liable on account of the independent or unauthorized actions of other associated partners. This is a unique feature as it shields the honest partners from joint liability which is created by the wilful misconduct, omissions and commissions of other partners. Discussed below is the step-by-step process of forming LLP in India.

Step 1. Fixation of partners and designated partners: The LLP Act, 2008, mandates that there should be at least two minimum partners for incorporation of an LLP firm in India. These partners can be 'individuals' or 'body corporate' represented through their nominees. The Act further mandates that there should be at least two designated partners out of the total partners for any LLP firm, of which there must be at least one Indian resident. The definition to qualify as an Indian resident is similar to that defined in the Income Tax Act, 1961, which stipulates that one should have stayed more than 182 days in India to be qualified as an Indian resident.

Step 2. Obtaining Director Identification Number (DIN): The LLP Act mandates the need for obtaining DIN for each designated partner in the firm from GOI. The procedure and guidelines for obtaining DIN are prescribed and laid down by the Ministry of Corporate Affairs, GOI, and can be accessed from its website.

Step 3. Need of digital signature: The procedure for registration of LLP has been made online and one needs to procure a 'digital signature certificate' before applying for registration for the same. Any of the designated partners can obtain the digital signature certificate and can sign the documents for registration, filing of annual returns, approvals and intimations and so on.

Step 4. Availability of LLP firm name: At the time of application for registration, an applicant has to evaluate the proposed name of LLP firm under the prescribed parameters and accordingly make an application to the registrar in the prescribed form (Form 1) of Rule 18(5) of the LLP Act, 2008, for reservation of the desired name. The LLP Act mandates that the name of LLP shall not be similar or identical with company or LLP already registered in India. It further mandates that the name of LLP should not contain words which are prohibited under the Emblems and Names (Prevention of Improper Use) Act, 1950. If the central government is of the opinion that the name proposed by the applicant is 'undesirable' or 'unfit' or 'inappropriate', then it can request for an alternative name in lieu of the name proposed.

Step 5. Drafting of LLP agreement: Partners in the LLP firm have to draft the LLP agreement which will guide about the mutual rights and duties of the partners including the governing and operations of LLP firm. LLP agreement must be notarized in India and it is recommended that the same should be drafted, agreed and signed by partners before incorporation of the LLP firm. If the same is not drafted and submitted to the registrar within 30 days of incorporation, the rights and duties of partners will be governed by Schedule 1 of the LLP Act. Elements presented in Figure 5.12 are integral part of an LLP agreement among partners.

Step 6. Filing of incorporation documents: Having drafted the agreement and finalized the name of LLP firm, partners are required to file the required documents for incorporation of firm and consent of each partner to this effect. The application procedure is online with the 'registrar of LLP' and the same can be completed on payment of prescribed fee which is based on the total monetary value of contribution of partners in the proposed LLP. Partners also have to give a declaration that their association is for lawful purposes and they will not carry out anything forbidden under any law in India. Partners are also required to subscribe their names along with signatures to the subscription sheet mandated under the LLP Act. Each partner has to declare his

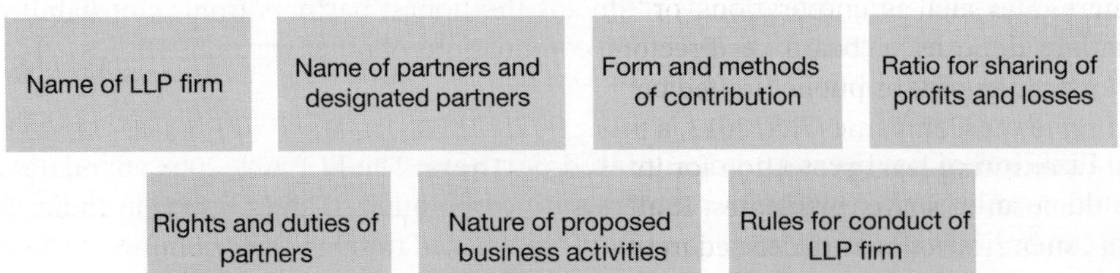

FIGURE 5.12 Essential elements of an LLP agreement among partners.

Source: Adapted from Limited Liability Partnership (LLP) Act, 2008.

consent that he/she is becoming partner to this firm without fear and awe and the same is witnessed by any chartered accountant/company secretary/advocate in practice.

Step 7. Issuance of certificate of incorporation: Once the registrar of the LLP is satisfied that the applicants have successfully completed all the formalities for incorporation of the LLP firm, he/she will issue a 'certificate of incorporation' which is usually within 14 days from the date of filing of documents. Partners can start their business under this legally created firm after having received the certificate of incorporation.

LLP is a new corporate structure for an emerging country like India which has a high cost of doing business. Its beauty lies in the fact that it combines the flexibility of a partnership and the advantages of limited liability of a company at a low compliance and operations cost. It is an alternative corporate business vehicle for foreign investors who want to start their business in a short span of time and shall be able to wind up without long legal hassles. The characteristics of LLP firm are unique in the sense that it provides the benefits of limited liability of a company, but at the same time allows its members the flexibility of organizing their internal management on the basis of a mutually arrived agreement, as is the case in a partnership firm. LLP can be a low-cost attractive vehicle for new SMEs as it is easy to register, flexible to manage and operate and yet has a separate legal status with limited liability for its partners. Small enterprises, especially in the services sector in India, are increasingly using this form of business to start domestic as well as international business.

5.2.4 Joint Stock Company

A joint stock company is an artificial person which is created by law and has perpetual succession. People may come in and people may go out, but the existence of such legally created company remains forever unless otherwise dissolved as per the procedure mandated under law. It is a separate business entity where share and securities can be bought, owned and sold by shareholders. The share of ownership of each shareholder is proportionate to contributed capital in such business formation and same is evidenced by his or her shares certificates. The ownership of each shareholder may vary from time to time as shareholders are free to buy and sell shares to other shareholders or new shareholders without causing any effects to the continued existence of such legally formed company. Synonymous to other contemporary legislations in the world, the Companies Act, 2013, also stipulates the separate existence of a joint stock company which has legal status having separate status from shareholders and limited liability. It means that shareholders of such business formation are liable only for the company's debts and the value of the money they have invested in the company. Joint stock companies are known by different names such as 'corporations' or 'limited companies'. The management and control of such companies are done by a 'board of directors' who are elected by the company stockholders. The company may be private or public limited company.

According to the Companies Act, 2013, a private limited company offers limited liability to its shareholders, thus ensuring legal protection for its shareholders that they are liable to extent of contributed capital in the form of share certificates. It also places certain restrictions on ownership among shareholders and such restrictions are defined in the company's bye-laws, takeover guidelines or regulations. These are meant to prevent any hostile takeover attempt to control the company. The Companies Act, 2013, stipulates three major ownership restrictions on private companies in India. *First*, shareholders of a private company are not allowed to sell or transfer their shares without offering them first to other shareholders for purchase; *second*, shareholders are not allowed to trade freely their shares in the stock exchange and cannot offer their shares to the general public and *third*, there is a restriction of minimum 2 and maximum 50 shareholders for any private company in India. The key features of a private limited company are as follows:

1. **Independent legal existence:** A private limited company is a separate legal entity created under the Companies Act, 2013, and is formed as per procedure prescribed under law. Group of individuals interested to form a private limited company should approach the 'Registrar of Companies' (ROC) who is appointed for this purpose with specified jurisdictions for various states and union territories and is responsible for registering companies falling under his/her jurisdictions under established procedure and law.
2. **Ease in operations:** It is relatively easy to form a private limited company than a public limited company. A private limited company is relatively less cumbersome to organize and operate. There are many exemptions granted to a private limited company which make it easy for directors to do desired business activities. Figure 5.13 illustrates some of such exemptions.
3. **Limited liability:** The liability of shareholders in a private limited company is limited to the shares allotted to its members. These shares are not freely transferable among them and shareholders cannot invite general public for sale, purchase and transfer of such shares and debentures.
4. **Perpetual existence:** The existence of a private limited company is perpetual and it enjoys continuity of its existence. A company continues to exist even if all its members die or desert it until it is dissolved as per procedure prescribed under law.

In the light of the above-mentioned points, a private limited company is a preferable business form for those interested individuals who prefer limited liability, privacy of operations but can control the business within a limited circle. The key advantages and disadvantages of a private limited company are explained in Figure 5.14.

A public limited company is also a legally incorporated, voluntary association of people, having separate legal status and limited liability of associated people. The shares of a public company are freely traded in stock exchanges and such shares can also be traded, transferred and sold to any member of the public. The Companies Act, 2013, prescribes the rules and regulations regarding the conduct of business which is carried out under a set of strict procedures and rules. Strict rules are must as a public company must publish a true financial position to its investors and they can determine the exact worth of any shares that they hold in such a legally incorporated company. Public limited companies are also

FIGURE 5.13 Exemption enabling ease in business operations under LLP.

Source: Adapted from Limited Liability Partnership (LLP) Act, 2008.

FIGURE 5.14 Advantages and disadvantages of private limited company.

known as 'Plc' in the United Kingdom and 'Inc' in the United States. The key features of a public limited company arc as follows:

1. **Separate legal existence:** A public company has a separate existence as it is a legally created artificial person. Its legal existence is apart from its members who created it under law.
2. **Created by law:** The formation, functioning and dissolution procedures of a public limited company including governance of its business operations are strictly governed by rules and regulations as prescribed under the Companies Act, 2013. This Act contains the legal formalities for setting up of a public limited company and explains procedure for working and winding up. ROC having specified jurisdictions of various states and union territories as mandated under rules is vested with powers and duties with regard to all these formalities.
3. **Membership:** The Companies Act, 2013, mandates that there should be minimum seven members for forming a public limited company; however, no upper limit on members is prescribed in the statue, meaning they could be as high as the number of issued shares.
4. **Share capital:** The share capital of a public limited company is raised by the issuance of shares which are sold to the general public, freely traded in stock exchanges and transferred from one member to another.
5. **Transferability of shares:** The shares of a public limited company are freely transferable and are freely tradable. Transferability and trading of shares of a public limited company can be done without the prior consent of other shareholders or without subsequent notice to the company.
6. **Limited liability:** The liability of any shareholder is limited to the face value of the shares that he or she owns in the company. No one can claim the personal assets or other business assets of shareholders in case of loss/insolvency of the company. Alternatively, shareholder risks are limited only to the face value of contributed share capital in such business formation.
7. **Management and control:** The management and control of the company are taken care of by the board of directors who are elected by the shareholders. All decisions vis-à-vis functioning of company for its business operations are taken by the board of management, and it ensures unity in direction, command and control of business operations. Shareholders of a company have no right to participate in the day-to-day functioning of the company as they vest their rights to elected directors in thc board of management. It is a unique feature of the public limited company as it ensures separation of ownership from management.
8. **Perpetual succession:** A public limited company has perpetual succession. It is an independent and legally created artificial person. The existence of the company is not affected by death, migration, retirement or insolvency of any of its shareholders and it continues to survive as an artificial person (Table 5.1).

TABLE 5.1 Distinction between a Private Company and a Public Company

Bases of Differences	Private Limited Company	Public Limited Company
Minimum paid-up capital	The paid share capital of a private company must be ₹100,000	The paid share capital of a public company must be ₹500,000
Minimum members	There should be minimum two members in case of a private limited company	There should be minimum seven members in case of a public limited company
Maximum members	The maximum number of members cannot be more than 50	The maximum members can be equivalent to number of shares issued
Issue of prospectus	Private companies are not allowed to issue the prospectus	Public companies can issue the prospectus
Transferability of shares	Shares cannot be transferred, sold or bought without the knowledge of existing members and board of management	Shares are freely transferable. They are freely traded, and general public can buy and sell the shares at stock exchanges
Number of directors	There has to be at least two directors for a private company	There should be at least three directors in case of a public company
Consent of directors with Registrar of Companies	There is no need to give the consent by the directors of a private company	Directors of a public company must file with the Registrar a consent to act as director of the company
Qualification shares	Directors of a private company need not sign an undertaking to acquire the qualification shares	Directors of a public company are required to sign an undertaking to acquire the qualification shares of the public company
Commencement of business	A private company can commence its business immediately after its incorporation	A public company cannot start its business until a certificate to commencement of business is issued to it
Shares warrants	A private company cannot issue share warrants against its fully paid shares	A public company is allowed to issue share warrants against its fully paid shares
Further issue of shares	A private company does not need to offer the further issue of shares to its existing shareholders	A public company has to offer the further issue of shares to its existing shareholders as right shares
Statutory meeting	A private company has no obligation to call the statutory meeting of the members	A public company must call its statutory meeting and file statutory report with the Register of Companies
Quorum	The quorum in the case of a private company is two members present personally	The quorum in the case of a public company is five members present personally. Higher quorum strength can be mandated under the article of association
Managerial remuneration	Total managerial remuneration in the case of a public company cannot exceed 11 percent of the net profits	There is no such restriction in case of public company
Special privileges	A private company enjoys some special privileges	Public company cannot enjoy special privileges and is governed as per established law and procedure

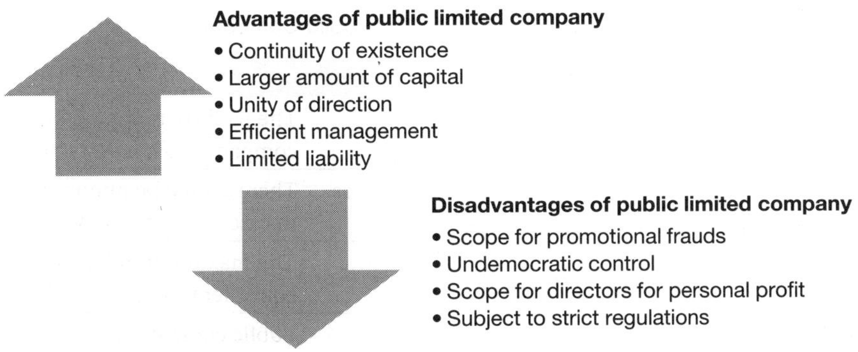

FIGURE 5.15 Advantages and disadvantages of public limited company.

The advantages and disadvantages of a public limited company are depicted in Figure 5.15.

5.2.4.1 Procedure for Setting Up a Company in India

Discussed below is the step-by-step procedure for setting up a joint stock company in India.

Step 1. Interested individuals should select a few suitable names, at least three or four, in order of preference and prepare an indicative list of main objectives of the company. They should ensure that the name(s) does not resemble with the name of any of the already registered company and does not violate the provisions of the Emblems and Names (Prevention of Improper Use) Act, 1950, of GOI.

Step 2. Interested individuals should apply in prescribed form to the concerned ROC so as to ascertain the availability of selected name. The application fee is ₹500. If the proposed name is not available or is already registered or is in violation of the established law, they can suggest the second name in order of preference. In case of electronic filing, one must have digital signature for the same.

Step 3. Once the name is approved by ROC, interested individuals can apply for registration of the new company by filing the required forms within six months from the date of approval of name by ROC.

Step 4. Applicants should arrange for drafting of the memorandum and articles of association (AOA) which can be completed with the help of chartered account/advocates or solicitors for vetting of the same to ROC and printing of the same for information to other stakeholders. They shall also arrange for stamping of the memorandum and articles with the appropriate stamp duty.

Step 5. It is the duty of applicants to get MOA and AOA signed by at least two subscribers with details such as father's name, occupation, address and the number of shares subscribed for. Same should also be witnessed by at least one person. Applicants should also ensure that the MOU as well AOA are dated on a date after the date of stamping.

Step 6. Applicants have to pay the registration fee and filing fee to the office of ROC and have to submit the documents mentioned in Figure 5.16 as well.

Step 7: After having completed the required formalities, he/she should obtain certificate of incorporation from the office of ROC. It is issued only after the satisfaction of ROC that all formalities for the incorporation of the company are successfully completed. The company shall be deemed

- Duly stamped memorandum of association and self-authenticated duplicates thereof
- Duly stamped AOA and self-authenticated duplicates thereof
- The agreement among members for appointment as its managing or whole-time director or manager
- A copy of the agreement regarding AOA and power of attorney, if any, along with applicable stamp fees
- Approval letter from ROC intimating the availability of the proper name
- Application form in e-Form No. 1 along with prescribed stamp fees for incorporation of a company
- Application form e-Form No. 18 in case of change of address of registered office
- Prescribed application form e-Form No. 32 and e-Form 32 Addendum for directors' particulars
- TR Challan or GAR 7 document evidencing payment of prescribed registration and filing fee

FIGURE 5.16 Procedure for setting up a company in India.

Source: Adapted from Companies Act, 2013.

to be incorporated from the date of issue of such a certificate by the ROC. A private company can start business operations immediately after having received the certificate of registration; however, there are additional formalities in case of a public limited company.

5.2.5 Hindu Undivided Family

HUF business is a distinct type of business formation which is unique to India. There are variants of HUF business practices even within India. For example, under the Dayabhaga system which is prevalent in West Bengal and Assam, the father is the sole owner and the exclusive possessor of the joint family property and no member of such joint Hindu family can enforce the partition of HUF so long as the father lives. Another system is known as 'Mitakshara law' which stipulates that the property of such undivided joint family rests with HUF itself as a business unit and not with any individual member of the family. Hence, such property can be partitioned within the lifetime of the father among family members. Mitakshara law is prevalent and practised in all states except in West Bengal and Assam. The business decisions under this form are taken jointly by the family members under the control of the head of the family who is known as the *karta*. Other members of HUF are known as 'coparceners'. The salient features of HUF are discussed as follows:

1. **Eligibility for HUF:** HUF business form comes into existence by the operation of the Hindu law. Jains, Buddhists and Sikhs in India fall under the definition of Hindus, while Muslims, Parsis and Christians do not fall under the definition of Hindu law, hence, cannot form HUF.
2. **Business formation:** One has to get married to be qualified for the formation of HUF. Husband and wife can form HUF. Newly born children from such a family can join HUF and their membership is the result of status arising from the birth in the family and its legality is not affected by the minority. The Hindu law mandates that only three successive generations in the male line that are grandfather, father and son are deemed to be members of HUF. With amendment in the

Hindu Succession Act, 1956, a female relative of a deceased male is eligible for a share in lieu of husband, father and brother.

3. **Management and control:** The chief of HUF is called *karta*, its members are called coparcener and there is no legal limit to the maximum number of members. The rights and liabilities of coparceners are decided upon the general rules and practices mandated under the Hindu law. The chief or *karta* has full control and command on all decisions of HUF and his words are considered as final decision; however, he can consult his family members for all decisions. He has all powers in the formulation of all policies and in their execution and has unquestioned authority in the conduct of the family business.
4. **Nature of liability:** There is unlimited liability of *karta* in HUF but the liability of coparceners is limited to the extent of the value of their individual interests in the joint family. *Karta* has the authority to obtain loans against the family property or through other means. Other members of the family cannot exercise such rights.
5. **Perpetual succession:** HUF business formation has perpetual succession and its existence is not subject to the death or insolvency of a coparcener or even of the *karta* himself.
6. **Tax benefits:** HUF enjoys tax benefits both under the Income Tax Act, 1962, and the Wealth Tax Act, 1957. There are several advantages to HUF in tax liability as it is treated as a separate business unit. There is need of a separate permanent account number (PAN) card and bank account in name of HUF to be eligible for such tax benefits.
7. **Ancestral property:** The unique feature of HUF is that there must be some property to be jointly managed by HUF.

In the light of the above characteristics of HUF, Figure 5.17 explains the advantages and disadvantages of HUF business formation for international trade.

5.2.6 Cooperative Society

One can form a cooperative society to get started in EXIM business. This kind of business formation is owned by a group of individuals and is operated for their mutual benefit. The persons who constitute or form such a cooperative society are called members. There exist a variety of cooperatives in India, some of them are incorporated; however, many other are unincorporated. For example, milk cooperative, electricity cooperative, farmer cooperatives and so on are usually registered; however, many others such as cooperative mandi, cooperative banking, cooperative credit unions and housing cooperatives

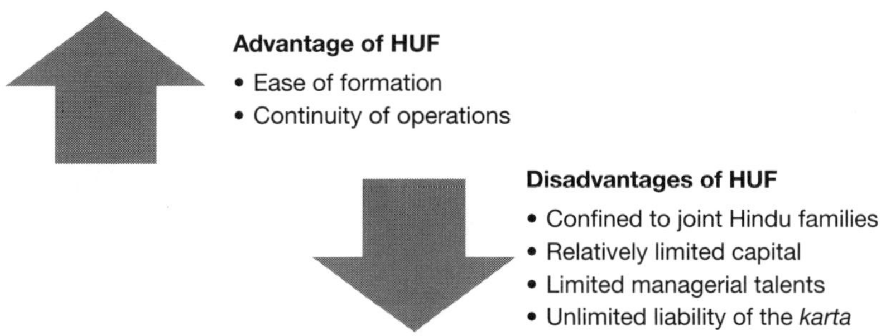

FIGURE 5.17 Advantages and disadvantages of HUF business in India.

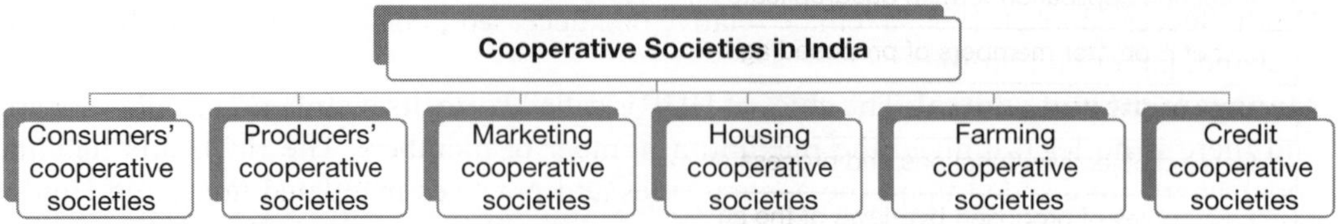

FIGURE 5.18 Types of cooperative societies in India.

are unregistered. Business formation such as sole proprietorship, partnership, LLP, joint stock company and HUF are aimed at generating profits for members but cooperatives are formed for the purpose of providing services to its members. Profit is not the main motto, but cooperatives can earn reasonable profits to promote the interests of their members in future. Various types of cooperatives in India are given in Figure 5.18.

The formation of a cooperative society is done according to the provisions of the Co-operative Societies Act, 1912, and under the Co-operative Societies Acts of the respective states. Majority of the states in India have their cooperatives legislation and following are the common requirements prescribed for registration of a cooperative society in India.

Step 1. There has to be a minimum of 10 interested individuals to form a cooperative society with certain objectives aimed at maximizing the services to its members. They should constitute a 'provisional committee' and elect a 'chief promoter' who shall act on behalf of them. In case of interstate cooperative, the minimum requirement of members is 50.

Step 2. Chief promoter in consultation with provisional committee/open house should decide the name the of the 'cooperative society' and move an application to Registrar of Society of concerned state. On receipt of the application, if the registrar is satisfied, he/she will issue a letter for 'reservation of name' and chief promoter should collect such a letter of confirmation of the name of the cooperative society. The name once reserved is valid for three months.

Step 3. Members have to contribute their share capital for the formation of such society and there is an entrance fee as well to be collected from the prospective members.

Step 4. The chief promoter has to open a bank account in the name of the proposed society which is done as per directions of the registration authority. The chief promoter shall deposit all full share capital and membership fees so collected in the bank account. The bank manager will issue a certificate for such a bank account and bank balance.

Step 5. The chief promoter shall now move an application for registration of the society to the Registrar of Societies of the concerned region/zone/municipal ward. The list of documents to be submitted for registration of the cooperative society are given in Figure 5.19.

Step 6. The Registrar of Societies will appraise the documents and, on his/her satisfaction, will enter the particulars in the register of application. He/she will give the serial number of society registration and issue an acknowledgement to this effect.

Step 7. Upon the completion of these formalities, the registrar will notify the registration of the society in the Official Gazette and issue registration certificate.

A cooperative society is a voluntary association of persons who with common interest and objectives intend to form a cooperative society which acts on the principles of self-help and mutual help. Salient features of the cooperative society are explained as follows:

- Prescribe application form in quadruplicate duly signed by 90 percent of the promoter members
- List of promoter members of proposed agri-society
- Bank certificate
- Detailed objectives/functions and process of working of society
- Four copies of proposed bye-laws of the agri-society
- Proof of payment of registration charges
- Other documents such as affidavits and indemnity bonds
- Any documents specified by the Registrar of Societies

FIGURE 5.19 Procedure for setting up the cooperative society in India.

Source: Adapted from Co-Operative Societies Act, 1912.

1. **Voluntary association:** Members have common interests and goals while forming a cooperative society and their association is also by their own choice. There is a service objective that creating welfare out of desired objectives binds volunteered members for such association. Members are free to leave, resign and new members can join in lieu of them.
2. **Open membership:** Membership of cooperatives is open to all framers who have a common economic interest, that is to find out a low-cost solution to their problems and extend public service to all associated members. The Indian Constitution mandates that there can be no discrimination among members on the basis of caste, creed, ethnicity, social status, gender, religion, colour and so on.
3. **Limit of membership:** There is a minimum requirement of 10 interested members for forming a society and in case of multi-state cooperative societies, the law mandates the need of a minimum 50 members. There is no upper limit on membership of a cooperative society which can be specified by cooperative itself at the time for incorporation.
4. **Registration of the society:** Cooperative societies have to get registered under the Co-operative Societies Act, 1912, or under respective State Co-operative Societies Act. In order to facilitate the formation of interstate or multi-state cooperative societies, GOI has enacted the Multi-State Co-operative Societies Act, 2002. Any of the registered society becomes a separate legal entity which has perpetual succession and management and control of chief promoter with the help and assistance of a committee created for this purpose. Internal management may vary from society to society and is specified in bye-laws. The benefits of registered cooperative society in India are given in Figure 5.20.

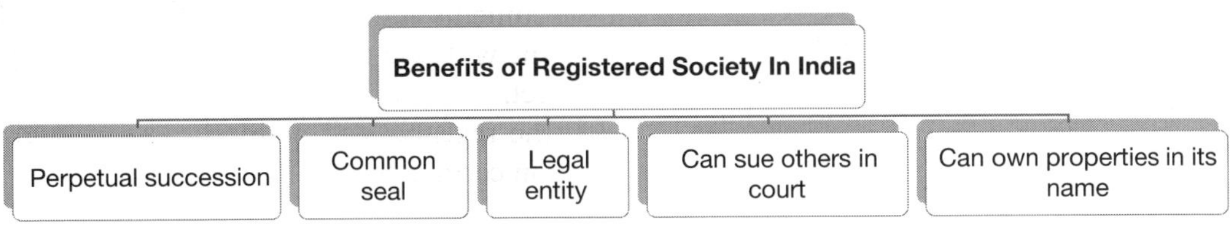

FIGURE 5.20 Benefits of registered society in India.

Source: Adapted from Co-operative Societies Act, 1912.

5. **State control:** It has been made mandatory that all cooperative societies should be registered with the registrar of the concerned state and shall be regulated under the control and supervision of the concerned state government. It should get its accounts audited for each financial year and submit the report to this effect to the concerned Registrar of Societies. Societies not cooperating for the same shall face legal actions for non-compliance to this effect.
6. **Sources of capital:** Sources of capital to the cooperative society are the members who buy the share certificate and also contribute membership fees. Cooperative societies are also financed and assisted by state governments in case of shortage of funds of societies. In other cases, societies are also allowed to take loans from banks as well as from government. Societies also seek grants from state governments to keep their business running.
7. **Democratic set-up:** The management and administration of cooperative societies are done in a democratic manner, whereby each member of the society exercises his/her vote to elect a representative body, general secretary and chairman/patron. All decisions are taken by majority vote and are governed by the by-laws of the society.
8. **Service motive:** Cooperative societies are set up for the purpose of providing intended services to the community and are primarily aimed at the welfare of the associated members of the society.
9. **Reserves and dividends:** Profits, if any, are maintained as reserves in order to meet the exigencies or shortage in future and are usually kept as reserves in form of fixed deposits or any other form. In case of sustained, continuous and higher profits, the same are distributed among the associated members of the society in the form of dividend.

5.3 Understanding Tariff Classification System

There are thousands of varieties of manufactured goods which are traded among nations across national boundaries. All goods so traded do not necessarily carry the same rate of duty payable or the amount of duty. Practically, it is also not possible to identify all products individually by the assessors and appraisers while applying such tariff on the goods imported and exported. Hence, it is necessary that there should be a mechanism to identify the numerous products through groups and subgroups so that the applicable duty on them can be decided on the basis of each group/subgroup. In international trade parlance, it is called 'classification' of a product, meaning each product will be covered under a heading or subheading. There are more than 200 countries which use harmonized trade classification system representing almost 98 percent of world trade.

Trade classification, thus, is the act of placing import and export goods into categories by describing them under headings and subheadings. Earlier, each country used to have its classification system which created problem as the classification system of importing and exporting countries used to differ. Accordingly, efforts were made by trade enthusiastic nations to harmonize the trade classification system. Now, HS known as ITC(HS) is followed by majority of the countries in international trade. Harmonization of trade classification has helped nations, companies, MNCs, exporters and importers by letting them know in advance how much customs duty or other applicable taxes they have to pay for exporting and importing these products. Exporters can accordingly decide what price they should fix in order to have an anticipated profit on the products. It has also helped the customs and duty drawback

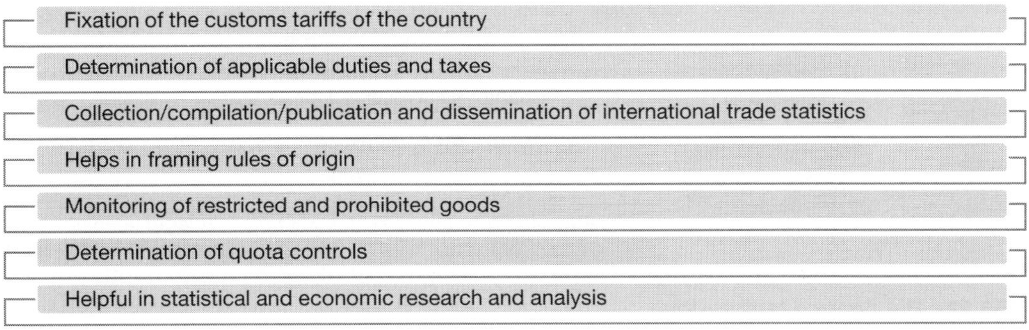

FIGURE 5.21 Uses of ITC(HS) classification.

departments of various countries as the assessment of duty and drawback/incentives/benefits has become easy and standard procedure can be fixed by the government for this purpose on an annual basis. Trade classification helps in the following areas (Figure 5.21).

The Harmonized Commodity Description and Coding System (HS) of tariff nomenclature is maintained by the World Customs Organization (WCO) and customs departments from each country who are always involved in reviewing imported and exported goods so as to make sure that import tariffs or export tariffs are declared properly. WCO, Brussels, Belgium, discusses classification of individual products and gives opinion on them based on inputs of national representatives of all countries. The opinions so rendered by WCO are not binding in the legal sense for the countries, but nations usually follow them as they provide a useful guideline for classifying goods. Accordingly, trade classification is updated periodically so as to accommodate the new changes into the system because some newly developed advanced products may attract a higher rate of duty which may not have been possible under the existing system as these products were not classified there. Improper declaration of the products may affect nations' revenue collections, as newer products are not classified under the existing system and may result to issues such as higher applicable duty rates, import/export prohibitions and restrictions, licensing requirements, country of origin issues, commodity inspection, safeguard measures, risk management and trade statistics. Thus, proper classification of tariffs (trade classification) is a herculean task because there are so many categories, and wrong classification may lead to over/lower payment of duties. Even after thoughtful classification by government of products under ITC(HS), exporters and importers should take due diligence to classify their products in intended products' category/group only, failing which their goods may be seized/held or even forfeited by the customs authorities.

At the international level, harmonized trade classification extends to the first six digits of the tariff. In other words, goods imported into any country using ITC(HS) are classified under the same first six digits in their respective tariffs. However, countries are free to extend it further to ensure their national interests and most developed countries have expanded the international system by adding more digits. For example, the United States and Canada have HS classification up to 10 digits and India has up to 8 digits only. As a result, HS classification may vary from country to country at 6-, 8- and 10-digit level. Products are classified under 98 chapters divided into 21 sections. Indian tariff classification is done in two schedules. Schedule 1 is import policy and Schedule 2 is export policy. Chapter 77 of Harmonized Tariff Schedule nomenclature is blank and is reserved for future use. There are over 1,000 tariff headings and 2,000 subheadings and more than 11,500 tariff lines in the Indian nomenclature. Structure of tariff classification can be understood through Figure 5.22.

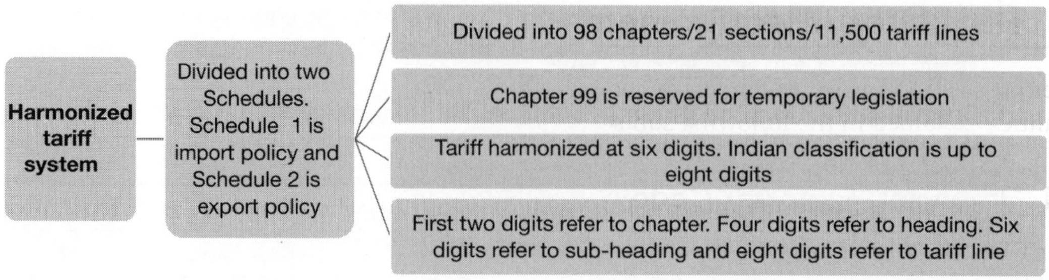

FIGURE 5.22 Harmonized tariff system.

Source: Adapted from Director General of Foreign Trade, Ministry of Commerce & Industry, GOI.

5.4 Preparing for EXIM Business

After having formed the business unit under any of the above-discussed business formations, an exporter has to prepare himself/herself for export and import of products. In order to start the import–export of commodities/allied inputs, he/she should properly read the guidelines/rules governing the export or import in domestic as well as in intended country of export or import. It is a must to properly understand the foreign market, nature of competition, methods of entry, export planning, product planning, pricing, promotional and distributional strategies and should appraise and analyse the necessary import–export data of intended commodity for export and import. He/she should also check whether India has any foreign trade agreement with such country, thus facilitating preferential or zero tariff regimes. The exporter should also evaluate his/her firm's 'export readiness' and assess the financial and human resource needs of the firm.

It is important to analyse the business environment of country of export or import and one should accordingly plan his/her risk-hedging strategy. Several kinds of risks are associated in case of foreign trade, the prominent being transport risks, credit risks and forex risks. Exporter or importer should accordingly prepare the plan to handle such risks, and such plan should be practical and flexible for profitable and sustainable export business. In order to manage the transport risks, he/she can avail the transit insurance/cargo insurance from the general insurance company. For managing the payment risks, the exporter should ensure that his/her firm has proper cover from ECGC, and for managing the forex risks, he/she can take the forward cover from bank to manage the fluctuations of foreign exchange to his/her favour or not to adversely affect his/her firm.

An exporter should also study the various incentives and benefits given to exporters for export promotion; for example, GOI is supporting the exporters with Vishesh Krishi & Gram Udyog Yojana. Similarly, exporters are entitled to export incentives under Focus Market Scheme, Focus Product Scheme and Market Linked Focus Product Scheme. GOI also neutralizes various duties and taxes either by exemptions or by remissions. Advance Authorization, Duty Free Import Authorization and Duty Drawback are some of the schemes which can make an export order either profitable or loss-making in international markets. For enhancing the production capacity of Indian exporters, GOI allows duty-free imports of capital goods provided they export six times the duty saved over the period of six years.

5.5 Regulatory Requirement for Getting Started

For getting started into export–import of goods and services in India, one has to complete the regulatory formalities explained in the following sub-sections.

5.5.1 Importer–Exporter Code Number

As per FTP of India, export and import of goods as well as services from India and into India are not allowed without an Importer–Exporter Code (IEC) number. The Foreign Trade (Development and Regulation) (FTDR) Act, 1992, vests powers to DGFT as a competent authority to issue IEC on prescribed application by the exporter or importer. DGFT acts under the administrative control of Ministry of Commerce and Industry, GOI, and is authorized to grant such licence to the exporter. The procedure for getting IEC from DGFT is explained as follows:

1. **Application for grant of IEC number:** An exporter or importer shall make an application for grant of IEC number as mandated under ANF 2A of Aayat Niryat form to DGFT or its regional offices located in 36 places throughout the country. An IEC code is a 10-digit code number issued to an exporter or importer by the regional office of DGFT. Application should be moved from the registered head office of the firm/company. Application shall be made to the jurisdictional regional authority of DGFT where the registered office or head office of the firm/company is located. It is mandatory to have a bank account and income tax PAN number. All other documents can be generated at the time of application. Box 5.1 depicts the step-by-step procedure including documentation therein for issue of IEC.

BOX 5.1 ► Step-by-Step Procedure for Issue of IEC

One must apply on a prescribed application in ANF 2A. Each page of the application must be duly signed by the applicant or the person authorized for this purpose under partnership deed, AOA. The application must be accompanied by documents as per details given below:

1. Bank certificate endorsing that the proprietor, partnership firm, company, HUF or cooperative society holds a saving or current account with the bank under Appendix 18C.
2. Self-certified copy of PAN issued by the income tax authorities.
3. Two copies of passport-size photographs of the applicant/authorized signatory.
4. Photograph on the banker's certificate should be attested by the banker of the applicant.
5. Demand draft of ₹250 evidencing payment of application fee in favour of the concerned regional office of DGFT. In case of electronic transfer, there is rebate of 25 percent and online application attracts additional 25 percent rebate.
6. Self-addressed envelope and stamp of ₹40.
7. These documents may be kept secured in a file cover.

Source: Adapted from Director General of Foreign Trade, Ministry of Commerce & Industry, GOI.

In the case of Software Technology Parks of India (STPI)/Electronic Hardware Technology Park (EHTP)/Biotechnology Park (BTP) units, the regional offices of DGFT having jurisdiction over the district in which the registered/head office of the STPI unit is located shall issue or amend the IECs. Only one IEC can be issued against a single PAN number. It has been made mandatory that one must have a landline number in the name of the applicant firm as no IEC is issued without having a landline number to this effect. Any proprietor can have only one IEC number and in case of more than one IECs allotted to a proprietor, the same may be surrendered to the regional office for cancellation. Online application can also be provided, proprietor/partner/director/*karta* must have digital signature on website www.dgft.delhi.gov.in

2. **IEC statements and validity:** Authorized officials at DGFT or its regional offices shall issue an IEC number in the format as given in Aayat Niryat form after having appraised the authenticity and truthfulness of the documents submitted by the applicant. He/she will also endorse a copy of such IEC to the concerned banker where the applicant holds bank account and requisite column and space is provided to this effect in Ayat–Niryat Application Form. DGFT officials are also required to send the consolidated statement of IEC number issued by the regional authority to the offices of the Exchange Management Department of RBI and the Central Board of Indirect Taxes and Customs (CBIC) for registration of same at www.icegate.gov.in. IEC is valid in any part of the country for all branches/divisions/units/factories as indicated by exporter in the application form. IEC once issued is permanent and renewal is required only for modification that may so happen because of change in address, business formation, change of directors, correspondence details, bank account number, PAN card number and so on.
3. **Duplicate copy and surrender of IEC number:** In case an IEC number allotted to an applicant is lost or misplaced or stolen or is untraceable, one has to apply for duplicate IEC to the issuing authority along with an affidavit to this effect. Issuing authority on its satisfaction may consider requests for grant of a duplicate copy of IEC number. In case an IEC holder does not wish to operate the allotted IEC number, he/she may surrender the same by informing the issuing authority. On receipt of such intimation, the issuing authority shall immediately cancel the same and electronically transmit it to DGFT for onward transmission to RBI, customs and regional authorities.
4. **Modification in IEC:** One should apply for modification of an IEC number to the concerned issuing authority from where the original IEC was issued. Form ANF 2A shall be used for modification of IEC details such as name, address and constitution. It is important to note that the application for modification should be filed within 90 days of the modification, otherwise penalty as prescribed in *Handbook of Procedures* (Volume 1) shall be charged as additional application fees. In case of change in ownership of firm or business formation or business is sold to some other individuals or any other reasons, the new application should be moved in prescribed format so as to incorporate such details of change along with PAN details of the new ownership. The application must be made from where the earlier IEC was issued.
5. **Exemption from IEC:** FTP of India exempts certain individuals, transactions and categories from IEC. These are as follows:
    a. Importers covered by Clause 3(1) (except sub-clauses (e) and (l)) and exporters covered by Clause 3(2) (except sub-clauses (i) and (k)) of the Foreign Trade (Exemption from Application of Rules in Certain Cases) Order, 1993.
    b. Ministries/Departments of the central or state government.

c. Persons importing or exporting goods for personal use not connected with trade or manufacture or culture.
d. Persons importing/exporting goods from/to Nepal provided the cost, insurance and freight (CIF) value of a single consignment does not exceed Indian ₹25,000. Persons importing/exporting goods from/to Myanmar through Indo-Myanmar border areas provided the CIF value of a single consignment does not exceed Indian ₹25,000.
e. However, the exemption from obtaining IEC number shall not be applicable for the export of special chemicals, organisms, materials, equipment and technologies (SCOMET) as listed in Appendix 3, Schedule 2 of ITC(HS) except in the case of exports by category (b) above.

5.5.2 Registration-cum-Membership Certificate

FTP of India mandates that no restricted category licence such as 'special import licence for restricted items' and 'special export licence for restricted items' shall be issued by DGFT until an application to this effect is not endorsed by applicant through CB/EDA/EPC. EPC/EDA/CB shall endorse the application only if the exporters or importers have their membership and registration. Additionally, exporter or importer cannot claim any incentives/benefits as prescribed in FTP unless he/she has not obtained registration-cum-membership certificate (RCMC) to this effect from the concerned EPC/CB/EDA/FIEO. RCMC is issued by concerned EPC/EDA/CB/FIEO as per the following procedure.

1. **Authorities issuing RCMC:** EPCs/CBs/EDAs/FIEO are the mandated authorities for issuance of IEC. An exporter desiring to obtain RCMC shall declare his/her main line of business in the application, which shall be made to the concerned trade promotion agency relating to his/her line of business. However, a status holder has the option to obtain RCMC from FIEO except in case of exporter or importer of drugs and pharmaceuticals and under this case he/she shall obtain RCMC from Pharmexcil Export Promotion Council only. It is further mandated that exporters of minor forest produce, and their value-added products, shall obtain RCMC from Shellac Export Promotion Council. In respect of exporters having their head office/registered office in the State of Odisha, RCMC may be obtained from FIEO office in Bhubaneswar irrespective of the product being exported by them. Services exporters of IT and IT-enabled services shall take RCMC from EPC for IT and IT-enabled services and other services exporters shall take RCMC from Services Export Promotion Council. Additionally, an exporter has the option to obtain RCMC from FIEO or any other relevant EPC if the products exported by him/her do not relate to any of the established EPC/CB/EDA.
2. **Issuance of RCMC:** Each EPC/CB/EDA has its own prescribed application form. The list of various EPCs/CBs/EDAs is provided in Appendix 2B of FTP 2009–2014; the list of important trade promotion bodies related to Indian culture sector is provided in Table 5.2. An exporter should apply on such prescribed application to get registered to become the member of EPC/CB/EDA. Documentation and fee for each of the trade promotion body varies; hence, one must consult the website of the concerned trade promotion body before applying for RCMC. Online registrations are also possible in some of the trade promotion bodies. The list of trade promotion bodies is given in Appendix 2B. In case an exporter desires to get registration as a manufacturer exporter, he/she shall furnish evidence to that effect. Prospective/potential exporters may also, on application, register and become an associate member of EPC provided they have IEC issued to this effect by DGFT.

TABLE 5.2 List of Trade Promotion Bodies for Agricultural Products Exports

1. APEDA	**11.** Shellac and Forest Products Export Promotion Council
2. MPEDA	**12.** Wool & Woollens Export Promotion Council
3. Cashew Export Promotion Council of India	**13.** Coffee Board
4. The Cotton Textiles Export Promotion Council	**14.** Coir Board
5. Council for Leather Exports	**15.** Tea Board
6. Export Promotion Council for Handicrafts	**16.** Tobacco Board
7. Jute Products Development & Export Promotion Council	**17.** Coconut Development Board
8. The Indian Silk Export Promotion Council	**18.** Spices Board
9. Handloom Export Promotion Council	**19.** Rubber Board
10. Indian Oilseeds and Produce Export Promotion Council	

3. **Validity and modifications:** RCMC once issued shall be deemed to be valid from 1 April of the licensing year in which it was issued to five years ending on 31 March of the licensing year, unless otherwise specified. Some trade promotion bodies mandate the validity for the period of three years. However, an exporter has to pay the required membership fees every year. In case of change in business formation, ownership and constitution of firm or name or address of an exporter, it shall be obligatory on the part of RCMC holder to intimate such change to the registering authority within a period of one month from the date of such change. The registering authority, however, may condone delays if it is satisfied with the reasons for delay on merits.
4. **De-registrations and appeal against de-registration:** If RCMC violates the provisions of FTP or brings disrepute to the country or acts with malafide intentions, EPC/CB/EDA/FIEO can de-register such RCMC holder for a specified period for violation of the conditions of registration. RCMC holder is given a show-cause notice by the registering authority for reasons of de-registration and is also provided an adequate and ample opportunity to make a representation against the proposed de-registration. If the de-registration is done, same is communicated to all concerned regional authorities of DGFT for necessary action. If RCMC holder feels that he/she is not satisfied with reasons of de-registration or is not heard in proper context, such aggrieved RCMC holder can make an appeal to DGFT or an officer designated in this behalf within 45 days against the said decision and the decision of the appellate authority shall be final.
5. **Furnishing of returns:** An RCMC holder is required to furnish quarterly returns/details of his/her exports of different commodities to the concerned registering authority. The filing of timely returns by the exporter helps design proper polices and training programme in required areas by concerned the trade promotion bodies. They can also lobby with GOI for grant of assistance, support and other additional benefits for export promotion from such affected areas.

5.5.3 Registration with Indian Customs

In order to promote paperless trade and provide transparent and fast custom clearance services to Indian trading community, Indian customs has implemented the e-commerce portal www.icegate.gov.in aimed at online processing of trade documents with associated stakeholders. In order to clear the goods from customs, an exporter can submit the 'shipping bill' and for imports, a document called 'bill of entry' is filed which is processed online in 95 percent of the cases. Hence, each IEC holder has to get registered on Indian customs online portal 'www.icegate.gov.in' and one cannot file the documents online without being registered. Following are the few benefits of registration at customs' e-commerce portal 'ICEGATE':

1. Once registered at ICEGATE, an exporter, importer or other stakeholders such as shipping lines, airlines, customs house agent (CHA, custom broker), console agents, airline agents and banks can file all documents online, thus cutting business time and cost, reducing red tape and reducing scope for corruption, if any, at any level with regulatory authority.
2. Exporter and importer or their CHAs can see the status of their jobs online via document tracking system, whether the documents submitted are processed or not, and if not, then the reasons therein for corrective action.
3. Exporter and importer or their CHAs can get positive or negative acknowledgement along with shipping bill and bill of entry numbers of their jobs on their registered email ID with various customs authorities with direct contact, thus saving business time and costs.
4. Exporter and importer or their CHAs can raise any query and get reply of the same online.

Registration is a simple process. Either of the party as discussed above intending for registration should log on to ICEGATE website www.icegate.gov.in and click on the registration link on the home page or follow the link services register and fill up the registration form providing all the details required in the same. All the users are advised to use their digital signature (Class 3 individual type) token plugged into their systems before starting the registration process. It is mandatory for all the users to upload their digital signature certificates at the time of registration. Remote EDI System software as implemented by Indian customs also mandates for validation of PAN of IEC holder and it is done online at the time of registration itself as particulars of PAN of registrant shall be verified online from PAN data of the Income Tax Department. For meeting the requirement of identify proof of IEC holders/other stakeholder, only driving licence or passport or Aadhaar card or voter ID card are considered as valid proof of identity of IEC holder or another involved stakeholder. The registrant should also upload a copy of PAN. Documents mandatory at the time of registration are given in Table 5.3.

Customs department does not issue any identification number of exporters and importers but uses IEC issued by DGFT as an essential requirement for the creation of 'business identification number' at ICEGATE.

5.5.4 GST Registration

Tax is an essential evil which each government uses so as to generate revenue for public welfare. India being a developing country has to resort to several levels of taxation, for example, excise duty on manufacture of goods, custom duty on import of goods, value-added tax (VAT) on sale of goods, octroi on movement of goods, services taxed on services used in manufacturing, transportation or in process of sale. As a result, goods were taxed (taxation upon taxation) multiple times without setting-off of tax or refunds, thus making goods expensive in the market. The basic principle for taxation is that 'tax' must be consumption based. More so, before implementation of GST, Indian taxation system was an amalgamation of central, state and local level taxes, thus increasing red tape and compliance cost for any manufacturer in India. By subsuming more than a score of taxes under GST, the road to HS of indirect tax has been paved making India an economic union, thus providing transparent and facilitative tax regime for doing business in India. In the Goods and Services Tax, the concept of 'input credit' is

TABLE 5.3 Documents Required for Registration with Indian Customs

Users/Documents	Scanned Copy of Authorization Letter (.pdf)	Scanned Copy of Licence/ Permit (.pdf)	Scanned Copy of Driving Licence, Passport, Aadhaar Card, Voter ID Card (.pdf)	Scanned Copy of Authorization to F Card/ G Card (Employee)	Authorization Letter/ Order of Commissioner
F card custom broker/ CHA (firm)	✓	✓	✓		
F card custom broker/ CHA (individual)		✓	✓		
F card/G card custom broker/CHA (employee)	✓		✓	✓	
IEC holder		✓	✓		
IEC authorized person	✓		✓		
Shipping lines	✓		✓		✓
Shipping agents	✓		✓		✓
Airlines	✓	✓	✓		
Air agents	✓	✓	✓		
Console agents	✓	✓	✓		
Others (banks/custodians)	✓	✓	✓		

Source: Central Board of Indirect Taxes and Customs, Ministry of Finance, Government of India.

introduced wherein the purchasing firm can claim the input tax credit of the taxes paid. It facilitated business with less capital, following the golden rule 'goods are taxes; taxes are not'. The benefits achieved by the implementation of GST are shown in Figure 5.23.

India has adopted dual GST model because of its unique federal nature. Under this model, tax is levied concurrently by the centre as well as the states on a common base, that is, supply of goods or services or both. GST to be levied by the centre is called Central Goods and Services Tax (central tax/ CGST) and that to be levied by the states is called State Goods and Services Tax (state tax/SGST). SGST is called Union Territory Goods and Services Tax (UTGST) in union territories without legislature. CGST and SGST/UTGST are levied on all taxable intrastate supplies.

In order to address the problems of interim tax where it is yet not fixed who will collect tax, whether state or centre, and which state among them all, the concept of interim tax is introduced. Accordingly, interstate supply of goods or services shall be subject IGST. The IGST model is a unique contribution of India in the field of VAT. The IGST model envisages that centre would levy IGST which would be CGST plus SGST on all interstate supply of goods or services or both. The interstate supplier will pay IGST on value addition after adjusting available credit of IGST, CGST and SGST on his/her purchases. The exporting state will transfer to the centre the credit of SGST used in payment of IGST. The person

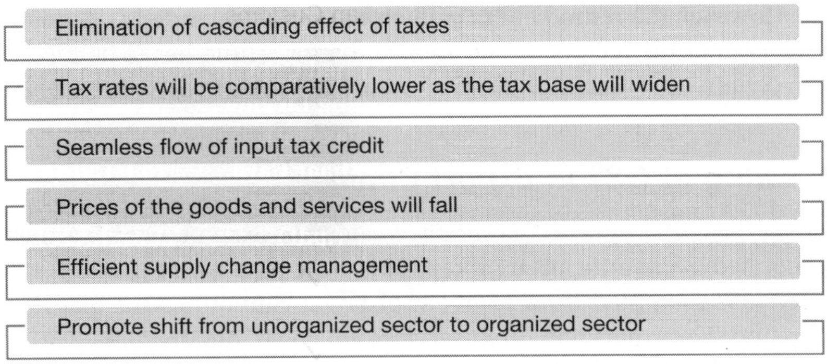

FIGURE 5.23 Benefits of implementation of GST.

Source: Central Board of Indirect Taxes and Customs (CBIC). https://www.cbic.gov.in/ (accessed on 24 May 2023).

based in the destination state will claim credit of IGST while discharging his/her output tax liability in his/her own state. The centre will transfer to the importing state the credit of IGST used in payment of SGST. The relevant information will also be submitted to the central agency which will act as a clearing house mechanism, verify the claims and inform the respective governments to transfer the funds. The major advantages of the IGST model are as follows:

1. Maintenance of uninterrupted input tax credit chain on interstate transactions
2. No upfront payment of tax or substantial blockage of funds for the interstate supplier or recipient
3. No refund claim in exporting state, as input tax credit is used up while paying the tax
4. Self-monitoring model
5. Model takes B2B as well as B2C transactions into account

Owing to unique Indian socio-economic milieu, four rates, namely 5 percent, 12 percent, 18 percent and 28 percent, have been adopted. Besides, some goods and services are also exempted. Rate for precious metals is an exception to 'four-tax slab rule' and the same has been fixed at 3 percent. In addition, unworked diamonds, precious stones and so on attract a rate of 0.25 percent. A cess over the peak rate of 28 percent on certain specified luxury and demerit goods such as tobacco and tobacco products, pan masala, aerated water and motor vehicles is imposed to compensate states for any revenue loss on account of implementation of GST. The list of goods and services in case of which reverse charge would be applicable has also been notified.

5.5.4.1 *Deemed Exports and GST*

'Deemed exports' refer to supplies of goods manufactured in India (and not services) which are notified as deemed exports under Section 147 of the Central Goods and Services Tax (CGST) Act, 2017. The supplies do not leave India. The payment for such supplies is received either in Indian rupees or in convertible foreign exchange. Deemed exports are not zero-rated supplies by default, unlike the regular exports. Hence, all supplies notified as supply for deemed export will be subject to levy of taxes, that is, such supplies can be made on payment of tax and cannot be supplied under a bond/letter of undertaking (LUT). However, the refund of tax paid on the supply regarded as deemed export is admissible to either the supplier or the recipient. The application for refund has to be filed by the supplier or recipient (subject to certain conditions) of deemed export supplies, as the case may be.

5.5.4.2 *Zero Rating of GST in Export Chain*

As per Section 2(47) of the CGST Act, 2017, a supply is said to be exempt when it attracts nil rate of duty or is specifically exempted by a notification or kept out of the purview of tax (i.e., a non-GST supply). But if a good or service is exempted from payment of tax, it cannot be said that it is zero rated. The reason is not hard to find. The inputs and input services which go into the making of the good or provision of service have already suffered tax and only the final product is exempted. Moreover, when the output is exempted, tax laws do not allow availment/utilization of credit on the inputs and input services used for supply of the exempted output. Thus, in a true sense, the entire supply is not zero rated. Although the output suffers no tax, the inputs and input services have suffered tax and since availment of tax on input side is not permitted, that becomes a cost for the supplier. The concept of zero rating of supplies aims to correct this anomaly. What is zero rating? By zero rating it is meant that the entire value chain of the supply is exempt from tax. This means that in case of zero rating, not only is the output exempt from payment of tax but also there is no bar on taking/availing credit of taxes paid on the input side for making/providing the output supply. Such an approach would in the true sense make the goods or services zero rated. All supplies need not be zero rated. As per the GST law, exports are meant to be zero rated. The zero-rating principle is applied in letter and spirit for exports and supplies to SEZ. The relevant provisions are contained in Section 16(1) of the IGST Act, 2017, which states that 'zero-rated supply' means any of the following supplies of goods or services or both, namely:

1. Export of goods or services or both.
2. Supply of goods or services or both to an SEZ developer or an SEZ unit. As already seen, the concept of zero rating of supplies requires the supplies as well as the inputs or input services used in supplying the supplies to be free of GST. This is done by employing the following means:
    a. The taxes paid on the supplies which are zero rated are refunded.
    b. The credit of inputs/input services is allowed.
    c. Wherever the supplies are exempted or the supplies are made without payment of tax, the taxes paid on the inputs or input services, that is, the unutilized input tax credit is refunded.

The provisions for the refund of unutilized input credit are contained in the explanation in Section 54 of the CGST Act, 2017, which defines refund as refund of tax paid on zero-rated supplies of goods or services or both or on inputs or input services used in making such zero-rated supplies, or refund of tax on the supply of goods regarded as deemed exports or refund of unutilized input tax credit as provided under Subsection 3. Thus, even if a supply is exempted, the credit of input tax may be availed for making zero-rated supplies.

A registered person making zero-rated supply can claim refund under either of the following options:

1. He/she may supply goods or services or both under bond or LUT, subject to such conditions, safeguards and procedure as may be prescribed, without payment of integrated tax and claim refund of unutilized input tax credit.

2. He/she may supply goods or services or both, subject to such conditions, safeguards and procedure as may be prescribed, on payment of integrated tax and claim refund of such tax paid on goods or services or both supplied, in accordance with the provisions of Section 54 of the CGST Act, 2017, or the rules made thereunder. As per Section 54(3) of the CGST Act, 2017, any unutilized input tax credit in zero-rated supplies can be refunded, wherever such supplies are made by using the option of bond/LUT.

5.5.5 FSSAI Registration

The Food Safety and Standards Authority of India (FSSAI) came into existence in the year 2006 with the enactment of the Food Safety and Standards Act, 2006, by the parliament of India. FSSAI is unique in the sense that it consolidates various acts and orders with regard to food-related issues in various ministries and departments. In order to strengthen the regulatory regime for food items, FSSAI is established so as to lay down the science-based standards for food goods and items and regulate their manufacture, processing, storage, distribution, sale and import. FSSAI is aimed at ensuring the availability of safe and wholesome food for human consumption all over the country and ensuring the basic right of quality food to human life. The Acts mentioned in Figure 5.24 have been repealed with the passing of the Food Safety and Standards Act, 2006.

For an agriculture exporter and importer, it is mandatory to get registered with FSSAI as this legislation aims to establish a single reference point for all matters relating to food safety and standards, by moving from multi-level, multi-departmental control to a single line of command. Following are the key objectives of FSSAI:

1. Primary objective of FSSAI is to frame the regulations governing the conduct of standards of food articles and guidelines therein.
2. FSSAI is also mandated for specifying an appropriate system of enforcing various standards notified under the Food Safety and Standards Act.

FIGURE 5.24 Mandatory requirement of FSSAI for food products.

Source: Based on inputs from the Food Safety and Standards Act, 2006. https://www.indiacode.nic.in/bitstream/123456789/7800/1/200634_food_safety_and_standards_act%2C_2006.pdf (accessed on 27 April 2023).

3. FSSAI lays down the mechanisms and guidelines for accreditation of certification bodies engaged in certification of food safety management system for food businesses.

The functions of FSSAI have got an extension. As proposed under the 'Draft of Food Safety and Standards Regulation, 2010' it is mandatory for all food business operators in India to get registered with FSSAI or have a licence issued for this purpose under the provisions of the Food Safety and Standards Act. The procedure for registration with FSSAI is discussed as follows:

1. Proprietor/Partner/Director/*Karta*/Trustee, as the case may be, must fill the application form as prescribed in 'Form-B' and duly complete and get it signed in duplicate from all partners/directors/coparceners. It is mandatory to submit the blueprint/layout plan of the processing unit showing the dimensions in metres/square metres and operation-wise area allocation (mandatory for manufacturing and processing units only). It is also mandatory to attach the list of names of directors with full address and contact details and list of equipment and machinery along with the number, installed capacity and horse power used (mandatory for manufacturing and processing units only). Applicants for FSSAI registration are required to submit the photo ID and address proof issued by the governmental authority of proprietor/partner/director(s)/authorized signatory along with the application.
2. It is mandatory for the manufacturers to provide the list of food category desired to be manufactured. In case of processing unit, the applicant should also attach an authority letter with the name and address of the responsible person nominated by the manufacturer along with an alternative responsible person indicating the powers vested with them. Such authority letter shall clearly specify the role of the concerned persons who shall be responsible for assisting the officers in inspections, collection of samples, packing and dispatching and so on.
3. Applicant shall also mandatorily provide an analysis report (chemical and bacteriological) of water to be used as an ingredient in food from a recognized/public health laboratory to confirm the portability. He/she should also give an affidavit along with registered paper of property/lease deed where such factory is located and proof of possession of premises duly evidenced by sale deed, rent agreement, electricity bill and so on.
4. Applicants have to provide the copy of partnership deed in case of partnership firm, memorandum of understanding (MOU) in case of joint stock company, an affidavit in case of proprietor firm, society registration in case of cooperative society as proof towards the constitution of the firm.
5. In case of re-labelling or repacking of already manufactured food material, it is a must to provide a copy of no objection certificate (NOC) from manufacturer. Applicant should also provide for a food safety management system plan or certificate (if any).
6. It is mandatory to provide the source of milk or procurement plan for milk including location of the milk collection centre in case of milk and milk products processing units, wherever applicable. Similarly, it is mandatory to provide the source of raw material for meat and meat processing plants, wherever applicable. For potable water units, it is necessary to provide the pesticide residues report of water in case of units manufacturing packaged drinking water, packaged mineral water and/or carbonated water from a recognized/public health laboratory.
7. FSSAI also mandates for recall plan, wherever applicable, with details on which the product is distributed in certain cases and NOC from the municipality or local body where such goods will be warehoused for distribution.

5.6 Summary

For getting started in international business in cultural goods, it is a must that one should have an organization such as sole proprietorship, partnership firm, joint stock company and LLP. A sole proprietorship is the simplest and easiest form of doing business as any business activity under this model is owned, operated and managed by only one person. The partnership firm is formed to overcome the disadvantages associated with sole proprietorship. Under partnership form of business organization, the business is owned and operated by two or more persons who contribute financial resources in the agreed proportion into the entity. The persons who create such business form are called partners and divide the profits or losses among themselves in the proportion of their contributed capital. LLP uniquely combines the best features of both joint stock company and partnership. Under LLP, one partner is not responsible or liable for misconduct or negligence of another, thus protecting each business partner from unlimited partnership. A joint stock company is an artificial person which is created by law and has perpetual succession. It is a separate business entity where share and securities can be bought, owned and sold by shareholders. The share of ownership of each shareholder is proportionate to contributed capital in such business formation and same is evidenced by his or her shares certificates. HUF business is a distinct type of business formation which is unique to India. There are variants of HUF business practices even within India. One can form a cooperative society to get started in EXIM business. This kind of business formation is owned by a group of individuals and is operated for their mutual benefit. The persons who constitute or form such cooperative society are called members.

As per FTP of India, export and import of goods as well as services from India and into India are not allowed without an IEC code number. The FTDR Act, 1992, vests powers in DGFT as a competent authority to issue IEC on prescribed application by the exporter or importer. FTP of India mandates that no restricted category licence such as 'special import licence for restricted items' and 'special export licence for restricted items' shall be issued by DGFT until an application for restricted license is endorsed by the concerned CB/EDA/EPC.

Tax is an essential evil which each government uses so as to generate revenue for public welfare. India being a developing country has to resort to several levels of taxation, for example, excise duty on manufacture of goods, custom duty on import of goods, VAT on sale of goods, octroi on movement of goods, services tax on services used in manufacturing, transportation or in process of sale. Consequently, goods, in the pre-GST regime, were taxed multiple times at various stages of manufacturing/value addition without set-off of the tax being paid, thus making goods expensive in the market with a taxation upon taxation. Basic principle for taxation is that 'tax' must be consumption based. More so, before implementation of GST, Indian taxation system was an amalgamation of central, state and local-level taxes, thus increasing red tape and compliance cost for any manufacturer in India. By subsuming more than a score of taxes under GST, road to HS of indirect tax has been paved making India an economic union, thus providing transparent and facilitative tax regime for doing business India. The introduction of the concept of 'input credit' removed the cascading burden by expanding the coverage of credit for all inputs, including capital goods, thus paving the way for goods should be taxed and there should not be tax on tax, as prevalent under the pre-GST regime. This is in sync with golden rule of 'taxes must be consumption-based' and there is 'no tax upon tax' as in the case of pre-GST regime.

In addition to the above, an exporter or importer may require trade-specific registration like if he/she is dealing in food items, he/she needs FSSAI registration and in case of car, it is registration with Automotive Research Association of India and in case of helmets, it is registration with Bureau of Indian Standards.

Review Exercises

Multiple Choice Questions

1. Why is sole proprietorship considered the preferred form of getting started in exports and imports?
   a. Few legal formalities and simple to form
   b. Ease in business operations
   c. Faster decision-making and total control over the business
   d. Enhanced motivation as the proprietor gets 100 percent profits
   e. All of the above
2. Which of the following is not a key advantage of a partnership firm?
   a. Shared and lower exposure of any kind of losses
   b. Benefits of specialization
   c. Inability in decision-making leading to weak decision mechanism
   d. Easy to form and flexibility in operations
   e. Better decision-making for complex business operations
3. Which of the following is the key feature of a joint stock company?
   a. Independent legal existence
   b. Ease in operations
   c. Limited liability
   d. Perpetual existence
   e. All of the above
4. What are the prime reasons for introducing the LLP Act in India for forming LLPs?
   a. Globally accepted form of business, easy to form and easy to manage and operate
   b. Lower cost in forming an LLP and easy to dissolve or wind up the business operations
   c. Minimum regulatory compliance and lower need for maintenance of statutory records
   d. All of the above
   e. None of the above
5. Which of the following is the main advantage of HUF?
   a. Confined to joint Hindu families
   b. Relatively limited capital
   c. Limited managerial talents
   d. Ease of formation and continuity of business operations
   e. None of the above
6. Which of the following is the main purpose of business formation under cooperative societies?
   a. Enhancing mutual cooperation and benefits
   b. Pooling funds as a group
   c. Serving the society
   d. Proving self-management is better
   e. None of the above
7. Name the body that issues IEC.
   a. Ministry of Commerce/Regional offices of Ministry of Commerce
   b. Controller of exports and imports

c. DGFT/Regional offices of DGFT
d. Commissioner (exports)/Development commissioner (SEZ)

8. What is the prime reason for availing RCMC?
   a. To avail all government benefits, incentives and authorizations
   b. To avail special import or special export licence for restricted items
   c. To enhance the reputation of the company
   d. To increase the goodwill of the company
   e. Both a and b

9. RCMC stands for
   a. Registration-cum-magistrate certificate
   b. Recompilation-cum-memorandum certificate
   c. Registration-cum-membership certificate
   d. Recompilation-cum-membership certificate
   e. None of the above

10. Exporter should apply for GST because
    a. Export supplies under GST rules are zero rated
    b. Exports are taxable
    c. Exporter needs it for compliance and business
    d. Exporter must have it as it adds to the status symbol

Critical Thinking Questions

1. Explain the key advantages and disadvantages of getting started in exports and imports under sole proprietorship.
2. Explain the process of business formation under a partnership firm. What are the key advantages and disadvantages of partnership?
3. Explain step by step the process of business formation under an LLP firm.
4. Explain the key advantages and disadvantages of getting started in exports and imports under a joint stock company.
5. Explain the procedure of getting registered for IEC in detail. What are the benefits of taking RCMC?
6. Why is GST registration so important for export–import transactions? Explain the regulatory framework of Zero Rating of Export Transactions under GST legislations.

Further Readings

1. Central Board of Excise and Customs, Ministry of Finance, Government of India.
2. Central Board of Indirect Taxes and Customs. Ministry of Finance, GOI. 2017.

CHAPTER 6

Product Selection and Adaptation for International Markets

CHAPTER OBJECTIVES

- To explain the concept of product for international markets.
- To explain the steps involved in export product planning.
- To discuss the need of adapting a product for international markets.
- To explain the selection process of export for international markets.
- To discuss the international product policy and life cycle stages in international markets.

6.1 Introduction

Selection of exportable products is one of the most important decisions an exporter has to deal with in export management. Product, in international marketing, is anything that can be offered to a market and should satisfy a want or need of overseas customers. The concept of product for international marketing has two components: first, 'tangible' or 'physical' and, second, 'intangible' or 'non-physical'. In today's competitive business environment, international sales essentially entails some services (intangibility) in a firm's overall marketing strategies. Sale of product in international markets is not merely a 'sales transaction' but a 'complete bundle of benefits' or satisfactions that an importer or buyer perceives he/she will obtain if he/she imports such a product. An exportable product, thus, is the sum of all physical, psychological, symbolic and service attributes that a potential buyer is looking for and is not mere the physical merchandise. Selection of such a bundle of satisfaction involves careful planning, research and due diligence for any exporter to succeed in international markets. Product planning, design and selection for export markets is a complex process as the creation of a bundle of such benefits for target buyers has to be done in the context of the local market. Indian exporters, for instance, have less frequently understood the importance of truly 'localizing' or 'adapting' the content of a product for export markets. An exportable product has to be made localized or adapted so as to meet the tangible as well as intangible requirements of target markets, wherein tangible requirements include changing colour, contents, sizes, dimensions, weights, labelling and marking, and intangible requirements include the product adaptations for linguistic, cultural and other requirements. In short, for export markets, there can be need for product adaptations which include understanding and accommodating cultural nuances such as differences in colour association, symbols, size and weight and payment preferences among consumers. Export firms addressing product adaptation concerns early on in their global strategy will be far more competitive in the international markets. For example, adaptation of measurement units, such as kilometres or miles, is an obvious area requiring adjustments for an automobile company selling cars or other vehicles anywhere in the world. A software development company should understand if there are different date formats in different regions of the world and should use different notational conventions for writing time, date, numbers and currency as it develops software for specific markets. The date is written in the sequence YY/MM/DD for software development from Japan but is written MM/DD/YY for the similar kind of order coming from a firm based in the United States. Any firm planning to export must have knowledge of a country's social and cultural idiosyncrasies such as jokes, symbols and colours, as what may be acceptable in one market may cause offence in another foreign market. For example, while selling a beauty cream to the female segment, Unilever had to change its name from 'Fair & Lovely' to 'Dark & Lovely' in African countries as dark colour of skin is considered a sign of beauty in many African countries. Similarly, a US company tried to sell its toothpaste in certain Southeast Asian markets by emphasizing that the core benefit of the toothpaste is that it 'whitens your teeth', whereas in many Southeast Asian countries people chew betel nuts to blacken their teeth, as they see it as a sign of beauty, thus contradicting the core benefit desired by consumers. Another company marketed its cologne for men with an advertisement featuring a man and his dog which was considered as offensive, unhygienic and unclean by consumers of many Islamic countries as they consider the dog as not only unclean but also as a sign of bad luck. Localization of product or services offered is particularly very important for IT companies as the majority of web contents and software they make are designed in English while it is not the largest spoken language of the world and hence requires adaptations for local users in many parts of the world, for example, China, Japan, South Korea and Bangladesh.

6.2 Concept of Product for International Markets

Product is defined as a bundle of physical service and symbolic attributes which provide the benefits to a user or buyer for which it is designed, manufactured, sold, purchased, used and consumed. It yields the desired satisfaction to the customer. A product is a combination of 'physical attributes' such as size, shape, dimensions, weight and contents and 'subjective attributes' such as brand equity, quality and image. Any customer, when he/she buys a product, analyses both the dimensions. With increasing competition in the global markets, customers are increasingly getting aware about the services, especially product-related services, such as after-sales services, recall service, and replacement and repair service and firms are increasingly competing with each other on the basis of service quality. For example, Maruti Suzuki in India boasts about its car service network for marketing its products in India. With increasing consumer awareness, firms are scaling up their levels of engagement by highlighting symbolic attributes as an important element of marketing strategy. For example, when someone buys a Honda car, he/she just does not buy a car but an assurance of quality, unique features and efficiency. Understanding of the concept of any product for any exporter is very important as 'symbolic product' offer is not just aimed at fulfilling the core benefits for which it is purchased but beyond that for 'experience creation' for target consumers or users; for example, selling mineral water may not be enough to just quench the thirst or assure the best quality of minerals in water but beyond that to make a customer feel great by mentioning that it has been bottled at a freshwater source at the Himalayas.

In order to exactly understand the nature of the exportable product, one should conceptually understand what the product stands for. Various marketing gurus have explained the different layers of product attributes (Figure 6.1). The first level is a 'core product' which is intangible, and one cannot touch it because the core product is the 'benefit' of the product that makes it valuable to consumers. For example, a car offers convenience, medicine offers relief, a hotel offers comfort and air travel offers speed with which one can travel quickly. The second level of product is the 'actual product' which is tangible and is a physical product, what is delivered to a customer. One can get some use out of it; for example, one can use a car and one can take a joy ride on an aeroplane. 'Augmented product' is the third stage and is the non-physical part of the product. Augmented product usually consists of lots of added value for which one may or may not pay a premium; for example, paracetamol is of two types, one which gets diluted very fast, thus immediately provides relief from pain, and other is normal which takes time to get diluted in the stomach and takes time to offer functional benefit to the consumer. Similarly, business-class travel in aeroplane is an augmented product which is non-physical but offers extended comfort and convenience in air travel along with the actual benefit of quick travel. Another example is when a car dealer offers extended repair and parts warranty and other after-sales services, they become an augmented product. Marketers are exploring on the fourth level which is a potential product so as to further address the problems of consumers. So when you buy a car, part of the augmented product would be the warranty, the customer service support offered by the car's manufacture and any after-sales service.

In addition to understanding the bundle of product attributes and levels, one also needs to understand the stages of product in global markets. One can classify the products according to their degree of potential for international marketing. Broadly, the products for international markets can be classified into the following four categories:

1. **National products:** National products are suitable for one single market and are usually marketed within one country. National products are usually developed so as to cater to the marketing needs of the specific national market. National products are also referred to as local products and are developed as a result of addressing the product needs of local consumers, for example, Dabur Mustard Hair Oil so as to address the need of North Indian consumers. It is easy to develop these products and brand them at the national level as firms know well the product needs of local consumers.

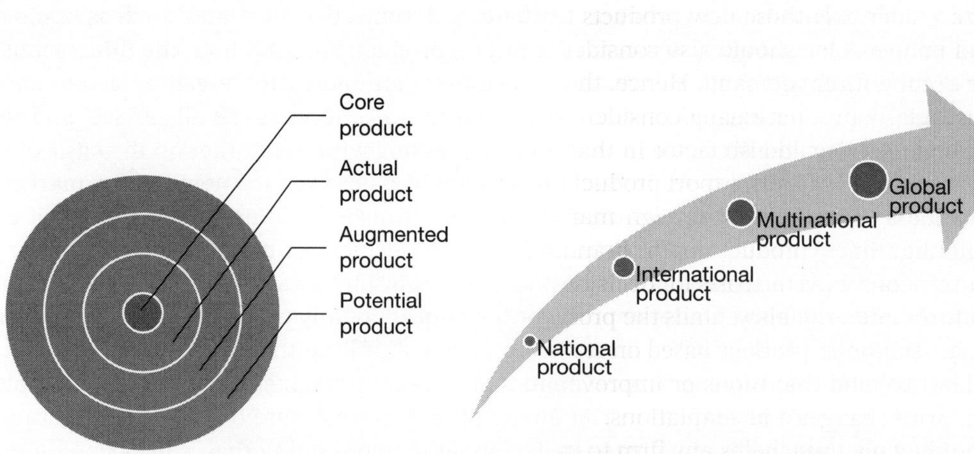

FIGURE 6.1 Level of products and stages of product adaptation for international markets.

2. **International products:** When products are exported from one country to nearby countries as an extension of the same product portfolio to nearby markets, they are called international products. Such markets are usually similar to cultural and other attributes of a national market. International products are usually the extension of national products which become international products when they are exported from one country to another. International product is only being nationally distributed and marketed but is usually exported to the countries without significant adaptation to other markets. International products are owned and advertised by a national manufacturer, wherein a manufacturer can make small changes in a national product so as to make it compatible for exports to similar kinds of international markets. Firms, after having established themselves in specific national markets, may sell national products in international markets on account of the reputation of their brands to get the greater market share.
3. **Multinational products:** When the business operations of the firm expand and diversify to several markets across more than one continent, a firm has to develop and adapt the perceived unique characteristics of a product as per the specific market needs and may have to invest in such countries so as to manufacture the products as per consumers' needs there. A firm may develop standard products but is more focused on adapting its products and services to each individual local market.
4. **Global products:** Global products are designed to meet the needs, desire and demand of consumers all over the world by catering to different segments and ensuring product adaptation to specific global segments. Global products are marketed through the use of the same coordinated image or brand in all the markets. Firms usually have one corporate office that is responsible for global product development and launch strategy. Global product strategy always emphasizes on sales volume, cost management and efficiency so as to generate more profits and increase investor's wealth.

6.3 Export Product Planning

Export product planning is a systematic process that helps an exporter to understand the products that can be exported in international markets. It is an important step in export planning and execution, and one should consider only those new products that are unique, different, innovative, superior in quality and cost-competitive. One should also consider those products for exports which can be produced on a larger scale to fulfil global demand. Hence, there must be sufficient supply of raw material for production or produced goods after having considered the requirements of the domestic market. While planning for exports, one should also factor in that quality and timely delivery of goods are very important in international business. Thus, export product planning is a continuous process of identifying, adapting and articulating the products for foreign markets, thus generating additional business for a firm by extending product lines, product depth, branding and product uses in international markets. Export product planning serves as the basis for decisions about pricing, distribution and logistics and promotion in international markets. It also entails the process of managing the product life cycles and leveraging its different stages in foreign markets based on stages of development by using appropriate marketing strategies including product extensions or improvements, stages of introduction, enhanced promotion and distribution, price changes and adaptations.

Export product planning helps any firm to understand the new products which can be introduced in prospective countries including nature of modifications, brand name changes, new product features, packing, guarantees and warranties and after-sale services which it has to offer so as to successfully establish the products in these markets. As international markets differ from each other, one should base his/her export product planning on sound informational inputs and develop different market scenarios and mechanisms to address uncontrollable market forces. For example, there are differences in trade rules, languages, currency, taxation, tariffs, inflation and so on, and one has to manage all this through proper export product planning. Some of the key steps one should factor in while devising a plan for exportable products are explained in the following sub-sections.

6.3.1 Clarity in Internationalization Commitment

Venturing into international markets requires long-term vision and managerial commitment for any firm as there is no guarantee of success at the time of entering into any such markets. Internationalization of sales operations of a firm does not begin with an enquiry from a distributor or customer from another country but with a long-term commitment, clarity in business vision and continuous follow-up for improvements in the business process. Accordingly, one must have a look at his/her competitors, suppliers and current customers and accordingly plan the firm's export strategy.

6.3.2 Compliance with Standards of Target Country

It is very important that export firms plan for compliance of business standards of target country and export planning process should be central to designing the products conforming to international standards. Improved quality of goods with the best of industry standards help the export firms to expand and diversify effectively in the potential market and grow greatly. Firms can devise an export plan of standardizing only the core products or a large part of them, and the same products can be subsequently retrofitted for compliance of local standards in any country.

6.3.3 Identify the Areas of Product Adaptation

In addition to compliance with local standards, an export firm should identify the areas of product adaptations due to technological, cultural and economic differences in target country with that of domestic product. Export planning should include various levels of product adaptation; for example, some products may need only different-language packing, labelling and marking or EXIM documentation, whereas others may require technological adaptations so as to make them fit as per the local standards or merely have to change the pricing by introducing cost-effective products in low-income countries.

6.3.4 Anticipation of Level of Competition

Export planning must factor in the level of competition so as to design suitable responses to handle competition in international markets. Export planning helps the firm to react quickly to such business challenges in foreign markets when new products are introduced. Understanding the nature of competition provides a number of tangible benefits to product managers of any export firm which is better able to develop new products with required standards and specifications complying with international scale.

6.4 Designing the Products for International Markets

Designing the products for international markets is not only the cross-functional, inter-departmental, inter-country function but is also a knowledge-intensive work. Designing new products through technological innovations has been the prime business strategy for any internationally engaged firm as for any firm which fails to innovate, its survival becomes tough. Internationally engaged firms consider it as a key strategic business activity as the new product development contributes significantly to sales revenue and profits with increased market share in today's globally competitive environment. Any export can command premium pricing and other business terms if it develops distinctive products. Developing new product design has become a critical factor for any export firm because it sets the characteristics, features and performance of the service or good that global consumers demand. For example, Samsung enjoys great market share and revenue in mobile sales only with new product design and product features. The prime objective of product design team of any export firm is to create a good or service with excellent functional utility and sales appeal at a reasonable cost, time and improved quality. The product design team of various export-oriented firms has to constantly develop not only the high-quality products and low-cost materials but improved methods for handling such products post exports. It is the constant endeavour of any product design team to make the resultant products competitive with similar kinds of products in the market in terms of quality, appearance, performance, service life and price.

Waves of economic globalization have raised expectations of consumers the world over as manufacturers are competing with each other to gain greater market access in the global market with improved product design and product features. New product designs have become more important, especially for firms which are doing business internationally as the customers are demanding greater product variety and if firms are unable to offer extended product features, consumers are switching more quickly to rival products which may be offering the state-of-the-art technology. This is a new business reality, especially for the firms which offer greater product variety with a shorter product life cycle. For example, a few years ago, if a mobile manufacturer had to produce four different products and each product may have had a product life cycle of 5 years, it may have to design only 4 new products every 5 years, but today, in order to be competitive and relevant in the market in globalized set-up, it has to develop a new product every year, thus it has to develop 20 new products every 5 years. It is a prime reason that designing new products for the international market is no more an ad hoc and intermediate activity but has become a regular and continuous business activity for any firm with global business motivations. In the following sub-sections we understand the prime reasons for increasing the scope of product design in changing the business environment for any export-oriented firm.

6.4.1 Product Design for Compliance in Global Supply Operations

Waves of globalization have opened the gates of global markets for many firms and compliance with product design and standards as per the requirements of global customers can also be an important mechanism for coordinating international sales. With increasing specialization and shifting of manufacturing activities to low-cost centres, many firms are outsourcing production of sub-assemblies and components. These firms are increasingly demanding that their suppliers should also participate in product design and development. With outsourcing of product design capabilities to these low-cost production centres, it is important for these global firms to manage and coordinate the flow of information with their supply chain participants. As product standards and specialization vary from market to market, it is extremely important for such outsourcing firms to have regular interface with their two or more suppliers as devoted product design discussion and interfaces ensure not only low product costing but also ensure timely designs and compliance in product design, specification, standards and quality.

6.4.2 Product Design for Global Business Success

In the era of globalization, product design is an essential activity for any firm as it is product innovation that leads to the firm's business success in international markets. New product designs directly and significantly impact nearly all the critical determinants for the firm's global business success. With increasing proliferation of new product designs, customers have also become demanding and ask for greater product variety and are ready to quickly shift to new, innovative, full-featured products. Aware global customers make purchase decisions based on a growing list of factors that are affected by product design, features, specification, cost and quality (Caselet 6.1). Additionally, global customers have also started factoring issues such as customizability, order-to-delivery time, product safety, and ease and cost of maintenance in their purchase decisions. Educated customers are also looking at environmental concerns as per the impact of production on the environment during the product's operating life and at the end of its life, that is, recyclability. An internationally engaged firm must address global customers' concerns on defective products, product liability losses, after-sale services, enhanced warranty provision and so on. To address these product design and development challenges, any export firm must be ready with plans and activities to address these dimensions. Accordingly, global firms are increasingly embracing concepts such as mass customization, design for manufacturing and assembly, product disposal, quality function deployment and time-based competition. Internationally engaged firms now have dedicated business team so as to examine the environmental, legal and ethical issues in product design as well as the impact of product design on the contemporary business environment.

CASELET 6.1

China Mass Customization Product Strategy for Global Markets

The huge success of China as the world leader in export of value-added goods and as a leading importer of raw material is entrenched in its philosophy of 'mass production and mass consumption'. As China lacked in intellectual property rights, it added a new dimension to its manufacturing success, 'mass customization'. China's mass customization product strategy for global markets is based on the process of delivering wide-market goods and services which are modified to satisfy a specific customer's need. Mass customization has been the Chinese strategy towards winning global markets as Chinese marketers and manufactures resorted to combining the flexibility and personalization of custom-made products with the low unit costs associated with mass production. In the academic field, mass customization is also known as 'made to order' and 'built to order'. Mass customization allows a manufacturer to design certain features and manufacture a product while still keeping costs closer to that of normally produced products. Chinese manufactures have rolled out mass customized products in the global fashion industry and achieved huge success as the components of the product are modular. This flexibility allows the client to mix and match options to create a semi-custom final product so as to fill the needs and wants in different segments of fragmented global markets.

6.4.3 Product Design for Mass Customization

With integration of global markets, internationally engaged firms are designing products for mass customization to fulfil the needs of core product benefits to global customers as mass customization product strategy is not only low cost but also allows the production of high-quality goods at large volume with greater economies of scale, thus increasing more market share for sustainable business operations. Product design strategy is aimed towards the firm's ability to quickly design and produce customized products at a large scale at low cost so as to cater to global markets. Mass customization product strategy has been used by Chinese firms and as a result China has become not only the global factory for almost all kinds of products but also the largest exporter of goods in the world economy. Indian policymakers are also aiming the same kinds of economic dividends through the 'Make in India' campaign, wherein India is positioned as the global centre for mass production of cost-effective and highly differentiated products at a very low cost. Speed in product design, development, production, transportation and logistics to global markets is an indispensable criterion for any exporter to pursue mass customization strategy.

6.5 Selection of Product for Export

An export firm should always aim to select the right product at the right price for a right market as firm's success in the overseas market largely revolves around the quality products at competitive prices and timely cost-effective delivery of products. An export firm should factor in the points discussed in the following sub-sections while selecting products for exports markets.

6.5.1 Product Profiling of Prospective Exportable Products

A firm with export motivations should scan the prospective product, profile its export trends in international markets, analyse its sales and growth potential so as to understand the suitability of the product for international markets. One can do this by analysing the past export data of possible markets, wherein appraising issues such as 'country-wise' and 'commodity-wise' export trends over a period of time. An analysis of the past four-year trends of any market growth provides very important results; for example, Table 6.1 provides us with profiling and selection of key products from India's ceramic products for exports, explicitly illustrating the product segment with high and low product growth in the last four years.

6.5.2 Domestic Demand and Surplus for Exports

While selecting a product for export, one should consider the fact that there is adequate production capacity not only to meet the domestic demand but also to fulfil the export orders. If there is not adequate production of goods, the regulatory authority like DGFT may declare the products restricted for exports, thus affecting exports. Hence, the steady supply base is required not only to cater to domestic demand but also to fulfil export orders as per the agreed delivery schedules.

6.5.3 Ease in Product Adaptability

Easy adaptation of any product for international markets makes it suitable for exports as there may be strong reasons to adapt the products to local needs; for example, differences in physical conditions, cultural

TABLE 6.1 Product Segment with High Export Growth in India's Ceramic Industry

ITC-HSN	Product Name	Value Exported in 2018 (USD Thousand)	Trade Balance 2018 (USD Thousand)	Annual Growth in Value between 2014–2018 (%, per annum)
6904	Ceramic building bricks, flooring blocks	2,718	1,753	75
6907	Unglazed ceramic flags and paving, hearth	463,110	440,293	52
6912	Tableware, kitchenware, other household articles	34,362	14,272	39
6910	Ceramic sinks, washbasins, washbasin pedestals	129,945	20,021	16
6905	Roofing tiles, chimney pots, cowls, chimney liners	1,115	–16,572	16
6908	Glazed ceramic flags and paving, hearth or wall tiles	549,920	520,766	12
6902	Refractory bricks, blocks, tiles and similar refractory	188,588	6,747	12
6914	Ceramic articles, n.e.s.	26,840	–15,104	6
6911	Tableware, kitchenware, other household articles	17,066	–2,999	3

Source: UN Comtrade.
Note: Not elsewhere specified.

factors, tastes and preferences, functional requirements of the product, levels of skill, levels of technical development and so on may necessitate for making a product adaptable for target market. If there is a significant cost of such adaptations, such products should be avoided as break-even time may be longer. Product adaptations are real-time business need so as to make them suitable for exports such as changes in product design, colour, size and dimensions, taste and preferences, packaging, labelling and marking.

6.5.4 Mapping Realistic Export Potential

Mapping of realistic export potential and level of demand for a product in the target markets is an important factor in the selection of the product for export. An exporter should map the realistic export potential of a market by factoring various aspects such as political, economic, demographic and socio-cultural environment and looking at infrastructural and market access issues for the identified products. One should consider the dimensions mentioned in Figure 6.2 of various aspects for the identification of appropriate products for international markets.

6.5.5 Level of Import Tariffs

Tariffs refer to a customs duty or any other tax that is imposed on goods and services traded internationally across borders (Figure 6.3). For example, custom duty or entry duty or border tax that is imposed

Demographic Environment	Physical Environment	Political Environment	Economic Environment	Socio-Cultural Environment	Product Potential	Market Access
• Size and growth of population • Population density, scattered or spatial • Demographic profile of population by targeted age groups for identified product • Distribution of population by urban, sub-urban and rural areas • Clustering of target groups and mapping the scalable target groups for identified product	• Compatibility of climate and weather conditions for identified product • Transport distances from point of production to potential markets • Nature of the physical and virtual infrastructure required for exports • Adequacy and timely availability including cost of transportation, packaging, distribution, stevedoring and other logistics	• Conduciveness of present political system for business • Level of government interference in conduct of business • Government attitude towards foreigners including imports • Stability of political system • Trade openness in government policy such as elimination of tariff and non-tariff barriers, FTAs • Level of political engagement for opening up economy for trade and investment	• Project economic growth • Size of GNP • Position of balance of payment and foreign exchange reserves • Interest rates, inflation and currency volatility • Growth in exports and imports including changes in share and structure • Per capita income, disposable income and growth in income levels • Saving rates, consumer spending, tax rates and credit availability • Foreign exchange regulations	• Literacy level of target consumers and quality of education • Size of different consumers groups, that is, middle class, high net worth individuals and below poverty line • Similarity of target consumers with domestic market in terms of tastes and preferences • Key differences in consumers groups, cultural differences and need for product modification and adaptation	• Potential market size and scope of identified product in target market • Gap in demand and supply • Percentage of imports in fulfilling domestic supply • Growth in imports and demand structure • Customer attitude towards imported products • Level of competition in the foreign market for the product • Level of preparedness of competitors including commitment to stay	• Level of regulation of distributorship in the foreign market • Documentary requirements, licences to operate • Licences for technical and environmental compliance • Import regulations for identified product • Tariff and non-tariff restrictions • Intellectual property issues and protection laws • Commercial dispute and redressal mechanism • Transparency and non-discrimination in trade law • Issues of repatriation of profits

FIGURE 6.2 Elements of market scanning of international product selection and exports.

Source: Adapted from S. Carter (1997). *Global Agricultural Marketing Management*. (*Marketing and Agribusiness texts-3*). FAO Regional Office for Africa.

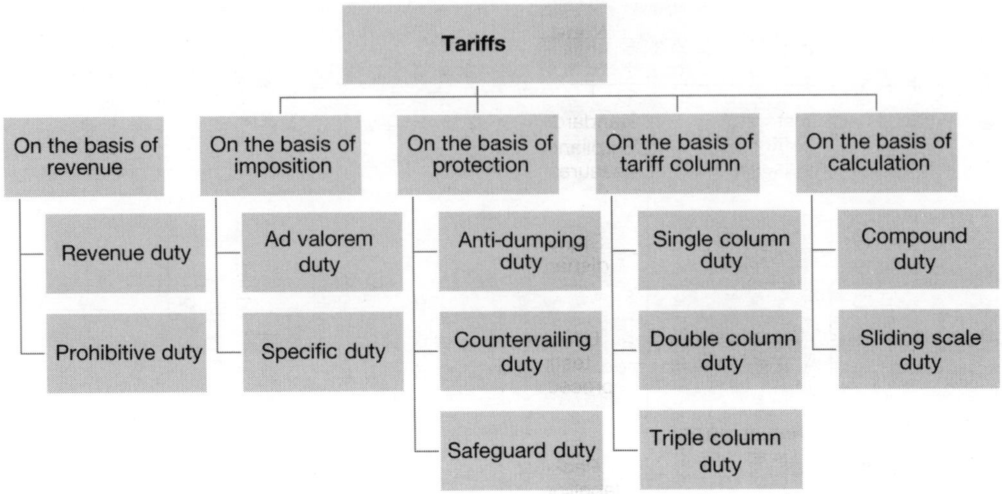

FIGURE 6.3 Kinds of tariffs.

Source: Adapted from United Nations Conference on Trade and Development. https://unctad.org/ (accessed on 24 May 2023).

by a country on the imported goods and services will be referred to as 'tariff barrier'. While selecting the potential markets for exports, one should consider the level of custom duty, that is, import tariffs that are imposed by country of imports. Import tariff may include any duty, tax, cess, octroi and so on that is imposed on movement of goods across territorial border of the country for the purpose of restricting the imports from other country, aimed at either collection of revenue or protecting domestic industry from foreign competition. Imposition of tariff in case of import is higher and multi-layered, exports are usually free from tariff. On selected exported items, government can impose tariff for purpose of maintaining demand and supply equilibrium, development of industry, discouraging export and in case of monopoly or strategic supplies. The kinds of tariffs imposed on imports are given in Figure 6.3.

6.5.6 Non-tariff Restrictions for Trade

Any country can impose non-tariff restrictions on the import of products originating from other countries in various forms such as licensing, standards compliance, government subsidies, local content requirements, minimum import price and quantitative restrictions. Although the negotiated trade regime under WTO provides for the elimination of such non-tariff barriers (Figure 6.4), they are used by countries in a proliferated form so as to restrict imports from other countries. One should check that identified potential product may not be facing non-tariff restrictions in target markets by certain regulations aimed at protecting the environment, child labour, public health, public safety and so on. Potential markets for trade may use these non-tariff barriers as 'policy instruments' aimed at restricting and prohibiting imports into the country. The tariff measures always bring revenue to the government by making imported goods expensive vis-à-vis domestically produced goods. Non-tariff barriers, on the other hand, restrict/prohibit imports implying that imported goods have either high compliance costs for import clearance or may not be cleared at all. The types of non-tariff barriers used as policy instrument to restrict trade even in WTO borderless trade regime are given in Figure 6.4.

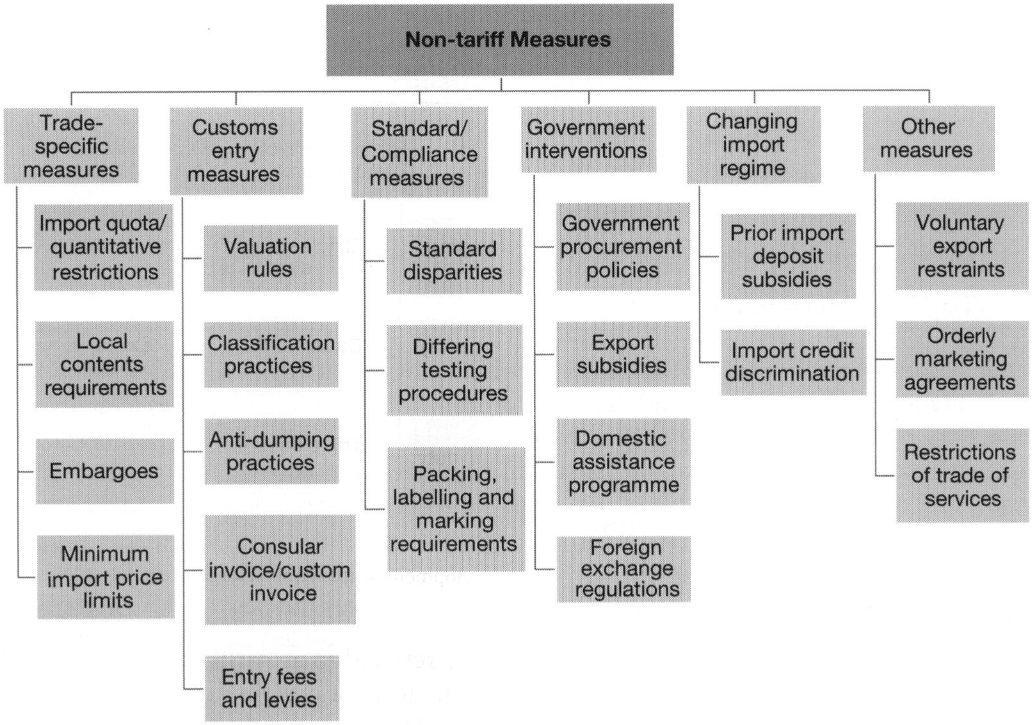

FIGURE 6.4 Kinds of non-tariff measures.

6.5.7 Level of Incentives and Export Benefits for Export Promotion

An exporter should check the level of incentives, export benefits and assistance, and duty neutralization offered by the government to promote the export of particular products in international markets. He/she may consider these benefits and incentives while selecting a product for export as it may make the export of these products attractive in international markets. For example, exporters in India enjoy several schemes announced by the DGFT in its FTP aimed at export promotion from India. In addition to these benefits, there may be sector-specific benefits offered by other departments as well which are largely aimed at export promotion and employment generation in the country. An exporter should factor these subsidies, incentives, assistance, benefits and duty neutralization schemes while selecting a product for exports.

6.5.8 Maintaining High Quality and Launching Innovated Products

An exporter must pay attention to the quality of goods and the introduction of innovated products in international markets. There are several studies on export–import which indicate that firms with innovation and quality complied products not only have better market access but also have witnessed sustained increase in their sales and overall profits. An exporter should select niche products of high quality so as to differentiate his/her products in proliferated international markets. One should consider the fact that traditional marketing techniques such as price cut, timely delivery and credit extensions are no longer as effective as they used to be and one needs to constantly upgrade the quality and launch the innovated products in niche market segments so as to ensure export success. Japanese manufacturers have established themselves as leading exporters only because they never compromised with the quality of goods and always insisted on innovated and differentiated products for global markets.

6.6 International Product Policy: Standard versus Adapted Product

International product policy of any global firm is primarily aimed at exploring the kinds and types of products it intends to offer to global markets. Product manager of any such firm has to define whether to introduce the standardized product or it has to be adapted to local market needs. Product adaptations may come up in several forms, for example, technical adaptation, cultural adaptation, price adaptation, quality adaptation and many more; this is also called 'product differentiation' or 'product localization' or 'product customization'. Product standardization is the process that aims at manufacturing generally uniform characteristics for a particular good or service. Product standardization can be good business technique, especially for technology-based industries, as it provides the best quality products to consumers and promotes competition on other market variables such as service and cost among various suppliers. For varied international markets, the product manager has to address the socio-cultural differences and other peculiarities of the local market and it is considered necessary to adapt the products to the needs of such markets. Product adaptation can be voluntary or mandatory, wherein voluntary product adaption fosters flexibility, addresses customer expectations and helps generate additional sales and profits; mandatory adaptations, on the other hand, involve changes that have to be made before the product can be introduced to any foreign markets. For example, Indian automobile companies have to factor in the homologation norms while manufacturing a vehicle as there are some countries where vehicles are driven by following right-side traffic rule unlike in India where vehicles are driven on the left side. Similarly, electronic devices such as computer and mobile phones must factor the different voltages in different countries of the world and may accordingly fulfil this mandatory requirement of the country of import. There are scenarios when the products need not be adapted in either way and only a standard product is introduced by the firm in international markets. The rationale of product standardization is based on the globalized approach of firm aimed at making one global standard product in the belief that the same product can be sold across markets without any modification. This helps the firm achieve the economies of scale as the focus of the firm is mass production for mass selling so as to cover the costs of development before the product becomes technologically obsolete. The key differences in product standardization and adaptation for export operations are summarized in Figure 6.5.

While foraying into international markets for the first time, it is advisable for any firm to begin with the launch of domestic products without introducing any changes in design and specification. The introduction of standardized products helps the firm to gauge the market expectations and changes expected from customers in different areas of product specifications. This will reduce the cost of changes as the firm will introduce only those changes which are required for the target market. Introduction of standardized products in export operations results in lower costs and larger economies of scale from the stage of production to final sales. Following are the key arguments given in favour of product standardization in international markets.

Basis of Difference	Standardization	Adaptation
Application in marketing means	Companies should apply the four basic marketing instruments (4P) in the same way world wide and ignore national specialties in individual markets.	It is supported by strong market variety, especially by market individualism and market uniqueness.
Reason for application	MNC should think globally and apply integration access world wide.	Almost every international company takes into account (in higher or lower level) regional or local conditions which are typical to the differentiation.
Product offered	Complete standardization would involve designing a product that is identical in every relevant way for geographical market in which the product will be sold.	Altering relevant feature of the product in significant ways for each and every individual geographical market.
Characteristics	A standard product does not need to have all the characteristics of the other products buyer requires.	A product is different from competitor's product and further the products produced by particular company.
Approach	Standardization of product is the approach for increasing commonality of product in the supply chain management.	Adaptation is an approach of detailing the differentiation that exists between products and services.
Fulfilment of needs	Satisfy the heterogeneous needs of the buyer.	Satisfy a particular need of buyer.
Economies of scale	Commonality in products results in higher productivity due to higher demand, having an impact on economies of scales which lowers the total cost.	Unique aspects in product result in different quality, thus increasing cost of production and lower economies of scale.
Final outcome of marketing efforts	Often the product management drives this very important question.	Show sense of value to the buyer but they have to pay more for such product.

FIGURE 6.5 Basis of difference between product standardization and product adaptation.

1. **Low cost of standardized product:** There is one-time product development cost in case of a standardized product while there can be higher cost attached for adapting it to different market needs. This high cost of product adaptation can make it difficult to sell, especially in price-sensitive and low-volume markets. Exporting standardized products can allow any firm larger economies of scales at lower cost per unit, thus resulting in more sales and profits from target markets.
2. **Standardized industrial products:** Another argument in favour of standardization is that industrial goods tend to be more standardized as they focus on delivering the core function adhering to best technical principles, thus ensuring the best quality products to customers all over the world. Industrial products rarely need to be people-centric. They need to fulfil the core function effectively for which they are designed, hence, standardized products are more cost-effective for international markets.
3. **Convergence of tastes and preferences in globalized markets:** With globalization of world markets, there is convergence in consumer's tastes and preferences all over the world. More so, markets tend to converge with identical income levels, thus standardized products are more suitable for such markets. As the world market is a 'melting pot' with increasing similarities in dressing, eating pattern and lifestyles, there are more reasons for product standardization than product customization.
4. **Increasing level of urbanization:** The waves of globalization have resulted in higher trade and investment from one country to another, resulting in speedier economic growth of developing countries. People tend to settle in urbanized set-up when income level increases and this has resulted in similarities in buying pattern across the world markets. Firms with global business operations identify such markets with similar characteristics and offer standardized products to their customers. Standardized global product is suitable to cater to such urbanized markets.
5. **Centralized export division and operations:** In order to cater to a large number of clients, firms have set up a centralized export division which has to serve large global markets with products having shorter product life cycle. The focus of the export division is to recover the developmental costs of products by exporting the products to each nook and corner of the world. Any firm will prefer to sell standardized core product so as to generate faster sales and profit for the firm. Centralized export division tends to maximize sales with standardized products, thus reaps the benefits of economies of scale in business operations.
6. **Made of country's effect:** There are some countries which are globally known for their quality or performance or other aspects. Products manufactured in these countries are accepted in the same form in other countries as consumers like to buy the standard products so as to be assured of the quality and performance. For example, consumers world over prefer to buy Made in Japan goods as they are assured of the quality of such goods. Marketers use this as a potent marketing tool and retain the standardized features of a product with domestic market focus and use it strategically to enhance their sales in overseas markets. Japan auto manufacturers have successfully leveraged this strategy to sell second-hand cars and other utility vehicles in African markets, where consumers trust second-hand Japanese vehicles more than the new ones from any country.
7. **Economies in business operations:** Standardized products along with standardized business operations tend to generate higher economies of scale as a firm can use an identical marketing approach globally and reduce the cost of business operations significantly.

Product adaptation, on the other hand, is the process of modifying an existing product or altering its features so as to make it suitable for different markets. As customs vary from each other culturally, socially and economically, it is important for any marketer to bring changes in products as desired by customers in overseas markets. Product adaptation is particularly important for those export firms that want to penetrate each market segment by complying product features with local cultural and regulatory requirements. It is a vibrant market tool for those firms which cannot develop a new product for each market but can adapt the existing standard product for various markets, thus expanding their business and profits with low investment. There are many compelling reasons for product adaption in the international market such as differences in culture, stage of market development, level of competition and regulatory compliance. Any firm has to develop a product adaptation strategy in order to address these challenges and fulfil customer needs with adapted products. However, a firm must base a sound research based on primary and secondary research to introduce any modification in the existing standardized products. Following are the key arguments in favour of product adaptation in international markets.

1. **Varying technical standards:** The level of technological development varies (Caselet 6.2) world over and as a result, there are differences in technical standards in different markets of the world. One cannot do anything except to comply with local technical standards to sell products and services in such markets.

CASELET 6.2

Auto Industry to Comply with Bharat Stage VI

The Indian automotive industry is reeling under the impact of varying technical standards as India introduced Bharat Stage (BS) VI emission standards on 1 April 2020. Coupled with ongoing economic slowdown, the cost of introducing new technology is putting pressure on an already depressed Indian automobile industry. This transition to BS VI norms has been the topic of discussion among echelons of the Indian automobile industry and policymakers including government machinery which was trying its best to demystify its implications as the deadline for roll-out of BS VI norms was closer. BS VI is the new emission standard that all vehicles in the country will have to adhere to from 1 April 2020. The Government of India has made it clear that the sale of BS IV vehicles will also cease from 31 March 2020. The apex court of the country has also confirmed that only BS VI vehicles would be sold with effect from 1 April 2020. It is pertinent to note that BS VI norms will lead to a sharp reduction in emission of hazardous contents which make Indian cities unworthy for living, especially during winters. The sulphur content of BS VI fuel shall be mere 20 percent to that of BS VI norms, which is the major contributor of air pollution in the country. In order to double up government efforts for access to cleaner air to common public, it is mandated that there will be onboard diagnostics and real driving emission on all vehicles so as to facilitate real-time tracking of emissions. The Indian automobile industry is already grappling with one of the worst slowdowns in recent times and it has to further escalate its efforts first on selling the inventory of BS IV vehicles coupled with technological upgradation for rolling out the BS VI stage vehicles in the country. Automobile industry is waking up to product adaptation to simultaneously invest in building BS VI engines and ramp up the production of BS VI vehicles.

2. **Different product uses by customers:** Product uses may vary for the same products or consumers may demand additional features in the product so as to fulfil local problems. Firms may have to adapt their products in order to address such concerns. For example, a mini truck called TATA ACE is promoted for different uses by Tata Motors in India and abroad.

Fresh vegetable van

Cafeteria

Goods carrier

Delivery van

Cash van

Milk van

Source: Pinterest, Just Dial, IndiaMart, Alibaba.

Adapted product fulfils the varying needs of customers as the usage conditions may vary in different markets and one needs to adapt the product so as to cater to local needs.

3. **Varying income pattern:** Countries vary in terms of per capita income globally and marketers need to understand the fact that firm should design the products so as to cater to the differing needs of consumers with varying income pattern in different markets of the world. The firms engaged in export operations have to factor these differences in income pattern and accordingly cater their products to global consumers.
4. **Socio-cultural differences:** Consumers vary the world over based on their socio-cultural background (Caselet 6.3), and an export firm has to adapt its products so as to address these cultural differences from one market to another. Socio-cultural differences may well affect the buying criteria of customers based on their local needs, usage pattern, tastes, preferences and habits, and a firm has no other alternative than to adapt the products according to target market needs.
5. **Local content requirement:** Sometimes, product adaptation is dictated by government policies of country of imports which may forbid the sale of wholly imported product and may mandate the use of local products for product development. Countries suffering from problems of balance of payments usually dictate such terms and conditions wherein they may regulate that imported products must have specified minimum local content requirements. India has used such a strategy in the automobile sector so as to develop the ancillary industry for its growing automobile sector and as a result, India has emerged as the second largest auto-component manufacturer in the world.

CASELET 6.3

Localization Strategy of Product Adaptation Helps Dabur Grow in MENA Region

Dabur started its business with a humble beginning as a small clinic for making Ayurvedic medicine in 1884 in the Indian city of Kolkata. In the last 132 years, Dabur has transformed itself to a transnational FMCG company with its business operations spread into 120 countries of the world. As part of its business expansion, Dabur ventured into the Middle East and North Africa (MENA) market as Dabur found these markets to be very similar to the Indian culture and where customers have preference and taste for natural and Ayurvedic products. Banking on its strong product portfolio in Ayurvedic and natural care segments, Dabur tried to focus on specific consumer categories that can be tapped such as skin care, oral care, home care and foods through brands such as Dabur Vatika, DermoViva, Fem, Hajmola, Sanifresh and Odonil. Dabur has already established these brands as household names in many parts of the world. Dabur wanted to duplicate its South Asian success in the markets of MENA region.

To fulfil its dream of market expansion in the MENA region, it banked upon a multi-tiered strategy which was aimed at first localizing existing products range for the MENA market. The research team at Dabur, with first-hand market inputs from the marketing team, decided to offer products specifically formulated and developed to cater to the consumer needs of this region. Dabur banked on the local knowledge of herbs used for treatment of health problems and integrated this knowledge in its product development programmes. Accordingly, a different range of products was developed and offered in different geographies of the MENA Region. For example, Dabur's hair oil brand called Dabur Amla which was launched in 1940 and has acquired a special place in the hearts of women in India is adapted to local needs. During the course of these adaptations, the research team focused on local herbs used for making hairs long and black and accordingly innovated products such as Hammam Zaith and Snake Oil. The marketing team mobilized its efforts for localized marketing campaign for promotion of these products and it was done through prominent Arab celebrities. By effectively leveraging these product adaptation strategies, Dabur considerably gained brand equity in shampoos and conditioners' category by leveraging its Vatika brand which is launched in a range of shampoos and conditioners under the brand Amla, Snake Oil, Keratin and Vitamin variants. Under product Vatika Naturals, it adapted products with traditional herbs used extensively by the local Arab populace and launched a new range of ingredient-based shampoos and conditioners in the MENA region. Arab people used traditional products such as argan, black seed and garlic for hair and Dabur used these products to its favour. It further launched an innovative Vatika hair mayonnaise range shampoos. This helped Dabur to increase its business from a mere 200 million dirham in 2006 to over 1 billion dirham by 2011 in a time span of just 5 years. To further penetrate deep into the market, it banked on acquiring local companies and has acquired Hobi Kozmetik in Turkey and Namaste Laboratories based in Chicago, United States, but having a leading business portfolio in African-American hair care. This product adaption strategy coupled with strategic acquisitions helped Dabur emerge as a leading Ayurvedic product company in the MENA region.

6. **Leveraging adapted products as the firm's corporate strategy:** In today's fast-changing proliferated market segments, firms are increasingly leveraging the adapted product launch as the corporate strategy so as to outsmart their competitors with aggressive marketing attack. Global mobile markets witness several product launches mainly aimed at capturing the niche market segment and outcompete the competitors in marketing warfare.

6.7 Leveraging Product Life Cycle Stages in Exports

With increased speed of technological innovations in product design and development by product manufacturers, there are proliferations of new product designs in international markets. Development of new products cost a lot in terms of innovation and research and financial investments for any internationally engaged firm. Hence, it is the constant endeavour of any export firm to reap the dividends of such product innovation, new design and development in international markets so as to recover the developmental cost of the firm. The product life cycle of any internationally launched product consists of four stages: introduction, growth, maturity and decline. Table 6.2 illustrates the stages of the product life cycle in international markets. It is the constant endeavour of any internationally engaged firm to leverage each of these stages to its favour as the determination of a product's stage in its life cycle is not based on age, but on the relationship of sales, costs, profits and number of competitors operating in the market. Each of these stages is important for an international market. One should understand the various aspects explained in the following sub-sections of leveraging each stage of product for enhanced business opportunities in international markets.

6.7.1 Introduction

When a new product is introduced in the international market, a firm may spend a lot on marketing of the product in target segments. There can be a small group of people usually referred to as 'innovators' who may be aware of the new product. Sometimes, it is a new product in this product category and there is a possibility that customers may not know what the product's uses are or what the product is meant for. The key characteristics of this stage of the product are: the sales volumes are very low, only innovators know about the product, marketing costs are high and there is sometimes resistance even from distribution networks about the possible profit margins. Under this stage, the manufacturer enjoys the market monopoly, level of competition is low and sales usually do not result in profits. It is the constant endeavour of international marketers to adapt the production strategy to local markets' condition and leverage every possible business initiatives to recover the developmental cost of the product. Firms may have to leverage aggressive marketing strategy to push sales and factor in the feedback of customers in product design as no international marketer can sustain the introduction stage for too long. Accordingly, marketers make every possible effort to scale up sales of the product and recover developmental costs and profits, if possible.

TABLE 6.2 Examples of Product Life Cycles of Various Products

Product Segment	Introduction	Growth	Maturity	Decline
1. Book writing	Smart mobile phones	Laptops	Desktop	Typewriters
2. Personal communication	Videoconferencing	Email	Faxes	Handwritten letters
3. Bank transaction system	Iris-based personal identity cards	Smart cards	Debit and credit cards	Cheque books
4. Lighting	LED bulb	Mercury bulb	Electrical bulb	Kerosene lamp

6.7.2 Growth

Exports sales expand at growth stages and firms also start getting profits on the sales. If the product succeeds the introduction stage, the product enters the growth stage and if it fails, the firm may have to bring in necessary changes to product design and usage. The key characteristics of the growth stage are that firms have increasing sales, resultant profits, expanding market base with early adopters and market monopoly. An international marketer must observe how the product is responding to market competition and is establishing itself in the market. He/she must factor in the promotional efforts, changes required and tools to handle the emerging competition. The product must be profitable at this stage as the growth stage manifests the increasing sales, hence, more retailers are interested in marketing this product. Marketer must constantly endeavour to enhance not only the sales but should also focus on gaining customer preference for the product, only then the product can establish itself as a mature product in the market.

6.7.3 Maturity

Each exporter always wishes to achieve this stage of product cycle as product sales as well as profits touch almost the highest possible level, but the market competition also becomes very high as lots of competitors start marketing similar kinds of products. Due to market expansion and consumer knowledge, even the inefficient firms may make money as bigger firms may not be able to operate in each product segment. An exporter has to offer differentiated products so as to tap the maximum possible sales. As a result, the market becomes proliferated with a large number of products models. There can be business scenario when total sales continue to grow but the profits keep on shrinking as there is intense competition and firms have to compromise on profits margin so as to operate with higher market share. The declining profits is an indication for any firm that the product has reached its maturity stage and it is time to introduce a new product to beat its competitors.

6.7.4 Decline or Obsolesce

Any export firm will be interested to abandon the market at this stage of product as export sales continue to decline and profits become negligible. Firms always endeavour to accelerate the decline process as firms may have launched a new product which they want to market aggressively. The decline stage of any product is not time-bound and it is the changes and advances in technology which play a crucial role in bypassing and replacing a product. There is no permanent phasing out of the product by some manufacturers as they can make profits from sales because some laggard consumer may be resisting to switch to newer alternatives. Over a period of time, even the laggards will switch to newer product alternatives and product groups will be completely phased out by manufacturers.

6.8 Summary

A product is defined as a bundle of physical, service and symbolic attributes which provide the benefits to a user or buyer for which it is designed, manufactured, sold, purchased, used and consumed. It yields the desired satisfaction to the customer. A product is a combination of ‘physical attributes’ such as size, shape, dimensions, weight, contests and subjective attributes such as brand equity, quality and image. Thus, an exportable product is the sum of all physical, psychological, symbolic and service attributes that a potential buyer is looking for and is not merely a physical merchandise. Selection of such bundle of satisfaction involves careful planning, research and due diligence for any exporter to succeed in international markets. Product planning, design and selection for export markets is a complex process as creation of a bundle of such benefits for target buyers has to be done in the context of the local market.

Export product planning is a systematic process that helps an exporter to understand the products that can be exported in international markets. It is an important step in export planning and execution, and one should consider only those new products that are unique, differentiated, innovative, superior in quality and cost-competitive. One should also consider those products for exports which can be produced on a larger scale to fulfil global demand. Hence, there must be sufficient supply of raw materials for production or produced goods after having considered the requirements of the domestic market. Export planning of any product must factor the following key concerns:

- Clarity in internationalization commitment
- Compliance with standards of target country
- Identifying the areas of product adaptation
- Anticipation of the level of competition

An export firm should always aim to select the right product, at the right price for a right market as firm's success in the overseas market largely revolves around quality products at competitive prices and timely cost-effective delivery of products. While selecting a product for exports, one should consider the fact that there is adequate production capacity not only to meet the domestic demand but also to fulfil the export orders. If there is no adequate production of goods, the regulatory authority like DGFT may declare the products restricted for exports, thus affecting exports. The exporter should check the level of incentives, export benefits and assistance, and duty neutralization offered by government to promote the export of particular products in international markets. Exporter may consider these benefits and incentives while selecting a product for export as it may make the export of these products attractive in international markets.

The international product policy of any firm with motivation to sell in the international markets is aimed at identifying the types of products to sell abroad. Product manager of any such firm has to define whether to introduce the standardized product or to adapt it to local market needs. Product adaptations may come up in several forms, for example, technical adaptation, cultural adaptation, price adaptation, quality adaptation and many more and are also called 'product differentiation' or 'product localization' or 'product customization'. Development of new products costs a lot in terms of innovation and research and financial investments for any internationally engaged firm. Hence, it is the constant endeavour of any export firm to reap the dividends of such product innovation, new design and development in international markets so as to recover the developmental cost of the firm. The product life cycle of any internationally launched product consists of four stages: introduction, growth, maturity and decline.

Review Exercises

Multiple Choice Questions

1. The concept of a product for international marketing has which of the following as an integral part?
   a. Tangible
   b. Intangible
   c. Both a and b
   d. None of the above
2. Sale of a product in international markets is not merely a 'sales transaction' but a
   a. Complete bundle of benefits
   b. Complete bundle of incentives
   c. Complete bundle of assistance
   d. Complete bundle of support
   e. None of the above
3. Mass customization product strategy aims to cater to which of the following types of products to global customers?
   a. Core product
   b. Actual product
   c. Augmented product
   d. Potential product
   e. None of the above
4. Which of the following are important market access issues for an automobile exporter while accessing the Kenyan market for car exports from India?
   a. Import regulations for identified products
   b. Tariff and non-tariff restrictions
   c. a and b
   d. Similarity of target consumers with domestic market in terms of tastes and preferences
   e. a, b and d
5. Which of the following are important areas of appraising economic environment of a South American market for opening a bank in Brazil?
   a. Project economic growth
   b. Interest rates, inflation and currency volatility
   c. Per capita income, disposable income and growth in income levels
   d. Foreign exchange regulations
   e. All of the above
6. A vehicle exporter from India must comply with homologation norms in the country of import for guaranteed market access and interrupted export operations. Homologation refers to which of the following?
   a. Level of regulation of distributorship in the foreign market
   b. Documentary requirements, licences to operate
   c. Licences for technical and environmental compliance
   d. Import regulations for identified product
   e. Tariff and non-tariff restrictions

7. Which of the following trade measures is used by a country as a non-tariff instrument to restrict import, hurting the domestic industry?
   a. Import quota/Quantitative restrictions
   b. Local contents requirements
   c. Embargoes
   d. Minimum import price limits
   e. All of the above

8. An international product refers to which of the following?
   a. Product is a bundle of services with tangible goods
   b. Product is a physical good with all its intangible services
   c. Product is a need-satisfying offering of a firm
   d. Product refers to any good traded internationally
   e. Product means well-packaged goods with a popular brand name

9. Which of the following is not a stage of product life cycle in international markets?
   a. Market maturity
   b. Market penetration
   c. Market introduction
   d. Sales decline
   e. Market growth

10. In export operations, when a product moves through its product life cycle, which of the following characteristics can be observed in the product life cycle?
   a. Operational profits of the firm may decrease while industry sales increase as the cycle advances
   b. Nature of business competition moves towards pure competition or oligopoly as cycle advances
   c. Newer and differentiated product segment becomes the business reality for increasing sales
   d. Product may require customer-specific adaptation based on the attitudes and needs of the customer
   e. All of the above

Critical Thinking Questions

1. Critically examine the concept of product for international markets. Discuss practical examples to support your answer.

2. Critically examine the process of export product planning for global export operations.

3. Explain the process of selection of products for international markets. What specific issues require an exporter's attention in decision-making for international product selection?

4. Discuss the international product policy. What are the pros and cons of introducing standard and adapted products in international markets?

5. Critically examine the stages of international product life cycle. What are the key marketing mix decisions an exporter has to leverage at various stages of international product life cycle?

CHAPTER 7

Regulation of Foreign Trade in India

CHAPTER OBJECTIVES

- To explain the legal framework regulation of foreign trade in India.
- To discuss the salient features of legislation governing exports and imports.
- To understand the trade policy regime and guidance note for regulation of foreign trade.
- To explain the regulation of foreign exchange for foreign trade in India.
- To explain the regulation of foreign trade by Indian customs.

7.1 Introduction

One of the distinctive features of EXIM operations is that an exporter or importer has to deal with different legal systems as the law of India does not apply beyond India's territorial waters. In fact, India, being a party to various international conventions, treaties and agreements, has to abide by commitments and obligations as agreed and ratified from time to time, and exporters and importers in India have to comply with those rules and regulations even if not enacted by the Government of India. Even within India, there is a comprehensive law governing the different aspects of foreign trade, and an exporter and importer must be well aware of the laws, rules, regulations and notifications issued thereunder, public notices, guidance note and trade policy regime governing exports and imports. If an exporter fails to abide by these rules and regulations, then he/she will be subject to prevalent Indian laws as well as to the jurisdiction of Indian courts. In addition to this, exporters and importers should also be aware of the key obligations and responsibilities that may arise due to their business interactions with involved trade intermediaries such as shipping companies, airlines, custom house agent, packing and fumigation agent, insurance companies and banks involved in an international trade transaction. These trade intermediaries are from different countries and accordingly may be governed with laws of different countries or international law to which an exporter or importer may become a party in some cases. For example, an Indian exporter based in Mumbai failed to declare the hazardous nature of goods to an airline and handed over goods for international transportation to Amsterdam. The cargo burst in the air as soon as the aeroplane took off from Mumbai and caught fire in air, posing extreme risks to the lives of passengers, aircrew and staff, and the aeroplane itself. Quoting International Air Transport Association guidelines, the exporter was sued in the court of law, as he negligently did not declare the hazardous nature to goods; instead, he submitted false information, owing to which the airline could not take necessary steps to protect such cargo from external risks and causing the event. The court ruled in the favour of the airline and imposed a huge penalty on the exporter. Similarly, the International Convention for the Safety of Life at Sea (SOLAS) mandates carrying of all kinds of dangerous goods to be in compliance with the International Maritime Dangerous Goods Code, failing which the vessel captain has the right to throw away the cargo at sea without any obligations to cover the loss of property. Even the insurance company does not pay if the exporter or importer is found negligent in the declaration of the nature of cargo, especially if it poses danger to the life of the personnel on a ship. SOLAS is an 'international maritime treaty' to which India is a party; it mandates for Indian exporters and importers to follow rules and regulations as required for the safety of ship's personnel. The list of key conventions and treaties regulating foreign trade is depicted in Figure 7.1.

Even the domestic law governing foreign trade has many obligations for exporters and importers; for example, the FTDR Act, 1992, provides for an orderly and systematic development of foreign trade in India and public officers are allowed to make required decisions to ensure orderly development of trade and commerce in India. Accordingly, various public notices, trade policies and circulars are issued by the regulatory authority DGFT so as to ensure that exporters and importers may not be able to contravene the provisions of prevalent other laws in India and if found doing so, shall be brought to jurisdiction of the Indian court including penal action as mandated under the FTDR Act, 1992. FEMA, 2000, and rules and regulations issued thereunder prescribe reasonable restrictions for compliance of Indian exporters and importers failing which suitable action can be initiated by the nodal agency 'Enforcement Directorate'. Indian customs is the nodal agency for orderly and systematic movement of goods into and outside India and an exporter or importer has to do the necessary documentation in order to export or import goods in India including compliance of trade policy regime, other acts in force and payments of required duties, if any, failing which the Indian customs is authorized to take legal actions against such offenders as mandated and provided under the law. FTP provides the general guidelines for the regulation of exports and imports, export incentives, duty neutralization mechanism, capacity-building

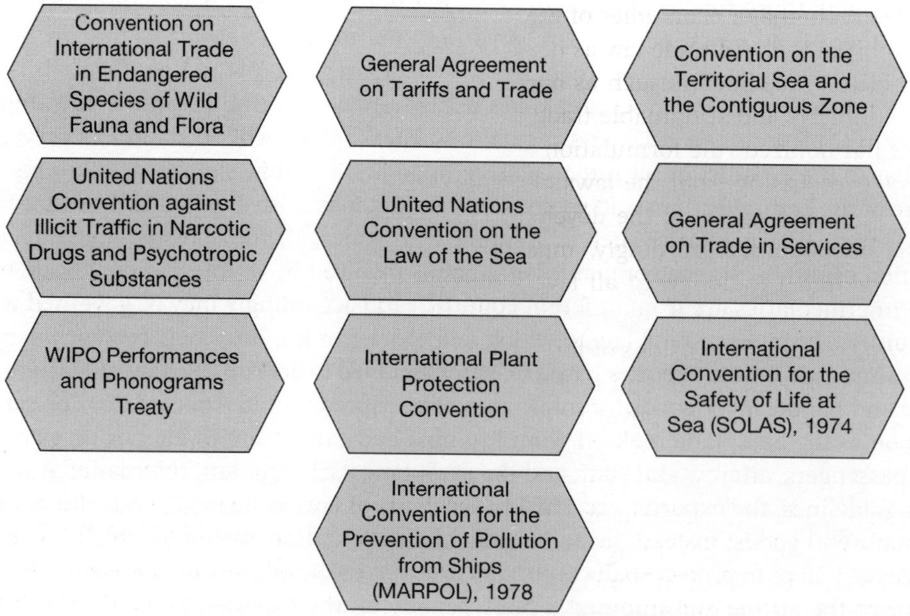

FIGURE 7.1 List of key conventions and treaties regulating foreign trade.

schemes and policy for dedicated exports enclaves and criteria and procedure for deemed exports benefits. In exercise of the powers conferred under Section 5 of the FTDR Act, 1992, DGFT, Department of Commerce, GOI, notifies FTP for the period of five years incorporating salient provisions, exemptions, incentives and other export promotion schemes. More so, DGFT reserves the right in public interest to make any amendments to this policy in exercise of the powers conferred by Section 5 of the Act by issuing required notifications and circulars which have the same regulatory impact as mandated under any legislation, policy and regulations. The key legislation regulating the foreign trade of India are exhibited in Figure 7.2.

Even the foreign trade agreement that India signed with partner countries has significant obligations on Indian exporters in terms of compliance to rules of origin and other non-tariff issues. It is the duty of an exporter to comply with rules and regulations governing the fulfilment of eligibility for any goods to qualify as manufactured in India in compliance to letter and spirit of clauses on rules of origin. India has signed several trade agreements aimed at India's export promotion and increasing its share in world trade and facilitating required imports, thus making goods available at competitive price to local customers and taming inflation. It also helps Indian exporters to source required raw material from partner countries without payment of duties or at a lower rate of duties. Table 7.1 depicts the list of existing, ongoing and trade agreements which are under consideration for negotiation by GOI.

7.2 Legal Dimension of Foreign Trade

Laws regulating foreign trade, whether domestic, international, bilateral or multilateral, play an important role in systematic and sustainable development of foreign trade of a country. With waves of economic globalization in major economies of the world creating a 'single market', it is important to have harmonized and standardized trade law as it will help the industry, exporters and importers, investors and other associated stakeholders such as banks, insurance companies, shipping companies and airlines to conduct orderly and sustainable trade and commerce. Hence, policymakers must take coordinated steps for harmonized rule formulation at regional and international levels, and for elimination of those divergences arising from the laws of different countries in matters relating to international commerce that create obstacles to the development of cross-border trade and commercial relations. Trade-enthusiastic nations, accordingly, must take necessary steps to continuously improve and strengthen international trade law at all levels—within country, bilateral, regional, multilateral and international.

Understanding of legal dimensions of foreign trade is indispensable for both exporters and importers and contemporary legislation, and its impact on business environment reflects upon the policy framework and the mindset of the governmental structure and bureaucracy with regard to regulation and facilitation of foreign trade from that country. Regulating agencies always constantly endeavour that firms and individuals engaged in exports and imports must function as per the statutory framework of the country. Hence, each firm or company wishing to start an EXIM business must take into account this legal set-up while framing the basic aims and objectives of the firm or company. This is necessary for efficient and healthy functioning of the organization and helps it to know about the rights, responsibilities as well as the challenges that it may have to face while doing EXIM business. In India, some of the major legislations which are important and should be taken care of are the

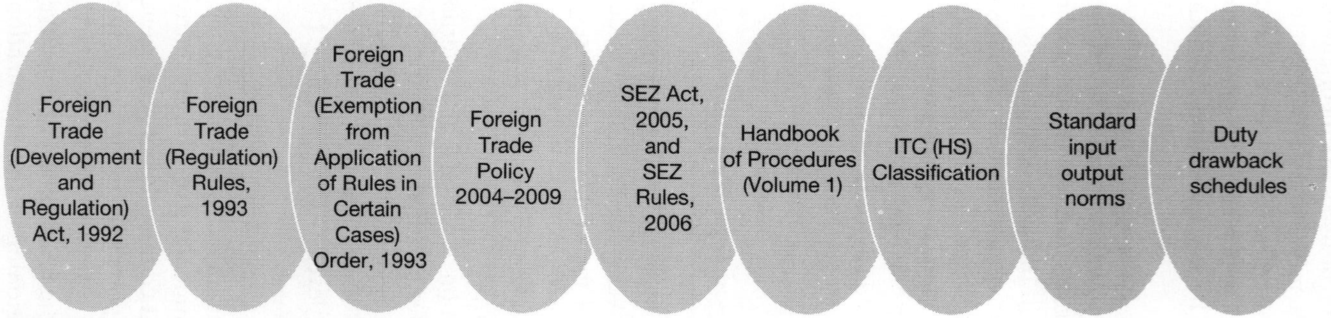

FIGURE 7.2 Key legislations and policy documents regulating India's foreign trade.

Source: Director General of Foreign Trade, Ministry of Commerce and Industry, GOI.

TABLE 7.1 India's Trade Agreements at a Glance

Existing Trade Agreements	FTAs /PTAs under Study and Consideration
1. ASEAN–India Comprehensive Economic Cooperation Agreement	1. India-Gulf Cooperation Council Free Trade Area
2. Asia–Pacific Trade Agreement	2. Bay of Bengal Initiative for Multi-Sectoral Technical and Economic Cooperation Free Trade Area
3. India–Afghanistan Preferential Trading Agreement	3. India–Australia Free Trade Agreement
4. India–Bhutan Trade Agreement	4. India–Canada Comprehensive Economic Partnership Agreement
5. India–Chile Preferential Trading Agreement	5. India-Customs Union of Russia, Belarus and Kazakhstan Free Trade Agreement
6. India–MERCOSUR Preferential Trade Agreement	6. India–Egypt Preferential Trade Agreement
7. India–Singapore Comprehensive Economic Cooperation Agreement	7. India–European Union Free Trade Agreement
8. India–Sri Lanka Free Trade Agreement	8. India–Indonesia Comprehensive Economic Cooperation Arrangement
9. India–Republic of Korea Comprehensive Economic Partnership Agreement	9. India–Israel Preferential Trade Agreement
10. Indo–Nepal Treaty of Trade	10. India–Mauritius Comprehensive Economic Cooperation and Partnership Agreement
11. Japan–India Comprehensive Economic Partnership Agreement	11. India–Southern African Customs Union Preferential Trade Agreement
12. Malaysia–India Comprehensive Economic Cooperation Agreement	12. New Zealand–India Free Trade Agreement
13. South Asian Free Trade Area	13. Regional Comprehensive Economic Partnership
14. Global System of Trade Preferences	
15. Generalized System of Trade Preferences	

Source: Ministry of Commerce and Industry, Government of India.

Industries (Development and Regulation) Act, 1951; the Competition Act, 2002; FEMA, 1999; the Trade Unions Act, 1928; the Arbitration and Conciliation Act, 1996; laws related to intellectual property rights as well as laws related to labour welfare. Having set up a company or firm, one has to get registered for IEC, RCMC, excise control code, service tax registration and VAT. The procedure for availing these licences is explained in Chapter 10. The legal framework for the regulation of foreign trade is mainly provided by the FTDR Act, 1992, the Export (Quality Control and Inspection) Act, 1963, the Customs and Central Excise Duties Drawback Rules, 1995, FEMA, 1999, and the Customs and Central Excise Regulations.

7.3 Foreign Trade (Development and Regulation) Act, 1992

The main legislation concerning foreign trade is the FTDR Act, 1992, which replaced the Imports and Exports (Control) Act, 1947, and gave GOI enormous powers to control it. The FTDR Act provides for the development and regulation of foreign trade by facilitating imports into and augmenting exports from India and for matters connected therewith or incidental thereto. A comparison of the nomenclature of the two Acts makes it very clear that there is a shift in the focus of the law from control to development of foreign trade. This shift in the focus is the outcome of the emphasis on liberalization, privatization, globalization and marketization as a part of the process of economic reforms initiated in India since June 1991. As per the provisions of the Act:

1. The FTDR Act, 1992, is enacted with the objectives of development and regulation of foreign trade by facilitating essential imports which are vital to India's growing economic needs and augmenting the exports capacity across various sectors of the Indian economy. This Act replaced the erstwhile legislations named the Imports and Exports (Control) Act, 1947, which was highly prohibitory and controlled the orderly development of both imports and exports.
2. Section 3 of the FTDR Act, 1992, enables the Department of Commerce and its attached office DGFT, which is constitutionally set up under this Act, to ensure systematic development and regulation of foreign trade and prohibit, restrict or otherwise regulate import and export of goods for creating the welfare in India's economic system. Restrictions to exports and imports should be based on either to ensure supply of goods to the domestic market on priority or to manage demand–supply equilibrium and on certain principles as drafted in FTP 2020. Principles of restrictions are given in Figure 7.3.
   Foreign Trade Policy and Handbook of Procedure (Vol. 1) as issued in Official Gazette by DGFT, New Delhi, mandates that exports and imports shall be free, except in cases where they are regulated by the provisions of this policy or any other law for the time being in force. The item-wise export and import policy shall be, as specified in ITC(HS), published and notified by DGFT, as amended from time to time. DGFT regulates exports and imports of goods through ITC(HS) Schedules 1 and 2 wherein it prescribes goods as 'free' or 'restricted' or 'state trading enterprise' and 'prohibited'. Usually, the import or export of goods which are prohibited through licensing or otherwise, or canalized, falls under the negative list and freely importable and exportable

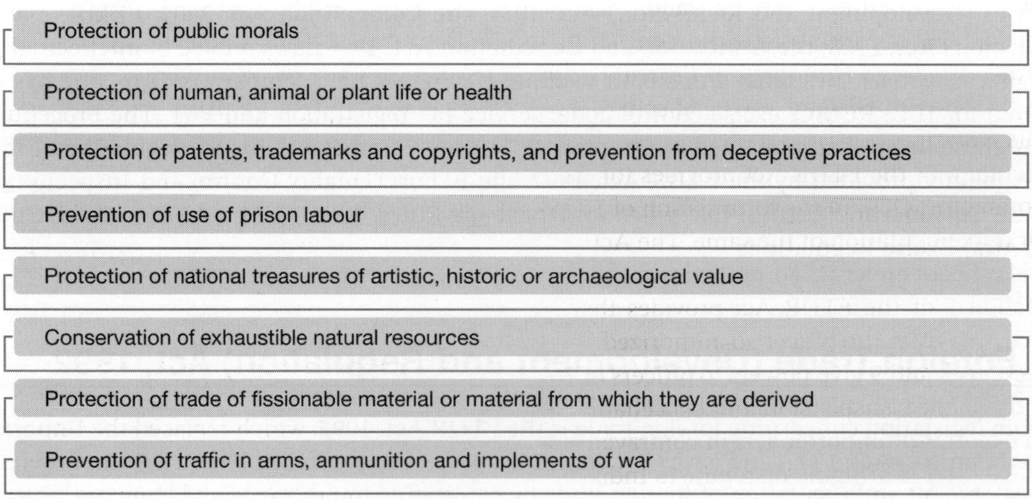

FIGURE 7.3 Principles of export–import restrictions.

Source: Ministry of Commerce and Industry (2020).

TABLE 7.2 Trade Policy Provisions Regarding the Conduct of Foreign Trade

Trade Regime for Regulation	Policy Decision for Trade	Industry People Expression of Trade Regime	Impact of Trade Regime
Positive list	Free goods	Open general licence	The goods allowed as freely exportable and importable can be imported by IEC holders subject to fulfilment of an authorization, if so required without any restrictions.
Negative list	Prohibited goods	Banned goods	Prohibited items in the negative list either for exports or for imports cannot be exported or imported at all.
	Restricted goods	Special export or import licence (SEL or SIL)	Any goods, the export or import of which is restricted through licensing, may be exported or imported only in accordance with a licence as required against application as prescribed in Aayat–Niryat Form.
	State trading enterprise	Canalized goods	Any goods, the import or export of which is canalized, may be imported or exported only through the canalizing agency specified in against the trade regime. Concerned nominated agency may, however, grant an NOC to any other person to import or export any canalized goods.

Source: Adapted from Director General of Foreign Trade, Ministry of Commerce & Industry, GOI.

goods fall under positive list. Table 7.2 explains the nature of the trade regime as prescribed by DGFT for equation of foreign trade.

3. The FTDR Act authorizes the central government to formulate and announce the *Foreign Trade Policy and Handbook of Procedure* and amend the same from time to time by notification in the Official Gazette. DGFT discharges such reasonability as mandated under Section 5 of this Act.
4. Section 6 of the FTDR Act provides for the appointment of DGFT to advise the Department of Commerce, GOI, in the formulation of FTP, procedures and allied guidelines and be responsible for implementation of the same. The Act defines the role, responsibilities and functions of DGFT and officers under its administrative control throughout the country.
5. Section 7 of the FTDR Act provides that every importer and exporter must obtain IEC from DGFT or from the officer so authorized.
6. Sections 8 and 9 give powers to officers of DGFT for suspension and cancellation of IEC number and issuance, suspension and cancellation of various authorizations, certificates and licences if an exporter or importer acts in contravention to objectives of this Act or it is in public interest or an exporter is bringing disrepute to India or is a hindrance in friendly and cordial trade relations with partner countries.

7. The FDTR Act provides powers to DGFT and its offices for search, seizure, penalty and confiscation but not to interfere with other punishments. DGFT is also the adjudicating authority for any disputes arising out in the areas of domain of FTP, procedure and associated rules and regulations thereunder by providing an appropriate opportunity to the owner of the goods on the said disputes. Sections 10–14 of the said Act provide legislative provisions for the same.
8. Sections 15–17 of the said Act provide for appeal, revision and powers of adjudicating of DGFT and officers under its administrative control throughout India.
9. Finally, Sections 18–20 of the Act are aimed at taking protective action if so desired in public interest in good faith of the officers of DGFT and constitutionally allow GOI to make rules or repeal existing rules and ensure savings.

As per provisions of this Act, DGFT has been made the nodal officer responsible for all functional and operational issues with regard to the issue of licences, granting permission for import of capital goods under the Export Promotion Capital Goods (EPCG) scheme and issuing licences under the duty exemptions and remissions schemes. This can be done either by DGFT or any other officer so authorized by it. It also ensures that export or import of goods to and from India is in accordance with the Act. It is also quasi-judicial authority as it settles the disputes that emerge from issue, cancellation of such licenses, authorizations and so on. Every exporter or importer shall comply with the provisions of the FTDR Act, 1992, the rules and orders made thereunder, the provisions of this policy and the terms and conditions of any licence/certificate/permission granted to him/her, as well as provisions of any other law for the time being in force. All imported goods shall also be subject to domestic laws, rules, orders, regulations, technical specifications, environmental and safety norms as applicable to domestically produced goods. If any question or doubt arises in respect of the interpretation of any provision contained in this policy, or regarding the classification of any item in ITC(HS), the said question or doubt shall be referred to DGFT whose decision thereon shall be final and binding. If any question or doubt arises whether a licence/certificate/permission has been issued in accordance with this policy or if any question or doubt arises touching upon the scope and content of such documents, the same shall be referred to DGFT whose decision thereon shall be final and binding.

Foreign Trade (Regulation) Rules, 1993

Section 19 of the FTDR Act, 1992, provides that rules can be made for regulation of foreign trade and accordingly, these rules are made by GOI. There are 18 rules which support the existing act and empower the officers of DGFT to take appropriate regulatory decisions vis-à-vis development of foreign trade in India. Salient features of the Foreign Trade (Regulation) Rules, 1993, are discussed as follows:

1. Rule 3 enables DGFT and its regional authorities across the country to issue 'special licences' to persons whose IEC numbers have been suspended or cancelled.
2. Rule 5 specifies the scale of fees to be paid towards applications for licences and categories which are exempt from payment of fees. Every application for a licence to import shall be accompanied by the fee specified in the Schedule. It accordingly provides for following schedule of fee for licences on imports.

S. No.	Particulars	Amount of Fee
1.	Where the value of goods specified in application does not exceed ₹50,000	₹200
2.	Where the value of the goods specified in the application exceeds ₹50,000 but does not exceed ₹10 million	₹2 per thousand or part thereof subject to a minimum of rupees ₹200.
3.	Where the value of the goods specified in the application exceeds ₹10 million	₹2 per thousand or part thereof subject to a maximum of ₹150,000
4.	Application for grant of duplicate licence	₹200
5.	In case where import licence and other correspondence are required by speed post	₹200
6.	Application for issue of an identity card	₹200
7.	Application for issue of duplicate identity card in the event of loss of original card	₹200
8.	Extension of the period of shipment of an import licence	₹200
9.	Application for grant split-up licences	₹1,000 per split-up licence

Source: Director General of Foreign Trade, Ministry of Commerce & Industry, GOI.

3. Rule 6 of the said rules provides the general conditions applicable to licences for exports and imports issued by DGFT. Rule 6(4) provides for import certificates issued under the Indo-US MOU.
4. Rules 7 specifies the circumstances under which a licence can be refused by DGFT wherein the designated authority must document the circumstances of such refusal or rejection in writing, and further Rule 8 enables the licensing authority to amend a licence if so desired and required in public interest.
5. Rule 9 deals with suspension of licences issued to an exporter or importer in accordance with FTP 2015–2020. Rule 10 lays down the reasons and procedure for cancellation of licences, if so desired by a competent authority.
6. Rule 13 indicates the manner of utilization of goods allotted by State Trading Corporation (STC) or any other agency recognized by the central government in a manner and for the purpose of canalized trade of goods as detailed in ITC Schedules 1 and 2 as framed by DGFT for the regulation of trade regime. An importer of the goods shall not dispose of any goods imported by him/her against a licence such as Advance Authorization, Duty Free Import Authorization and EPCG scheme and Gold Replenishment scheme except in accordance with the terms and conditions of such licence or FTP in force.
7. Rule 15 provides the procedure for search, seizure and Rule 16 provides the mechanism and system for settlement of matters, disputes, if any, in accordance with established procedures.
8. Rule 17 provides for redemption of imported goods and material subject to fulfilment of export obligations as mandated and Rule 18 provides for confiscation of goods materials if they are imported in contravention of established trade regime in force.

Foreign Trade (Exemption from Application of Rules) Order, 1993

This order has been issued under the FTDR Act and is aimed at exempting the application of foreign trade legislation and rules on certain categories of imports and exports. Any request for relaxation of the provisions of this policy or of any procedure on the ground that there is a genuine hardship to the applicant or that a strict application of the policy or the procedure is likely to have an adverse impact on trade may be made to DGFT for such relief as may be necessary. DGFT may pass such orders or grant such relaxation or relief as it may deem fit and proper. DGFT may, in public interest, exempt any person or class or category of persons from any provision of this policy or any procedure and may, while granting such exemption, impose such conditions as it may deem fit. Important exemptions for exports and imports are detailed in Figure 7.4.

It is provisioned under the *Handbook of Procedure* that no export or import shall be made by any person without an IEC number unless specifically exempted under the policy. An IEC number shall be granted on application to the competent authority and procedure for availing IEC has been detailed in Chapter 10. The following categories of importers or exporters are exempted from obtaining an IEC number:

1. Importers covered by Clause 3(1) and exporters covered by Clause 3(2) of the Foreign Trade (Exemption from Application of Rules in Certain Cases) Order, 1993, with some exceptions.
2. Ministries/Department of the central or a state government.
3. Persons importing or exporting goods for their personal use not connected with trade or manufacture or agriculture.
4. Persons importing/exporting goods from/to Nepal provided the CIF value of a single consignment does not exceed Indian ₹100,000.
5. Persons importing/exporting goods from/to Myanmar through Indo-Myanmar border areas provided the CIF value of a single consignment does not exceed Indian ₹100,000.

In addition to above, permanent IEC numbers as listed in Table 7.3 shall be used by the categories of importers/exporters mentioned against them for import/export purposes.

Imports

- Imports for defence purposes
- Import by central/state government or public sector undertaking through the India Supply Mission at Washington and London
- Imports for transit to other countries
- Imports under the Baggage Rules
- Personal imports
- Imports by diplomatic personnel
- UN officials
- Temporary imports for fairs, exhibitions and so on

Exports

- By or under the authority of central government
- Ship stores
- Baggage
- Transshipment
- Goods imported without a valid licence and ordered to be re-exported
- Goods manufactured by 100 percent export-oriented units or units in export processing zones

FIGURE 7.4 Important exemptions for exports and imports under foreign trade (exemption from application of rules) Order, 1993.

Source: Foreign Trade (Exemption from Application of Rules) Order, 1993.

TABLE 7.3 Permanent IEC Numbers for Use by Importers/Exporters

S. No.	Code Number	Categories of Importers/Exporters
1.	0100000011	All ministries/departments of the central government and agencies wholly or partially owned by them.
2.	0100000029	All ministries/departments of the state government and other agencies wholly or partially owned by them.
3.	0100000037	Diplomatic personnel, counsellor offices in India and the officials of the UNO and its specialized agencies.
4.	0100000045	Indians returning from/going abroad and claiming benefit under the Baggage Rules.
5.	0100000053	Persons/Institutions/Hospitals importing or exporting goods for their personal use not connected with trade or manufacture or agriculture.
6.	0100000061	Persons importing/exporting goods from/to Nepal provided the CIF value of a single consignment does not exceed Indian ₹100,000.
7.	0100000070	Persons importing/exporting goods from/to Myanmar through Indo-Myanmar border areas provided the CIF value of a single consignment does not exceed Indian ₹100,000.
8.	0100000088	Ford Foundation
9.	0100000096	Importers importing goods for display or use in fairs/exhibitions or similar events under the provisions of ATA carnet.
10.	01000000100	Director, National Blood Group Reference Laboratory, Bombay, or their authorized offices.
11.	01000000126	Individuals/Charitable Institutions/Registered NGOs importing goods, which have been exempted from customs duty under the notification issued by the Ministry of Finance for bona fide use by the victims effected by natural calamity.
12.	01000000134	Persons importing/exporting permissible goods as notified from time to time, from/to China through Gunji, Namgaya Shipkila and Nathula ports, subject to value ceilings of single consignment as given in Para 2.8 (iv).
13.	01000000151	The Directorate of Purchase and Stores, Department of Atomic Energy, Government of India
14.	01000000169	Non-commercial imports and exports by entities who have been authorized by RBI.

Source: Chapter 2 of Foreign Trade Policy (2015–2021) Director General of Foreign Trade, Ministry of Commerce & Industry, GOI.

7.4 General Provisions Regarding Imports and Exports

Appraising and understanding the FTP is essentially for those planning to head the trade operations division of a firm as it helps them to understand the trade policy, procedure and guidelines governing the conduct of India's foreign trade vis-à-vis other countries. Knowledge of trade policy is essential to enable the exporters and importers to deliver and get the contracted goods in international trade and also help them to know the various export promotion schemes, incentives, subsidies, capacity development programme, duty remission and exemption schemes as given in trade policy to facilitate Indian exporters to stand up in international markets. In other words, FTP serves the major perspectives of enlightening the prospective and existing traders about the international trade transactions in today's complex and ambiguous global environment.

7.4.1 Policy on Approved Exporter Scheme for Self-certification of Certificate of Origin

India has signed a number of bilateral and multilateral FTAs for the purpose of expansion and diversification of its foreign trade and integration of its economy with other global economies. Certificate of origin acts as the quasi-financial instrument in extending the relief in payment of lower rates of duties in the country of import, thus making such goods attractive and competitive vis-à-vis other countries and resulting in enhanced export activity. Currently, India has preferential and zero duty regime under various PTAs, FTAs, comprehensive economic cooperation agreements and comprehensive economic partnership agreements, wherein the designated agencies issue certificate of origin as per Appendix 2B of FTP 2015–2020. It is sometimes seen that Indian exporters are not using the benefit of these agreements as they find the documentation for availing certificate of origin to be too cumbersome. Hence, a new optional system of self-certification known as 'Common Digital Platform for Issuance of Certificate of Origin' is being introduced with a view of reducing transaction cost in India's foreign trade and making Indian goods competitive in the international markets. Accordingly, DGFT has provisioned in FTP 2015–2020 that Indian manufacturer-exporters who are also status holders shall be eligible for the 'Approved Exporter Scheme'. Any manufacturer-exporter who enlists under this scheme shall be entitled to self-certify his/her manufactured goods as originating from India with a view to qualifying for preferential treatment under different FTAs signed by India. Self-certification will be permitted only for the goods that are manufactured as per the Industrial Entrepreneur Memorandum (IEM)/industrial licence (IL)/letter of intent (LOI) issued to manufacturers. It is important that such manufacturer-exporter must have required infrastructure, capacity and trained man-power as prescribed in Appendix 2F of FTP 2015–2020. A manufacturer-exporter who is also a status holder can take benefit of this scheme but must comply with the provisions of the agreed and negotiated agreement with partner countries, failing which such exporter shall be liable to penalty provisions, which are provided in Appendix 2F of Foreign Trade Policy (2015–21) and will come into effect only when India incorporates the scheme into a specific agreement with its partner/s and the same is appropriately notified by DGFT.

7.4.2 Policy on Import of Samples

In the changing dynamics of world trade, it has become extremely necessary for exporters to carry samples of manufactured goods or to send samples of manufactured goods to buyers in other countries which will act as demonstration, prototype, display and so on to prospective customers to get familiar with product features, thus enabling importers to solicit purchase orders from such customers. India has signed the global convention for harmonized trade procedure for movement of sample cargo in 1952 and it is known as 'Convention to Facilitate the Importation of Commercial Samples and Advertising Material'. Indian customs issue notifications from time to time on the harmonized procedure as negotiated at a global level which enables duty-free import of genuine 'commercial samples' into the country for smooth flow of trade. Convention for facilitation of import of samples and advertising material was aimed at smooth and orderly development of trade and commerce among countries and by no means should be used as an instrument to avoid paying customs duty through repeated imports of samples in smaller lots.

The commercial samples refer to 'specimens of goods' that may be imported by the Indian traders so as to understand the specific product requirements of an importer. Sometimes, the authorized export agents of big retail chains or the representatives of big exporters based in India also import samples so as to know exactly the product characteristics, its usage requirements and to assess its marketability in India. Samples are always imported duty free and may include consumer goods, consumer durables, prototypes of engineering goods or even high-value equipment, machinery and their accessories. The import of samples in India shall be subject to prevailing foreign trade regime and one has to fulfil all licensing required, if so mandated, and prohibited goods shall not be imported in any circumstances. For example, samples of wild animals, wild birds and parts of wild animals and birds, ivory, arms and ammunitions, and narcotic drugs. Any firm or individual or trade body or research institute or laboratory fulfilling the licensing requirements for imports such as IEC and RCMC is allowed to import duty-free samples.

FTP of India specifies the value limit for import of bona fide trade samples for both importers and export promotion councils/commodity boards. For example, the Export Promotion Council for Handicrafts imports samples on behalf of individual small exporters, thus helping them save their time and cost in foreign trade. There is value limit for import of duty-free samples, and it should not exceed ₹300,000 per year or 50 units of samples in a year except in the gems and jewellery industry where it can be 0.25 percent of FOB value of last year's export. Import of samples regulations, however, allow duty-free import only up to ₹300,000 and remaining imported samples, if any, must be re-imported within a period of 12 months or any other such extended period as the assistant commissioner of customs may allow. Further, there is provision that high-valued samples can be cleared after payment of due duties with undertaking for their re-import within nine months wherein such deposited duty is refunded when the machinery is exported out of India. The value limit for duty-free import of samples is excluding the local refundable taxes like VAT in the country of dispatch. Each importer is required to declare correctly and adhere to the undertaking of the limit of yearly value and quantity as specified by regulatory authorities and if any person is suspected to contravene the limit or undertaking deliberately, then he/she is liable to be investigated, penalized or prosecuted. In addition to this general rule for import, the following are specific rules for import of samples in India:

1. DGFT, through FTP, allows 100 percent export-oriented units (EOUs), SEZ units, EHTP units, STPI units and BTP units to import samples, without any limit, of all types of goods duty-free subject to other conditionalities for positive exchange earner as specified.
2. Duty-free import of samples is also allowed without any limit for events sponsored by GOI.
3. Import of samples is also allowed for 'private commercial exhibition' for display or demonstration with the prior permission of the Ministry of Commerce and ITPO.
4. Duty-free import of samples is also allowed for promotion of tourism equipment and ancillary goods.

7.4.3 Policy on Exports of Samples

In order to allow Indian exporters a red-tape-free export regime and access to potential and prospective customers, DGFT has decided not to impose any limit on export of samples, thus bona fide trade and technical samples can be exported 'without any limit' subject to compliance of other conditionalities of FTP. For example, if an item is restricted for exports, an exporter should file an application to DGFT as per ANF 2Q for export of samples, exhibits and so on.

7.4.4 Policy on Import and Export of Gifts Items

Import as well as export of gifts shall be 'free' where such goods are otherwise freely importable under 'open general licence' as prescribed in Schedules 1 and 2 of ITC(HS). In other cases, such imports as well as exports shall be permitted against an authorization issued by DGFT to this effect. FTP prescribes the value limit for export of gifts (including edible items. if any) not exceeding ₹500,000 in a licensing year. However, items mentioned as restricted for exports in ITC(HS) shall not be exported as a gift without an authorization to this effect issued by DGFT or its regional office under the laid-down procedure. For clearance of gifts from customs authorities, an importer must comply with provisions as prescribed under FTP and should file for custom clearance permit (CCP) for import of gifted items. In case where the recipient of a gifted item is a charitable or religious or an educational institution registered under any law in force, the gift can be allowed for import clearance without CCP issued by DGFT, at the satisfaction of custom officials.

7.4.5 Policy on Re-import of Goods Repaired Abroad

FTP allows that capital goods, equipment, components, parts and accessories, which were imported by an actual user or procured from the domestic supplier, if so required, can be sent for repairs, testing, quality improvement or upgradation or standardization of technology and re-imported without an authorization. If such a good or material is declared as restricted good, an exporter has to take special export licence from DGFT; however, prevailing import regimc may not apply on such goods sent abroad for repair, testing quality improvement and so on. The exporter may have to pay the import duty on the amount of value added or invoice of repair, whichever is higher, on such imported goods (returning after repair abroad). Other provisions of FTP will apply mutatis mutandis on such re-import of goods repaired abroad but the requirement of an authorization is waived off by DGFT.

7.4.6 Policy on Import of Goods Used in Projects Abroad

Project exports are vital for a developing country like India and accordingly the government encourages Indian firms to procure project works abroad and facilitate them at all levels as earnings from them are the exports of India. FTP mandates that project contractors may import goods without an authorization, including capital goods used in the project, after completion of projects abroad, provided they have been used for at least one year abroad.

7.4.7 Policy on Import of Prototypes

India is fast emerging as a designing centre and major companies are basing their operations for design and development in India. Accordingly, DGFT has allowed the import of new or second-hand prototypes and second-hand samples on payment of duty without an authorization to an actual user (industrial) engaged in production or having IL or LOI for research. An importer of such prototype, however, has to satisfy the custom authorities about its design capabilities through industrial literature and any other documentary evidence or through a self-declaration as the case may be.

7.4.8 Policy on Export and Import through Courier Service

Exports as well as imports through a registered courier service are permitted as per notification of the Department of Revenue. In order to regulate the import and export through courier, GOI had framed the Courier Imports (Clearance) Regulation in 1995 which was subsequently revised by incorporating the provisions for courier exports as well and was pronounced as the Courier Imports and Exports (Clearance) Regulations in 1998. According to these regulations, the facility of courier clearance of both imported and exported courier goods from India is available at select customs airports and land customs stations of India. These are shown as follows.

Airports	Land Custom Stations
1. Mumbai	**1.** Petrapole
2. Delhi	**2.** Ghojadanga
3. Chennai, Kolkata	
4. Bangalore	
5. Hyderabad	
6. Jaipur	

Source: Courier Imports and Exports (Clearance) Regulations, 1998.

Courier exports and imports from these customs stations shall be subject to compliance of FTP and importability as well as exportability of such items are regulated in accordance with this FTP/ITC(HS). The facility of imports and exports through courier mode can, however, be only affected through those courier companies which are registered with the Customs Department. Any courier company intending to engage in international shipment, dispatch and receipt of courier cargo should apply for registration to the jurisdictional commissioner of customs. Commissioner of customs on his/her satisfaction of fulfilment of eligibility conditions can grant registration for three years and same has to be renewed every three years by the courier company. An authorized courier company can get registration at more than one airport or land customs station if it is falling under different custom jurisdictions. Applicant courier company/firm needs to furnish a separate bond and security at each airport and land customs station. The applicant courier company has to produce a certificate from any scheduled bank in proof of possessing the assets of value not less than ₹0.5 million and also needs to execute a bond with a security of ₹0.2 million for registration at Mumbai, Calcutta, Delhi and Chennai and security deposit of ₹0.1 million at other airports and land customs stations. Further, the Courier Imports and Exports (Clearance) Regulations, 1998, mandates that the following goods cannot be allowed for exports and imports through couriers.

Perishables	Animals and plants	Drugs and pharmaceuticals	Publications containing maps depicting incorrect boundaries of India	Precious and semi-precious stones, gold or silver in any form

Source: Courier Imports and Exports (Clearance) Regulations, 1998.

Similarly, rules restrict the export and import of goods which are not under the licensing regime of DGFT, canalized for exports and imports and prohibited for exports and imports. The rules also prescribe the value limit for export through courier which should not be more than ₹25,000 per transaction.

7.4.9 Generalized System of Preferences

Generalized system of preferences (GSP) is a non-contractual and non-reciprocal tariff preference instrument wherein the industrialized and developed countries unilaterally extend tariff concessions to developing countries so as to provide level playing field and promote exports from developing countries which will act as catalyst for enhancing economic growth of these countries. The United States has withdrawn this facility from India; other countries which offer GSP benefits to India are New Zealand, Belarus, the European Union, Japan, Russia, Canada, Norway and Switzerland. GSP schemes of these countries are available to specific tariff lines of India's exports products. Further, a certificate of origin in compliance with laid-down rules and regulations is required to avail this benefit. GSP scheme has been revised several times by developed countries and is modified from time to time so as to address the changing business needs. GSP benefits are now largely available to LDCs. An exporter has to furnish the certificate of origin in Form 'A' (prescribed for GSP rules of origin) and get it certified by authorized agencies. DGFT specifies the list of such agencies and Export Inspection Council (EIC) of India is one of them.

7.4.9.1 Policy on Duty-free Tariff Preference Scheme for LDCs

Duty-free tariff preference (DFTP) scheme is similar to GSP scheme. Under this scheme developing countries offer the non-reciprocal tariff preference to LDCs. The mandate for duty-free, quota-free access to LDCs is provided under the Hong Kong Declaration of WTO (2005). Initially, developed countries, especially from Europe, Japan and the United States, offered this benefit to LDCs and India became the first developing country to extend this facility. India offered DFTP scheme to LDCs in the year 2008 and extended tariff reductions which comprise 92.5 percent of global exports of all LDCs. Out of 49 LDCs, 28 LDCs are availing this scheme and it was modified to increase its coverage as well as to simplify the procedure in 2014. With the DFTP scheme, the exports originating from LDCs get better market access in India, thus promoting the process of faster economic development of these countries.

7.4.9.2 Policy on Denomination of Export Contracts

1. All export contracts and invoices shall be denominated in either freely convertible currency or Indian rupees, but export proceeds shall be realized in freely convertible currency.
2. Export proceeds against specific exports may also be realized in rupees, provided it is through a freely convertible vostro account of a non-resident bank situated in any country other than a member country of Asian Clearing Union (ACU) or Nepal or Bhutan. Additionally, rupee payment through vostro account must be against payment in free foreign currency by the buyer in his/her non-resident bank account. Free foreign exchange remitted by the buyer to his/her non-resident bank (after deducting bank service charges) on account of this transaction would be taken as export realization under export promotion schemes of FTP.

3. Contracts for which payments are received through ACU shall be denominated in ACU dollar. The central government may relax provisions of this paragraph in appropriate cases. Export contracts and invoices can be denominated in Indian rupees against EXIM Bank/GOI line of credit.

7.5 Foreign Exchange Management Act, 1999

FEMA has been enacted by the Indian Parliament in the year 1999 and it came into force from 2000. FEMA, 2000, replaces the erstwhile draconian act legislating the law of foreign exchange in India, the Foreign Exchange Regulation Act (FERA) 1973. FEMA, 2000, has been legislated so as to ensure conservation and proper utilization of the foreign exchange resources of the country in the changing era of economic liberalization and globalization. FEMA is an umbrella legislation for managing foreign exchanges in India including certain aspects of the conduct of business outside the country by Indian companies and in India by foreign companies. As Indian business is increasingly becoming global with more exports and imports including the flow of investment both into Indian economy and outflow to other business destinations, there is a greater need to regulate and facilitate such business operations. FEMA provides the guiding principles, allied rules and regulations for management of 'foreign currency' and includes deposits, credits and balances payable in any foreign currency. It also includes drafts, cheques, letters of credit or bills of exchange, expressed or drawn in Indian currency but payable in any foreign currency. The prime purpose of FEMA, 2000, is to consolidate and amend the law relating to foreign exchange with the objective of facilitating merchandise exports and imports, services trade, bilateral flows of investments, foreign currency payments and for promoting the orderly development and maintenance of foreign exchange market in India. FEMA empowers the Enforcement Directorate, a body under RBI with an important role of managing and regulating the foreign exchange in India. RBI is the nodal agency for framing rules, regulations and norms pertaining to several sections of the Act, in consultation with the central government and other associated stakeholders in the management of foreign exchange in India. FEMA provides the powers to the central government to appoint as many officers of the central government as adjudicating authorities for holding enquiries pertaining to contravention of foreign exchange in India and abroad by Indian enterprises and individuals.

7.6 Export (Quality Control and Inspection) Act, 1963

EIC is responsible for planning, execution and implementation of mandatory and voluntary EXIM inspection in India and is appointed under this Act. Under the Act, a large number of exportable commodities have been notified for compulsory pre-shipment inspection as there were regular complaints received from overseas buyers against the supply of these goods. The quality control and inspection of various export products is administered by EIC through a network of more than 55 nodal officers located all over the country. These nodal offices are either close to port towns or in the vicinity of production centres. Additionally, the Act provides the mandates for appointing of other organizations/agencies for export quality inspection and quality control. In order to promote the agro-exports from India, agricultural, foods and fishery products are exempted from compulsory pre-shipment inspections, provided importer gives an undertaking that he/she does not want these products to be mandatorily inspected. It is the constant endeavour of GOI to emerge as a quality-conscious supplier of goods and accordingly this act of parliament plays an important role in achieving that objective. Some of the mandatorily inspected goods under this Act are listed as follows:

1. Food and agricultural products
2. Chemicals and allied products
3. Engineering goods
4. Textiles
5. Coir, jute and leather products like footwear

Further, the Export (Quality Control and Inspection) Act, 1963, empowers GOI to:

1. Notify commodities which shall be subject to quality control or inspection or both, prior to the export.
2. Specify the type of quality control or inspection which will be applied to a notified commodity.
3. Establish, adopt or recognize one or more standard specifications to a 'notified commodity'.
4. Prohibit the export in the course of international trade of a notified commodity, unless it is accompanied by a certificate under Section 7 that the commodity satisfies the conditions related to quality control or inspection or it has affixed or applied to it a mark or seal accepted by the central government that it conforms to the standard specifications applicable to it.

Inspection of cargo for quality control can take place at three stages in any EXIM transaction. It can be mandated by the country of exports or by the country of imports and finally foreign buyers can also lay down their own standards and specifications, which may be higher than the Indian standards. Export inspection will take place as per agreed terms between exporter and importer; however, if the goods are mandatorily regulated for inspection, it will take place either in the country of exports or country of imports as the case may be. FTP of India mandates that import transactions will be subject to all those rules and regulations mandating quality compliance, inspection and adherence to the Indian standards. An importer must be registered with aligned quality assurance agency; for example, a food importer should be registered with FSSAI. Indian customs is vested with the task of carrying out physical as well as documentary check on all the goods crossing the Indian customs frontier. All export consignments will be checked by the customs authorities at port or airport with a view to ascertaining that the goods being shipped are those which are declared in the documents and that no under or over invoicing is involved.

7.7 Customs Act, 1962

In ancient times, merchants used to trade goods mainly through silk routes, wherein goods were exported and imported from China and India to Europe and vice versa. There was a 'customary practice' of gifting a part of their merchandise to the king while entering a kingdom and such a practice has been formalized by the modern states into the practice of collecting duties known as 'customs duty'. Customs duty is a kind of indirect tax which is levied on goods when they cross the territorial boundary of a country, that is, when goods are traded internationally, custom duties are levied mainly on imported goods and few exports goods. Taxes and duties levied and collected on imported goods are known as 'import duty' and taxes and duties levied and collected on the export goods are called 'export duty'. The authority which collects such duties is known as 'customs authority'. There is an act in India called the Custom Act, 1962, which empowers customs authority on levying, collection, adjudication and preventive actions of Indian customs. In addition to the Customs Act, 1962, there is an Indian Customs Tariff Act, 1975, which provides the framework for rates of duties to be levied on exportable and importable goods. The laws governing the Custom Act have evolved under the deliberations and negotiations of the WCO. The Indian government has framed the Indian customs law, rules and regulations based on WCO framework, guidelines and principles. Accordingly, the Customs Act, 1962, and the Customs Tariff Act, 1975, have been framed to regulate the movement of imported goods into India and exported goods out of India. For effective administration of indirect taxes in India, the central government has constituted the Central Board of Indirect Taxes and Customs (CBIC) which is the apex body for administration of Indian customs and GST. CBIC acts under the Department of Revenue of Ministry of Finance, GOI. CBIC deals with the task of formulation of policy concerning levy and collection of customs duties and overall administration of collection of indirect taxes in India. In order to perform these functions effectively, CBIC discharges various tasks with the help of its field formations, namely the Customs, Customs (Preventive) and CGST Zones, Commissionerates of Customs, Commissionerates of Customs (Preventive), Commissionerates of CGST, Central Revenues Control Laboratory and Directorates.

7.8 Summary

One of the distinctive features of EXIM operations is that an exporter or importer has to deal with different legal systems as the law of India does not apply beyond India's territorial waters. In fact, India, being a party of various international conventions, treaties and agreements, has to abide by commitments and obligations as agreed and ratified from time to time, and exporters and importers in India have to comply with those rules and regulations even if not enacted by GOI. Even within India, there is a comprehensive law governing the different aspects of foreign trade, and an exporter and importer must be well aware of the laws, rules, regulations, notifications issued thereunder, public notices, guidance note and trade policy regime governing exports and imports. Law regulating foreign trade, whether domestic, international, bilateral or multilateral, plays an important role in systematic and sustainable development of foreign trade of a country. With waves of economic globalization in major economies of the world creating a 'single market', it is important to have harmonized and standardized trade law as it will help the industry, exporters and importers, investors and other associated stakeholders such as banks, insurance companies, shipping companies and airlines to conduct orderly and sustainable trade and commerce. Hence, policymakers must take coordinated steps for harmonized rule formulation at regional and international levels and elimination of those divergences arising from the laws of different countries in matters relating to international commerce that create obstacles to the development of cross-border trade and commercial relations.

In fact, the main legislation concerning foreign trade is the FTDR Act, 1992, which replaced the Imports and Exports (Control) Act, 1947, and gave GOI enormous powers to control it. The FTDR Act provides for the development and regulation of foreign trade by facilitating imports into and augmenting exports from India and for matters connected therewith or incidental thereto. Appraising and understanding FTP is essentially for those planning to head the trade operations division of a firm as it helps them to understand the trade policy, procedure and guidelines governing the conduct of India's foreign trade vis-à-vis another country. Knowledge of trade policy is essential to enable the exporters and importers to deliver and get the contracted goods in international trade and also help them to know the various export-promotion schemes, incentives, subsidies, capacity development programmes, duty remission and exemption schemes as given in trade policy to facilitate Indian exporter to stand up in international markets. Salient policy schemes under the Indian FTP are listed as follows:

1. Policy on approved exporter scheme for self-certification of certificate of origin
2. Policy on import of samples
3. Policy on export of samples
4. Policy on import and export of gift items
5. Policy on re-import of goods repaired abroad
6. Policy on import of goods used in projects abroad
7. Policy on import of prototypes
8. Policy on export and import through courier service
9. Generalized system of preferences
10. Policy on DFTP scheme for LDCs
11. Policy on denomination of export contracts

FEMA has been enacted by the Indian Parliament in the year 1999, and it came into force from 2000. FEMA, 2000, replaces the erstwhile draconian act legislating the law of foreign exchange in India, FERA, 1973. FEMA, 2000, has been legislated to ensure conservation and proper utilization of the foreign exchange resources of the country in the changing era of economic liberalization and globalization. In ancient times, merchants used to trade goods mainly through silk routes, wherein goods were exported and imported from China and India to Europe and vice versa. There was a 'customary practice' of gifting a part of their merchandise to the king while entering a kingdom and such a practice has been formalized by the modern states into the practice of collecting duties known as 'customs duty'. Customs duty is a kind of indirect tax which is levied on goods when they cross the territorial boundary of a country, that is, when goods are traded internationally. Customs duties are levied mainly on imported goods and few exports goods. EIC is responsible for planning, execution and implementation of mandatory and voluntary EXIM inspection in India and is appointed under this Act. Under the Export (Quality Control and Inspection) Act, 1963, a large number of exportable commodities have been notified for compulsory pre-shipment inspection as there were regular complaints received from overseas buyers against supply of these goods. The quality control and inspection of various export products is administered by EIC through a network of more than 55 nodal officers located all over the country.

Review Exercises

Multiple Choice Questions

1. Which of the following Acts regulates foreign exchange in India?
   - **a.** FTDR Act, 1992
   - **b.** FEMA, 1999
   - **c.** Export (Quality Control and Inspection) Act, 1963
   - **d.** Customs Act, 1962

2. How many commissionerates of the Indian customs are there?
   a. 59
   b. 60
   c. 57
   d. 93
3. Which of the following Acts provides for levy and collection of customs duties in India?
   a. FTDR Act, 1992
   b. FEMA, 1999
   c. Export (Quality Control and Inspection) Act, 1963
   d. Customs Act, 1962
4. The policy on approved exporter scheme for self-certification of certificate of origin in India specifies for
   a. Exporter himself/herself can issue certificate of origin
   b. Importer himself/herself can issue certificate of origin
   c. Agency can issue online certificate of origin
   d. Third party can issue certificate of origin
5. The policy on export and import through courier service mandates that exports and imports through courier cannot take place for more than
   a. ₹35,000
   b. ₹25,000
   c. ₹50,000
   d. ₹15,000
6. The policy on DFTP scheme for LDCs provides
   a. Non-reciprocal preferential market access to notified LDCs in India
   b. Reciprocal market access to notified LDCs in India
   c. Waiver of most-favoured-nation clause
   d. Special status to LDCs in India
7. Which Act provides the legal framework for export quality control and pre-shipment inspections?
   a. FTDR Act, 1992
   b. FEMA, 1999
   c. Export (Quality Control and Inspection) Act, 1963
   d. Customs Act, 1962
8. GSP provides for
   a. Non-reciprocal preferential market access to developing countries in developed countries
   b. Reciprocal market access in developed countries
   c. Most-favoured nation status of all developing countries
   d. Special status to LDCs for market access
9. FTP is drafted and circulated by which of the following agencies?
   a. DGFT
   b. CBIC
   c. RBI
   d. EIC

10. Which of the following Acts promotes, facilitates and regulates foreign trade in India?
  a. FTDR Act, 1992
  b. FEMA, 1999
  c. Export (Quality Control and Inspection) Act, 1963
  d. Customs Act, 1962

Critical Thinking Questions

1. Write a short note on the legal framework for regulation of foreign trade in India.
2. Critically discuss the salient features of legislation governing exports and imports.
3. Critically examine the trade policy regime for any two of the following schemes:
  a. Policy on re-import of goods repaired abroad
  b. Policy on import of goods used in projects abroad
  c. Policy on import of prototypes
  d. Policy on export and import through courier service
4. What is the legal framework for management of foreign exchange in India?
5. Examine the legal framework for administration of the Indian customs.

Further Readings

1. Directorate General of Foreign Trade. 2009. *Foreign Trade Policy and Handbook of Procedure*. Vol. 1. New Delhi: Ministry of Commerce and Industry, Government of India.
2. Government of India. 1993. *Foreign Trade (Regulation) Rules, 1993*. New Delhi: Government of India.
3. ———. 1998. *Courier Imports and Exports (Clearance) Regulations, 1998*. New Delhi: Government of India.
4. Ministry of Commerce and Industry, Government of India. https://commerce.gov.in/ (accessed on 1 May 2023).
5. Ministry of Commerce and Industry. 2020. *Foreign Trade Policy, 2020*. New Delhi: Ministry of Commerce and Industry, Government of India.

CHAPTER 8

Understanding INCOTERMS 2020

CHAPTER OBJECTIVES

- To understand the purpose and scope of shipping terms in international trade and logistics operations.
- To explain the factors influencing the choice of shipping terms in international trade operations.
- To explain the various types of shipping terms drafted under the International Chamber of Commerce publication 2020.
- To explain the risks and cost responsibility of shipper or consignee for each trade term.
- To describe the leveraging of INCOTERMS with different modes of transport in international logistics.
- To brief about the selection criteria for different types of shipping terms in international trade logistics.

8.1 Introduction

The trade relationships among nations are multilateral trade systems, which are fast changing in the globalized and liberalized era. The competitive, comparative and factor endowment advantages have compelled firms from developed countries to locate their production facilities at places where they enjoy maximum cost and business advantages. Although the integration of emerging countries in the global production chain and their subsequent emergence as low-cost suppliers have enabled sourcing firms globally to procure cost-effective products, dealing with poor regulatory legislations in these countries for distribution of responsibilities and liabilities vis-à-vis cost and risk sharing in logistics operations is a great challenge. As we know, there are a number of intermediaries in international trade and logistics operations which make the business relationships complex, cumbersome and open to litigations in countries with weak domestic legislations, any exporter and importer shall be willing to get out of such unforeseen situations and wish to govern their trade relationships, distribution of responsibilities for risks and costs in a transparent, mutually accepted and as per internationally recognized rules and regulations so that they can approach an independent arbitrator in case of disputes.

International commercial terms, in short known as INCOTERMS, and also known as 'terms of delivery' or 'shipping terms' or 'trade terms' or 'INFOTERMS', help overcome these challenges. Shipping terms are an integral part of any EXIM transaction between an exporter and an importer. They help define the roles and responsibilities of the exporter and the importer in a trade deal, as these demarcate the functional activities to be performed by the exporter and the importer such as getting the insurance cover, reserving shipping space, loading and unloading of cargo, and customs and excise clearance. INCOTERMS (shipping terms) are the internationally accepted standard benchmark and are most commonly and popularly used in ISCs for describing the responsibility of both the parties regarding the risks and costs in a trade deal. These INCOTERMS are universally accepted, recognized, adhered and administered by all the signatory member countries of the International Chamber of Commerce (ICC). INCOTERMS are the most 'commonly accepted terms' (not legislation) of sale in international business. They have been adopted by most countries; however, India is not the signatory country so far, but they are popular in India and are widely used. Also, if once incorporated into a sales contract, then they have arbitrary and quasi-judicial sanction. They were first set out in 1936 and were subsequently revised in 1953, 1967, 1980, 1990, 2000 and 2020. However, earlier references to unpublished INCOTERMS date back as early as 1923 in the United States. The latest version of INCOTERMS is known as INCOTERMS 2020. The main differences in INCOTERMS 2020 and earlier versions of INCOTERMS of 2000 and 2010 are provided in Figure 8.1.

The interpretation of shipping terms gives the exporter and importer some suggestions and recommendations, and enlightens them as to how to use these terms in international trade transactions. Through shipping terms, the responsibilities and obligation of both exporter and importer become clear and they can take necessary precautions to minimize their risks associated in particular trade transactions through careful planning and execution. This is the reason why INCOTERMS have been considered of such high significance in international trade logistics. Trading parties in international

INCOTERMS 2000	INCOTERMS 2010	INCOTERMS 2020
• INCOTERMS are 13 • There are seven multimodal and six water transport INCOTERMS • Not valid for domestic sales • Confusing on which party will bear the terminal handling charges • Does not recognize electronic communication • Confusion during 'string sales', especially on high sea • Silent on information duties for insurance cover • INCOTERMS are silent on which party will bear charges for security-related clearances	• INCOTERMS are 11 • There are seven multimodal and four water transport INCOTERMS • Have equal force of law if incorporated in domestic sales contract. This clause is not relevant to India • Guidance notes incorporated like on terminal handling charges • Recognizes electronic communication • String sales allowed/procure • Explicitly define the obligations of parties on insurance cover and information duties • Explicitly define the obligations of party for security-related clearances	• INCOTERMS are 11 • There are seven multimodal and four water transport INCOTERMS • DPU Replaces DAT, meaning delivery can take place anywhere at terminal, warehouse, importer's place • Under CIP, mandatory requirement of insurance to ICC(A), however, not in case of CIF, thus facilitate warehouse-to-warehouse trade • 'Stopgap' solution to banks' insistence on asking for on-board bills of lading for containers, in case of INCOTERMS FCA/FOB • Transit clearance of customs • Buyer or seller can transport the goods using their own vehicles • Clarity on security-related obligations

FIGURE 8.1 Key differences in INCOTERMS 2000, 2010 and 2020.

Source: International Chamber of Commerce (2019).

trade transactions many times do not know the kinds of trading practices adopted in different countries, regions and economic environments. For example, carriage and insurance paid (CIP) for an Australian trader may have a different connotation than for an Indian trader. This usually results in confusion and misunderstanding and in some cases, it has been seen that disputes arise between exporter and importer resulting in costly litigation. INCOTERMS are framed to avoid such kind of misinterpretations in international trade transactions, as INCOTERMS are globally accepted as benchmarks in determining the responsibilities and obligations of various trading parties involved in international trade operations. Distribution of responsibilities, rights, obligations and duties under INCOTERMS are acceptable to all parties as they are framed, designed and administered on the basis of a standardized process based on mutual agreement, acceptance and accession of concerned parties. Figure 8.2 depicts the evolution process of INCOTERMS in a changing global regulatory and business environment.

Due to different legal systems of participating countries in a trade transaction, such relationships are getting increasingly complex, complicated and sub-operated by various other rules and regulations. INCOTERMS, at least, in such a complex environment helps the trading parties to decide the risks and

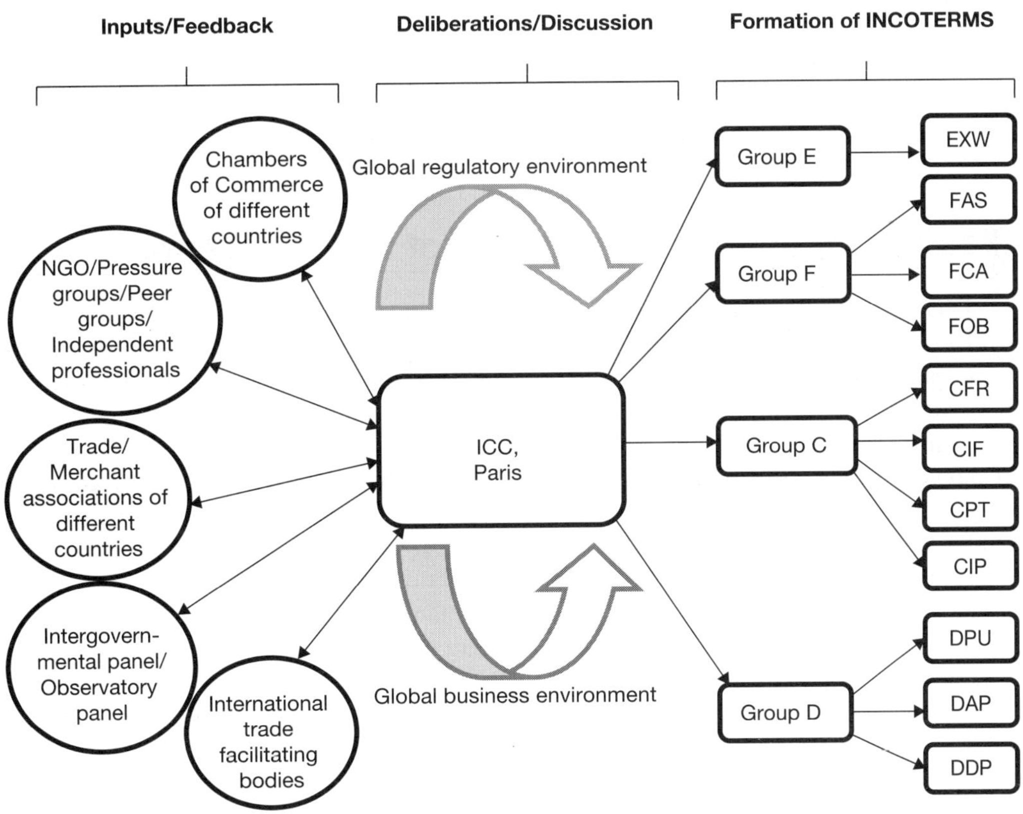

FIGURE 8.2 Process of formation of terms of delivery at ICC.

Source: International Chamber of Commerce (2019).

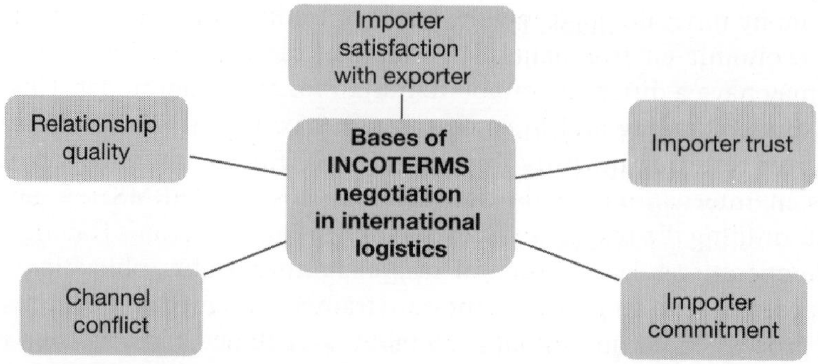

FIGURE 8.3 Study framework for appropriate INCOTERMS negotiation in international logistics.

Source: International Chamber of Commerce (2019).

responsibilities. The choice of trade terms may be affected by a variety of reasons such as volume of cargo, nature of cargo, relationship between seller and buyer, conflict situations in trade deals, value of cargo, regulatory obstacles and trading practices of the participating countries in international trade transaction. Choice of a particular INCOTERM usually depends on the kind of relationship the exporter and importer have as INCOTERMS are a guiding factor about the distribution of risk and responsibility between two trading parties. Figure 8.3 depicts the factors which become the basis for negotiation of appropriate INCOTERMS in international trade logistics.

8.2 Factors Influencing the Choice of Delivery Terms

Terms of delivery are an important managerial decision-making tool in any importing or exporting company. The revision of INCOTERMS in 2020 has made them legal trade instruments to be accepted as law if two partners have mutually agreed to base the distribution of their responsibilities and liabilities as per particular INCOTERMS. Hence, the exporter as well as importer should be aware of their obligations and consequences of using particular INCOTERMS 2020. The major function performed by terms of delivery is to clarify that costs and risks are split between the exporter or consignor and importer or consignee in a mutually agreed manner by providing the clarity of financial implications involved in a trade deal to both the parties and the same shall be included in ISC to provide it a legal sanctity for future purposes. In international trade transactions, it is possible to use different modes of transport such as trains, trucks, marine vessels and aeroplanes. All these modes of transport are of different capacities, size and can be used only after having analysed the conditions such as nature of cargo, delivery date and regulatory obstructions as items such as gems and jewellery in India are not allowed to be exported by sea routes beyond a certain limit. The Indian meat and sea food are usually exported by aeroplanes. Iron ore can either be exported by road or railway transport to neighbouring countries or otherwise necessarily to be transported by marine vessels. Hence, the factors influencing the choice of transport mode are the volume, location, destination and desirable speed of delivery. The choice of mode of transport is essential for the use of a particular INCOTERM and vice versa. Some of the INCOTERMS 2020 can only be used for water transport (e.g., free alongside ship [FAS], FOB, cost and freight [CFR], CIF), the rest are suitable for all means of transport (e.g., ex works [EXW], free carrier [FCA], carriage paid to [CPT], CIP, delivered at place unloaded [DPU], delivered at place [DAP], delivered duty paid [DDP]).

The initial factor which governs exporter–importer decision dyad for the choice of delivery terms is the geographical location of countries and access to them. For example, Sri Lanka and New Zealand do not have land borders, and thus the carriage of goods, whether importable or exportable, is possible only either by sea or by air. In case of sourcing of goods from such maritime nations, the following delivery terms theoretically can be used: EXW, FAS, FOB, FCA, CFR, CIF, CPT, CIP, DPU, DAP and DDP. On the contrary, India has land borders with Bhutan (though no railway connection exists); hence, transportation by either air or road is possible. Thus, INCOTERMS used in water transport cannot be used in case of export and import between India and Bhutan. Figure 8.4 lists the factors of consideration for both exporter and importer which can act as base for selecting the appropriate INCOTERMS keeping in mind the other associated factors.

The choice of term of delivery between exporter and importer is subject to negotiations and largely depends on the relationship between exporter and importer in international trade operations. 'Risk distribution matrix' plays an important role in choice of an INCOTERM and it varies among diverse INCOTERMS, for example, under shipping terms EXW, risks shift to an importer at the time of delivery of goods to his/her appointed vehicle at the warehouse or factory gate of an exporter. Similarly, under Group 'F', an exporter is relieved of all risks and responsibilities as soon as exporter delivers the cargo to the carrier nominated by the importer. Although the exporter pays for the export licence and customs formalities for export, this group represents the next advantageous terms of delivery for the exporter. In this case, the exporter bears less responsibility for carriage of goods, risks and costs than in the case of Groups 'C' and 'D'. The delivery terms of Group 'C' also relieve the exporter from the responsibilities and risks as soon he/she delivers the goods to the carrier, though here in some cases the exporter is also responsible for minimum insurance (CIF and CIP). Group 'D' is more advantageous for the importer as the exporter bears all responsibilities vis-à-vis cost and risks until the delivery of goods to importer's country. Value and volume of cargo are also a guiding factor for choice of INCOTERMS in international trade logistics. For example, INCOTERMS FOB, CFR and CIF cannot be used in case of 'less than container load' (LCL) cargo. Under such circumstances, possibly the INCOTERMS FCA, FAS, CPT and CIP suit the business requirements more precisely. Similarly, certain INCOTERMS cannot be used from country hinterland. For example, one cannot use FOB (New Delhi) or CIF (Kathmandu) as these INCOTERMS can be more precisely used only from the port town.

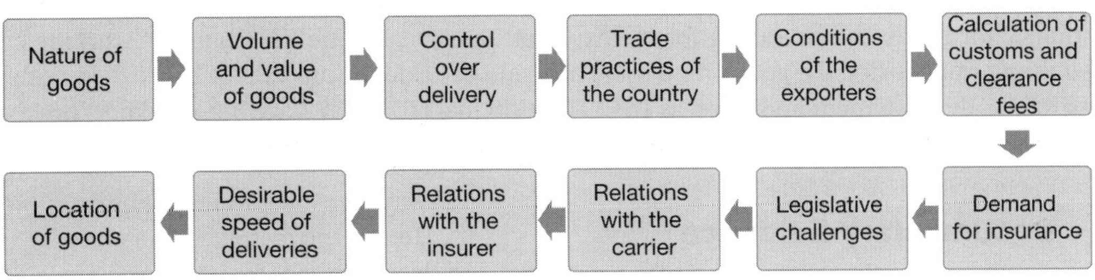

FIGURE 8.4 Main factors affecting the choice of INCOTERMS in export management.

Source: International Chamber of Commerce (2020).

8.3 Purpose and Scope of Shipping Terms

As discussed above, the main objective of INCOTERMS is to provide a base of understanding and interpretation to an international trader about the determination of the responsibilities of exporter and importer vis-à-vis distribution of costs and risks associated in international logistics of goods. Thus, INCOTERMS provide the clarity in execution of international trade and logistics operations to both the parties. In the following sub-sections we discuss the main purposes of shipping terms in international trade logistics.

8.3.1 Clarity in Interpretation of Trade Terms and Rules

INCOTERMS are globally accepted standard and harmonized rules which provide clear-cut interpretation of risks and costs to negotiating parties in a trade deal. Both exporter and importer become clear on their responsibilities and obligations with regard to international trade and logistics operations and know the financial implications of the trade deal.

8.3.2 Minimization of Losses

Due to the clarity provided by INCOTERMS, international trade disputes become less, and it reduces the transactional cost of international trade. Shipping terms provide an exporter and importer a well-defined structured mechanism for sharing of responsibilities and obligations in international trade logistics of goods from one country to another. Hence, INCOTERMS help reduce the scope of uncertainties due to different interpretations of such trade terms in various countries and avoid costly litigations.

8.3.3 Base of Contract of Sale

INCOTERMS are the base of any trade relationship and are an integral part of the contract of sale. Some people misinterpret it as the base of contract of carriage only, but INCOTERMS have wider connotations with regard to various aspects of trade deals and their scope is not limited only to clarify the responsibilities and obligations with respect to the carriage or transport of goods. INCOTERMS help in not only deciding the export price to be offered in the quotation but also help in explaining the other responsibilities and obligations of exporters and importers with regard to arrangement of insurance, mode of shipment, customs and excise clearance, payments of duties and so on. It is the main reason that ICC has clearly underlined and explained that INCOTERMS deal with the relationship between the exporter and importer in the contract of sales and that even in a very distinct manner. INCOTERMS, being the base of ISC, also help in contracts of carriage for delivering the goods to the buyers, arranging the insurance for goods and financing for the exporter. Banks calculate the finances (working capital) required for manufacturing the goods for a trade deal and exclude the amount to be used on transportation, insurance, duty payment and so on as INCOTERMS like DDP may have higher export price quotation due to the various duties and obligations to be performed by the exporter.

8.3.4 Documentary Evidence

In case exporter and importer have agreed for the use of CFR- or CIF-based ISC, the exporter will have a problem in sending the goods by any other mode of transport except by water transport. If the exporter sends goods by any other mode of transport, he/she will have a problem producing the bill of lading which is possible only in the case of ocean transport and bill of lading carries the title of goods which is not possible in any other document used in other modes of transport such as air waybill (AWB), combined transport document, multimodal transport document and customs transit challan. It is well known that document carrying the title of goods such as 'Bill of Lading' or 'Multimodal Transport Document' is preferred for documentary collections (documents against acceptance [D/A] and documents against payments [D/P]) and payment under a Letter of Credit (L/C).

8.3.5 Provide Solid Base to Contract

As INCOTERMS provide a solid base in contract execution in international trade transactions, domestic traders in case of large-scale contracts are also using them as they are very clear and specific in differentiating the responsibilities of seller and buyer. The reason of increased use of INCOTERMS in purely domestic transactions is the larger clarity provided by them in the exercise of role and responsibilities of seller and buyer. That is why, some people have rightly referred to INCOTERMS as INFOTERMS.

8.4 Various Types of INCOTERMS

As per ICC's revision of INCOTERMS in the year 2020, there are 11 types of INCOTERMS and these are divided into four distinct groups. Group E of INCOTERMS indicates that the goods shall be made available to the importer at the exporter premises, for example, at the factory gate or warehouse of an exporter. Group F indicates that the exporter must deliver the goods to a carrier which has been appointed by the importer for carrying the goods to destination. Group C indicates that the exporter is liable for losses and damages only up to the port of shipment and all losses and damages subsequent to exporter delivery of cargo to the shipping company and any additional cost or charges and so on shall be borne by the importer. Exporter takes the obligation of all risks of losses or damages to the cargo only before the start of the journey of the cargo. The INCOTERMS under Group D indicate that the exporter will be having obligations and responsibility to incur all the costs, charges and other risks which may be associated in the course of the journey from exporter country to the importer country. This is the riskiest trade term for exporter and more beneficial for importer. Table 8.1 depicts the macro-level snapshot of sharing of risks and responsibilities of costs and risks between an exporter and importer in international trade logistics.

In addition to the above macro-level snapshot, various types of INCOTERMS are explained in the following sub-section in detail, outlining roles, responsibilities and obligations of exporter and importer in international trade and logistics operations. Immense care is to be taken in the use of these INCOTERMS keeping in mind which mode of transport/carriage will be suitable for the transportation of the goods to a particular country and region. The various INCOTERMS provide us with the opportunity to choose the best one to be incorporated in ISC and contract of carriage.

8.4.1 EXW (Named Place of Delivery)

The exporter shall place the goods at the disposal of the importer at his/her premises which can be factory or his/her warehouse or any other named place. Such goods are yet to be cleared for export and are yet to be loaded on any collecting vehicle of the importer at his/her own expenses. In this way EXW

TABLE 8.1 Sharing of Responsibilities under Different INCOTERMS between Seller and Buyer in International Trade Logistics

	Group E (Departure)	Group F (Main Carriage Not Paid By E)			Group C (Main Carriage Paid By E)				Group D (Arrival)		
Responsibility and Charges Service	EXW	FCA	FAS	FOB	CFR	CIF	CPT	CIP	DPU	DAP	DDP
Exporter warehouse/factory/works place or storage at cargo origin point	E	E	E	E	E	E	E	E	E	E	E
Labour expenses at warehouse (cargo origin point)	E	E	E	E	E	E	E	E	E	E	E
Export packing of cargo (cargo origin point)	E	E	E	E	E	E	E	E	E	E	E
Stuffing of cargo in boxes and loading of cargo on carrier (cargo origin point)	I	E	E	E	E	E	E	E	E	E	E
Inland freight charges (in exporter's country)	I	I	E	E	E	E	E	E	E	E	E
Terminal handling along with other charges relating to port (port of departure)	I	I	E	E	E	E	E	E	E	E	E
Forwarders fee (in exporter country)	I	I	E	E	E	E	E	E	E	E	E
Loading on ocean carrier (departing port)	I	I	I	E	E	E	E	E	E	E	E
Ocean and air freight	I	I	I	I	E	E	E	E	E	E	E
Port charges (arrival port)	I	I	I	I	I	I	E	E	E	E	E
Customs duties and taxes	I	I	I	I	I	I	I	I	I	I	E
Delivery charges at final destination	I	I	I	I	I	I	I	I	I	I	E

Source: International Chamber of Commerce (2019).
Note: E = Exporter and I = Importer

INCOTERMS indicate the minimum involvement of risks of losses and damages to the exporter and the maximum involvement of losses and damages to the importer. Under EXW INCOTERMS, the importer is responsible for all expenses associated with customs duty clearance, insurance, transportation, documentation work, pre-shipment inspection and so on from the factory, warehouse or premises of exporter to his/her country. All obligations vis-à-vis costs and insurance are on the part of the importer and are given in Table 8.2.

Having understood the obligations under EXW, let us understand how to leverage them in international trade and logistics operations. An exporter should remember the following points while incorporating the EXW INCOTERMS in an international trade contract:

1. EXW INCOTERMS can be best used for domestic sales. Alternatively, the buyer does not intend to transport these goods to the country of destination and may sell them to a third party in India or may keep goods for an indefinite time in a warehouse in India. The export of goods is not guaranteed under these INCOTERMS.
2. The importer would prefer to buy goods if he/she has better logistical expertise than that of exporter and save on freight and insurance charges.
3. The importer would prefer EXW INCOTERMS when he/she wants to maximize his/her control on international logistics operations for the speedy delivery of cargo at destination.
4. The exporter can dictate this term to the importer if he/she enjoys monopoly in the market or buyer is ignorant of market conditions.
5. This INCOTERM is widely preferred for deemed export sales in India.
6. The exporter wishes to sell on EXW as he/she is averse to risk and does not want to involve himself/herself in lengthy logistics operations.

TABLE 8.2 Obligations under the EXW Term (I: Importer)

Who Burdens the Responsibility Under E Group	EXW
Inland freight of cargo in India and delivery of cargo to the carrier at frontier	I
Export customs clearance including export duty, if any	I
Payments of any cesses/octroi, if any, along with payment of customs charges in exporter's country	I
Loading charges for the outbound cargo in exporter's country including payments of port charges/terminal-handling charges	I
Payments of carriage or freight to the departing vehicles/vessels/carriers/aeroplane	I
Cargo insurance/marine insurance for the Cargo	I
Payment of expenditure relating to unloading of cargo at destination port including payment of port charges/terminal-handling charges	I
Payment of expenditure relating to import authorization/special import licences/documentation expenditures on filing of bill of entry/CHA charges and so on	I
Payment of import duty/cesses/entry taxes/octroi and so on in the importer country	I
Payment of inland transportation costs in the importer's country	I
Any other costs and risks not covered as above in the importer's country	I

Source: International Chamber of Commerce (2019).

7. The exporter should leverage payment terms such as payment in advance under this INCOTERM or take custody of documents for routing through proper banking channels for payments under D/A, D/P and L/C.
8. In the cases where the exporter is not a manufacturer exporter, the actual point of delivery of cargo to importer may vary from the place where exporter operates his/her own business.
9. Under INCOTERMS EXW, payment of loading charges is the duty of importer. Exporter cannot claim such charges if he/she does so at his/her own; however, he/she can claim such loading expense from the buyer if he/she instructs him/her to do so.
10. The exporter will provide packing to the goods which is provided in the normal course of action in this segment of the industry. If importer requests for seaworthy packing, the exporter can demand payable charges for that from the importer.
11. Any mode of transport can be engaged for transportation of goods to destined markets.
12. INCOTERMS EXW is not a competitive term to win customers in the global competitive markets.

8.4.2 FCA (Named Place)

In the FCA shipping term, an exporter is under obligation to take the responsibility of all risks and costs which are involved in trade transactions and associated with the cargo until the cargo is not delivered to the named place of shipment and the same has to be collected by the carrier nominated by the importer. Under Group F of INCOTERMS, the responsibility of export customs clearance is on the exporter. Sometimes, under FCA INCOTERMS, the carrier of cargo may have to collect the goods from the premises of exporter, but exporter shall bear the cost of delivering the goods up to the point of place or port of shipment (inland container depot [ICD]/container freight station [CFS] or port) as agreed in the export sales contract. Sometimes, exporter premises are the 'named place' in the contract, the exporter may have to load the goods onto the truck, but the cost of such loading shall be borne by the importer. The obligations vis-à-vis costs and risks under Group F are listed in Table 8.3. Following points are important for leveraging the FCA INCOTERMS in international trade logistics:

1. Exporter and importer should place emphasis on clearly specifying the named place as it may entail cost implications for either party.
2. Exporter shall be responsible for all custom-related expense including the export duties, if any.
3. Seller is under obligation to load these goods on arriving means of transport if it comes within the date of shipment. If the importer fails to appoint a vehicle for loading, exporter should handover documents for loading of cargo to the person nominated by the buyer.
4. The exporter will be responsible for 'special export licence' in case of restricted category exports under ITC(HS) nomenclature Schedule 2 which specifies the export regime for various goods in India. Any additional clearance certificate shall also be at the cost of the exporter.
5. Any mode of transport can be engaged for transportation of goods.
6. FCA INCOTERMS can be best leveraged for 'deemed export sales' as published under Chapter 8 of the Foreign Trade Policy 2009–2014.
7. FCA INCOTERMS can be best used when buyer wants to maximize his/her control on international trade and logistics operations.
8. FCA INCOTERMS are best suited for air shipments in international trade logistics.

TABLE 8.3 Obligations under the F Terms (E: Exporter, I: Importer)

Who Burdens the Responsibility Under E Group	FCA	FAS	FOB
Inland freight or carriage of Cargo in India and delivery of Cargo to the carrier at frontier	E	E	E
Export customs clearance including export duty, if any	E	E	E
Expenditure relating to any cesses/octroi along with payment of customs duties (if applicable) in exporter's Country	E	E	E
Expenditures relating to loading of cargo in the exporter country including payments of ICDs/CFS or port charges/terminal-handling charges	E	I	E
Expenditure on carriage or freight of goods from departing ports to post of destinations	I	I	I
Expenditure on cargo insurance/marine insurance for the cargo	I	I	I
Expenditure relating to unloading of cargo at destination port including payment of port charges/terminal-handling charges	I	I	I
Expenditure relating to import authorization/special import licences/documentation expenditures on filing of bill of entry/CHA charges and so on	I	I	I
Expenditure on import duty/cesses/entry taxes/octroi and so on in the importer country	I	I	I
Expenditure relating to inland carriage of goods in the importer's country	I	I	I
Any other costs and risks not covered as above in the importer's country	I	I	I

Source: Adapted from International Chamber of Commerce (ICC), Paris France. https://iccwbo.org/ (accessed on 24 May 2023).

8.4.3 FAS (Named Port)

FAS INCOTERMS were previously known as free on wharf as per the INCOTERMS 1990 version. The exporter is responsible for delivery of cargo to the named port. This port can be port of departure or may not be as there may well be ports behind the main port of departure in case of countries which have strong inland water transportation system. For example, the port of Cologne or Dusseldorf at Rhine river in Germany feeds cargo for gateway ports of Hamburg and Bremerhaven. The exporter is responsible for preparing EXIM documents, getting goods inspected and custom clearance of cargo and all freight charges unto named port in the contract. Unloading of cargo at the named port shall be the responsibility of the exporter and any subsequent loading and unloading shall be the responsibility of the importer. The obligations vis-à-vis costs and risks under Group FAS are listed in Table 8.3. Following points are important for leveraging this shipping term in international logistics operations:

- FAS INCOTERMS can be best used in case of delivery of goods at named port which is a port behind the main ports from where the mother vessel will depart for international voyage. Named port under FAS INCOTERMS is this port located in the inland water transport system of the country.
- One can use FAS INCOTERMS with equal ease at gateway port for international water transportation. However, these INCOTERMS in no case can be used from country hinterland, that is, place. For example, FAS Kanpur or FAS Pune. Named port means a maritime port.

- FAS INCOTERMS can be used only in case of water transportation of goods.
- Bill of lading is a prerequisite document as no other mode of transport can be used for international trade logistics.
- FAS INCOTERMS should be avoided in case of charter party contracts in international logistics of goods.
- Risks and costs both transfer to importer once goods are delivered at named ports and buyer shall be responsible for all costs and risks from this point to point of destination.

8.4.4 FOB (Named Port of Shipment)

FOB is the most popular term used in international trade logistics. It is the most favoured and widely used INCOTERM by international marketers in the liberalized era. Under this INCOTERM, the exporter shall be responsible for delivering goods to the named port of shipment and loading the goods on the arriving ship appointed by the importer. Once the goods are loaded on the buyer's appointed ship, all costs and risks shift from exporter to the importer. The exporter is under obligation for all responsibilities before loading of goods on the ship such as preparing EXIM documents, getting goods inspected, export customs clearance, payment of export duties and other taxes, if any, and carriage of goods from factory to port of departure. Any risk related to the cargo before the loading of cargo on the vessel shall be borne by the exporter. The obligations vis-à-vis costs and risks under Group FOB are listed in Table 8.3. Exporter and importer should consider following points while leveraging FOB INCOTERMS:

1. Shipping term FOB is monomodal like FAS and such INCOTERMS can be used when the transportation of goods is by sea route only from the country of origin to the country of destination.
2. Bill of lading is a prerequisite document to be used during transportation under FOB INCOTERMS. No other mode of transport documents such as AWB, road consignment note and railway receipt will be acceptable for negotiation of documents under FOB INCOTERMS.
3. The handling, loading, stowage and other port charges of cargo under FOB shall be the responsibility of the exporter.
4. FOB is suitable for both trading parties in an ideal competitive situation as the exporter is responsible for covering all responsibilities of logistics in his/her country and subsequent obligations are that of the importer.
5. One should consider that FOB INCOTERMS cannot be used from 'place', for example, FOB New Delhi or FOB Lucknow, as these INCOTERMS entail main carriage by sea only and that is possible only from gateway ports such as FOB Chennai and FOB Kandla.
6. FOB should be avoided for air transport as the exporter will not get the bill of lading in case of air freight and trade documents will not be complied for negotiation under L/C payment term.
7. FOB INCOTERMS establish ideal business relationships between exporter and importer.

8.4.5 CFR (Named Port of Destination)

Under these INCOTERMS, the exporter is required to cover all costs related to customs clearance of export shipment, appointing carriers, paying the freight charges and unloading the goods at named port of destination. The exporter is responsible for all charges until the discharging of cargo from the ship, including all port and terminal charges. However, the risks of the exporter shall be limited to port of loading, that is, once the cargo is loaded at the named port of departure, all risks shift from the exporter to the importer. Hence, exporter procures insurance cover only up to the port of departure. It is port-to-port INCOTERM, meaning insurance by the exporter is up to the port of loading and freight and unloading charges up to the port of destination. This INCOTERM is monomodal and, hence, can be used only in case of water transportation between two ports of the involved countries. However, it can be used in case of inland water transportation.

Table 8.4 depicts the obligations of exporter and importer at various stages of logistics operations in international trade. The exporter and importer should consider the following points while leveraging CFR INCOTERMS:

1. CFR INCOTERMS can be best leveraged for bulk cargo such as coal, cotton bales, iron ore and fertilizers as this type of cargo requires special loading and unloading equipment which can be best considered while booking the ship for international transportation.
2. CFR INCOTERMS is also suitable for 'stand-alone shipments' or when the buyer has his/her own means of transportation.
3. CFR INCOTERM is suitable for a full container load (FCL) cargo, meaning it is either full container load or full ship for one kind of cargo like transportation of gas from Oman to India.
4. The buyer should take insurance cover from the port of loading to port of destination to mitigate associated risks during international transportation.

TABLE 8.4 Obligations under the C Terms (E: Exporter, I: Importer)

Who Burdens the Responsibility Under E Group	CFR	CIF	CPT	CIP
Inland freight or carriage of cargo in India and delivery of cargo to the carrier at frontier	E	E	E	E
Export customs clearance including export duty, if any	E	E	E	E
Expenditure relating to any cesses/octroi along with payment of customs duties (if applicable) in exporter's country	E	E	E	E
Expenditure relating to loading of cargo in the exporter country including payments of ICDs/CFS or port charges/terminal-handling charges	E	E	E	E
Expenditure on carriage or freight of goods from departing ports to ports of destinations	E	E	E	E
Expenditure on cargo insurance/marine insurance for the cargo	I	E*	I	E*
Expenditure relating to unloading of cargo at destination port including payment of port charges/terminal-handling charges	E	I	E	I
Expenditure relating to import authorization/special import licences/ documentation expenditures on filing of bill of entry/CHA charges and so on	I	I	I	I
Expenditure on import duty/cesses/entry taxes/octroi and so on in the importer's country	I	I	I	I
Expenditure relating to inland carriage of goods in the importer's country	I	I	E	E
Any other costs and risks not covered as above in the importer's country	I	I	I	I

Source: Adapted from International Chamber of Commerce (ICC), Paris France. https://iccwbo.org/ (accessed on 24 May 2023).
**Note*: Depends on the sales on contract.

5. Cost of unloading will be the responsibility of the seller; however, haulage will be at the end of the importer. Terminal charges will be paid by the exporter including security clearances, if any.
6. Customs duties including custom clearance procedure will be taken care of by importer.
7. It is monomodal like CFR and can be used in case of water transportation only. Bill of lading is an essential transport document when CIF INCOTERM is used.
8. CFR INCOTERMS are preferred in tramp shipping involving charter party contracts for engaging ships for international transportation of goods.

8.4.6 CIF (Named Port of Destination)

Seller is responsible for making goods available at named port of destination but not unloaded from the ship. It means exporter is responsible for all expenses from point of origin to port of destination such as export clearance, freight forwarder charges, export duties, if any, freight to ship and cargo insurance to the port of destination. Cargo insurance under CIF is minimum insurance, meaning importer is under obligation for all risks and must take measures to mitigate them. Under CIF, seller procures marine insurance against buyer's risk of loss; hence, the seller is required to obtain insurance only on minimum cover. CIF INCOTERM is monomodal, meaning it can be used only in water transportation. Table 8.4 depicts the obligations of exporter and importer under CIF INCOTERMS in international trade logistics. Exporter and importer should consider the following points while leveraging CFR INCOTERMS:

1. CIF is one among the most preferred INCOTERMS for importers and is widely used in international trade. Importers are assured of delivery of cargo in their country.
2. Like CFR, it is most suitable for port-to-port shipment, whereby exporter pays for freight and insurance up to the port of destination and risks belong to the buyer from the port of loading, meaning importer must take necessary measures to mitigate associated risks from port of loading to port of destination.
3. CIF cannot be used from a place, for example, CIF New Delhi or CIF Lahore. The destination should be a maritime port.
4. It is monomodal like CFR and can be used in case of water transportation only. Bill of lading is an essential transport document when CIF INCOTERM is used.
5. CIF INCOTERM is ideal for competitive business relations to win competing markets as both exporter and importer share almost equal obligations in trade relationship.
6. CIF INCOTERMS are suitable for both FCL/LCL cargo, and they are widely used in containerized trade.

8.4.7 CPT (Named Place of Destination)

The shipping term refers to the responsibilities of exporter up to the delivery of the goods at named place of destination which can be CFS, ICD, frontier or terminal, land custom station and so on. Exporter and importer should be specific about incorporating the named place of destination as it may entail cost implication for either party. The exporter shall be responsible for all expenses related to carriage of goods from point of origin to place of destination; however, the importer shall be responsible for all risks from point of origin to place of designation. All expenses after delivery of goods which have not been unloaded since arriving shall be at the importer's end such as filing of bill of entry, terminal charges, custom clearance, import duties and haulage. CPT INCOTERM can be used irrespective of mode of transport, that is, in case of multimodal transport as well. Table 8.4 depicts the obligations vis-à-vis costs and risks of both exporter and importer under CPT INCOTERM. Exporter and importer should consider following points while leveraging CPT INCOTERM in international trade and logistics operations:

- CPT INCOTERM is most suitable for 'warehouse-to-warehouse shipment'. CPT is widely used when intent is to get cargo in country hinterland at dry ports or at buyer warehouse in country hinterland.
- Buyer must take care of risk-mitigating mechanism for protection against various transport risks from the first warehouse itself.
- This INCOTERM cannot be used from ports such as Jawaharlal Nehru Port (JNPT), Kandla and Vizag. The final place of delivery must be a place; for example, it can be Santacruz, Bombay, but not the JNPT port as Santacruz is a place and JNPT is a maritime port.
- This INCOTERM can be used for all types of cargo, that is, bulk, containerized, break bulk and so on.
- This INCOTERM is ideally used for standardized trade operations between B2B trade operations.
- Any mode of transport can be engaged for international transportation including more than one mode of transportation, that is, multimodal transportation.

8.4.8 CIP (Named Place of Destination)

The shipping term CIP has the same set of cost and risk responsibilities between exporter and importer as in case of CPT INCOTERMS discussed above. The only difference in CPT and CIP is that CIP INCOTERM entails the responsibility of 'minimum insurance' to the exporter from first warehouse to warehouse in the importer's country. The exporter shall be fully responsible for all costs such as carriage, export custom clearance, packing labelling marking and stowage to cargo CHA charges up to the named place of destination. He/she is also fully responsible for all damages up to the first warehouse or dry port in exporter's country. He/she will procure cargo insurance from the first warehouse to the second warehouse or dry port in the importer's country but will not be responsible for the losses. Hence, exporter procures insurance against the buyer's risks of loss. The exporter usually procures minimum insurance to save on premium. It means that importer should have requisite risk mitigation in place to safeguards his/her business interest which can be by taking an additional insurance policy from exporter's warehouse to warehouse in importer's country. Alternatively, he/she may request exporter to take higher risk coverage policy and importer will pay him/her any additional premium which comes as a difference between minimum insurance policy and the one recommended by the importer. CIP term can be used irrespective of mode of transport, that is, it is a multimodal trade term. Table 8.4 depicts the obligations of both exporter and importer at various stages of international trade logistics under CIP shipping term. Exporter and importer should pay attention to the following points while incorporating CIP INCOTERMS in their international trade and logistics operations:

8.4.9 DPU (Named Place of Destination)

DPU INCOTERMS have been incorporated in 2020 revision for the first time. Under DPU trade term, an exporter delivers the goods to the importer after having unloaded them from arriving means of transport at the place of destination. Buyer and seller should agree specifically about place of unloading in the importer's country. Goods once unloaded are at buyer's dry port or at a maritime port and all expenses including internal haulage shall be at the end of the importer. Seller is responsible for the costs and risks to bring the goods to the point specified in the contract. The seller should ensure that their forwarding contract mirrors the contract of sale. Seller is responsible for the export clearance procedures and the importer is responsible to clear the goods for imports, arrange import customs formalities and pay import duty. Importer can leverage this point if he/she does not have suitable unloading facilities in his/her country. Table 8.5 depicts the obligations of both exporter and importer under DPU term in international trade logistics. Exporter and importer should consider the following points while leveraging the DPU shipping term in international trade operations:

- The seller delivers the goods to the importer once unloaded from the arriving means of transport.
- The goods are placed at the disposal of the buyer at the named place of destination which can be maritime port or dry port. The place may include quay, warehouse, container yard or road rail or air terminal.
- It is highly recommended that both parties should agree about the place of destination in advance and, if possible, a point within the terminal at which point the risks will transfer from seller to the buyer of the goods.
- If it is intended that seller is to bear all the costs and responsibilities from the terminal to another point, it is recommended to use DAP INCOTERMS.
- All terminal charges at the port of departure as well as at port of destination shall be at the end of the exporter.
- Exporter shall also be responsible for all security-related expenses at both ends.

TABLE 8.5 Obligations under the D Terms (E: Exporter, I: Importer)

Who Burdens the Responsibility Under E Group	DPU	DAP	DDP
Inland freight or carriage of cargo in India and delivery of cargo to the carrier at frontier	E	E	E
Export customs clearance including export duty, if any	E	E	E
Expenditure relating to any cesses/octroi along with payment of customs duties (if applicable) in exporter's Country	E	E	E
Expenditures relating to loading of cargo in the exporter country including payments of ICDs/CFS or port charges/terminal-handling charges	E	E	E
Expenditures on carriage or freight of goods from departing ports to ports of destinations	E	E	E
Expenditures on cargo insurance/marine insurance for the cargo	E	E	E
Expenditure relating to unloading of cargo at destination port including payment of port charges/terminal-handling charges	E	E	E
Expenditure relating to import authorization/special import licences/documentation expenditures on filing of bill of entry/CHA charges and so on	I	I	E
Expenditure on import duty/cesses/entry taxes/octroi and so on in the importer's country	I	I	E
Expenditure relating to inland carriage of goods in the importer's country	E	E	E
Any other costs and risks not covered as above in the importer's country	E	E	E

Source: Adapted from International Chamber of Commerce (ICC), Paris, France. https://iccwbo.org/ (accessed on 24 May 2023).

- DPU INCOTERM has been designed to fulfil the requirements of increasing containerization in international trade. It also simplifies the documentation needs vis-à-vis compliance for L/C terms for an exporter or importer.
- A risk-averse importer can use these terms and exporter with logistics expertise can use them to win competitive markets.

8.4.10 DAP (Named Place of Destination)

Under DAP INCOTERMS, the seller is responsible for all costs and risks until the delivery of goods to the named place of destination which is always in importer's country. It is advised that the seller should always obtain the contract of carriage that matches the contract of sale. The importer is responsible for all costs and risks from point of unloading of cargo at the place of destination such as haulage, customs clearance imports duties and subsequent transfer to his/her factory or warehouse. Transport carrier will be appointed and paid for by exporter; however, unloading charges shall be borne by the importer. It should be noted that such carrier should be ready for unloading of cargo at the named place of destination. Table 8.5 depicts the obligations of both exporter and importer at various stages of international trade logistics under DAP INCOTERMS. Following are the points of consideration for both exporter and importer while incorporating DAP INCOTERMS in international logistics operations:

- If the seller incurs unloading cost at named place of destination, unless previously agreed, he/she is not entitled to recover any such costs from importer.
- Trading parties, both exporter and importer, are advised to specify as clearly as possible the point within the agreed place of destination, because risks transfer at this point from seller to the buyer.
- All responsibilities including licences/authorization for import clearance are of the importer.
- If the carrier will move through landlocked country to the named place of destination, the exporter should check in advance the various levies and entry taxes for such movements including whether transit access is allowed or not.
- DAP can be best leveraged to deliver goods at the frontier of two countries and can be used in place of DAF of INCOTERMS 2000 version.
- Exporter should use DAP INCOTERMS, if he/she knows the fact that the terminal at the destination does not have proper unloading facilities for this type of cargo.
- Detention charges including demurrage, if any, will be on part of the importer.
- If the intent is to deliver the goods duly cleared from customs (import duty and procedure), DDP should be used.

8.4.11 DDP (Named Place of Destination)

Under this INCOTERM, the exporter has highest obligations and responsibilities as he/she has to bear all the costs and risks involved in delivering the cargo to a named place of destination which is ideally the warehouse or factory of the importer. All expenditures from point of origin of cargo to point of destination such as customs clearance (both in exports and imports), cess/octroi/local taxes (both in exports and imports), insurance, transport of goods and risks (both in exports and imports) are to be borne by exporter. The exporter must offer price rates which are sufficient to incur for ensuring safe and secure delivery of cargo at importer's premises. This is the riskiest shipping term for an exporter in international trade logistics as he/she is under legal obligation to provide the services at his/her cost until goods are delivered at the premises of importer. Table 8.5 lists the obligations of exporter which are all from point of origin to point of destination. Exporter and importer should keep the following points in mind while leveraging the DDP INCOTERMS in international trade logistics:

- The exporter should specifically check whether this item is allowed for import in the country of destination or not (prohibited for import); if not, then this trade transaction cannot be completed.
- If an item is under 'restricted category', the exporter should negotiate in advance with importer for taking 'special import licence' from a competent authority, for example, DGFT in the case of India.
- In addition to these import regime restrictions, there may be need of additional authorization(s) or import permit for custom clearance. The exporter should check all these requirements in advance.
- The exporter should check the applicable rates of import duties including subsequent cess and so on as slabs for imposition of duties and taxes vary from country to country, and he/she should factor this while quoting export prices.
- The exporter should also check the attitude of customs authority in customs clearance and level of corruption, delay in clearance and so on and factor this in his/her export price.
- DDP INCOTERM is best leveraged in case of online sales, teleshopping, value payable exports and goods imported through posts.
- DDP is a widely accepted trade in case of export goods where there is a trend of 'vendor-managed inventory'.
- DDP is also ideal for 'consignment basis sales' transactions as the seller has better logistical knowledge.
- DDP INCOTERM is known as 'Franco Domino' in Francophone countries. In India, traders refer it to as 'door-to-door' INCOTERMS.

8.5 Applicable INCOTERMS in Different Modes of Transportation

There are certain INCOTERMS which can be used with any mode of transport or with combinations of transport in international trade logistics, while there are certain other INCOTERMS where the mode of transport of goods should be only sea or inland water. While negotiating and incorporating INCOTERMS in the contract of sale and subsequent contracts such as contract of carriage, contract of insurance and L/C contract, one must check whether he/she will be in a position to complete the desired transport documentation with INCOTERMS incorporated. An international trader shall take care of which particular INCOTERM is suitable for conducting the business as such decision will also be based on buyer's and seller's bargaining power. Choosing FOB term for a landlocked country like Turkmenistan shall have implications for the exporter as it shall be considered as discrepancy in negotiations of documents while recovering the payment through documentary credit. Figure 8.5 lists the applicability of various modes of transport for the main carriage under various INCOTERMS.

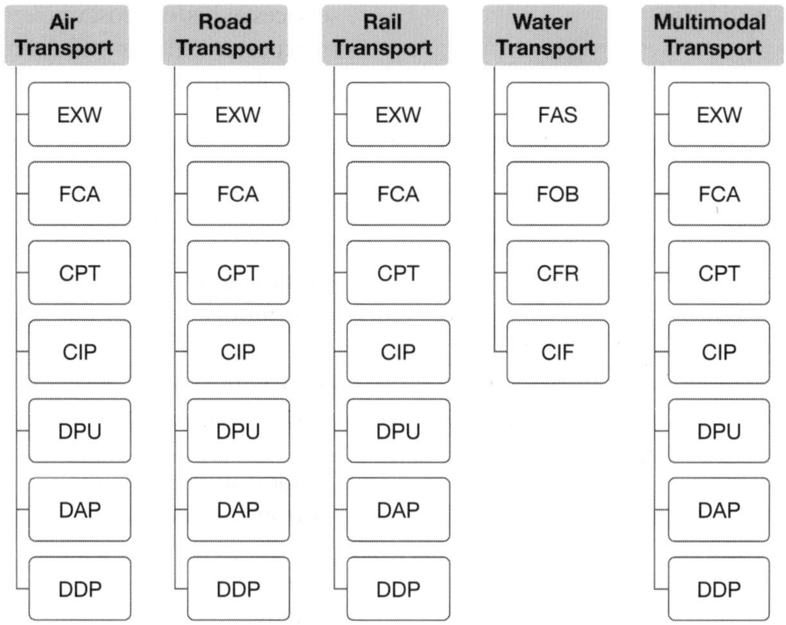

FIGURE 8.5 Applicable INCOTERMS in different modes of transportation.

8.6 INCOTERMS and Transfer of Risks

Each INCOTERM used in the sales contract and contract of carriage of cargo indicates the importer's obligations and responsibilities regarding the risks and costs and specifies the point when the responsibilities and obligations are shifting from exporter to the importer, thereby making responsibility clear about the cost and risks associated in trade transactions. INCOTERMS are particularly very helpful in deciding the point when the risks associated with transportation of cargo shall transfer from exporter to the importer. Table 8.6 indicates the transfer of responsibilities and obligations between exporter and importer.

8.7 Leveraging Payment Mode with INCOTERMS

Payment terms such as documentary collections, documentary credit, open credit and advance payments are typically negotiated between the exporter and importer for settlement of a trade transaction. Agreed payment terms imply the mode of payment including credit period, if any, payment date, currency of payment and how it will be settled, that is, banking channels. Payment terms and INCOTERMS are interrelated in the sense that elements of costs and risks associated with transportation of goods have their bearing on the payment term. In export operations, payment terms commonly incorporate one or the other agreed-upon INCOTERM such as EXW, FCA, FOB, CFR, CIF, DPU and DDP which spell out clearly where the responsibilities of the exporter and importer lie in respect of transportation of goods from country of export to country of import. For example, with

TABLE 8.6 Transfer of Risks

EXW	Importer's risks start from the point of loading of cargo at exporter factory or warehouse or any other agreed place. Exporter is responsible only to make goods available at named place of delivery.
FCA	Risks shift from exporter to importer once goods are cleared from customs and are loaded on carrier appointed by importer. If importer fails to appoint carrier within scheduled date, exporter will handover requisite trade documents for loading of cargo to person nominated by importer.
FAS	Risks shift from exporter to importer once goods are placed alongside the ship at named port by exporter. Exporter intimate about unloaded goods to person nominated by importer.
FOB	Risks shift from exporter to importer when goods are loaded on ship appointed by importer at port of departure. Proof of loading is mate's receipt.
CFR	Risks shift from exporter to importer once goods are loaded at named port of departure.
CIF	Exporter procures insurance for buyer's risks of loss up to named port of destination, however, exporter's risks are limited only up to point of cargo loading at named port of departure. Buyer must take appropriate risks mitigation measures to protect himself/herself as insurance procured by exporter is minimum cover unless otherwise agreed.
CPT	Risks shift once goods are delivered to the carrier at dry port or warehouse in exporter's country. Importer's risks start from this point.
CIP	Exporter procure minimum insurance up to place of destination; however, exporter's risks are limited only up to delivery of cargo to carrier at named place of departure which is usually a dry port or warehouse of exporter. Importer should take risks' mitigation measures from first warehouse itself.
DPU	Risks shift from exporter to importer once goods are unloaded at named place of destination. It is advised that exporter and importer should specify the exact place to avoid disputes.
DAP	Risks shift from exporter to importer once carrier reaches at named place of destination in importer's country. Buyer's risks start from the time of unloading of cargo.
DDP	Exporter is responsible for all risks until the carrier does not reach at named place of destination, that is, doorstep of an importer. Any damages during unloading at destination will be that of the importer.

Source: Adapted from INCOTERMS 2020, International Chamber of Commerce.

EXW, the exporter is responsible to deliver the goods at the named place of delivery which can be factory or warehouse of an exporter in India. Similarly, in term CFR, the seller is responsible for the cost of transportation up to the port of destination but insurance only up to port of departure. It is rightly said that in international trade, one does not get what he/she deserves but what one negotiates. INCOTERMS, being trade terms for allocating of cost and risks in trade, form the basis of responsibility of either party of trade and have their important bearing on payment terms.

8.8 Choosing INCOTERMS for International Trade Deal

Shipping terms, no doubt, help in fixation of responsibility as well as obligation of both the trading parities in international trade operations. As nature of international logistics operations is complex involving several parties at various stages of logistics operating from different jurisdictions, one has to be careful in understanding each other well. Additionally, there are differences between trading parties due to different cultures, trading practices and languages. Hence, exporter and importer should be careful while incorporating shipping terms for their international business operations. In the following sub-sections we discuss some of the areas of precautions for both the trading parties.

8.8.1 Responsibility Shifts at 'Named Port or Place'

Exporter and importer while signing the ISC shall take care to mention the 'named place' where the goods are to be handed over to the importer or his/her authorized carriage. For example, if it is FOB shipping term and the place of handover of goods is JNPT, Mumbai, then it shall be mentioned as FOB (JNPT, Mumbai) in the ISC. Name of each INCOTERM can be abbreviated into three words which are to be written in 'capital letters' in the ISC. Figure 8.6 depicts the sharing of costs of carriage and risks (insurance, pilferage and transit losses) between exporter and importer in international logistics operations.

8.8.2 Mention of INCOTERMS Edition

Exporter and importer shall also take care of the mentioning of the particular edition of INCOTERMS while quoting them in the sales contract and contract of carriage. For example, for FOB INCOTERMS, it shall also be mentioned that it is the 2020 version of INCOTERMS and shall be quoted as FOB 2020 Mumbai. As per ICC, Paris, the 'INCOTERMS shall not apply unless the particular edition of shipping term is not incorporated into the ISC by clearly mentioning that this particular shipment is governed by INCOTERMS 2020'.

8.8.3 Clarity on Additional Clauses, if Any

There has to be clarity on any additional clauses incorporated along with INCOTERMS for a trade transaction. For example, if it is agreed that seller will bear the expenses for the loading of cargo at origin point under INCOTERMS EXW which is not a case as per standard practices, it should be clearly incorporated as 'EXW, Kolkata loaded on truck' in the ISC. Similarly, if it is agreed that exporter will provide 'seaworthy packing' under INCOTERMS EXW, it should be clearly incorporated with INCOTERMS used to avoid confusions and disputes.

8.8.4 Explicit Understanding of Cost and Risks

An exporter has to clearly and minutely understand the cost and risks obligation under each INCOTERM. For example, if DPU term is used which is applicable to 'named place of destination', then it means that seller is responsible for carriage as well as risks up to named place of destination including unloading of cargo at destination. Term DPU mandates similar responsibilities for the seller except the case that he/she is not responsible for unloading at named place of destination (Figure 8.6). Similarly, under term CIF, seller procures insurance against buyer's risk of losses, hence he/she is supposed to procure minimum insurance unless otherwise agreed, meaning buyer must take risk mitigation measures to protect against transit risks.

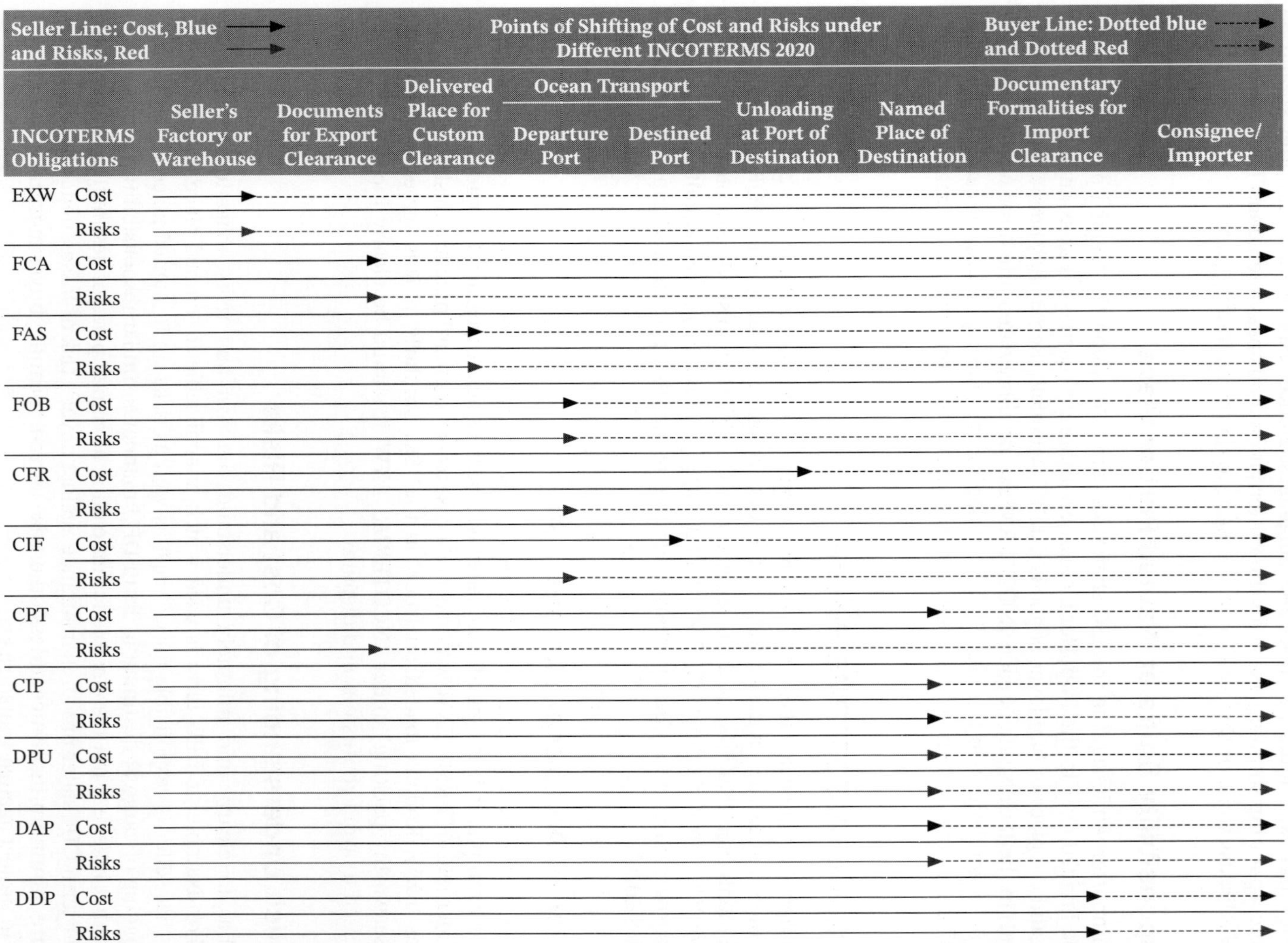

FIGURE 8.6 Points of shifting of cost and risks under different INCOTERMS 2020.

Source: International Chamber of Commerce (2019).

8.8.5 Avoid Risky INCOTERMS

Both contracting parties are advised not to incorporate extreme INCOTERMS in trade transactions; for example, terms EXW, FCA DPU, DAP and DDP are considered extremely risky. Thus, it is recommended that exporter and importer should trade-off and select INCOTERMS whereby their cost, risks, obligations and responsibilities are distributed in an equitable manner and shall be acceptable to both exporter and importer.

8.8.6 Reciprocity for Each Other's Concerns

The exporter should understand that the same INCOTERMS may not be suitable for each importer. Both exporter and importer need to discuss and appraise prevailing circumstances along with each other's concerns while selecting INCOTERMS. INCOTERMS are negotiable and must be facilitative to both contracting parties in the reduction of costs, risks and time in international trade logistics.

8.8.7 Compatibility with Rules and Regulations of Importer's Country

The exporter should appraise the rules and regulations of importer's country as some countries in the world have restrictions for the incorporation of certain INCOTERMS in case of procurement by GOI agencies. The Director General of Shipping gives preference to Indian shipping lines, hence requests all public sector undertakings (PSUs) to incorporate INCOTERMS only from E and F groups and use Indian ships for transportation from the country of export to India. Similarly, many underdeveloped African countries, which are suffering from the problem of foreign exchange and balance of payments, prefer domestic carriers. These countries save precious foreign exchange by using domestic carriers. Contracting parties to a trade deal should take care of all such implications.

8.8.8 Standard Practices of Country or Region

Some countries and regions have certain standard INCOTERMS practices in place; for example, many European countries prefer that the goods shall be delivered to the country destined by the exporter. The exporter is at risk under such INCOTERMS practices.

8.8.9 Mode of Transport

Certain shipping terms are used for sea transport only and some other are applicable for any mode of transport. Contracting parties to a trade deal should take care of such INCOTERMS while incorporating them in ISC or quoting export prices in proforma invoice.

8.8.10 Knowledge of Trade Regime

Contracting parties should have all the information about the rules and regulations regulating export and import such as what items fall under restricted or prohibited category and then negotiate the INCOTERMS. For example, an exporter has agreed to deliver the goods on DDP terms. Once the goods have arrived at the place of destination, custom department of importer's country refuses to allow the entry of the goods as these goods are under prohibited list, hence, cannot be imported. Similarly, an importer should not negotiate and incorporate EXW INCOTERMS if goods are under restricted or prohibited category.

8.8.11 Competitive Shipping Helps Win New Markets

An exporter shall choose shipping terms which offer the most competitive price to the importer. He/she shall consult importer and enquire what kinds of shipping terms will be convenient to his/her logistics needs. Competitive shipping terms can help an exporter explore new markets and retain satisfied customers.

8.9 Summary

International commercial terms, in short known as INCOTERMS, and also known as 'terms of delivery' or 'shipping terms' or 'trade terms' or 'INFOTERMS', help overcome challenges. Shipping terms are an integral part of any EXIM transaction between an exporter and an importer. Shipping terms help define the roles and responsibilities of the exporter and the importer in a trade deal as these demarcate the functional activities to be performed by the exporter and the importer such as getting the insurance cover, reserving shipping space, loading and unloading of cargo, customs and excise clearance. INCOTERMS were published for the first time in 1936 by ICC, Paris, and have been revised several times. Recent revision was in 2020 which prescribes the following set of INCOTERMS for international trade operations.

1. EXW Ex works (Named place of delivery)
2. FCA Free carrier (Named place)
3. FAS Free alongside ship (Named port)
4. FOB Free onboard (Named port of departure)
5. CFR Cost and freight (Named port of destination)
6. CIF Cost, insurance and freight (Named port of destination)
7. CPT Carriage paid to (Named place of destination)
8. CIP Carriage and insurance paid (Named place of destination)
9. DPU Delivered at place unloaded (Named place of destination)
10. DAP Delivered at place (Named place of destination)
11. DDP Delivered duty paid (Named place of destination)

Terms of delivery are an important managerial decision-making tool in any importing or exporting company. The revision of INCOTERMS in 2020 has made them legal trade instruments to be accepted as law if two partners have mutually agreed to base the distribution of their responsibilities and liabilities as per particular INCOTERMS. Hence, the exporter as well as importer should be aware of their obligations and consequences of using particular INCOTERMS 2020. The major function performed by terms of delivery is to clarify that costs and risks are split between the exporter or consignor and importer or consignee in a mutually agreed manner by providing the clarity of financial implications involved in trade deal to both the parties and the same shall be included in ISC to provide it a legal sanctity for future purposes. Contracting parties to trade deal are advised to exercise due diligence while negotiating and incorporating INCOTERMS for international trade and logistics operations.

CASE STUDY Application of INCOTERMS 2020 in Real-life Business Scenario

Mr Sharma, based in Delhi, runs a handicraft export business. He has got an export order for supplies of variety of handicraft items from a buyer based at Vienna, Austria. The agreed payment mode is document against payment. The cargo is around 8 tons with a volume of around 20 cbm. The value of cargo is around $85,000. The cargo has some of the items which are fragile, meaning there is requirement to exercise precautions at loading and unloading points as tumbling or jerking of container or unit load device (ULD) may potentially result in damages to cargo.

Questions

Mr Sharma seeks your advice for negotiating an appropriate INCOTERMS 2020 in these trade transactions under the following conditions:

1. When the cargo is to be routed by water transport. Assuming the agreed port of origin is Mundra, India, and the port of destination is Hamburg, Germany. The final destination is Vienna, Austria, which will be completed by either rail or road from Hamburg to Vienna.
2. When cargo is to be routed by air transport. Assuming the agreed airports are New Delhi and Vienna. Further, on enquiry it has come to the notice of Mr Sharma that there is huge shortage of ULDs at Delhi airport.
3. When the buyer wants to maximize his/her control on trade supply chain of cargo from point of origin to point of destination.
4. When the buyer wants the cargo to be delivered at Austria frontier as he/she does not intend this cargo in Austria but is importing to tap an emerging opportunity in a trade fair in Geneva, Switzerland.
5. When the seller, Mr Sharma, is highly risk-averse and does not want to engage in foreign trade operations as he has no knowledge of foreign trade.
6. When the buyer and the seller have agreed to let Mr Sharma complete all the export-related formalities that are specific to India and once goods are cleared from Indian authorities, the buyer will manage all elements of remaining logistics.

Review Questions

Multiple Choice Questions

1. Terms of delivery (INCOTERMS) used in export contracting and pricing are prepared and written by which of the following agencies?
   a. UNCTAD, Geneva
   b. ICC, Paris
   c. Under the WTO Agreement as adopted in 1995
   d. Under the United Nations Convention for the International Sale of Goods (Vienna Convention)
2. Who among the following shall be responsible for completing the 'export formalities' in CIF?
   a. Seller
   b. Consignor but not the seller
   c. Buyer
   d. Freight forwarder
   e. Third party
   f. Consignee but not the buyer
   g. Subject to buyer and seller mutual consent
   h. Indian law governing goods transport

3. Who among the following shall be responsible for completing the 'import formalities' in FCA?
   a. Seller
   b. Consignor but not the seller
   c. Buyer
   d. Freight forwarder
   e. Third party
   f. Consignee but not the buyer
   g. Subject to buyer and seller mutual consent
   h. Indian law governing goods transport
4. Where does delivery occur under the CPT terms of delivery?
   a. Named place at origin
   b. Named port at origin
   c. Named port at destination
   d. Named place at destination
   e. The buyer's facility at destination
5. Which of the following modes of transport can be used in the case of CFR INCOTERMS-based contract between two parties in international trade transactions?
   a. Only sea and inland waterway transport
   b. Only road transport
   c. Only air transport
   d. Only rail transport
   e. Surface transport, that is, road and rail
   f. Surface and water transport
   g. All modes of transport
6. In international logistics operations, terms of delivery (INCOTERMS) 2020 must be incorporated into which of the following?
   a. Contract of carriage
   b. Negotiable bill of lading
   c. Sales contract
   d. The shippers export declaration
   e. Shipping bill
7. Who among the following shall be responsible for completing the 'import formalities' in FOB?
   a. Seller
   b. Consignor but not the seller
   c. Buyer
   d. Freight forwarder
   e. Third party
   f. Consignee but not the buyer
   g. Subject to buyer and seller mutual consent
   h. Indian law governing goods transport
8. Where does delivery occur under the CIP terms of delivery?
   a. Named place at origin
   b. Named port at origin
   c. Named port at destination

d. Named place at destination
e. The buyer's facility at destination

9. Who among the following shall be responsible for completing the 'export formalities' in FOB?
   a. Seller
   b. Consignor but not the seller
   c. Buyer
   d. Freight forwarder
   e. Third party
   f. Consignee but not the buyer
   g. Subject to buyer and seller mutual consent
   h. Indian law governing goods transport
10. Which of the following modes of transport can be used in the case of DPU INCOTERMS-based contract between two parties in international trade transactions?
   a. Only sea and inland waterway transport
   b. Only road transport
   c. Only air transport
   d. Only rail transport
   e. Surface transport, that is, road and rail
   f. Surface and water transport
   g. All modes of transport

Critical Thinking Questions

1. What do you mean by terms of delivery (INCOTERMS)? What role do they play in the formation of an ISC? How are the INCOTERMS evolved?
2. Discuss the various INCOTERMS used in ISC and pricing. What is the scope of terms of delivery in an international trade transaction?
3. Discuss in detail the delivery terms under 'F' group. What are the obligations, responsibilities and risks for an exporter and importer under 'F' group delivery terms?
4. Discuss the various terms of delivery from their applicability in different modes of transportation. On what basis are INCOTERMS chosen for an international trade transaction?
5. Discuss in brief the following:
   a. INCOTERMS under 'C' group
   b. INCOTERMS and transfer of risk in international trade transaction
   c. INCOTERMS under 'D' group
   d. INCOTERMS and transport mode

Further Reading

1. International Chamber of Commerce. 2019. *INCOTERMS 2020 (ICC Publication Number 723)*. Paris: International Chamber of Commerce.

CHAPTER 9

International Sales Contracts

CHAPTER OBJECTIVES

- To brief about ISC.
- To discuss the key provisions of ISC under the Vienna Convention.
- To explain the legal dimensions affecting the formation of ISC.
- To explain the important elements of contract formation and execution in a sales contract.
- To explain the important legal terms and issues including sharing of responsibilities in a sales contract.

9.1 Introduction

International business in today's volatile and ambiguous times is far more complex and riskier primarily due to varying 'legal regime and jurisdictions' governing the conduct, control and regulation of two or more trading parties in a trade transaction. Exporters as well as importers are unknown to each other's regulatory environment and accordingly take measures to mitigate their associated business risks in trade transactions. In order to arrive at a mutually accepted solution(s) on rules and regulations governing their trade transactions, the exporter and importer have to negotiate and agree on a mutually acceptable harmonized and standardized trade regime which is agreed among countries through treaties, conventions and protocols either through the UN or through ICC, Paris. Trading parties in today's ambiguous trade regime avoid accepting any legal and trading regime favouring either party to trade as it exposes them to potential business risks arising out of misinterpretation, judicial corruption and bureaucratic anarchism. Trading parties always prefer the harmonized trade regime like the Convention on International Sales of Goods (CISG), facilitating the sale and purchase of internationally traded goods in a transparent and fair manner among the trading parties.

With the elimination of tariff and non-tariff barriers under the General Agreement on Tariffs and Trade (GATT) negotiations coupled with the evolution of transparent, non-discriminatory and standardized trade regime under WTO, trade expanded significantly and accordingly the nations world over realized the need to strengthen and improve the regulatory framework governing foreign trade, that is, sale and purchase of goods. Accordingly, several initiatives (Figure 9.1) have been taken to evolve a transparent and standardized regime for contract formation of internationally traded goods. Global trade institutions such as the United Nations Commission on International Trade Law (UNCITRAL), ICC, UNCTAD, WCO, International Maritime Organization (IMO), WTO and United Nations Centre for Trade Facilitation and Electronic Business (UN/CEFACT) have played a key role in evolving, improving, framing and strengthening the international regulatory framework governing the sales of

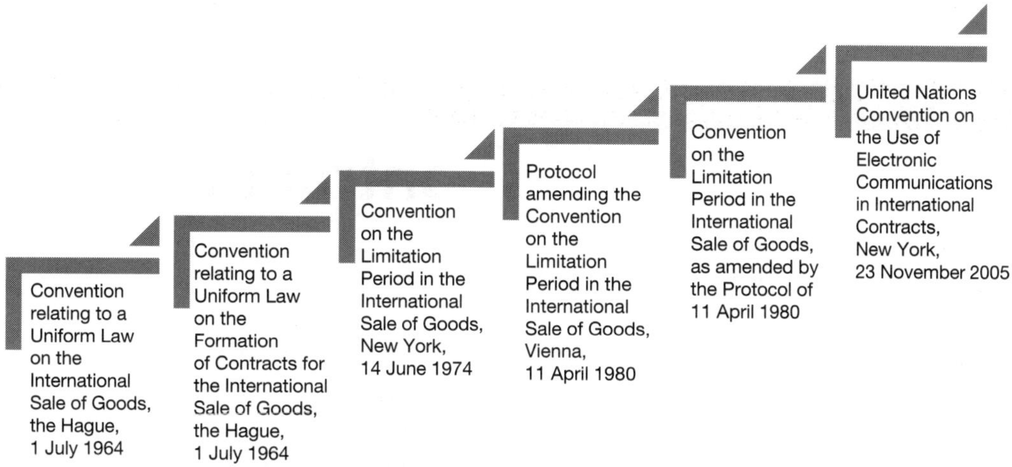

FIGURE 9.1 Evolutionary initiatives for CISG.

Source: Adapted from United Nations Commission on International Trade Law (UNCITRAL). https://uncitral.un.org/ (accessed on 24 May 2023).

internationally trade goods. Accordingly, on the basis of consensus among contracting parties in the Vienna Convention,[1] a final draft of CISG (Figure 9.2) is prepared by UNCITRAL. This text explains the terms and conditions of ISC to be used by exporters and importers for defining their responsibilities and obligations so that terms and conditions of trade deals are clear to each trading party and are enforceable in the court of law in the case of dispute between parties. The Republic of India has so far not ratified the model code of conduct of ISC, but such contracts are enforceable in India if incorporated under the model sales contract of the Vienna Convention on CISG.

For ISC, there has to be at least two parties who are intending to engage themselves in an international trade transaction. Such parties in any trade transaction (sales contract) are known as 'exporter' or 'consignor' and 'importer' or 'consignee'. Trading parties, that is, exporter and importer can be operating as a proprietor, partnership firm, a registered company (private, public or government), HUF, LLP, trust or society intending or consenting for the international trade deal. Trading parties sign ISC so as to provide clarity in sharing of various risks, responsibilities and obligations in trade transactions. As a result, the contents, terms and conditions of ISC are of immense significance to the contracting parties as they help build trust and confidence among trading parties regarding issues such as settlement of payment, transfer of title, sharing of cost and risks of freight, carriage, insurance, quality compliance, packing labelling, marking issues and timely delivery, thus facilitating the smooth conduct of trade and commerce among trading parties. Moreover, ISC also helps the contracting parties in avoiding any disputes in the process of international trade transactions. ISC between trading parties is framed in light of certain rules and regulations which are globally acceptable, harmonized, standardized and are transparent, thus facilitating the international trade among nations in a friendly manner by protecting the interest of their trading communities. International trade transactions are conducted on the basis of the terms and conditions as negotiated between exporter and importer in ISC. By negotiating the terms and

[1] ICC has standardized ISC on the basis of CISG among nations, the convention was held in Vienna in 1980 and 71 countries have signed it.

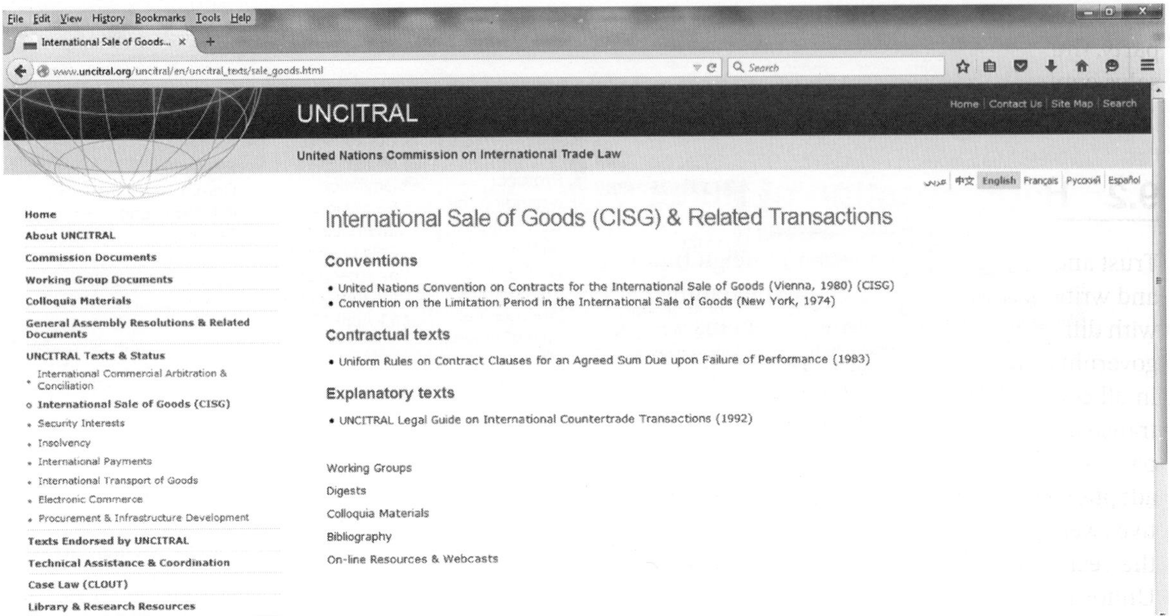

FIGURE 9.2 Snapshot of CISG at UNCITRAL.

Source: Screenshot from United Nations Commission on International Trade Law (UNCITRAL). https://uncitral.un.org/ (accessed on 24 May 2023).

conditions in ISC, an exporter or importer not only secures the business deal but manages (minimizes) the associated risks carefully and also protects his/her firm from potential trade disputes, claims and legal actions. UNCITRAL has framed the standard terms and conditions through CISG and the exporter and the importer can make necessary changes if so desired, negotiated and agreed so as to clearly define the risks, responsibilities and obligations for each trading party.

ISC contains all important terms and conditions of any sale transaction between trading parties such as place and date of delivery, delivery schedule, terms of payments, INCOTERMS, packing and packaging standards, labelling and marking norms, price of goods, port of shipment, port of destination, inspections, quality compliance requirements and responsibility for procuring insurance cover. The nature and contents of the sales contract may vary, and it may be a one-page document or spanning into many pages explaining the exact nature of responsibilities and obligations of each trading party. Explained and properly documented sales contract is important in the long run as a business environment changes very fast and can make a profitable business deal loss-making over a period of time, thus opening scope for trade disputes between trading parties. A sales contract can be written or implied (construed); it depends on some factors such as exporter–importer relationship, nature of business, size of the trade deal, export turnover time and business environment of trading countries involved. However, it is always advisable to have a written sales agreement which might include some additional costs and time as it protects both trading parities from potential confusions, ambiguous understanding of trade terms and complexity of dispute resolution. A written sales agreement has several benefits such as it helps avoid uncertainty, reduces scope of litigation, defines place and process of arbitration or reconciliation between trading parties. Above all, if both trading parties have any disputes, the third party exactly understands the nature of contracts and obligations of each party, thus scope of uncertainty, mistrust and trade disputes is almost wholly eliminated with written sales contract.

9.2 Harmonization of Rules on International Sales of Goods

Trust and confidence to engage in foreign trade cannot arise between trading parties until there is formal and written sales contract as both the trading parties are unknown to each other, from different countries with different language, business customs and practices and above all with different economic legislation governing their business. In this context, ISC is rightly referred to as the backbone of international trade in all countries, irrespective of their legal tradition or level of economic development as it provides the transparent, legally sound and trustworthy base for engaging into export and imports with unknown party(ies). Hence, CISG is considered one of the core international trade conventions where universal adoption of this law among world countries is most desirable. After the end of the First World War, initiatives were made for harmonization and standardization of law governing international sales of goods, but the real efforts for harmonization of sales law came with the adoption of 'Convention Relating to a Uniform Law on the Formation of Contracts for the International Sale of Goods' at the Hague on 1 July 1964, which provided a careful balance between the interests of the buyer and of the seller for the first time. This convention acted as a catalyst for reforms on standardization of legislation governing international sales even at the national level.

The adoption of the present model sales contract under 'Convention on the Limitation Period in the International Sale of Goods' as amended by the Protocol of 11 April 1980 provides modern, uniform legislation for the international sale of goods. If a sales transaction is negotiated incorporating sales contract under this convention, it will apply whenever contracts for the sale of goods are concluded between parties with a place of business in contracting states. Hence, if a contract of sale is negotiated and contracted under CISG, it would apply directly without any reference to private international law to determine the law applicable, thus clearly defining the certainty and predictability of ISCs. The international law of sales as drafted under the Vienna Convention will also apply to contract(s) of international sale of goods in cases when the legislation and rules of private international law of contracting state also point to reference on applicability of CISG law as the applicable one regardless of place and venue of business. This indicates the global acceptability of law on international sales as the Vienna Convention provides not only harmonized and standardized set of rules governing the contract of sales but also a neutral one having acceptability among contracting parties. Model sales contract as drafted under the Vienna Convention offers insights into the interpretation of these rules to any contracting party, thus simplifying the rules for greater usage among global trading community. Hence, CISG fulfils the purpose of providing a fair, transparent, uniform, modern, harmonized and standardized regime for contracts for the international sale of goods. Thus, CISG contributes significantly in bringing the certainty and neutrality on contracts of sales among trading parties, promoting trade and commercial exchanges in global trade regime and helps in decreasing the scope of disputes and associated transaction costs. This is significant for small- and medium-sized exporters and importers of developing countries who are usually apprehensive about engaging in international trade in absence of strong contractual arrangement coupled with reduced access to legal advice. These exporters and importers always feel that they are more vulnerable to various risks associated with international trading, resulting in low participation in trade, thus not leveraging the potential of trade to act as catalyst for speeding up the economic growth of their countries.

CISG governs contracts related to export and import of merchandised goods only and that too between private parties clearly excluding sales to consumers, sales of services and specified sales, if any. The Vienna Convention does not specify the validity of the contract and the effect of the sales contract on transfer to title. It, however, deals with the process of formation of the sales contract, which is concluded by the exchange of offer and acceptance. It also deals with the obligations of each contracting party which includes on seller's part to deliver the goods in conformity with the quantity and quality as stipulated in the contract, related trade documents including documents related to title (ownership) of goods. The key obligations of the buyer are timely payments on agreed price and taking delivery of goods once they arrive at the place of destination. The Vienna Convention provides fair and transparent rules for possible remedies for breach of the contract by either party or the aggrieved party can either ask for performance of agreed sales contract or can claim emergent damages. The Vienna Convention of Sales of Goods also provides a fair mechanism to regulate for passing of risk, anticipatory breach of contract and resultant commercial damages, if any, and exemption from execution of the contract. Last but not least, CISG provides freedom to either contracting party to form the sales contract. CISG has 101 articles so as to define, execute and regulate the sales contract. Following are some of the significant provisions of CISG:

1. Details interpretation of sales agreement between trading parties.
2. The role of business practices, customs including their usages in international trade transactions.
3. Key features of the sales contract, duration and revocability clause of the sale offer.
4. The manner, timing and effectiveness of acceptances of sale offer.
5. Provisions aimed at bringing changes in sales terms as well as the process of acceptance of such changes including brining modifications to ISCs.
6. The seller's obligations with respect to the quality compliance of the goods.
7. Provision explaining explicitly the time and place for delivery including clarity on sharing of costs and risks.
8. Provision explaining explicitly the place and date for payment.
9. Provision mandating explicitly the buyer's obligations to take delivery of goods.
10. Provision explaining the procedure of cargo inspection and examination of delivered goods including intimation on any claimed lack of conformity in quality and quantity.
11. Provision aimed at buyer's remedies for breach of contract by the seller including buyer's rights to demand delivery of goods or repair or replacement of non-conforming goods or to avoid the performance of sales contract or to recover damages and to reduce the price for non-conforming goods.
12. Provision aimed at seller's remedies for breach of contract by the buyer including rights to obligate the buyer to take delivery of arrived goods at destination and obligate him/her to pay the invoiced amount or to avoid the performance of sales contract and to recover the resultant damages, if any.
13. Provision aimed at transfer of costs and risks in the goods sold through appropriate INCOTERMS as negotiated and agreed.
14. Provision for reconciliation through litigation or arbitration from any anticipatory or potential breach of sales contract.

15. Provision aimed at explicitly expressing the ways and means for recovery of interest on sums in arrears for either party to trade deal.
16. Provision providing the exemption from liability for failure to perform, including force majeure.
17. Provision obligating the role of each trading party to preserve goods that are to be sent or returned to the other party.

CISG applies only to international trade transactions, that is, EXIM transactions taking place between two contracting countries. It does not apply to the purely domestic sale contract which remains to be regulated by domestic law unless otherwise agreed. More so, ISCs which are negotiated and agreed under any valid private law would also not be affected by CISG. For countries which have signed CISG, there are no financial implications arising out of its ratification and such countries do not require any dedicated body for administration of such contracts, reporting and other associated obligations. The countries shown in Figure 9.3 have signed CISG.

Albania	Argentina	Armenia	Australia	Austria	Bahrain	Belarus	Belgium
Benin	Bosnia Herzego vina	Brazil	Bulgaria	Burundi	Canada	Chile	China (PRC)
Colombia	Croatia	Cuba	Cyprus	Czech Rep.	Denmark	Republic	Ecuador
Egypt	El Salvador	Estonia	Finland	France	Gabon	Georgia	Germany
Greece	Guinea	Guyana	Honduras	Hungary	Iceland	Iraq	Israel
Italy	Japan	South Korea	Kyrgyzstan	Latvia	Lebanon	Lesotho	Liberia
Lithuania	Luxembourg	Macedonia	Madagascar	Mauritania	Mexico	Moldova	Mongolia
Montenegro	Netherlands	New Zealand	Norway	Paraguay	Peru	Poland	Republic of Congo
Romania	Russian Federation	San Marino	Serbia	Singapore	Slovakia	Slovenia	Spain
Sweden	Switzerland	Syria	Turkey	Uganda	Ukraine	USA	Uruguay
			Uzbekistan	Zambia	Saint Vincent and Grenadines		

FIGURE 9.3 Names of signatory countries of CISG.

Source: United Nations Commission on International Trade Law (UNCITRAL). https://uncitral.un.org/ (accessed on 24 May 2023).

As on today, 83 countries excluding India[2] have signed, adopted and ratified the CISG. Countries from both developed and developing world have signed CISG, and success of the convention can be witnessed from the fact that countries which have signed the Vienna Convention contribute almost 2/3 of the world trade. In this context, it can be said that CISG is an outstanding success in the legal harmonization of the law governing, facilitating and regulating the international sale of goods among nations. However, CISG lacks the role of an independent body free from all national jurisdictions and having a non-partisan role in trade promotion through a body of uniform rules that may have been more acceptable to emerging powers such as India, Indonesia and South Africa. Some of the other features which made the convention unattractive were that it provides the neutral right to the contracting parties for accepting these rules and regulations. Hence, the application of the Vienna Convention depends completely on the willingness of the contracting parties. Parties are free to exclude it completely or apply it partially on the basis of their mutual agreement. The significant point to be taken care of is that the contracting parties must give emphasis to the jurisdiction of their countries while framing ISC along with the rules and regulations in making of ISC as given in the Vienna Convention.

9.3 ISCs: The Legal Dimensions

The sale of goods in international markets entails a number of legal and regulatory challenges for an exporter which may arise out of 'conflict of law' and the legal formation of contract. For example, various local rules and acts may be in conflict with ISC, thus one has to not only consider the legal and regulatory issues related to ISC but also associated laws such as rules governing the relationships between the exporter and agents or distributors, trademarks, patents product liability, promotion and payment terms particularly for L/C which is governed by not only contract law but also by the Uniform Customs and Practice for Documentary Credits 600 (UCPDC 600). Hence, one should consider the aspects discussed in the following sub-sections related to the formation and execution of ISCs.

9.3.1 Conflict of Law

The conflict of law is common in international sales transactions as the operating business environment and allied legislation of both exporter and importer countries are usually different from one another. Exporter and importer may be well versed to understand the domestic law regulating business but are usually unaware about the business legislation of other countries. Exporter and importer both are prone to commit inadvertent mistakes while dealing in trade operations in different countries and fail to comply with the legislation, rules and regulations of the host countries. For example, tax and tariff usually vary from country to country including the mechanism of imposition. Additionally, countries in today's ambiguous and volatile business environment resort to restricting imports by imposing non-tariff barriers in the form of SPS and technical barriers. Imposition of these non-tariff barriers

[2] India has not signed the Vienna Convention due to the factors such as the government not viewing the ratification of CISG as a legislative priority, a lack of interest from the trader community in supporting the ratification, opposition from a number of large and influential organizations, a lack of public service resources and a danger that such convention will expose small Indian exporters to a costly international litigation and arbitration which they cannot afford as either they are ill-informed about the international regulatory system or they do not have financial might to withstand the costly process.

usually leads to disputes and litigation between contracting parties. Cunning traders may intentionally resort to incorporate litigant elements in ISC so that their country's law may have some influence while settling these disputes. Such an influence of another country's regulatory system on ISC is known as 'conflict of laws', and such conflict of law can be settled and taken care of in advance by incorporating some specific provisions with respect to the jurisdiction and applicability of law in that sales contract. Disputes and litigation are common in EXIM operations but can be minimized through fair negotiation and model sales contract formation. In addition to unique efforts of UNCITRAL for the Vienna Convention on CISG, nation states are also bringing uniformity, harmonization and standardization in the interpretation of trade law, quality and health standards, transportation rules and so on. The problems of conflict of law become grave due to unique features of international trade which are long distance involved between trading parties, large use of trade intermediaries in the trade process, different languages and business practices and so on, which essentially add to confusion, ambiguity and variation in explaining the various trade terms to both trading parties. Problems become even greater when there is no written sales contract between trading parties.

In the absence of mutually agreed harmonized law between trading parties, rules of 'private international law' are used to resolve any of the trade disputes arising between the trading parties. Trading parties should mutually agree upon the place of litigation, and it is normally advisable to sue in the country where the defaulting party resides or is incorporated and has headquarters of the company. This is primarily because the defendant can be more easily compelled to go to court and answer the case as his/her image is under question and in case, he/she is out of court jurisdiction, he/she will use every tactic to avoid the litigation and will not respond to a court of law. The prime question that one should also consider is which type of law will apply and one should weigh the following scenarios for applicability of law:

1. **Lex foci:** Under *lex foci*, the applicable law will be of the country in which the case is tried for.
2. **Lex loci solutions:** Under *lex loci solutions*, the applicable law will be of the place where the contract is performed.
3. **Lex situs:** Under *lex situs*, the applicable law will be of the place where the property is situated.
4. **Lex loci contractus:** Under *lex loci contractus*, the applicable law will be of the country where the contract is made.

Considering all these difficulties on conflict and applicability of law, various treaties, protocols and conventions have been signed in order to unify the law relating to international sales, thereby avoiding the difficult task of weighing various factors in deciding which law to apply between trading parties in case of disputes. These are the Uniform Law on the Formation of Contracts for the International Sale of Goods and the Uniform Law on the International Sale of Goods.

9.3.2 Written versus Constructed Contracts

As a matter of rule, all large export as well as import orders including the orders which are for a long-term supply of raw materials, goods and services are usually inked between exporter and importer so as to avoid any kind of ambiguity and make the trade deal fruitful in its execution and implementation. Lengthy trade documentation involving the process of explaining and quoting the various trade terms is signed in written agreement between an exporter and an importer (Figure 9.4). This is specifically true in case of contracts which are project or services exports as the scope of disputes is much higher

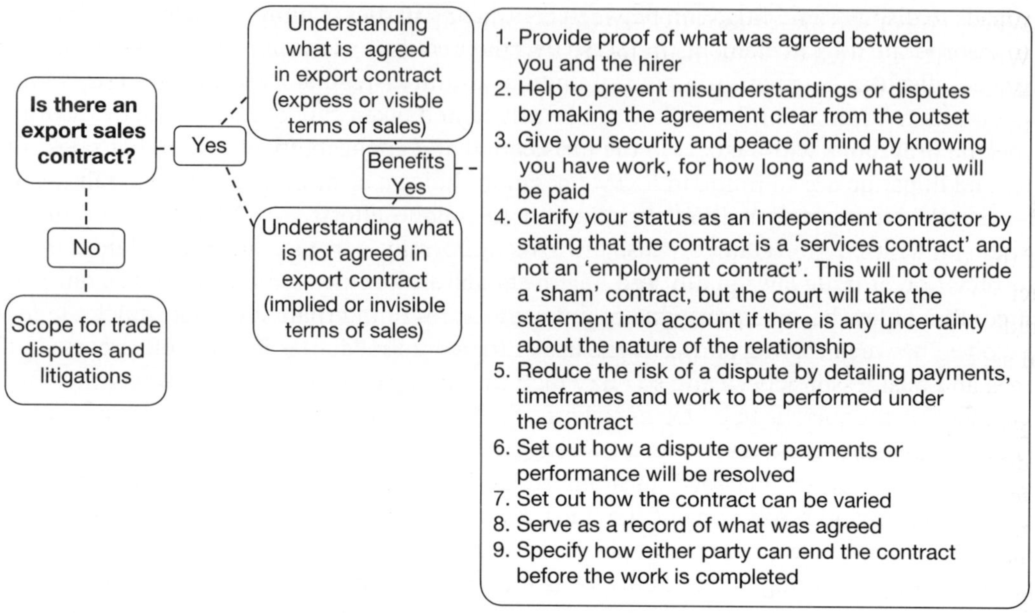

FIGURE 9.4 Rationale of written export sales contract.

Source: Adapted from https://business.gov.au/Products-and-services/Contracts-and-tenders/Types-of-contracts (accessed on 10 May 2023).

due to the nature of exportable services involving various stages of execution and implementation of contract. Indian companies, particularly dealing on a regular basis in the areas of export activities such as gems and jewellery, petro products, textiles, electronics, services exports including exports of IT, outsourcing activities, consultancy and so on, prefer a written sales contract with the trading partner.

In case an exporter does not have a written sales contract with the importer, he/she can establish the existence of a contract on the basis of various commercial and regulatory documents, communication with importer through email, fax, telex and so on in the court of law if any dispute with the importer arises. The Indian Evidence Act recognizes commercial as well as regulatory documents as an evidence in the court of law provided exporter shall prove it through the various communications he/she had with importer through email, fax, telex, telegram, bill of exchange and L/C. Such an unwritten contract so proved in a court of law shall be referred to as 'construed contract' and shall have same relevance and effect as in case of written contract in execution of legal order if any dispute arises between exporter and importer. It is always better to have your contract in writing, no matter how small the job is. Any contract with a hirer that involves a significant risk to your business should always be carefully considered and put in writing. This is advisable even if it means delaying the start of the work. A written contract is essential:

1. When the contract price is large enough to make or break your business if you do not get paid.
2. Where there are quality requirements, specifications or specific materials that must be used.
3. Where there is some doubt that the hirer has enough money to pay you.
4. When you must have certain types of insurance for the type of work you are doing.
5. Where the contract contains essential terms like a critical date for the completion of the work before payment can be made.

6. Where you or the hirer needs to keep certain information confidential.
7. When it is required by your insurance company for professional indemnity purposes.
8. Where there is a legal obligation to have a written contract (e.g., trade contracts for building work in Queensland).

9.3.3 Regulatory Compliance of Local Legislations

One of the key challenges for exporters as well as importers is that they have to ensure that their trade contract should be in compliance with local rules and regulations, especially the one dealing with foreign trade. Following are some of the key legislations in India which one should consider while looking at legal aspects affecting the formation and execution of ISCs:

1. **FTDR Act, 1992:** Under Section 5 of the FTDR Act, 1992, DGFT brings out FTP of India which determines and prescribes the do's and don'ts to the exporter as a policy is a guiding instrument for any exporter and importer intending to get started in international trade. FTP is revised every five years and updated on an annual basis with an annual supplement. *The Handbook of Procedure* (Volume 1) is issued under FTP. FTP determines, among other things, whether the particular commodity is in the open category, restricted or canalized category, or the prohibited category. In case of open category, the exporter is free to export and import, an order from DGFT has to be taken in case of restricted category and the exports and imports are prohibited completely if policy allows otherwise.

   FTP and allied policy instruments prescribe the policy for various kinds of export benefits, duty credit scrip, incentives, assistance, duty neutralization, authorizations and licences. One has to understand the FTP directions regarding issuance of restricted import licence, export obligations, second-hand items' imports and agriculture export as FTP is dynamic and keeps on changing in coherence with geo-economic business realities. DGFT can change FTP and allied procedure through notification(s). For example, if DGFT fixes the 'minimum export price of a commodity', then one has to consider its impact in formation and execution of sales contract. FTP may disallow trade with certain countries and may prescribe other measures for controlling the export and import in public interest; an exporter must remain updated about all such information and accordingly frame the terms and conditions in ISC by taking notes from *Foreign Trade Policy and Handbook of Procedures* which provides explanation to FTP. In addition to FTP, one must also understand some of the key features of the FTDR Act, 1992, as they may also have their bearing on the formation and execution of ISC.

   a. Action can be initiated against the exporter under Clause 7 of the Export (Control) Order, in case of non-payment of commission, supply of sub-standard goods, non-adherence of delivery schedules, indulgence in unethical commercial dealings or any other activity which amounts to breach of ISC.
   b. DGFT, if satisfied that the exporter has committed an economic offence as specified by the government or has made an export/import business or has entered in connivance into ISC which is gravely prejudicial to the trade relations of India with any foreign country or to the interests of other persons engaged in imports or exports or has brought disrepute to the credit or the goods of the country, then it can initiate action against such traders under Section 8 of the FTDR Act, 1992.
   c. DGFT or the officer authorized by it is empowered under Section 9(4) to grant licence to suspend or cancel any licence granted under the Act if it believes that the licence has been

obtained by fraud, suppression of facts or misrepresentation and where the licensee has contravened any law relating to custom or foreign exchange or the rules and regulations. Rule 10 of the Foreign Trade (Regulation) Rules, 1993, lays down the conditions for such cancellation of licence to the international trader.

d. A fiscal penalty can be imposed in cases where a person makes or abets or attempts to make any import or export in contravention of any provisions of the FTDR Act, any rules or orders made thereunder or FTP 2004–2009. The authority to DGFT is given under Section 11(2) of the FTDR Act.

e. Under Rule 11 of the Foreign Trade (Regulation) Rules, 1993, an exporter is made responsible to state the shipping bills or any other documents prescribed under the Customs Act, 1962. An exporter has to declare the value, quality and description of export goods to the best of his/her knowledge and belief and is required to certify that the quality and specification of the goods are in accordance with the terms of ISC. In order to make it legally binding, it is ensured that the exporter must subscribe and accept that the above-mentioned facts and details are true and best of his/her knowledge in a declaration at the end of such documents.

2. **FEMA, 2000:** FEMA, 1999, came into effect from 1 June 2000. FEMA has replaced FERA which was considered to be outdated in the contemporary global business environment. FEMA is very comprehensive, business-friendly and captures all amendments made to the laws pertaining to foreign exchange from time to time to meet the changing business requirements of exporters, investors, non-resident Indians, industry and trading community. RBI has been empowered under FEMA to grant general or special permissions for all foreign exchange related activities related to trade or individual investments. RBI has a controlling agency called 'Enforcement Directorate' so as to execute its regulatory compliance for various rules and regulations enacted under FEMA, 2000.

   Various rules issued under FEMA, 1999, such as FEM (Authentication of Documents) Rules, 2000, FEM (Current Account Transactions) Rules, 2000, FEM (Export and Import of Currency) Regulations, 2000, FEM (Realization, Repatriation and Surrender of Foreign Exchange), 2000, FEM (Manner of Receipt and Payment) Regulations, 2000, and FEM (Export of Goods and Service) Regulations, 2000, have an important bearing on terms used in ISC regarding the realization of payment, manner of payments, declaration of exports, agency commission in trade, filing of statutory documents, export on elongated credit terms, export of goods on lease, hire, project exports and so on. Hence, it is advisable to make a reference to the country's foreign exchange rules and regulations while framing ISC. The key provisions of FEM (Export of Goods and Services) Regulations, 2000, are given in Table 9.1.

3. **Export (Quality Control and Inspection) Act, 1963:** Export (Quality Control and Inspection) Act, 1963, is the prime regulatory measure by GOI to take measures for quality control. Various export inspection agencies (EIAs) have been set up so as to implement the quality control mechanism in India. This has been largely done to protect the image of the country in the international market by offering quality products to customers. Provisions with regard to technical standards of quality are laid down under this Act and no one can export an item unless a designated agency certifies that the quality of the product being exported is as per the standards laid down by either government or as per importer requirements. Usually, the standards being asked by the importer are higher; hence, an EIA must take note of the same while issuing the certificate of inspection to the exporter. In certain cases, the pre-shipment inspection has been made mandatory and exporter essentially has to get it done irrespective of the fact whether the importer has asked for

TABLE 9.1 Foreign Exchange Management (Export of Goods and Services) Regulations, 2000: Key Provisions Governing Conduct of Foreign Trade

Para	Heading	Rule
3 (1)	Declaration as regards export of goods and services	Every exporter of goods or software in physical form or through any other form, either directly or indirectly, to any place outside India, other than Nepal and Bhutan, shall furnish to the specified authority, a declaration in one of the forms set out in the Schedule and supported by such evidence as may be specified, containing true and correct material particulars including the amount representing: **1.** the full export value of the goods or software **2.** if the full export value is not ascertainable at the time of export, the value which the exporter, having regard to the prevailing market conditions expects to receive on the sale of the goods or the software in overseas market, and affirms in the said declaration that the full export value of goods (whether ascertainable at the time of export or not) or the software has been or will within the specified period be, paid in the specified manner.
6A	Declaration in Form EDF/SDF	**1.** The declaration in form EDF/SDF shall be submitted in duplicate to the Commissioner of Customs. **2.** After duly verifying and authenticating the declaration form, the Commissioner of Customs shall forward the original declaration form/data to the nearest office of the Reserve Bank and hand over the duplicate form to the exporter for being submitted to the authorized dealer.
8	Manner of payment of export value of goods	Unless otherwise authorized by the Reserve Bank, the amount representing the full export value of the goods exported shall be paid through an authorized dealer in the manner specified in the Foreign Exchange Management (Manner and Receipt and Payment) Regulations, 2000.
9	Period within which export value of goods/software to be realized	The amount representing the full export value of goods or software exported shall be realized and repatriated to India within 270 days from the date of export.
11	Export on elongated credit terms	No person shall enter any contract to export goods on the terms which provide for a period longer than six months for payment of the value of the goods to be exported.
14A	Export of goods on lease, hire and so on	No person shall, except with the prior permission of the Reserve Bank, take or send out by land, sea or air any goods from India to any place outside India on lease or hire or under any arrangement or in any other manner other than sale or disposal of such goods.
18	Project exports	Where an export of goods or services is proposed to be made on deferred payment terms or in execution of a turnkey project or a civil construction contract, the exporter shall, before entering into any such export arrangement, submit the proposal for prior approval of the approving authority, which shall consider the proposal in accordance with the guidelines issued by the Reserve Bank from time to time.

Source: Reserve Bank of India (Exchange Management Department) (2000).

a quality certificate or not. Hence, an international trader has to take care of all such precautions while framing ISC.

4. **Customs Act, 1962:** The Customs Department under CBEC is empowered with the task of carrying out physical as well as documentary check on all goods which are being exported from and imported into India. All EXIM consignments are supposed to be examined and checked by the customs authorities at port or airports with a view to ascertaining that the goods being shipped are those which are declared in the documents and are not prohibited or restricted goods. In the changed geopolitical environment, customs officials' role has increased a lot due to smuggling of narcotics and weapons and customs officials check all trade documents including ISC in order to verify the authenticity of the goods being exported or imported. Customs department also verifies whether exporter and importer have entered an under-invoiced deal to avoid higher duty and if so, then it takes necessary actions. The exporter should know about all documents and procedure as prescribed by CBEC and accordingly frame the terms and conditions in ISC.
5. **Customs Tariff Act, 1975:** The Customs Tariff Act, 1975, lays down the procedure on the levy of customs duty to be imposed on exported and imported material and there are some exceptions on the levy of duty in cases when GOI has entered PTA or FTA with the partner country. The additional excise duty to be charged is also prescribed under the provisions of this Act. The exporter shall know such relevant provisions which may help in reducing the transaction cost and accordingly frame ISC.
6. **International commercial practices:** Besides the Indian laws and regulatory procedure, there are certain international commercial practices and conventions to which India is a signatory party and such commercial practices and conventions may have a bearing on ISCs. Three documents which are prepared by ICC, Paris, are widely used in international business. These are (a) UCPDC 600, 2006, (b) the Uniform Rules for Collections 522 (URC 522), 1995, and (c) INCOTERMS, 2010. The UCPDC 600 is a document which is used by the banks for the negotiation of EXIM documents for realizing payment through L/C. URC 522 of ICC lays down the procedure for collection of bills under D/P and D/A terms for realization of payments and INCOTERMS 2010 explain the various trade terms such as EXW, FCA, FAS, FOB, CFR, CIF, CPT, CIP, DAT, DAP and DDP and define the respective rights and obligations of the exporter or consigner and importer or consignee in ISC. All such international commercial practices and conventions have an important bearing in framing of ISC.

As ISC involves exporter and importer only, the state does not intervene in the execution and implementation of such contract provided such contract shall not have been entered upon for a malafide intention of either party and such contract shall not be in contravention of public order, social and moral values of India people. The contract agreed upon between exporter and importer shall be in line with the various acts promulgated by GOI as tabled in Figure 9.5 for promotion, facilitation and regulation of international trade irrespective of the fact whether it is written or constructed.

9.4 Elements of ISC

The elements of ISC may vary depending upon the nature of the products and the country to which goods are exported; hence, there is no single format of model sales contract and one can amend and supplement additional clauses so as to cater to their business needs. However, there are some standard

FIGURE 9.5 Various trade legislations affecting the formation and execution of ISC.

terms and conditions which are part of any contract and are essential and integral to fulfilment and execution of any sales contract. These terms and conditions are almost universal in their application worldwide in all trade transactions (Box 9.1). In order to ensure sustainable, long and enduring relationship between the exporter and importer, it is important to have a written ISC. The key elements (Figure 9.6) of any such contract signed and agreed for international sales transactions are discussed in the following sub-sections.

9.4.1 Seller's and Buyer's Names

A sales contract is signed between two trading parties namely exporter and importer; hence, it is advisable that the full names of 'exporter' and 'importer' (proprietor/partnership/LLP/company/trust or society) should be written in ISC as given in respective legislation incorporating any such entity. For example, 'Sher-a-Punjab Export Company Pvt. Ltd' or 'Rajasthan Export Company Pvt. Ltd' shall be mentioned under the column trader's name (consignor or consignee). The exporter and importer are also required to mention their IEC number as issued by DGFT and name of the Act under which the business firm is registered, for example, the Companies Act, 2013, the Indian Partnership Act, 1932, and the LLP Act, 2009.

One should thoroughly examine whether there legally exist a company as exporter or importer as there are plenty of fake companies existing in this world for defrauding the exporters. One should be extra cautious while negotiating a trade deal, especially in developing countries particularly in Africa, Asia and the Caribbean. Some of the countries from these regions have emerged as potential and attractive buyers but have weak regulatory framework and law enforcement systems. More so, these countries also suffer from very high economic and political corruption. RBI usually issues circular(s) cautioning Indian exporters to remain vigilant to negotiate trade deals with genuine buyers and many Indian exporters have been defrauded by such kinds of companies in the past. It is also very tough to sue such companies as these are fake companies and flee away once they have done their job. One can

BOX 9.1 ▸ Brief Specimen of Sales Contract for International Trade Transactions

I. Name and address of the parties.......(state correct appellation and complete address of the parties)

II. We, the above-named parties have entered this contract for the sale/purchase, etc. .... (state briefly the purpose of the contract) on this ....(date) at ....(place)..... subject to the following terms and conditions:

a. Goods ....

b. Quantity ....Quality.. (Describe the quantity, quality and the other specifications of the goods precisely as per the agreement. An agency for inspection/certification of quality and/or quantity may also be stipulated).

c. Price.. Mode of payment ....(Quote the price, terms, i.e., ex-works/FOB (free on board) CIF (cost, insurance and freight) etc. in the currency agreed upon and describe the mode of payment, i.e., payment against L/C (letter of credit)/D/A (document against acceptance)/D/P(document against payment) etc. It is also desirable to mention the exchange rate.)

d. Shipment...(Specify date of delivery and the maximum period up to which delivery could be delayed and for which reasons, port of shipment and delivery should be mentioned).

e. Packing and marking.......................................(Requirements to be specified precisely)

f. Insurance .... (State the type of insurance cover required, i.e., FPA (free from particular average)/WA (with average)/all risks, etc. State also the party responsible for insurance)

g. Brokerage/Commission ....(if any payable may be mentioned)

h. Passing of the property and of risk. The property or ownership of the goods and the risk shall finally pass to the buyer at such stage as the parties may agree, i.e., when the goods are delivered at the seller's place of work/pass the ship's rails/are covered by insurance, etc. as per agreed terms).

i. Arbitration clause recommended by the Indian Council of Arbitration, 'All disputes or differences whatsoever arising between the parties out of or relating to the construction, meaning and operation or effect of this contract or the breach thereof shall be settled by arbitration in accordance with the Rules of Arbitration of the Indian Council of Arbitration and the award made in pursuance thereof shall be binding on the parties' (or any other arbitration clause that maybe agreed upon between the parties).

j. Any other special condition, prevalent in or relevant to the particular line of trade or transaction, may also be specified.

.... Sd/ - Seller .... Sd/ - Buyer

Source: Adapted from Indian Council of Arbitration, GOI.

check the accuracy of genuine buyers by seeking an advice on credit rating from ECGC and ask for a data universal numbering system number as issued by Dun & Bradstreet which is a private consulting firm for providing a fact sheet on the exporter and importer globally.

9.4.2 Unit Price

International business, although risky, offers greater returns and better prices on commodity and services. Hence, the exporter should quote such prices in ISC that he/she must be in a position to cover all expenses and risks after making provision of profits for his/her export firm. While quoting unit prices,

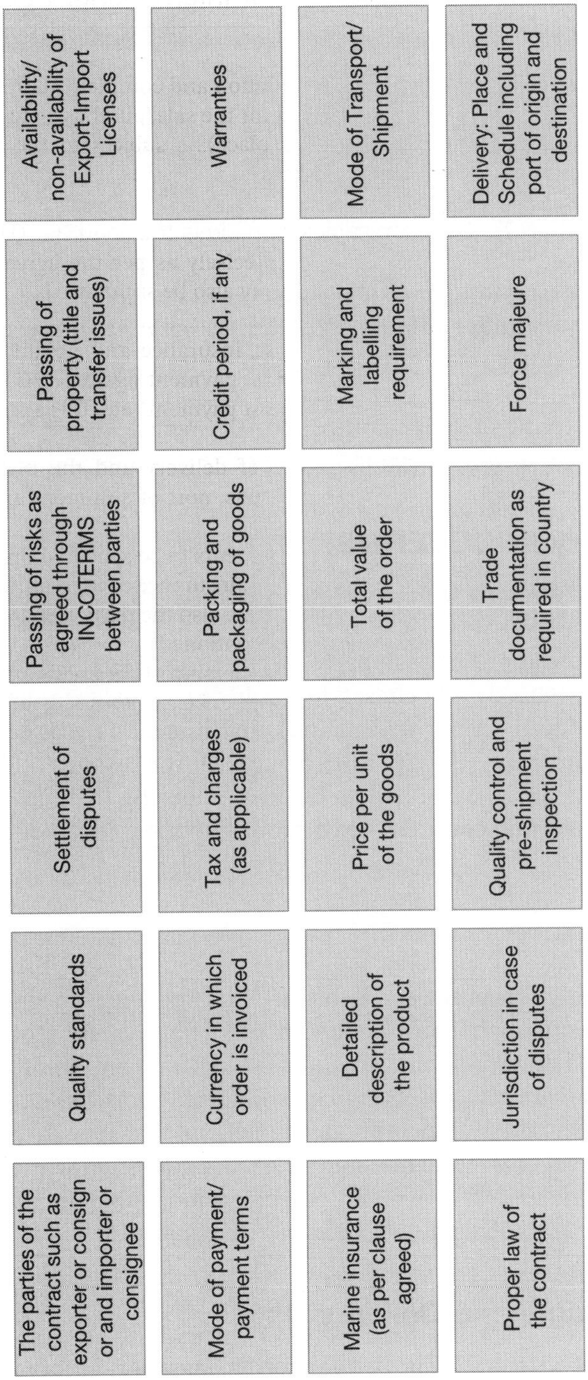

FIGURE 9.6 Key elements of ISC.

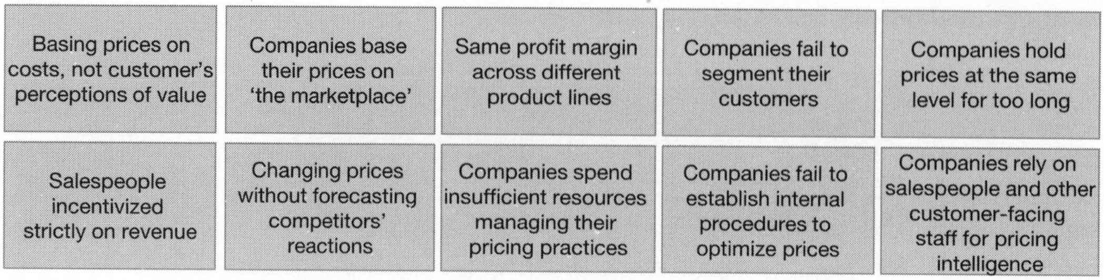

FIGURE 9.7 Common mistakes made in framing ISC.

an exporter should refer the pricing in light of obligations as under agreed INCOTERMS as costs and risks coverage responsibilities vary under different INCOTERMS of ICC. Hence, an exporter shall quote a competitive price in light of other trade terms like payments so as to attract more customers in a globally competitive environment. Trading parties should also clearly indicate how prices have been indicated, in kilo, gram, *tola*, tonne or other unit of measurements. Figure 9.7 depicts the common mistakes that an exporter can make while negotiating the price of goods and services internationally.

9.4.3 Terms of Delivery (INCOTERMS)

ICC, on the basis of long deliberations with associated stakeholders, publishes INCOTERMS almost every decade and recent publication was made in the year 2010. INCOTERMS 2010 publication has 11 INCOTERMS explaining obligations of each party (exporter and importer) on sharing of costs and risks in export operations. The INCOTERM chosen for trade deal by exporter and importer must indicate the named port or place (discharge of destination), and it shall be written as 'CIP Berlin' if the goods are destined to Berlin, Germany. INCOTERMS make clear the responsibilities and obligations of exporters as well as importers; hence, care shall be taken in choosing them as an error may result in financial losses which are the beyond control of exporter or importer. Terms of delivery are separately covered in detail in the book.

9.4.4 Payment Terms

An exporter has to be particularly concerned about the method of payments negotiated for the sales deal and to incorporate an appropriate method of payment in ISC. The payment term shall be clearly mentioned; for example, it can be D/A with 30 days credit or L/C without any credit period or sight L/C. If it is confirmed L/C at sight, the same is to be written as 'confirmed irrevocable L/C at sight' in the sales contract. Both trading parties should also incorporate the general and specific conditions for payment settlement; for example, what set of documents shall be needed for settlement of payment under L/C. Clear and specific terms of payment help in avoiding confusion and ambiguity in ISC. Figure 9.8 depicts the various safe and unsafe methods of payments for both trading parities, that is, exporter and importer.

9.4.5 Shipment Schedule and Delivery Date

An exporter should ensure that he/she shall be in a comfortable position to supply the goods or services to the importer on the delivery date as agreed and incorporated in ISC. In case the exporter is

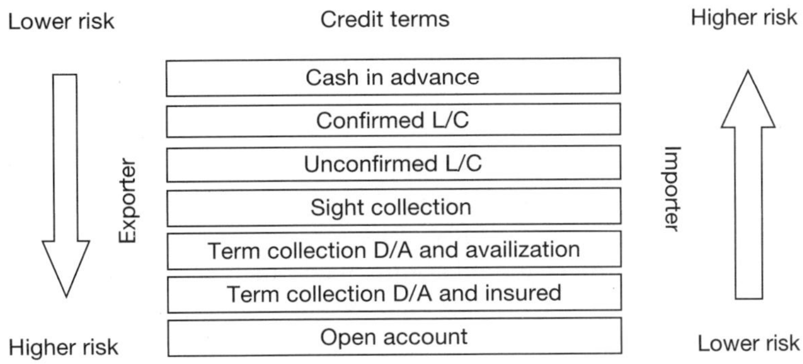

FIGURE 9.8 Payment–Risks matrix in international trade.

manufacturer exporter, he/she must keep a margin of at least 10 days in manufacturing and shipment date as sometimes the production schedules may suffer unexpected delay because of reasons which are beyond the control of an exporter. In case the exporter is merchant exporter, even then he/she is required to keep a margin of at least 15 days as he/she has to procure the goods only as per quality standards as agreed with the importer. Trading parties should also clearly incorporate the delivery schedule; for example, whether 'part' of 'partial' shipment is allowed are not. One must consider the fact that if the shipment is after the 'due date', then the importer will consider it as breach of contract and can make his/her reservations in accepting the delivery of goods or making the payments to the exporter. The delivery date should be clearly mentioned with date and day of month along with the year. Ambiguous words such as 'early as possible' or 'within 25 days from the receipt of order' shall be avoided as such words have no legal sanctity in case of disputes in the court of law. An exporter shall also ensure that he/she can arrange shipping space within delivery date and keep in touch with his/her freight forwarder for arranging the shipping space for the shipments.

9.4.6 Claims Clause in Sales Contract

One of the important concerns for both the trading parties is to bring clarity in settlement of claims with an insurance company in cases of losses occurred during the course of transit from point of origin to point of destination. As the international trade is full of risks exposing both the parties' business interests to various kinds of maritime hazards, damages, perils and losses, INCOTERMS help bring clarity about obligation regarding which party will bear the cost and risks in a trade transaction. Accordingly, trading parties can get their risks covered through insurance cover procured from an insurance company. Trading parties should be careful in explaining the claims procedure in ISC. Making claim procedure clear in ISC helps both trading parties to determine the responsibility of loss and settle the claims.

9.4.7 Arbitration Clause in Sales Contracts

There are three ways for dispute settlement in international trade: litigation, mediation and arbitration. Arbitration is preferred due to a variety of reasons such as least costly, least impact of differing legislation and clarity of scope of rules governing the conduct of the arbitration process. Litigation is more costly and one should follow the principle of 'no litigation in international trade', and mediations, especially in international trade, have scope for ambiguity and further result in litigation. International business disputes are settled in a completely different manner because the jurisdictions of exporter and importer are different. Disputes occur during trade transactions but what is important is that such disputes shall be determined in an amicable manner without having any large financial commitment by the exporter and importer. Hence, it is advisable that exporter as well as importer shall make clear the arbitration process or negotiations in ISC. ICC, Paris, is an international body working for devising, designing and synchronizing the international commercial practices and procedure norms related to trade mechanism; the regulatory framework has detailed some precautions for entering an arbitration clause which are explained as follows:

1. In case there is any dispute regarding the terms and conditions of ISC between the contracting parties of an international trade deal, the same has to be settled as per the provisions of ICC by one or more appointed arbitrators and such arbitration process of the disputes between the parties shall take place as per ICC rules in the International Court of Arbitration, Paris, for a speedy, transparent and amicable ruling without having any larger financial commitment by either of the contracting party.
2. ICC has specially told in its model code of conduct for arbitration process that the language of ISC shall be made clear, particularly in cases where the importers are from non-English-speaking country.
3. The contracting parties while framing ISC shall clearly incorporate in the contract that 'the decision made by the Court of Arbitration shall be final and binding upon all parties concerned'.
4. In countries having a poor legal and regulatory system of governance, it is advisable that the exporter shall take advice of legal experts regarding precautions shall he/she take to make the arbitration process enforceable on either party.

9.4.8 Force Majeure Clause

Force majeure literally means the occurrence of those events, damages or losses which are beyond the control of exporter, importer and insurer. 'Force majeure' clauses are also known as 'Acts of God' as the exporter, importer and insurer are helpless to perform the contract obligations due to events such as war, rebellion, tsunami, earthquake and floods. Some examples of events which fall under force majeure are as follows:

1. Natural disasters such as lightning, floods, earthquakes and hurricanes, such as administrative break-down of public order due to heavy floods in Chennai in 2015.
2. Wars between two countries or more countries or groups, riots such as sectarian, communal, religious and ethnic, or other major upheavals like the Gulf War or rebellion in Thailand by the military Junta.
3. Government restrictions as imposed by India in 1991 during balance of payments crisis or in case of international restriction for export to Iran as mandated under Security Council Resolution.
4. Other such failures of contracting parties which are beyond their control. Such performance failures may include failure on the part of subcontractors, suppliers and carriers, for example, failure of Gujarat exporters to send their shipments on time due to nationwide strike of truck operators.

The important point to be noted down is that 'force majeure' clauses are intended as an excuse of the party only in case it is seeable that exporter or importer has taken sufficient measures to avoid the mishappening, but such circumstances are really beyond his/her control.

9.4.9 Other Miscellaneous General Conditions of Sales Contract

Some other issues, terms and conditions may be included in ISC by the exporter and importer on the basis of their mutual agreement. For example, the responsibility of availing trade licences from DGFT for items which may become 'restricted or canalized' due to changes in foreign trade regime by DGFT. Usually, trading parties assist each other in getting these licences as no export or import can take place without these licences. *First*, trading parties can also provide the terms and conditions for frustration of contract on the failure of either party in availing these licences from regulatory authority. *Second*, trading parties should also clearly incorporate general conditions that the sales contract will automatically supersede the previous clauses in ISC once it is mutually agreed, accepted and signed by exporter and importer on any amendment and supplement to it. *Third*, trading parties should also agree that neither party will delegate or transfer their rights or obligations under the existing ISC to any third party without the written consent of the other party. *Fourth*, trading parties should clearly mention the name of the place where the parties have signed such contracts; for example, in the case of signing of a contract in New Delhi, it shall be clearly mentioned that 'New Delhi, India, is the place of signing of the present contract between the parties'. *Fifth*, trading parties should incorporate an additional clause on avoiding any kind of uncertainties and minimizing the losses, damages and risks in international trade transactions. *Finally*, both parties should agree to incorporate in future any other clause or terms or conditions which the exporter and importer find are mandatory in the execution of the contract and should be included in ISC.

In addition to the above, ISC has to be signed by all the contacting parties of the trade deal and such parties may include consignor or exporter and consignee or importer and any third party, that is, middlemen or agent or canalized agency. Both exporter and importer shall devote time and energy in reading, comprehending, explaining and in making of ISC as it is rightly said that 'prevention is better than cure'.

9.5 Professional Tips for Incorporating Sales Contract

In this section, we will discuss some of the professional tips which one should consider while incorporating ISC with another party to trade. Either party to trade deal must essentially give emphasis on the most important points such as price, conditions of payment, period of delivery and modalities connected with settlement of legal disputes.

9.5.1 Use Simple and Straight Language in Draft Sales Contract

Sales contracts in India are usually made in English language as it is globally accepted language for business. The use of proper English is important as its use in different parts of the world may have altogether different connotations for business people. It is advisable to use clear, simple and straightforward language, preferably English, in ISCs. Both parties should take care to avoid the use of poetic, slang and artistic language. The use of expressions, idioms, slang or any vernacular word shall be avoided as it will put ambiguity in the contract text regarding the executions of various terms and conditions by either party. One should also avoid the use of lots of abbreviations and if necessary, then they should be properly explained when incorporated in ISC.

9.5.2 Different Date Formats

Different date formats are used globally, for example, 01/04/16 in India is April 1, 2016; however, in some countries like European countries, the same shall be known as January 4, 2016. Hence, one should use the proper date format which offers clarity in understanding to either party irrespective of cultural and social differences in the use of date format in different parts of world. Such confusion can be avoided by putting the date in complete in numerical and alphabetical form. For example, in India, the DD-MM-YY is the predominant short form of the numeric date usage. Almost all government documents need to be filled in the DD-MM-YYYY format. An example of DD-MM-YYYY usage is the passport application form. Although not yet a common practice, the Bureau of Indian Standards of GOI introduced the standard named 'IS 7900:2001 (Revised in 2006) Data Elements and Interchange Formats—Information Interchange—Representation of Dates and Times' which officially recommends use of the date format YYYYMMDD, for example, 20150910 or 2015 09 10, or 2015-09-10 for the date 10 September 2015. Table 9.2 illustrates the different types of date formats used in some of the key trade partners of India which are YMD (year, month and day), DMY (day, month and year) and MDY (month, day and year).

9.5.3 Units of Measurement

The unit of measurement is different in some countries as compared to India. India follows the metric system of measurement which is popularly known as MKS (metre, kilo and second), while Britain follows the FPS System which means foot, pound and second. An exporter shall be careful in quoting the weight measurement, otherwise it may create problem in converting the price as per the importer's national measurement criteria. Additionally, it has also been seen that importers have problems in marketing and selling such products with different units of measurement as they are not aware about other country's measurement criteria. Table 9.3 illustrates the different types of units of measurements in world markets.

TABLE 9.2 Date Format in Various International Markets

	Format		
Country	**YMD**	**DMY**	**MDY**
India	No	Yes	No
China	Yes	No	No
Japan	Yes	No	No
The United Kingdom	Yes	Yes	No
The United States	Yes	No	Yes
United Arab Emirates	No	Yes	No

TABLE 9.3 Measurement Types Used in International Business

	Inches	Feet	Yards	Statue miles	Centimetres	Meters	Kilometres
Inch	1	0.83333	0.0277		2.54005	0.0254	
Foot	12	1	0.333		30.48006	0.304801	
Yard	36	3	1	0.00568	91.44018	0.914402	0.000914
Statute mile	63.360	5,280	1,760	1		1,609.347	1.609347
International nautical mile		6,076.10	2,025.36	1.150777			
United Nations nautical mile		6,080.20	2,026.73	1.51553			
Centimetre	0.3937	3.280833	1.093611		1	0.01	
Metre	39.37				100	1	0.001
Kilometre				0.62137		1000	1
Decimetre	3.037	0.328				0.1	
Decametre	393.7	32.8				10	
Hectometre		328.1					0.1
Myriametre				6.213712			10

9.5.4 Currency

Usually, the international trade transactions are conducted in freely convertible foreign exchange. In India, FEMA, 2000 and allied rules thereunder clearly specify the realization of export proceeds only in 'freely convertible foreign currency'. The point to be considered is that currency chosen shall not be volatile in the market; for example, if US dollar is the currency of exporter contract, an exporter will have lower realization from export proceeds in case Indian rupee appreciates and vice versa, meaning higher realization of export proceeds if rupee depreciates. Hence, an exporter should trade in hard currency, which is less volatile in the international market and incorporate such currency as 'currency of invoice' in ISC. An exporter should select a suitable and stable foreign currency for invoicing which should also be highly liquid in the foreign exchange market, for example, euro, dollar and yen. Table 9.4 illustrates the list of some currencies with their alphabetic code and numeric code.

TABLE 9.4 List One: Currency, Fund and Precious Metal Codes

Entity	Currency	Alphabetic Code	Numeric Code
China	Yuan renminbi	CNY	156
India	Indian rupee	INR	356
Indonesia	Rupiah	IDR	360
Malaysia	Malaysian ringgit	MYR	458
United Arab Emirates	UAE dirham	AED	784
UK	Pound sterling	GBP	826
USA	US dollar	USD	840

9.5.5 Interpretation or Translation

It has been seen that in some cases importer or consignee is requesting that ISC shall be bilingual, for example, in Chinese and English language. Efforts shall be made that there is no ambiguity in translation of language from one to another in ISC to the contracting parties. Maintenance of accuracy of business translation is crucial for effective and efficient execution of contract between the parties. The point of caution is that different languages in different countries can have an entirely different meaning and can result in costly disputes. Hence, one should be cautious while translating the sales contract from one language to another.

9.5.6 Signing of the Contract

In case there are more than one pages in ISC, all pages should be signed by contracting parties as per the mandatory requirement of ICC. It is seen that trading parties sometimes sign a sales contract without understanding the key clauses and resultant business obligations. A faulty agreement of international sale may lead to unnecessary delays and frustration of contract. The agreement is not only the initial point of the international business process but also the critical point around which an international sale of goods and services between trading parties revolves. When the time comes to sign the sales agreement, it should be ensured by trading parties that they understand everything written in ISC and should not sign if they have any doubt or uncertainty about any of the clauses or meaning thereof. The bottom line is that both trading parties should ensure that they are fully and satisfactorily aware of their respective business obligations in terms of the sales agreement.

9.6 Preparation of the Export Sales Contract

While preparing ISC, the exporter shall take the advice or legal opinion of a legal expert or lawyer in case he/she has any doubt regarding any terms and conditions as engrained in ISC. Contracting parties have to ensure that all terms and conditions which are to be included in ISC are well negotiated, precisely discussed, overtly informed and mutually agreed between the parties Table 9.5. If an exporter feels that there is any ambiguity/uncertainties/misunderstanding, he/she should contact the importer and clarify those terms and conditions. As already mentioned, litigation in international trade is a costly process; hence, each effort shall be aimed to avoid misunderstanding as it will cost exporter money, time and energy in unnecessary litigation arising out of such ambiguity/uncertainties.

Utmost care is required while preparing ISC, particularly regarding the various trade terms to be agreed upon between the contracting parties. Some of the elements which are very important and may have adverse repercussions in distribution of responsibilities and obligations are mode of payments, delivery date, credit period expected by the importer, quality issues, port of shipment, post of destination, mode of transit, insurance policy clauses and any preferential benefits, if available.

Export pricing of international consignment is based on various trade terms, particularly the INCOTERMS being used in quoting a sales deal. An exporter has to choose an INCOTERM which maximizes his/her profit, reduces his/her responsibilities, risks and obligations. Any INCOTERM in E and F categories shall be acceptable to any exporter but importer will always try to ask the exporter to accept any INCOTERM from Categories C and D. However, every trade decision, in the globalized era, is based on a trade-off between exporter and importer in deciding the various terms to be used in

TABLE 9.5 Distribution of Responsibility for ISC under Commonly Used INCOTERMS

Determination Criteria	EXW	FAS	FOB	CFR	CIF	DDP
Exporter's factory or premises	EBI	I	I	I	I	I
Invoice and packing list and certificate of origin	ER	ER	ER	ER	ER	ER
Load on to carrier, inland transport/insurance costs, demurrage charges, export documents formalities, unloading cargo at port	I	ER	ER	ER	ER	ER
Payment of port dues	I	ERBI	ER	ER	ER	ER
Notice of name of vessel/sailing date, loading berth, delivery time	I	I	I	ER	ER	ER
Load on ship	I	I	ERBI	ERB	ERB	ERB
Bill of lading/Airway bill	I	I	ER	ER	ER	ER
Marine/Air insurance charges	I	I	I	I	ER	ER
Cost of ocean/Air shipment	I	I	I	ER	ER	ER
Unload at port of import, port authority charges, customs duties and taxes, demurrage charges at port of destination, import documentation formalities	I	I	I	I	I	ER

E: Exporter's expenses
R: Exporter's responsibility
B: Point where importer assumes risks
I: Importer's responsibility

Source: The author.

a sales contract. Once the export quotation involving various elements as discussed above has been agreed upon, it will be tough for either party to ask for change as each party shall try to demand some favour under such circumstances from another party.

Errors and omissions of word or language, although shall be avoided to the best, can happen during the process of preparation of export quotation by the exporter. Under such circumstances, some importers may try to force the exporters to make a reduction in price or increase in quality of goods on the basis of such omission and errors. It is advisable that as a precautionary measure, it is desirable to add the acronym E&OE which stands for 'errors and omissions excepted', and exporter shall also make it clear that all typographical errors are subject to error and omissions.

9.7 Summary

International business in today's volatile and ambiguous times is far more complex and riskier, primarily due to varying 'legal regimes and jurisdictions' governing the conduct, control and regulation of two or more trading parties in a trade transaction. Trading parties, in today's ambiguous trade regime, avoid accepting any legal and trading regime favouring either party to trade as it exposes them to potential business risks arising out of misinterpretation, judicial corruption and bureaucratic anarchism.

Trading parties always prefer the harmonized trade regime like CISG facilitating the sale and purchase of internationally traded goods in a transparent and fair manner among trading parties. Global trade institutions such as UNCITRAL, ICC, UNCTAD, WCO, IMO, WTO and UN/CEFACT have played a key role in evolving, improving, framing and strengthening the international regulatory framework governing the sales of internationally traded goods. Accordingly, on the basis of consensus among contracting parties in the Vienna Convention, a final draft of CISG (Figure 9.2) is prepared by UNCITRAL. The adoption of the present model sales contract under 'Convention on the Limitation Period in the International Sale of Goods' as amended by the Protocol of 11 April 1980, provides modern, uniform legislation for the international sale of goods. If sale transaction is negotiated incorporating sales contract under this convention, it will apply whenever contracts for the sale of goods are concluded between parties with a place of business in contracting states. CISG governs contracts related to export–import of merchandised goods only and that even between private parties clearly excluding sales to consumers, sales of services and specified sales, if any. The Vienna Convention does not specify the validity of the contract and the effect of the sales contract on transfer to title. It, however, deals with the process of formation of the sales contract, which is concluded by the exchange of offer and acceptance. CISG has 101 articles so as to define, execute and regulate the sales contract. The sale of goods in international markets entails a number of legal and regulatory challenges for an exporter which may arise out of 'conflict of law' and legal formation of the contract. For example, various local rules and acts may be in conflict with ISC, thus, one has to consider the legal and regulatory issues not only related to ISC but also associated laws such as rules governing the relationships between the exporter and agents or distributors, trademarks, patents product liability, promotion and payment terms particularly for L/C which is governed by not only contract law but also by UCPDC 600. Domestic trade legislations such as FEMA, 2000, the Customs Act, 1962, the FTDR Act, 1992, Export (Quality Control and Inspection) Act, 1963, and allied international commercial practices have their impact on the formation and execution of ISC. Sales contract incorporates important clauses such as the name of trading parties, quality standards, settlement of disputes, passing of risks under agreed INCOTERMS, passing of property (title and transfer issues), availability/non-availability of EXIM licences, mode of payment or payment terms, currency in which order is invoiced, tax and charges (as applicable), packing and packaging of goods, credit period, if any, warranties, marine insurance (as per clause agreed), detailed description of the product, price per unit of the goods, total value of the order, marking and labelling requirement, mode of transport/shipment, proper law of the contract, jurisdiction in case of disputes, quality control and pre-shipment inspection, trade documentation as required in a country, force majeure, cargo delivery place and schedule including port of origin and destination.

Review Exercises

Multiple Choice Questions

1. Model sales contract for international sales of goods is proposed under which of the following conventions?
   a. Paris Convention
   b. Vienna Convention
   c. London Convention
   d. Basel Convention
   e. None of the above

2. Draft of model sales contract is prepared by which of the following international bodies?
   a. ICC
   b. International Banking Institute
   c. London Institute of Underwriters
   d. UNCITRAL
   e. None of the above
3. CISG was signed in which of the following years?
   a. 1980
   b. 1964
   c. 1974
   d. 1996
   e. None of the above
4. How many countries in the world have signed CISG?
   a. 83
   b. 73
   c. 63
   d. 85
   e. None of the above
5. For applicability of law, the term *lex foci* means
   a. The applicable law will be of the place where the contract is performed
   b. The applicable law will be of the place where the property is situated
   c. The applicable law will be of the country in which the case is tried for
   d. The applicable law will be of the country where the contract is made
   e. None of the above
6. For applicability of law, the term *lex loci* solutions means
   a. The applicable law will be of the place where the contract is performed
   b. The applicable law will be of the place where the property is situated
   c. The applicable law will be of the country in which the case is tried for
   d. The applicable law will be of the country where the contract is made
   e. None of the above
7. Which of the following is the main legislation regulating the conduct of foreign trade in India which can be sometimes in conflict with sales contract?
   a. FTDR Act, 1992
   b. FEMA 2000
   c. Export (Quality Control and Inspection) Act, 1963
   d. Customs Act, 1962
   e. None of the above
8. Which of the following is the main legislation regulating the conduct of foreign exchange in India which can be sometimes in conflict with sales contract?
   a. FTDR Act, 1992
   b. FEMA, 2000
   c. Export (Quality Control and Inspection) Act, 1963
   d. Customs Act, 1962
   e. None of the above

9. The term 'force majeure' in sales contract refers to
   a. Acts of God
   b. Acts of devils
   c. Acts of negligence
   d. Acts of caution
   e. Acts of terrorism

10. Which of the following commercial rules are most important for sharing of risks and responsibilities in international sales transactions?
   a. INCOTERMS 2010
   b. UCPDC 600
   c. URC 522
   d. International Standard Banking Practices 15
   e. None of the above

Critical Thinking Questions

1. Write an introductory note on the significance of ISC in EXIM operations.
2. Critically explain the rules aimed at harmonization of ISC under the Vienna Convention.
3. What are the key legal dimensions which affect the formation of ISC? Examine.
4. What are the important elements of contract formation and execution in sales contract? Appraise critically.
5. What are the professional tips one should consider while preparing ISC? Explain.

Further Reading

1. Reserve Bank of India (Exchange Control Department). 2000. *Foreign Exchange Management (Export of Goods and Services) Regulations, 2000*. Mumbai: Reserve Bank of India.

CHAPTER 10

Processing of an Export Order

CHAPTER OBJECTIVES

- To explain the nature of an export order in international trade transactions.
- To discuss the process of negotiation, receipts and acknowledgement of an export order.
- To discuss the process of scrutiny, examination, clarification and confirmation of an export order.
- To explain the various steps in the processing of an export order.
- To discuss the post-export documentation for realizing payments and claiming incentives.

10.1 Introduction

The initiation of any trade deal in international trade begins with the formation of an 'export order' between two trading parties. Hence, an exporter order is an important document as it works as the base for other documents to be prepared during the stage of processing of an export order aimed at the transport of goods from one country to another, including the transfer of title/ownership and realization of payments. The formation of an export order begins with certain commercial documents shared between an exporter and an importer. In case an exporter wants to sell his/her goods abroad as he/she has surplus domestic supply, he/she will approach an importer; similarly in the case of domestic demand, an importer approaches the exporter for supply of goods. The forces of demand and supply shape any trade transaction. Once an initiative for sales or purchase is made by either party and is negotiated and agreed by another, the export order is made between two trading parties. The processing of an export order entails further documentation as goods have to move from boundaries of one territorial country to another involving EXIM clearance from customs authorities. An exporter or importer has to book the carrier (ship/aeroplane/rail/truck) depending on INCOTERMS agreed and has to procure insurance cover so as to minimize the transport risks.

The processing of an export order involves several steps at both pre-export and post-export stages. Both the trading parties have to carefully examine and scrutinize the terms and conditions of the export order before confirming it to the other party. Each trading party has to consider certain areas of trade negotiations very carefully before confirming the export order. Once a trade order is received by either party, the first task is to acknowledge the receipt of the export or import order to the other party. Acknowledging an export order is different from confirming it, and it is advised that the exporter must make proper scrutiny of the export order before confirming it to the foreign buyer.

Scrutiny of the export order is also important as it provides a last chance to make necessary changes in an export order. An exporter must evaluate that the export order is conforming to the terms and conditions as communicated to the importer. The exporter should examine important issues such as mode of payments, price of goods or services, delivery date and schedule, product standards and specifications, pre-shipment inspection and quality compliance, special packaging and cargo packing, labelling and marking, freight and insurance issues, number of items, size of ordered quantity, handling instructions and marks, issues of tariff preference and number of documents required for documentary compliance. If an exporter has any doubt or confusion, then he/she can seek clarification from the importer in that regard and accordingly renegotiate the terms and conditions to amend the export order. Once the scrutiny of the export order is over and if the exporter is satisfied that he/she can honour the terms and conditions of the export order, he/she can confirm the export order to the importer with his/her thanks.

Initiation of a trade deal between two trading parties is purely driven by forces of demand and supply. When an importer contacts an exporter, he/she approaches him/her through 'purchase quotation' and when an exporter approaches an importer to sell something, he/she sends a 'proforma invoice'. Based on trade negotiation between trading parties, either party can confirm the EXIM order and both the parties should take necessary steps to enter a formal ISC. UNCITRAL has framed standardized clauses for the formation of ISC. Both exporter and importer are free to make necessary changes in model sales contract and accordingly ISC can be just a one-page document and in some other cases, it may be a very complex 15-page booklet including many appendices, additional conditions and so on. Sometimes, exporter and importer execute the trade transaction merely on the basis of trade documents, thus having an implied or construed contract. However, it is advisable that exporters must enter international sales contract with importer as international trade is full of risks and sales contract ensures legal protection through accepted trade documents during litigation or arbitration in case of disputes. ICC also advises exporters and importers to pen down the sales contract in order to avoid disputes and if disputes even occur, ISC helps in the arbitration process to be progressed easily with strong evidence. In some countries, it is mandatory to enter ISC. All these issues need the attention of an exporter in advance to avoid any unforeseen situation in the future.

In reality, an EXIM transaction is deemed to be successfully concluded only after the exporter has been able to deliver the consignment in accordance with the export contract and has received payment from the importer and claimed all the incentives, drawbacks and other benefits from the government. In order to successfully conclude the trade transactions, one should understand the complete export chain from procurement of raw material to designing and processing of goods, finding out buyers and then successfully executing the trade transaction. One should have sound knowledge of product, trade channels, trade rules and regulations, commercial practices, contemporary business environment, business cultures, etiquettes and business practices of countries involved to successfully process the EXIM transactions. Both the parties should be extremely well versed about micro-level issues in EXIM management which are trade documentation practices, regulatory compliance, payment terms, terms of delivery, packing and marking standards, price terms, delivery schedule, product specifications, pre-shipment inspection and quality compliance, nature of goods, suitability of transport mode including managing associated marine insurance, trade reference issues and understanding of banking channels. Both exporter and importer should exercise due caution before confirming any EXIM transaction. If they cannot spare time for all this, they should appoint/assign a trusted manager so as to take care of all issues related to the management of EXIM operations from place of dispatch to place of consumption.

10.2 Formation of an Export Order

Any EXIM transaction is purely a demand–supply transaction between two countries (Figure 10.1). Demand of goods and services can be due to natural reasons such as some countries do not produce rice and import it from rice-producing countries. Demand can be due to other economic reasons such as factor endowment, comparative cost advantages and absolute advantages. For example, India has more skilled labour; thus, majority of India's exports contain a significant part of labour, for example, gems and jewellery, handloom, handicraft, carpets and so on. Similarly, some countries enjoy comparative cost advantages in the supply of certain goods, thus become low-cost suppliers and other countries in the world economic system import these goods from such low-cost suppliers. Various trade theories propound the reasons for trade with the end result that international trade transaction is purely a demand–supply transaction. An exporter from country with excess production of agro-produce is bound to contact buyers from countries where such produce is in demand. Hence, when an exporter approaches an importer for supply of certain goods or services, he/she approaches the buyer(s) with 'proforma invoice'. Similarly, when an importer approaches the suppliers (exporters) to buy or procure something, he/she sends the 'purchase or import quotation'.

Hence, trade transaction may begin from either side depending on demand and supply forces. The proforma invoice or import quotations are the starting point of contact and negotiation between an exporter and importer on terms and conditions of the sales contract. It is rightly said that processing of an export order starts with the receipt of an export order which can be written or implied implying that when contracted, negotiated and agreed in a model sales contract, it becomes written sales contract or when executed on the basis of trade documents (invoice, packing list, bill of lading), it is considered as an implied sales contract. Any of the following forms can be types of export order between two trading parties:

1. An exporter initiates the trade deal through 'proforma invoice'. Exporter and importer negotiate and agree on certain terms and conditions of business to which importer accepts, stamps and signs, and acknowledges to the exporter. Proforma invoice is an auxiliary commercial document which has standardized contents as per the UN layout key containing information on name and address of the exporter, name and address of the consignee, exporter's IEC number, proforma invoice number and date, port of loading, place of loading, port of destination, place of destination, cargo description, price, rate and total amount, number and size of containers, buyer's order

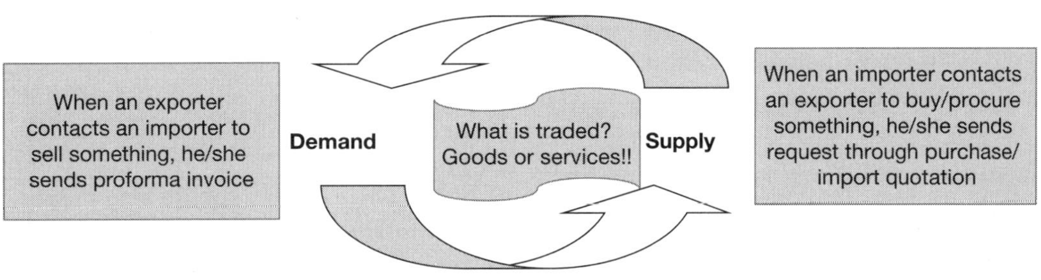

FIGURE 10.1 Demand and supply forces shape the formation of EXIM order.

number and date, trade terms like INCOTERMS and payment terms as agreed between exporter and importer.

2. Import quotation or purchase order is placed by the importer. Both parties negotiate and agree on certain business terms of sales deals which the exporter accepts, signs and stamps with seal and sends it to the importer, thus confirming export order. It has all commercial aspects of a trade deal such as name and addresses of consignor and consignee, IEC number of importer, import quotation number and date, quantity demanded, cargo description, quality issues, payment mode, INCOTERMS, price, rates, number of units, port of dispatch and destination, and total amount.
3. Trade negotiation can begin formally with either instrument or informally through email/telephone, web query and so on between exporter and importer. As confirmation of export order, the importer opens L/C in favour of the exporter. L/C is a contractual agreement whereby the issuing bank undertakes the responsibility of making payment to an exporter on behalf of an importer subject to fulfilment of agreed terms and conditions of L/C.

Any of the above forms of initiation of trade deal leads to the conclusion of the export order when agreed and accepted by another party. In the case of a long-term contract, it is advisable to draft and sign a model sales contract either under local trade rules or under model sales contract as agreed among countries in the Vienna Convention on international sales of goods.

10.3 Negotiation, Receipt and Acknowledgement of an Export Order

In export operations, the processing of an export order starts with the receipt of an export order which may be initiated by either party, exporter or importer. When an exporter approaches a buyer, he/she communicates a willingness to sell through 'proforma invoice' and in case buyer approaches seller for imports, he/she sends him/her 'import quotation' or 'purchase quotation'. Based on negotiation between exporter and importer, an export order is placed by the importer to exporter indicating his/her wiliness to import the agreed goods or services as per negotiated terms and conditions of imports. Hence, an export order, in a form, is an agreement between two trading parties (importer and exporter) before the exporter actually starts producing or procuring goods for exports. An export order can be in the form of a written ISC or L/C or 'purchase order' or simply 'singed proforma invoice' by the importer in favour of the exporter. Each form of these export orders has different legal standing and are used as per the established trading practices, nature and size of export order and trust between trading parties. Once an export order is received by the exporter, he/she should acknowledge the receipt of export order. The exporter should indeed thank the importer for placing trust in him/her for this export order and indicate his/her enthusiasm to serve importer's expectations better. The exporter should simply write a letter or email to importer acknowledging and thanking him/her for the export order. The exporter should also mention that he/she will come in touch with importer shortly after scrutinizing the export order. Letter of thanks shall be formal and shall not be too long. The draft of the letter of acknowledgement and thanks is exhibited in Box 10.1.

BOX 10.1 ▸ Specimen of Letter of Acknowledgement and Thanks from Exporter to Importer

REF No.: ....
Date: ....

Dear .... (Name of Importer)

I hereby solemnly confirm the receipt of your export order no. ....dated .... for supply of cotton shirts as per following details as mutually negotiated and agreed.

1. Quantity.......................................: .... Shirts
2. No. and size specification ....: ....
3. Date of delivery............................: ....
4. INCOTERMS................................: ....
5. Payment terms ....: ....
6. Quality specification......................: ....
7. Packing and labelling....................: ....
8. Any other issue

I extend you warm thanks and deep appreciation for reposing faith in my firm through this order. We shall work rigorously and come true to your expectations and trust.

With warm regards

Exporter (Name)
Firm (Name)

10.4 Scrutiny, Examination and Clarification of an Export Order

On receipt of export order, an exporter should examine its terms and conditions and scrutinize the various clauses of the contract so as to understand the overt and covert intricacies involved in the execution of this export order. Any mistake by the exporter at this crucial stage can make an order a loss of an important buyer. The exporter should exercise due caution for examination and scrutiny of export order and if required, can take help from an expert to understand the business intricacies as all subsequent actions and reactions shall depend on the terms and conditions of the export order. The key areas of scrutiny are product description (HS code of product), product specification, terms of delivery and payment, delivery date, insurance and inspection clauses, documents required for payment settlement, port of loading, port of destination, choice of mode of transport, currency of invoice, exchange regulations and associated financial risks and so on. The exporter should also examine issues such as packing, labelling and marking non-tariff issues such as sanitary–phytosanitary, technical barriers to trade (TBT), the attitude of custom official(s) in the country of import, involved maritime risks and contemporary business environment of country of import. In case of satisfaction to these aspects, the exporter should confirm the export order and in case of doubt, he/she should ask for clarifications from an importer. If the importer fails to constructively respond to the exporter's concerns and is engaged in fraudulent practices, the exporter should refuse to execute the export order. In the following subsections, we will discuss the specific areas of precautions while examining the export order.

10.4.1 Product HS Code, Size and Specification

As HS codes are harmonized only up to six digits globally, the products' classification may vary up to eight digits from one country to another. More so, there are some countries having HS code nomenclature up to 10 digits and 12 digits. The actual description of ordered cargo may vary from what an exporter meant to sell from a country following 8-digit harmonized nomenclature. Hence, an exporter should examine the ITC(HS) practices of both the countries, that is, home country and country of import before confirming the export order and make sure that he/she has received the order for the same product for which he/she has sent proforma invoice or has received the import quotations. There is always a scope of misunderstanding as the exporter may have sent two or three quotations for other purchase orders to the same importer and may mean confirmation of one order instead of what importer means to import, hence, the exporter should examine the proforma invoice number or quotation number with export order, letter reference and date. Following are specific areas that an exporter must scrutinize in harmonized trade nomenclature:

1. Whether goods are allowed for export, that is, free for export; if restricted, an exporter must avail the 'special export licence' as mandated from DGFT. If the goods are under 'state trading enterprise' trade regime, then an exporter should enter 'letter of intent' with nominated canalizing agency and should never enter the export contract with foreign buyer if the ordered goods are classified as 'prohibited'.
2. Whether goods are regulated for exports, that is, have restriction of 'minimum export price' or 'maximum export packing size' or 'maximum export quantity'. An exporter should examine the second schedule of ITC(HS) nomenclature (export policy) to check that ordered goods are not falling under any price or quantity quota.
3. Whether an export authorization is required from a specific agency; for example, exporters of medicine require special authorization from the Central Drugs Standard Control Organization or exporters of dual use technology require SCOMET authorization from SCOMET committee of Ministry of Commerce and Industry, GOI. Similarly, those dealing in radioactive goods (e.g., X-ray machine, ECG, ultrasound and so on) should have authorization from the Department of Atomic Energy or other mandated bodies to this effect and an exporter of seeds of any type should check with Plant Quarantine Department that there is no additional authorization required for exports.
4. Whether country of import is under any international sanctions which restrict the free export or import with the country including restrictions on settlement of payments; for example, United Nations Security Council (UNSC) Resolution mandates for international sanctions from member countries of the Islamic Republic of Iran due to its nuclear energy programme. Similarly, Ivory Coast also has international sanctions for export and imports. Iran also faces international sanctions from UNSC for no trade in arms and ammunition from any member country of the UN.
5. In addition to country-specific trade sanctions, there can be firm-specific or process-specific international sanctions from multilateral organizations under the aegis of the UN. For example, Kimberley agreement as agreed among countries at the UN mandates for international trade of only those diamonds which are genuinely extracted by sovereign countries or authorized firms

and blood diamonds which are extracted by unauthorized terror group should never be allowed for sale in international markets. Similarly, the UN continuously updates the list of certain firms that are debarred from engagement in international trade and commerce as they are charged against funding terrorism, civil war activities or have links with a military dictator, thus dictating genuine democratic aspirations of people.

In addition to these policy issues, an exporter should also scrutinize the issues related to sizes and specifications; for example, there can be a mistake by an exporter to misunderstand the trousers for men instead for women where the sizes can be the same but fitting specifications and design patterns are always different. Following are some other examples of common mistakes that an exporter can make while negotiating the size and specifications of goods:

1. An Indian pharmacy exporter has supplied the non-Food and Drug Administration (FDA) rules complied medicines and drugs to an US importer which will never be cleared by the US customs for imports.
2. A leading Indian truck manufacturer gifted trucks to UNICEF Afghanistan without changing the driver's seat to 'right side' as Afghanistan is a right-side driven country while Indian road norms mandate for left-side driven transport vehicles. Afghan customs refused to clear the trucks which were finally called back as these gifted trucks fail 'homologation norm' of the Afghan government.
3. An export firm based at Hyderabad supplied meat to a firm in the United Arab Emirates. Exporter checked all specifications but forgot to get a certificate from the local 'Maulvi' to certify that it is 'Halal' meat meaning fit for use in Islamic countries. Importer refused to make payments knowing the fact that meat is biologically fit for consumption, is of best quality and priced at industry standards but not complying with the Islamic way of eating.
4. An Indian exporter gets an order from a German importer for supply of iron pipes. As per proforma invoice, the circumference size was given 0.5 cm; however, the importer requested for circumference size of 0.50 cm in the export order. Exporter makes a mistake in judging that 0 is a limiting factor here and supplied pipes having circumference 0.51. Importer refused to make payments as goods supplied are not as per order. It is to be noted that 0 acted as a limiting factor in this case. Hence, it is advisable that exporter should read between the lines and may take inferences from 0 as well.

10.4.2 Quality Standard and Inspection Agency

An exporter should examine the quality standards as quoted in the export order and make sure whether he/she will be in a position to comply with these standards or not. Second, whether the mandated inspection agency has its office in India as sometimes importer may ask for inspection agency other than Export Inspection Council (EIC) and other allied Indian agencies, for example, Bureau Veritas, Intertek, SGV, Alex Stewart International, NQAQSR North America and so on. GOI has prescribed mandatory export quality inspection in certain cases as there has been increased complaints against Indian consignment for non-compliance, for example, honey, basmati, spices, eggs and egg powder, red chilli powder, milk products, mangoes and so on. If the name of the agency is other than EIC or allied agency as prescribed in Appendix 2G of FTP 2015–2020, then exporter should also verify whether he/she will be in a position to get the required inspection done from mandated agency and costs therein as sometimes the cost of quality inspection may be very high, especially in case of European quality inspection agencies. In case of the buyer's nominated agency, it is advisable to get the agency name incorporated in the 'export order' itself so as to resolve any subsequent disputes for quality compliance and financial implications therein.

10.4.3 Currency of Invoice, Credit Period and Payment Terms

FTP 2015–2020 mandates that currency of invoice for export order can be Indian rupee or any 'freely convertible foreign currency' but payment realization must be in freely convertible foreign currency. FEMA, 2000, and allied regulations known as FEM (Export of Goods and Services) Regulations, 2000, mandate for realization of export proceeds strictly in freely convertible currency except in cases of export to Nepal, Bhutan and ACU countries where payment can be realized in rupees subject to rules and ceiling as mandated under FEMA. Rupee settlement is also allowed for exports if such payment is realized from the nostro account of foreign banks located in India in compliance with RBI rules and regulations. More so, FEM (Exports of Goods and Services) Regulations mandate maximum credit period of 270 days except in cases of prior permission from RBI to this effect. In addition to this, an exporter should check whether the terms of payment are the same as negotiated and agreed between exporter and importer. Advance payment is considered the safest followed by L/C, D/P and D/A. Open account is the most unsafe method from exporter's point of view.

An exporter must scrutinize the authenticity of L/C, credit standing of issuing bank and financial condition of importer's country. He/she should also examine the transactional cost involved in presentation, negotiation and settlement of payment under L/C. He/she should leverage the appropriate method of payment keeping in mind the credit-worthiness of the importer, banking channel and economic-politico environment of the country of import (Box 10.2). Open account payments are not advisable as jurisdictions of countries vary and there is no international convention protecting exporters through arbitration for getting payments. Following are some issues of minute investigation by an exporter while accepting a particular mode of payment, as international sale is considered as a gift until the payment for such sale is not guaranteed.

BOX 10.2 ▸ Areas of Precautions in International Payment Settlement

- L/C even after being considered a safe method is open to vagaries of rules and regulations governing it, for example, UCPDC 600 and ISBP 15 norms. The exporter should always prefer L/C available with Indian bank and confirmed by the Indian bank. Exporters shall also check the credit-worthiness of the issuing bank through world banks almanac.
- Terms and conditions of L/C can comply with or not especially the documentary compliance as banks deal in documents and not the goods. Settlement of payment is by negotiation or by honour.
- The exporter has to look whether the credit validity period is sufficient for the collection of all relevant documents or not, if no, it is advisable to get it extended by the buyer in the beginning itself.
- Under documentary collections, an exporter should examine whether draft (bill of exchange) is drawn at sight or 'usance'. Whether it is drawn on the bank of the importer or the buyer himself/herself.
- What are exchange control regulations of the buyer country? It is possible that the buyer may be interested to make payments but due to the importer's country balance of payment problems, the exporter may not receive payments in freely convertible currency as per Indian regulations.

10.4.4 Managing Risks in Export Operations

There are a number of risks involved in export operations. First and foremost is the credit risk and others include carriage risk, currency risk and country risk (Figure 10.2). Credit risk can be insured to a great extent by insisting upon payment terms under irrevocable L/C from the foreign buyer. An appropriate policy from ECGC can also be obtained for this purpose. The country risks can also be covered by ECGC regarding currency risk, that is, possible loss due to adverse fluctuation in the exchange rate can be avoided by obtaining forward cover from the bank authorized to deal in foreign exchanges, alternatively you can obtain export order in Indian rupee. Carriage risk, that is, possible loss of cargo in transit can be covered by taking a marine insurance policy from general insurance companies.

Additionally, the exporter is under credit risk of non-payment by the buyer, his/her bank or any other bank involved in the process of payment settlement. Country of import may suddenly impose foreign exchange restrictions controlling the flight of capital from the country, thus impacting exporter's payment realization. Sometimes, import may default or may even become insolvent; hence, an exporter is always exposed to credit risks. The exporter should examine whether there is need for procuring a credit insurance cover under a relevant policy from ECGC.

10.4.5 Terms of Delivery and Obligations

Terms of delivery or INCOTERMS are rules framed by ICC, Paris, which define the sharing of costs (for transport and carriage) and risks between exporter and importer and associated obligations of each party. The risk coverage (cost of insurance) and cost of carriage may vary as per agreed INCOTERMS. Hence, an exporter must examine INCOTERMS prior to confirmation of export order. Figure 10.3 depicts the risk–costs matrix of 11 INCOTERMS between exporter and importer.

An exporter shall examine the terms of delivery and his/her risks, costs and responsibilities under the agreed INCOTERMS. He/she should examine the possibility of taking cost-effective but appropriate

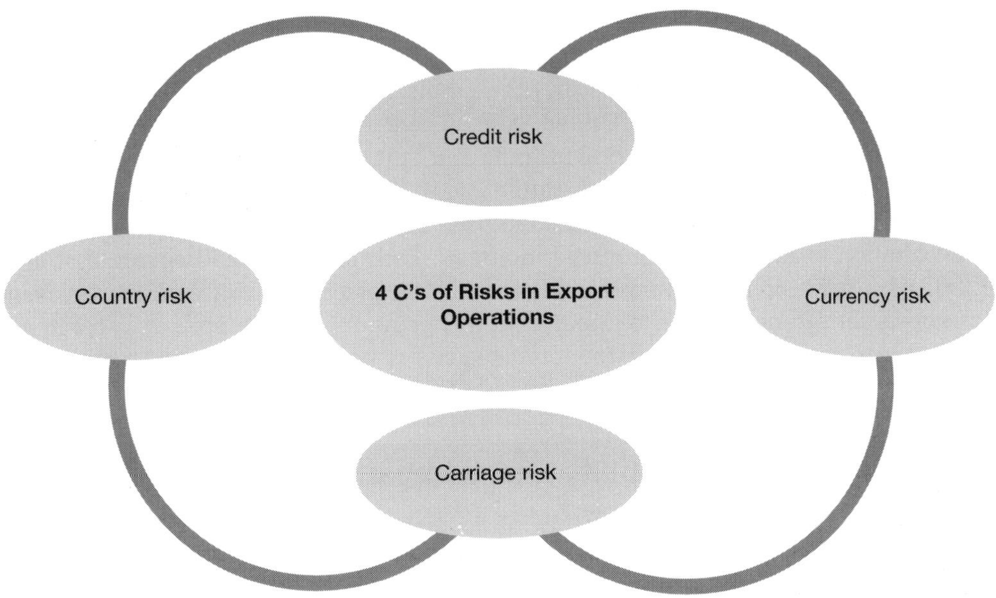

FIGURE 10.2 Managing 4C's of risks in export operations.

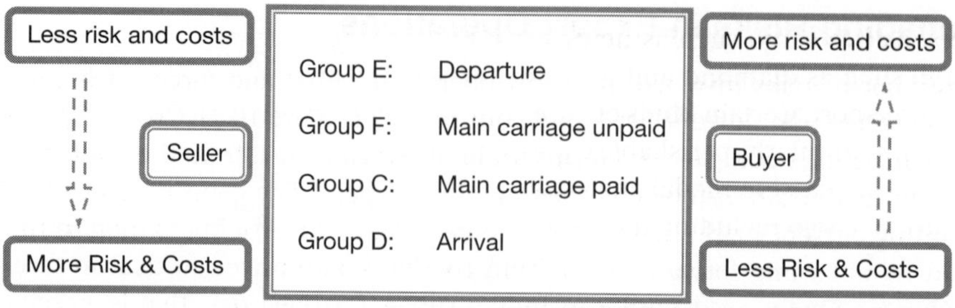

FIGURE 10.3 Risk–costs matrix under INCOTERMS 2010 for exporters and importers.

insurance cover for the goods, if responsibility falls on him/her under agreed terms of delivery. Under INCOTERMS 2010, both trading parties are obligated to coverage of insurance policy so that each trading party can take necessary measures to protect his/her risks, take additional covers, if required. An exporter should also discuss from where insurance has to be taken, that is, in India or from the country of import or from a third country keeping in mind the relevant rules and regulations governing the procurement of insurance policies for export transactions. Insurance policies are mainly divided into three types, A, B and C, under institute cargo clauses and risk coverage may vary from one clause to another. There are additional clauses as well, for example, war clause, terrorism clause and so on. There can be cost implications for either party, hence, cargo insurance clause must be examined before export order confirmation.

10.4.6 Port of Shipment, Destination and Place of Delivery

An exporter should examine the port of shipment agreed and negotiated for shipment of goods and port of final destination for unloading of cargo. He/she should examine the availability of required infrastructure such as stevedoring arrangements for agreed exportable consignments, restrictions, if any, and costs therein. He/she should be sure about location of port, airport and dry ports involved in logistics operations and ask the importer to completely mention the name of the port including the name of the country and port code so as to avoid any confusion as there exist in the world more than two ports with the same name but in different countries, for example, Port of Plymouth is located in Australia as well as in the United Kingdom and the United States. There are two Santiago, one in Chile and other in Brazil and there are two Hyderabad, one in India and other in Pakistan. Entry restrictions vis-à-vis seaworthiness of ship, ship-type, flag of registration and so on should also be examined in case of charter party contract. An exporter should ensure that 'place of delivery' is agreed which can be a place at a port of destination or far away in country hinterland. Both parties should ensure that appropriate INCOTERMS are used keeping in mind the location of place of delivery. Place of delivery is important as risks and costs shift from exporter to importer at this point. It is also important as cargo movement may be restricted to country hinterland due to inadequate or poor-quality road pavement, inadequacy of railway infrastructure and dry port facilities at country hinterland.

10.4.7 Modal Choice, Availability and Compatibility

Trading terms including regulatory compliance of documentation are affected by choice of mode of transport in international trade. Accordingly, an exporter must appraise the modal choice along with documentary compliance, availability of chosen mode of transport including frequency of services and costs therein and compatibility of modal choice with the nature of goods to be transported. For example, time-sensitive cargo such as newspaper and magazines are always moved by air transport. High-value cargo such as diamond and gold are also air transported due to increased scope of piracy and theft by sea transport. Certain kinds of cargo are sensitive to air pressure and hence, are transported by sea transport only. Similarly, perishable cargo such as flowers are always air transported. An exporter must appraise issues related to modal choice, its availability and frequency of services and its compatibility with nature of cargo including the issues of costs and risks before confirmation of export order.

10.4.8 Delivery Date and Schedule

Whether the exporter will be in a position to comply with scheduled delivery as desired and communicated by an importer. An exporter should appraise issues such as whether he/she can manufacture goods or procure from someone else before the date of shipment, arrange finances for manufacturing and arrange logistics including the availability of means of transport within the agreed date. He/she should negotiate the definite date of delivery as words like as early as possible, prompt delivery, within a fortnight, at the earliest, immediate delivery, good quality or prompt shipments used in export orders have scope for disputes at the later stage. He/she should also negotiate and agree on a definite delivery schedule as to how goods will move from country of export to country of import. Whether 'part or partial shipment' is allowed or not and whether 'trans-shipment' is allowed or not and so on are the issues that should be addressed in the delivery schedule.

10.4.9 Packaging, Packing and Labelling

An exporter shall examine the nature and kind of packing and packaging of exportable goods desired by the importer. Sometimes, an importer may request for special packing requirements, for example, seaworthy packing, palletization, unitization, shrink wrapping of cargo, use of special kinds of containers and other protective types of packing. For example, perishable goods require use of reefer container, breakable cargo requires cushioning and proper stowage and so on. Additionally, there exist country-specific or region-specific norms for cargo labelling; for example, Japan mandates for mandatory usage instructions of imported cargo in the Japanese language as 98 percent of Japanese cannot speak English or any other languages. EU countries have several special labelling requirements, for example, eco-label and CE labelling. Similarly, ship marking practices vary from country to country or region to region and have to be clearly understood by exporter based on negotiation with the importer. There exist restrictions for use of certain kinds of material for packing; for example, Germany restricts the use of plastic in imported cargo even for cushioning and stowage or outer packing. Australia and New Zealand restrict the use of wooden pallets for imported cargo and the United States mandates for only heat-treated or chemically treated pallets for use in imported cargo. There also exist specific colour preferences for packing material and the exporter should make himself/herself aware about all such choices before confirmation of the export order. There also exist preferences and disliking(s) for use of certain numbers and shapes due to cultural taboos. Exporters must cross-check all such issues and accordingly decide his/her price involving all such hidden costs of special packing, labelling and marking requirement mandated by the importer.

10.4.10 Shipping and Handling Precautions

An exporter should examine the shipping and handling marks communicated by the importer in export order as correct and complete marking of exportable packages help to prevent incorrect handling of cargo in exports operations, thus saving goods from potential accidents, physical damages, incorrect delivery, loss of weight and volume and customs fines, if any. Ship marking must be clear and precise, communicating the information and instructions for handling of goods and its colour and symbols should stand out clearly from that of the exportable package. Shipping marks are usually black in colour on white background and should be legible and durable to bear the transport hazards during loading and unloading. European countries, for example, have strict compliance for shipping and handling marks failing which objections may be raised by the customs authorities and fines are imposed for non-compliance. An exporter should examine three parts for compliance of shipping and handling marks in export management as indicated in Figure 10.4.

In order to overcome the language problems, specific shipping and handling instructions are given through symbols which are internationally standardized by International Organization for Standardization, Geneva. These symbols help the labours to understand the handling instruction at ports who either are illiterate or know only local language. The list of such symbols along with explanation is given in Table 10.1.

10.4.11 Compliance of Trade Documents

Export documents as requested by the importer are same as per quotation particularly those documents which are required with the bill of exchange or L/C for purchase/discount or negotiation of trade documents. For example, the commercial invoice does not require any specific notation like legalization or visaed from an embassy or a specified chamber. One should also check whether any 'consular invoice' is also required or certification by any authority of the commercial invoice is required. If so, an exporter should enquire about the name of certifying body, if any, and associated costs for certification. Second,

Shipping Mark

- Identification mark
- Identification number
- Total number of items in the complete consignment
- Number of the package in the consignment
- Place and port of destination

Information Mark

- Country of origin
- Indication of weight of package
- Dimensions of packages

Handling Instructions

- Handling marks
- Whether the package is sensitive to heat or moisture
- Whether it is at risk of breakage
- Where the top and bottom are and where the centre of gravity is located
- Where loading tackle may be slung

FIGURE 10.4 Shipping and handling precautions in export business.

TABLE 10.1 Internationally Standardized Symbols

Designation	Symbol	Explanation
Fragile, handle with care		The symbol indicates that cargo is fragile and should be handled with utmost care.
Use no hooks		The symbol indicates no use of hooks in the cargo.
Top		This symbol signifies that packages must always be transported, handled and stored in such a way that the arrows always point upwards.
Keep away from heat (solar radiation)		This symbol signifies that this cargo should be protected from solar radiation in order to prevent losses.
Protect from heat and radioactive sources		This symbol signifies that cargo should be protected from heat and radioactive substances.
Sling here		The symbol signifies the point where the cargo should be slung.
Keep dry		This symbol signifies that cargo bearing this sign must be protected from excessive humidity. Such cargo must be protected by tarpaulin as it is sensitive to humidity and rainwater.
Centre of gravity		This symbol signifies that product has centre of gravity at the point as indicated through this sign.
No hand truck here		The symbol signifies that one should seek permission to use a hand truck on them before doing so.
Stacking limitation		The symbol signifies the maximum stacking load which must be stated as '...kg or tons max.'.
Clamp here		The symbol signifies that packages may be clamped at the indicated point.
Temperature limitations		The symbol signifies that the product inside has temperature limitations. The exporter should note down the corresponding temperatures or temperature limits on the consignment note.

(Continued)

TABLE 10.1 (*Continued*)

Designation	Symbol	Explanation
Electrostatic sensitive device		This symbol signifies that one should avoid the contact with packages bearing this sign and one must be insulated by wearing the footwear.
Tear off here		This symbol intends that receiver of the cargo should tear the carton/packet from this place so as to prevent the damages which otherwise may be caused to cargo.

an exporter should specifically examine the transport document(s) desired in the export order, that is, bill of lading, AWB, road consignment note, rail consignment note, multimodal transport document or forwarder certificate of receipt (FCR) and specific types and kinds of such transport document; for example, the bill of lading has to be 'straight' or 'to order' and 'shipped on board' or 'received for shipment' or 'direct' or 'through'. Third, an exporter needs to check whether the certificate of origin required is non-preferential as issued by a trade association(s) or chamber of commerce such as Federation of Indian Chambers of Commerce, PHD Chamber of Commerce or preferential, for example, GSP, Generalized System of Trade Preferences (GSTP), India–ASEAN FTA, India–Sri Lanka FTA and so on which are issued by government-mandated agencies like EIC or development commissioner(s) of SEZ. Fourth, packing list or cargo manifest, as the case may be, if any special thing is required, it has to be examined by the exporter. Fifth, an exporter should examine the requirements of marine insurance policy as requested by importer, risks coverage, obligations and responsibilities and what are his/her responsibilities vis-à-vis cost and risks under chosen INCOTERMS. The general policy, coverage therein, time duration and so on are the issues to be looked into. Figure 10.5 explains the kinds of documentary compliance challenges that an exporter has to face pre- and post-exports and accordingly should be taken care of before confirmation of an export order.

In case an exporter is not satisfied with the terms and conditions of export order, he/she can request for clarification to the importer and solicit for changes in those clauses and conditions. This can follow on the basis of mutual discussion and negotiation between exporter and importer. The exporter usually does not put any time limit in getting the clarification and expect that he/she shall get such clarification from the importer in due course of reasonable time. But there is no harm if the exporter puts a time limit of say 15 days or so for getting these clarifications from the importer for speeding up the work. Once the exporter has received the clarifications from the importer, he/she must confirm the same to the importer and can start work. The confirmation is to be sent in the printed form or on a simple letter. There is usual practice to repeat the broad terms on which the export order is accepted by the exporter to get the things clarified thoroughly.

10.4.12 Confirmation of Export Order

In case the exporter is satisfied with different aspects of the export order as discussed above, he/she shall send a confirmation of the export order to the buyer. In fact, there is no standard format to be used for an export order confirmation. It is just a letter to be sent by the exporter to the importer that he/she is satisfied with all the terms and conditions as mentioned in the order and he/she shall deliver the goods as per the agreed schedule. Now importer is required to open a L/C in favour of exporter so that exporter can start his/her work on export order and can avail the necessary packing credit from the bank.

Discrepancies in L/C	• L/C has expired as shipper cannot ship the goods within scheduled date of delivery or shipper has made late shipment or late presentation of documents to bank.
General discrepancies in trade documents	• Documents required under export order are non-compatible or inconsistent or contradictory to each other/L/C order mandates for original documents not marked 'original' or 'marked unsigned'. Time for submission of documents to bank not specified or is clear as banks in India will not accept documents presented to them later than 21 days under FEMA rules or state ambigious language such as submit after date of shipment.
Discrepancies in commercial invoice	• Confusion over sharing of risks and responsibilities under INCOTERMS, invoice states wrong amount or for an amount greater than the credit value, invoice does not state payment terms and currency of invoice, invoice is not signed or certified by authorized signatory or is not legalized but L/C terms demand so, invoice omits the goods description (HS code) as detailed in the credit and shipping marks and handling instructions differ from transport documents.
Discrepancies in bill of lading	• Bill of lading does not indicate the name of the carrier or specify clearly the name of consignee, shipper or notifying party and weights and measurements in bill of lading differ from other documents. Bill of lading is not signed as desired and mandated under terms of L/C or UCP 600 or ISBP. Bill of lading is either stale or claused (dirty or foul) showing defective goods or packaging (e.g., rusty, leaking, bumped, defective drums and so on) or indicating that goods are shipped on deck of ship.
Discrepancies in insurance	• Certificate of insurance is presented in lieu of an insurance policy and date is after the date of shipment on insurance certificate, thus indicating that risks coverage is effective after the transport date. Certificate does not specify the risks covered or is of insufficient insured value or is not endorsed in favour of importer or certificate of insurance as submitted is under an expired policy. Certificate is not issued in negotiable form and does not specify whether the premium is paid or not whether paid in full or in part and so on.
Discrepancies in certificate of origin	• Certificate of origin requested should be in name of other party than buyer, with change in HS code and not signed by shipper.
Discrepancies in certificate of inspection	• Copy of invoice omitted. • Copy of invoice not authenticated by inspection agency.
Discrepancies in telex advices	• Not sent within the time scales laid down in the credit. • Incomplete or incorrect information provided.
Discrepancies in legalization of invoice	• Omitted or not completed for all documents (and copies) where this is a requirement.
Miscellaneous documents	• Exporter fails or forgets to present certificate of origin as required by L/C or export order, forgets to sign or seal of chamber is missing or not duly signed by authorized signatory of chamber. Proforma of requested packing list does not conform to the exporting country's requirement. Bill of exchange should be drawn to other party than buyer and should be drawn for higher amount than actual export value.
Other common discrepancies	• Goods shipped by sea instead of air (or vice versa). • Amount claimed exceeds the credit value. • Partial shipment or transhipment effected when not allowed.

FIGURE 10.5 Common discrepancies in compliance of trade documents in export management.

10.5 Steps in Processing of an Export Order

After confirmation of export order and receiving L/C or any other documentary proof of export, an exporter has to sequentially follow these steps to execute the export order:

1. **Availing export finance from bank:** GOI offers liberal interest rates to Indian exporters; hence, the interests are lower for meeting the working capital requirement of exportable goods in both cases, when availed in Indian rupee and foreign currency. Commercial banks in India are directed via notifications of RBI, wherein commercial banks in India have to offer export credit as per RBI Master Circular in both pre-shipment and post-shipment stages. An exporter can avail the finance(s) under these schemes from any commercial bank to finance working capital needs for purchase of raw materials, processing them and converting them into finished goods for the purpose of export. Banks demand the copy of 'export order' which can be an L/C or 'written sales contract' or 'duly singed copies of proforma invoice' by the importer. Banks offer pre-shipment and post-shipment stage liberal credit on the basis of procedures as laid down in RBI circular.
2. **Reserving space for shipment:** An exporter should book the shipping space with a carrier on an agreed mode of transport for definite delivery on agreed schedule to the buyer. In order to overcome the problems of shipping space for transporting cargo, responsible party (exporter or importer) should book the shipping space in advance. An exporter can avail the services of freight forwarder who offers specialized transport and logistics services as he/she acts as 'travel agent of cargo' in export operations. An exporter can give shipping instructions to the freight forwarder and ask him/her to make available the information for the arrival of the ship at least 10–15 days in advance so as to complete the custom clearance formalities on time. In case of special caution to protect cargo from maritime hazards, the exporter should intimate the freight forwarder about the need of seaworthy packing for certain kinds of cargo, for example, reefer cargo, roll-on/roll-off cargo and insulated cargo. Appointed freight forwarder should be experienced, specialized and updated so as to handle all these issues.
3. **Procuring or manufacturing the goods:** After availing the export credit, an exporter can start production so as to ship the goods to the importer on the agreed schedule and date. He/she should forward a delivery note (Figure 10.6) to production department for understanding the various issues of the exporter, that is, quantity to manufacture, quality issues, sizes, specification and dimensions, packing material, labelling and any other issue which is important for this export order. In case of merchant exporter, the exporter should tie up with a manufacturer so as to get the material produced for shipment on time. The exporter should place a copy of purchase note with a tied-up manufacturer so as to ensure compliance in quality, quantity, delivery date and other issues. Merchant exporter should carefully examine the production process, progress for production and quality as he/she does not have direct control on the staff of such a tied-up manufacturer. Exporter should coordinate the whole export operations with export order execution team which should be formed by taking the right persons from finance, logistics, documentation handling and production department as these business operations are interrelated and need coordination for timely delivery of exportable cargo. For example, without finances, production of exportable goods will suffer and without production, logistics team cannot do anything. On completion of the production schedule, an exporter can pack the material for overseas transport.

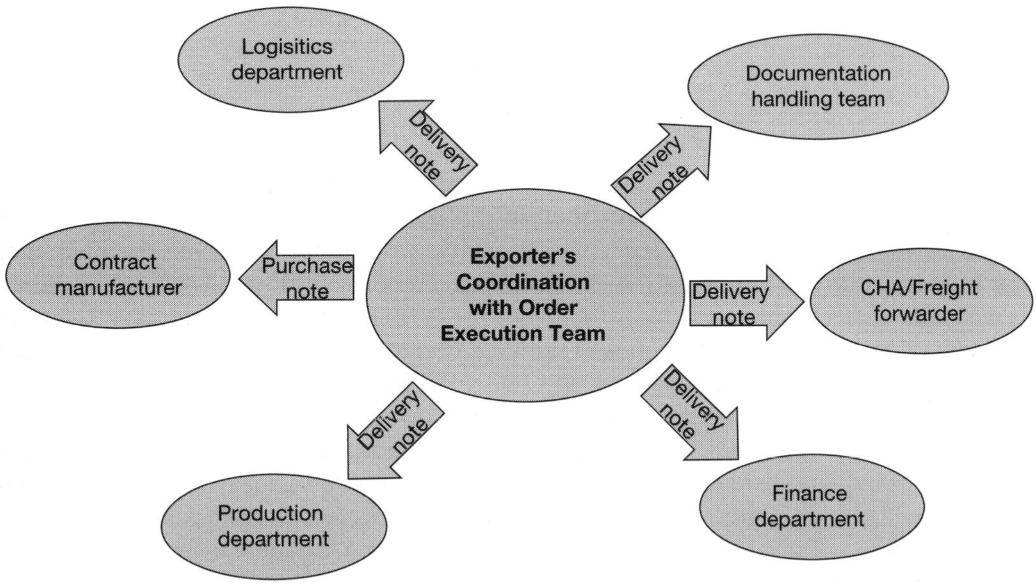

FIGURE 10.6 Exporter's coordination with order execution team.

4. **Procuring exchange fluctuation cover:** As the invoiced currency is usually freely convertible foreign currency (US dollar/euro/yen/pound), an exporter will receive the payments in foreign currency which will be converted into equivalent Indian rupees at the time of realization. Since trade cycles in international trade are longer due to longer distance involved leading to longer transportation time, customs clearance, loading and unloading time and credit period, payment is realized after some time unlike in case of domestic trade where the trade cycles are shorter. The value of currencies keeps on changing due to psycho-economic pattern and as a result depreciate or appreciate, thus exposing an exporter to 'exchange rate fluctuation risks'. Currency movements, upwards or downwards, can have severe repercussions for an exporter. If rupee is depreciating, it is good for the exporter as he/she will realize more Indian rupee vis-à-vis foreign currency. In case rupee is appreciating, the exporter will realize less Indian rupees, hence, such a situation has a foreign exchange fluctuation risk for an exporter. In order to overcome such challenges, an exporter must take necessary steps to mitigate foreign exchange fluctuation risks. An exporter can use any of the instruments shown in Figure 10.7 to manage such types of risks.

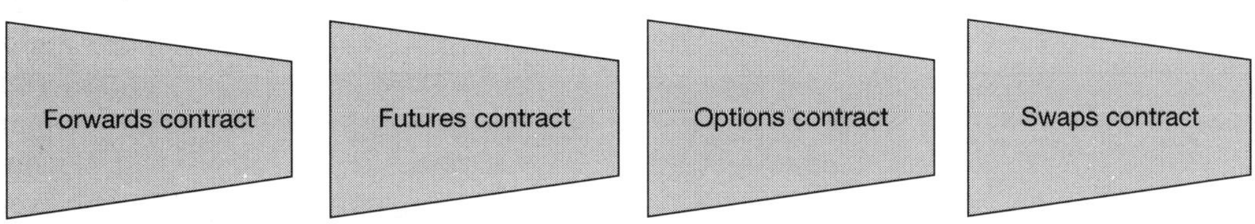

FIGURE 10.7 Instruments for hedging foreign exchange fluctuation risks in export operations.

5. **Clearance from GST:** An exporter has to clear the goods from GST department under Zero Rating Mechanism by filing the Legal Undertaking (LUT) or Bond as provided under GST Refund Rules 2017 and GST-RFD-11.
6. **Pre-shipment inspection of foods:** EIC mandates for quality control inspection of certain goods before they are shipped irrespective of the fact whether the buyer has requested for quality control inspection or not. This is done on the basis of a series of complaints received about Indian exporters shipping substandard goods, thus impacting the image of Indian goods in international markets. Sometimes, importer demands for quality control and pre-shipment inspection and sometimes country of import necessarily mandates that only those goods which are adhering to established quality control norms of their country shall be cleared for imports into the country. In cases where mandatory inspection is required under GOI rules/notification, Indian customs authorities will clear the goods for exports only after having received the copy of certificate of inspection issued by a competent and designated authority. Hence, goods cannot be exported without compliance to notified pre-shipment inspection norms and should be exported only in compliance with requested quality norms of importer or country of importer as in this case either the importer will not pay or goods will not be cleared by customs for import at destination. Figure 10.8 depicts the types of inspection carried out for exportable goods depending on circumstances.

   Usually, export inspection certificate is issued in triplicate, wherein the original copy is retained by Indian customs after verification, other two copies are stamped by customs and one is sent to the importer and the third copy remains with the exporter for his/her future reference.
7. **Appointment of clearing and forwarding agents:** An exporter should appoint a freight forwarder for completing the formalities related to GST, custom clearance, FEMA compliance, service tax clearance and documentation, VAT/CST-related documentation, booking of shipping space, railway/lorry booking, payment of port charges, terminal handling charges (THCs), payment of haulage, carrying out stevedoring operations at multiple point(s), arranging for packing, labelling and marking, container stuffing, freight payment and allied documentation leading to completion of the export process. The freight forwarder will seek the following documents from the exporter for successful completion of this job at the initial stage of export operations.

   These documents help the freight forwarder to understand the nature of goods, HS classification and associated customs clearance procedure, nature of incentives, duty neutralization, export benefits, issues related to trade policy compliance and need of special licences/approvals

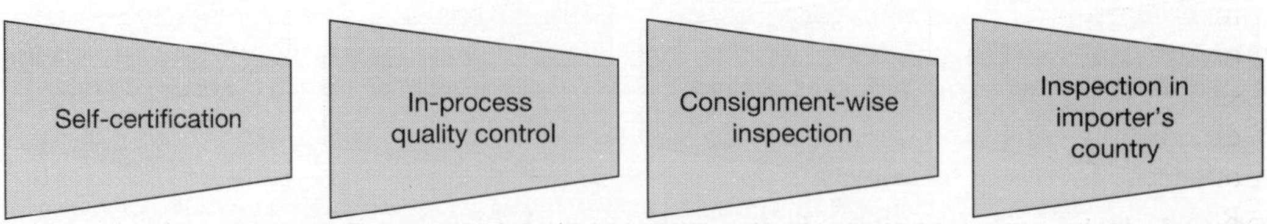

FIGURE 10.8 Types of quality control inspection for exportable goods.

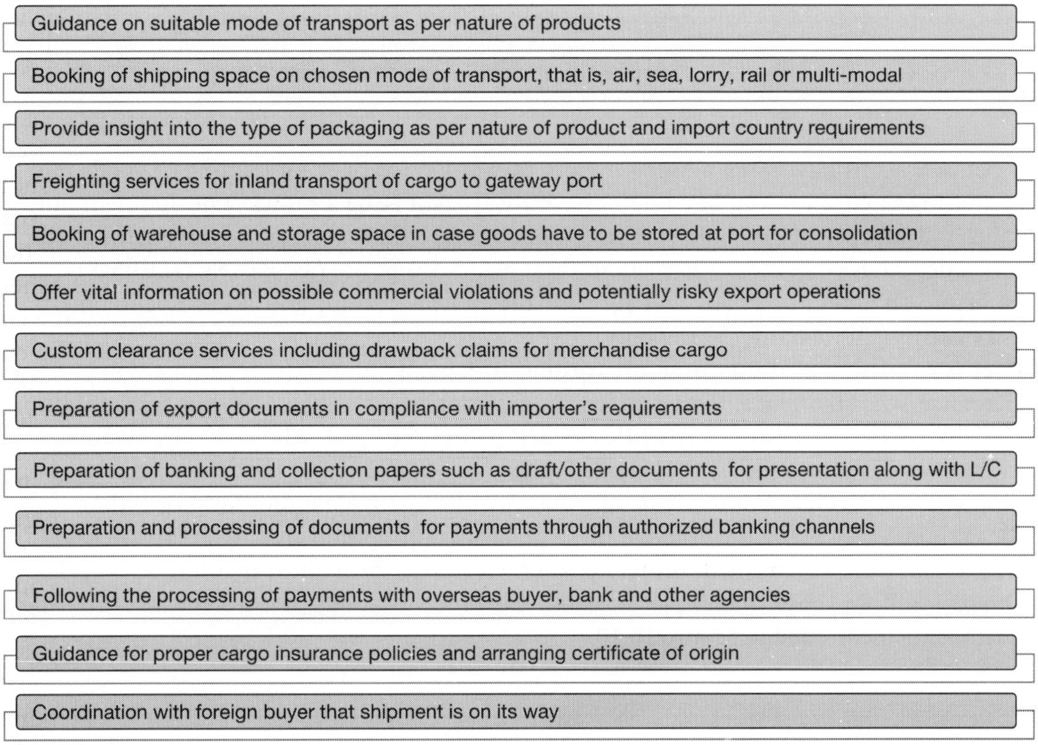

FIGURE 10.9 Functions of freight forwarder in export operations.

therein, nature of export packing, labelling, marking and handling requirement(s) for this consignment, quality inspection compliance, booking of right shipping space with low cost-effective service carriers. With this information at hand, he/she can handle the issues related to various clearances better at the stage of shipment of goods. Freight forwarder offers the specialized services related to export transaction management (Figure 10.9).

8. **Transport of goods to port:** Once formalities related to GST clearance and pre-shipment inspection are done, goods are packed, marked and labelled as per the negotiated terms and conditions between exporter and importer. Freight forwarder arranges for container, gets it fumigated and ensures compliance of suitable use of packing material by clearly understanding international conventions such as FIATA (International Federation of Freight Forwarders Associations) rules for dangerous goods and International Air Transport Association (IATA) rules for dangerous goods and European conventions; goods are stuffed into container with proper handling marks for their quick and safe transportation. Freight forwarder in coordination with logistics department of exporter takes steps for reservation of shipping space for both in-country transport and onward transport (depends on INCOTERMS). He/she secures a proof of reservation of shipping space through a document known as 'shipping order'. For in-country road movements, no additional formality is required as it is contracted service from private players; however, in the case of goods movement by railway to port town, freight forwarder has to book the space with Indian Railway and secure the allotment of wagons. Freight forwarder submits the following documents for railway booking and wagon allotment.

Forwarding note (A railway document)	Copy of IEC/RCMC (for wagon booking preference for exports)	Shipping order	Copy of packing list/packing note	Wagon registration fee receipt

Once wagons have been allotted, freight forwarder arranges for loading of goods into wagons or stuffing-in-cum-loading of containers. Railways will issue a railway consignment note usually called railway receipt as proof of receipts and non-negotiable contract of carriage of goods. Freight forwarder guides exporter's team about right insurance policy (as per INCOTERMS) which must be before shipment of goods and forward the railway receipt and other documents to his/her associate freight forwarder at the port town.

9. **Port formalities and customs clearance:** It depends on export locations where the custom clearance will take place; for example, an exporter based in country hinterland will prefer to complete export clearance formalities at dry port (ICD/CFS). Alternatively, customs clearance formalities are completed at CFS located at gateway port. Freight forwarder associate at gateway port will take receipt of documents and custody of cargo from either lorry or Indian Railway (as the case may be). He/she will lodge these goods at appropriate staking area/warehouse/shed of CFS at gateway port and will initiate custom clearance formalities by filing appropriate type of shipping bill. In order to complete custom clearance of goods, the freight forwarder needs the documents mentioned in Figure 10.10.

- Shipping bill or bill of exports
- Export order or purchase order or ISC or L/C
- Commercial invoice in 8–10 copies
- Packing list in 8–10 copies
- Inspection certificate (original)
- GATT declaration
- Special export licence, if needed
- SDF or EDF form for exchange control (in original and duplicate)
- BG/LUT under GST RFD-11 vide Rule 96A
- Shipping order (original)
- Railway consignment note/Road consignment note/Lorry way bill, as the case may be

FIGURE 10.10 Documents required for export processing.

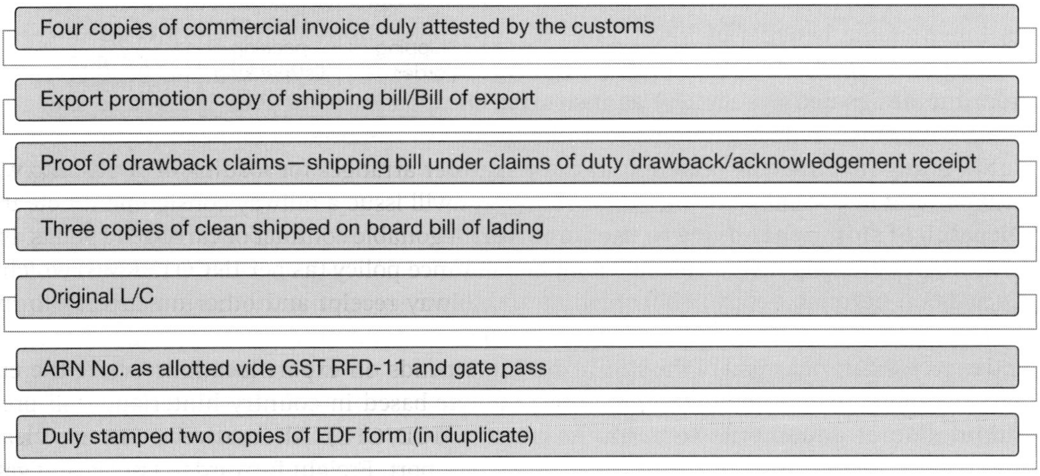

FIGURE 10.11 Documents submitted by freight forwarder after custom clearance to exporter.

Once shipping bill is appraised and stamped with LEO, freight forwarder presents the port trust document to the shed superintendent of the port for loading order. He/she obtains the 'carting order' for loading of goods to appointed ship. Customs can physically examine the goods at this stage if desired so by dock appraiser. Goods remain in the transit yard until loaded on the appointed ship for onward movement of cargo to destination. Once goods are loaded on the appointed vessel, the captain of the ship or his/her mate issues a receipt known as 'mate's receipt'. The freight forwarder takes the receipt and examines that it should be clean, that is, clearly indicating that goods are received in an apparently good condition for onward transport to destination; if mentioned in the clause, he/she should discuss the issue with the captain and take preventive measures as instructed by the ship captain for a clean mate's receipt. He/she should also pay the port charges as mandated by port authority for use of port and terminal services. He/she submits the mate's receipt to shipping company and requests for issuance of bill of lading, which is a vital transport document indicating rights of title or ownership, contract of carriage and negotiable instrument.

10. **Dispatch of documents by the freight forwarder to the exporter:** After procuring the bill of lading from the appointed shipping company, the freight forwarder submits these trade documents to exporter for submission to bank as mandated under FEMA rules either for purchase/discount or negotiation. Figure 10.11 depicts the documents that are handed over by the freight forwarder to the exporter for submission to the bank.

10.6 Post-export Documentation for Realizing Payments and Claiming Benefits

Once goods are shipped to the destination, an exporter has to execute the following activities for compliance with regulatory authorities and processing of trade documents through proper banking channels for the realization of payments:

1. **Application for certificate of origin:** In case of preferential or free trade regime between contracting countries, an exporter has to apply for 'certificate of origin' to the designated

chamber or government body. Certificate of origin is a 'quasi-financial instrument' which offers an importer the benefits of lower rates of applicable duties in the country of import, thus making these goods available at lower cost. An exporter has to procure the certificate of origin from the designated agency(ies) as instructed in appendices of FTP 2015–2020 and route it along with other trade documents to an importer. An importer is liable to pay a lower rate of duties if any free trade or preferential trade regime exists between such involved countries of exporter and importer.

2. **Dispatch of shipment advice to the importer:** An exporter should send the 'shipment advice' to the importer along with principal commercial document such as commercial invoice, packing list and non-negotiable copy of bill of lading and shipment advance, thus intimating the importer that goods have been shipped as per agreed terms and conditions on the appointed named ship and expected date of arrival of the ship at destination is around (date/month/year). This helps the importer with the information as mentioned in Figure 10.12.
3. **Submission of documents to bank:** As mandated under FEMA regulations, an exporter submits the documents listed in Figure 10.13 to the bank for realization of export proceeds from the importer and regulatory compliance under FEMS, 2000. The bank either purchases or discounts the trade documents or negotiates them with issuing bank for payment settlement.
4. **Claiming export incentives and benefits:** An exporter is entitled to various benefits, incentives and duty neutralization authorization from GOI and accordingly has to claim these benefits and incentives to the designated office of DGFT. An exporter can claim any of the benefits, incentives and duty neutralization in one transaction as listed in Figure 10.14.

- Inform him/her about the arrival of goods as ordered.
- Alert him/her to take necessary steps for payment to exporters.
- Help coordinate with his/her freight forwarder for import clearance.
- Help find out alternate buyers and execute sales on high seas, if so desired.
- Help make warehouse arrangements, if so desired.
- Help find out local buyers.

FIGURE 10.12 Benefits of sending a shipment advice note to buyer.

- Commercial invoice
- Packing list
- L/C, if payment agreed under L/C
- Certificate of insurance
- Certificate of origin
- Certificate of inspection, if applicable
- EDF/SDF form
- Bill of lading/Airway bill/Multimodal transport document
- Bill of exchange
- Bank certification

FIGURE 10.13 List of documents to be processed to bank for payment realizations.

FIGURE 10.14 Checklist of incentives for exports in India.

5. **Issuance of bank realization certificate (BRC):** BRC is a regulatory document which an exporter has to prepare post export and submit to various regulatory authorities as 'proof of export'. BRC is now processed by banks online through e-commerce support of DGFT and is called e-BRC; it is based on the realization of export proceeds from the foreign buyer. As a part of the B2B message exchange initiative, it is now decided to exchange BRC information electronically through EDI with banks. This will provide accurate and updated information about BRC and reduce the hardship for Indian exporters as furnishing of physical copy of BRC has been dispensed with from 2013. Any exporter has to furnish e-BRC copy(ies) in order to apply for benefits under FTP and it acts as a proof of realization of export proceeds. An exporter has to furnish the details such as invoice number, shipping bill number and date, exchange control document number (export declaration form [EDF]/statutory declaration form [SDF]), freight paid, insurance declaration and agency commission, if any. BRC is submitted as proof of export payment realization to various trade regulatory bodies such as DGFT, RBI, Indian customs, GST clearance, service tax and VAT department so as to claim export benefits, incentives and duty neutralization.

10.7 Summary

Any trade deal in international trade initiates with the formation of an 'export order' between two trading parties. Hence, an exporter order is an important document as it works as base for other documents to be prepared during the stage of processing of an export order aimed at transport of goods from one country to another including transfer of title/ownership and realization of payments. The formation of an export order begins with certain commercial documents shared between an exporter and an importer. Any EXIM transaction is purely a demand–supply transaction between two countries. Demand of goods and services can be due to natural reasons such as some countries do not produce rice and import it from rice-producing countries. Demand can be due to other economic reasons, for example, factor endowment, comparative cost advantages and absolute advantages. Trade transaction may begin from either side depending on demand and supply forces. The proforma invoice or import quotations is the first point of contact and negotiation between an exporter and importer on terms and conditions of sales contract. It is rightly said that processing of an export order starts with the receipt of an export order which can be written or implied, meaning when contracted, negotiated and agreed in model sales contract, it becomes written sales contract or when executed on the basis of trade documents (invoice, packing list, bill of lading), it is considered as implied sales contract.

When an exporter approaches a buyer, he/she communicates willingness to sell through 'proforma invoice' and in case buyer approaches seller for imports, he/she sends 'import quotation' or 'purchase quotation'. Based on negotiation between exporter and importer, an export order is placed by importer indicating his/her wiliness to import the agreed goods or services as per negotiated terms and conditions of imports. Hence, an export order, in a form, is an agreement between two trading parties (importer and exporter) before the exporter actually starts producing or procuring goods for exports. An export order can be in the form of a written 'international sales contract' or L/C or 'purchase order' or simply 'singed proforma invoice' by the importer in favour of exporter. Each form of these export orders has different legal standing and are used as per the established trading practices, nature and size of export order and trust between trading parties. Once export order is received by exporter, he/she should acknowledge the receipt of export order.

Review Exercises

Multiple Choice Questions

1. Which of the following organizations has framed ISC?
   a. UNCTAD
   b. UNCITRAL
   c. The World Bank
   d. International Law Commission
   e. None of the above
2. An exporter contacts an importer with an offer to sell something with which of the following documents?
   a. Customs invoice
   b. Proforma invoice
   c. Commercial invoice
   d. Legalized invoice
   e. None of the above
3. An importer approaches an exporter to purchase something with which of the following documents?
   a. Import quotation
   b. Email request for supplies
   c. Purchase letter
   d. Import order
   e. None of the above

4. FEMA rules in India mandate that export proceeds should be realized in
   a. Any currency of the world
   b. Only dollar
   c. Any freely convertible foreign currency
   d. Only Indian rupees
   e. None of the above
5. Who among the following assists an exporter or importer in logistics operations and is known as a travel agent of cargo?
   a. Custom broker
   b. Sea agent
   c. Freight forwarder
   d. Non-vessel operating common carrier
   e. None of the above
6. The certificate of origin facilitates the importer with lower rate of duties in country of imports due to agreed tariff preference regime between trading countries and is also known as
   a. Non-negotiable instrument
   b. Negotiable instrument
   c. Financial instrument
   d. Quasi-financial instrument
   e. All of the above
7. Who among the following issues the carting order?
   a. Appoint carrier
   b. Port authority
   c. Surveyor of cargo
   d. Inspection agency
   e. None of the above
8. Which of the following is not the trade regime for exports and imports in India?
   a. Free
   b. State trading enterprise
   c. Prohibited
   d. Restricted
   e. Preference trade regime
9. BRC is now electronically processed so as to reduce
   a. The hassles exporter faces in manual processing
   b. To cut the transaction cost and time
   c. To reduce the paperwork of exporter
   d. To enhance increased compliance of export benefits and incentives
   e. All of the above
10. Handling marks in export operations help to ensure that greater care is taken with cargo handling in long logistics operations and such marks must be able to communicate with the involved stakeholder that
   a. This package is sensitive to heat or moisture
   b. This package is at risk of breakage

c. Where the top and bottom are and where the center of gravity is located
d. Where loading tackle may be slung
e. Where loading tackle may be slung

Critical Thinking Questions

1. Critically explain the process of formation of an export order in international trade transactions.
2. What is the process of negotiation, receipt and acknowledgement of an export order? Critically appraise the process of scrutiny, examination, clarification and confirmation of an export order.
3. What are the various steps in the processing of an export order? What are the benefits of appointing a clearing and forwarding agent in export operations?
4. Critically examine any two of the following:
   a. Availing export finance from bank
   b. Procuring exchange risks cover
   c. Reserving space for shipment
   d. Procuring or manufacturing the goods
   e. Clearance from GST
5. Explain step-by-step post-export documentation in the processing and execution of an export order vis-à-vis realizing of overseas payments and claiming incentives from government agencies.
6. Examine any two of the following:
   a. Pre-shipment inspection of goods
   b. Appointment of clearing and forwarding agents
   c. Transport of goods to port
   d. Port formalities and customs clearance
   e. Dispatch of documents by freight forwarder to exporter

CHAPTER 11

Export–Import Documentation

CHAPTER OBJECTIVES

- To understand the role of EXIM documentation in foreign trade.
- To appraise the legal aspects of trade documentation practices in EXIM operations.
- To explain the commercial documents used in EXIM operations.
- To describe the regulatory documents used in EXIM operations.
- To explain the procedure of preparation and handling of various documents in logistics.

11.1 Introduction

A number of EXIM documents are required at various stages of international trade operations as trading parties deal with various parties involved in trade transactions through trade documents only. It is rightly said that in international trade, one deals in documents and not the goods, as the ownership of goods, transportation, payments, sharing of costs and risks, tariff preference and so on is governed by trade documents only. EXIM documents are rightly referred to as the 'soul of international trade transactions', as trade documents fulfil various commercial and regulatory requirements for involved trading parties. An EXIM transaction begins with the 'proforma invoice' and ends with the negotiation of trade documents with the banks for payments of export transactions. Preparation and execution of trade documents in EXIM operations serve various purposes; for example, the proforma invoice helps communicate the willingness to sell something with tentative prices and other terms and conditions, the commercial invoice helps realize foreign exchange from the foreign buyer, certificate of origin ensures that goods enjoy tariff preference in the country of imports, bill of lading carries the title of goods, a contract of carriage and proof of ownership tells the origin and destination of goods. Similarly, the certificate of insurance helps protect either party of trade from various maritime risks, AWB is used when goods are transported by air and the packing list explains the cargo details and helps customs properly classify the cargo. Sound knowledge of the EXIM documents is essential for a successful international marketer. Meticulous planning and care are required on the part of exporters and importers while preparing these documents; otherwise, there may be problems for the exporter in negotiation of trade documents with banks in the realization of payments. Discrepancy in trade documentation at any stage for both commercial and regulatory documentations carries several potential business risks including the non-realization of export proceeds from foreign buyers. Importers can also be at risk due to incomplete or discrepant trade documents as this creates problems and can even result in non-delivery of goods. The process of preparing EXIM documents involves various stages and parties such as exporter and importer, customs and GST officials, shipping company, freight forwarder, banks,

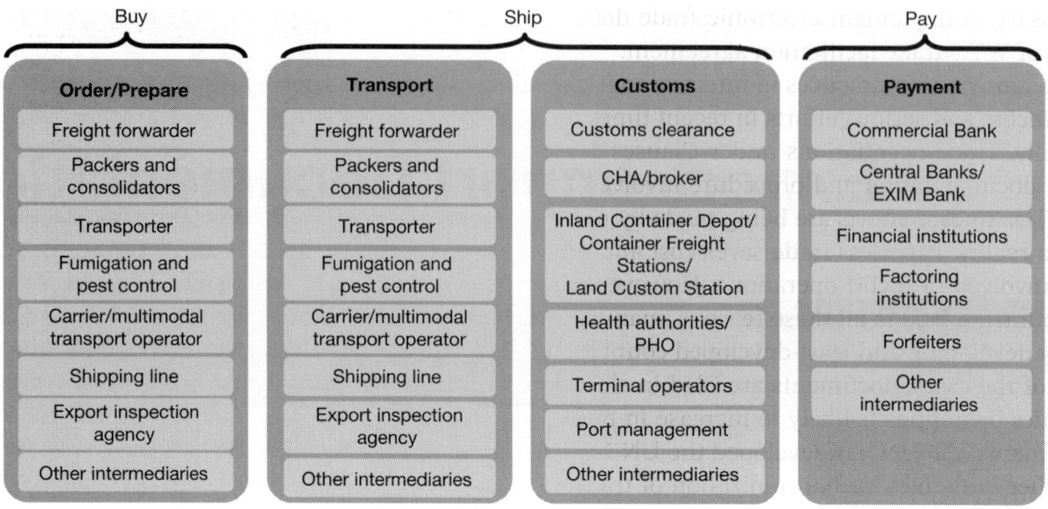

FIGURE 11.1 List of various parties in international trade operations.

Source: Adapted from National Board of Trade, Sweden, 2003.

insurance company, quality control and pre-shipment inspection agency, chamber of commerce and ECGC. Figure 11.1 provides the list of involved parties in the trade value chain at three stages, that is, buy, ship and pay.

In the era of free trade regime, the world has become a 'global village' as both developing and developed countries are dependent on each other for exchanging goods, services and ideas so as to speed up the process of economic development, control inflation, reap benefits of factor advantages, accumulate foreign exchange reserves and enjoy other spillover benefits associated with free and flourishing trade. The waves of globalization under WTO and recent initiatives such as Transatlantic Trade and Investment Partnership and Trans-Pacific Partnership have well extended the scope of business beyond the boundary barriers as associated stakeholders in trade, that is, policymakers, trade community and society, at large, have realized the need of efficient and speedy execution of transactions and orders which calls for flawless EXIM documentation, so as to reap the greater benefits of growing trade. EXIM documentation has various applications, not limited only to exchange of goods and services between two trading parties and settlement of payment, but much beyond as an instrument of proof in the court of law, collection of trade statistics, future reference for trade negotiations and understanding terms and conditions of trade between involved parties. In fact, EXIM documents are the core means of exchanging information among involved parties in international trade operations. Accordingly, countries have accepted standardized trade documentation system under 'aligned trade documentation system' which is based on internationally negotiated, accepted standards and best practices for efficient information exchange in international trade. The prime aims of aligned trade documentation were: to facilitate both exporters and importers with standardized information and to ensure the efficiency and security of the trade transaction itself. WTO Agreement on Trade Facilitation has been a step forward for all involved countries to consider aligned trade document system as the main step towards the implementation of GATT Article 8 on fees and formalities connected with importation and exportation of goods among member states. Standard aligned paper documents are also extremely important and necessary to implement electronic trade documentation as envisaged under 'single window' mechanism of WTO trade facilitation agreement.

Documentation practices in international trade operations may vary from country to country. There are sincere and serious efforts in recent times for synchronizing and streamlining the trade documents globally. Trade negotiations under Clauses 5, 8 and 10 of GATT, which are aimed at simplifying the trade documentation and procedure involved in international trade operations, are already underway at WTO. Sincere efforts are being made by negotiating countries to make electronic trade documentation a reality. Paperless trade saves cost and time and is of immense help in reducing the transaction cost involved in EXIM operations. However, these trade facilitation measures need huge investments by countries. Due to all these reasons, manual trade documents are still in use not only in India but in many developing and least-developed countries in Asia, Africa and Latin America. In India, in 95 percent of the cases, documents are filed in electronic form and it is expected that the use of IT in trade logistics operations is likely to increase in near future. In order to simplify and standardize the EXIM documents, the UN has developed the UN Layout Key for Trade Documents. This is further supported by other initiatives for harmonization of trade documentation practices such as related standards and tools for paperless trade, UN Trade Data Elements Directory, ITC(HS) and list and box completion guidelines for the preparation of these trade documents. Most of the advanced trading nations including India have been using these harmonized trade documentations; for example, DGFT has prepared a single document for trade, the EU single administrative document, Lloyd's Certificate of Insurance, TIR (Transports Internationaux Routiers) Carnet and the IATA AWB. The need of export–import may vary from product to product and country to country on the basis of mode of transportation, determination of duty, any other regional trade arrangements, but major commercial and regulatory documents will remain the same as standardized by UN/CEFACT. It has prepared the UN Layout Key in 1988 by dividing the trade documents into Master Documents 1 and 2. India has also streamlined its documents on the basis of the UN Layout Key in 1991 and divided the documents into two categories of Master Documents 1 and 2. There are some documents which may be required keeping in mind the nature of products and the destination of the country to which they are exported. Some products may be under preferential tariff treatment and such trade deal may require documentations as prescribed under that preferential scheme. There are special documents which are required for inspection under SPS and TBT regime of quality control and inspection. For example, food, fruits and pharmaceutical products are subject to SPS measures and TBT and special certification from the drug authority of importing country. Indian pharmaceutical companies file application for certification from FDA of the United States for making exports of pharmaceuticals to the United States.

11.2 Legal Framework for EXIM Documentation

EXIM documentation has legal dimensions as goods cannot be moved into or outside the territorial waters of India without the permission of the Indian customs. For any carriers such as aeroplane, ship, truck, lorry and rail to arrive in India, a notice of arrival has to be given to the Indian customs under Section 29 of the Customs Act, 1962. Any carrier must file Import General Manifest (IGM) as prescribed by the Indian customs under Section 30 of the Customs Act and imported goods cannot be unloaded from the vessel/any other carrier until 'entry inwards' is granted by the Indian customs under Section 31 of the Customs Act, 1962. The person in charge of the carrier (captain/driver/master) is not allowed to unload any cargo in India unless it is mentioned in IGM as stipulated under Section 32 and no goods can be either loaded or unloaded to any carrier (rail/ship/aeroplane/truck) except under the supervision of custom officer as mandated under Section 34 of the Customs Act, 1962. The Customs Act, 1962, also imposes reasonable restrictions like loading and unloading of cargo on Holidays (Section 36) and any other foreign boat cannot be move into territorial waters of India even for coastal shipping without proper intimation to Indian customs. In practice, however, the coastal ship moves beyond territorial waters for smooth navigation but with proper intimation to the Indian customs. No carriers from India can load goods unless a permission of 'exit outwards' is granted by the Indian customs under Section 39, and no stevedore or terminal operator can load the goods on board unless such goods are duly cleared for exports by the Indian customs under established procedure as given under Section 40 of the Customs Act, 1962. Section 40 of the Customs Act, 1962, says that export goods are subject to the approval of proper officers of customs before being loaded to the ship or airlines and cannot be loaded without their permission. As per the Act,

> The person-in-charge of a conveyance shall not permit the loading at a customs station—
>
> **a.** of export goods, other than baggage and mail bags, unless a shipping bill or bill of export or a bill of transshipment, as the case may be, duly passed by the proper officer, has been handed over to him by the exporter;
> **b.** of baggage and mail bags, unless their export has been duly permitted by the proper officer.

Any carrier must file 'Export General Manifest (EGM)' with the Indian customs before leaving the ship beyond the territorial waters of India (Section 41), and such permission for any conveyance to leave from India must be in writing to the notified officer of the Indian customs. Similarly, there is an established procedure for where the carriers have to embark and disembark which are always notified to customs stations under Section 8 of the Customs Act. No exporter can export the goods outside India unless he/she files a 'shipping bill/bill of export' as mandated under Section 50 of the Customs Act. Similary, no importer can clear the goods from the custodian of cargo unless a 'bill of entry' under the specified category is not filed with the Indian customs subject to successful appraisement, assessment and order of customs which can 'let export order (LEO)' for exports and 'out of charge' order for imports. Table 11.1 illustrates the flow of a ship carrier coming into and going out of India with required documentation.

In addition to the Customs Act, FEMA, 1999, and rules and regulations issued thereunder deal with the documents which are to be submitted by the exporters for realizing the export proceeds within the prescribed time. FEM (Export of Goods and Services) Regulations mandate that an exporter has to file a form called 'statutory declaration form' for goods exported beyond $25,000 and export proceeds must be realized within 270 days from date of export, that is, date of issuance of bill of lading. More so, export proceeds can mandatorily be realized only through proper banking channels. For manual exports, an exporter has to file EDF and for services export, it is 'Softex'. Similarly, for imports, there is a form called 'A-1' which has three variants. Export (Quality Control and Inspection) Act, 1963, mandates for compliance of quality through cargo inspection if goods are notified for mandatory export inspection. Transport documents like bill of lading are governed by the Indian Bills of Lading Act, 1953; Airway Bill (AWB) is governed by the Carriage by Air Act, 1972; and similarly, other transport documents are governed by stipulated legislative procedure. If a bill of exchange is used as an instrument to settle the payments, law relating to the Indian Negotiable Instruments Act, 1881, comes into play. Hence, it is mandatory for an exporter or his/her agents or freight forwarder to understand the role and importance

TABLE 11.1 Concept of Territorial Waters and Documentation for Movement of Carrier

Documentation Flow of Ship Coming into India	Territorial Waters of India	Documentation Flow of Ship Going Out of India
Person in charge of carrier (vessel/airline/truck/rail) files IGM with the Indian customs (Section 30 of the Customs Act)	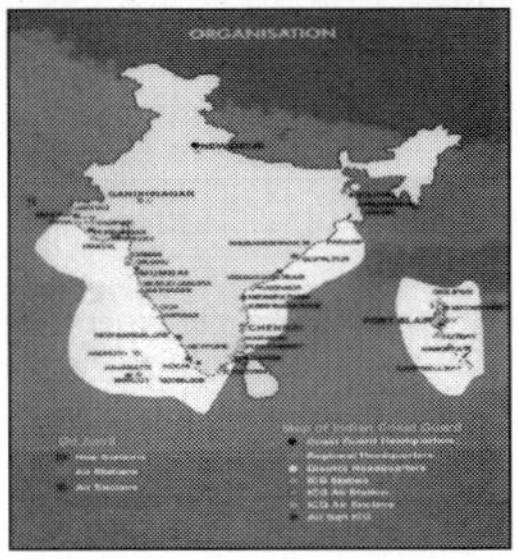	Person in charge of carrier should file EGM before departure of ship for onwards transit for exports (Section 41 of the Customs Act, 1962)

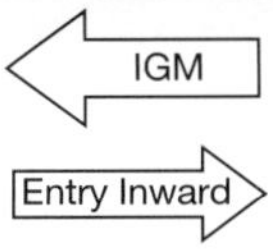		
No ship can unload the cargo unless entry inwards is granted by the customs (Section 31 of the Customs Act)		No ship can load the goods unless exit outwards is granted by the customs under Section 39 and order for loading is received from the customs under Section 40 of the Customs Act, 1962.

of these documents used in export operations in the beginning itself, so as to avoid any problems that may crop up during the prolonged trade operations.

11.3 Role of EXIM Documentation

Trade documentation is necessary and an integral part of EXIM operations due to variety of reasons. When an exporter sells his/her goods in international markets, he/she has to prepare various documents as transportation of cargo from one country to another is full of various regulatory and commercial requirements. Another country may have some legislation in place for quality control and inspection of certain items such as SPS requirements and TBT. When an exporter gives goods to a shipping company, he/she must have some documents to prove the delivery of goods and retain the title of goods. Such goods have to be insured and cross-checked by the customs official for which the exporter is again required to submit some documents such as invoice, packing list, insurance certificate and shipping bill. The various reasons for careful understanding of trade documentation in export operations are given in Figure 11.2.

In addition to the above-mentioned points, some of the important aspects of documents in EXIM operations are explained as follows:

1. There are certain documents which are essentially required as they are needed as per the regulations of importing and exporting country and other international conventions for the transportation of goods from one country to another. Such essential documents in international trade operations

FIGURE 11.2 Role of trade documents in export operations.

are bill of lading, packing list, commercial invoice, import licence, certificate of origin, inspection certificate, insurance certificate and so on.

2. Transfer of ownership of cargo from exporter to importer is done through transport documents under the established procedure, wherein trade documents are routed through proper banking channels. For example, a bill of lading is a document of title and ownership which helps in transfer of ownership of cargo from exporter to importer.
3. Countries maintain their database of imports of various items and commodities so as to keep track of avoidable imports to control the outflow of foreign exchange. Such information is of prime importance to the statistical department of a country. Failure to submit such documents or forms properly may invite a fine or punitive action or both, and may cause unnecessary delay in clearing and transiting the goods to destination through foreign customs stations; for example, many countries like Mali request for customs invoice as it helps Mali customs administration in not only easy collection of revenue but also check, control and record the necessary information for avoiding sensitive imports in a foreign exchange deprived country.
4. Risks are an integral part of foreign trade and can never be controlled but can be effectively managed with an insurance cover. Sharing of risks in foreign trade is agreed by INCOTERMS and either party to trade has to take an insurance cover so as to mitigate the associated physical, climatic and biological risks to goods during the course of transportation from one country to another. Hence, the certificate of insurance issued by the insurance company against payment of premium plays an important role in risk mitigation in foreign trade.
5. Trade documents provide complete information about the goods and services such as HS code, description of goods, price, quality and quantity of goods to be exported, mode of payments, INCOTERMS and date of shipment. This helps the customs department of importing countries in easy cross-checking, duty assessment and clearance of goods to the importer. It also saves time and cost in export operations and helps exporters, importers and end users in getting low-cost products for trade, use and consumption. Trade documents, in certain cases, also help in furnishing the information required by importing country so as to administer the exchange control regulations or import quotas of the country.
6. In certain cases, importing country demands certain documents so as to arrive at a conclusion regarding the safety of public and animal health and to ensure that such commodities shall not

be imported which may cause the spread of plant diseases. Such documents are furnished for control of SPS and TBT. For example, Germany imposed restrictions on import of honey from Nepal as Nepalese honey was considered to have pesticides due to the high use of pesticides and insecticides by farmers on their agricultural crops. It also has more than permissible limit of antibiotics. Recently, Pakistan did not allow a passage to Indian trucks carrying wheat, which was to be exported to Afghanistan, due to the fear that some pilferage, spillage, theft on the way may spread botanical diseases in Pakistan agriculture.

7. Article 4 of UCPDC 600 clearly and lucidly points out that banks deal in trade documents only when undertaking the responsibility to pay under L/C, further clearly highlighting that banks do not deal in goods. It can be understood from this statement how important are trade documents for the bank for settlement of payment instead of goods, and ownership of goods lies with trade documents.
8. Customs officials' job is not only the evaluation, determination and collection of EXIM duties on the cargo being exported/imported, but they have a wider spectrum of functions like looking after whether the goods are permitted for export/import or not. Nowadays, customs department acts in tandem with other federal crime prevention agencies such as the police, intelligence services, paramilitary forces and coast guard as there is a greater threat to national and international security due to international smuggling of radioactive items, opium, RDX and other hazardous materials. Customs officials have to comply with FTP of the country on the open/channelized/prohibited/restricted trade categories of export and import. Accordingly, an exporter or importer has to get his/her goods checked by customs officials and get a 'let export seal' or 'out of charge order' proving that goods meant for export and imports are as per country's rules and regulations. The exporter is duty-bound to provide such information to customs through export documents. Customs officials ask the exporter or importer to authenticate the trade documents submitted by him/her and ask for certificates. If documents submitted are found to be false, the exporter or importer shall be subject to penalty and even in certain cases, his/her goods may be confiscated. Trade documents help the customs to see, verify and inspect the cargo of exporter and importer.
9. With emerging free trade regime across the countries, exporters enjoy tariff preference in the country of imports, thus reducing the landed cost of goods and making them attractive to buyers in the foreign country. The certificate of origin issued by a chamber or other mandated trade body plays an important role in claiming the benefits of a preferential tariff in a foreign country. Hence, documentation is extremely important for any exporter.
10. An exporter has to declare that these goods are meant for exports through trade documents. This helps him/her get the right insurance cover for safe and secure transportation of goods to another country. An exporter has to submit such export documents indicating that goods are insured to the shipping company, importers and banks while negotiating the documents for the realization of export proceeds.
11. There are certain countries which, in order to control their imports, keep a check on them through a sound information system. Accordingly, these countries ask for furnishing the information as per their regulatory requirement. In international trade, such forms are known as customs invoices. On the contrary, certain other countries demand the consular invoice along with the commercial invoice or legalization/visa of commercial invoice so as to get the details of export shipments coming to their country. Such documents create several non-tariff barriers for exporters. Such countries demand it so as to control their imports from certain countries.

Knowledge of such invoices, which have to be prepared, is essential for the exporter for smooth and systematic export operations.

12. Certain documents like 'short shipment certificate' are required so as to prove that only a part of goods has been shipped, provided it was either agreed in ISC or mentioned in L/C. Short shipment certificate helps the exporter to realize even partial payment, hence, it is an important and integral part of international trade operations.

It can be said that trade documentation is an integral and essential part of EXIM operations and no trade activity between two countries can be harmonious, sustainable and continuously growing until the exporters and importers are not well trained and informed on trade documentation practices of the country. GOI has paid great attention to the same and has asked several trade promotion organizations and institutions to provide training to exporters and importers in trade documentation. IIFT, set up under the Ministry of Commerce, has been playing a vital role in this regard since its foundation in 1963.

11.4 Aligned Documentation System

For enjoying maximum benefits of economic globalization in the world economy, it is important that traders world over must provide information on goods, their transport, clearances and payment in a harmonized and standardized manner. The aligned documentation system is aimed at eliminating the multiple documents and forms, other trade documents and provides trade-related information to various stakeholders in a standardized manner. Accordingly, negotiations under GATT agreement were started among countries to arrive at a consensus for an aligned documentation system incorporating the perspective of each party, avoiding duplication of trade information and ensuring that traders are able to complete the documentation formalities in a timely manner. The aligned documentation system is aimed at streamlining the different definitions of trade information, reducing various formats of trade documents and harmonizing the presentation of data in trade documents. Accordingly, different layouts and paper sizes of trade documents are streamlined in a standard format for all traders in the world. Aligned documentation system has reduced the scope of errors and delays and reduced the time required to prepare the trade documents. It has also simplified the process across the EXIM operations, thus reducing redundancy and duplication of information.

Initiatives for standardization of trade documents started as early as in 1960 by the United Nations Economic Commission for Europe. Trade documents were divided into two categories: Master Documents 1 and 2, known as the UN Layout Key. In a short period of time, it has become the most important tool for document alignment across the globe and most of the customs authorities started using UN Layout Key in their electronic processing system such as Automated System for Customs Data (ASYCUDA) and United Nations Electronic Trade Documents. The UN Layout Key provides a model form that defines specifications such as paper size, margins and form's design sheet. Figure 11.3 indicates the organizations which have played an important role in standardization of aligned trade documents through 'United Nations Layout Key for Trade Documents'.

Efforts were further mobilized to develop a paperless trade documentation system by using these standardized trade documents as traditional paper-based systems were too slow, costly and unable to cope with the rising amount of international trade transactions in the world economy. Aligned documentation system based on UN Layout Key facilitated these efforts and national custom authorities along with associated stakeholders in the EXIM chain started moving towards e-commerce portal

- ICS standard bill of lading (International Chamber of Shipping)
- CMR road consignment note (Convention sur le contrat de transport international de marchandises par route)
- CIM international rail consignment note (Convention internationale concernant le transport des marchandises par chemins de fer)
- IATA air waybill (International Air Transport Association)
- UPU post parcel compendium documents (Universal Postal Union)
- CCC customs export, import and transit declarations (Customs Co-operation Council, now World Customs Organization)
- FIATA freight forwarding documents (Fédération Internationale des Associations de Transitaires et Assimilés)

FIGURE 11.3 Organizations involved in standardization of trade documents.

aimed at cutting the cost and time involved in the processing of trade documents and bringing transparency to the system. The experience of regulatory bodies, policymakers and exporters and importers in India has been that electronic processing of trade documents with Indian customs, GST council, DGFT, RBI and port authorities has resulted in substantial reductions in document processing costs and turnaround time of goods from/into India. Aligned documentation system in electronic form has brought the benefits shown in Figure 11.4 to the Indian trade community.

Trade facilitation agreement as negotiated and agreed to by member countries provides for the creation of 'single window system' for required trade information to EXIM community including the trade documentation practices of a country and duty structure therein. It further mandates the member states to create online e-commerce facilities, thus moving towards paperless trade by processing the trade documents electronically. Member state has required huge investments to create

- Real-time processing of trade documents resulting in faster release of goods
- Speedier and increased revenue collection as exporters and importers can pay faster than the traditional system
- Faster compilation of trade statistics for policymaking and records
- High level of accuracy in trade documentation and increased post-export compliance
- Transparency and predictability of services to trade community
- Reduced corruption and red tape and improved regulatory and procedural compliance
- Reduced transaction costs of business and enhanced service levels

FIGURE 11.4 Benefits of electronic aligned trade documentation system to Indian exporters and importers.

such platform and needs to train customs officials in regulatory and procedural requirements and documentation therein in electronic form. Many countries in the world trade have introduced automation of trade procedures known as ASYCUDA. The Indian government has created an e-commerce portal called www.icegate.gov.in which is linked to other regulatory agencies such as GST (www.gst.gov.in), DGFT (www.dgft.org), RBI (www.rbi.org) and various Indian ports. It is expected that electronic trade documentation will eliminate the procedural hurdles, bring transparency, reduce public interface and above all cut the costs of doing business and promote foreign trade, thus generate increased government revenues substantially owing to more efficient formalities and documentation processing.

11.5 Various Aspects of Export Documentation

The major concern of importing as well as exporting countries in international trade is the accuracy of export documents as it helps the importer in making prompt duty payments which comes to doldrums if export documents are not correct or discrepant. Banks may not purchase or discount the trade documents under the documentary collection method of payment if documents are not complied and L/C issuing bank may not negotiate the documents for payment if the exporter has submitted non-complied trade documents. Similarly, exporting country also emphasizes that the exporter shall submit accurate documents to the customs department with the right description so that customs may take least time in assessing for duty, if any, and for clearing the goods promptly. Hence, it is advisable that new exporters should consider obtaining the training, advice or suggestions or outsource services to a freight forwarder for preparation and handling of trade documentation. It is extremely important to have right, accurate and proper documentation for smooth transfer of title of goods, transport of goods, clearance of goods and settlement of payments including the realization of export proceeds through involved banks. It is usually advisable that an exporter should take the services of reliable, competent and dynamic freight forwarder so as to ensure compliance in essential documents in international trade. Freight forwarder provides an invaluable source of information and helps the exporter regarding the information on markets and packing trend keeping in mind nature of goods, shipping costs, as well as documentation and procedure for trade transactions. Interestingly, the role of freight forwarder has significantly increased and is continuously increasing in the previous some decades due to the rapid expansion of trade not only in India but globally.

Documentation is of prime importance in the financing, transport/carriage and control of goods in international trade. It is only through documents that financing of shipments, transportation of cargo and ensuring of payments is possible. Export documents help in implementing completion and transfer of goods to the importer. Hence, export documentation is mandatory in order to ensure that exporter's cargo shall arrive at destination on time and exporter may realize his/her payment for the consignment promptly and safely. It is the duty of exporter to ensure correct and accurate documents in trade transactions so that the whole cycle of trade may run smoothly without any legal, regulatory or commercial hiccups. Several aspects of export documentations are as follows:

1. **It is an easy process:** Small and first-time exporters are usually worried about the trade documentation practices as they find it a very complicated and cumbersome process. But the fact is, it is very easy to understand and prepare EXIM documents and the trader himself/herself can use his/her own expertise in preparing them provided he/she has gone for a training

programme on trade documentation practices for a hands-on knowledge on various aspects of trade documentation. Several trade promotion organizations established under the Ministry of Commerce help the start-ups and first-time exporters. These organizations conduct short-term awareness programme and management development programme for exporters and importers so as to make them aware about trade documentation framework. As the volume of trade grows, exporters can engage a shipping and forwarding agent who is supposed to take care of the job of documentation preparation, reservation of shipping space, clearance of cargo from customs and getting all documents prepared for negotiation with the banks for payments.

2. **Documentation is an integral part of international trade:** As already mentioned, trade documentation is an important and integral part of EXIM business. Correct filing of documents and other regulatory procedures must be followed when a trader exports or imports the goods and services in the foreign market. Undoubtedly, international trade involves lots of documentation and it is advisable that exporters should be well informed about preparing them rather than considering it clerical and cumbersome. Export documentation is one of the major differences between trading in the home country and trading with a foreign country as no major documentation is required in domestic business but in international trade it is a must as the regulatory environment of the foreign market is different.
3. **Correct documentation essential:** A number of documents as specified under rules and regulations of importer's country must accompany each export shipment. They must be correct, precise, non-discrepant. It is not an easy exercise as export documentation practices differ from country to country, product to product and region to region. In case the trade documents are found to be incorrect, incomplete and discrepant, an importer cannot get the custody of cargo from 'custodian of cargo' as and when they arrive. He/she may have to request for fresh, complete and non-discrepant documents and pay the demurrage charges to port authorities or a penalty to customs, as the case may be. Under such circumstances, an importer will think twice before giving repeat orders to same exporter, hence, the knowledge of trade documentation is essential for an exporter.
4. **Helpful in transportation:** Trade documents such as the bill of lading, AWB, road receipt, rail receipt and courier receipt are proof of transportation of goods from the place of origin to place of destination. Bill of lading carries the title of goods as it is a contract of carriage of cargo. In case of loss/misplacement of cargo, these documents help in claiming the cargo insurance from the insurance company. These documents also help the exporter in claiming credit insurance from ECGC in case of non-payment/default by the importer. Hence, trade documents not only help in smooth transportation but also are corroborative evidence of shipment from the originating country to the destined country.
5. **Provide clarity in export deals:** Trade documents provide clarity and transparency in international sales deals. One major purpose of the trade documentation is to provide a specific and complete description of the goods to customs officials, shipping company, banks duty drawback directorate and importers.

Conclusively, we can say that whether or not the exporter uses a 'shipping and forwarding agent' for preparation and handling of EXIM documentation, he/she must be well-informed about each document involved in foreign trade because it plays such an extensive role in international trade transactions.

11.6 Trade Documentation Practices in India

With the onset of a new political environment in India with the slogan 'maximum governance and minimum government', policymakers in India are constantly trying to reduce the trade documents in foreign trade as India inherited these documentation practices from the British empire and there had been an increase in red tape and bureaucratic controls in the initial years of economic planning and implementation. There has been harmonization of commercial documents as envisaged by UN Layout Key but unfortunately, regulatory documentation is the area that has attracted least attention of concerned regulatory authorities. Excessive regulatory documentation and allied procedure resulted in high cost of doing business in India. With the new government at the helm, the Department of Commerce has set up an inter-ministerial committee under the chairmanship of DGFT in July 2014 to study and recommend ways to reduce the number of mandatory documents required for export and import. The concerned regulatory authorities such as customs, central excise/service tax/port authority, RBI and DGFT held detailed discussions with all stakeholders and the concerned departments/ministries/agencies and visited several ports and dry ports to study the ground situation and find ways to minimize the number of documents and reduce transaction costs and time for exports and imports. DGFT submitted its report on cutting red tape and involved documentation entitled as 'Trading across Borders' to Prime Minister's Office in December 2014. DGFT panel recommended that certain trade documents can be merged with other documents without compromising the purpose for which they are generated and required for regulatory compliance. It was agreed with RBI to do away with the 'foreign exchange control form (SDF)' by incorporating the declaration in the 'shipping bill' (for exports) and also dispensing with the 'foreign exchange control form (Form A-1)' (for imports). Similarly, the Indian customs have also agreed to merge the 'commercial invoice' with the 'packing list'; however, in practicality, it has not been implemented at various customs stations in India. Port authorities both at major and non-major ports have also agreed to do away with the requirement of 'terminal handling receipt' in manual form by hosting the process online at respective ports. Accordingly, concerned involved regulatory authorities took some of the historic steps to improve the 'ease of doing business' in India as foreign investors consider it an important yardstick to plan their investment forays in India. India took a significant jump from 142 rank to 130 within a year of these steps aimed at reducing documentation in trade operations. At the announcement of new FTP 2015–2020, the minister of commerce announced that there are only three mandatory documents (Figure 11.5) required for export and import in India.

However, the ground story of contemporary trade documentation practices in India is far from reality as shown by regulatory bodies. Even the World Bank, while appreciating the efforts to reduce the trade documentation in India, has highlighted a completely different story. According to the World Bank's 'Trading across Borders' report, Figure 11.6 indicates the mandatory documents required for export and import in India.

There is always a gap between what policymakers propose as good documentation practices and present ground realities when we interact with exporters and importers on the ground. In order to provide a first-hand picture of present ground reality of trade documentation practices in India, one can divide the documents into three broad categories: first being the trade documents, which are harmonized, standardized and designed as per the UN Layout Key which are being used in India since 1991. These documents fulfil the commercial purposes of both exporters and importers in a trade transaction, for example, effecting physical transfer of goods and its 'title' from the exporter to the

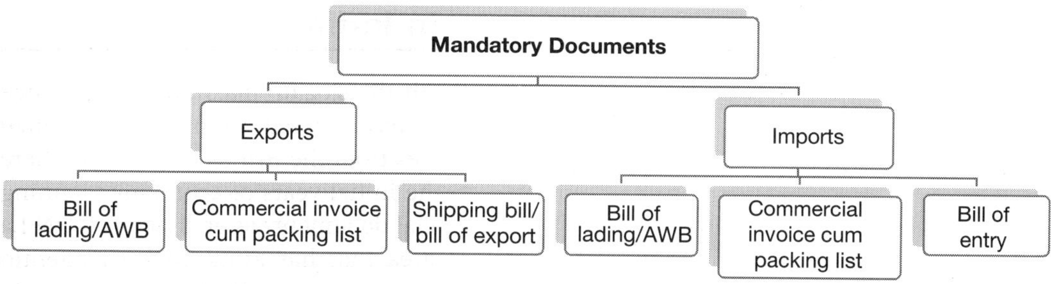

FIGURE 11.5 Mandatory documents for export and import.

Source: Adapted from Chapter 2 of Foreign Trade policy, 2015–21, Director General of Foreign Trade, New Delhi.

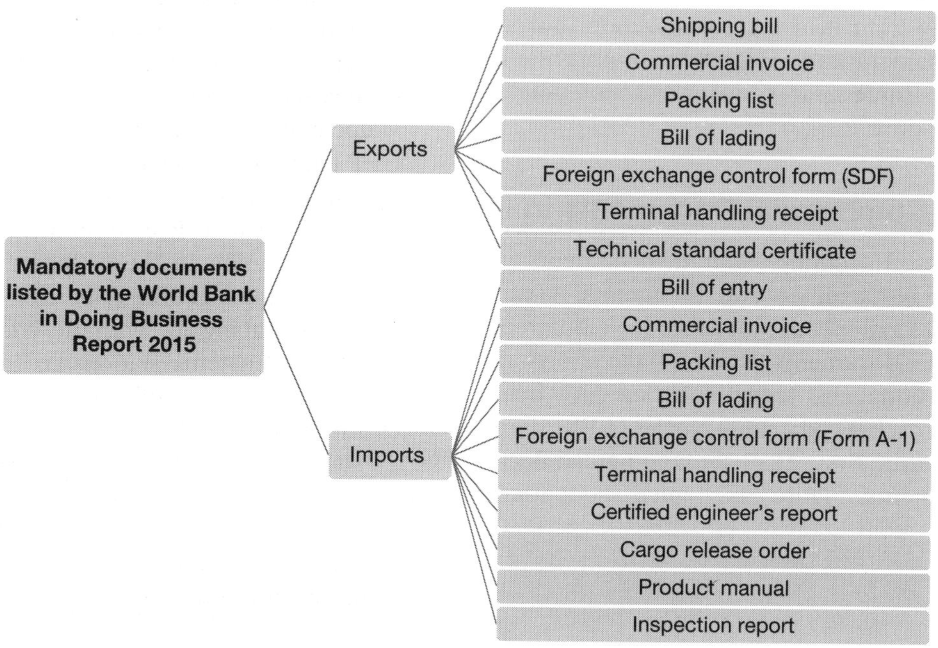

FIGURE 11.6 Mandatory documents listed by the World Bank in Doing Business Report 2015.

Source: Adapted from Trading Across Borders, Ease of Doing Business Report of India, 2018.

importer, tariff preference and cargo risks management, quality compliance and realization of payment. Such documents involve the full process of trade deals from the stage of transportation, negotiation and realization of sales proceeds. The second category of documents is known as regulatory documents which an exporter or an importer has to file with regulatory authorities such as the Indian customs, central excise, service tax, VAT/central sales tax (CST), port authorities and authorized bank. These are prescribed under relevant laws such as FEMA, 1999; the Customs Act, 1962; the Central Goods and Services Tax Act, 2017; the FTDR Act, 1992; the Customs Tariff Act, 1975; the Major Port Trust Act, 1963 and CGST Rules, 2017. In the third category, there are documents which may not be

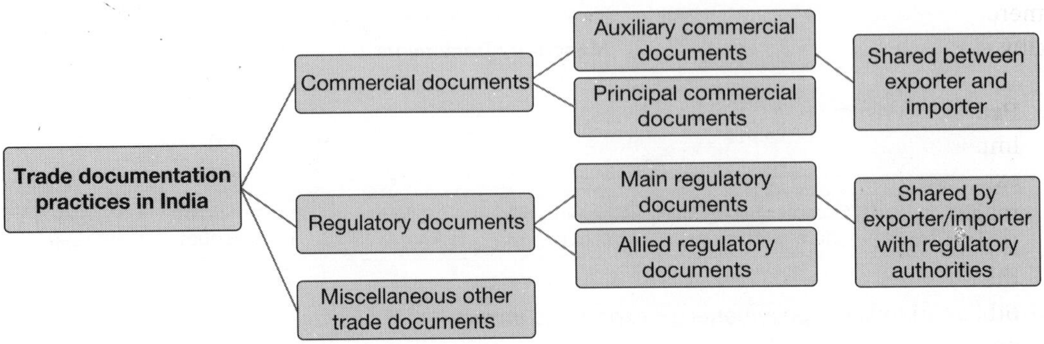

FIGURE 11.7 Trade documentation practices in India.

specifically used in a trade transaction, but an exporter/importer should know about as they are required sometimes in trade operations. For example, short shipment certificate, shut-out certificate and so on. Contemporary documentation practices in India as used in the industry can be understood through Figure 11.7.

11.6.1 Commercial Documents in International Trade

Out of these 16 commercial trade documents as discussed below, 14 have been either standardized or aligned to one another. Two documents, namely the bill of exchange and shipping order, cannot be standardized simply because they have different data elements and are quite different from the other commercial documents. However, the efforts are still on to standardize the documents as it will help in transactional cost reduction in an era when documents are usually electronically generated, prepared and exchanged among parties of EXIM operations. Commercial documents are sub-divided into two categories: first, 'auxiliary commercial documents' which help us prepare the 'principal commercial documents'. Figure 11.8 depicts sequentially which auxiliary documents help generate principal

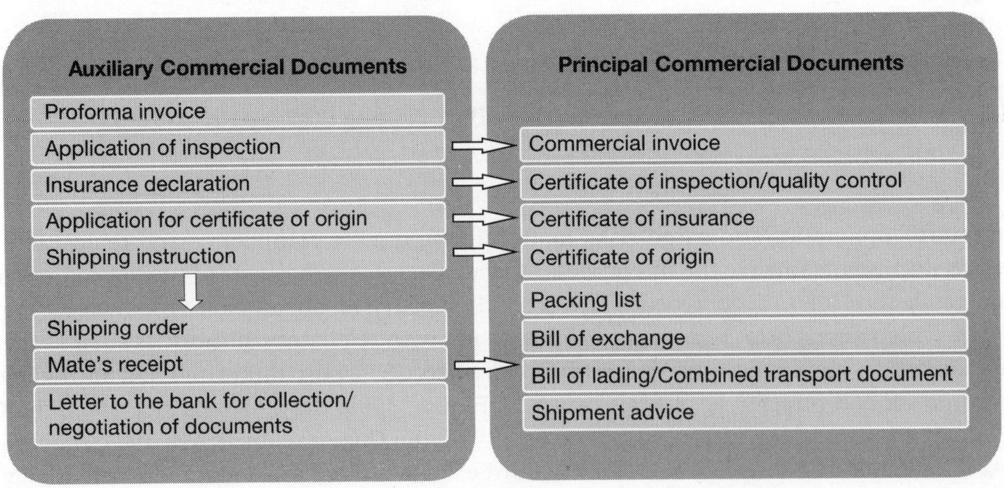

FIGURE 11.8 Flow of creation of commercial documents.

commercial documents. Only principal commercial documents are routed to importer through proper banking channel by an exporter.

1. **Proforma invoice:** An EXIM transaction begins either from the side of the exporter or from an importer based on forces of demand and supply. If importer demands any supply from an exporter, the contact or willingness is communicated through 'import quotation' and if exporter makes an offer to sell something to the importer, it is called 'proforma invoice'. Proforma invoice is prepared by an exporter willing to sell merchandise internationally and is aimed at informing the buyers of the kinds and quantities of goods available for export, price per unit, total value and other cargo specifications such as ITC(HS) code, weight, quality standards, country of make, size and dimensions, place of exports, INCOTERMS and payments terms. An exporter provides all the information with respect to export purposes to the importer and such information may include the elements mentioned in Figure 11.9.
2. **Commercial invoice:** Exporter and importer negotiate the various terms of trade such a quantity, quality, price, delivery terms, payment terms, currency of invoice, delivery date, port of loading and discharge, place of delivery and other associated issues on the basis of proforma invoice. An exporter prepares commercial invoice basically as an instrument to bill the importer for the goods exported. Commercial invoice is a formal 'demand note' issued by an exporter to an importer for payment of goods sold under a sales contract. Commercial invoice is also extremely important for customs clearance of goods as Indian customs cannot clear the goods without atleast three mandatory documents as listed in Figure 11.6. An exporter also has to submit the copy of the invoice to the authorized bank along with exchange control documents for compliance of FEMA rules. An exporter, sometimes, prepares it in advance and shares with other concerned departments for execution of export order, for example, with production department so as to inform about the quantity to be produced and quality to be complied with, logistics department so as to inform about booking of shipping space and finance department for arranging the required working capital. The UN Layout Key has prescribed the standard format of commercial invoice. Governments around the world use the commercial invoice so as to restrict/control imports as the commercial invoice will often specify the whole description about the export and import. The commercial invoice includes important information such as the dates of shipping of cargo, packing and shipping marks as per importer's country requirements, IEC and name of exporter, terms of payments, name of the consignee, trade terms like INCOTERMS, description of goods including HS classification, number of units to be sold, the total price of the cargo, mode of transportation, per unit price and any other important information which is required in the importer's country. Commercial invoice is the first and foremost principal commercial document and it serves as documentary proof in case of disputes between exporter and importer. The court takes due cognizance of agreed terms and conditions of the

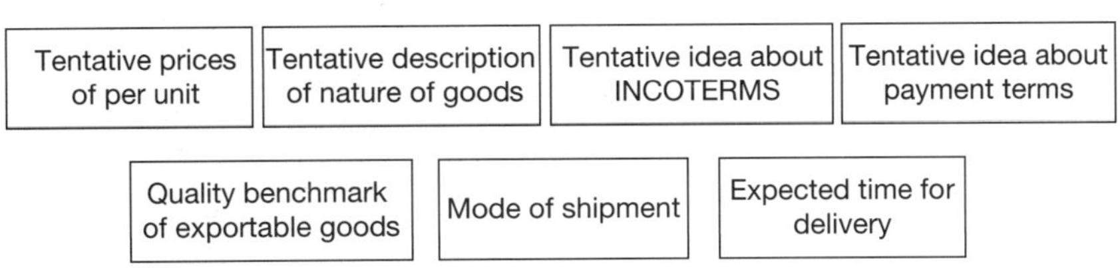

FIGURE 11.9 Key information elements in proforma invoice.

commercial invoice so as to construe the events leading to dispute between parties, for example, quality non-compliance, changes in quantity and other terms and so on. An exporter uses the copy of a duly signed invoice to claim export benefits and incentives from DGFT, settle the export compliance with regulatory bodies such as income tax and GST for exemptions claimed. Hence, an exporter should maintain and preserve a copy of the commercial invoice for further purposes such as income tax audit and duty drawback audit. Commercial invoice acts a basis for the preparation of other export documents like the shipping bill or bill of export for clearance of goods from customs. An exporter also has to submit a copy of the commercial invoice to EIA or any other mandated inspection agency for quality compliance and similarly to the chamber of commerce or other notified body for the certificate of origin. In a standard transaction, a minimum 12 copies of commercial invoice are required. Any commercial bank in India, while sanctioning the export finance, asks for commercial invoice so as to understand the financing needs of an exporter. Commercial invoice is issued by the exporter for the full realizable amount of goods as per the terms of trade and shows the value of goods. There are countries which require a special type of invoice (Figure 11.10) in addition to commercial invoice.

As a matter of practice, some exporters use the same invoice (commercial invoice) for domestic and international trade operations. This invoice is required in the United States, Canada and Australia. In some cases, importing countries insist on legalization/ visaed commercial invoice and such invoice is known as consular invoice. When the commercial invoice is duly verified (sign) by the embassy/consulate of the importer country based in the country of the exporter, it is called a consular invoice. Embassy/Consulate attested invoice becomes legalized/consular invoice. This type of invoice is required in countries like Mexico and the Middle East countries. This is done by the importing country so as to keep the record of sensitive imports to the country. If at any point of time, a country realizes that imports are increasing, and it does not have the foreign exchange to make payment, it can control/restrict certain items from the importing list. Such an arrangement is also used to provide preferential tariffs to friendly countries and to avoid the enemy countries for trading. It has sometimes been used as a diplomatic weapon to settle other issues with trading countries through the use of non-tariff barriers. The countries which require the commercial invoice to be legalized/visaed, do so in order to maintain the actual database of various imported goods into the country. In case of some countries, there is a demand for consular invoice or legalized/visaed commercial invoice as they make assessment of duty payable on the basis of such visaed commercial invoice. Legalized invoices are demanded in countries such as Turkey, Liberia, Taiwan and Latin American countries. Such practices are used in landlocked and island nations as they want to control/regulate imports in their porous borders. In

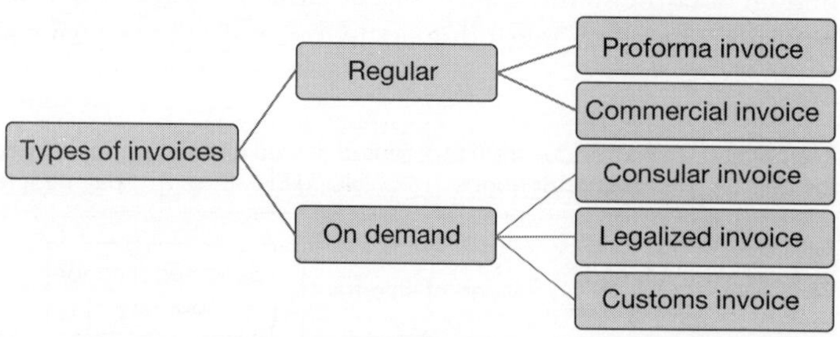

FIGURE 11.10 Types of invoice in international trade.

majority of the countries there is no need of a consular invoice as such countries make the assessment of duty payable on the basis of a commercial invoice. Commercial invoice is the principal commercial document and must be signed and dated.

3. **Application for certificate of inspection:** Quality of exportable goods is an important issue that every exporter has to keep in mind while exporting goods to international markets. Importers from developed countries are very particular about quality issues. Inspection of exportable goods for quality compliance can take place at three levels: First, country of export may mandate the compliance of quality in exports of certain goods; for example, EIC, which was established under the Export (Quality Control and Inspection) Act, 1963, is the nodal agency for quality compliance, wherein GOI has notified the goods for mandatory quality compliance such as honey, basmati rice, eggs and certain engineering products. An exporter has to make an application in duplicate in the prescribed form for intimating EIA to carry out the pre-shipment inspection work. Such inspection may be carried out at the exporter premises or at a prescribed export agency. The intimation for the same purpose has to be given to EIA through 'intimation for inspection' as per standardized pre-shipment export document. Second, the inspection of goods may be carried out by the inspection agency notified by the importer which may be an independent EIA. DGFT has compiled the names and addresses of certain inspection agencies of international repute in Appendix 10 of FTP 2015–2020. Third, sometimes, export inspection may not be desired by the exporter's country or an importer, but by the country of imports; for example, the US FDA does not allow import of any eatables without proper inspection for quality compliance and authenticity. Based on negotiated INCOTERMS, an exporter or importer has to intimate the agency concerned for export inspection and while filing the application for export inspection, either party to trade is required to attach the following documents to be the submitted along with application to concerned EIA:
   a. Copy of sales contract and in absence of sales contract, a copy of proforma invoice or commercial invoice clearly providing the description of goods and agreed quality standards.
   b. Copy of L/C if payment is to be settled through L/C.
   c. Requisite fees for inspection of cargo in a crossed cheque/draft or Indian Postal Order.
   d. Description of packing specifications as instructed by importer.
   e. Any other documentary evidence which mandates for quality compliance.

   EIA, on the satisfaction that goods to be exported are in compliance with negotiated and agreed quality standards and norms, may issue a certificate of inspection within 2–3 days from the date of receipt of application of the exporter.
4. **Certificate of inspection:** Based on information provided by the exporter or importer in application for the certificate of inspection, pre-shipment inspection is undertaken by EIA which may be under the administrative control of EIC or any other independent notified inspection agency by importer or importer's country. The list of notified independent inspection agency is compiled in Appendix 10 of FTP. While conducting the pre-shipment inspection, export agency factors in issues such as the nature of products, standards of quality or agreed quality norms and other importer specifications which may be related to packing material, labelling and marking. Such inspection usually takes place on 'consignment to consignment' basis at the premises of exporter or a sample collected for inspection in the lab. In some cases, there can be in-process quality control where the quality control becomes a process of manufacturing for assured quality compliance of exportable goods. Sometimes, inspection is also done by

concerned CB officials such as tea board and coffee board due to the specific nature of goods requiring specialized expertise. In cases where the pre-shipment inspection is made mandatory, export inspection must take place essentially by the agency as named by the importer. If quality control facilities are not available at the exporter premises, the inspections of consignment can be done at the port of the shipment. On the submission of the above documents along with application for certificate of inspection as listed above, EIA requires at least 2–3 days to conduct a quality test of the consignment of exportable goods. On its satisfaction about the exportable quality of consignment as per importer requirement/standards, it issues five copies of the certificate of inspection to the exporter in the prescribed proforma. The exporter submits the original copy of such inspection certificate to customs authorities along with shipping bill/bill of export at the time of export consignment clearance by the Indian customs. Second copy of export inspection is to be sent to the importer along with various export documents. Third copy shall be retained by the exporter for any future reference. Fourth copy is to be sent to EIC at its headquarters at New Delhi and fifth copy shall be retained by the concerned EIA for future references.

5. **Application for certificate of insurance:** Risk is an integral part of international trade operations due to factors such as long distance, long duration, no physical control on goods, various involved trade intermediaries, external threats like piracy, terrorist attacks and natural calamities. Risks can never be controlled but can be managed by taking an insurance cover. Accordingly, an exporter or importer needs to apply to the insurance company for insurance cover and has to declare the cargo details. He/she should intimate the cargo destination of exports and other details through the standard insurance declaration which is part of standardized documents and is based on the format which is approved by the Institute of London Underwriters. It is suggested that open cover/policy holders may be supplied with blank forms of these documents. Such forms can be reproduced from the standardized master document which can be sent by exporter/importer to the nearby office of the General Insurance Corporation for declaration of cargo so as to get the insurance cover for the exportable goods. The general insurance company should issue the certificate of insurance to the exporter after completion of necessary entries and certification by the company.
6. **Certificate of insurance:** As international trade transportation is full of risks, ocean carriers do not take any responsibility for loss, piracy, damage, pilferage and so on to the cargo if the cargo is shipped without the insurance cover. Ocean carriers consider it negligence on the part of exporter. Hence, it is mandatory for the exporter to arrange the cargo/marine insurance for his/her export shipment. Certificate of insurance is an insurance document that indicates the type and amount of insurance coverage in force on a particular shipment in EXIM operations. Insurance is must in a trade transaction as either party to trade is exposed to risks and insurance certificate is used to assure both the parties that insurance is provided to cover loss of or damage to the cargo while in international transit. Regular exporters usually take a master policy, wherein shipper of goods may issue a document that certifies that a shipment has been insured under a given open policy, and this certificate represents and takes the place of such open policy and shall also be accordingly governed by the provisions of open policy. A certificate of insurance is issued upon the exporter's intimation for the insurance to the insurance company. The insurance certificate indicates the amount insured of the shipments and also describes that what kind of risks are covered under the particular policy of various Institute Cargo Clauses A, B and C. Certificate of insurance is always issued by an insurance company, certifying the existence of the

contract between the insurer and insured and shows an abstract of the most important provisions of the insurance contract. In marine insurance where cargo is insured against a floating insurance policy, certificate of insurance acts to assure the consignee that insurance is in effect for the internationally traded goods and proper policy will be followed to protect either party to trade against maritime risks.

7. **Application for certificate of origin:** Certificate of origin is a 'quasi-financial instrument' which has got immense importance in an environment of free trade/regional economic grouping. Certificate of origin helps us in establishing evidence of the origin of goods which in turn helps the nations to decide whether the product is eligible for duty preference/duty-free entry or not. Importing countries mandate it for the exporters to certify the 'origin of goods' in order to make goods eligible for such preferential duty regime. Hence, complying with the origin of goods is essential for exporters in order to avail the duty preference in international trade operations. There are several agencies including EIC that have been mandated by GOI to issue a certificate of origin. An exporter has to apply to these agencies to get certificates of origin. Certificate of origin is of two types—preferential and non-preferential. Figure 11.11 depicts the various preferential schemes of certificates of origin available to Indian exporters.

   These PTAs and FTAs prescribe rules of origin, which the exporter has to follow so as to become eligible for tariff preference. Various agencies authorized for this purpose charge some fee for issuing a certificate of origin, providing the details regarding rules of origin, list of items covered by an agreement, extent of tariff preference, verification and certification of eligibility. Preferential certificate of origin is issued only by EIC and FIEO. Non-preferential certificate of origin is issued by several chambers of commerce, industry associations and merchants organizations, the details of which can be accessed from appendices to FTP 2015–2020. The exporters desiring preferential or non-preferential certificate of origin may apply to the concerned agency along with following documents:

FIGURE 11.11 Preferential scheme available to Indian exporters.

Source: Ministry of Commerce & Industry, Government of India. https://commerce.gov.in/ (accessed on 24 May 2023).

a. A covering letter to EIA/FIEO/chamber of commerce for issue of the certificate of origin. The letter should also indicate that the information furnished in the relevant documents is true and correct.
b. Details of quantum/origin of inputs/consumables used in export products.
c. Two copies of invoices.
d. Indemnity bond.
e. Packing list in duplicate for concerned invoice.
f. Nine copies of the certificate of origin duly completed along with one copy of the invoice.
g. Declaration from the exporter with the words 'We hereby declare that the goods mentioned in this invoice are of Indian origin and manufacture'.
h. Fee not exceeding ₹100 per certificate or as may be prescribed by the concerned agency.

The authorized agency would ensure that goods to be exported are of Indian origin or seem to be of Indian origin as per general principles governing the rules of origin before issuing non-preferential certificate of origin. The certificate shall be issued as per format given in appendices to FTP 2015–2020. Applicants should not make any kind of overwriting or typing errors while submitting the certificate as certificate of origin. It is a quasi-financial instrument and agencies take immense care and caution while issuing the certificate of origin as it offers lower duty on importable goods, thus making goods attractive in the country of imports.

8. **Certificate of origin:** Certificate of origin is issued to an exporter by the authorized chamber or trade promotion body as enunciated in appendices to FTP 2015–2020. An exporter sends the certificate of origin along with other principal commercial documents to an importer who uses it to avail the preferential tariff under applicable PTAs/FTAs such as India–Sri Lanka Free Trade Agreement and India–ASEAN Free Trade Agreement and other non-reciprocal arrangements such as GSP and GSTP. Certificate of origin indicates that the goods have been manufactured from the originating country material; hence, they shall be entitled to preferential rates of tariff in the country of imports as agreed in any FTA or other arrangement. In certain cases, countries which are giving such preferential treatment require legalization of the document from their country consular in order to make such consignment for preferential benefits. Certificates of origin are issued by trade promotion bodies such as EIC, CBs, SEZ commissioners and various chambers of commerce.
9. **Shipping instruction:** In today's globalized world, export operations have become so complex that an exporter is required to get specialized services from a freight forwarder to complete the trade logistics operations successfully. In order to communicate the details related to smooth and systematic transportation of cargo from origin to destination, an exporter has to communicate the negotiated terms and conditions such as delivery date, mode of transport, documentary compliance, hazardous goods compliance, effective freight rates and other issues to a freight forwarder who arranges for shipment of goods and looks after issues such as custom clearance, movement of cargo, packing, labelling, marking, fumigation, palletization, terminal charges and booking of ship at cost-effective rates. An exporter outsources these activities as the rules governing the international transportation are not only complex but extremely dynamic, changing every day and spanning over the various regulatory authorities. It is advisable to engage a trade specialist like freight forwarder to offer such specialized logistics solution services to an exporter. Appointing a freight forwarder is considered as an extension to the exporter's export department. Accordingly, freight forwarder has to be apprised of the various aspects of international shipment through shipping instructions. A freight forwarder needs to know as much about the transaction

as the exporter knows so as to comply with all of the importer's requirements for successful and effective execution of contract and for keeping the importer loyal for future purposes. In case an exporter makes an error or mistake in furnishing the exact and accurate shipping instructions to the freight forwarder, following types of unnecessary problems may come in international trade operations:

a. There may be documentary non-compliance resulting in problems in negotiation of trade documents with issuing bank under an arrangement of payment settlement through L/C. A freight forwarder may make a mistake in preparing the certain essential documents which are important for L/C negotiation as he/she would have thought that the exporter would prepare them.

b. One must understand that each mode of transport has its own regulations for compliance requirements and freight forwarders, as a logistics professional understands that the carriage of dangerous goods is subject to compliance with national and international regulations such as 'Carriage of Dangerous Goods and Use of Transportable Pressure Equipment Regulations, 2009', which apply to the carriage of dangerous goods by road, rail and internal EU waterways, European Agreement Concerning the International Carriage of Dangerous Goods by Road, International Maritime Dangerous Goods Code as mandated by FIATA and International Civil Aviation Organization and other international conventions aimed at the safety of seamen at works (SOLAS).

c. In absence of accurate shipping instructions, a freight forwarder may make a mistake in shipping the goods on wrong INCOTERMS like freight prepaid instead of collect basis, thus making transaction unprofitable.

d. A freight forwarder may make a mistake in returning the original documents to the shipper so as to distribute them, instead of sending them to a bank and/or consignee for payment negotiation/purchase or discounting of export proceeds.

f. A freight forwarder may book the cargo by sea route while air transportation was agreed with the importer.

In order to provide proper and exact information, it is recommended that the list provided in Figure 11.12 may be used by an exporter to brief the freight forwarder about smooth transportation and logistics operations and help in availing best freight rates and saving time in international logistics of goods.

10. Shipping order: Shipping order is issued by the shipping line for intimating the exporter about the reservation of space of shipment. It also describes the name of specific ships calling at a port of departure on the possible date of arrival and subsequent departure. It is an alert for any consignor to get his/her cargo cleared from customs authority as no shipping company/carrier will load the cargo without customs clearance. It is also referred to as ticket of cargo for transportation of goods from origin to destination. A shipping order issued by a shipping line generally contains the order number, date, name and address of the shipper, customs broker or forwarder name, shipping and receipt dates, vessel and voyage number, sailing time, delivery date and location, name of local sea agent, customs closing date, number and type of packages to be transported and manner of freight payment. An exporter must check that 'shipping order' issued by a shipping line must be in line with 'shipping instructions'.

11. Packing list: Packing list is also known as cargo manifest in many countries and is a 'principal commercial document' which shows the number and kinds of packages being shipped, total of

Shipper/ Consignor name: Name of exporting firm/company	Pickup party: Operating customer at origin	Origin: City/State for the rail origin	Consignee name: Company name (owner of the goods in the equipment)	Notify party (if notified): Care of party, that is, operating customer at destination
Account of party at destination: Loading/ Unloading customer at destination	Destination: City/State for the rail origin	STCC: Standard transportation commodity code (7-digit number)	Payment method: Prepaid or collect	Weight code (i.e., shipper's scale weight, RR scale weight, agreement weight, no weight)
Hazmat information if hazardous commodity (UN/NA number, primary hazardous class, proper shipping name, packaging group and so on)	Payer of freight: Company name and full address information	If a Rule 11 move – the follow information is Required:	Payer of freight: Company name and full address information	Restriction on use of particular flag of ship registration, for example, Pakistani ship for Indian goods
Additional requirements for intermodal customers only	Quote number	Notify party: Company name and contact number	Any other business partners that need to be identified on the bill of lading (i.e., beneficial owner, account of, release to and so on)	Price authority: Contract, quote or tariff
	Special handling options	Route, carrier and junction abbreviations (include origin and destination delivery switch carriers when applicable)		

FIGURE 11.12 Checklist of required information for shipping instructions.

Source: Adapted from BNSF Railway, Canada.

gross, legal and net weights of the packages, and marks and numbers on the packages. It should always be a unique document and not combined with any other document and its description must be in sync with other trade documents. A detailed packing list requires a listing of the contents of each package, carton and so on, and other relevant information. Customs officials use packing list to check what is being exported or imported while importer uses it to know without opening the carton/packing that goods are of specified nature as requested by the importer in export order. The key contents of the standard packing list document are illustrated in Figure 11.13.

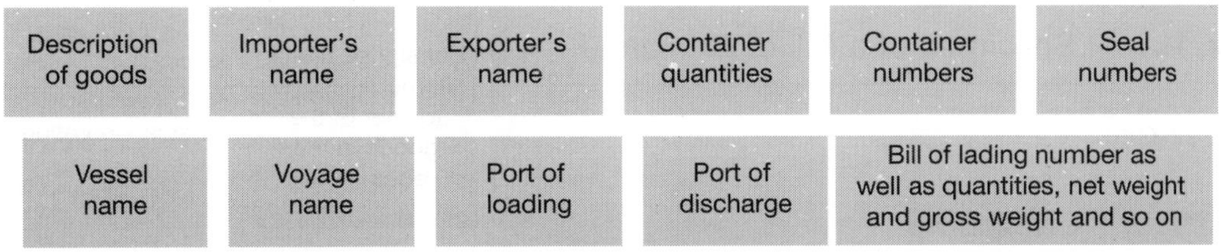

FIGURE 11.13 Key contents of standard packing list.

Cargo manifest or packing list provides all the information with respect to all the items in the box, crate, pallet and container including their type, dimensions and weight of the container so as to help the customs authorities to know what is inside the carton or packet. It is important to note that in cases where quantities, weights or contents of the various packing cases vary in an export shipment, it is mandatory for an exporter to prepare a separate packing list for each carton mentioning its colour, contents, weight and measurements. A packing list usually includes the outside dimensions of each carton/pack, the total cubic content and total weight of the shipment to be exported. In some countries, cargo manifest or packing list is not a mandatory document required by the customs authorities, but it serves the important purposes of cross-checking the cargo by customs officials from various importing countries in addition to supplementing the commercial invoice which accompanies the export shipment. Usually, the export packing list is more detailed and informative than a domestic packing list, as it summarizes the material in each individual carton/packet and describes the type of package such as a box, crate, drum or carton. A packing list is also important for inventory management for both exporter and importer as each party knows what type of cargo is going out of the factory or coming into the warehouse. It is extremely important for logistics companies as they classify the cargo for safe and secure transportation on the basis of the packing list.

12. **Bill of exchange:** A bill of exchange is always prepared by the exporter. It is a 'negotiable instrument' similar to the cheque, hundi or promissory notes. It is an unconditional order in writing, in which the importer is addressed and required by the exporter to pay on demand or at a future date a certain amount of money to the order of a person or bearer. It is a non-interest-bearing written order which is used in international trade as it provides a sort of guarantee to the exporter to get a specified and fixed sum of money from importer at a predetermined future date as has been agreed between exporter and importer in export sales contract. It can be withdrawn by individuals or banks. It is also transferable by endorsements of exporter. The specimen of bill of exchange is shown in Box 11.1.

    There are three parties involved in a bill of exchange. These are drawer, drawee and payee. Figure 11.14 explains the parties in a bill of exchange.

    Due to negotiable nature of bill of exchange, a drawer can also draw a bill in his own name. Thus, he/she himself/herself becomes the payee. The language to be used in such bill of exchange shall be 'Pay to me or on my order'. If the time period is mentioned in the bill of exchange, then it shall be known as time bill (Box 11.1). If it is payable on demand, then it shall be known as demand bill. Figure 11.15 shows the features of a bill of exchange.

13. **Mate's receipt:** Mate's receipt is a declaration/intimation which is issued by an officer of a vessel whereby he/she indicates that the goods have been received on board on his/her vessel for shipment to the destined country or port of destination. It is a document which is signed by the

BOX 11.1 ▶ Specimen of a Bill of Exchange

USD 5,00,000/- .... New Delhi

.... November 11, 2018

Three months after date pay to Order (To me or to the Order of me) the sum of USD Five Hundred Thousand Only for value received.

To Nepal Petroleum Company ....
Stamp Zorawar Exports India Limited

Kathmandu .... New Delhi

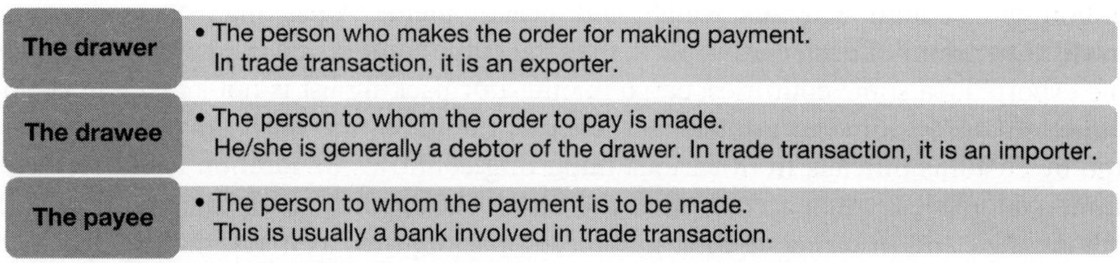

FIGURE 11.14 The parties to a bill of exchange.

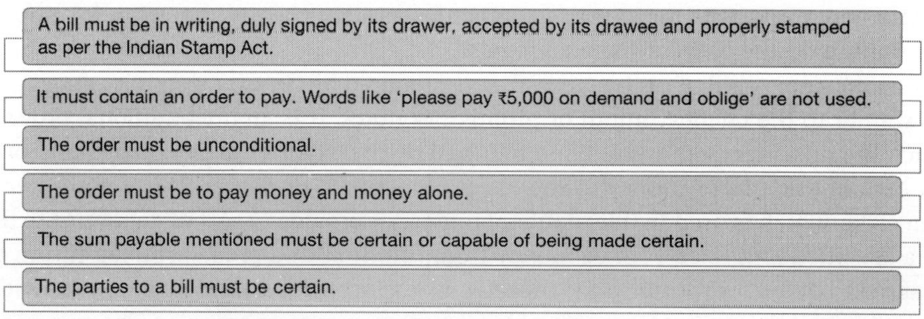

FIGURE 11.15 Features of bill of exchange.

mate of a vessel whereby he acknowledges receipt of cargo on board ship. The one who has the 'mate's receipt' is entitled to get a bill of lading from the contracted shipping line. Thus, mate's receipt issued by the officer of the ship is exchanged to get bill of lading at a subsequent stage. The mate of the ship marks the claused or clean receipt of goods meaning whether 'goods are received in apparent good condition and order'. If goods received have improper packaging or leaking or damaged or have incomplete documentation, the mate will issue a claused or dirty mate's receipt. If mate's receipt is dirty or claused, the bill of lading shall also carry dirty title as the mate's receipt is supposed to indicate/acknowledge that the shipping company has received the cargo in what condition stated therein. Mate's receipt is an auxiliary commercial document. It is also a document of title as long as it is not marked 'non-negotiable'.

14. **Bill of lading and AWB:** Around 92 percent of the world trade goods are transported either by sea or by air transport. In fact, water transport is the most favourable mode of transport used in international trade operations. If goods are exported through sea routes, the shipping company issues a transport document called 'bill of lading' and, alternatively, if goods are exported by air transport, airlines or appointed agent issue a transport document called 'air waybill'. Bill of lading can be negotiable or non-negotiable. In fact, 'negotiable bill of lading' is the most vital and important document in successful execution of international trade operations. A negotiable bill of lading plays a key role in facilitation and execution of free, smooth and fast international trade and commerce. It is issued by carriers upon the receipt of exportable cargo or in lieu of mate's receipts issued for this purpose. It has three vital characteristics: *first*, it is an acknowledgement by the carrier that goods as mentioned in the bill of lading have been received and are in physical possession of carriers for transport and delivery to the consignee. Acknowledgement through bill of lading by the shipping company for receipts of cargo acts as an 'evidence' of delivery of goods to carrier for export. If the cargo is lost or stolen or misplaced during the voyage or transshipment or at destination port, exporter or importer can demand compensation from carrier for such losses. *Second*, bill of lading provides details or evidence of relevant terms of 'contract' between consignor and carrier. These commercial terms again help in establishing the costs and risks which shall be borne by either of the party. Bill of lading has details of consignor, consignee and notifying party that helps in faster, smoother and secure evacuation of cargo at destination. *Third*, and most important, the negotiable bill of lading acts as a 'transferable document' for ownership and title of goods between two trading parties. This is the most important aspect of the bill of lading and it sets it apart from other transport documents, be it non-negotiable seaway bill, AWB, road consignment note, courier receipts, post parcel receipts and rail receipts. The key features of bill of lading are illustrated in Figure 11.16.

    Bill of lading as a 'document of title' provides its holder with the exclusive right to demand delivery of cargo from the shipping company. No shipping company will release the cargo to

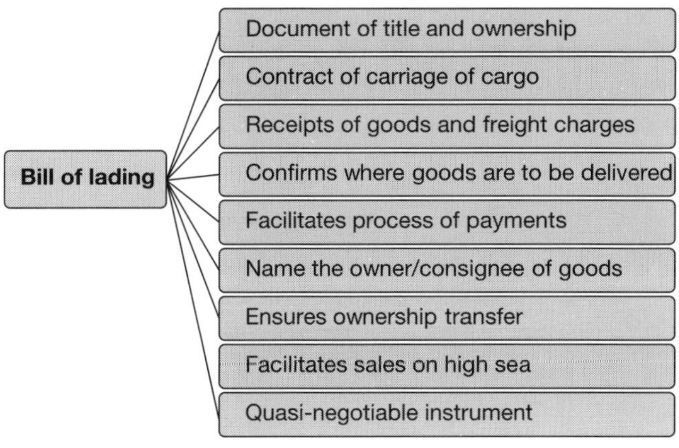

FIGURE 11.16 Features of bill of lading.

Source: Adapted from Indian Bill of Lading Act, 1856.

anyone without a negotiable bill of lading or certificate of indemnity. Cargo at destination can only be received at the presentation of negotiable bill of lading along with full set of trade document by the consignee. Negotiable bill of lading thus establishes the constructive ownership and ensures transfer of cargo to the right person. There are two kinds of bill of lading. It can be 'straight' or 'to order'. The characteristics of each of them are given in Figure 11.17.

Mostly, 'to order bill of lading' is used as it facilitates the 'string sale' or 'sale on high sea'. This is a unique feature of a negotiable bill of lading as it helps the consignor or subsequent buyer to transfer the ownership of cargo or sell the goods to another party without actual physical transfer of goods; that is, goods may still be on board with the carrier for the transportation to destination. This is executed by way of pledge of this negotiable bill of lading to a bank and the same is used as a security to raise finance. On the contrary, if the word 'straight' is added before the negotiable bill of lading, then the custody and possession of such goods can only be received by the named party and string sale or sale on high sea cannot be executed by such bill of lading. There are several types of bills of lading used in international trade operations and are accordingly discussed as follows:

a. **Shipped bill of lading:** The Carriage of Goods by Sea Act, 1925, in India gives right to the consignor of the cargo to demand from the shipping company a 'shipped' or 'shipped on board' bill of lading which proves that cargo has actually been shipped. The shipping company under such circumstances is bound to deliver the cargo at destination to the consignee. As a practice in the shipping industry, the term 'shipped (on board) in apparent good order and condition' is printed on the bill of lading itself. This is a confirmation on the part of shipping company under contract of carriage that these goods are actually loaded on board ship and shipping company promises to hand over these goods at intended destination. If the importer does not receive cargo at destination, he/she can call surveyor and can claim compensation for any losses. From consignor's point of view, it is the most satisfactory type of receipt and consignee will also be happy as he/she will get the delivery of cargo on presentation of original bill of lading to this effect.
b. **Received bill of lading:** Sometimes, the goods are received by the freight forwarder or agent of the shipping company for shipment. These shipments are usually from country hinterland at ICDs and CFS. Freight forwarder or agent of shipping company issues the bill of lading to consignor with term 'received for shipment in apparent good condition and order'. If the word 'shipped' does not appear on the bill of lading, then it is understood that goods have been handed over to the freight forwarder or agent of shipping for shipment. If goods have

Straight bill of lading	• A straight bill of lading is a non-negotiable document. It is prepared to a named consignee. It is also an acknowledgement of payment of freight and shipping company ensures that it shall transport the goods to destination.
'To order' bill of lading	• A to order bill of lading is a document that is prepared to the foreign importer or its bank for the payment and custody of goods. It is negotiable.

FIGURE 11.17 Kinds of bill of lading.

not been actually shipped so far and are in the custody of freight forwarder or agent of carrier, then such received cargo is usually at dock or ICD or CFS or warehouse or in transit or received for consolidation or at 'CONCOR depot' or at rail yard, but essentially yet to be loaded on the ship for shipment. Such bill of lading if not subsequently stamped with term 'shipped on board' has no value as it does not guarantee that goods have actually been shipped from India. No importer will release payments if the bill of lading is stamped 'received for shipment' instead of 'shipped on board' because importer is not assured of the guaranteed delivery of cargo at the port of destination. Banks usually avoid handling bill of lading stamped as 'received for shipment' for their clients.

c. **Groupage/master bill of lading:** In India, 35–40 percent exporters and importers are of small scale having LCL shipments. Accordingly, the government has allowed freight forwarders and logistics companies to 'consolidate' cargo. Compatible cargo from various small-scale exporters is consolidated into one container meant for several small-scale consignees located usually in the same country/area. Thus, various small lot shipments are consolidated into one and are dispatched in one container. Such an arrangement helps small-scale exporters to get competitive and lower freight charges for their LCL cargo and make their products' price attractive in international markets. The shipping company issues to such freight forwarder or logistics company a single 'master or groupage' bill of lading evidencing the details of each type of cargo consolidated into the container. Freight forwarder or logistics company in turn issues split bill of lading to each consignor(s).

d. **Split bill of lading:** Split bill of lading is also known as 'freight forwarder bill of lading' or 'house bill of lading' and is issued by the freight forwarder. Freight forwarder accepts the LCL cargo from two or more small shipment consignors and consolidates it into one container for consignment usually as FCL. Such consolidated cargo, that is, FCL is handed over to shipping company which issues the groupage/master bill to freight forwarder, who in turn issues split bill of lading to each party whose cargo has been consolidated evidencing the details of the cargo. Split bill of lading has all other details such as name of consignor and consignee, commercial terms, port of loading and discharge and place of destination. Split bill of lading is not a complete document of title, but it has a legal standing similar to that of a normal carrier's bill of lading. If the terms and conditions of L/C do not restrict such split bill of lading, then it is capable of being negotiated for payments.

e. **Transshipment bill of lading:** Usually, there is transshipment of cargo in international trade operations due to variety of reasons, for example, not direct service by ship to destination, lower freight rates, scheduling problems and so on. In case of transshipment, a bill of lading has to be issued for each voyage; for example, if cargo from India destined to Germany has three transshipment during the course of transportation, three separate bills of lading will be issued. More than one bill of lading in single transportation involving transshipment in course are known as transshipment bill of lading.

f. **Through bills of lading:** Through bill of lading is an improvement on transshipment bill of lading. Under through bill of lading, a consignor will get one bill of lading evidencing the transshipment in transportation of goods. Carrier employs two or more than two carriers for transportation of goods but issues only one bill of lading. Under a single contract for carriage of goods, an exporter can get lower freight rates. Freight forwarders also offer competitive freight rates for through transshipment of goods to destination involving various transshipment. For example, first carriage may be from port of Vizag to port of Singapore and second voyage may be from port of Singapore to port of Hamburg but the consignor will get one bill of lading evidencing both voyages, thus limiting the possibilities of discrepant documents for negotiation, purchase or discounting through banks.

g. **Clean bills of lading:** If the bill of lading states and acknowledges the receipts of cargo by term '............ (number of boxes) received on board for shipment in apparent good order and condition', it will be known as a clean bill of lading. By such an acknowledgement, the shipping company undertakes the full responsibility of safe and secure transport of cargo and safe and secure delivery of cargo at destination. If not done so, shipping company shall be liable for compensation to affected party under claim of insurance. An importer always insists for a clean bill of lading and banks also favour a clean bill of lading for financial settlement of documents under any of the payment terms used.

h. **Claused bill of lading:** If the cargo received on board by a carrier is damaged or less on quantity than what documents say, or is improperly packed, marked and labelled or have any other irregularities, the shipping company may mark the mate's receipts as well as bill of lading as claused by incorporating the term 'received on board 10 containers, 3 containers received not in apparent good condition or order'. Such bill of lading is referred to as 'claused' bill of lading as shipping company has notified the negligence on the part of the consignor in terms of improper packing, inappropriate marking, unprotected palletization, loose unitization, use of second-hand cases/cartons or wet and stained cartons, short shipment, three containers leaking or found damaged and so on. In various regions of the world, these types of bill of lading may be known by different names, for example, in the United States, as 'foul' bill of lading and in India as 'dirty' bill of lading. In European countries, the term 'claused' bill of lading is popular.

i. **Stale bill of lading:** Another term 'stale bill of lading' is used particularly in cases when the last date of shipment has passed and cargo cannot be shipped. Under such circumstances, shipping companies usually insert the clause 'shipped on deck at owner's risk'. If the bill of lading is claused or dirty or foul or stale, insurance claims cannot be demanded from the insurance company. There is a fundamental principle of insurance that is 'good faith' in cargo insurance which the consignor has broken by sending the damaged or improperly packed cargo or shipping it after the date of shipment. Banks also do not accept such bill of lading for settlement of documents and realization of payments under D/A, D/P and L/C payment terms.

j. **BOLERO bill of lading:** As the world is moving towards paperless trade due to variety of reasons, several international organizations comprising world's leading banks, shipping companies, insurance companies, logistics companies, export management companies and so on have come together to set up the Bill of Lading Electronic Registry Organization (BOLERO). It has paved the way for safe, secure and smooth transfer of trade documents like bill of lading in an electronic form or paperless mode. BOLERO provides services for digital bills of lading. In addition to the digital bill of lading, it also offers other paperless allied trade documentation services involving areas such as banking, insurance and certification. BOLERO bill of lading and other associated documents are based on the open standards such as EDIFACT and XML and can be operated all around the world on any technology such a Linux, Microsoft and Solaris. This electronic registry organization employs a patented legal infrastructure and a secure messaging system in association with SWIFT. BOLERO aims at following objectives as explained in Figure 11.18.

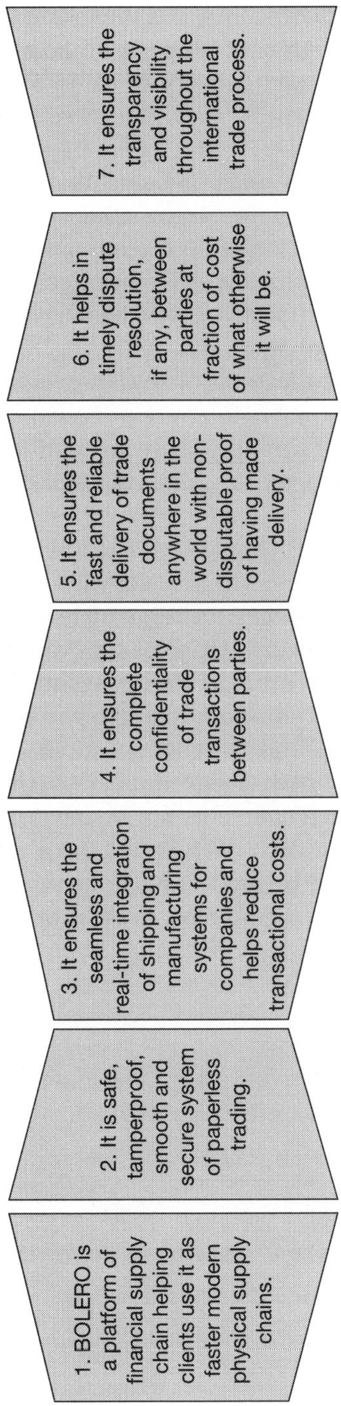

FIGURE 11.18 Salient objectives of Bill of Lading Electronic Registry Organization.

Concluding the discussion on bill of lading, it is important that it should not only be negotiable but should also be 'clean', 'through' and 'shipped on board'. Such a bill of lading enables the consignor to ensure the carriage and delivery of cargo to the point of destination under one transport document, and it also ensures safe and secured delivery of cargo to consignee.

AWB: AWB is a non-negotiable instrument meaning that it does not carry the title of goods as in case of a bill of lading. It is issued by the cargo airline carrier or by consolidator of the cargo. It refers that the airlines/carrier has accepted the goods, and it obligates to the carrier to carry the consignment to the airport of destination of importer country. It is also documentary evidence that the contract has been executed. It also serves the purposes of providing guidance to airline's/carrier's staff for handling, dispatching and delivering of the shipments to destined port in importer country. Some important features of AWB are highlighted in Figure 11.19.

AWB or air consignment note refers to a receipt issued by an international airline for goods and an evidence of the contract of carriage. There are total 12 copies of AWB issued by an airline. Table 11.2 lists the distribution scheme of various types of AWB for various stakeholders in international trade operations.

Original copy number 1 of AWB should be signed by the consignor of the cargo or his/her agent if so authorized for this purpose. Original copy number 2 has to be signed by both the carrier company responsible for transporting the cargo up to the destination and the consignor of the cargo or his/her agent on his/her behalf. Original copy number 3 has to be signed by the carrier and is given to the consignor of the cargo or his/her agent which is the proof that cargo has been accepted by the carrier airlines for transport up to the port of destination. If the payment term in a particular transaction under L/C and L/C contract stipulates the full set of original documents, then an exporter can present the original copy number 3 to the bank along with other commercial documents while negotiating the documents for payment under L/C contract. The numbering of AWB is done in a manner that each AWB issued has a unique identification number. AWBs have 11-digit numbers which can be used to make bookings, check the status of delivery and current position of the shipment. The number consists of the first three digits of airline prefix.

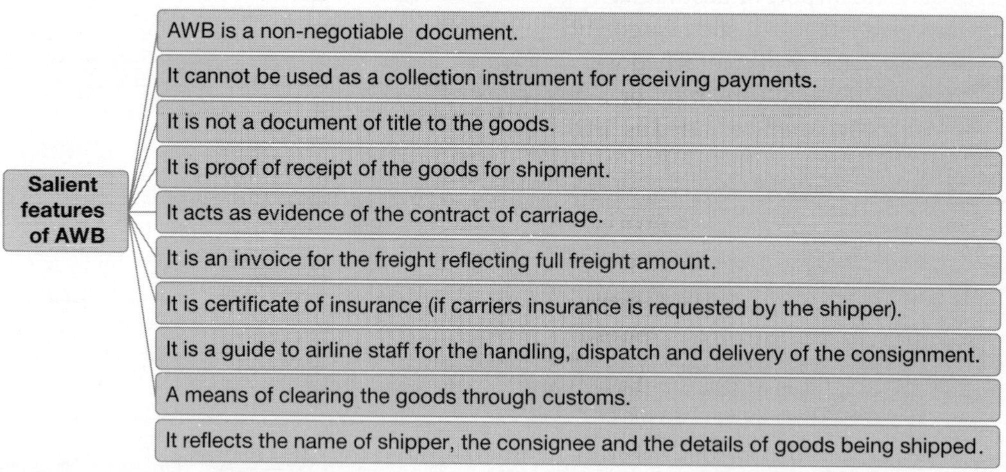

FIGURE 11.19 Salient features of AWB.

TABLE 11.2 Recipient of Various Copies of AWB in Export Operations

Number	Copy	Recipient	Colour Scheme
1	Issuing carrier accounting	Airlines cargo billing	Blue
2	Original for consignee	Consignee	Orange
3	Original for shipper	Shipper	Blue
4	Airport of origin	Origin gateway domestic: Maintain for one year International: Maintain for five years	
5	Delivery receipt/Airport of destination	Domestic: Maintain for one year International: Maintain for five years	Yellow
6	Extra copy	Can suffice as origin or delivery receipt/ airport of destination copy for gateway or CFS	White

Note: Origin or destination CFS must make a copy of MAWB and attach it to the AC12 register of air freight or work order to retain for their records.

Each airline has been assigned a three-digit number by IATA, so from the prefix, it can be judged that which airlines has issued AWB. The next seven digits are the running numbers. The last digit is known as 'check digit'. It is arrived at in the following manner (Figure 11.20).

a. **Master versus house AWB:** A total of 35–40 percent of exporters from India are small-scale exporters, usually not having FCL of cargo for shipment at a time. Alternatively, the items exported are of low volume but high-value cargo and shipper does not need a full container to ship his/her cargo to destination. Such LCL cargo is consolidated by freight forwarder or logistics companies along with other cargo moving to the same country of destination. Exporters of such low-volume cargo deliver their cargo to freight forwarder/logistics companies who consolidate their cargo in container/unit load devices. Logistics companies or freight forwarder, in turn, handover such consolidated cargo to the airlines for transportation of cargo to airport of destination. Airlines/air carriers issue a consolidated AWB encompassing the details of all such cargo and this is known as master air waybill (MAWB). A copy of packing list(s) is also attached with MAWB evidencing the details of each type of cargo consolidated. Freight forwarder or logistics company, in turn, issues each consignor of cargo a transport document entitled as 'house air waybill' (HAWB) or freight forwarder AWB usually

The AWB number has 11 digits and 3 parts

The first three digits are the airline prefix

The next seven digits is the serial number of AWB

The last digit is the check digit

The check digit is derived by dividing the 7-digit serial number by 7.
The remainder determines the check digit. Example: Serial number 8114074 divided by 7 is 1159153 remainder 3. Therefore, the serial number + check digit is 81140743.

FIGURE 11.20 Numbering of AWB.

with the name of freight forwarder/logistics company at the top. HAWB will have details of cargo shipped by each consignor. For a freight forwarder to be eligible to issue HAWB, it must be registered with IATA. Thus, the HAWB is same as 'split bill of lading' issued by logistics company/freight forwarder in case of sea transportation and MAWB is similar to 'groupage/ master bill of lading'. The characteristics of such AWB (house or master) remain as that of AWB discussed above.

b. **Clean versus foul AWB:** When the cargo to be air transported is received without damages, irregularities and short shipments, there will be mention of words 'number of...containers received on board in apparent goods condition and order', and it will be signed by the air carrier. Such AWB is referred to as 'clean AWB' as goods are received 'clean on board' for shipment to the airport of destination. Sometimes, cargo received by airlines may be damaged externally or internally, maybe leaking, pilfering or stinking, have irregularities in documentation or insufficient packing, safety seal missing on cargo containers, absence of fumigation certificate, short shipments and so on. Airlines under such circumstances mark AWB with words 'number of ... container received/...containers are not received in apparent good condition and order'. Such AWB is referred to as 'foul' AWB or 'unclean' AWB or 'dirty' AWB or claused AWB.

15. **Shipment advice:** Shipment advice is an important document mandated under aligned documentation system aimed at bringing more transparency in smooth and systematic documentation by an exporter. It is a sort of alert given by shipper to consignee before the arrival of goods at destination containing the details of shipment and providing list of compliance of documentation agreed in the sales contract. Once the goods are loaded on the vessel and required documentation is completed, an exporter prepares the shipment advice mentioning the details of shipment with the name of vessel/flight details, expected time arrival at the destination port, name of load port and discharge port and named place of destination, transshipment detail, if any, and so on. An exporter scans the copies of commercial invoice, packing list, insurance certificate, bill of lading and attach them with shipment advice and sends them to the overseas buyer, thus alerting him/her or appointed care party about the shipment details and its arrival at the destination, so as to enable them to plan for taking delivery of goods. Shipment advice is also known as 'shipping alert' in some countries. This document is sort of intimation to the importer that goods have been shipped to importer as per agreed terms and conditions in sales contract and commercial invoice. While preparing shipment advice, an exporter must include the information given in Figure 11.21 as mandated in the aligned documentation system.

    Shipment advice is important information for any consignee, as it helps to track arrival of shipment at the destination port for smooth planning to take delivery of goods. There are many cases where the consignee failed to know about arrival of goods and happened to pay exorbitant demurrage and detention to the authorities. An importer can track the cargo on a real-time basis and need not to wait for 'cargo arrival notice' from the carrier, thus saving time and cost in the clearance of goods. In case the importer has good relationship with the exporter, he/she can settle the payment through telegraphic transfer, thus saving the bank charges in collection/ negotiation of trade documents.

16. **Letter to bank for collection/negotiation of documents:** It is an auxiliary commercial document written by the exporter to the bank, whereby the request is made by the exporter to the bank for negotiation of documents with the L/C issuing bank for payments. Alternatively, if the

FIGURE 11.21 Information element of shipment advice.

payment term is under documentary collection method, the exporter will request to his/her bank through this letter for routing of these documents to importer's bank for payments. An exporter requests for either purchase or discounting of these trade documents which again can be with recourse or without recourse. Banks act on exporter's request of collection or negotiation as per general commercial agreement or the standard terms for banking facilities/standard terms for trade-related services.

11.6.2 Regulatory Documents in International Trade

Regulatory documents are the documents which are required in compliance with various rules and regulations governing trade and are prepared by either exporter or an importer and are submitted to regulatory authorities. For example, various statues such as FEMA, 1999; the Customs Act, 1962; Central Goods and Services Tax Act, 2017; GST Rules, 2017; the Major Port Act, 1963, and allied rules and regulations thereunder prescribe for documentation for customs clearance, GST clearance, port handling, foreign exchange clearance and so on, wherein an exporter has to submit prescribed documents to various government departments and bodies such as RBI, Indian Customs, Central Excise and Indian Port Authority. The regulatory documents are also subdivided in two broad categories: major regulatory documents and allied regulatory documents (Table 11.3).

Regulatory documents, unlike the commercial documents, are not standardized in India under the aligned documentation system. Ministry of Commerce, in consultation with the Ministry of Finance, is taking a keen note in streamlining these documents. For effective regulation of Indian foreign trade, following regulatory documents have been specified by the government.

TABLE 11.3 Regulatory Documents Used in India

Main and Important Regulatory Documents	Allied Regulatory Documents
1. Shipping bill/Bill of export	1. THC
2. Bill of entry	2. Gate pass
3. GST-RFD 1 and GST-RFD 11, GSTR 3B	3. Freight payment certificate
4. Exchange control declaration (EDF/SDF/Softex) forms	4. Insurance premium payment certificate
5. e-BRC	

1. **Shipping bill/Bill of export:** The Customs Act, 1962, lucidly provisioned that goods cannot be loaded on board the carrier unless permission from the customs authorities has not been obtained. Such permission to the exporter is accorded on a document prescribed by the customs authorities. In cases where the goods are sent by sea, this document is known as shipping bill and when goods are sent by land/rail, it is known as bill of export. Bill of export is also known as application for export. The contents of shipping bill/bill of export form are given in Figure 11.22.

   Export consignment through post parcel requires customs declaration form to be filled in by the exporter. Shipping bill/bill of export is a document which is essentially required by the customs authority/officials for allowing shipment for export purposes with let export seal. The various types of shipping bills are mentioned in Figure 11.23 for various kinds of exports taking place from India.

   An exporter has to submit the documents in Figure 11.24 in normal course for processing of shipping bill in international trade operations.

   For the goods which are cleared by land customs, bill of export is used instead of shipping bill. Bill of export is used when goods are cleared from a land customs station, SEZ and surface transport is used to transport the goods. Different number of copies of shipping bill/bill of export are to be prepared in different cases.

2. **Bill of entry:** A bill of entry is a regulatory form mandated for clearance of imported goods, wherein an importer makes a formal declaration describing goods which are being imported. The bill of entry (BoE) is of three types, BoE for home consumption, BoE for warehousing and BoE for home consumption/ex-bond, wherein an importer can file bill of entry for home

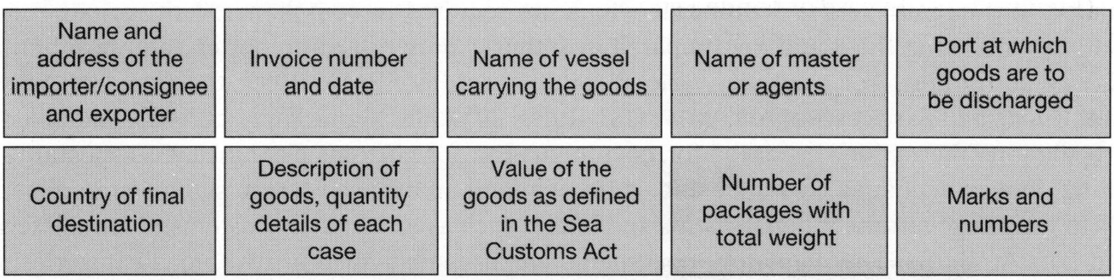

FIGURE 11.22 Key information elements of shipping bill.

Source: Central Board of Indirect Taxes & Customs (1976).

FIGURE 11.23 Various types of shipping bills or bills of export.

Source: Central Board of Indirect Taxes & Customs (2016).

Five copies of invoice which contains all relevant particulars such as number of packages, quantity, unit rate, total FOB/CIF value, and correct and full description of goods to be exported

Five copies of the packing list or cargo manifest mentioning the contents, quantity, gross and net weight of each package of the cargo to be exported

SDF or EDF forms (in duplicate) for shipment to all the countries

Export sales contract, L/C, and purchase order of the overseas buyer as the case may be

ARE I or II (both original and duplicate) and commercial invoice/legalized invoice/customs invoice (as the case may be)

Pre-shipment inspection/Examination certificate of quality control

FIGURE 11.24 Documents to be submitted along with shipping bill.

Source: Central Board of Indirect Taxes & Customs (2016).

consumption or warehousing only at the time of imports which is examined by customs officials to confirm that the contents of a shipment conform to the Indian customs and other rules and regulations in force and to determine which taxes, tariffs and restrictions apply to the imported goods as per prevalent law in force. Bill of entry is always prepared by the importer or by CHA on behalf of the importer. With implementation of electronic data interchange system through e-commerce portal www.icegate.org, bills of entry are usually filed online (Figure 11.25). In case of bonded goods, third type of bill of entry is filed for clearance of goods

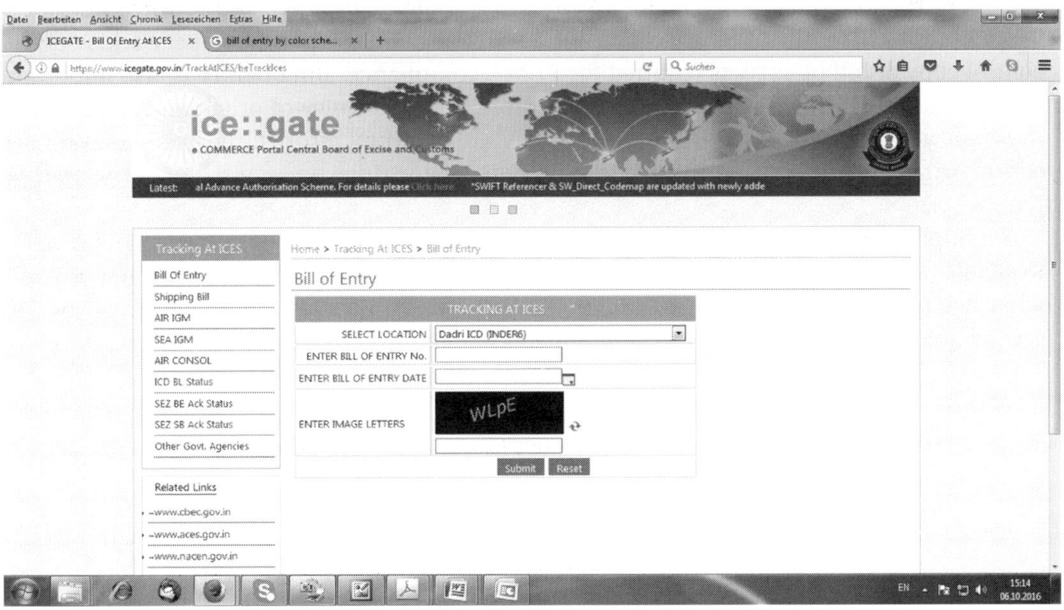

FIGURE 11.25 Electronic filing of bill of entry at ICEGATE.

Source: Screenshot of Icegate.

for home consumption/ex-bond. Bill of entry is a declaration on a prescribed form by an importer to the customs authorities about the exact nature, precise quantity and value of goods that have landed or entered the country. An importer files bill of entry along with principal commercial documents to custom authorities (custodian of cargo) to clear his/her cargo after having assessed the duty payable on them. Customs authorities examine its accuracy and conformity with the country tariff and regulations and grant 'out of charge' order after having collected all dues and duties on goods assessed.

Any type of bill of entry includes commercial as well as regulatory details such as description of the imported goods, quantity of the goods and estimated value of imported goods. The Indian customs reserves the right to inspect the shipment based on risk management system, thus pursuing first appraisement of goods so as to determine whether or not the goods are consistent with the bill of entry. While filing the bill of entry, an importer also files the GATT declaration which provides a basis to Indian customs to start legal proceedings against importer or his/her CHA if there are discrepancies in goods imported and details of bill of entry. Appraising officer of customs executes the secondary examination of documents, passes noting on bill of entry and if found in compliance with established procedure and norms, goods are cleared by imports subject to payment of duties as assessed by customs officials. If imported goods are prohibited for import or not imported through canalizing agency, if so mandated, or restricted goods imported without special import licence, then the Indian customs has the right to confiscate the goods. There are specific rules in India called the Bill of Entry (Electronic Integrated Declaration) Regulations, 2011, and Bill of Entry (Forms) Regulations, 1976, for how bills of entry should be formatted and presented to customs officials. Non-compliance of established procedure as mandated under these rules including documentation therein can result in delay or holding of goods by the Indian customs. If customs withhold the goods due to documentary non-compliance, there can be spoilage or destruction to the goods including demurrage and detention charges. Any importer must keep copies of filed bills of entry on record as part of his/her financial paperwork as exchange control copy of bill of entry is required for FEMA compliance. Bill of entry is also important for policymakers as it explains the trends of imported goods, country of origin and value imported, thus policymakers can take note of these facts while planning future tariff rates, rules for certificate of origin and other trade defence instruments. The various types of bill of entry are listed in Figure 11.26.

An importer of goods must submit the trade documents required by customs authorities so as to enable them to first check the goods and see if they are allowed for imports or not, if yes, with what documentation and licences under the prevailing trade regime as mandated by DGFT, second, to decide value and classification of goods and; third, to ensure that the import is legally

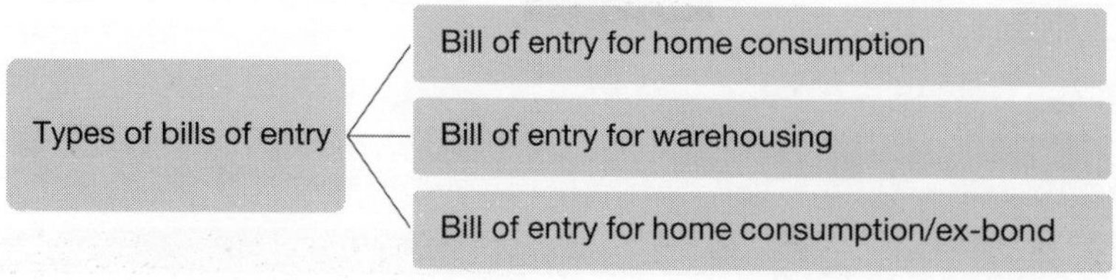

FIGURE 11.26 Types of bills of entry.

Source: Central Board of Indirect Taxes & Customs (2016).

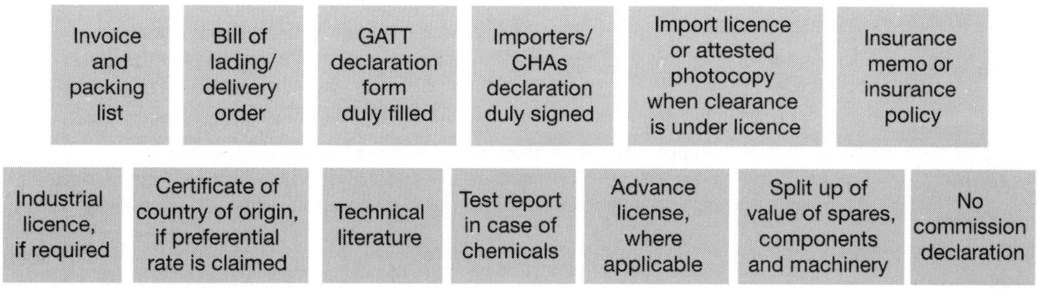

FIGURE 11.27 Documents to be submitted along with bill of entry.

Source: Custom Manual, 2018.

permitted and nature of authorization required, if any. An importer should submit the documents listed in Figure 11.27 along with the bill of entry to customs officials.

3. **GST-RFD 1/GST-RFD 11/GSTR 3B:** RFD-01 is an application mandated for refunds of Input Tax Credit and is submitted online for the processing of refund under GST. GST Refund Rules 2017 provides the following ground for Input Tax Credits:
   a. taxes, cess and interest paid in case of zero-rated supplies
   b. balance of excess cash paid into the electronic cash ledger
   c. unutilised input tax credit accumulated in your Electronic Credit Ledger due to Inverted duty structure

   There are other grounds of refunds also.

   Similarly, all GST registered tax payers who are involved in export of goods and services from India, are required to furnish Letter of Undertaking (LUT) in GST RFD-11 form on the common portal of GSTN in order to make exports without payment of IGST. Rules 96a provides for zero rating of export transactions.

   GSTR-3B is the monthly return of all GST Assess and is also known as monthly returns. It is vital for refunds and zero-rating of export of goods and services.

4. **Exchange control declaration forms:** Foreign exchange regulations in India mandate for documentary compliance if goods are exported beyond $25,000 per transaction and accordingly an exporter has to file a declaration in the format prescribed by RBI and submit the same to the Indian customs. Duly stamped with let export seal, such declaration in the prescribed form which is either SDF (electronic filing) or EDF (manual filing) must contain the information about sender, consignee, description of goods and full export value of goods in foreign currency and must be handed over to authorized dealer (exporter's bank) for FEMA compliance. FEM (Export of Goods and Services) Regulations, 2000, clearly mandate that export proceeds must be realized within 270 days from the date of export of goods which is the date of transport documents, that is, bill of lading/AWB or date of stamping of courier receipt. An exporter submits a duplicate SDF/EDF to his/her bank along with shipping documents and the bank endorses the copy of same after realization of sales proceeds and sends it to RBI. The original copy submitted at customs is also directed to RBI by the customs. The RBI confirms the realization of the proceeds as per full export value after comparing the two copies. It is to be noted that declaration has to be made with appropriate forms as mentioned in Figure 11.28 for all exports as per FEMA rules and regulations to RBI.

SDF form

- Under the present FTP, this document has been merged with electronic shipping bill by incorporating the requisite details in electronic filing of shipping bill through www.icegate.gov.in.

EDF form

- EDF form shall be applicable in all other cases of merchandise goods exports. It replaces the earlier used PP form in case of export of goods by post, GR used in case of manual shipping and VOP/COD used for value on payment and cash on delivery sales.

Softex form

- Softex form is used in case of export of services as mandated under appendices of FTP 2015–2020.

FIGURE 11.28 Various types of exchange control documents.

Source: Reserve Bank of India. www.rbi.org.in (accessed on 24 May 2023).

Requirement of submission of SDF has been dispensed with amendment in the Shipping Bill (Electronic Integrated Declaration) Regulations, 2000, as SDF is merged with shipping bill. The key contents of exchange control declarations for SDF/EDF are listed as follows:

a. Name and address of exporter, IEC number and description of goods.
b. Name and address of authorized dealer through whom the proceeds of the exports have been, or will be, realized.
c. Details of commission due to foreign agent or buyer should be correctly declared. Otherwise, difficulties may arise at the time of remittances of such commission/payment. An exporter should note this point very carefully.
d. It should be clearly indicated whether the export is on 'outright sale basis' or 'on consignment basis'.
e. An exporter is required to give an analysis of full export value, a break-up of FOB value, freight, insurance, discount, commission and so on.
f. An exporter has to mention the period within which he/she will realize the full export value of transaction. If the shipment is on D/A terms, then an exporter has to bring foreign exchange within that period. However, normally, the maximum period allowed is 270 days.

5. **Bank realization certificate:** BRC is an important proof of exports and is issued by the bank to their customers against the exchange control declaration always after the realization of export proceeds from overseas buyer. On request of export in the prescribed application format which is given in appendices to FTP 2015–2020, banks issue BRC to their exporter clients. Any export firm claiming any of the export benefits/incentive/duty neutralization under FTP is required to furnish valid BRC as a proof of realization of export payments from the overseas buyer as FEM (Export of Goods and Services) Regulations mandate for realization only in freely convertible foreign currency except of Nepal and Bhutan. The current procedure for furnishing BRC is made in electronic form through an e-commerce portal maintained by DGFT. An IEC holder, after realization of the payment, should submit the online application at DGFT website for e-BRC and accordingly should submit the requisite details of exports as mandated in BRC form. As a part of B2B message exchange initiative by DGFT, export realization related information of an exporter is shared electronically using EDI system with commercial banks in India. DGFT server transmits this information to the concerned bank which issues the e-BRC after verification and compliance of exports claims for BRC. This is a unique arrangement for export facilitation by DGFT

and reduces the hardship faced by Indian exporters in getting BRC by furnishing the physical copy of BRC. In fact, DGFT has dispensed with the system of physical processing of BRC and each BRC issued after 15 September 2012 must be e-BRC. It is signed by an authorized signatory of the bank with his/her name and designation. Bankers affix certificate number and date and mention the authorized foreign exchange dealer's code number allotted to the bank by RBI. For this purpose, this certificate must be accompanied by the following documents:

a. A copy of invoice

b. A copy of customs attested export promotion copy of the shipping bill

c. A copy of bill of lading/PP receipt/AWB

d. A copy of the insurance certificate/insurance policy/cover

An exporter can furnish BRC as proof of exports to close the entries of availed incentives, import duty exemptions and other financial assistance from various EPCs/DGFT and Indian customs. Various export promotion bodies ask for proof of export and an exporter can submit the documents such as export promotion copy of shipping bill (EP copy of shipping bill), mate's receipt/bill of lading issued by the carrier and BRC issued by the respective bank to claim the benefits offered by these bodies to an exporter.

6. **Terminal handling charges:** THC refer to the charges and fees collected by terminal authorities at each port for providing services related to cargo handling, loading and unloading. There are two types of maritime ports in India, the first category is called major ports which are maintained by the central government and the second category is called non-major ports which are maintained by respected state governments where such ports are located. Airports are managed by either the central government or by private players and so is the case for management of various dry ports. Ports, whether maritime or air or dry, require huge capital investment for erection of required infrastructure for loading, unloading, temporary storage, maintenance and safety of cargo. The tariff rates of terminal handling vary from port to port within the country and even different tariff rates are there for different types of cargo at the same port. An exporter has to pay THC for exports to shipping lines at the time of release of the bill of lading once the formalities for export customs clearance procedures are completed. INCOTERMS define the party of trade which has to pay the THC, which are collected at load port for exports and at the port of destination for imports. The import THC are collected by shipping carriers at the time of issuing delivery order to the consignee to take delivery of goods at the port of discharge. THC are for use of port infrastructure and services and should not be confused with inland haulage charges which refer to transportation costs from inland ports to maritime port of India for exports and from maritime port to dry port for import.
7. **Gate pass:** In order to optimally use the port stevedoring facilities, customs clearance, stuffing-destuffing and aggregation-disaggregation of cargo is shifted from maritime ports to nearby located CFSs which are treated as off-dock facility for all these logistics activities. Similarly, in case of country hinterland, customs clearance facility is provided at both ICD for FCL cargo and at CFS for LCL cargo. For exportable goods, all the factory or warehouse stuffed-in containers which will be sealed by GST officials (factory stuffing) or by customs officers (for ICD/CFS clearance) are required to enter to any of the designated CFSs/buffer yards at gateway ports in sealed containers with the relevant trade documents. Based on the endorsement of document by the gate officer of CFS/buffer yards and examination of documents such as commercial invoice, examination report (reverse side of invoice), packing list and transport documents (road receipt/rail receipt), shipping bill is registered at ICEGATE system and LEO is granted. Three copies of

the shipping bill are generated, first is the exporter's copy, second is for exchange control and third is customs copy. Officer in charge at CFS/buffer yard issues the 'gate pass' and customs cleared (LEO) stuffed-in containers are moved from CFS to the port terminal, wherein the gate officer of the port verifies the details of the shipping bill and LEO on EDI system and if satisfied with the documents, gate officer at gateway port will retain the 'gate pass' issued by the custodian of CFS indicating the container number, seal number, time of departure from CFS and so on. This is done by the terminal gate officer so as to verify the time of departure of the container from CFS and its arrival at the terminal gate.

Similar to exports where 'gate pass' is an important document for onward transit of cargo, gate pass is also important in import operations. As per customs procedure in India, once the bill of entry is assessed and appraised, it is passed to shed appraiser or superintendent of customs for physical examination of goods. The shed inspector or customs examiners, after examining the goods, would give order for 'out of charge', meaning the goods are cleared for imports and custody of importer. Once the 'out of charge' order is granted on bill of entry, the importer or his/her CHA presents the same to the custodian who in turn issues the 'gate pass' after verification of correctness of bill of lading and number of packages. It is mandatory for an importer/CHA to present the importer's copy of the bill of entry and custodian gate pass to the customs officer at the gate while taking the goods out of the customs area. Hence, gate pass as an allied document plays a crucial role in taking into the goods in the terminal port for exports and release of cargo from customs area post imports clearance. In short, goods will not be allowed to customs areas for both exports and imports without gate pass.

8. **Freight payment certificate:** Any transport document, be it bill of lading, AWB, courier receipt, rail receipts, road receipt and forwarder certificate of receipt, has a column for freight to be charged by the transport company. Freight is either usually prepaid or freight collect basis, wherein if freight is paid in advance, it will be referred to as 'freight prepaid' which can be by either party depending on INCOTERMS, and if freight collect is mentioned, it means that transport company, that is, shipping line, airline, road line, railway and so on will collect freight at destination. This transport document acts as proof of payment of freight. However, in practice, a freight payment certificate may be required by either party of trade for complying with other trade documentation. For example, an exporter requires 'freight payment certificate' as he/she has to fill the details in e-BRC, which is the final 'proof of exports' and an importer requires it for the purpose of compliance of documentation in the bill of entry in cases where customs has to arrive at CIF value of goods, by adding or deducing freight value. Freight payment certificate indicates the amount of freight to be paid/payable by an exporter. It is issued by shipping company/steamer line which indicates that the freight for the consignment has been paid to the shipping company. It can also be useful in case the original bill of lading is lost and duplicate is required. It has to be given along with indemnity bond to shipping line for another set of bill of lading.
9. **Insurance premium payment certificate:** Marine insurance policies are usually issued in three forms. First, as the 'specific policy' which is mainly issued for covering a specific import/export consignment. The second type is called the 'open cover' which is issued for a period of one year and is also sometimes known as 'master policy'. Open cover indicates the rates of premium, terms and conditions agreed upon by the insured and insurer for covering the EXIM consignments. Under this policy, an exporter has to declare to the insurance company the shipment made within the agreed period and accordingly has to pay the premium for cargo insurance

at the agreed rate. On receipt of premium, the insurance company issues insurance premium payment certificate, thus contracting to cover the risks as agreed in the open insurance cover for the declared consignment. The third type of cargo insurance is for 'custom duty cover' and is aimed at covering the loss of customs duty paid in case goods arrive in damaged condition. Insurance premium payment certificate is applicable in case of open cover and customs duty cover. Any liner company/Indian railways always asks for 'certificate of insurance or insurance premium payment certificate' before they accept the goods for international transport. The carriage of goods through ship is full of risks and the company usually does not want to be responsible in case of pilferage/loss/piracy and insists that insurance cover shall be taken by the exporter/importer for the goods to be exported or imported.

11.6.3 Miscellaneous Trade Documents

Commercial as well as regulatory trade documents are an integral part of any EXIM operation. In addition to these documents, an exporter or importer may come across various other miscellaneous trade documents which are prepared on specific demand of either party of trade or to serve any other purpose in trade and logistics operations. Following are some of the miscellaneous trade documents used in foreign trade:

1. **Blacklist certificate:** Blacklist certificate is required in scenarios where a country has strained political relation with another country and mandates for that exporter to produce a certificate from the shipping line/shipowner/aircraft transporting the goods to such country that it has not touched the territorial water of a country with which it has strained political relations. For example, South Korea insists that any goods imported into South Korea should not be originating from North Korea and even if originating from a third country, the ship/aircraft should never touch any ports of North Korea or even the territorial waters of North Korea. If an importer mandates for blacklist certificate, it is the duty of exporter to ensure that he/she should caution the shipping line with which cargo is booked for transport/carriage not to call on ports of such adversary country. Blacklist certificate can also be issued by agents of airline or shipping line. If the same is not produced in the country of imports, regulatory authority like customs will not allow the cargo to be cleared for imports.
2. **Weight note:** Weight certificate is a document usually issued by customs authorities of the exporting country certifying the correct gross weight of the goods being shipped. It is required to confirm the packets or bale or other form are of a stipulated weight. For example, in India, the Legal Metrology Act, 2009, and Standards of Weights and Measures Act, 1976, mandate reasonable restrictions on harmonized and standardized packing so to enlighten the Indian consumers. Globally, weight practices vary from country to country; for example, Indians follow the metric system while the United Kingdom follows foot-pound-second system, thus creating confusions about the weight of goods being imported. Standards of Weights and Measures Act, 1976, and allied rules thereunder prescribe specification of measuring instruments used in commercial transaction, industrial production, any other measurement involved in public health and human safety in India and FTP mandates that domestically applicable rules and regulations will mutatis mutandis apply to imports transactions. Department of Consumer Affairs, GOI, mandates the specifications listed in Table 11.4 under the Standards of Weights and Measures (General) Rules, 1987.

TABLE 11.4 Specifications under Weight and Measurement Rules in India

Unit	Abbreviation
Mass	Kilogram (kg), gram (g), milligram (mg)
Length	Metre (m), centimetre (cm), millimetre (mm)
Area	Square metre (m^2)
Capacity	Kilolitre (kl), litre (l or L), millilitre (ml)
Temperature	Degree Celsius (°C) or degree Kelvin (°K)
Volume	Cubic metre (m^3), cubic centimetre (cm^3), cubic millimetre (mm^3)

Source: Department of Consumers Affairs, Government of India.

In consonance with directions under FTP 2015–2020, the Indian customs demands for weight certificate so as to comply with regulation of interstate trade and commerce in weights and measures and commodities sold, distributed or supplied by weights or measures and control and regulation of export and import of weights and measures and commodities in packaged form. The Indian customs is empowered to search, seize and forfeiture of non-standard weight or measure and file case in the court for prosecution and can also prescribe a fee for various services rendered for compliance of these rules. There is a dedicated weight and measurement department in each state of India which issues the weight certificate.

3. **Verified gross mass (VGM) weight certificate:** In order to ensure cargo safety as well as the safety of sea workers, amended SOLAS, 1974, mandates 'VGM weight certificate' from 1 July 2016 for each container meant for international transportation. VGM weight refers to the total weight of a packed container including packing and securing materials such as pallets and wires and container tare weight. Thus, VGM weight of container is different from the 'cargo weight' which means weight of the cargo weight. Considering the risks involved for sea workers and ensuring safety to their life and that of ship as well, SOLAS provides that all containerized cargo shall have VGM weight certificate prior to loading of container on the vessel. Amended provisions of SOLAS came into effect from 1 July 2016 and new regulations will be enforced globally. In order to ensure compliance with the SOLAS amendment, governments world over are advised to issue their own regulations and guidelines. In compliance with this, Maersk Shipping Line issued the following order to all exporters, wherein mandating all shippers to submit a VGM weight certificate for every export container before the vessel cut off. In consideration of this, the following implications are to be observed effective 1 July 2016:
   a. Shippers need to ensure they provide a VGM certificate for every container before the vessel cut off.
   b. The responsibility to ensure the provision of accurate and not estimated weight of the container lies with the shipper.
   c. Failure to provide VGM certificate will result in the container not being loaded on the vessel.

   This requirement is in line with the recommendation of the IMO's Maritime Safety Committee that is being adopted globally. It serves to reduce the risk to cargo, vessels, equipment and workforce which are currently more prone to accidents due to incorrect container weight being provided to prepare the load list. VGM certificate is issued by independent weighing machine operators located near the port towns.

4. **Manufacturer's certificate:** There are certain cases where an importer or importer's country may ask for certificate of manufacturer so as to understand from where the goods are actually originating. Manufacturer's certificate is required in addition to the certificate of origin in some countries to show that the goods shipped have actually been manufactured and are available. Manufacturer's certificate can in some cases be an authenticated or notarized document certifying that the goods ordered have been produced by the manufacturer so as to satisfy the documentary requirement of importer's country or that of importer. Sometimes, manufacture issues it on company letterhead only.
5. **Certificate of chemical analysis:** Certificate of chemical analysis or chemical composition may be required in addition to certificate of inspection. It is required to ensure that the quality and grade of certain items such as metallic ores and pigments are in compliance with what has been agreed in sales contract. A certificate of analysis is a document issued by the quality assurance specialist or metal surveyor that is aimed at ensuring that the traded product meets its product specification as agreed between exporter and importer. Certificate of chemical analysis is issued by EIC, other specialized lab and certified independent surveyors specializing in the area.
6. **Certificate of shipment:** Certificate of shipment is issued by an exporter or by agent of shipping line indicating that a certain lot of goods have been shipped. An exporter is responsible for the truthfulness of certificate of shipment. Such a documentary practice is common in the United Kingdom and certain landlocked African countries.
7. **Health/Veterinary/Sanitary certification:** Health/Veterinary/Sanitary certification is required for export and import of eggs, ovum, ova, semen, foodstuffs, marine products, hides, livestock such as dogs and cats and so on and is aimed at ensuring that communicable diseases do not get carried by these traded items from one country to another. For example, in India, the Plant Quarantine (Regulation of Import into India) Order, 2003, regulates import and prohibition of import of plants and plant products into India. Similarly, India, a member state of the World Health Organization (WHO), has adopted the International Health Regulations aimed at ensuring the maximum security against the international spread of communicable diseases such as yellow fever, Zika virus, H1N1 cold flu virus and Ebola virus. Each member state is required to maintain as many of the sanitary ports and airports as practicable with organized medical and health service with adequate staff, equipment, premises and so on under the WHO commitment for health safety. Accordingly, port health organizations are set up at each international airport/maritime port and land ports and to comply with it, an exporter or importer has to take a veterinary or sanitary certificate for livestock and other items. One can access these documents by contacting Port Health Organization or Directorate of Plant Protection, Quarantine & Storage.
8. **Certificate of conditioning:** Certificate of conditioning is issued by the competent office designed for this purpose by GOI. They certify the compliance with humidity factor, dry weight and so on for certain exportable or importable commodities, such as wine, basmati rice and jaggery. Certificate of conditioning can be accessed from EIC and some designated test houses.
9. **Certificate of antiquity measurement:** Certificate of antiquity is issued by the Archaeological Survey of India in case of export of non-antiques as antique items cannot be exported and are the property of GOI either in various museums or with public in temple, museums, private property, and other trusts or bodies. An exporter has to make an application for the issuance of certificate of non-antiquity for the export of art objects, arms and submit the same in duplicate in respect of each category of object such as wood, bronze, brass, paintings, ivory, coins, medals and

manuscripts exporter should also submit the photograph of such items in the size of 8″ × 6″. Customs is the controlling authority and may ask for antiquity certificate in exports of these goods. Application form for certificate of antiquity can be accessed at the website of Archaeological Survey of India.

10. **Cart/Lorry/Vehicle ticket:** Cart ticket or vehicle ticket is issued by the port authority personnel for admittance of the cargo through the port gate and includes the shipper's name, cart/lorry number, marks on packages, quantity and so on.
11. **Carting order:** Carting order is the final clearance given by the customs authorities after the goods are cleared for export or import with either LEO or 'out of charge order'. In case of export, carting order is meant for permission to load the cargo on vessel/other carrier and for imports, it is to transport the cargo out of customs area to the owner's premises. Carting order is a very important document as it determines whether goods can be loaded or not or can be removed from bonded customs area or not.
12. **Shut-out advice:** Sometimes, cargo cleared for export cannot be exported due to reasons like ship has a technical problem or importer's country is facing an embargo or any other reasons. Goods cleared for exports are called back and an exporter has to surrender all original documents with customs authorities which includes shipping bill with LEO seal, exchange control copy of SDF/EDF, copy of GST-RFD 11, bill of lading/AWB and so on as an exporter becomes eligible for export incentives and other benefits with these trade documents. If the exporter has availed any incentive/benefit, then same has to be surrendered. On surrender of these documents, customs authority will prepare the shut-out order which will facilitate the custody of exported cargo to an exporter.
13. **Dock receipt/Warehouse receipt:** A dock receipt at a maritime port and warehouse receipt at dry ports are the documents issued by a sea freight carrier to acknowledge receipt of sea freight shipment at the carrier's shipping terminal which can be CFS with LCL or container yard with FCL, carrier's pier in roll on/roll off, break bulk and so on. In case of LCL cargo, dock receipt or warehouse receipt also verifies weight and measurement of cargo received by the shipping terminal (CFS).
14. **Short shipment form:** Short shipment certificate is a document issued by customs authorities which describes that the actually exported quantity is less than what has been mentioned in the shipping documents. For example, Mr Ram wants to export 1,000 pairs of shoes to the United Kingdom, but at the time of export clearance, shed appraiser informs that actual number of loaded shoe pairs are only 980 meaning there is a shortage of 20 pairs of shoes than what Mr Ram has mentioned in documents such as shipping bill/commercial invoice and packing list. Customs will issue a short shipment notice of 20 pieces and same is also marked in shipping bill that there is short shipment of export quantity. Short shipment form is attached to the new shipping bill for export of remaining 20 pairs of shoes to importer. Exporters engaged in foreign trade and settling their payment through L/C need to cautious with Shot-shipment Certificate as many a times, the L/C contract does not allow the shot-shipment of cargo.
15. **Destination control statement:** Destination control statement is a legal statement, wherein an exporter has to declare in the commercial invoice itself that these goods are restricted for imports in the destination country as per the trade administration regulations of country of imports and the International Traffic in Arms Regulations. An exporter must state about 'destination control statement', thus alerting the customs authorities of country of imports about such goods. In India, such a statement is required for SCOMET. It is a necessary legal boundary clarifying

what happens to shipments, and it essentially states no other person except as mentioned in destination control statement/commercial invoice/bill of lading is going to take the goods and forward them to another country.

16. **Fumigation certificate:** The fumigation certificate in EXIM operations is also known as 'pest control certificate'. Countries across the world impose reasonable restrictions so as to protect their fauna and flora; for example, there is restriction on use of wooden pallets without fumigation or heat treating as per the International Standards for Phytosanitary Measures (ISPM-15). Fumigation certificates in EXIM operations contain details such as purpose of treatment, the articles in question, temperature range used and chemicals and concentration used. The fumigation certificate, in international trade documentation practices, is not a mandatory document but may be required if so demanded by importer or mandated by importer's country's rules and regulations as it assists in quarantine clearance of an imported cargo upon the arrival to the destination.

11.7 Summary

A number of EXIM documents are required at various stages of international trade operations as trading parties deal with various parties involved in trade transactions through trade documents only. It is rightly said that in international trade, one deals in documents and not the goods as the ownership of goods, transportation, payments, sharing of costs and risks, tariff preference and so on are governed by trade documents only. Trade documentation is necessary and an integral part of EXIM operations due to variety of reasons. When an exporter sells his/her goods in international markets, he/she has to prepare various documents as transportation of cargo from one country to another is full of various regulatory and commercial requirements. Aligned documentation system is aimed at streamlining the different definitions of trade information, reducing various formats of trade documents and harmonizing the presentation of data in trade documents. Accordingly, different layouts and paper sizes of trade documents are streamlined in a standard format for all traders in the world.

Aligned documentation system has reduced the scope of errors and delays and reduces the time required to prepare the trade documents. There has been harmonization of commercial documents as envisaged by the UN Layout Key, but unfortunately, regulatory documentation is an area that has attracted least attention of concerned regulatory authorities. Excessive regulatory documentation and allied procedure resulted in high cost of doing business in India. Out of the 16 commercial trade documents as discussed in the chapter, 14 have been either standardized or aligned to one another. Two documents, namely bill of exchange and shipping order, cannot be standardized simply because they have different data elements and are quite different from the other commercial documents. However, the efforts are still on to standardize the documents as it will help in transactional cost reduction in an era when documents are usually electronically generated, prepared and exchanged among parties of EXIM operations. Commercial documents are subdivided into two categories: first, 'auxiliary commercial documents' which help us prepare 'principal commercial documents'. Auxiliary commercial documents include proforma invoice, application of inspection, insurance declaration, application for certificate of origin, shipping instruction, shipping order, mate's receipt and letter to the bank for collection/negotiation of documents. Principal Commercial Documents include commercial invoice, certificate of inspection/quality control, certificate of insurance, certificate of origin, packing list, bill of exchange, bill of lading/combined transport document and shipment advice.

Regulatory documents are the documents which are required in compliance with various rules and regulations governing trade and are prepared by either exporter or an importer and are submitted to regulatory authorities. For example, various statues such as FEMA, 1999; the Customs Act, 1962; the Central Goods and Services Tax Act, 2017; the Major Port Act, 1963, and allied rules and regulations thereunder prescribe for documentation for customs clearance/GST clearance/port handling/foreign exchange clearance, wherein an exporter has to submit prescribed documents to various government departments and bodies such as RBI, Indian Customs and Central Excise and Indian Port Authority. The regulatory documents are also subdivided into two broad categories: main regulatory documents and allied regulatory documents. Main and important regulatory documents are shipping bill/bill of export, bill of entry, GST-RFD 11, exchange control declaration (EDF/SDF/Softex) forms, BRC and allied regulatory documents are THC, gate pass, freight payment certificate and insurance premium payment certificate. In addition to these documents, an exporter or importer may come across various other miscellaneous trade documents which are prepared on specific demand of either party of trade or to serve any other purpose in trade and logistics operations. These include blacklist certificate, certificate of chemical composition, manufacturer's certificate, short shipment form, shut-out order, destination control statement, weight certificate, VGM weight certificate, dock receipt/warehouse receipt, carting order, cart/lorry/vehicle ticket, certificate of conditioning, certificate of antiquity measurement, health/veterinary/sanitary certification, certificate of shipment, fumigation certificate and so on.

Review Exercises

Multiple Choice Questions

1. Which of following types of bills of entry is filed for bonded warehousing of imported goods?
   a. Bill of entry for ex-bond clearance for home consumption
   b. Bill of entry under ATA Carnet
   c. Bill of entry for warehousing
   d. Bill of entry for home consumption
   e. None of the above
2. Which of the following documents is filed with the customs department to get clearance for exportable cargo?
   a. Shipping bill
   b. Bill of entry
   c. IEC
   d. Packing list
   e. None of the above
3. Which of the following documents is mandated for foreign exchange declaration under manual filing of shipping bill under FEMA rules?
   a. SDF
   b. EDF
   c. Softex
   d. None of the above

4. Which of the following bills of entry is filed to get cleared the goods warehoused in bonded warehouse?
   a. Bill of entry for warehousing
   b. Bill of entry for home consumption
   c. Bill of entry for ex-bond clearance for home consumption
   d. Advance bill of entry
   e. None of the above
5. Which of the following exchange control documents is filed in case of exports of services?
   a. SDF
   b. EDF
   c. Softex
   d. Exchange control declaration
   e. None of the above
6. In order to claim the refund of input duties paid on manufacture of exportable goods, which of the following types of shipping bill is filed?
   a. Shipping bill under ATA Carnet
   b. Shipping bill under claim of duty drawback
   c. Shipping bill for dutiable goods
   d. Shipping bill for duty-free foods
   e. Shipping bill for duty-free goods ex-bond
7. Which of the following types of regulatory documents is filed for immediate clearance of goods once imported in India?
   a. Bill of entry for ex-bond clearance for home consumption
   b. Bill of entry under ATA Carnet
   c. Bill of entry for warehousing
   d. Bill of entry for home consumption
   e. None of the above
8. Which of the following documents is called final and most acceptable proof of exports?
   a. Shipping bill
   b. Bill of lading
   c. Certificate of insurance
   d. SDF/EDF/Softex
   e. BRC
9. Which of the following documents is used for payment of port charges?
   a. Port charges receipt/Dock challan
   b. THC
   c. Vehicle chit
   d. Freight payment certificate
   e. Insurance premium payment certificate
10. Which of the following documents is filed for clearance of exported goods when transported by road or rail to adjoining land customs station?
    a. Bill of export
    b. Bill of entry

c. Shipping bill
d. Customs declaration certificate
e. None of the above

11. Which of the following is a principal commercial document?
a. Commercial invoice
b. Customs invoice
c. Consular invoice
d. Performa invoice
e. None of the above

12. Which of the following is sent by an exporter to an importer to show his/her willingness to sell something or offer to sell something?
a. Commercial invoice
b. Customs invoice
c. Consular invoice
d. Performa invoice
e. None of the above

13. Which of the following is not a feature of bill of lading?
a. Non-negotiable instrument
b. Contract of carriage
c. Receipt of cargo
d. Title of goods
e. None of the above

14. Which of the following is not a feature of AWB?
a. Contract of carriage
b. Contract of affreightment
c. Negotiable instrument
d. Receipt of cargo
e. None of the above

15. Ideally, how many parties are there in a bill of exchange?
a. 4
b. 3
c. 2
d. 5
e. None of the above

16. Which of the following documents is used to get the preferential or zero tariff in country of imports?
a. Certificate of inspection
b. Certificate of origin
c. Certificate of insurance
d. Importer certification for zero duty clearance
e. None of the above

17. Which of the following documents is received from the ship captain while handing over the goods to shipping company at the time of loading of cargo?

a. Bill of lading
b. Seaway bill
c. Ocean bill of lading
d. Mate's receipt
e. None of the above

18. Packing list is important as it describes
a. Cargo features
b. Cargo size and dimensions
c. Stock management and customs compliance
d. All the above
e. None of the above

19. Master AWB is issued by which of the following?
a. Airlines/Air cargo freighter
b. IATA approved agent
c. FIATA approved agent
d. Freight forwarder or CHA
e. None of the above

20. An exporter conveys about the shipping instructions to a freight forwarder or shipping company through which of the following documents?
a. Shipping order
b. Shut-out order
c. Short shipment certificate
d. Shipping instructions
e. None of the above

Critical Thinking Questions

1. Critically explain the role of EXIM documentation in foreign trade. What are the key legal aspects of consideration for an exporter in trade documentation practices?
2. Critically examine the role and use of commercial documents used in EXIM operations. Also list the auxiliary and principal commercial documents.
3. Explain the various regulatory documents used in EXIM operations. Critically examine the role of shipping bill and bill of entry for an exporter and importer.
4. Explain the various miscellaneous trade documents used in foreign trade. Also explain the procedure of preparation and handling of various documents in international trade operations.
5. Write short notes on any two of following:
a. Aligned documentation system
b. Transport documents in foreign trade
c. Various types of invoice and their role
d. Types of exchange control documents

Further Readings

1. Central Board of Indirect Taxes & Customs. 2016. New Delhi: Ministry of Finance, Government of India.
2. ———. 1976. *Bill of Entry (Forms) Regulations, 1976*. New Delhi: Ministry of Finance, Government of India.
3. ———. 2016. *Customs Manual 2016*. New Delhi: Ministry of Finance, Government of India.
4. Department of Consumers Affairs. New Delhi: Ministry of Consumer Affairs, Food & Public Distribution, Government of India.
5. National Board of Trade. 2003. *Trade Facilitation from a Developing Country Perspective*. Stockholm: National Board of Trade.
6. Reserve Bank of India. *Foreign Exchange Manual*. New Delhi: Reserve Bank of India.

CHAPTER 12

Pre-Shipment Export Credit Scheme

CHAPTER OBJECTIVES

- To describe the rationale and need of export finance.
- To describe various export financing facilities available.
- To elaborate the need of pre-shipment finance for exports and process and procedure therein.
- To explain the instruments and channels under which the pre-shipment finance is extended.
- To brief on the special cases of pre-shipment financing in India.

12.1 Introduction

Export financing is one of the most important factors for successfully engaging in international trade operations. The need for export finance begins when an exporter gets an export order after the successful contract negotiation. As finances are the lifeblood of any organization, exporters are increasingly concerned for timely export credit so as to execute international orders as per agreed schedules. If the agreed payment terms extend credit to importers in competitive markets, exporters necessarily have to arrange the export credit so as to procure the raw material for manufacturing and sale. Hence, an exporter should be fully aware of the financing need of export transactions after factoring the agreed payment terms in the international sale. The exporter has to essentially arrange for export finance if the agreed payment terms are an open account, a documentary collection and an L/C. It is only the payment in advance when the exporter need not arrange the export finance. In India, there is a considerable effort by the central government to extend the liberal export credit to facilitate Indian exporters so as to provide them level-playing field vis-à-vis their competitors in international markets. Accordingly, RBI frames the necessary policy directions to the scheduled banks in India except the regional rural banks to facilitate the liberal export financing for Indian exporters. An Indian exporter needs to understand the following factors while availing the export credit facilities for export operations:

1. **Need for export financing:** An exporter needs to understand the need for export financing for international sales as in some cases, favourable payment terms such as the 'payment in advance' negates the need of export financing, and in some cases, competitive payment terms such as 'D/C' or 'time L/C' can help an exporter to win the competitive markets.
2. **Tenure of export financing:** An exporter should determine the tenure of export financing, for example, the export credit period is usually longer in case of export of capital goods and shorter in case of sale of normal goods. The exporter should estimate the time period of export financing based on payment terms and credit involved therein.

3. **Cost of export financing:** An exporter should also factor the cost of financing the export transactions. One can negotiate lower prices of exports so as to get favourable payment terms in case the cost of export financing is higher. In India, for example, the cost of financing is relatively higher in comparison to developing countries, and one can estimate the pros and cons of cost financing while availing the export finance facility. The exporter should also factor the various hidden costs of financing such as processing charges, one-time fees and the nature of interest rates, fixed or floating, as they affect the cost of financing significantly and the resultant price of goods and profits.
4. **Risks associated with export financing:** Banks charge the interest rates based on risks perception attached to an export transaction. The riskier the export transaction, the harder and costlier it will be to finance in India. Banks may ask for additional coverage of risks if they find that the political and economic stability of the importer's country can also be an issue. For example, banks insist on the most secure method of payments so as to provide financing for either account receivable or the production or purchase of the product for the international sale. Sometimes, banks may ask for ECGC's credit cover so as to provide the export financing. Hence, one should factor the risks associated before taking the export credit to finance export transactions.
5. **Nature of export order:** The need for export credit is directly linked to the nature of export orders as production or manufacturing for an unusually large order may necessitate a larger volume of funds and vice versa. The export order of capital goods always necessitates larger needs of funds and interest which may usually be higher if export credit limit is beyond the exposure limit of an exporter. Banks will charge higher rates of interest rates if the exporter avails exports credit beyond his/her approved credit limits.

In view of the importance of export credit in maintaining the pace of the export growth, RBI has initiated several measures in the recent years to ensure timely and hassle-free flow of credit to the export sector. These measures, inter alia, include rationalization and liberalization of export credit interest rates, flexibility in repayment or prepayment of the pre-shipment credit, a special financial package for large value exporters, liberal export finance for agricultural exports, the Gold Card Scheme for exporters and so on. Further, banks have been granted freedom by RBI to source funds from abroad without any limits, exclusively for the purpose of granting export credit in foreign currency. This has provided additional leverage of business extension of Indian commercial banks as Indian exporters are increasingly looking for export credit in foreign currency first to hedge their foreign exchange fluctuation risks and second to avail the benefit of lower interest rates that exist in foreign currency export credit. The export financing scheme by RBI was first introduced in 1967, specifically for meeting the exporter's credit requirements and helping this sector grow faster. Prior to this, Indian exporters were compelled to avail normal commercial loans from various banks to fund their export operations, which not only attracted a higher rate of interest but were tough to avail as well. With the nationalization of Indian banks in 1969, the landscape for export financing in India changed significantly as exporters need not approach private banks and money lenders who used to charge exorbitant rate of interest from exporters. RBI has systematically endeavoured its master directive guide to commercial banks in India to design the export credit products both for fulfilling the needs of short-term export finances and long-term finances. The nationalization of banks in 1969 provided further leverage to RBI and GOI to devise schemes for exporters for export credit in a liberal way in order to enable them to remain competitive vis-à-vis their competitors from other countries. Under the scheme, banks extend working capital loans to exporters at pre- and post-shipment stages. The credit limits sanctioned to exporters are based upon the financing bank's perception of the exporter's creditworthiness and past performance. The export financing may be denominated either in Indian rupees or foreign currency. For both stages of export financing, RBI sets a ceiling on the interest rate that banks can charge to borrowers under the scheme. Since RBI fixes only the ceiling rate of interest for export credit, banks are free to fix lower rates of interest for exporters on the basis of their actual cost of funds, operating expenses and taking into account the track record and the risk perception of the borrower, that is, the exporter. Figure 12.1 illustrates the declining trend in export credit in India in recent years.

Policymakers in today's globalized set-up understand it very well that the contribution of the external sector, especially of exports, is vital for the Indian economy. Globally, many countries which witnessed the higher growth trajectory in the economic growth have given much importance to export operations as they foresee the international business as a potent instrument in availing competitive, comparative and factor endowment advantages that an economy enjoys. Many countries, including China, have used export operations as an engine of economic growth of the nation. In the era of economic globalization, both merchandise and services exports are important for foreign exchange accumulation, accelerating economic growth and employment generation. One of the integral aspects of the international trade financing is that the degree of risks in international trade operations is significantly higher. An awareness and understanding of export risks on the part of the exporter coupled with the appropriate risk-mitigation strategy can help him/her develop the design and implement his/her financing options better and can also determine his/her success or failure in the export business. Although export-related risks (Caselet 12.1) are similar to domestic risks, they differ in scope and allied business implications for the firm. One has to be smart enough to assess, analyse and appraise successfully many additional factors of international commerce and accordingly has to employ the techniques that can be used to manage these risks. It is critical for Indian exporters dealing in international trade transactions to identify and seek ways to mitigate the major risks involved in the EXIM business. A

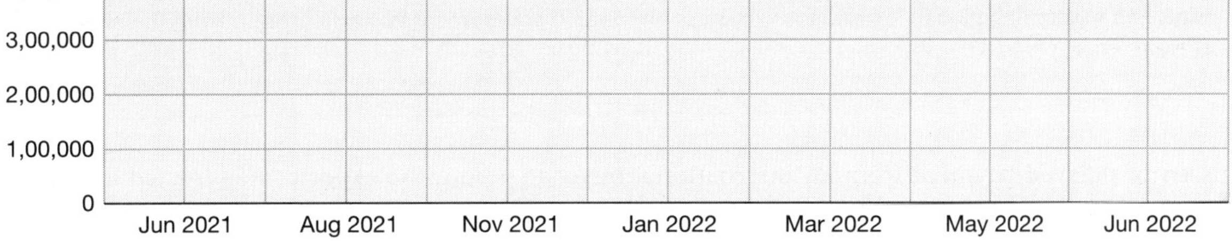

FIGURE 12.1 Outstanding as on Trade Credit in India (June 2021 to June 2022 in INR Crores).

Source: Reserve Bank of India. www.rbi.org.in (accessed on 24 May 2023).

CASELET 12.1

Rising Cost of Export Credit: Government Mulls Extension in Interest Equalization Scheme

Russia–Ukraine war coupled with economic sanctions and the blockage of financial channels has led to the disruption in the supply chain. These events have the spiralling impact on the rising cost of fuel, food, and fertilizers, thus leading to the catalytic impact of price rise across the sectors. To tame inflation, the central banks, world over, are increasing their banks' rates to restrict the money supply in the markets. The increase in FED rates has led to its spiralling impact all across the world, and interest rates are historically high in the world economy, especially in the context of the developed countries. Reserve Bank of India (RBI) has consistently followed the global trends and accordingly kept on increasing the interest rates. For instance, on 30 September 2022, the Monetary Policy Committee (MPC) increased interest rates by 50 basis points, as anticipated, to 5.90 percent. The rising cost of credit is making Indian exporting firms worried as it can make their products and services uncompetitive in international markets.

Additionally, exporting companies are concerned about the persistent volatility of the US dollar, ongoing monetary tightening, rising inflation, and worries about a global financial market recession because these factors could have a negative impact on emerging market economies and seriously jeopardize India's prospects for the development of its external sector. RBI will continue its endeavour to maintain financial stability in order to prevent persistent inflation, and it is well known that a rise in key rates causes banks to raise their lending rates, which has a highly negative influence on the business plans of companies engaged in export operations. The industry, already struggling with a slump in demand from important export markets, would face higher borrowing costs as a result of the consecutive repo rate increases. Additionally, the repo rate hike and the tight liquidity conditions would result in a huge increase in the cost of finance, which would have an effect on pre-shipment and post-shipment loan rates.

In an effort to lessen the burden of rising interest rates on small and medium exporters, the government is thinking about increasing the interest equalization or subsidy benefit provided to them. The decision to offer financing at interest rates below market rates comes at a time when Indian exporters are struggling due to sluggish demand in important countries, record inflation, and the possibility of a global recession. The government wants to raise the interest subsidy for micro-, small-, and medium-sized manufacturers from 3 to 5 percent, as well as for manufacturer-exporters, merchant-exporters, and exporters under tariff line 410 from 2 to 3 percent. The plan will be formally submitted to the ministry of finance by the department of trade, which is also estimating the cost of the exercise. The programme enables exporters to access capital more affordably. In the wake of the central bank raising interest rates repeatedly, exporters have been urging the government to reinstate the interest equalization advantages. Due to the burdensome high interest rates and weakening global demand for exporters, the Indian government is considering raising the interest subsidy rates.

missed or delayed payment from an international buyer to whom the exporter has trusted a lot can irreparably damage the future of his/her business. The solution for such challenges lies in a well-considered approach of export financing at various stages and by using all available mechanisms to ensure that the risk of the proposed transaction can be well and effectively managed if need arises. Due to all these reasons, a well-planned, synchronized and systematic export financing strategy is overemphasized for the success in the intentional trade.

12.2 Need for Export Finance

Liberal export credit is vital for smooth conduct of export transactions. Recognizing the fact that exports are extremely important not only for accelerating economic growth but also for the generation of employment for a developing country like India, RBI is playing an instrumental role in drafting the policy guidelines for liberal financing opportunities to Indian exporters in both Indian rupee and foreign currency. Scheduled commercial banks in India are mandated to extend these liberal financing facilities for the export promotion. Liberal export financing and the introduction of the Interest Equalization Scheme have provided a level-playing field to Indian exporters vis-à-vis their competitors. Indian exporters feel that timely credit is one of the most influencing factors for the scheduled export delivery and retaining satisfied customers. The commercial banks provide short-term export finance mainly by the way of pre- and post-shipment credit in both Indian rupee and foreign currency. Figure 12.2 explains the need for export finance in international trade operations.

Export credit facilities of RBI are largely aimed at not only providing the export financing facilities to existing exporters but also expanding and diversifying Indian exporters in the international markets. Project financing in the export of services and extending export credit for the long term through negotiated lines of credit is one such way for facilitating Indian exporters to win new projects in emerging markets of Africa and other developing countries. Liberal export financing helps Indian firms in exploring and funding new export venture(s) and also to switch their business orientation from domestic to mainly export based. In today's globalized era, each firm wishes to extend its activities to various markets due to variety of reasons such as generating economies of scale, higher profits margins, better returns, increased productivity and technological development and enhanced business experiences from international buyers. Firms may need finance in order to successfully process the export orders. This can be achieved by ensuring proper planning and execution of a financial plan for the successful conduct of the international business. The need for export finance can be due to a variety of reasons and some of them are explained further:

1. The export firm may be extending the credit to its buyers in internationally competitive markets so as to get more orders. Alternatively, the firm may have shipped the goods, granting extended payment terms to its buyers, importers and now requires short-term financing until the payment is received from such buyers.

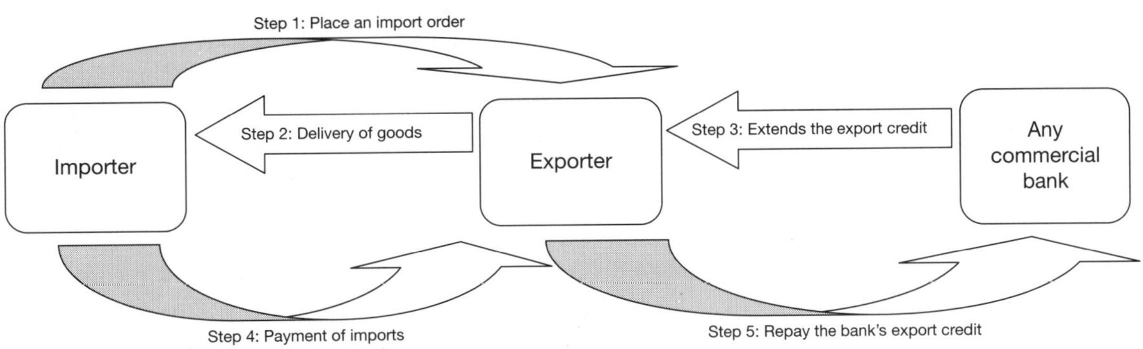

FIGURE 12.2 Need of Export Finance.

Source: Adapted from RBI Master Circular on Export Credit in INR & Foreign Currency.

2. The export firm may need the finances so as to pay its suppliers upfront in order to procure the raw material, semi-processed goods or finished goods which are intended for international sales either after required value addition or purely as merchandise.
3. The export firm may be concerned about the customers' creditworthiness and accordingly wish to improve cash flow.
4. The export firm might require export financing in order to refine or adapt its product or services for differentiated and heterogeneous export markets.
5. Any firm, aspiring to go global, may require funds in order to conduct the market study or feasibility analysis for its products and services in various international markets or may need funds to organize the fact-finding trips, international marketing or other pre-shipment activities in targeted markets abroad.
6. The firm may have to plan better export financing models if it is operating or likely to operate in the markets that are politically and economically unstable and uncertain but highly lucrative and growing. In such circumstances, the firm may have to plan better to optimize or mitigate risk.

Each of these situations requires a corresponding set of export financing requirements for a firm dealing in international trade. Keeping this in mind, commercial banks in India have designed various financing options for Indian exporters so that they can effectively withstand the competition as well as have the operational capability to deal in globally competitive markets.

12.3 Export Financing Facilities

Export finance refers to the liberal commercial credit extended by banks and other financial institutions to Indian exporters so as to fund their business for exports of goods and services outside the country. Export financing enables Indian exporters to expand their reach and presence to the global markets. Exporters require a liberal export credit for purchasing, processing, packaging and their day-to-day activities. Export financing facilities in India are designed to the needs of both the pre-shipment stage and post-shipment stage. The credit facilities are offered for meeting different purposes such as packing credit to sub-supplier, running account facility, packing credit in foreign currency, packing credit for deemed exports, packing credits for consulting services and advance against cheques/drafts received as advance payments. One of the crucial aspects is that export financing facilities should be designed so as to resolve the finance needs both at the pre-shipment and post-shipment stages. Figure 12.3 provides the framework of stages of export financing in India.

With the changing business needs, RBI has to adapt its credit schemes accordingly. There has been a lot of changes in export financing facilities in India from the time when the scheme was introduced by RBI in 1967. The Master Circular of RBI dated 1 July 2015 is aimed to make short-term working capital finance available to exporters at internationally comparable interest rates. Under the earlier scheme in force up to 30 June 2010, RBI used to fix only the ceiling rate of interest for the export credit while banks were free to decide the rates of interest within the ceiling rates keeping in view the benchmark prime lending rate (BPLR) and spread guidelines and taking into account the 'track record of the borrowers' and the risk perception. In order to enhance transparency in banks' pricing of their loan products, banks were advised to fix their external benchmark lending rate (EBLR) after taking into account the factors exhibited in Figure 12.4.

BPLR was introduced in 2003 but fell short of its original objective of bringing transparency to lending rates. This was mainly because banks could lend below BPLR under the BPLR system. Due to all these

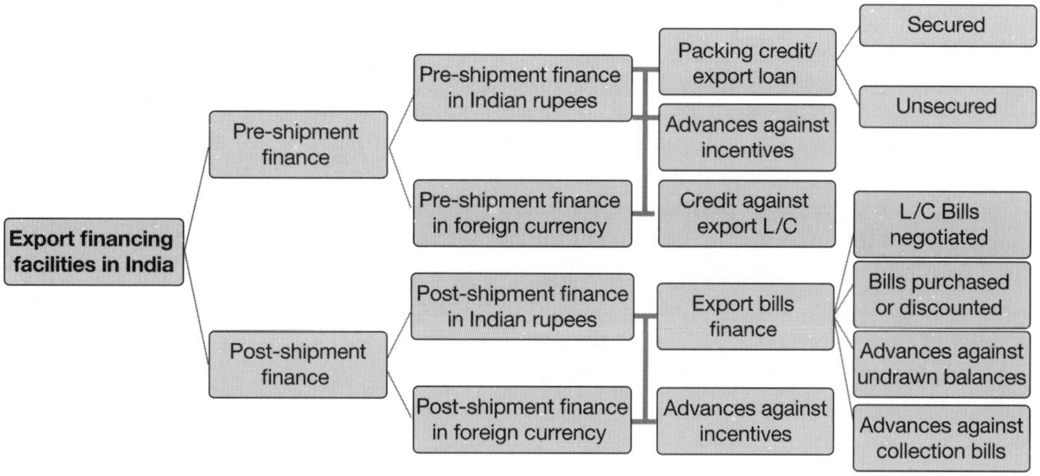

FIGURE 12.3 Export financing facilities in India.

Source: RBI (2011).

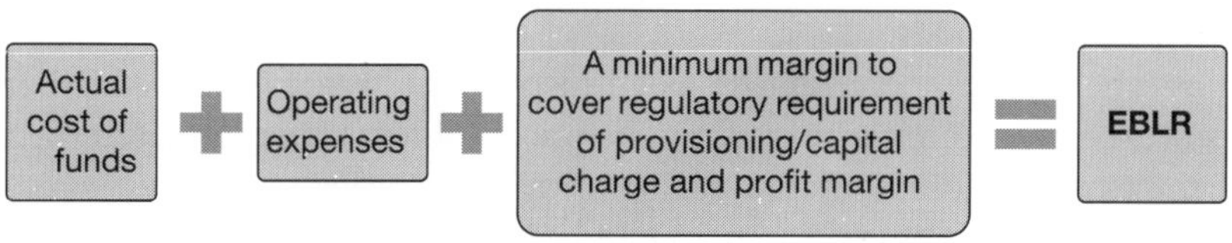

FIGURE 12.4 External Bank Lending Rates (EBLR).

Source: RBI (2011).

reasons, there exists unhealthy competition among banks, difficulty in assessing the transmission of RBI policy rates, assessing what are the actual costs of fund of exporters and so on. Keeping these factors in mind, RBI appointed a committee under the chairmanship of RBI Deputy Governor Anand Sinha to look into the issue of transparency in the export credit pricing and functioning of BPLR system. Anand Sinha Committee recommended the introduction of base rate system after studying the efficacy of base rate with respect to the transmission of the monetary policy. The existing system for export financing is called EBLR.

12.4 Pre-Shipment Finance for Exports

The 'pre-shipment credit' also known as the 'packing credit' means any loan or advance granted or any other credit provided by a bank to an exporter for financing the purchase, processing, manufacturing or packing of goods prior to shipment of goods to overseas market. The pre-shipment scheme is also available to fund the working capital expenses for rendering of services. In order to avail packing credit, there should be proof of export order which can be a sales contract signed between the exporter and importer or an L/C opened by the importer's bank in the favour of an exporter. The packing credit can also be extended to supporting manufacturer provided that there is a transferable L/C to his/her favour or back-to-back L/C or original credit mandates for part of credit to be rendered to such supporting supplier. Such L/C has to be either a confirmed or an irrevocable order for the supply of goods or services from India. Banks are allowed to waive off the requirement of the export order or L/C as a 'proof of exporter order' if they are satisfied with other material evidence to this effect that the exporter will use these funds only for meeting out the working capital requirement of the potential future order. The main purposes of pre-shipment finance are as follows:

1. There is a long gestation period of manufacturing of goods or rendering of services, and firms need to fund the manufacturing of such longer delivery of product or services.
2. The firm has to procure raw materials from various other suppliers for subsequent processing and manufacturing. The business is cyclical in nature, and the firm has to procure such cyclical supply of raw material for executing the export order.
3. The pre-shipment credit is also required so as to pay the expenses such as payment of salary, labour wages and electricity bills to carry out other manufacturing activities.
4. There is a need for the fund for internal processing and subsequent packing of goods for the export consignment. Additionally, the fund may be required so as to pay the freight and carriage expenses for shipping the goods to the buyers.
5. The exporter always needs the fund of buyers who are unable to make the payment in advance or have negotiated a payment term with export credit. The export credit may even be required in case of part payment in advance necessitating the firm to raise funds to procure the raw material for manufacturing the goods.
6. Firms can use the pre-shipment finance as an instrument to tide over the challenges of exchange rate risks and exchange controls by availing the pre-shipment export credit in the foreign currency.
7. Above all, the export credit is offered at liberal rates, in order to engage firm's own capital as it can be used for further business expansion and diversification.

The pre-shipment finance scheme as announced by RBI enables Indian commercial banks to provide the financing that an exporter needs to purchase or produce a product for exports of both goods and services. The scheme can also be used to finance short-term accounts receivable on exports. The main purpose of the pre-shipment scheme is to guarantee the working capital requirement to an exporter so as to facilitate the export sales or to meet a temporary need for cash flow arising from a single export transaction. The pre-shipment export finance scheme is offered at liberal interest rates so that exporters can increasingly make use of it for export growth, expansion and diversification. The pre-shipment finance in India is extended in both the ways as packing credit to eligible exporters in Indian rupee and in foreign currency. The pre-shipment credit is offered for both secured and unsecured transactions, advances against cheques and advances, advances against export incentives and against export L/C in favour of the exporter.

12.4.1 Eligibility for Availing Packing Credit

RBI has the eligibility criteria for extending the pre-shipment credit to exporters so as to ensure the credit flow only to desirable exporters and discretion in export credit lending can be eliminated. In India, the pre-shipment export credit is provided to an exporter who satisfies the following criteria:

1. The exporter should have a bank account with the bank where he/she wants such export credit and such branch of the bank should be authorized to deal in foreign exchange in compliance with RBI/FEDAI rules and procedures.

2. The exporter should have an import–export code issued by DGFT or regional authority. Import–export code has 10 digits indicating that the exporter has been authorized to export and import goods and services from and into India.
3. The exporter should be having the 'RCMC' issued by the concerned EPC or commodity board or export development authority. In case exportable products do not fall with any of the above-mentioned export promotion bodies, he/she should get registered with the Federation of Indian Exporters Organization. Services exporters are mandatorily required to get registered with Services Export Promotion Council.
4. As the part of the bank's due diligence for any credit, banks must examine that the exporter should not be in the caution list of RBI.
5. The exporter should not be in the list of ECGC mandating for 'specific approval required' for the extension of export credit.
6. In case the exportable goods are not under an open general licence, the exporter should have the required special export license issued for this purpose by DGFT. In the case of canalized items, he/she should have the permit (NOC) from authorized state trading enterprise clearly indicating the clearance for quantity and value of goods to be exported and imported.

In addition to the above mandatory requirements of due diligence for extending export credit, banks also examine the following areas while granting the pre-shipment credit to an exporter:

1. The bank is satisfied with the formal application of the exporter for releasing the packing credit on the basis of undertaking to the effect by the exporter that he/she would ship the goods to the overseas importer within stipulated due date as communicated by the exporter. The exporter ensures to submit the relevant shipping documents to the banks within the prescribed time limit or other documentary evidence of having shipped the goods such as the bill of lading or AWB.
2. The exporter should have to confirm the order of exports under a negotiated international business contract from the buyer or have irrevocable L/C issued in his/her favour by a foreign bank at the request of the importer. Banks accept it as documentary evidence for extending export credit. In exceptional cases, if banks find that the exporter has a very good track record of export business, they can extend export credit merely on the production of original cable, email, fax, telex message that are being exchanged between the exporter and the importer. It should be noted that the confirmed order as received by the exporter from the overseas buyer should reveal the information about the full name and address of the overseas buyer, description quantity and value of goods (FOB or CIF), destination port and the last date of payment.
3. If the exporter produces a special export licence issued to him/her by DGFT for the export of restricted goods or a NOC issued by the notified canalizing agency, banks, on their satisfaction, can provide pre-shipment finance as they become satisfied about the export prospects of goods.
4. If the exporter order is in the name of two parties as wherein the first is a 'main supplier' and the second is 'sub-supplier' or 'allied supplier', banks in India has been authorized to provide the export credit on the basis of shared percentage of export order between two more than two exporters.

12.4.2 Period of Advance

The period of advances for the pre-shipment credit is dependent on business circumstances of each individual exporter, and the credit period may vary; for example, the industry cycle of each business varies and banks are given the discretion to decide the time required for procuring, manufacturing or processing and shipping the relative goods or the rendering of services for each exporter when he/she applies for such credit. Banks factor various issues in arriving at the decision to grant the time period of pre-shipment credit such as the nature of the business, the supply of raw material, supply of ancillary services and shipment issues to an exporter to ship the goods or render the services. RBI directives mandate that if pre-shipment advances are not adjusted by the submission of export documents within 360 days from the date of advance, the advances will cease to qualify for the concessive rate of interest to the exporter from the date of grant of such export credit. It further mandates that RBI would provide refinance only for a period not exceeding 180 days.

12.4.3 Appraisal and Sanction of Limits

Banks check the various aspects while making an appraisal and sanction of export credit to exporters. Some of the important aspects that banks check are the product profile of the exporter in the international market and the political and economic environment of the country of import. Banks also look into the creditworthiness and solvency report of the prospective buyer, with whom the exporter proposes to do the business. In order to arrive at a fruitful conclusion about the creditworthiness and solvency position of buyers, banks consult various credit rating agencies such as ECGC or private consulting agencies such as SMERA, Vistas and Dun & Bradstreet. The sanction of pre-shipment export credit is based on the satisfactory appraisal of the following:

1. The exporter is of good track record or is a regular customer of the bank. He/she is a bona fide exporter and has a good standing in the market vis-à-vis his/her creditworthiness.
2. The exporter has all necessary licences/permits and volume permit as mandated in Schedule II of the ITC (HS) classification of FTP for the export.
3. The country to which the exports are to be made is not under UN watch list or is not the restricted cover countries or is not facing any kind of international sanctions for transfer of funds such as Iran, Ivory Coast, Somalia, Iraq and Syria.

12.4.4 Quantum of Finance

The pre-shipment export finance facility in India is based on the principle of 'need-based financing principle'. The quantum of the export finance cannot be more than the amount as indicated in the irrevocable L/C or export order. Banks also consider the percentage of margin (as profit) along with the factors illustrated in Figure 12.5 while sanctioning the packing credit to exporters.

The quantum of pre-shipment export finance is fixed depending on the FOB value of export order or value of irrevocable L/C or the domestic values of goods, whichever is found to be lower. The bank may consider the inclusion of marine insurance and freight charges at subsequent stages when the confirm order has come and the goods are ready to be shipped. Banks are also particular about the disbursals of export packing credit, particularity in cases when the disbursal is to be made in stages. Banks disburse the amount of credit possibly through to cheque/draft/bankers and so on and not in cash directly to the supplier of raw material to the exporter. The bank usually decides the duration of packing credit based on the export cycle or manufacturing cycle of the product. As per RBI guidelines, the maximum period of the packing credit period in India is 180 days. However, the banks are authorized to use their discretion in providing a further 90 days extension in packing to the exporter on their satisfaction.

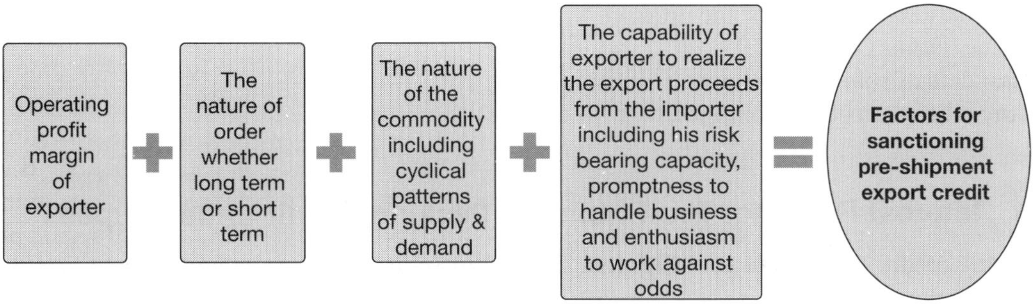

FIGURE 12.5 Factors for sanctioning pre-shipment export credit.

Source: RBI (2011).

12.4.5 Disbursement of Packing Credit

The RBI master circular provides for guidelines to be followed in the disbursal of credit wherein the guidance to banks is that banks should maintain a separate account for each account of the pre-shipment credit extended so as to monitor the period of sanction and end use of funds. Banks should ensure that funds so allocated should only be used for meeting the financing requirements of export transactions by exporters. Banks, at their satisfaction about the nature of business of an exporter, may release the pre-shipment export credit as a lump sum or in stages as per the requirement of an exporter. For the exporter availing the export credit for different export transactions, banks should maintain different accounts at various stages of processing, manufacturing and so on depending on the types of goods or services to be exported such as by hypothecation or pledge. It is the duty of the bank to ensure that outstanding balance in export credit accounts are adjusted either by transfer from one account to the other or by proceeds of relative export documents on purchase or discount when an exporter submits the bills after shipment of goods. To ensure proper compliance of effective use of the liberal credit to the exporter for export promotion, it is the duty of banks to keep a close watch on the end use of the funds and ensure that credit at lower rates of interest is used for genuine requirements of exports only. Banks should also monitor the progress made by the exporters in timely fulfilment of export orders so that pre-shipment credit can be liquidated within the time period as mandated.

On the completion of the successful appraisal of various aspects for the disbursal of export credit, banks must check that the exporter should have executed the list of documents as stipulated by it for this purpose. Disbursement of export credit is normally allowed only after the successful submission of all documents by the exporter. Sometimes, an exporter may not have the confirmed order but is anticipating it coming on festivals such as Christmas, Holi and Id-ul-Fitr and need finances to keep his/her goods ready by the time orders comes in. Under such circumstances, RBI has allowed banks in India to provide a special packing credit facility. This special facility is known as running account packing. Banks specifically check for the following particulars while processing the running account facility to the exporter:

1. Name of buyer
2. Commodity to be exported
3. Quantity
4. Period of the credit

5. International demand for the product
6. Value (either CIF or FOB)
7. Last date of shipment/collection/negotiation
8. Any other terms to be complied with

12.4.6 Interest Rates for Pre-Shipment Packing Credit under Rupee

The packing credit, that is, the pre-shipment finance to Indian exporter is available in both Indian rupee and foreign currency. Prior to 1 July 2010, the BPLR system was in place whereby it was recommended by RBI that banks should charge interest on the pre-shipment credit up to 270 days at the rate BPLR minus 2.5 percentage basis. Under this system, the period of credit is to be reckoned from the date of advance. This system has been revamped in order to make it compatible with geo-economic realities, and the 'base rate' system has been introduced by RBI with effect from 1 July 2010. The BPLR system has been abolished and was applicable only up to 30 June 2010. RBI circular on export credit makes it clear that if pre-shipment export credit is not liquidated from proceeds of bills on the purchase, discount and so on, on the submission of export documents within 360 days from the date of advance, such export credit as given to the exporter ceases to qualify for the concessional rates of interest as indicated in Table 12.1. In circumstances where the packing credit is not extended beyond the original period of sanction and exports take place after the expiry of the sanctioned period but within a period of 360 days from the date of advance, the exporter would be eligible for concessional credit only up to the sanctioned period. For the balance period, the exporter will have to pay interest rate prescribed under the category 'Export Credit Not Elsewhere Specified'. Banks are advised to explain with reasons to the exporter why such credit has been extended up to 360 from the sanctioned period of credit.

In cases where exports do not take place within 360 days from the date of pre-shipment advance, such credits will be termed as 'Export Credit Not Elsewhere Specified', and banks are free to charge interest rate as prescribed under ECNOS category. If exports do not take place at all, banks should charge on relative packing credit domestic lending rate plus penal rate of interest, if any, to be decided by the banks on the basis of a transparent policy approved by their Board. The applicable rate of concessional/preferential interest for lending on export credit is given in Table 12.1.

In the case of pre-shipment credit in foreign currency (PCFC), applicable interests were applicable as mentioned in Table 12.1. Due to increased pressure on India's foreign exchange reserves, banks are made free to charge the interest rates as per their economic interests. No ceiling rates on pre-shipment in export credit in foreign currency are applicable for any banks. However, applicable interest should be fixed with reference to ruling London Interbank Offered Rate (LIBOR), EURO LIBOR or Euro Interbank Offer Rate (EURIBOR).

TABLE 12.1 Pre-Shipment Credit in Indian Rupee from the Date of Advance

1. Up to 270 days	Base rate or over & above base rate
2. Against incentives receivable from the government covered by ECGC up to 90 days	Base rate or above base rate

Source: RBI (2011).

12.4.7 Follow-up of Packing Credit Advance

Banks usually hypothecate the stock of the exporter, and the exporter is required to submit stock statement providing all the necessary details about the stocks. Banks use such stock as a guarantee for securing the pre-shipment export credit in advance. Banks may demand such information from the exporter at the time interval as they deem fit keeping in mind the exporter's reputation and creditworthiness. In addition to this, banks also physically inspect the stock at regular intervals at the premises of exporter.

12.4.8 Liquidation of Packing Credit Advance

Pre-shipment export credit has to be liquidated out into post-shipment credit after the submission of export bills by the exporter or alternatively on the realization of export proceeds relevant shipment. The liquidation of pre-shipment export credit can also be done by the payment receivable as export benefits/incentives/subsidies from GOI. In India, some of the export benefits/incentives/subsidies received from GOI include the duty drawback, duty credit scrip under MEIS or SEIS, the payment under the 'Interest Equalization Scheme', export assistance under the MDA of the central government or from any other relevant source.

If the exporter has failed to make the export or export cannot take place due to the cancellation of the order or any other reasons, banks are authorized to recover/realize the entire advance from exporter along with a certain interest rate. In some cases, the RBI master circular allows some flexibility in the use of packing credit whereby the exporter is allowed and permitted to substitute the exportable commodity. Thus, the pre-shipment export finance can be repaid by export proceeds of another commodity, which can be exported to the same or another buyer. This is to be done with the prior approval and satisfaction of banks; banks usually discourage such substitution but allow it in cases where market circumstances have compelled the exporter to do so, or the exporter is of a good track record or is a long-standing client of the bank with good reputation.

12.4.9 Overdue Packing

In some cases, banks may have to consider the pre-shipment export finance as an overdue as the exporter fails to liquidate the packing credits as per stipulated rules and regulations of RBI. Banks are allowed to grant overdue in bona fide cases, but if the condition persists and exporter fails to liquidate the packing credit even after such overdue period, then the banks can take the necessary actions to recover such dues as per normal recovery procedure.

12.5 Pre-Shipment Credit in Foreign Currency (PCFC)

PCFC is aimed at making credit available to Indian exporters at internationally competitive rates so as to enable them to compete with their counterparts from developed countries where interest rates are far lower than what is changed in India. RBI has permitted the authorized dealers, dealing in foreign exchange under the FEMA rules to extend PCFC to exporters for the procurement of domestic and imported inputs to be used of exportable goods. Risk-free rates, or RFRs, are likely to replace LIBOR. RFRs are overnight interest rate benchmarks that the FCA and other regulators believe are more representative and reliable than LIBOR. These benchmarks can be calculated using actual transactions

TABLE 12.2 New Risk-Free Interest Rate Regime in lieu of LIBOR Currencies

Libor Currencies	Proposed Replacement	Transaction Types
USD	Secured Overnight Funding Rate (SOFR)	Secured
GBP	Sterling Overnight Index Average (SONIA)	Unsecured
Euro	Euro Short-term Rate (ESTR)	Unsecured
CHF	Swiss Average Rate Overnight (SARON)	Secured
JPY	Tokyo Overnight Average Rate (TONAR)	Unsecured

Source: SBI-LIBOR Transition Compendium, 2022 https://sbi.co.in/documents/16337/16538/241221-SBI-LIBOR_Transition_Compendium_-_Booklet_Digital+-Ver+3-Dec+2021.pdf (accessed on 11 April 2023).

because they are intended to be based on liquid markets. In order to identify alternative RFRs for the relevant currency, several RFR working groups were formed in a variety of countries. In India, a system of Alternate Reference Rates (ARRs) is introduced based on the globally accepted concept of RFR and ARR are proposed as shown in Table 12.2 for each currency. Several currencies have additional IBORs in addition to the RFRs described above, such as EURIBOR in the Eurozone and TIBOR in Japan. Market participants may occasionally decide to utilize these rates in addition to the pertinent RFR and instead of the Euro LIBOR or Japanese Yen LIBOR, respectively. But, as was already indicated, several of these IBORs are up for reform because they have LIBOR-like problems; therefore, market players might choose to utilize RFRs in their place. The Reserve Bank of India in one of its Master Circulars has fixed the spread to be charged on the pre-shipment in foreign currency as LIBOR rates stand phased out in the light of the LIBOR scandal of 2013. The packing credit in foreign currency is an additional window to Indian exporters to get working capital for export transactions at internationally competitive rates of interest. Rules and regulations for the conduct of this credit are similar to the packing credit in Indian rupee unless otherwise specified, and such credit is allowed only for cash exports meaning the foreign currency packing credit is not applicable where the exporter has extended the payment credit to the foreign buyer. PCFC can be availed in any of the following business scenarios by an exporter:

1. The exporter is allowed to avail the pre-shipment credit in rupees and then the post-shipment credit either in rupees or discounting/rediscounting of the Export Bills Abroad (EBR) Scheme.
2. The exporter is allowed to avail of PCFC and discount/rediscounting of the export bills in foreign currency under the EBR Scheme.
3. The exporter is allowed to avail the pre-shipment credit in rupees and then convert withdrawals into PCFC at the discretion of the bank.

The exporter availing the packing credit in foreign currency is allowed to take the export credit in any of the freely convertible foreign currency such as US dollars, pound sterling, Japanese yen and Euro. There are operational flexibility in availing this scheme for the exporter wherein the packing credit is allowed in currency (Table 12.3) other than the invoiced currency in export order, for example, an auto manufacturer in India has got the export order from the United Kingdom invoiced in pound sterling where in for making a car, this manufacturer has to procure or import all of auto components from its mother plant located in Japan. Banks are advised to allow packing credit in Japanese yen and risks and cost of cross-currency conversion in this whole transaction will be that of the exporter. Further, banks are allowed to extend PCFC for exports to Asian clearing unit countries.

TABLE 12.3 Pre-Shipment Credit in Foreign Currency (PCFC)

1.	Up to 180 days	Not exceeding 200 basis points over LIBOR/EURO LIBOR/EURIBOR
2.	Beyond 180 days and up to 360 days	Rate for initial period of 180 days prevailing at the time of extension plus 150 basis points, that is, 1 above plus 150 basis points

Source: RBI (2011).

12.6 Special Cases of Pre-Shipment Financing

As the nature of credit varies with the different exportable products, there are special schemes designed so as to cater to business needs of such sectors and industries. These are explained in the following sub-sections.

12.6.1 Packing Credit to Sub-supplier

The pre-shipment export finance can be shared between the actual export order holder and the manufacturer of export goods on the basis of the disclaimer. Such a disclaimer should be signed by the actual export order holder by clearly indicating that he/she himself/herself is not utilizing any credit facility against the export order, which has been transferred to a manufacturer for manufacturing the goods for export order. Such a disclaimer should also be signed by the bankers of actual export order holder. In such circumstances, an inland L/C can be opened in favour of the manufacturer of the goods; thus, the sub-supplier becomes eligible for packing credit. The pre-shipment export credit is also available to manufacturing firm and the individual who supplies his/her exports routed through canalizing agencies such as State Trading Corporation/Minerals and Metal Trading Corporation/other export houses and agencies. Banks are also allowed to extend the pre-shipment credit to manufacturer suppliers who do not have export orders/L/C in their own name because goods are declared as canalized, and export can take place only through the nominated canalizing agency such as State Trading Corporation/ Minerals and Metal Trading Corporation or other export houses, agencies unless an export is allowed against NOC from such notified agency.

12.6.2 Running Account Facility

Running account facility is provided by the bank to those exporters who deal in multiple items of exports. It helps them keep ready their various goods for the purpose of exports. This may be the case when the availability of raw material is seasonal, and exporters have to procure raw material, manufacture the export product and keep the same ready for the shipment, in the anticipation of the receipt of L/C/firm export orders from the overseas buyers. Running account facility may also be required by exporters where the time taken for manufacture and the shipment of goods is more than the delivery schedule as per export contracts. Usually, the bank sanctions such kind of export credit only to those exporters who have a good track record and impeccable reputation in the eyes of the banker. Such an exporter is also required to produce the L/C/export order as and when he/she gets it from his/her international clients. Considering the innumerable challenges that such exporters face in availing of adequate pre-shipment credit, scheduled banks in India have been authorized to extend the pre-shipment credit through 'running account' facility in respect of any commodity, without insisting on prior lodgment of L/C/firm export orders. Banks usually consider the following conditions while granting the running account facility to Indian exporters:

1. Banks may extend the 'running account' facility only to those exporters who have a good track record in the past vis-à-vis liquidation of packing credit on time in compliance with established statutes and guidelines.
2. Banks can extend 'running account facility' to EOUs, STPI, BTP, units and so on located in SEZs and AEZs.
3. Banks should clearly guide such account holders to submit the 'proof of exports order' such as 'an irrevocable L/C' or 'confirmed import order' or 'negotiated and signed sales contract' within a reasonable period of time as decided by the banks from time to time.
4. Banks are advised to mark off individual export bills when submitted by the exporter whether under negotiation or collection. Banks should mark such export bills against the earliest outstanding pre-shipment credit on the 'first-in, first-out' basis. It is the duty of banks to ensure the compliance vis-à-vis time period for the utilization of packing credit and should ensure that the individual pre-shipment credit does not go beyond the period of sanction or 360 days as stipulated by RBI from the date of advance, whichever is earlier.
5. Banks can liquidate the packing credit with export proceeds of export documents against which no packing credit has been extended to the exporter. For example, if an exporter has not taken any export credit for this transaction and he/she submits the export documents for liquidation of other packing credit availed for some other export transaction, banks are duty-bound to accept such document for liquidation of export credit.

RBI guidelines mandate that running account facility cannot be granted to sub-suppliers, and if banks find at any stage or bank official are of preview that the exporter is involved in the misuse of these funds for other purposes or such funds are not directly used for fulfilling the export transactions, they can withdraw such facility to such exporter. Further, if banks find that there is a compromise of agreed terms and conditions of packing credit as mandated by RBI by the exporter, it can terminate the running account facility and may change commercial rates of interest on remaining credit if any.

12.6.3 Packing Credit for Export of Services

Considering services export is extremely vital for the Indian economy, especially the employment generation, banks are allowed to extend both the pre-shipment and post-shipment export credit to exporters of all the 161 tradable services covered under the General Agreement on Trade in Services. The only condition is that the payments must be realized in freely convertible foreign exchange as mandated under FTP 2015–2020. Banks are advised to do the due diligence vis-à-vis avoidance of double financing for the same export of services, and the export credit can be liquidated with remittances from abroad of services export realization. While extending credit, banks may take into account the track record of the exporter or overseas counterparty. Banks may ask for matching of the statement of export receivables of service providers with that of the statement of payables receivable of overseas party. As services exports are tangible with any documentary evidence of having crossed India's territorial water, it results in the confusion, especially on evidencing the services export with 'proof of export'. RBI has allowed banks to make their own rules and parameters to conduct due diligence

- The proposal is a genuine case of export of services. The item of service export is covered under Appendix 10 of the Handbook of Procedures, Volume I.
- The exporter is registered with the electronic and software EPC or services EPC or with Federation of Indian Export Organizations, as applicable.
- There is an export contract for the export of the service. invoices are raised and inward remittance is received in foreign exchange.
- There is a time lag between the outlay of working capital expense and actual receipt of payment from the service consumer or his/her principal abroad. There is a valid working capital gap, that is, the service is provided first while the payment is received some time after an invoice is raised.
- Banks should ensure that there is no double financing/excess financing, and the export credit granted does not exceed the foreign exchange earned less the margins if any required, advance payment/credit received.
- The company will raise the invoice as per the contract. Where the payment is received from the overseas party, the service exporter would utilize the funds to repay the export credit availed of from the bank.

FIGURE 12.6 Areas of consideration for due diligence while granting packing credit to services exporters.

Source: Adapted from Master Circular-Rupee/Foreign Currency Export Credit and Customer Service to Exporters, Reserve Bank of India.

before extending the pre-shipment export credit to service exporters. Exporters of services are eligible (Figure 12.6) for availing the working capital need through export credit (pre- and post-shipment) for consumables, wages, supplies and so on. The specific issues that a bank considers while granting the pre-shipment export credit to services exporter are listed in Figure 12.6.

12.6.4 Packing Credit Facilities to Deemed Exports

Deemed exports are the exports which do not leave the territorial boundary of India. Such export supplies are usually made to multi-lateral aid agencies and programme such as UN and Asian Development Bank. The beauty of such exports is that the supplies are made on the basis of the international competitive bidding process, and payments are received in freely convertible foreign currency as stipulated by the FEMA, 2000. Such deemed exporters are eligible for concessional interest rate both at the pre- and post-shipment stage of an export transaction.

12.6.5 Advance against Cheques/Drafts Received as Advance Payment

The pre-shipment credit is also available in places where the exporter receives direct payments from abroad by means of cheque/drafts and so on. Scheduled commercial banks can extend the pre-shipment credit against cheques and drafts at a concessional rate to those exporters who are of a good track record. Such a credit facility shall be available only till the time of realization of export proceeds of cheque/draft from abroad. The banks usually offer such services at the discretion and track record of the exporter and after satisfying themselves that such credit is against an export order and is as per trade practices of the country. Banks also ensure that the realization of export proceeds against such pre-shipment credit should be in accordance with the approved method of realization of export proceeds as per extant rules. If an exporter has availed the financing under normal commercial rates as he/she fails to comply with terms and conditions for packing credit against cheques and drafts, banks may give effect to the prescribed rate for the export credit rate retrospectively once the aforesaid conditions have been complied with and refund the difference to the exporter.

12.6.6 Pre-Shipment Credit to Floriculture, Grapes and Other Agro-based Products

Considering the time-consuming nature of India's agriculture sector and cutting down the cost of the transaction, RBI has guided banks in India to extend the pre-shipment credit to floriculture sector where the credit is allowed for the purchase of cut flowers and all post-harvest expenses, such as packing, labelling and marking and unitization, incurred for making flowers shipment abroad. Banks can also extend export credit for meeting out the working capital requirements for export-related activities of all agro-based products including the purchase of fertilizers, pesticides and other inputs for growing flowers, grapes and so on. Banks are allowed to frame their own internal rules so as to clearly identify such activities as export-related and satisfy themselves of the export potential. Banks are also required to check that there should not be double financing of same activities as National Agricultural and Rural Development Bank (NABARD) also implements various direct and indirect schemes aimed at the promotion of the Indian agriculture sector through scheduled commercial banks. RBI has framed the policy guidelines which are aimed at promoting export of floriculture, grapes and other agro-based products, and accordingly, pre-shipment credit is not only liberal but also eligible to the 'Interest Equalization Scheme' of GOI. Other terms and conditions of such packing credit such as period, quantum and liquidation remain the same. Banks are allowed to extend credit only for the working capital requirements and such facility should never be extended for capital investments, such as import of foreign technology, equipment and land development.

12.6.7 Export Credit to Processors/Exporters in AEZs

GOI has set up AEZs in the country to promote agricultural exports. This scheme is implemented by the state government wherein the product-specific zones are identified in the country for the focused agro-export promotion of identified crops. For processing value-added products, one can set up the processing units within and outside, provided that the production and processing of goods must be integrated as one activity. To comply with this, an agro-processing unit has to enter into 'contract farming' with farmers and has to ensure supply of quality seeds, pesticides, micro-nutrients and other material to the group of farmers. The agro-processing unit shall be purchasing the products as raw material for the production of the final products and shall export it outside India. RBI, therefore, has directed scheduled banks to extend pre-shipment credit facilities to such agro-processing units for the purpose of procuring and supplying inputs to the farmers so that quality inputs are available for the purpose of exporting agro-export production. The pre-shipment credit to such agro-processing unit or agro-output exporters will enable them to purchase or import inputs in bulk with greater economies of scale.

Banks can consider the 'inputs supplied to farmers' by exporters as collateral for extending pre-shipment credit facilities and can also sanction the lines of credit/export credit to processors/exporters to cover the cost of such inputs required by farmers to cultivate such crops to promote the export of agro-products. This arrangement will not only ensure economies of scale in agro-operations but will help in promoting the agro-sector both in terms of higher per-unit value realizations and employment generation. The agro-processing unit or an output exporter can make the bulk purchases of the inputs and supply the same to the farmers in AEZs as per a pre-determined arrangement. Banks should verify the end utilization of the fund and should also do the due diligence to check that there exists a contractual arrangement between the agro-unit and the farmer and the agro-unit and the overseas buyer for resultant exports. Banks are required to continuously monitor the situation that exists for such a loan extension in case of agricultural exports as first, there is no definite proof of exports orders; second, agro-products are perishable in nature; third, there is significant quality rejection(s) in agro-exports, and fourth, the profit margins are not that great.

12.7 Summary

Exports play an important role in accelerating the economic growth of developing countries like India. In view of the important role played by exporters, several initiatives have been taken by the RBI and GOI. The commercial banks provide short-term export finance mainly by the way of the pre- and post-shipment credit. RBI first introduced the scheme of export financing in 1967. The scheme is intended to make a short-term working capital finance available to exporters at internationally comparable interest rates. The BPLR system fell short of its objectives of cost-effective transparent export credit. Accordingly, RBI appointed a committee under the chairmanship of RBI Deputy Governor Anand Sinha to look into the issue of transparency in the export credit pricing and the functioning of the BPLR system. Anand Sinha Committee recommended the introduction of the base rate system after studying the efficacy of the base rate with respect to the transmission of monetary policy. The 'pre-shipment credit' also known as 'packing credit' means any loan or advance granted or any other credit provided by a bank to an exporter for financing the purchase, processing, manufacturing or packing of goods prior to shipment or working capital expenses for the rendering of services and so on. The following are the types of pre-shipment finance offered by banks and financial institutions in India:

1. Packing credit
2. Advance against cheques/draft and so on representing advance payments

The pre-shipment export finance facility in India is based on the principle of 'need-based financing principle'. The quantum of export finance cannot be more than the amount as indicated in the irrevocable L/C or export order. Banks should also consider the percentage of margin (as profit) along with the following factors while sanctioning the packing credit to exporters. These are:

1. The nature of order, whether long term or short term.
2. The nature of the commodity including cyclical patterns of supply and demand.
3. The capability of the exporter to realize the export proceeds from the importer including his/her risk-bearing capacity, promptness to handle business and enthusiasm to work against odds.

The applicable rate of concessional/preferential interest for lending on export credit is determined by RBI in its master circular. RBI prescribes the periodic interest rates which are shown in the table on the next page.

The following are the stages at which the pre-shipment export finance in India is given to the exporter and includes appraisal and sanction of limits, disbursement of packing credit advance, follow-up of packing credit advance, liquidation of packing credit advance and overdue packing. Similarly, there are special cases under which the pre-shipment finance is available to an Indian exporter. The schemes are as follows:

1. Packing credit to sub-supplier
2. Running account facility
3. PCFC
4. Packing credit facilities to deemed exports
5. Packing credit facilities for services export
6. Advance against cheques/drafts received as advance payment

Pre-Shipment Credit in Indian Rupee from the Date of Advance

1. Up to 270 days	Base rate or over & above base rate
2. Against incentives receivable from government covered by ECGC up to 90 days	Base rate or above base rate
Pre-Shipment Credit in Foreign Currency	
1. Up to 180 days	Not exceeding 200 basis points over LIBOR/EURO LIBOR/EURIBOR
2. Beyond 180 days and up to 360 days	Rate for initial period of 180 days prevailing at the time of extension plus 150 basis points, that is, 1 above plus 150 basis points

Source: RBI (2011). https://www.rbi.org.in/scripts/NotificationUser.aspx?Id=6515&Mode=0 (accessed on 27 August 2020).

Review Exercises

Multiple Choice Questions

1. What can be the maximum period for the extension of packing credit at concessional rates by a scheduled commercial bank in India?
   a. 360 days
   b. 180 days
   c. 270 days
   d. Any period
   e. None of the above
2. Which of the following types of banks are not allowed to extend the pre-shipment credit in India?
   a. Private scheduled bank
   b. Public scheduled bank
   c. Foreign scheduled bank
   d. Regional rural bank
   e. All of the above
3. Banks have changed to a new system of extending concessional export credit as previously used BPLR system was not competitive enough. What is the new system called?
   a. Base rate
   b. Bank rate

c. Repo rate
d. Commercial rate
e. None of the above

4. As part of the bank's eligibility criteria for extending concessional export credit, which of the following is not of active consideration?
   a. The exporter should have an IEC from DGFT
   b. The exportable items should not be prohibited or restricted or canalized for exports
   c. The exporter should not be in caution list of RBI
   d. The exporter should have a track record of at least 10 years of export business
   e. The exporter should have an export order or irrevocable L/C in his/her favour
5. Running account facility is useful for which type of the exporter?
   a. Status holder exporter
   b. Registered MSME exporter
   c. Exporter with confirmed L/C
   d. Exporter having multiple orders at a time from different client based in different countries
   e. None of the above
6. Banks in India started extending concessional export credit from which of the following year?
   a. 1968
   b. 1969
   c. 1965
   d. 1967
   e. None of the above
7. Banks, while extending the packing credit to service the exporter, do not consider which of the following point as part of their due diligence?
   a. Exportable service is allowed for exports under the list of exportable services of DGFT.
   b. The exporter has RCMC issued by either from electronic and software EPC or Services EPC or with Federation of Indian Export Organizations as the case may be.
   c. There is an export contract for the export of the service and irrevocable L/C as well.
   d. The company must be ranked as the top 25 company in India in the services it deals with.
   e. All of the above
8. Banks usually consider which of the following conditions while granting the running account facility to Indian exporters?
   a. Banks can extend 'running account facility' to EOUs and units located in other dedicated export enclaves.
   b. Banks should consider that the exporter has genuine 'proof of exports order' such as 'irrevocable L/C' or 'confirmed import order' or 'negotiated and signed sales contract'.
   c. Banks may extend the 'running account' facility only to those exporters who have a good track record.
   d. Such exporter should not be in caution list of RBI/customs/central excise/services tax and denied entity list of DGFT.
   e. All of the above
9. In compliance with ensuring the need-based export financing, banks consider which of the following factors while sanctioning the quantum of export finance to an exporter?
   a. Operating profit margin of the exporter
   b. The nature of order whether long term or short term
   c. The nature of the commodity including cyclical patterns of supply and demand

d. The capability of the exporter to realize the export proceeds from the importer including his/her risk-bearing capacity

e. All of the above

10. What is the maximum spread that banks can charge on packing credit in Indian rupee?

a. 1 percent

b. 2.5 percent

c. 3.5 percent

d. 1.5 percent

e. None of the above

Critical Thinking Questions

1. Explain the rationale and need for export finance for an Indian exporter foraying in international markets.
2. 'Export finance is the blood for a country's exports.' Explain this quote and discuss the need for export finance for promoting the exports of the country.
3. What are the various export financing facilities available in India at various stages of the export cycle? Discuss.
4. What are the important things a bank should check in an exporter while extending his/her export credit under the pre-shipment finance facility?
5. What are the interest rates that RBI charges under concessional financing to Indian exporters under Indian rupee and foreign currency?
6. Write a short note on the following:
   a. Quantum of export finance
   b. Disbursement of packing credit advance
   c. Follow-up of packing credit advance
   d. Liquidation of packing credit advance
7. Explain the process and procedure for disbursal of packing credits in India. What are the various instruments and channels for availing pre-shipment finance for an Indian exporter?
8. Explain any two of the following:
   e. Running account facility
   f. Packing credit facilities to deemed exports
   g. Packing credit facilities for consulting services
   h. Advance against cheques/drafts received as advance payment
9. Discuss the various schemes as enshrined by RBI in the master circular for the special pre-shipment financing in India.

Further Reading

1. RBI. 2011. 'Master Circular on Rupee/Foreign Currency Export Credit & Customer Service to Exporters. Available at: https://taxguru.in/rbi/rbis-master-circular-dated-172011-rupeeforeign-currency-export-credit-customer-service-exporters.html (accessed on 4 May 2023).

CHAPTER 13

Post-Shipment Export Finance Scheme

CHAPTER OBJECTIVES

- To elaborate the need of post-shipment finance for exports.
- To explain the instruments and channels under which the post-shipment finance is extended.
- To explain the procedure of crystallization of overdue export bills in EXIM trade transactions.
- To discuss the mechanism for disbursal of post-shipment finance.

13.1 Introduction

RBI has framed the policy document guiding scheduled banks to extend the post-shipment credit to Indian exporters in both Indian rupee and foreign currency. Once the goods are shipped out of the country, there may be a delay in realization of export proceeds, as sometimes the exporter extends credit to importers. While extending pre-shipment finance, banks usually mortgage the stock of such firms as collateral for the loan. Once goods are dispatched out of India, banks extend post-shipment credit in lieu of 'trade documents' submitted by an exporter and adjust the loan of pre-shipment finance. Hence, post-shipment credit refers to an 'advance or a loan' that is extended to the exporter by a scheduled bank in India after the goods have been shipped to the importer. Post-shipment credit may take a different form; for example, it can happen through discounting of trade documents or by purchase or by negotiation. Post-shipment credit is occasionally executed by any scheduled bank in lieu of a full set of 'trade documents' including the transport document (as a proof of shipment), commercial invoice, packing list, certificate of insurance and L/C or draft (as applicable). Any Indian exporter availing pre-shipment finance can approach his/her bank for extending the post-shipment finance so as to fulfil his/her working capital needs until the payment is received from an overseas importer. Post-shipment credit is very popular in international trade transactions as an exporter is entitled to get assured export credit at a very liberal rate of interest. An exporter approaches a bank (exporter's bank) with trade documents after having dispatched the goods to an overseas buyer. The exporter's bank extends post-shipment credit in lieu of trade documents and sends these documents to the importer's bank. Post-shipment credit can be extended 'with recourse' or 'without recourse'. When it is extended as 'without recourse', banks keep the trade documents as collateral for non-funded limits or pre-approved credit lines. Post-shipment finance can be extended in both Indian rupee and freely convertible foreign currency to an exporter. In addition to RBI guidelines for export credit, banks also have their internal guidelines aimed at ensuring due diligence while extending such credit facility to exporters. Post-shipment export credit supports the trade supply chain of the exporters for meeting out the working capital needs, and its advantages are quite similar to that of pre-shipment finance. An exporter needs funds at both pre-shipment and post-shipment stages. An exporter has to finance the procurement of raw material and other inputs at the pre-shipment stage and extend credit to the buyer or to wait for the payment as export realizations take time due to long distance, different banking procedures and invoiced different foreign currency. The process of export credit in EXIM operations is provided in Figure 13.1.

Liberal export finances are very important for Indian exporters, as the interest rates in India are higher when compared with their counterparts in international markets, and as a result, Indian goods become priced out vis-à-vis their competitors in the international market. Realizing these inherent challenges of the Indian banking system, RBI had introduced the scheme of export financing in 1967 for both pre-shipment and post-shipment purposes, wherein the purpose of post-shipment finance scheme was to ensure liberal credit to the Indian exporter until their export proceeds are realized, especially in cases where the credit is extended to overseas buyers so as to win the competitive international markets for enhanced exports. The post-shipment credit system has been revamped several times from 1967 to realign it with emerging economic realities and make it more efficient and effective for Indian exporters. Similarly, an attempt was made to reduce the cost of funds to Indian exporters by introducing the 'base rate system' in 2010, which is aimed at enhancing the transparency in export credit rates of different scheduled banks. The new system is supposed to ensure better assessment of transmission of the central bank's monetary policy as envisaged and contemplated by RBI and facilitate the cost-effective availability of funds to Indian exporters. RBI wants that there should not only be a priority in export credit to Indian exporter, but funds delivery mechanism should also be cost-effective, hassle-free and more transparent. For all, export credit advances in Indian rupee at both pre-shipment and post-shipment stages will now be at or above the base rate of banks.

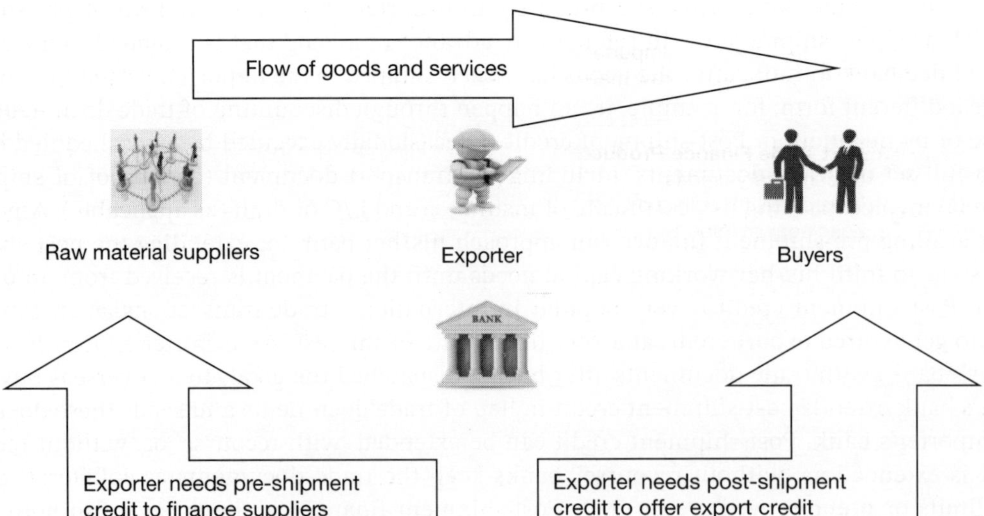

FIGURE 13.1 Foreign trade transaction cycle.

13.2 Need for Post-Shipment Finance

There is definitively a need for post-shipment finance to an Indian exporter, as there is a time gap between placing an order for goods and receiving receipt of the cash regarding export realization from an importer, and it can put a significant strain on the financial requirement of an exporter. Export transactions are usually manifested by seasonal peaks, long transit times and lengthy credit terms, and as a result, there are higher needs of working capital for export business. The exporter can negotiate favourable payment terms to reduce such risks, but many times export credit is the only way to get the export orders. Under such circumstances, it is important that the exporter should leverage other financing option at a liberal rate of interest. Post-shipment finance scheme of scheduled banks provides such leverage to Indian exporters wherein they can get their export bills financed for the period of 90 days under the present RBI guidelines. Post-shipment credit fulfils the financial needs of an exporter after goods have been shipped out of India. Figure 13.2 illustrates the trade cycle of export firms and needs of post-shipment credit after the dispatch of goods to an overseas buyer.

Post-shipment export credit by any scheduled bank can be extended in two ways: *first*, against the 'purchase' or 'discounting' of trade documents (export bills) submitted by the exporter after dispatch of goods to an overseas buyer and *second*, against the various incentives, duty drawbacks and other export benefits. The process of post-shipment credit under L/C is illustrated in Figure 13.3.

A bank extends credit (Figure 13.3) against export bills (non L/C Bills) submitted by exporter which will be by way of purchase if it is a sight payment (document against payment) and discounting of export bills if it is time or usance bill (D/A). A bank extends such post-shipment credit usually in cases of non-disputable international trade transactions against the proper sanctioned limit of export credit. Bank can extend credit either 'with recourse' or 'without recourse'; however, banks in India usually prefer to extend the post-shipment credit 'with recourse'. The process of extension of post-shipment credit under documentary collections is depicted in Figure 13.4.

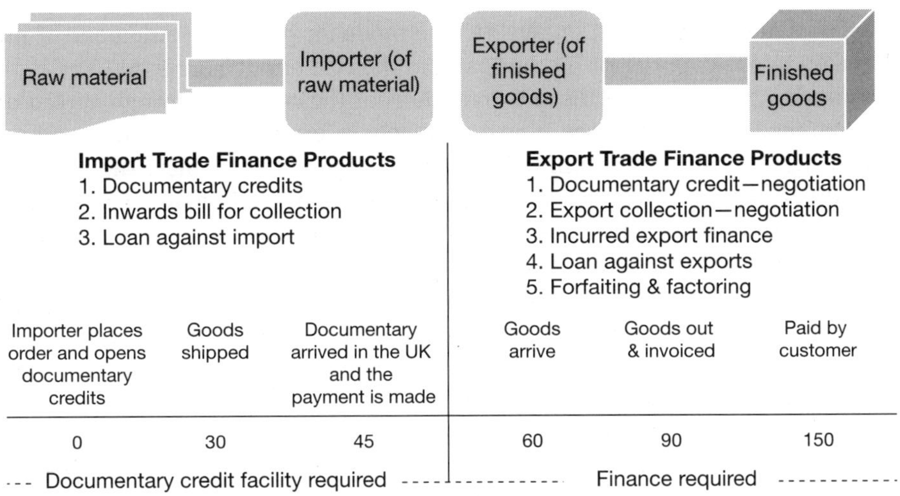

FIGURE 13.2 Trade cycle and financial products for EXIM operations.

Source: How to Access Trade Finance—A Guide for Exporting SMES, UNCTAD, 2009.

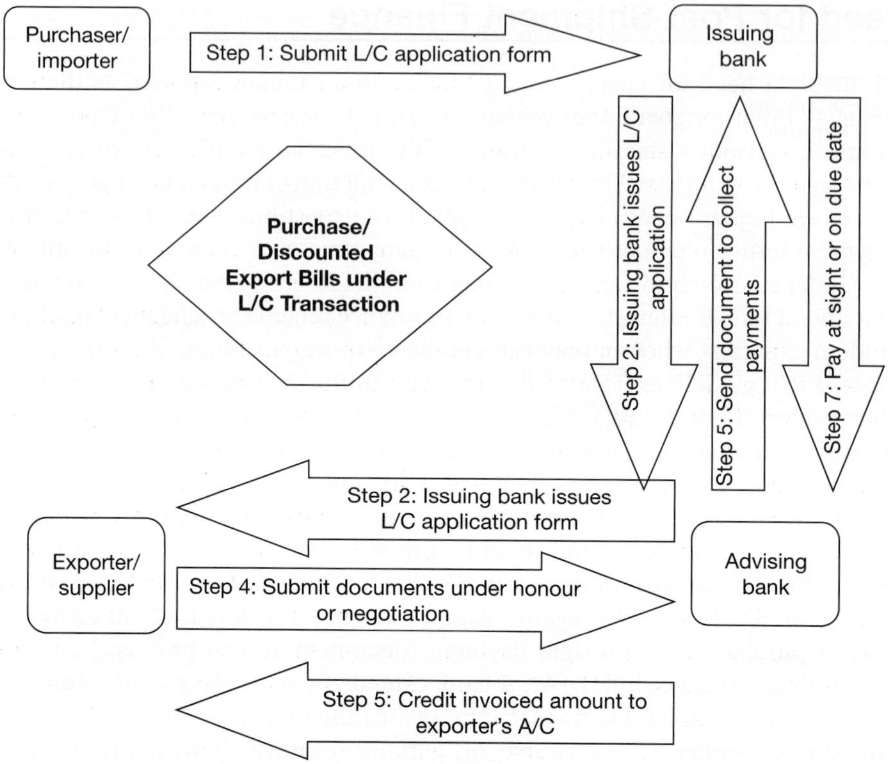

FIGURE 13.3 Process of post-shipment credit under L/C.

Source: RBI (2011).

The exporter faces relatively lesser risk under L/C as a mode for payment settlements if proper due diligence is undertaken by the exporter or his/her bank in the role of advising bank. The issuing bank is duty bound to make the payment if terms and conditions of the contract through agreed documentary evidence are complied with. Banks see it as a relatively safer mode of payment and extend the post-shipment credit against the bills submitted with L/C. Figure 13.4 depicts the process of post-shipment export credit against L/Cs. There is need for post-shipment credit to an exporter if the export bills are sent to the importer on collection basis which can be a scenario when the bills drawn under L/C have some discrepancies or the exporter wants to delay the receipt of payments anticipating the strengthening of foreign currency vis-à-vis local currency. Banks in India extend post-shipment credit against these collections of bills to an exporter with a concessional rate of interests depending upon the transit period in the case of 'sight bills' and transit period plus usance period in the case of 'usance bill'.

A bank can also extend post-shipment credit against the goods that are exported on 'consignment basis' at the risk of the exporter as the sale of such goods will take in near future, and export proceeds will also be realized at later date. Banks, in this scenario, usually instruct the overseas bank to deliver the document only against the trusted receipt/undertaking and transfer the sale proceeds by a specified date which is maximum 270 days unless specific permission to this effect is taken from RBI. Further, the post-shipment finance facility can be extended for a period of 15 months (concessional rate only up to 180 days) in case of export of goods through approved Indian-owned warehouses in the international

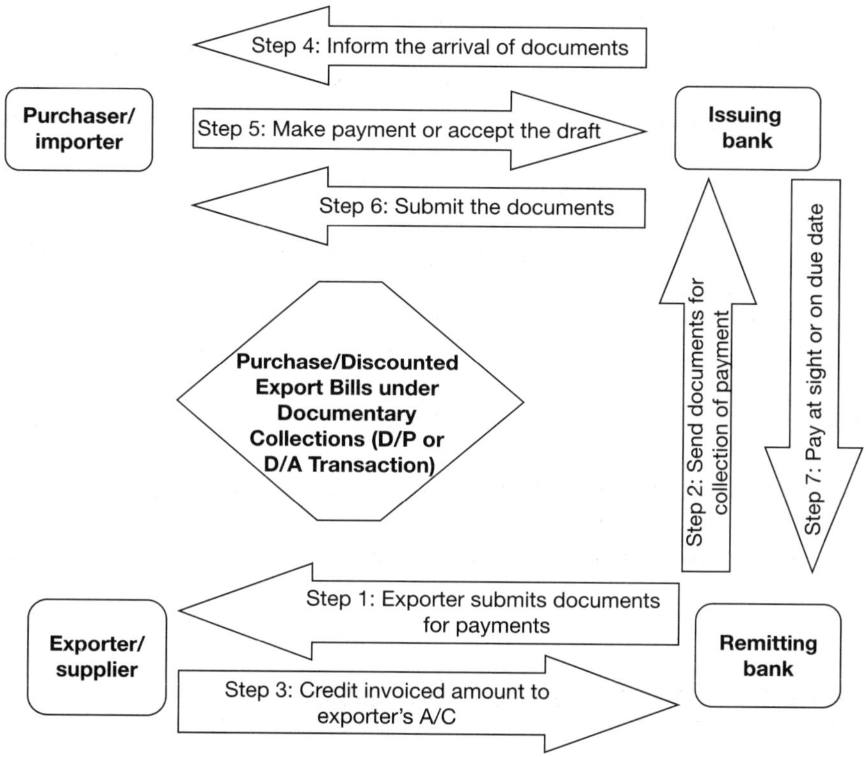

FIGURE 13.4 Process of post-shipment credit under documentary collections.

Source: RBI (2011).

market. Banks are also allowed to extend post-shipment credit against a small part of export bills that are 'undrawn for payment' after the adjustment due to the difference in rates, weight, quality and so on. Exporters are entitled to duty drawback after exports of goods which are usually given within three months from the date of exports. For the need-based export credit in such a situation, scheduled banks in India can grant post-shipment credit to exporters at a lower rate of interest for a maximum period of 90 days.

Post-shipment credit is extended against export bills or trade documents submitted by the exporter and can be availed in both Indian rupee and foreign currency so as to provide them with concessional trade financing and enable them to compete well in the international market. Post-shipment credit helps bridge the financial gap for Indian exporter from the date of shipment to actual receipt of payment from overseas buyer thereof. Similar to pre-shipment finance, the period, purpose, quantum of advance and so on of post-shipment credit is decided by RBI in its master circular from time to time. The significance of post-shipment finance for an Indian exporter can be summarized given below:

1. Post-shipment finance enables an exporter to pay to agents or distributors or anybody else in the export chain for their services.
2. Post-shipment finance helps Indian exporter to pay for publicity/sales promotion and advertising expenditures in the overseas markets.

3. Post-shipment credit facility helps an exporter to pay for post-shipment expenditures such as terminal handling charges, port charges, customs fee and shipping agents charges.
4. An exporter can pay export duty and other taxes, if any, through post-shipment finance. The exporter can also cover all expenditures at the destination of goods through post-shipment credit.
5. Post-shipment credit helps Indian exporter pay the ECGC premium in order to save him/her from credit risks if any.
6. Post-shipment credit helps Indian exporter pay to his/her freight charges, freight forwarder fee and other shipping expenses.
7. An exporter can pay his/her marine insurance premium under CIF, delivered at terminal (DAT), DAP and delivered duty unpaid (DDU) terms through post-shipment credit extended by the bank.
8. An exporter can meet the expenditures relating to 'after-sale service' through post-shipment credit.
9. Post-shipment credit helps exporters pay towards expenditures like participation in exhibitions and trade fairs in India and abroad.
10. Exporters can pay for expenditures relating to representatives abroad in connection with their stay abroad.

13.3 Post-Shipment Finances Scheme

Under priority sector lending to Indian exporters, post-shipment credit is offered by commercial banks in the form of any loan or advance after the shipment of goods or services from India. Post-shipment finance is offered in two ways, in either Indian currency or foreign currency. Foreign currency is usually extended in the invoiced currency of export order, but it can be any other currency also. Post-shipment finance is usually up to the date of realization of export proceeds after the shipment of goods or rendering of services. However, in order to fulfil exporter finance needs on a priority basis, liberal interest rates for post-shipment finance are only for the period of 180 days. As per RBI guidelines, post-shipment export credit can take forms among any of the shown in Figure 13.5.

Thus, post-shipment finance is sanctioned and offered to the exporter only after the shipment of goods/rendering of services and usually granted after the liquidation of pre-shipment finance on the

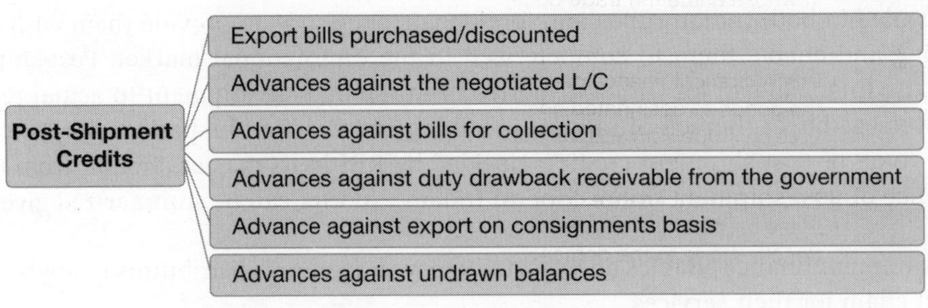

FIGURE 13.5 Types of post-shipment credits.

Source: RBI (2011).

submission of export documents by the exporter. Banks are also allowed under RBI rules and in mutual agreement with the exporter that post-shipment finance can be repaid or prepaid out of balances from exchange earners' foreign currency account (EEFC) of an exporter. Further, banks can allow the repayment and prepayment of such post-shipment credit against the proceeds of any other unfinanced (collection) bills of an exporter. FEMA and allied rules along with RBI guidelines mandate that such adjusted 'export bills' should, however, continue to be followed up for realization, and banks will maintain their record for compliance in the exchange control system (through XOS statement) until realization is not made. It has further endeavoured that the exporter can repay the interest accrued on their post-shipment finance through domestic rupees; however, the settlement of export realization shall be in strict compliance with FEMA rules and regulations. These relaxations are aimed at reducing the cost of business and facilitating exporter with the simplified regulatory regime but in compliance with established procedure and guidelines under different statutes, rules, regulations and guidelines as enacted. Some of the salient features of post-shipment finance are discussed in the following sub-sections.

13.3.1 Purpose of Finance

The purpose of post-shipment finance is to provide cheaper credit services to the exporter from the date of shipment of goods to the date of realization of export proceeds. Post-shipment finance is aimed at enabling vital finance to Indian exporters at concessional rates with a constant endeavour to enable them to compete effectively with their counterparts in international markets. Post-shipment finance in India is offered and granted by scheduled commercial banks for any of the three types of export illustrated in Figure 13.6.

13.3.2 Basis of Finance

Post-shipment finances are granted and extended to an exporter on the submission of EXIM documents by him/her after having shipped the goods to the overseas importer. Such export bills act as evidence of shipment of goods or supplies made to the importer or seller or any other designated agency.

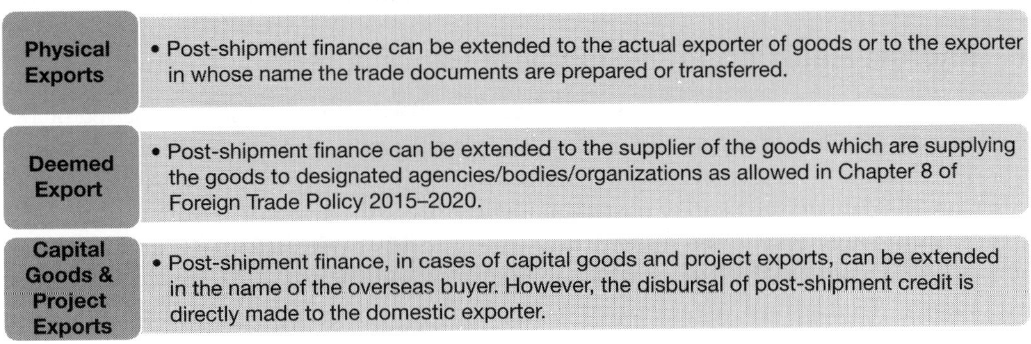

FIGURE 13.6 Trade financing for various types of export buyer's credit.

Source: RBI (2011).

13.3.3 Types of Finance

Post-shipment finance, in an international day transaction, can be both secured and unsecured. As such, finance is granted on the basis of evidence that the goods have already been shipped and export bills are submitted to the bank for the realization of payment. Such document retains the title of goods; thus, the bank provides post-shipment finance in cases of the documentary collection as well as documentary credit. This finance is usually provided to liquidate the pre-shipment credit of the exporter. In the circumstances, such finance is provided against undrawn balances and will be of unsecured nature.

13.3.4 Quantum of Finance

Post-shipment finance can be granted up to the 100 percent invoice value of exportable goods. In the circumstances when the domestic values of such goods are higher than the invoiced value of export order, banks can use their discretionary power to grant the post-shipment finance for the price difference. Post-shipment finance can also be given against the claim of duty drawback. Banks in India are allowed to determine the 'margin requirement' while sanctioning the post-shipment credit to the exporter.

13.3.5 Period of Finance

Post-shipment finance can be granted for short-term as well as for long-term purposes, depending on the export cycle, payment term and the nature of business. In the case of demand bills whereby the payment is settled under D/P, the period of post-shipment finance shall be the normal transit period (NTP). NTP (Box 13.1) as specified by Foreign Exchange Dealers Association of India (FEDAI) begins from the date of negotiation/purchase/discount of trade documents to the realization of export proceeds in the nostro account of the bank concerned. In the case where the payment is settled under D/A using 'usance bills', post-shipment credit can be granted for a maximum duration of 365 days from the date of shipment. This period also includes NTP and grace period, if any, as specified by FEDAI. RBI has advised banks that it should be a constant endeavour of banks to impress exporters to realize their export proceeds within a shorter time preferably within 270 days as mandated under FEMA rules. Export bill is declared as 'overdue bill' if it is not paid before the expiry of the normal transit period, plus grace period in case of payment under demand bill or D/P, and in the case of a usance bill or D/A, it becomes overdue if it is not paid on the due date.

13.3.6 Interest Rates on Post-Shipment Export Credit

RBI circular prescribes for concessional rate of interest for post-shipment credit for a period of 180 days. In the case of early payment of export bills, if the advances are against demand bills and the bills are realized before the expiry of NTP, it is prescribed that the bank should charge the interest at concessional rate of interest from the date of extension of post-shipment credit till the date of realization of export bills. A bank should accordingly charge the interest from the date of advances to the date of realization of demand bills which would be the date on which the proceeds get credited to the bank's 'nostro accounts'. For post-shipment credit against 'usance export bills', a bank can charge concessional rate of interest only up to the notional or actual due date of export bills realization from the buyer or the date on which export realization gets credited to the bank's nostro account abroad, whichever is earlier. A bank should not factor the date of post-shipment credit to the exporter's account in India. Further, in the business

BOX 13.1 ► FEDAI Rules for Calculation of Normal Transit Period

Concepts of NTP and notional due date are linked to the concessional interest rate on export bills. NTP comprises the average period normally involved from the date of negotiation/purchase/discount till the receipt of bills proceeds. It is not to be confused with the time taken for the arrival of the goods at the destination. NTP for different categories of an export business is laid down as below:

1. **Fixed due date:** In the case of export usance bills, where due dates are fixed or are reckoned from the date of shipment or date of bill of exchange and so on, the actual due date is known. Therefore, in such cases, NTP is not applicable.
2. Bills in foreign currencies—25 days.
3. Exports to Iraq under UN guidelines—maximum 120 days.
4. Bills are drawn in rupees under L/C:
   a. Reimbursement provided at the centre of negotiation—3 days.
   b. Reimbursement provided in India at the centre different from the centre of negotiation—7 days.
   c. Reimbursement provided by banks outside India—20 days.
   d. Exports to Russia under L/C where reimbursement is provided by RBI—20 days.
5. Bills in rupees not under L/C—20 days.
6. TT reimbursement under L/C:
   e. Where L/C provides for reimbursement by electronic means—5 days.
   f. Where L/C provides reimbursement claim after a certain number of days from the date of negotiation—5 days + this additional period.

Source: RBI (2011).

scenarios, where the 'correct due date' can be established before or immediately as the overseas buyer has accepted the export bills for payment and has transferred the funds to the account of the exporter before the notional date, applicable interest on such post-shipment credit in Indian rupee will be applied only up to the actual due date. Banks should not factor the 'notional due date' in such business scenarios provided the actual due date falls before the notional due date. In business scenarios where banks have collected the interest by calculating the entire NTP for demand bills or up to notional/actual due date for usance bills, banks are advised to refund the excess interest so collected, if any, for the period from the date of realization to the last date of NTP or notional due date or actual due date.

There is a separate procedure for charging the applicable interest on post-shipment credit which is adjusted from rupee resources as an exporter has not been able to realize the export bills on time, and banks are allowed to settle such export bills against rupee payment by exporter or ECGC so as to cut the transaction cost of the business of the exporter. Banks are guided by RBI to adopt the guidelines that ensure uniformity in charging interest on such post-shipment advances, and wherein, the rupee payment received as the post-shipment credit is not adjusted in an approved manner due to non-accrual of foreign exchange. Banks can settle the accounts from the funds received from the ECGC Ltd in the settlement of claims against the credit insurance policy as taken by the exporter against the relevant export consignment. In the case of business scenarios, buyers have paid in the local currency, but the payment (export realization) is not received as there is blockage of banking channels of such country due to international sanctions or failure of the country to not pay in 'freely convertible foreign currency' or failure of the banking system or inconvertibility or balance of payment crisis and so on. Banks can liquidate the post-shipment credit against the rupees so received from ECGC for the credit insurance cover taken by the exporter. Banks are free to charge interest rates on the basis of 'export credit not otherwise specified (ECNOS)'. Banks can do so even if the post-shipment credit may be outstanding beyond six months from the date of shipment. Banks are allowed to charge the applicable interest on the full amount of advance irrespective of the fact that the exporter has got the cover-up to the extent of 60 or 75 or 90 percent from ECGC. The exporter is duty-bound to repay the remaining balance if any from his/her own rupee resources. Banks are advised that in cases where they have charged the interest rates on post-shipment finance, liquidated through the exporter's own rupees or repayment from ECGC, banks are supposed to refund the excess interest charged, that is, the interest rate charged under ECNOS minus the concessional interest rates as specified by RBI, provided banks are satisfied that export proceeds are realized in an approved manner. Before refunding such excess amount representing the difference between the quantum of interest already charged and interest that is chargeable, banks should follow their internal standard banking procedures to ensure that there is genuine and bona fide evidence of export proceeds realization by the exporter. Above discussed procedure for implementing concessional interest rates is only for the timely realization of export bills. Liberal interest rates shall not apply in case export bills are not realized within the period of 180 days. Table 13.1 prescribes the rate of interests to be charged in normal circumstances to Indian exporter at post-shipment export credit both in Indian rupee and foreign currency.

13.3.7 Post-Shipment Credit in Foreign Currency

With declining exports, poor foreign exchange in an era of economic recession has impacted India's foreign exchange reserves. Accordingly, RBI has brought out changes in export credit in foreign currency both at the pre-shipment and post-shipment stage. Now, export credit at the both pre-shipment and post-shipment stages shall be at internationally competitive rates. Commercial banks are free to determine the interest rates on export credit in foreign currency with effect from 5 May 2012. However, up to 4 May 2012, banks may fix the rates of interest with reference to ruling LIBOR, Euro LIBOR or EURIBOR, wherever applicable as shown in Table 13.2.

TABLE 13.1 Post-Shipment Credit in Indian Rupee from the Date of Advance

1. On demand bills for transit period	As specified by FEDAI
2. Usance bills (for the total period comprising the usance period of export bills and the transit period) **a.** Up to 180 days **b.** Up to 365 days for exporters under the Gold Card Scheme.	As specified by FEDAI and grace period, wherever applicable
3. Against incentives receivable from the government (covered by ECGC) up to 90 days	
4. Against undrawn balances (up to 90 days)	
5. Against retention money (for supplies portion only) payable within one year from the date of shipment (up to 90 days)	

Source: RBI (2011).

TABLE 13.2 Post-Shipment Credit in Foreign Currency

1. On demand bills for the transit period (as specified by FEDAI)	Not exceeding 200 basis points over LIBOR/EUROLIBOR/ EURIBOR
2. Against usance bills (credit for the total period comprising the usance period of export bills, transit period as specified by FEDAI and grace period wherever applicable) up to six months from the date of shipment	Not exceeding 250 basis points over LIBOR/EUROLIBOR/ EURIBOR
3. Export bills (demand or usage) realized after due date but up to the date of crystallization	Rate for (2) above plus 200 basis points

Note: The bank should not levy any other charges over and above the interest rate under any name such as service charge and management charge except recovery towards out of pocket expenses incurred by banks as per Indian Banking Association (IBA) guidelines.

Banks are free to decide the rate of interest, being the rupee credit rate, for pre-shipment and post-shipment credit beyond the tenors prescribed above, keeping in view the guidelines on the base rate.

Source: RBI (2011).

13.4 Mechanism of Disbursal Post-Shipment Finance

Post-shipment credit is always after the shipment of goods and always against the export bills so submitted by the exporter.

13.4.1 Export Bills Purchased/Discounted (D/P and D/A Bills)

Post-shipment credit can be granted and sanctioned against the export bills (D/P or D/A) that are used in terms of sale contract or order whereby the exporter has undisputable faith about the overseas buyers. Banks in India can grant post-shipment finance against such export bills duly submitted by the exporter along with required documents after the shipment of goods by means of discounting (used in case of D/A bills) or by way of purchasing of export bills (used in case of D/P bills). It is used in indisputable international trade transactions, and the proper limit has to be sanctioned to the exporter for purchase of export bill facility.

India's Transition from LIBOR to Alternate Reference Rates: Key Takeaway

Reserve Bank of India has issued the guidelines for transition of LIBOR-based interest rates regime to a new system of alternate reference rates (ARRs). The key differences between the ARRs and LIBOR can be understood as under.

The Alternate Reference Rate concept is based on Overnight Risk-Free Interest Rates at the end of the overnight borrowing period, overnight rates or ARRs are published. This implies that they are 'retrospective'. On the contrary, LIBOR is a term rate (i.e., a rate to borrow for a set period such as three or six months) and published at the beginning of the borrowing period. Thus, LIBOR is 'forward-looking'. ARRs are based on fundamentals, while LIBOR are based on expectations and thus have a scope of manipulation as happened in the LIBOR scandal. Moreover, a premium for interbank credit risk is also factored into LIBOR (i.e., an additional sum to account for the possibility that the borrowing bank won't be able to repay the interbank borrowing), while ARRs, which are overnight rates and occasionally secured, do not or only partially incorporate this premium.

Furthermore, the same market is measured by LIBOR across all currencies (i.e., the unsecured interbank lending market), while ARR system of measure is far more robust and risks-free as it factors in the different marketplaces to measure the ARRs. For instance, the ARRs for the US Dollar and Swiss Franc are based on secured markets, but the ARRs for the British Pound, Japanese Yen, and Euro are based on unsecured markets. This implies that various ARRs may react slightly differently. ARRs are the need of hour to promote transparency as some market participants have stated that they require knowledge of the interest rate at the beginning of the borrowing term in order to properly price their interest rate products. On the contrary, certain public/private sector RFR working groups, who were in charge of selecting the ARRs, are currently debating whether it is possible to create versions of the ARRs that include forward-looking terms.

Source: SBI –LIBOR Transition Compendium. https://sbi.co.in/documents/16337/16538/241221-SBI-LIBOR_Transition_Compendium_-_Booklet_Digital+-Ver+3-Dec+2021.pdf (accessed on 11 April 2023).

13.4.2 Export Bills Negotiated (Bill under L/C)

L/C is considered a safe and secure instrument of realizing payments in international transactions, and the risk of payment is less under the L/C in comparison of other modes of payment. However, one should be well-versed with rules and procedures governing the conduct and negotiation process under L/C and Universal Customs and Practice for Documentary Credit (UCPDC). The issuing banks take the guarantee for making payment to the exporter on successful execution of exporter clearly as per the terms and conditions as laid down in L/C. As L/C is a secured mode of payment, banks in India extend post-shipment finance against 'time bills' under L/C.

13.4.3 Advance against Export Bills Sent on Collection Basis

Export bills can only be sent on collection basis if such export bills drawn under L/C have some discrepancies. Banks in India can grant advances against such export bills sent on collection basis. Alternatively, the exporter sometimes requests banks that his/her export bills should be sent on the collection basis as he/she anticipates that the invoiced currency will strengthen in the near future. Banks, as per RBI guidelines, can permit advances to the exporter against such export bills which are sent for the realization of the payment on collection basis. The bank can offer a concessional rate of interest depending on the transit period plus usance period of such acceptance/A. FEDAI rules (Box 13.1) in India define that the transit period under such circumstances shall be the date of acceptance of export bills, not the date of advance.

13.4.4 Advance against Export on Consignment Basis

Banks are also allowed to sanction post-shipment finance to Indian exporters who are exporting in international market on a 'consignment basis'. Banks in such circumstances instruct the foreign bank to hand over the document to the consignee only against trust receipt or an undertaking by the consignor to deliver the export proceeds by the specified date. Foreign exchange regulations in India allow the realization of export proceeds with a period of 15 months, provided such consignment basis export sales are made through approved Indian-owned warehouses abroad. In order to control the misuse of funds which has been reported to happen in consignment basis sales, RBI has instructed banks to extend concessional post-shipment credit only up to the notional due date (depending upon the tenor of the bills), subject to a maximum of 365 days.

13.4.5 Advance against Undrawn Balance

Sometimes, the exporter may request for advances against undrawn balance as he/she cannot submit the export bills for the total value of exporter goods due to factors such as weight, quality and different currency rates as per RBI guidelines; banks in India are allowed to grant post-shipment finance as in advances against undrawn balance (Caselet 13.1). However, such undrawn balance should be in conformity with the normal level of balance undrawn in that particular line of export. In no circumstances, the maximum permissible limit of advances against undrawn balance can be more than 10 percent of the invoice export value. Banks must seek an undertaking while granting such advances to the exporter that he/she will realize the export proceeds within six months from the date of payment or date of shipment of goods, whichever is earlier. The concessive rate of interest shall be applicable only to the maximum period of 180 days.

13.4.6 Advances against Retention Money

Large projects such as power projects, building of dams, commissioning of nuclear power stations and construction of oil refineries fall under the category of turnkey projects. Progressive payments, based on milestone completion of a project, are made to the turnkey company by the employer of such turnkey projects or construction contracts. At the completion of the project, the employer usually retains a small

CASELET 13.1

Live Case of 'Undrawn Balances'

Zoya Exports Private Limited is an export firm with 10 years of standing in the export sector and has got status holder certification from DGFT for continued export excellence in floriculture exports. The company exports floriculture to Amsterdam and export bills are invoiced to the extent of 75 percent only as the importer has negotiated the rest of 25 percent payment shall be subject to quality compliance, freshness, satisfactory packing and other transport compliances aimed at satisfactory delivery of flowers to the importer. Quality check of flowers takes place at public auction houses in Amsterdam where independent quality surveyors give a certificate of quality and remaining 25 percent export realization is paid by the importer after 30 days from such quality report. Zoya Exports is in a dire need of funds as it has further orders and has to make payments to several suppliers of flowers and other inputs. The manager of Zoya Export approaches the bank and seeks post-shipment credit under 'undrawn balances' category. As the payment of 'undrawn balances' is of contingent nature, scheduled banks in India usually consider granting advances against undrawn balances based on their commercial judgement, due diligence and track record of the buyer.

percentage of such total payments as 'retention money', which is payable after expiry of the stipulated period from the date of the completion of the contract. The employer usually releases such retained payments after commissioning of plant or facility and having undertaken necessary certificate(s) of compliance and NOC from competent authorities. The payment of retention money is contingent in nature as it is a 'deferred liability' in international trade operations. RBI, in its master circular, has advised the scheduled banks in India to follow certain guidelines before granting advances against retention money:

1. Banks should never extend the 'advances' for retention money for services portion of the contract as services are intangible and very tough to acknowledge the performance by documentary evidence, thus controlling scope for misuse of this facility.
2. It is better to advise exporters to arrange for the provision of suitable guarantees against the performance of remaining turnkey services instead of retention money. Banks should educate Indian exporters to leverage guarantees instead of retention money.
3. Banks, based on their own internal procedure for due diligence, may consider, on a selective basis, granting post-shipment export credit against 'retention money'. This should, however, be only for the 'supplies portion' of the turnkey contract factoring issues such as the size of the retention money accumulated, its impact on the liquid funds position of the exporter and the past performance regarding the timely receipt of retention money.
4. Banks should ensure that post-shipment export credit against retention money, wherever granted, should be secured by L/C or bank guarantee, where possible.
5. Concessional trade financing against advances for retention money shall be for the period of 90 days only, and banks should charge the interest rates as ECNOS to an exporter for the remaining 270 days of the year. This facility is only for the contract where the due date of the payment is within one year.
6. In cases where the 'retention money' is payable after a period of one year from the date of shipment, banks are allowed to extend post-shipment credit only for the period of one year under procedure as discussed above and should charge the commercial rates of interest for the period exceeding one year as it is treated as post-shipment credit given on deferred payment.

13.4.7 Advance against Claims of Duty Drawback

Duty drawback is given by GOI in order to neutralize the incident of duties that an Indian exporter suffers in our highly taxed economy. It is basically remission of such duties to an Indian exporter so that he/she can withstand international competition effectively and sell his/her goods at a lower cost. Banks in India are authorized to grant advances to the Indian exporter at a concessional rate of interest for the maximum period of three months. Banks may extend post-shipment credit to exporters against their duty drawback claims and covered by ECGC guarantee as provisionally certified by customs authorities in the shipping bill. Banks usually cross-check whether a relevant EGM has been issued by the customs department for the ship on which goods are loaded for onward transport. As the amount of duty drawback is given to the exporter within three months under Section 76 of the Customs Act, the concessional rate of interest shall be applicable only to the maximum period of 90 days. Financing banks, if find it necessary, may have their lien noted with the designated bank with which the exporter maintains an account for transfer to such duty drawback from customs and can make an arrangement with such designated bank to transfer funds to the financing bank as and when duty drawback is credited by the customs.

13.5 Special Cases of Post-Shipment Financing

In addition to the above mechanism of post-shipment finance, in the following sub-sections, we discuss some special cases of post-shipment financing.

13.5.1 Supplier's Credit

In order to promote Indian exports in international markets, GOI has come up with various schemes under various financial institutions including EXIM Bank of India. Supplier credit can be specific to the supplier or can be against lines of credit whereby such credit is offered by bank to the buyers for procuring/importing a large-scale contract. Once the bank approves loans to the overseas importer, the exporter shoulders all or part of the interests incurred in such deals.

13.5.2 Export of Goods for Exhibition and Sale

Indian exporters are increasingly facilitated by GOI to participate in exhibitions and trade fairs. It provides them with a requisite platform for enhanced export sales opportunities, tapping new customers and markets and identifying new trends, fashions and product segments. As per RBI guidelines, schedule banks can provide both pre-shipment and post-shipment finance to exporters against goods sent for exhibition and sale abroad. Banks will allow such post-shipment credit by maintaining separate accounts for such credits and by way of rebate after the sale of goods and overseas trade fair/exhibition is completed. The concessional rate of interest will, however, be up to the stipulated periods for both pre-shipment and post-shipment finance.

13.5.3 Export Credit for Export Domestic Tariff Area (DTA) Unit to SEZ Unit

The Special Economic Zone Act, 2005, and the Special Economic Zone Rules, 2006, consider such units located in SEZ to be foreign territory; hence, export from a DTA unit to an SEZ unit will be treated as exports. Banks are instructed to extend post-shipment credit to such DTA units supplying goods and services to SEZ units in accordance with the procedure laid down for normal post-shipment credit.

13.5.4 Deemed Exports Credit

FTP 2015–2020 specifies the categories of exports which will qualify as 'deemed exports' as export under this category does not leave the territorial waters of India, and the payment may be in freely convertible foreign currencies or Indian rupees. Scheduled banks are allowed to extend rupee pre-shipment and post-shipment rupee export credit to parties against orders for supplies in respect of orders defined as deemed exports. Banks may also extend rupee in pre-shipment credit and post-supply credit for a maximum period of 30 days or up to the actual date of payment by the receiver of goods, whichever is earlier. Any credit advances under post-supply category would be treated as overdue after the period of 30 days. Banks can charge interest rates as 'export credit not else specified' rates for the period of 180 days and after that commercial rate as applicable.

13.6 Gold Card Scheme for Exporters

Exports play a very crucial role in a developing economy like India which attaches considerable importance to export promotion as it has to earn foreign exchange to service imports, generate additional economic activity and enhance employments for the country. The Ministry of Commerce and Industry, GOI, in consultation with RBI had introduced a Gold Card Scheme in the FTP 2003–2004 so as to provide easy trade financing to creditworthy exporters with a good track record and on best credit terms. RBI has time and again taken several steps to promote export through concessional trade financing, and Gold Card Scheme is one such endeavour aimed at not only export promotion but ensuring expeditious and timely provision of financial assistance at competitive rates of interest and remove involved procedural hassles in the lending process. The scheme is similar to the Kisan Credit Card scheme which has largely revamped the procedural lapses in extending timely and cost-effective credit to Indian agri-farmers. Accordingly, a Gold Card Scheme (scheme) has been worked out in consultation with selected banks and exporters so as to extend concession, timely and hassle-free export credit to exporters with a good track record and make them competitive in international markets. The eligibility criteria for the issuance of Gold Card are prescribed in Figure 13.7.

The Gold Card Scheme also offers certain additional benefits based on the previous track record of exporters, and they enjoy a simpler and more efficient credit-delivery mechanism under this scheme. Some salient features of the Gold Card Scheme are as follows:

1. Gold Card Scheme is available for all creditworthy exporters, including from MSME sector with a good track record. Banks are advised to devise their internal guidelines or criteria for this scheme for due diligence of exporters before extending this facility.

- All creditworthy exporters with good track record
- Exporters whose accounts have been classified as 'standard' continuously for a period of three years
- There are no irregularities/adverse features in the conduct of accounts
- Exporters who are not blacklisted by ECGC or included in RBI's defaulter's list/caution list
- Exporters who are not making losses for the past three years
- Exporters who are not having overdue export bills in excess of 10 percent of the current year's turnover
- A general preference to small- and medium-sector exporters

FIGURE 13.7 Eligibility criteria for issuance of Gold Card to exporters.

Source: RBI (2011).

2. Banks are instructed to clearly specify to the exporter the benefits which they would be offering to Gold Card holders on their website and promotion material.
3. Banks should process the requests from card holders for export credit as quickly as possible. Banks should prominently feature on their website and promotion material that exporters' request for the issuance of Gold Card will be handled within 25 days, for renewal of limits within 15 days and fixation of ad hoc limits within 7 working days.
4. Banks are instructed that they should fix 'in-principle' limits of export credit coterminous to Gold Card period which is three years and provide a stand-by limit of 20 percent to meet urgent credit needs, if any.
5. Banks should give priority to Gold Card holders in the matter of granting of packing credit in foreign currency.
6. Banks should develop internal guidelines for waiver of collaterals and exemption from ECGC guarantee schemes based on the credit-worthiness of cardholders and their previous track record in the liquidation of credit.
7. The concessive rate of interest on post-shipment rupee export credit, which is otherwise available for a period of up to 90 days, can be extended for a maximum period of up to 365 days for Gold Card holders.
8. Banks are instructed to charge a lower rate of interest on export credit extended to Gold Card holders and also specify the other banking charges and fee structure lower to what the bank otherwise charges in the normal course of action.
9. Banks are instructed by RBI to extend other assistance and benefits to Gold Card holders which enable them to cut their cost of doing business and making Gold Card an attractive instrument in the market. If possible, banks can allow relaxation of certain rules and regulations applicable to trade financing mechanism.

In the light of these salient features, we will discuss the key commercial areas of Gold Card Scheme in India in the following sub-sections.

13.6.1 Fixation of Export Credit Limit

Banks are instructed to ensure simple procedure for sanction and renewal of the export credit limits under the Gold Card Scheme. Banks, in compliance with their internal procedure, are advised to factor into account the 'anticipated export turnover' and previous 'credit track record' of the exporter while fixing the export credit limits. While doing so, a bank must consider that export credit at both stages is a 'need-based finance' and are accordingly advised to adopt a liberal approach in the sanction of export credit limits. The 'in-principle export credit limit' will be sanctioned for a period of three years with a provision for automatic renewal subject to fulfilment of the terms and conditions of the sanction. The following are areas banks consider while sanctioning an export credit under the Gold Card Scheme:

1. Banks are advised to follow liberal approach towards Gold Card holders in compliance with the terms and conditions of export credit in India and are also advised to offer liberal rates of interest but in a transparent manner in macro-compliance of established banking rules and procedure.
2. Banks should give priority to Gold Card holders over the normal exporter in the extension of pre-shipment and post-shipment export credit. Gold Card holders should also get priority in availing the export credit in foreign currency.

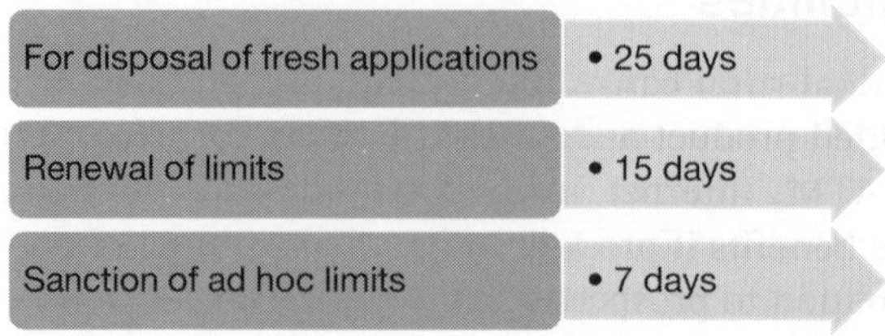

FIGURE 13.8 Period for issuance of Gold Card to Indian exporters.

Source: RBI (2011).

3. In the case where lines of credit for export business are available, banks should give priority to Gold Card holders.
4. Gold Card holders will get priority for disposal of applications received for the sanction of export credit. In order to ensure timely compliance, it is mandated to have citizen charter for the disposal of these applications and the sanction of export limit. Figure 13.8 stipulates the number of days allowed to scheduled banks in India to dispose of export credit application of Gold Card holders.
5. Gold Card holders shall further be entitled to a stand-by limit of not less than 20 percent of the assessed export credit limit. This has been allowed to enable timely and cost-effective export credit to Gold Card holders to execute urgent and sudden export orders, the export of seasonal commodities and address the problems of the peak and off-peak levels in complex export business.
6. Banks are instructed to streamline and simplify the information needed in the application for Gold Card holders. Banks can follow the best practices advised by the IBA for the same.

13.6.2 Interest Rates, Service Charges and ECGC Premium

In order to reduce the cost of credit and enable Indian exporters to do business at a lower cost to become competitive in international markets, the charges schedule and fee-structure in respect of export credit services provided by banks to exporters under Gold Card Scheme will be relatively lower than those provided to other exporters. Banks are advised to offer interest rates further reduced by at least 1 percent basis to Gold Card holders than interest rates charged to a normal exporter. Banks are instructed to offer export credit which is more competitive to Gold Card holders than otherwise available under any other option to the Indian exporter. Banks, on their discretion, are allowed to convert post-shipment credit from 90 days to 365 days. Further, to make foreign currency cheaply available, the service charge for purchase of a currency is fixed at a flat rate of 0.1 percent only by the bank on the interbank foreign currency borrowings. Gold Card holders may further be considered by banks for exemption from ECGC guarantee if banks are satisfied with their creditworthiness for both pre-shipment and post-shipment stage.

13.6.3 Tenure

RBI has allowed scheduled banks to issue a Gold Card for a period of three years. Banks are allowed to automatically renew it for a further period of three years unless there are adverse features or irregularities committed by such Gold Card holder exporter. If the bank feels that the exporter is not complying with terms and conditions of the card or it is used in violation of other statues/legislation, the bank will have the right to recall the card any time.

13.6.4 Additional Facilities

Schedule banks except regional rural banks can offer additional benefits in the Gold Card Scheme in order to offer it as value-added product and more sellable to Indian exporters. Banks can add supplementary services such as ATM, Internet banking and international debit/credit cards. Each bank should clearly lay down the benefits it proposes to offer to Gold Card holders on its website for wider dissemination of the information to prospective exporters.

13.7 Interest Equalization Scheme

In order to enable Indian exporters to compete at par with their counterparts from other countries, GOI has decided to provide export credit facilities at par with interest rates charges in countries which pose competition to Indian goods in international markets. Accordingly, in addition to the concessional rates of interest on pre-shipment and post-shipment finance, GOI has decided to offer 'interest subvention' so as to ensure interest equalization or parity in interest rates charged on Indian exporters with parity of their counterparts from competitors' countries. Accordingly, GOI has approved the 'Interest Equalization Scheme' for pre- and post-shipment rupee export credit with effect from 1 April 2015 for five years. The details of the scheme are as follows:

1. This scheme offers the interest equalization to Indian exporters availing rupee credit at the rate of 3 percent per annum at both pre-shipment rupee export credit and post-shipment rupee export credit.
2. GOI has decided that scheme will be in force for the period of five years beginning 1 April 2015; however, GOI reserves the right to modify or amend the scheme at any time so as to make it more relevant with changing geo-economic realities in the dynamic trade environment.
3. Interest Equalization Scheme has been extended to 416 tariff lines of ITC (HS) at 4-digit level (heading level) as per Annexure A (RBI 2016) as notified by RBI. However, exports made by MSMEs across all ITC-HS codes shall be entitled to the scheme.
4. It is further decided that the benefits of export must percolate to manufacturer's exporters scheme, and accordingly, the scheme would not be available to merchant exporters.
5. Scheduled banks in India are mandated to extend the benefits of interest equalization of notified eligible exporters in toto and as applicable and submit the claims to RBI for reimbursement. These claims should be duly certified by the external auditor as per procedure laid down by RBI.
6. This scheme will be funded by the Ministry of Commerce and Industry from the funds of consolidated funds of India, wherein the ministry will place funds in advance with RBI for a requirement of one month. RBI will release these funds to scheduled banks to reimburse Indian exporters for interest equalization with their counterparts in competitor's countries. This mechanism has been agreed between Ministry of Commerce and Industry and RBI and will operate on a monthly basis through a revolving fund system.
7. Exporters routed as transshipment or merchandising shall not be eligible for this facility. Hence, all eligible exports under the scheme would have to meet the criteria of minimum processing for the goods to be called as originating from India. Criteria and compliance for rules of origin for originating from India are laid down in the *Handbook of Procedures of FTP 2015–2020*.

13.8 Summary

RBI has framed the policy document guiding scheduled bank to extend the post-shipment credit to Indian exporters in both Indian rupee and foreign currency. Once the goods are shipped out of the country, there may be a delay in realization of export proceeds as sometimes the exporter has extended credit to importers. While extending pre-shipment finance, banks usually mortgage the stock of such firm as collateral for a loan. Once goods are dispatched out of India, banks extend post-shipment credit in lieu of 'trade documents' submitted by an exporter and adjust the loan of pre-shipment finance. Hence, post-shipment credit refers to an 'advance or a loan' that is extended to the exporter by a scheduled bank in India after the goods have been shipped to the importer. Post-shipment credit may take a different form; for example, it can happen either through discounting of trade documents or by the purchase or negotiation. Export transactions are usually manifested by seasonal peaks, long transit times and lengthy credit terms, and as a result, there are higher needs of working capital for the export business. An exporter can negotiate favourable payment terms to reduce such risks, but many times, export credit is the only way to get the export orders. Under such circumstances, it is important that the exporter should leverage other financing option at the liberal rate of interest. The post-shipment finance scheme of scheduled banks provides such leverage to Indian exporters wherein they can get their export bills financed for the period of 90 days under the present RBI guidelines. Post-shipment credit fulfils the financing needs of an exporter after the goods have been shipped out of India.

Under priority sector lending to Indian exporters, post-shipment credit is offered by commercial banks in the form of any loan or advance after the shipment of goods or services from India. Post-shipment finance is offered in two ways—in either Indian currency or foreign currency. The foreign currency is usually extended in the invoiced currency of the export order, but it can be any other currency also. Post-shipment finance is usually up to the date of realization of export proceeds after the shipment of goods or rendering of services. However, in order to fulfil exporter's finance needs on a priority basis, liberal interest rates for post-shipment finance are only for the period of 180 days. Post-shipment finance is sanctioned and offered to the exporter only after the shipment of goods/rendering of services and is usually granted after the liquidation of pre-shipment finance on the submission of export documents by the exporter.

Sometimes, the exporter may request for advances against undrawn balance as he/she cannot submit the export bills for the total value of exporter goods due to factors such as weight, quality and different currency rates. As per RBI guidelines, banks in India are allowed to grant post-shipment finance as in advances against undrawn balance. Duty drawback is given by GOI in order to neutralize the incident of duties that Indian exporters suffer in our highly taxed economy. It is basically remission of such duties to the Indian exporter so that he/she can withstand international competition effectively and sell his/her goods at a lower cost. Banks are also allowed to sanction post-shipment finance to Indian exporters who are exporting in the international market on a 'consignment basis'. Banks in such circumstances instruct the foreign bank to hand over the document to the consignee only against the trust receipt or an undertaking by the consignor to deliver the export proceeds by a specified date. Post-shipment credit can be granted and sanctioned against the export bills (D/P or D/A) that are used in terms of sale contract or order whereby the exporter has undisputable faith about the overseas buyers.

CASE STUDY Application of Concepts of Post-Shipment Finance for Exports

Mr Chopra from Mumbai has got an export order for the supply of engineering items to a buyer based in Kampala, Uganda. The following are details vis-à-vis the export order:

1. **Name of the seller:** Chopra Engineering Company, Mumbai, India
2. **Name of the buyer:** Ninja Import Company, Kampala, Uganda
3. **Cargo description:** Various engineering appliances falling under HSN 851010
4. **Value of order:** $1 million
5. **Port of departure:** JNPT, Mumbai
6. **Port of destination:** Mombasa, Kenya
7. **The final place of destination:** Kampala, Uganda
8. **Payment mode:** Time L/C 90 Days
9. **Issuing bank:** Stanbic Bank, Nakumatt Plaza Kampala
10. **The currency of the invoice:** USD
11. **Date of shipment:** 25 April 2020

In the above context, Mr Chopra manufactured the cargo and shipped it in complete compliance to terms and conditions of L/C on the specified date. He has got another big order from a buyer based in France. The value of the order is $10 million under confirmed sight L/C. The buyer and the bank are involved in the issuance of L/C of good reputation and exposure. The transaction is highly remunerative in terms of profitability, and Mr Chopra can execute this order but has one problem. Mr Chopra lacks working capital and has to arrange it. You are advising Mr Chopra to arrange funds for the next order so as to fulfil his working capital requirements.

Questions

1. In this context, discuss what is the post-shipment finance facility that Mr Chopra can use?
2. What is export bill discounting? How is it different from forfeiting?
3. Mr Chopra does not know the term 'Per Aval'? Guide him how it works in post-shipment financing of export transactions.
4. What are some of fintech developments in India for export bill discounting? Who are key players for such fintech platforms? How does system work? Explain these matters to Mr Chopra.

Review Exercises

Multiple Choice Questions

1. Post-shipment credit is extended on the concept and rationale of
   - **a.** Need-based financing
   - **b.** Working capital financing
   - **c.** Trade financing against export bills
   - **d.** Priority sector financing
   - **e.** None of the above
2. The collateral for the bank while extending post-shipment finance is
   - **a.** Trade documents submitted by the exporter
   - **b.** Assets of the exporter
   - **c.** Exposure limit of the exporter
   - **d.** Goodwill and relationship of the exporter with bank
   - **e.** None of the above

3. The maximum period of credit under post-shipment finance will be
   a. 90 days
   b. 120 days
   c. 360 days
   d. 180 days
   e. 270 days
4. Which of the following expenses cannot be financed under post-shipment financing to an exporter?
   a. To pay to agents or distributors involved in the export chain for their services
   b. To pay for publicity/sales promotion and advertising expenditures if any
   c. To help an exporter to pay for post-shipment expenditures such as terminal-handling charges, port charges, customs fee and shipping agents charges
   d. To pay export duty and other taxes
   e. To pay the raw material suppliers
5. What does FEDAI stands for?
   a. Foreign Exchange Dentures Association of India
   b. Full Earning Dentures Association of India
   c. Full Earning Dealers Association of India
   d. Foreign Exchange Dealer Association of India
   e. None of the above

Critical Thinking Questions

1. Discuss the need of post-shipment finance for exports and process and procedure therein for sanction of post-shipment finance.
2. Write a short introductory note on post-shipment export credit in India.
3. Explain the salient features of post-shipment export credit to the Indian exporter.
4. What was the BPLR system of lending? How were interest rates worked out under the BPLR system? Why did it fail?
5. What are the interest rates prescribed by RBI under liberal interest rates for post-shipment export credit in Indian rupee?
6. What are the interest rates prescribed by RBI under liberal interest rates for post-shipment export credit in foreign currency?
7. Write short notes on any two of the following:
   a. Purpose of finance
   b. Basis of finance
   c. Types of finance
   d. Quantum of finance
8. Comment on any two of the following:
   a. Advance against export bills sent on collection basis
   b. Period of finance
   c. Supplier's credit
   d. Financing for various types of export buyer's credit

9. What are the various instruments and channels under which the post-shipment finance is given to Indian exporters?

10. Write a note on interest rate subvention scheme of RBI. What was the rationale for launching such a scheme?

11. Write short notes on the following:
  a. Export bills purchased/discounted
  b. Export bills negotiated

12. Explain the procedure of post-shipment credit against the claim of duty drawback/export on a consignment basis and undrawn balances.

Further Readings

1. RBI. 2011. 'Master Circular on Rupee/Foreign Currency Export Credit & Customer Service to Exporters'. Available at: https://www.rbi.org.in/scripts/NotificationUser.aspx?Id=6515&Mode=0 (accessed on 19 August 2020).
2. RBI. 2016. 'Interest Equalisation Scheme on Pre and Post Shipment Rupee Export Credit'. Available at: https://pdicai.org/docs/RBI_322_12220161300112.PDF (accessed on 19 August 2020).

CHAPTER 14

Methods of Payment

CHAPTER OBJECTIVES

- To understand the overview of various methods of payment in international business.
- To describe the risk matrix of various payment terms.
- To explain factors affecting the payment terms in the export business.
- To explain each method of payment including the process of settlements.
- To discuss various methods of international fund transfers.

14.1 Introduction

In today's volatile and complex business environment, any export transaction is a gift until the payment for this has not been realized from the foreign buyers. More so, an exporter has to offer attractive sales terms, including payment terms, due to declining import demand coupled with increasing business competition in this recessionary and ambiguous environment. World's import demand, especially from developed countries of Europe and North America, is badly hit in post subprime and Greek sovereign crisis. Exporters have been doing business against all odds and have to negotiate attractive trade terms so as to woo importers for exports against other competitors. The choice for an appropriate mode of payment is very important for any exporter as he/she has to not only minimize his/her risks but also remain engaged and competitive in international markets. To do so, an exporter has to scan the business environment of the importing country, banks involved and credit-worthiness of the importer. There exist risks at three levels in export payments. *First*, it is the credit-worthiness of an importer. An exporter should appraise the credit-worthiness of an importer, especially his/her solvency position, previous payment history, financial standing and limit of financial exposure. *Second*, an exporter should appraise the solvency position, credit rating and payment history of banks involved in the payment settlement process; for example, an L/C opening bank may not be a bank of good credit history and may have engaged in fraudulent business practices in the past. If such involved bank fails and the importer may have settled the payment, the exporter is exposed to full payment risks. Hence, an exporter should appraise the financial standing, credit history and credit rating of banks involved in the payment settlement process. *Third*, an exporter should always appraise the business environment of the country of import, especially the level of foreign exchange reserves, socio-economic stability, soundness of banking regulations, international sanctions against the country, any other advisory for checks for association with terrorist organizations and so on.

There are five popular methods of payments in international trade. The *first one* is the payment in advance, wherein an exporter receives the 'payment in advance' and goods are shipped subsequently. In today's uncertain time, except in few cases, no importer is willing to pay in advance as it is extremely unfavourable for importers; hence, this method is not very popular for payment settlements. The *second method* is called an 'L/C' and is a contract between the issuing bank and the exporter for export payment subject to fulfilment of agreed terms and conditions of the contract. This method is safe for an exporter and is used when the importer's credit-worthiness is doubtful, and the exporter wants the risks of payment to be shifted to someone else to whom the exporter trusts, that is, the bank. The *third method* is 'D/P' wherein the exporter ships the goods and asks for the payment against the trade documents, which are routed through proper banking channels. This is an ideal method and is vastly used in export payment settlement globally. The *fourth method* is 'D/A' which is a risky method for the exporter wherein the process of payment settlement is same as in D/P except for the fact that the exporter has given credit period for payment to the importer; hence, the importer signs an acceptance with the bank and takes custody of documents so as to get them released from customs for domestic sales. The *last method* of export payment settlement is 'open account' and is a very risky method from an exporter's perspective in today's ambiguous and uncertain time. The exporter ships the goods and hands over the trade documents to the importer for the import clearance. The importer sells these goods in the domestic market and pays the exporter after the agreed credit period. This method entails a very high risk of non-payment for an exporter. The choice of each method of payment is dependent on certain factors which affect the decision criteria of an exporter. Figure 14.1 depicts the associated factors which an exporter should consider while negotiating and deciding upon a particular mode of payments.

An exporter should understand points of risks in the international payment settlement and appraise the nature of these risks. An exporter must appraise the country's risks while negotiating the payment terms in an export transaction. For example, the economic stability of a country of import,

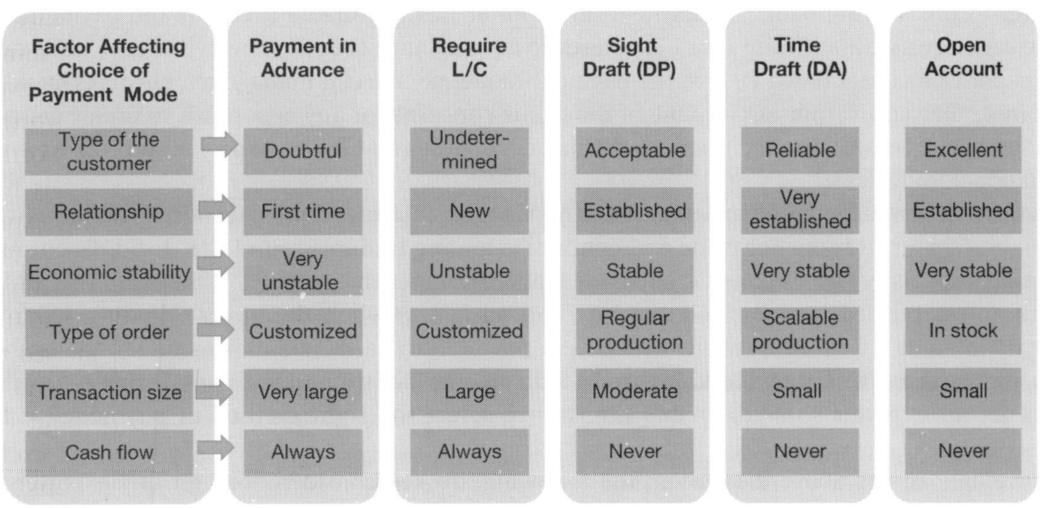

FIGURE 14.1 Factors affecting choice of payment mode for an exporter.

Source: Adapted from https://www.shippingsolutions.com/blog/seven-factors-for-determining-the-right-method-of-payment-for-your-exports (accessed on 5 May 2023).

sociopolitical stability, the legal system, business language, level of foreign exchange reserves and so on. Potential appraisable indicators in understanding the country's risks can be political instability, war or rebellion or civil disorder or military coup or dictatorship, economic embargoes by countries or international organizations, import license issues, potential risks of expropriation of cargo, import restrictions or high-tariff retaliations, convertibility of invoiced currency and exchange controls or currency restrictions and so on. The exporter should also understand the nature of involved commercial risks, which are import firm credential, financial performance, history of business and market share, past payment history, documentary risk, business regulations, customs and business practices and language barriers and so on. Appraisable indicators to understand the commercial risks are bankruptcy of the import firm, level of financial liquidity, involvement in disputes and frauds and history of slow payments. The exporter can evaluate these risks by taking help from other agencies so as to mitigate the risks of export payments. The exporter can take advice from his/her banks which specialize in assessing the country's risks exposures, trade associations or chamber of commerce, credit reports (ECGC, Dun & Bradstreet, Bureau Veritas and so on), newspapers and magazines, the Internet, credit-rating agencies and other traders based domestically and internationally.

14.2 Understanding the Risk Matrix in Payment Mode

In order to make a balanced decision on the payment mode, an exporter should understand the risk matrix of factors affecting his/her decision choice. In today's volatile and ambiguous trade environment, while choosing any mode of payment, the exporter has to assess not only the risk or degree of risk but also where this risk lies. If the exporter is successful in assessing and appraising the quantum and location of the risk, he/she can essentially reduce his/her risk by using an alternate mode of payment; for example, if an exporter feels that the importer does not have good credit-worthiness, he/she can choose an L/C as the mode of payment whereby the onus of payment shall be shifted from the importer to L/C issuing bank. Similarly, if an exporter has negotiated a D/P as the payment mode, he/she can negotiate any Group E or F incoterm so as to balance the risks involved in the trade deal, or if the exporter has negotiated D/A as the payment mode, he/she can manage his/her risks by taking a credit insurance cover from ECGC. One of the prime concerns for any exporter is to timely get paid in full. Figure 14.2 lists favourable methods for payment settlement for an exporter and importer in the international trade deal.

Payment in advance and open account methods are at extreme, that is, favouring either part, thus eliminating the great scope for trade and commerce among traders around the world. Documentary collection, especially D/P, is considered an ideal and a competitive method. Time drafts are preferred only in an established business relationship, and an L/C is when the buyer's credit-worthiness is under doubt, and the exporter wants the risks of payment to be shifted to someone to whom he/she trusts, that is, the L/C issuing bank. Figure 14.3 details the decision matrix considering each of these factors for an exporter so as to enable him/her to select the right method of payment for EXIM transactions.

In the light of the above discussion, the following are key considerations for any exporter while appraising the risks involved in the decision-making for international payment settlements. *First*, export operations offer different types, quantum and locations of risks, thereby confusing the exporter with uncertainty over the realization of payments and timing of payments between the exporter and importer.

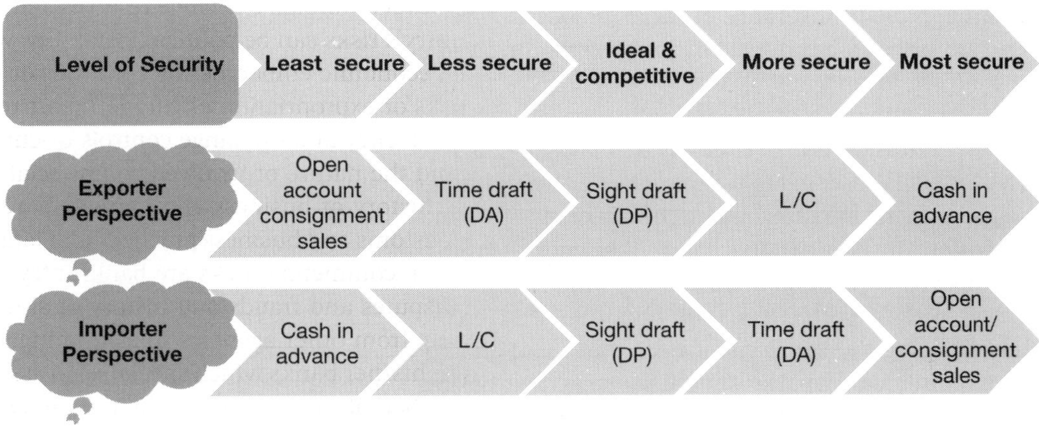

FIGURE 14.2 Mode of payment: a risk appraisal.

Factor	Payment in Advance	Documentary Credit	Documentary Collection	Open Account
Bank charges	Lowest	Highest	Medium	Lowest
Payment risk	Doubt on importer's ability to pay	Payment risks shifted to L/C issuing bank	Payment risk is mitigated through trade documents	Use if utmost good faith & trust with importer
Country risk	Low country risks for exporter	Lower country risks for exporter	Medium country risks for exporter	High country risks for exporter
Credit facilities	Not required	Required	Not required	Not required
Cash flow needs	Exporter needs cash as early as possible	Cash flow delayed	Delayed cash flow	Exports are gift until payment received
Goods price	Trade discount for payment in advance	Price can be negotiated at lower side	Effect on price depends on terms of collection	Premium pricing

FIGURE 14.3 Decision matrix for selecting a mode of payment.

It is important to understand the key locations of payment risks, which are with the importer's credit-worthiness and financial record, his/her bank and country. There is always a possibility of default, delay and insolvency of the importer or his/her bank. There is a possibility of default and insolvency of other involved banks as well, affecting the payment settlement. Additionally, there is always a scope of importer's country facing international sanctions for the settlement of payments, currency inconvertibility, exchange control restrictions and even country bankruptcy. *Second*, there are certain payment risks which can be mitigated by the exporter; however, there are certain ones which cannot be mitigated; for example, the credit risk which arises from a change in the credit-worthiness of the importer can be covered through credit insurance cover from ECGC. Similarly, risks arising out of fluctuations in the exchange rate can also be covered by hedging the invoiced currency through appropriate tools such as forward contract, futures and options. Payment risks arising out of acts of God (force majeure) cannot be covered, such as natural disaster crippling the economic system of the importer's country. Some other risks such as confusion due to difference in law, language or culture are also beyond the control of an exporter. *Third*, it is observed that exporters are always interested to receive the payments as soon as they send the goods to the importer, and an importer always wants to delay the payment as much as possible. For an exporter, any international sale will be equivalent to a gift until he/she has realized the payment from the importer, and for an importer, any import payment is a donation until he/she has received the cargo as sent by the exporter. It is, thus, important that the exporter and importer should negotiate mutually, understanding the concerns of each party and should arrive at a mutually benefitting payment decision. Exporter and importer should leverage their business decisions by dividing the payment mode as 'secure and unsecure' wherein they should negotiate payment options only falling under secure mode and cover additional risks by the insurance and bank guarantees. If any party feels that there is any exposure to risks, the same can well be covered by taking an insurance cover or guarantee from credit insurer or banks. *Last*, an exporter and importer must understand that even a secure mode of payment such as an L/C may not even be suitable for small-sized exporters due to high-processing charges of banks involved in the negotiation of trade documents.

14.3 Factors Affecting Choice of Payment Mode

As international business takes place in a different regulatory, cultural and business system, the possibility of misunderstanding in the payment settlement becomes very high. In such an ambiguous scenario, the exporter has to consider several factors (Figure 14.4) that affect the choice of payment terms in EXIM business. The nature of 'relationship' between the exporter and importer is very important as the exporter can negotiate unsecure payment terms such as D/A only in an established and trustworthy business relationship which has been tested over a long period. In the case of first-time order, the exporter should opt for either the payment in advance or L/C or at least D/P. The 'size of business transaction' is another factor affecting the decision choice of an exporter. If an importer's order is within tolerable 'credit exposure' of the importer, the exporter should consider the method such as D/P or L/C but should essentially avoid payment terms such as open account and D/A. The choice of payment term is also affected by the 'credit-worthiness of buyer' as exporters are willing to negotiate competitive business terms with importers of good credit rating and financial record. The choice of payment term is also affected by the 'nature of goods'; for example, for fast-moving consumer goods, one can consider payment terms with credit period wherein the importer can sell these goods and repay for after agreed credit period, but if these are capital goods such as export of customized ships, aeroplane, submarine, turbines, machines and project cargo, the exporter must consider at least part payment in advance or confirmed L/C supported by credit guarantees as well. An exporter cannot ignore the prevailing business environment while negotiating a trade deal and deciding upon particular payment terms. He/she has to factor the payment terms offered by his/her competitors, that is, the 'competitor's terms'. An exporter has to negotiate competitive payment terms in order to remain in the business; otherwise, he/she will lose the market to his/her competitors. The choice of payment terms is also affected by the 'cash flow needs' of an exporter. In case, the exporter has immediate 'working capital requirement', he/she cannot afford to

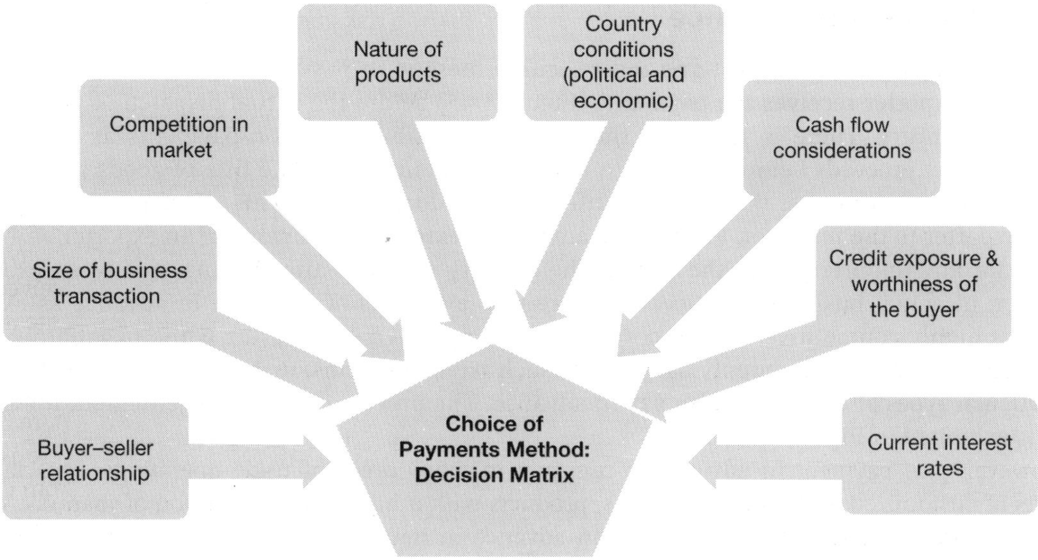

FIGURE 14.4 Choice of payments method: decision matrix.

negotiate the payment terms with credit period, for example, open account, D/A and time L/C. An exporter has to consider only payment in advance or sight L/C and D/P as a payment choice while entering into an EXIM deal.

The choice of payment term is also affected by 'profit margins' that a particular exportable product entails. An exporter can afford to negotiate unsecured methods of payment with high-profit margins and can take credit insurance cover from ECGC to mitigate his/her payment risks. In case profit margins are lower, an exporter cannot afford to negotiate unsecured payment terms (Figure 14.2), that is, consignment sale, open account and time drafts. The choice of payment term is also affected by 'current interest rates' as an exporter shall always be willing to negotiate payment terms such as payment in advance as the cost of financing working capital are higher and has to incur higher funds on pre-shipment financing so as to manufacture or procure the goods. In order to avoid higher interest rates, an exporter will always prefer payment terms with least credit period, that is, advance payment, sight L/C and sight draft (D/P). Last, an exporter always considers the contemporary economic, social and political 'business environment' of the importer's country. The exporter avoids unsecured method of payment in countries which are suffering from problems of balance of payments, high debt–GDP ratio, international sanctions, war-torn or rebellion.

14.4 Various Modes of Payment

There are five methods of payment in export operations, and the choice of particular payment mode is dependent on variety of factors affecting business decisions of negotiating parties, that is, the exporter and importer. Each of the payment methods along with process of payment settlement and key features is explained in following sub-sections.

14.4.1 Payment in Advance

Payment in advance is the safest and most secured method of payment realization of export proceeds as an exporter receives the payments (Figure 14.5) before the actual dispatch of goods to the importer's country. There is not even the remotest possibility of non-payments as an exporter receives export proceeds before shipment of goods to the importer. The title of goods also remains with the exporter even after the dispatch until the trade documents to this effect are not dispatched by the exporter to the importer. Payment in advance is extremely in favour of an exporter and is the riskiest for any importer as he/she solicits the delivery of goods after having paid to an exporter. However, in actual business practice, there are rare examples of payment in advance as export–import is highly competitive, and importers seek competitive trade terms while negotiating trade deals. Exporters having monopoly can ask for such payment terms, or an importer in urgent need of particular types of cargo may also pay in advance. The process of payment settlement under this term is exhibited in Figure 14.5.

However, part payment in advance is common in many areas of trade operations, especially in exports of customized and unique products, products with a high gestation period of manufacturing, high-value transactions and part payment in advance in lieu of other competitive trade terms, for example, lower price and competitive delivery term. Payment in advance is not a competitive term for winning new customers and even retaining existing good customers as it is highly in favour of the exporter. Those exporters, who insist that they would trade only with this term, may lose their foreign buyers to their competitors. This method of payment results in cash flow problems for importers, and they are at the mercy of the exporter who may even not send the goods. In today's volatile business environment, importers do not prefer this mode; however, they may pay in part in order to import customized, unique and high-value goods from suppliers having a monopoly. Hence, an exporter should weigh all such associated factors while negotiating and insisting on this payment term. This is a popular method of payment while shopping online and teleshopping as e-commerce usually demand payment in advance before sending the goods to their buyers. Key features of payment in advance term are discussed below:

1. Under this method, an exporter receives either full or partial payment from the importer prior to actual shipment of cargo from the country of exports. The payment can be remitted by credit card, wire transfer, international cheque, draft and so on by importer in favour of the exporter. The exporter must have received the payment either fully or partially before the actual transfer of ownership of the goods to the importer.

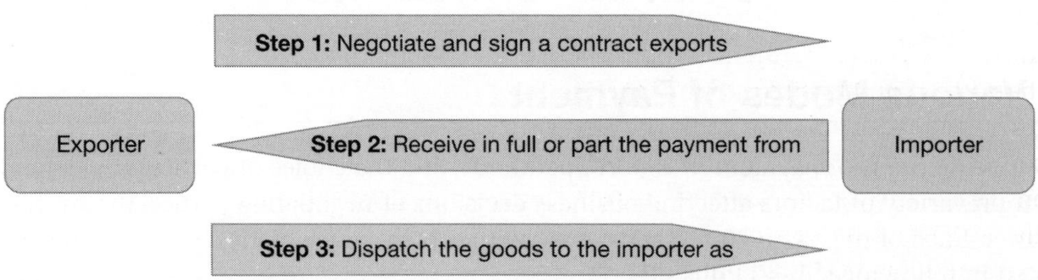

FIGURE 14.5 Process of payment settlement in payment in advance.

2. Trading under this term may result in losing important buyers to competitors as they may offer more favourable and attractive options of payment to importers in this globally competitive market.
3. Payment in advance term should be used in cases where the importer's credit-worthiness is either doubtful or cannot be ascertained and verified. The exporter should always demand payment in advance from the new, unknown and unestablished importers.
4. Payment in advance can be a suitable method of payment in cases where the political, economic and social environment of an importer's country are disturbed, thus resulting in the high-level of commercial risks for an exporter.
5. The exporter should always demand payment in advance from importers who are from countries facing inconvertibility, exchange control restrictions, low credit ranking, international sanctions, economic embargoes and so on. The exporter should also negotiate this term only if importers are from countries having poor regulatory regime, corruption, non-cooperative and disregarding attitude towards international business conventions and norms.
6. Importers are usually reluctant to negotiate this term as they are at the mercy of God in case of non-delivery of goods by exporters. More so, this term reduces their chances of greater cash utilization than other payment terms such as an open account, L/C and a documentary collection.
7. This is a popular mode of payment for e-commerce and teleshopping companies, petty sales, sellers enjoying monopolies, unique and customized products and high-risk business relationships.

14.4.2 Letter of Credit (L/C)

In today's financially uncertain and volatile times, L/C, also known as a documentary credit, is considered the safest method only next to the 'payment in advance' which most of the importers are unwilling to negotiate with. An L/C can be a secure and safe mode for payment, which ensures trust between two trading parties as it is not extremely in favour of either party unlike payment in advance. An L/C is widely used in cases of large business transactions, long period business deals, doubt on the importer credit-worthiness or lower credit rating, new and unestablished business relationships, country risks and so on. Under an L/C payment term, an importer asks his/her bank to make a contractual agreement with the beneficiary (exporter) for the supply of agreed goods and services in lieu of documentary compliance for having delivered or rendered such goods or services to an importer. In other words, the risk of payment passes from an importer to a bank (issuing bank) which undertakes a negotiable commitment for the payment to an exporter, on behalf of an importer, subject to the fulfilment of the terms and conditions as negotiated and agreed upon between the exporter and importer. The issuing bank issues a contractual agreement in favour of the beneficiary (exporter) through SWIFT message at the exporter bank, which is called an advising bank. An advising bank advises the exporter various terms and conditions of credit whether compliable or non-compliable, the credit rating of bank, risks associated with this credit both with the bank and importer's country and other associated risks. The exporter is free to accept or reject his/her bank's advice which is non-obligatory from the bank's perspective and may accordingly intimate his/her commercial decision to go ahead, seek an amendment in terms and conditions of an L/C or ask for an L/C from another bank with a credit rating or may even reject outrightly the proposal to export. In execution of the export order, the exporter ships the goods, prepares desired and agreed 'trade documents' and submits them to his/her bank (advising bank) for presentation, negotiation or honour. The issuing bank, on compliance of documentary evidence as negotiated in terms and conditions, releases the payment in favour of the exporter. In case of non-compliance of documentary evidence, the bank may ask for clarifications and resubmission for the compliance failures, and may reject the documents, thus resulting in non-payment to the exporter. Hence, in an L/C, banks deal in documents, not in goods, and subject of documentary compliance, the bank will release the payment to the exporter. Banking charges in execution of an L/C process are borne by trading parties as per agreed negotiated terms and conditions, sometimes jointly and sometimes by either party. An L/C, undoubtedly, is a reliable and secure mode of payment for both the exporter and the importer as one can trust the bank subject the fulfilment of documentary compliance. Hence, both trading parties should be well versed with the EXIM documentation, legislation governing documentation and credit, that is, UCPDC 600 and International Standard Banking Practice (ISBP). Key features of payment settlement under the L/C are explained below:

1. An L/C is a very safe and secure mode of payment provided the exporter cross-checks and verifies the financial standing of the issuing bank from his/her international banker or credit rating agency to avoid any kind of risks in trade deals. As the risk of payment shifts from the importer to the issuing bank, it is a viable option for payment in cases when the credit-worthiness of the importer is under doubt.
2. An L/C is a separate contract between the exporter and issuing banks, which is other than sales contract negotiated, agreed and signed between the exporter and importer. Under the L/C contract, the issuing bank undertakes the responsibility to pay the exporter subject to fulfilment of terms and conditions of the contract of an L/C, which is a mirror contract as these terms and conditions are communicated to the issuing bank by the importer based on terms of the negotiated sales contract.
3. The exporter manufactures or procures the goods and dispatches them to the importer. The exporter prepares agreed trade documents and submits them to the advising bank or confirming bank (as the case may be), which in turn, presents or negotiates these documents with the issuing bank for the payment realization.
4. The title of goods lies with trade documents; hence, an exporter is assured of receiving the payment once documents are accepted for the payment by the issuing bank.
5. An L/C can be at sight or time L/C whereby there is a credit period in time L/C and at sight payment by the issuing bank under at sight L/C. The exporter prefers sight L/C as it minimizes the risks for the exporter.
6. Essential features of an L/C are high-transaction cost in issuance, processing, presentation, negotiation, amendments and acceptance of trade documents, which are an integral and inseparable part of an L/C. As a result, small-sized export firms do not prefer the L/C as payment terms as it affects their profit margins.

14.4.2.1 Parties, Process and Papers in an L/C Transaction

The payment settlement under an L/C involves banks in addition to trading parties, that is, the exporter and importer. Banks deal in documents, and there is an established process of issuance, presentation, submission, amendment, acceptance and rejection, which is prescribed in UCPDC 600 and ISBP. For successfully leveraging an L/C as a payment mode, trading parties should be aware of the process, parties involved and papers, which are exhibited, step by step, in Figure 14.6.

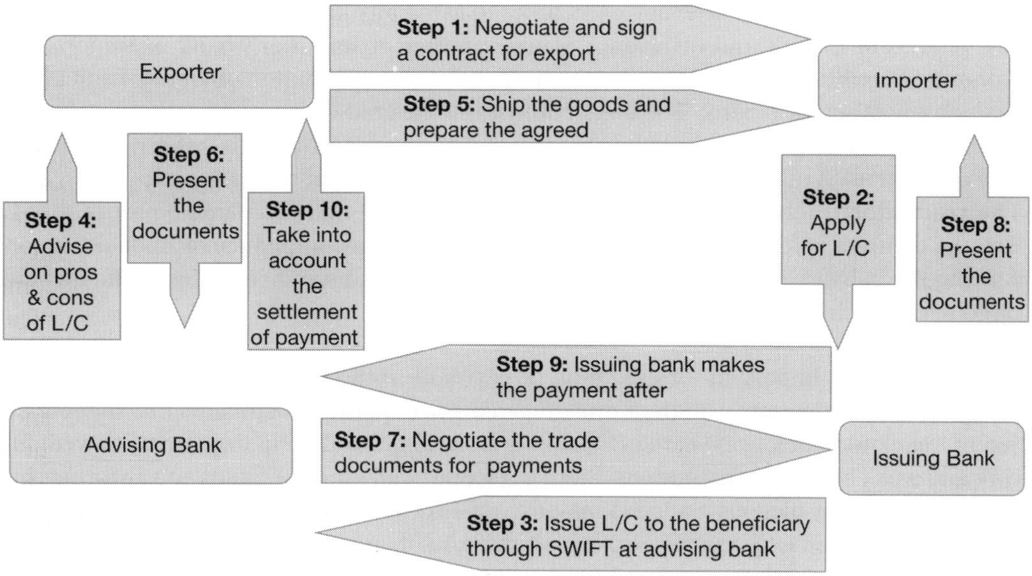

FIGURE 14.6 Process of execution for payment under L/C mode.

1. **The beginning:** For an L/C transaction, there has to be a trade deal between an exporter and an importer with agreed terms and conditions of the sale. Based on this sales contract/purchase quotation/singed proforma invoice, an importer request to his/her bank (issuing bank) for opening or issuance of the L/C in favour of an exporter.
2. **The issuing bank:** The issuing bank is a bank of the importer which opens an L/C in favour of the beneficiary (exporter) through SWIFT message at the advising bank, that is, the bank of the exporter.
3. **Letter of credit:** An L/C is a contractual arrangement between the issuing bank and exporter wherein the issuing bank commits to pay the exporter subject to the fulfilment of agreed terms and conditions irrespective of fulfilment of export sales contract.
4. **The beneficiary:** The exporter, also known as the beneficiary, is the party seeking payment for the export of goods or services with the documentary compliance to agreed terms and conditions of the L/C.
5. **The advising bank:** The advising bank is the bank of the exporter which advises the exporters about the status of credit, that is, the credit-worthiness and financial history of the bank, importer's country environment and associated payment risks, risks associated with currency, that is, inconvertibility, exchange control restrictions, international sanction and embargoes and so on. The exporter may act on the advice of the bank or seek amendment in an L/C based on the bank's advice or may even reject the export proposal. The bank's advice to the exporter does not attach any commercial obligations to the bank, all associated risks for payments will be that of the exporter only. As this bank corresponds with the issuing banks with all trade documents for the release of payment on behalf of the beneficiary, that is, the exporter, it is also referred to as the corresponding bank.

6. **The confirming bank:** The exporter, in order to avoid any kind of risks involved in the negotiation process or default and insolvency of an importer or importer's bank or importer country economic or political problems and so on, may seek the confirmation of an L/C from an advising bank or any other local bank. The bank confirming the credit is known as the 'confirming bank' meaning it promises to pay the exporter for export proceeds irrespective of any problems which may come in ways in the realization of export proceeds or even non-payment.
7. **The trade documents:** Trade documents are an integral and inseparable part of any L/C. In fact, the contract agreement to pay the exporter is based on compliance of trade documents evidencing the delivery of goods to importer as per agreed terms and conditions. The ownership of cargo lies with the trade document only.

As trade documents are important for execution of payment in the L/C transaction, it is important for both the exporter and importer to do their due diligence for requested documents for payments. Due to the different regulatory practices, careless banking officials, fraudulent importers, flawed financial framework and weak economic institutions, there is a scope of all kinds of frauds and cheatings by either party to trade. Some conspicuous trader(s) may use an L/C as an instrument for defrauding other(s). Similarly, some fraudulent experts may also exploit the rules to create discrepancies in trade documents so as to not make the payment. Discrepant trade documents accompanying an L/C, which may be having 'I-dot and T-cross', can negate the payment of export proceeds to an exporter. The following are the tips an exporter must understand to avoid the chances of discrepancy in the L/C:

1. The exporter and importer should communicate in detail the terms and conditions including documentary compliance therein before an importer applies for the L/C.
2. The exporter should always scan the business environment and if needed may ask for confirmed the L/C only.
3. The exporter should always ask for a copy of the L/C application to be faxed to him/her so that he/she can check for terms and conditions that may cause a problem in compliance at the presentation or negotiation stage.
4. The exporter should study the advising bank's advice on the L/C. The exporter should consult within the firm and with external experts whether firms' logistics team will be able to comply with terms and conditions of the L/C within the prescribed time limits.
5. Due diligence in documents' preparation is very important as many presentations of trade documents run into problems with time limits. Before the presentation of documents, an exporter must be aware of at least three 'time-constraints' which are the expiration date of the credit, the latest shipping date and the maximum time allowed between dispatch and presentation.
6. In case the L/C mandates for trade documents to be supplied by third parties, an exporter must make a reasonable allowance for the time the third party may take to process the documents.
7. After the shipment, the exporter should vouch for all the documents both against the terms of the credit and against each other for internal consistency.

According to UCPDC 600, all L/Cs issued after 1 July 2015 shall be irrevocable, which means the documentary credit cannot be revoked if once opened in favour of the exporter. An L/C can be a 'sight L/C' meaning that the issuing bank has to make the payments on the presentation of trade documents, or it can be a 'time or date L/C' which means that the payment has to be made at a future date as agreed between the exporter and importer. Sometimes, changes have to be made in terms and conditions of the L/C after it has been issued. Such changes are called amendments in L/C. There are banking charges for any amendment and are shared by either party based on their negotiation and agreement. An exporter can consider the precautions given in Figure 14.7 at the pre-shipment and post-shipment stage so as to avoid discrepancies for safe, secure and timely payment under the L/C transaction.

In order to serve the varying business needs of different traders in today's ambiguous and uncertain economic times, the documentary credit is used in different variants aimed at securing timely payments, cutting down transaction costs and meeting specific business needs. Accordingly, the following are the different types of L/C used in EXIM operations:

1. **Revocable L/C:** A revocable L/C is the one which can be amended, altered and cancelled at any point of time by the importer without seeking the consent of the exporter before the submission of documents to the issuing bank by the exporter. It is not a safe and secure mode for the payment realization for the exporter and is not allowed for the use as ICC, in its publication UCPDC 600, has clearly forbidden the issuance of any revocable L/C.

Precautions to Be Taken on Receiving the L/C

- The exporter should ensure whether it is L/C at sight, if not so what risks in dealing with time L/C?
- Can the exporter trust the issuing bank and paying bank, i.e., previous payment records of involved banks?
- The exporter should list the issues related to the currency conversion, exchange control, payment restrictions as per FEMA and other laws in force.
- The exporter should examine whether the value, quantities, trade terms and payment terms are same as negotiated and agreed.
- The exporter should list issues related to the documentary compliance as negotiated & agreed.
- Which party to trade will bear L/C fees, charges and amendment charges if any?
- Description of goods, applicable HS code and nomenclature is matching with the importer country or not as HS code may vary from country to country.
- Will the exporter be in position to comply with the date of shipment and date of expiration and date of presentation as agreed.
- The exporter must have clarity on other shipping issues, i.e., compliance of packing, labelling and marking, HAZMAT rules, dangerous goods rules and so on.

Precautions to Be Taken after the Shipment of Goods

- The exporter should avail the 'late presentation' of trade documents, i.e., after L/C has expired.
- The exporter should always ship the goods before the date of shipment as specified in L/C.
- The exporter should comply with terms & conditions of L/C, for example, never dispatch 'part good' or making partial shipment if not allowed in L/C.
- The exporter must ensure documentary compliance as mandated under L/C.
- The exporter complies by legalization of trade documents if so desired.
- The exporter should avoid issues related to claused, stale, dirty and foul bills of lading and non-compliance of insurance policy & premium and inspection of cargo.
- The exporter must submit the originals of agreed trade documents after the dispatch not later than 21 days.
- The exporter should avoid mispresentation of agreed facts, wrong quantity, value, named port of destination, named place and parties and other trade terms in documentation.

FIGURE 14.7 Tips for an L/C transaction.

2. **Irrevocable L/C:** An irrevocable L/C cannot be amended, altered and cancelled by either party without seeking the consent of other contracting party involved in a trade deal. In the UCPDC 600, as applicable from 1 July 2007, all L/Cs are irrevocable. This type of documentary credit is very safe and secure as the issuing bank gives a contractual undertaking to the exporter for making the payments subject to the fulfilment of terms and conditions of the L/C.
3. **Unconfirmed L/C:** An unconfirmed L/C is the one which is forwarded by the advising bank directly to the exporter without adding its confirmation. Under such L/C, the exporter's bank does not undertake or commit itself for making the payment to the exporter at a future date and only advises the exporter on the standing of the L/C. The bank, on behalf of the exporter, only presents and negotiates the documents with the issuing bank and does not guarantee the payment to an exporter.
4. **Confirmed L/C:** A confirmed L/C is the one in which the advising bank adds its confirmation that the payment will be made to the exporter provided trade documents are complied with and presented on time to the confirming bank. The confirmation can be added by the issuing bank, or the exporter can seek the silent confirmation. The confirmed L/C covers the risk of default and insolvency of the issuing bank or the unforeseen political conditions in the importer's country such as restrictions on the outflow of foreign exchange and inconvertibility; thus, it is preferred by exporters where they foresee the scope of country risks. The confirming bank will make additional charges for confirming an L/C and such changes, if not instructed by issuing bank, shall be borne by the exporter. The confirmed L/C is one of the most secure and the safest mode of payment in international business.
5. **Special or standby L/C:** The special or standby L/C is governed by the set of rules called International Standby Practices 98 (ISP 98)[1] of ICC, Paris. Such L/C is used as support in cases when a less secure mode of payment has been agreed between the exporter and importer. Alternatively, the exporter and importer want to use other modes of payment for cutting down transaction costs, documentary compliance, time saving, banking charges and so on, but an exporter seeks such standby L/C which gives him/her opportunity to negotiate documents, that is, if the exporter does not receive the payments from the importer under the agreed mode, he/she can claim the payment under the special or standby L/C. Essential trade documents required for requesting the payment under the standby L/C are shown in Figure 14.8.

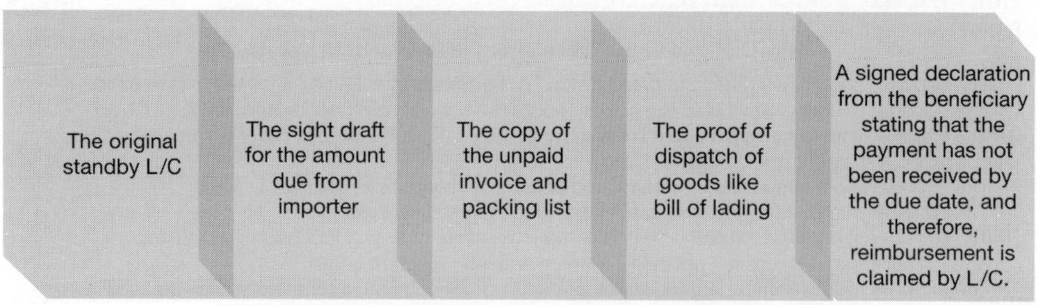

FIGURE 14.8 Essential trade documents for requesting payment under standby L/C.

[1] ICC Publication No. 590.

In today's volatile and uncertain times, special or standby L/C are considered important as the exporter is exposed to several commercial and country risks. The standby L/C assures payment to the exporter similar to 'demand guarantees', which are issued subject to the Uniform Rules for Demand Guarantees[2] of ICC.

6. **Revolving L/C:** The revolving L/C is popular among regular traders who deal in the same nature of goods and services round the year where, usually, goods have a very high turnover. This type of L/C is advisable for those traders who are dealing in the same product round the year, and they do not need to request, process and understand the terms and conditions of the L/C each time, as under the revolving L/C, the credit limit will be reinstated automatically for further regular shipments until the credit for the current shipment is fully drawn. The revolving L/C can be framed either on the 'time basis' or on 'value basis'. The most important feature of this type of L/C is that it reduces the time and transaction cost involved in opening the L/C again and again.
7. **Transferable L/C:** The transferable L/C is popular when there are middlemen involved in a trade deal. Under this type of L/C, an exporter has the right to request the confirming or negotiating bank to make a part of payment in favour of the agent or middleman or any other third party involved in the trade transaction. The exporter usually asks for such kind of L/C in cases when they have to procure raw materials, and major inputs of such exportable goods are sourced from a particular supplier.
8. **Back-to-back L/C:** In cases where transferable L/C cannot be availed, the exporter can leverage back-to-back L/C to pay his/her principal suppliers with inputs of exportable products. Sometimes, there are several suppliers or suppliers from many countries due to which transferring part of the payment is not practical and in workable position under the transferable L/C, then the back-to-back L/C is preferred. The back-to-back L/C is also popular when a merchant trader opens a new L/C in favour of the manufacturer in lieu of his/her L/C received from the overseas buyer so as to enable the manufacturer exporter to take pre-shipment finance at liberal rates of interest. Under the back-to-back L/C, the original L/C is used as security to establish a second L/C (back-to-back L/C) drawn in favour of supplier of inputs or raw materials or manufacturer exporter. The back-to-back L/C entails high-risk exposures, and thus, is not preferred by banks as well as suppliers.
9. **Inland L/C:** The inland L/C is popular in cases when back-to-back L/C cannot be opened as either the exporter does not have the L/C payment term or the advising bank refuses to open a back-to-back L/C. The inland L/C is very popular in domestic trade and also for merchant traders who procure the material from manufactures and export it to the overseas market. The original manufacturer may demand such type of L/C as he/she has to ensure pre-shipment finances under liberal interest rate as specified by RBI. The inland L/C is also used in units located in SEZ/EHTP/BTP/STPI/EOUs so as to procure goods from DTA suppliers and make them available to export the benefits as defined under 'deemed exports' of FTP 2015–2020. Additionally, an authorization holder under Advance Authorization Scheme or DFIA Scheme or Export Promotion Capital Goods Scheme also uses the inland L/C to procure raw materials, other inputs, plants and machinery and so on, thus offering deemed export benefits to a DTA supplier.

[2] ICC Publication No. 458.

10. **Red clause L/C:** The red clause L/C is also known as L/C with advance payment as the exporter can request the advance payment of an agreed amount which is negotiated and agreed in the terms and conditions of the L/C. This L/C is unique in the sense that a buyer extends an unsecured loan to a seller. Such advance is usually given by the correspondent bank against the red clause L/C issued by the issuing bank in favour of an agreed exporter. The red clause L/Cs are popular in the procurement of sheep wool from Australian suppliers as sheep keepers need some advance to feed their sheep and procure wool from them. The red clause L/C is primarily intended to fulfil the pre-shipment finance need of an exporter. The advance is normally paid out against the receipt which was earlier used to be marked with red ink, thus naming this L/C as the red clause. The advance is always given only against a written undertaking from the exporter that he/she will subsequently deliver the transportation documents to the corresponding bank by an agreed date for proof of having shipped the exportable goods. Table 14.1 illustrates the features of various types of Letter of Credit.
11. **Green clause L/C:** The green clause L/C is very similar to the red clause L/C with the prime difference that here the advance to an exporter is given under the specific confirmation with a documentary proof that the exportable goods have already been warehoused, that is, ready for the shipment, unlike the red clause where the advance payment is given against goods yet to be manufactured or produced and meant for the subsequent shipment.
12. **Bank's lines of credit L/C:** In order to promote foreign trade, the national bank offers a line of credit to the potential importing countries which are signed and agreed upon between two banks of the countries. A line of credit allows and facilitates an importer to purchase goods now but pay for them at the later stage. An importer can request his/her bank to open 'line of credit L/C' which will facilitate the import of goods from the country which has extended such line of credit to the importer's country. The line of credit L/C is a popular instrument to expand trade of capital goods, project exports and project with larger gestation period.

14.4.3 Documentary Collections

The documentary collection is one of the most preferred methods of payment settlement due to balanced risk exposure it offers to both trading parties. Under this method, the exporter and importer negotiate a trade deal, agree on terms and conditions including documentary requirements, date of shipment and so on. The exporter manufactures or procures goods and dispatches them to an importer through agreed mode of transport, delivery terms and cargo insurance policy. The exporter prepares the documents and submits them to his/her bank (remitting bank) as per procedure as laid down under FEMA, 2000, and regulations therein. The remitting bank processes the documents to the collecting bank which asks for the collection of payment from the importer against trade documents. Documentary collections are of two types. The *first* one is the 'D/P', also known as 'sight draft' or 'sight bill', wherein an importer pays to the collecting bank as soon as he/she collects the document from the collecting bank. The *second* type of documentary collection is known as 'D/A', also known as 'time draft/bill' or 'usance draft/bill'. The payment settlement under D/P method is safe for both trading parties; however, an exporter is exposed to unlimited risks under D/A similar to an open account method. ICC, Paris, has framed the universal rules for the payment settlement under the documentary collection to avoid confusions and problems arising out of differing regulatory framework of different countries. These rules are known as 'URC 555'. The process of payment settlement under documentary collection is exhibited in Figure 14.9.

TABLE 14.1 Risks Assessment for the Exporter and Importer with Different Types of L/C

Types of L/C	Time of Payment	Goods Available to Importer	Risk to Exporter	Risk to Importer
Irrevocable L/C	Payment at sight on presentation of documents to issuing bank or on specified date in case of time L/C	Goods available after payment	Risk lies with the confirming bank if L/C is confirmed	No credit risk. However, other commercial risks exist
Sight Draft L/C	On presentation of documentation once shipment is made	Goods available after payment	Risk lies with the local confirming bank if L/C is confirmed	Shipment of goods is assured; however, the importer is exposed to commercial risks, i.e., quality issues, different goods and sub-standard goods
Revolving L/C	Payment period is variable and subject of mutual negotiation	Variable	Same as in case of irrevocable L/C	No credit risk; however, other commercial risks exist
Back-to-back L/C	Same as in case of any irrevocable L/C	Goods available after payment	None	No credit risk; however, other commercial risks exist
Time Draft L/C	At maturity of draft or time draft can be discounted with the bank	Usually before payment	Risk lies with the local confirming bank	Assured shipment is made but relies on the exporter to ship goods described in the documents
Red Clause L/C	A percentage of total amount before shipment and rest as in case of any other L/C transactions	Goods available after payment	Same as in case of irrevocable L/C	Percentage of payment made in advance is full risks; however, other risks are same as in case of any other L/C transactions
Standby or Special L/C	Payment settlement after the delivery of goods	Usually before payment	Delay in payment is expected as standby L/C is used as last resort to realize the payment	No credit risk; however, other commercial risks exist
Transferable L/C	Same as in case of irrevocable L/C	Goods available after payment	Same as in case of irrevocable L/C	No credit risk; however, other commercial risks exist

Source: Adapted from Documentary *Risk in Commodity Trade*, UNCTAD.

FIGURE 14.9 Process of execution for payment under documentary collections.

Banks play an important role in the payment settlement under this method without directly assuming any risk and responsibility for the payment settlements. The collecting bank receives the export proceeds either at sight or against acceptance at future date from the importer and remits it to the remitting bank, which in turn, transfers the funds to the account of an exporter. Banks provide their banking services against their prescribed banking charges to both the exporter and importer, that is, both the remitting and collecting banks act as the facilitators and do not have any liability vis-à-vis payment to the exporter. The documentary collection does not require any kind of verification of documents by involved banks as in the case of L/C, but an exporter is required to submit the trade documents as agreed and negotiated with the importer along with the negotiable instrument, that is, the bill of exchange. The documentary collection method is much similar to the international cheques wherein an importer can dishonour the payment commitment if he/she so desires. The legal recourse under this mode is limited; however, an exporter can pursue the case under the Negotiable Instrument Act of the agreed jurisdictions, which can be a time-consuming and costly process. Even after these risks, trading parties prefer international payment settlement through the documentary collection as it is an effective and viable payment option to exporters and importers. It entails lower transaction costs, is more feasible, competitive and equally distributes the degree of risk between parties if used smartly. The key features of the documentary collection are discussed as follows:

1. The exporter and importer negotiate a trade deal and reach on consensus for terms and conditions of the trade deal. The exporter manufactures the goods or procures them from other manufacturer and ships these goods to an importer.
2. The exporter prepares and retails important documents such as invoice, packing list, bill of lading and bill of exchange, and submits them to his/her bank for collections from the collecting bank, which is usually in the importer country.
3. As trade documents are with an exporter, he/she retains title of goods irrespective of the fact that the goods have landed in the importer country and shall be in the custody of customs until an importer submits the trade document along with the bill of entry for the clearance from customs.

4. The collecting bank asks for the sight payment or acceptance for payment on the agreed future date as per the agreement of sales between the exporter and importer.
5. The collecting bank hands over trade documents to the importer against the sight payment and remits such funds to the remitting bank, that is, the bank of the exporter. The collecting bank asks for the payment to an importer on the agreed future date in case of D/A transaction.
6. An importer can refuse to pay at sight as well as after acceptance; thus, an exporter is exposed to payment risks under the documentary collection. The exporter must take risk-mitigation measures to protect from such payment risks.
7. In case of the importer's refusal, the exporter has three options to deal with such shipped goods. He/she can offer a rebate to an importer for the delivery and to find out another buyer; if these two options do not work, he/she can warehouse these goods for the future sale, and at worse, he/she has to transport these goods back to the home country.
8. The banks play an important role in facilitating the trade transaction between the exporter and importer without owning up the responsibility for payments.
9. The documentary collection is the preferred mode of payment in cases of established trade relationships and economically stable export markets as the exporter is at little more risk. However, this can be used by taking all credit risk protection measures.

Some degree of risks remains even in the D/A as the importer may change his/her mind or become insolvent or be unable and unwilling to make the payment due to reasons such as a decline in prices, decline in domestic demand and sudden changes in the business environment. The exporter can mitigate such risks through credit appraisal of an importer coupled with credit insurance cover or bank guarantees. Sometimes an importer may refuse to take the delivery of goods due to the change in trade regime, that is, goods declared prohibited or restricted for import. In case of restriction, if an importer fails to get special import licence from the regulatory authority, an exporter has no option except to sell the goods in another country or call them back. An exporter should always consult his/her international banker before entering into such a payment option for an international trade transaction. Figure 14.10 exhibits the assessment factors for the decision-making for documentary collections for both sight and time bills.

As exhibited, D/A is riskier for an exporter as he/she extends credit to an importer, delivers him/her goods as well as documents and asks for the payment at any future date. Exporters negotiate such trade

Assessment Factor	D/P (Sight Bill)	D/A (Time Bill)
Time of payment	After shipment but before documents are released	On maturity of draft at a specified future date
Transfer of goods	After shipment but before documents are released and after payment is made on sight	Before payment but upon acceptance of draft
Exporter risk	If draft is unpaid, goods may need to be disposed	As no control of goods and may not get paid at due date

FIGURE 14.10 Key features of D/P and D/A.

terms in order to win new buyers and penetrate new and unexplored markets. This can be a good strategy as this payment mode facilitates credit to an importer who can sell these goods in local markets and make the payments at a subsequent date, thus enabling the exporter to expand and diversify the business. On the negative side, an importer can default or deny making the payment; if not so, there may be issues of country risks such as inconvertibility, the imposition of exchange control restrictions, international sanctions and embargoes. Hence, this is a risky payment option for an exporter and should be used after thoroughly verifying and cross-checking the credit-worthiness of an importer, importer's country's economic and political situation. The exporter can smartly use this payment option by ensuring credit risk or by using the factoring or forfeiting services to hedge his/her risks in addition to the ECGC cover and bank guarantees. The parties in the documentary collection settlement are explained below:

1. **Drawer:** The drawer is basically an exporter who issues the bill of exchange for a trade transaction and to whom the payment is made. He/she sells goods and routes the documents through the remitting bank to the importer's bank and instructs for the payment. The collecting bank asks for the payment from the importer in lieu of documents if it is sight draft (D/P) or alternatively gives documents to the importer with a commitment from the importer to make the payment on the future date if it is a time draft (D/A). If he/she does not sell or discount the draft, he/she will also be known as a payee; if he/she discounts the draft to the bank, such discounting bank is entitled to payments and will be known as a payee.
2. **Drawee:** The drawee is basically the party who owes the money or agrees to make the payment and to whom the draft is addressed and made out. The drawee is an importer, a buyer, an acceptor and the payer of the draft in a documentary collection mode of payment. The importer makes the payments to his/her bank, that is, the collecting bank or presenting bank in this case in lieu of trade documents which have been received.
3. **Remitting bank:** A remitting bank is the exporter's bank to which he/she sends the bill of exchange along with all transport and shipping documents and instructions for the documentary collection. The remitting bank in turn sends these documents to the collecting bank so as to relay them to the importer and ask for payments as per instructions and agreed rules of payments between the exporter and importer for this trade transaction. The role of remitting bank is of a facilitator without any risk and responsibility for ensuring the payments from the importer or his/her bank.
4. **Collecting or presenting bank:** The collecting bank is the bank of an importer and facilitates in a trade transaction by getting the documents for the exporter bank, that is, the remitting bank. On receipt of trade documents, it informs the importer and calls for the payment as per agreed terms and conditions. The importer pays export proceeds to this bank in lieu of trade documents or in lieu of acceptance for payment at the agreed future date. The role of the collecting bank is also of a facilitator and does not entail any risk and responsibility for the payments of a trade transaction.

14.4.4 Open Account

An open account is the riskiest method of payment for an exporter and the safest for an importer, that is, extremely favourable to an importer and extremely unfavourable to an exporter. Under this method, an exporter negotiates and signs an export contract and ships the goods to an importer. The exporter also dispatches the trade documents evidencing the transfer of ownership from an exporter to an importer and asks for a 'sight' or 'time' payment. A sight payment is made as soon as the importer receives the documents and goods, whereas a time payment is made after the agreed credit period. This method of payment is used in case of extreme trust between the two trading parties, established trade relationship and sister firms. This method uniquely favours an importer as he/she can sell these imported goods in domestic markets, realize the payments and then pay to an exporter at the agreed future date. An importer can use other people's funds for his/her own business expansion and also does not have any product risk. An importer does not have to engage his/her working capital for doing business and has cash flow with him/her without any associated risks. An exporter is exposed to both commercial and country risks under this method. An exporter should use this method only with well-established customers with good credit rating and financial record, low country risks and competitive sales reasons. The process of payment execution under an open account method is exhibited in Figure 14.11.

The execution of payment under this method entails first, exporter shipping the goods to an importer and invoicing an importer through trade documents and bills for payment at sight or a future date. The exporter has full commercial as well as country risk, for example, no funds for meeting working capital requirements, the full cost of trade financing, delay or default or insolvency of an importer, inconvertibility, foreign exchange restrictions and country embargoes in today's volatile and uncertain times. This method can pose severe financial risks to an exporter and should be used only with well-established customers with a good credit rating. The exporters from emerging markets, especially from China, have been using this method to tap the unexplored new markets of Africa and Latin America and their government offer credit insurance at a nominal premium from state-run public insurance companies with the clear objectives of expanding and diversifying China's foreign trade. If the importer does not pay at sight or even an agreed future date, the exporter is exposed to a high degree of payment risks. An exporter can mitigate these risks by either credit insurance from ECGC or by availing a standby L/C. If the buyers are of sound credit-worthiness and have a strong and proven history of making timely and full payment, this can be a satisfactory mode of payment as it involves a least transactional cost (bank charge) in realizing the payments. In fact, many large organizations are using this method in India as well with the importer who has demonstrated long and positive records of timely payments to an exporter. Open account payments can also be negotiated in the case where exporters have thoroughly cross-checked the credit-worthiness of the importer and are found to be very positive.

This mode of payment has to be used smartly by an exporter as this is a very risky proposition for any exporter. The exporter loses both goods and payments as he/she hands over the documents

FIGURE 14.11 Process of execution for payment under open accounts.

evidencing the ownership of goods to an importer and that even without routing the documents through proper banking channels. Under this method, it is difficult for the exporter to pursue the legal enforcement for payment against the importer. The exporter has to pursue the claim for the payment at an individual level which is a very lengthy, costly, time-consuming and difficult process in a complex international economic and legal environment spanning between two countries. The exporter may also have a problem with regard to post-shipment financing as the receivables under such risky payment terms are usually not financed by the bank, and if so, banks charge a very high interest rate. Hence, it is advisable that the exporter properly and patiently verifies and cross-checks the political, economic and commercial risks involved in the deal and accordingly negotiate with an importer. The key features of this mode of payment are explained below:

1. This method is very unsafe for an exporter but very safe for an importer; hence, it should be used in cases where the exporter has very good trade relations with an importer, supported by credit insurance cover or special L/C or sovereign guarantee or trading with sister firms.
2. This method can be used in cases where the importer belongs to economically and politically stable markets with sound regulatory and legal framework.
3. This payments mode provides a competitive and hawkish strategy on the part of an exporter to win new and unexplored markets and also have significant exposure to non-payment risks and some additional cost of hedging payment risks.
4. Under this payment mode, the goods are shipped directly to the importer along with the agreed trade documents. The exporter orders through the bill of exchange an importer to pay at sight or on the date as agreed, which should be within 270 days as per FEMA rules unless otherwise permitted by RBI.
5. While using this method, an exporter should ensure risk mitigation through a credit insurance policy or guarantee as the facility of export factoring and forfeiting is not available under this payment mode.

14.5 Methods of Fund Transfer

In addition to methods of payment, one needs to understand the process of fund transfer from one country to another as fund transfer entails costs, time and risks and an exporter needs to understand the mechanism and process of fund transfer from one country to another in order to get assured export proceeds for the international sale. In an era of technological innovations, there have been some new developments for fund transfers as well, which facilitate timely, cost-effective and need-based international payment settlements. An exporter and importer should understand various options of funds transfer, and with increasing competition in foreign trade, they should leverage the cost-effective means so as to increase their profits margins. Cash in advance, through the wire transfer, is one of the safest, most attractive and favourable method of international trading for exporters, and as a result, the least secure and unattractive option for importers. The exporter should avoid the cash in advance through the international cheque as days required in the international collection of cheques are four–six weeks and may frustrate the original intentions of the exporter of realizing payment in advance and using the money for other purposes. Some methods of fund transfers in international payment are discussed in the following sub-sections.

14.5.1 Wire Transfer through Bank

Bank-to-bank wire transfer is the most cost-effective, widely used, highly secure and desirable method for fund transfer to international payments. It saves time, cost and even paper by reducing the need for cheques and deposit slips, thus making the payment process more environment friendly. In today's era of technology-driven business, banks facilitate importers and exporters to transfer money online using tools such as International Bank Account Number (IBAN), SWIFT and Corporate Identification Number (CIN). Wire transfer services require the importer and exporter to have a bank account with banks that operate on SWIFT or IBAN. The flow diagram along with step-by-step process on international money transfer under wire transfer is explained in Figure 14.12.

14.5.2 Personal Cheques

The process of international money transfer through personal cheque is similar to domestic cheques. Using cheque for fund transfer may result in delays as an exporter deposits this cheque with his/her bank which will process it to the corresponding bank in the currency of the invoice, which, in turn, will contact the collecting bank which will verify the cheque's details and if allowed, will process the payment to the corresponding bank, which in turn will process it to the bank of the exporter. In other words, US dollar-denominated cheques will be settled with US banks only, and Yen-denominated cheques will be settled with Japanese banks as currencies never leave their home country. The recipient of the cheque, that is, the exporter, in this case, has to pay a fee for encashing it and will also be exposed to exchange rate risks. It is a risky method as the buyer may also dishonour the cheque and is not an advisable method of money transfer for exporters. The step-by-step process of money transfer under foreign cheque is explained in Figure 14.13, and the process of cheque clearence is presented in Figure 14.14.

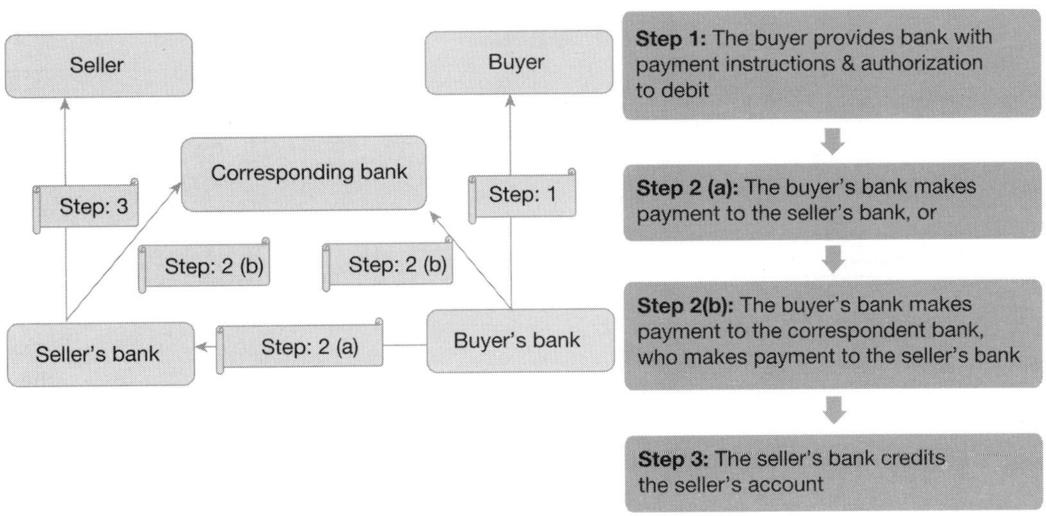

FIGURE 14.12 Step-by-step process of wire transfers.

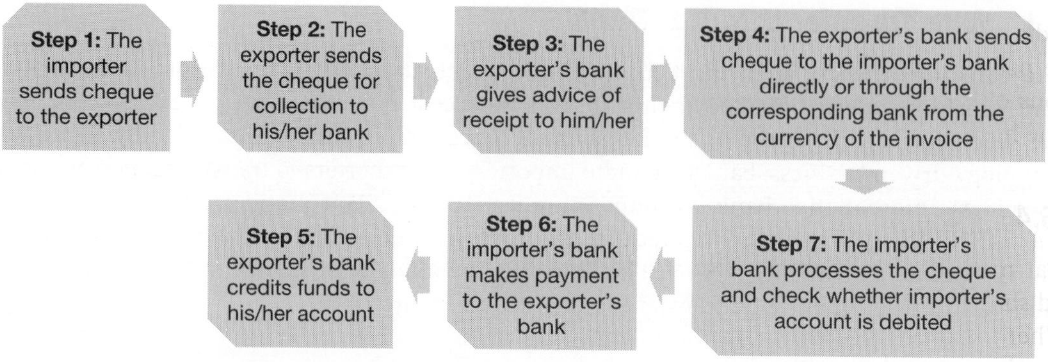

FIGURE 14.13 Step-by-step process of cheque payment.

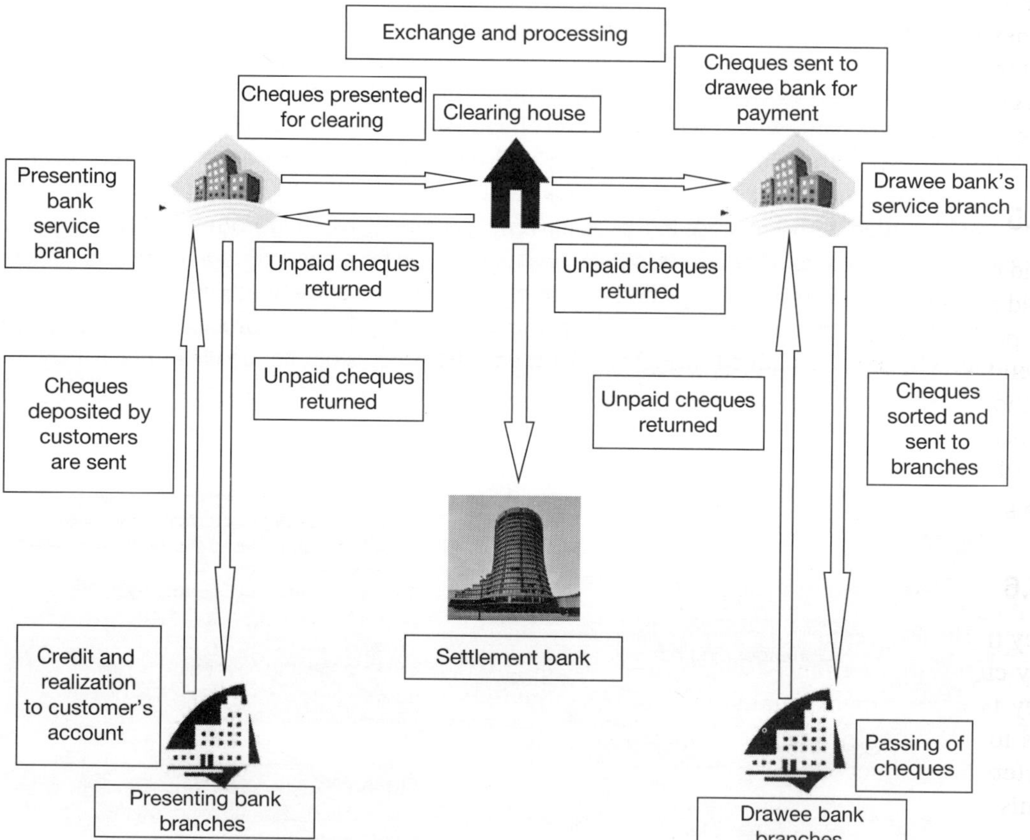

FIGURE 14.14 Process of cheque-clearing cycle.

14.5.3 Bank Drafts, Money Orders and Traveller's Cheques

Bank drafts/money orders and traveller's cheques are often great choices for international money transfers when it comes to physical transfers of funds that are being sent in foreign currencies. An importer can purchase bank drafts and money orders in the currency of the location, that is, if he/she is coming to India, it has to be freely convertible foreign currency or Indian rupees. It can be a useful method to settle petty expenditures mainly related to foreign travel and purchase of export samples. All these options of money transfer are often less expensive, and if someone does not use the funds abroad, he/she has the option to encash them back home in the local currency.

14.5.4 PayPal

PayPal method of payment settlement has been very popular in an era of teleshopping and web-based shopping (Figure 14.15). An exporter has to open a PayPal account with the bank, which allows him/her to transfer funds electronically from one PayPal account to another. PayPal is a very economical mode of payment settlements. An importer is usually not charged for sending money through PayPal, though the recipient is charged a fee when he/she withdraws cash from his/her account. PayPal can be a good method for small transactions as it saves time, documentation and is a very fast method of money transfer. The transfer fee varies between 2.5 and 3 percent for transfers up to $3,000, and there are some transaction charges. Transfer fees decrease slightly for larger transactions, it may be as less as 1 percent. Trade transaction under DDP, teleshopping, online shopping, personal gifts, donations, private remittances and so on can be best settled through PayPal mode.

14.5.5 Prepaid Money Cards

Prepaid cards have been another new development for international payment settlements (Figure 14.16). Prepaid money cards are fast getting recognized as a convenient alternative to the traditional methods of the payment settlement. Prepaid money cards are similar to 'credit card' or 'debit card' in operations and tend to have many benefits. A small-scale importer who wishes to participate in trade fairs/exhibitions and also wants to do some international buying can use prepaid money cards whereby he/she has to load funds onto the card before using it. He/she can only spend what amount he/she has on the card. Prepaid cards are best for online shoppers, international travellers and are also accepted at ATMs globally.

14.5.6 Money Transfer Operators

Money transfer operators are getting increasingly popular as they provide anyone to transfer money to any city, state or country where they have networks. They charge a flat rate as commission for money transfer that is usually based on the speed of the money transfer, the location where one wants to send money and the amount of transaction. This method can be suitable for small-scale exporters located in countries which do not have a sound banking system. Indian immigrant workers use this facility at large scale to send bank money to their families back home from abroad.

14.5.7 Email Money Transfers

In recent times, some large Canadian banks are offering this service. An email money transfer functions like an electronic cheque (Figure 14.17). Under this method, although the funds are not physically transferred by email, the transaction is initiated by an email. The recipient or exporter is notified by the email that the funds have been transferred to his/her account. The recipient requires a security question which is provided by the initiating branch to get him/her identified, and then, he/she can retrieve the

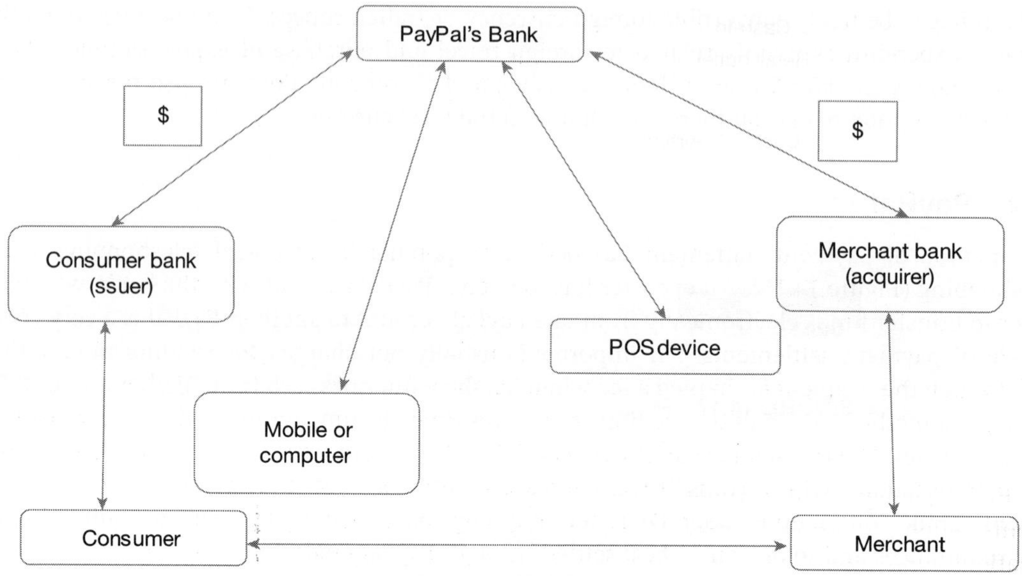

FIGURE 14.15 Process of payment settlement through PayPal.

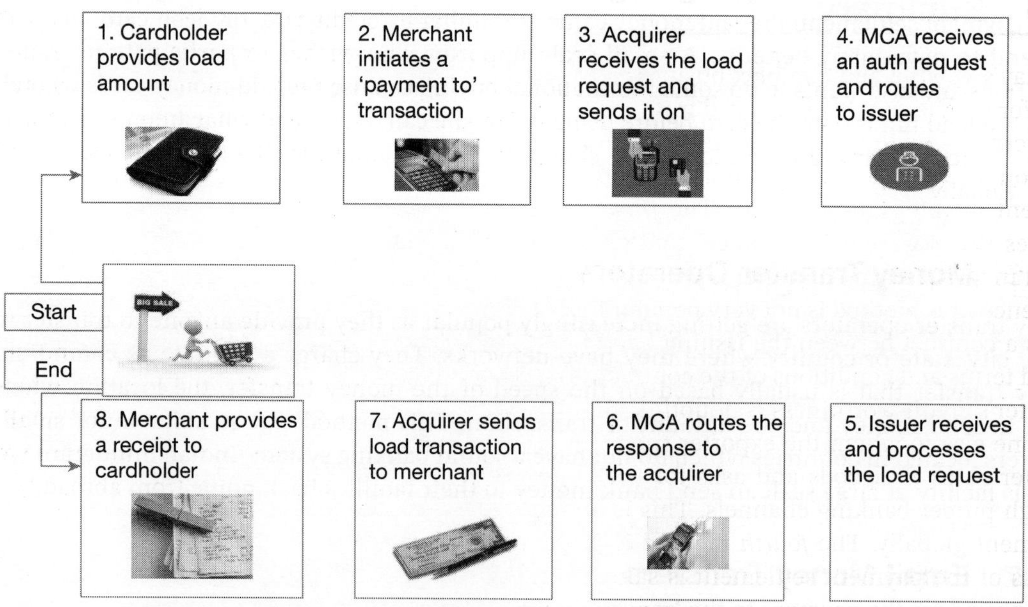

FIGURE 14.16 Process of payment through credit cards.

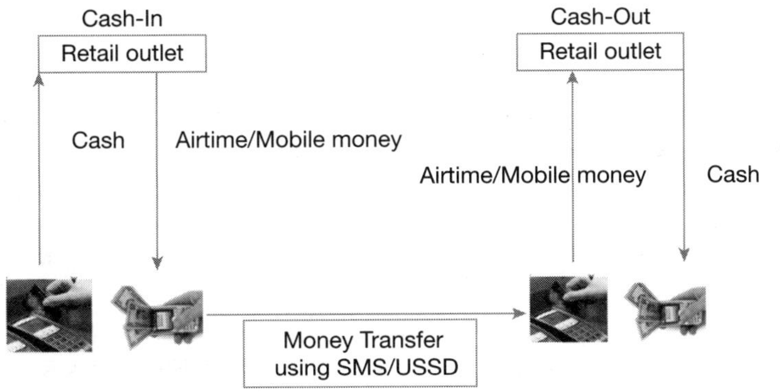

FIGURE 14.17 Process of payment settlement through emails.

funds. Email money transfer comes at a nominal cost and is a cheap option for settling international payments. Similar to this is 'TextPayMe' service for money transfer which has been started by telecommunications companies.

In the context of the above, some of popular means for realizing cash in advance for export operations are shown in Table 14.2.

14.6 Summary

In today's volatile and complex business environment, any export transaction is a gift until the payment for this has not been realized from the foreign buyers. More so, an exporter has to offer attractive sales terms including payments terms due to declining import demand coupled with increasing business competition in this recessionary and ambiguous environment. There are five popular methods of payment in international trade. The *first* method is the payment in advance wherein an exporter receives the 'payment in advance', and goods are shipped subsequently. In today's uncertain time, except in few cases, no importer is willing to pay in advance as it is extremely unfavourable for importers; hence, this method is not very popular for payment settlements. The *second* method is called 'L/C' and is a contract between the issuing bank and exporter for export payment subject to fulfilment of agreed terms and conditions of the contract. This method is safe for the exporter and is used when the importer's credit-worthiness is doubtful, and the exporter wants the risks of payment to be shifted to someone else to whom the exporter trusts, that is, the bank. The *third* method is 'D/P' wherein the exporter ships the goods and asks for the payment against the trade documents, which are routed through proper banking channels. This is an ideal method and is vastly used in the export payment settlement globally. The *fourth* method is 'D/A' and is a risky method for the exporter wherein the process of the payment settlement is same as in D/P except for the fact that the exporter has given credit period for the payment to the importer; hence, importer signs an acceptance with the bank and takes custody of documents so as to get them released from customs for domestic sales. The *last* method of the export payment settlement is an 'open account' and is a very risky method from the exporter's perspective in today's ambiguous and uncertain time. The exporter ships the goods and

TABLE 14.2 Pros and Cons of Various Types of Money Transfer in International Payment Settlement

Factor	Wire Transfer	Credit Card	Payment by Cheque
Cost involved	It is costly for the importer as the cost of remitting funds through wire transfers has to be borne by him/her, which is high in overseas transactions	It is a cost-effective method for small transactions; however, the card has fund transfer limits; hence, it is not very popular in exports and imports	It is a little costly as the collection charges for the export payment will be deducted by the collecting bank
Time	It takes the least time from one country to other country, around 16 seconds	It takes the least time and makes the funds available to the exporter well before the shipment	Payment through cheque takes time in collection of international cheques, usually 4–6 weeks
Safety	It is the safest mode of fund transfer	A credit card may result in fraudulent use as the mode of transfer is via online, telephone or fax methods	Cheques are safe, but the exporter has to check the whereabouts of the bank as fake banks are common in least-developed countries
Ease in use	It is very easy to use for large transactions	It is very easy to use	It requires some efforts at the end of exporter to deposit the cheque through collecting bank. Time is important in collection of cheque.
How it works	Wire transfer work through SWIFT system	A credit card works through online, fax and telephone system	The collecting bank sends the cheque to the importer's bank for transmittals of funds. Lengthy process as compared to other modes.

Source: The author.

hands over the trade documents to the importer for the import clearance. The importer sells these goods in the domestic market and pays the exporter after the agreed credit period. This method entails very high risks of non-payment for an exporter.

In addition to the methods of payments, one needs to understand the process of fund transfer from one country to another as fund transfer entails costs, time and risks. An exporter needs to understand the mechanism and process of fund transfer from one country to another in order to get assured export proceeds for international sale. Bank-to-bank wire transfer is the most cost-effective, widely used, highly secured and desirable method of money transfer for fund transfer to international payments. It saves time, cost and even paper by reducing the need for cheques and deposit slips, thus making the payment process more environment friendly. In today's era of technology-driven business, banks facilitate importers and exporters to transfer money online using tools such as IBAN/SWIFT/CIN. The process of international money transfer through personal cheque is similar to domestic cheques. Using cheques for fund transfer may result in delays as first an exporter deposits this cheque with his/her bank which will process it to the corresponding bank of the currency of the invoice, which, in turn, will contact the collecting bank which will verify the cheques' details and if allowed will process the payment to the corresponding bank, which in turn will process it to the bank of the exporter. Bank drafts/money orders and traveller's cheques are often great choices for international money transfers when it comes to physical transfers of funds being sent in foreign currencies. An importer can purchase bank drafts and money orders in the currency of the location, that is, if he/she is coming to India, it has to be a freely convertible foreign currency or Indian rupees. PayPal method of the payment settlement has been very popular in an era of teleshopping and web-based shopping. The exporter has to open a PayPal account with the bank, which allows him/her to transfer funds electronically from one PayPal account to another. PayPal is a very economical mode of payment settlements. Prepaid cards have been another new development for international payment settlements. Prepaid money cards are fast getting recognition as a convenient alternative to the traditional methods of payment settlement. Prepaid money cards are similar to a 'credit card' or 'debit card' in operations and tend to have many benefits. Money transfer operators are getting increasingly popular as they provide anyone to transfer money to any city, state or country where they have networks. Money transfer operators charge a flat rate as commission for the money transfer that is usually based on the speed of the money transfer, the location where one wants to send money and the amount of transaction.

CASE STUDY COVID-19 Pandemic: Impact on Payment under L/C Transaction

The COVID-19 pandemic has created a shock and awe among us all, putting two-thirds of the global population under lockdown. *Insaan*, *gyaan* and *vigyaan* stand challenged, posing socio-economic and political risks for the whole world. Contagion caused by COVID-19 resulted in unfathomable economic fallouts, zero economic activities, disruption of supply chains networks, falling global demands, supply gluts leading to price fall, loss of trust and confidence and fear of gloomy future. The pandemic started at a time when the global economic order was already under stress with rising trade protectionism, ongoing tariff wars, unilateral economic sanctions, standstill at WTO talks, crumbling economic and financial institutions and lack of mutual trust, wisdom and initiation among global leaderships.

COVID-19 pandemic is also affecting different financial instruments commonly used in trade and commerce globally. Exporters, across various sectors in India, are concerned with the fact that the L/C even being a safe instrument of payment realization is not covered under force majeure clause under UCPDC of ICC. Lockdown caused due to COVID-19 pandemic has disrupted the entire supply chain operations of exports operations in India. The date of shipment is a vital part of contractual conditions of L/C, which is a contract between the issuing bank and beneficiary (exporter) and is governed with the law of promise. As GOI has declared the banking services to be essential in the lockdown period, meaning no disruption of banking services, Article 36 of UCPDC will not offer any relief to an exporter.

Legally, various articles of UCPDC denote that L/C as a contractual arrangement is governed by banking laws and practices and predominates other contracts in an export transaction, that is, sales contract, bill of lading, certificate of insurance and so on. Article 36 of UCPDC states,

> A bank assumes no liability or responsibility for the consequences arising out of the interruption of its business by Acts of God, riots, civil commotions, insurrections, wars, acts of terrorism, or by any strikes or lockouts or any other causes beyond its control. A bank will not, upon resumption of its business, honour or negotiates under a credit that expired during such interruption of its business.

In this context, if an exporter fails to ship the cargo on the date of shipment, he/she has no option but to seek an amendment in the L/C and an extension in the period for presentation of documents under the L/C.

Since India's domestic laws have evolved from the English law, force majeure provisions imposed in domestic regulations will not apply to the L/C. The Code Law, as practised in France and Belgium, has its force on international law including that of ICC rules and regulations. In India, there will be relief of such to Indian exporters from the domestic law. Force majeure circumstances can apply on the L/C contract if expressly referred to and included in contractual conditions of the L/C. The prediction of an outbreak like COVID-19 is highly unlikely to be included; hence, there is no relief to exporters except to seek an extension of time from their counterparts. Indian exporters should keep in mind an anonymous quote saying, 'In business, we don't get what we deserve; but what we negotiate', and John F. Kennedy once said, 'Let us never negotiate out of fear. But let us never fear to negotiate'. It is the high time to re-negotiate with importers on amending the L/C so as to comply with terms and conditions for complied payments.

Questions

1. How has COVID-19 impacted the global economic order?
2. Why do not the rules of UCPDC extend any relief to an exporter?
3. What is the legal position of the domestic law impacting payment settlement under the L/C?
4. Do other countries have a different legal arrangement on the applicability of domestic law on the L/C contract?

Review Exercises

Multiple Choice Questions

1. Which of the following is the safest method for an exporter?
   a. Payment in advance
   b. D/P
   c. D/A
   d. L/C
   e. Open account
2. Which of the following is the most unsafe method for an exporter?
   a. Payment in advance
   b. D/P
   c. D/A
   d. L/C
   e. Open account

3. Which of the following methods is considered ideal and competitive as it distributes risks equally between an exporter and an importer?
   a. Payment in advance
   b. D/P
   c. D/A
   d. L/C
   e. Open account
4. Which of the following methods of payment is suitable when the importer's credit-worthiness is under doubt?
   a. Payment in advance
   b. D/P
   c. D/A
   d. L/C
   e. Open account
5. Exports offer competitive trade terms so as to win new and unexplored markets; which of the following term is the most competitive term for an importer?
   a. Payment in advance
   b. D/P
   c. D/A
   d. L/C
   e. Open account
6. The bank facilitates the payment settlements between trading parties without owning up any risk or responsibility for the payment under which of the following terms of payments?
   a. Payment in advance
   b. Documentary collections
   c. L/C
   d. Open account
   e. None of the above
7. Which of the following methods should be used only in the case of very established trade relationships?
   a. Payment in advance
   b. D/P
   c. D/A and open account
   d. L/C
   e. None of the above
8. An L/C is opened at the instruction of which party to trade?
   a. Importer
   b. Exporter
   c. Advising bank
   d. Negotiating bank
   e. None of the above

9. Who among the following is the drawer in documentary collection transactions?
   a. Importer
   b. Exporter
   c. Remitting bank
   d. Collecting bank
   e. None of the above
10. Who among the following is called the payee if an exporter discounts the export bills to a bank in documentary collection transactions?
   a. Importer
   b. Exporter
   c. Remitting bank
   d. Collecting bank
   e. Discounting Bank

Critical Thinking Questions

1. Describe various payments terms used in international trade transactions.
2. Briefly discuss the various instruments that are used in payment of international trade of goods.
3. What are the key considerations that an exporter should keep in mind while negotiating the payment terms for international trade transactions?
4. Explain the features of each mode of payment used in international trade.
5. Briefly explain the risk hierarchy in various modes of payment in international trade deals.
6. Diagrammatically explain the process of payment settlement under the L/C. Explain the various parties involved in the trade transactions under L/C payments.
7. What is the process and procedure of payments under documentary collections? What precautions should be taken by the exporter in documentary selections payment terms?
8. Explain the process and procedure of payments under the L/C. What precautions should be taken by the exporter in the payment under documentary credits?
9. Diagrammatically explain the process of payment settlement under D/P. Explain the various parties involved in the trade transactions under documentary collections payments.
10. What is the process and procedure of payments under cash in advance? What precautions should be taken by the importer in cash in advance payment terms?
11. Explain the process and procedure of payments under an open account method. What precautions should be taken by the exporter in payment under an open account method?
12. Explain the new developments in international payment settlements and how money transfer takes place in international business.

CHAPTER 15

Credit Insurance Policies and ECGC

CHAPTER OBJECTIVES

- To understand the concept of credit risks management in foreign trade.
- To explain the growing need of credit insurance for an exporter.
- To discuss the functions of ECGC.
- To explain the various credit insurance policies of ECGC.
- To brief up the principles of credit insurance and claim procedure.

15.1 Introduction

The GOI had established ECGC in 1957 for the purpose of strengthening and boosting the export promotion efforts by covering the risk of exporting on credit. ECGC, being essentially an export promotion organization for covering the credit risk so as to increase the exports from the country, functions under the administrative control of the Department of Commerce, Ministry of Commerce and Industry, GOI. ECGC is managed by a board of directors having expertise in the area of insurance, banking and management and comprises representatives from GOI, RBI, banking, insurance and exporting community of the nation. ECGC is ranked the fifth largest credit insurer of the world in terms of coverage of national exports, and the present paid-up capital of the company is ₹900 crore and authorized capital ₹1,000 crore. It has been playing an important role in the credit insurance and guarantee for 50 years since its inception and has emerged as an important pillar in the export promotion efforts of GOI. It has designed its policies keeping in mind the interests of various sections of exporters such as small exporters, large-scale exporters, IT services exporters and occasional exporters. It has one of the largest range of products and services to enable the exporter to choose among various available credit insurance products, keeping in mind the risks and exposures involved in particular transactions. It offers various policies based on the risk perception, and, usually, the premium is less in the case of lower-risk transactions and countries.

15.1.1 Main Functions of ECGC

Following are the main functions of ECGC:

1. ECGC provides a wide range of credit risk insurance covers and products to exporters so as to enable them against the losses in the export of goods and services in international transactions.
2. ECGC helps the exporters in financing their trade transactions by offering guarantees to commercial banks and financial institutions particularly in cases where exporters have risky

payment options and are having problems in pre-shipment and post-shipment finances for export transactions.

3. ECGC also provides overseas investment insurance to Indian companies which are investing in joint ventures abroad in the form of equity or loan, thereby covering their exposure to risks and enabling them to make a foray in international markets.

15.1.2 Specific Functions of ECGC

Following are the specific functions of ECGC:

1. ECGC helps the exporters by offering insurance coverage against the payment risks in a changing global economic environment when many Indian exporters are for the first time into international trade by taking benefits from the process of economic liberalization.
2. ECGC has first-hand information in export-related activities, particularly in the areas of potential risk associated with countries and mode of payment in a globally changing trade regime, and offers guidance to exporters to help them out to avoid risks in such deals.
3. ECGC, with its networks with other credit risk agencies in the world, occasionally publishes the information on the risk perception of different countries with its own credit ratings and helps the exporters to avoid them.
4. ECGC acts as a facilitator in obtaining the export finance from banks/financial institutions through various guarantees to banks and financial institutions.
5. ECGC assists the exporters in recovering bad debts from defaulters by helping them to precede legal and diplomatic channels.
6. ECGC maintains the database of domestic and international exporters and importers and shares it with other credit risk insurance agencies and provides information on the credit-worthiness of overseas and domestic traders.
7. ECGC offers a wide range of products and services to exporters, including customized products, to meet their requirement and needs for the export credit insurance.

As risk is an integral part of international trade transactions, payments for exports are always open to risks even at the best of times. Interestingly, such risks have assumed large proportions in today's globalized world due to the far-reaching political and economic changes that are sweeping every aspect of the world. An outbreak of war or civil war or political rebellion or public disturbances may block or delay payment for goods exported, thereby putting the exporter under the dock. A coup or an insurrection may also bring the economic and political system to a halt, and an exporter may face a potential problem. As new global economic order is getting formed, countries are increasingly facing the problems of economic difficulties or balance of payment problems, and such problems may lead a country to impose restrictions on either import of certain goods or transfer of payments for goods imported due to such economic reasons. For example, in a recent Iraq war, the new government has put a moratorium on the export and import due to the problem of balance of payments. Argentina is also facing the same problem as the country has, in recent past, witnessed an economic crisis resulting in the total breakdown of financial and banking system compelling the country to put the EXIM and overseas payment under moratorium.

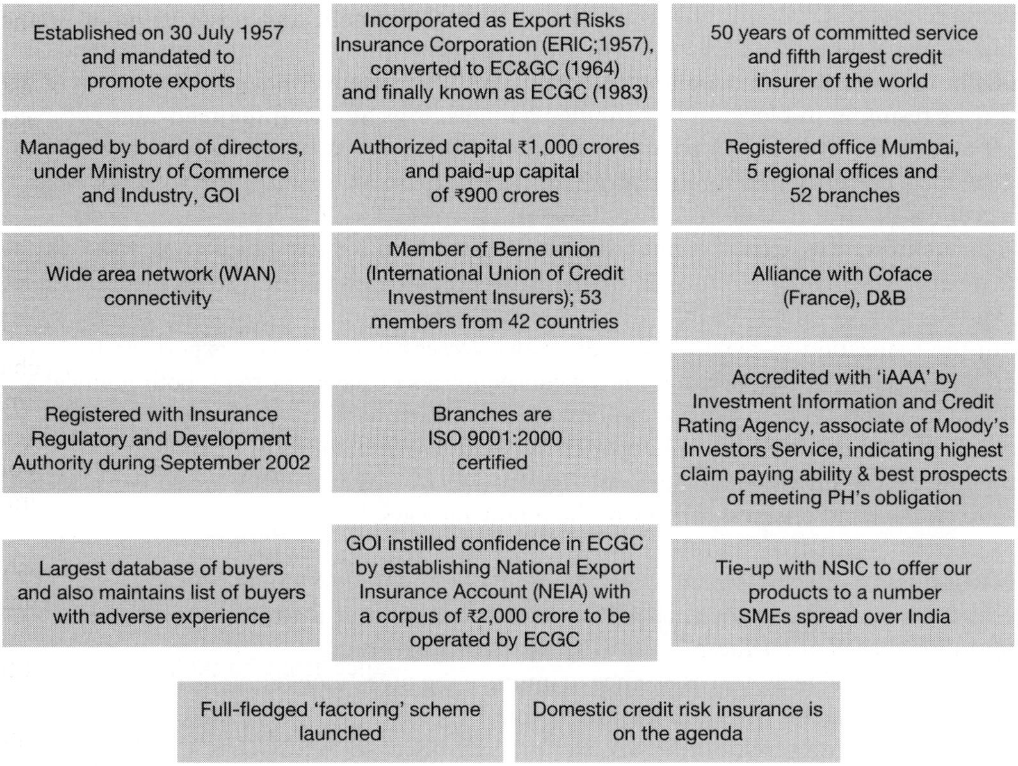

FIGURE 15.1 ECGC: Journey so far.

Source: Export Credit Guarantee Corporation of India.

In addition to the above, the exporters are also exposed to commercial risks of insolvency or protracted default of buyers. Political and economic uncertainties in the countries have aggravated the potential chances of the commercial risks of a foreign buyer whereby he/she can go bankrupt or lose his/her capacity to pay due to these circumstances. The very purpose of the export credit insurance is to protect exporters from such payment risks arising out of both political and commercial reasons and to provide them with a platform to cover such risks so that they can expand their overseas businesses without any fear of loss (Figure 15.1).

15.2 Growing Need of Credit Insurance

There are political risks which can be anticipated or predicted if not accurately with wild guesstimates such as a coup or an insurrection or possibility of civil disobedience, but newer waves of biological risks like the outbreak of coronavirus are beyond the comprehension of even best of scientists. Biological hazards like this are an undeclared war on mankind, hampering entire trade supply chain operations of the world economy. Economic challenges like an unfavourable balance of payment may lead a country to impose restrictions on either import of certain goods or transfer of payments for goods imported. Additionally, the exporters are open to commercial risks such as insolvency or protraction of buyers or country risks resulting in blocking of banking channels, thus affecting the realization of export payments. If a bank involved in the payment process becomes bankrupt or loses its capacity to pay or convert the local currency into foreign currency, it can expose an exporter to payments risks. The key objectives of credit insurance of ECGC are listed in Figure 15.2.

In such circumstances, export credit risks can be a solution for any exporter as 'risks can never be controlled but can be managed'. One way of managing credit risk is taking a credit insurance cover from ECGC. Various policies offered by ECGC help manage both political and economic uncertainties associated with the realization of export proceeds from overseas markets. The export credit insurance is designed to protect Indian exporters from the consequences of payment risks, both political and commercial, and to enable them to expand their overseas business without any fear of loss. ECGC works in close association not only with Indian exporters but with credit insurers of other countries and cooperates with Multilateral Investment Guarantee Agency (MIGA), an arm of the World Bank. MIGA assists Indian government and businesspersons in the following ways:

1. MIGA offers political insurance for foreign investment in developing countries, and ECGC benefits from such arrangement as MIGA offers protection at a strategic level and ECGC at the operational level of business.
2. MIGA offers vital technical assistance to improve the investment climate, thus indirectly helping ECGC to understand risks and manage them.
3. Dispute mediation service of MIGA is of vital significance to ECGC as it reduces litigation and prompts dispute resolution, thus helping ECGC.
4. Services of MIGA are of immense benefit to an exporter, a client of ECGC.
5. MIGA offers protection from political risks which are usually beyond the control of ECGC as it cannot control the events in foreign countries which have an adverse effect on India's exporters. Political risks in foreign countries include risks such as transfer restriction, expropriation, war, terrorism and civil disturbances.

By covering their commercial transaction under credit insurance schemes of ECGC, exporters safeguard themselves from potentially devastating effects of a loss caused by the insolvency or protracted default of one or more of their customers. In international trade, external factors such as import and trade restrictions can also interfere with the successful completion of the exporter contract of sale, resulting in a loss. The exporter in such circumstances may be exposed to insolvency, bad debts or even bankruptcy even without having any direct risk potential, which is why credit insurance is a must for an exporter as it helps him/her to put an end to all these worries, doubts and confusions and helps

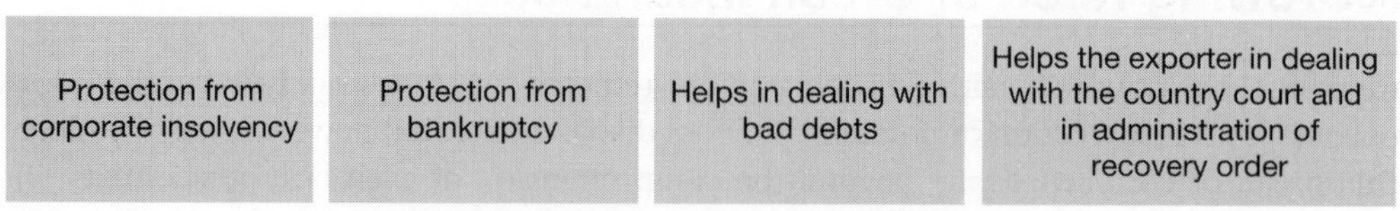

FIGURE 15.2 Key objectives of credit insurance.

Source: Export Credit Guarantee Corporation, GOI.

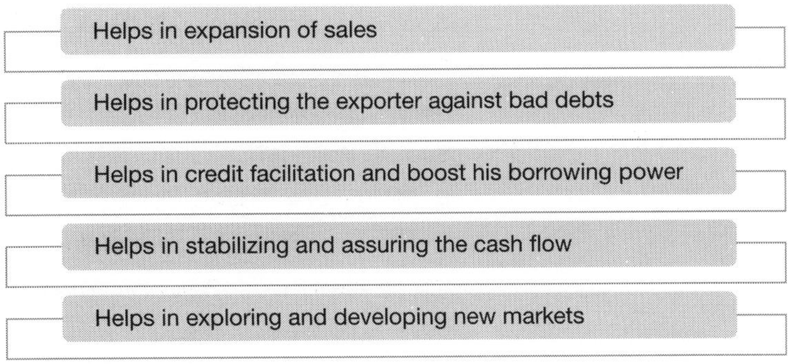

FIGURE 15.3 Role of ECGC in export promotion.

Source: Export Credit Guarantee Corporation, GOI.

him/her to concentrate on business-related activities rather than payments. Credit insurance helps the exporters to relax and get on with business-related activities. Hence, ECGC policies protect the exporters from a wide range of commercial and political risks and provide an exporter with a competitive edge in dealing in international trade. The role of ECGC (Figure 15.3) in export promotion is vital for India.

15.3 Credit Insurance Policies of EGCC

In order to address the risks involved at various levels of export payment chain, ECGC has designed multi-products and special services products for exporters and bankers. For example, credit insurance products for exporters are of different varieties such as short-term turnover-based, exposure-based and medium- and long-term-based products. Figure 15.4 details the various types of credit insurance products of ECGC.

15.3.1 Turnover-based Short-term Credit Insurance Products

ECGC offers a range of turnover-based credit insurance policies to exporters. Turnover policies are based on the total sales generated by an export business in a specific period. The export turnover of a firm is sometimes referred to as gross revenue or income. The turnover of an export firm is one of the key measures of its performance and scale of operations. Turnover-based policies are very popular and are explained below:

1. **SCR or Standard Policy:** This is one of the most popular policies of the ECGC, and this insurance product is suitable for exporters whose annual export turnover is more than ₹5 crore. An exporter below this export turnover is not eligible for this policy. The policy mandates that exporters to cover all their export shipment under this policy. Only exclusions permitted under this policy are exports made to associates and sister business concerns and export shipment, wherein the payment settlement is backed by the L/C. It is also known as 'Standard Whole Turnover Policy', and the period of the policy is 12 months. Risks covered under this policy include commercial risk, buyer risk, political risk and L/C opening bank risk. The percentage of

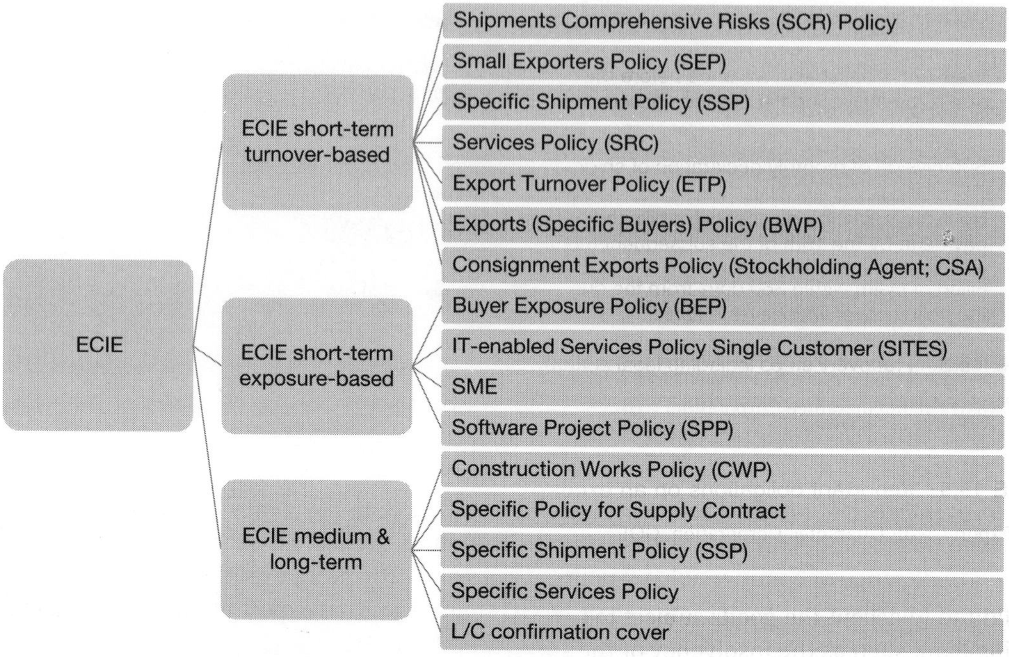

FIGURE 15.4 Export credit insurance for the exporter (ECIE).

Source: Export Credit Guarantee Corporation, GOI.

the cover is 90 percent under the Standard Policy. Any exporter is required to pay a minimum premium of ₹10,000 at the time of availing this policy, and such a premium will be subsequently adjusted towards premiums falling due on the shipments affected under the Standard Policy. If an exporter does not make even a single shipment in the financial year, the refund of the premium paid is not allowed. The Standard Policy mandates certain important obligations to an exporter as highlighted in Figure 15.5.

The Standard Policy offers credit insurance to Indian exporters at the lowest premium and is the largest selling policy of ECGC. Certain unique features make this policy very acceptable for India's trade community. For example, the Standards Policy is flexible and can offer a higher percentage of insurance cover from the standard limit of 90 percent. Premium rates under this policy are extremely competitive and similar to other insurance products; it offers no claim bonus (NCB) of 5 percent subject to no claim, up to a maximum of 50 percent. The Standard Policy also offers the discrepancy covers for L/C transactions subject to certain conditions. It provisioned for automatic cover for resale/reshipment up to 25 percent of the gross invoice value (GIV) of the export turnover if an exporter cannot sell it in the overseas market. It also provides the availability of discretionary credit limits to buyers on conditions. It offers cover for 'merchanting trade transactions (MTTs)' with prior approval by an endorsement.

Shipment (Comprehensive Risks) Policy or the Standard Policy of the ECGC covers risks from the date of shipment. The risks covered include 'commercial risks' which can be on the part of the overseas buyer such as insolvency of the buyer, failure of the buyer to make the payment due within a specified agreed period, which is normally four months from the due date, the buyer's

- Obtaining valid credit limit on buyers and banks from ECGC.
- Premium is payable in advance before the commencement of risks, and sufficient premium deposit is also to be maintained in advance based on the turnover projection at all times during the policy.
- Submission of monthly declaration of shipments by 15th of the subsequent month.
- Notifying/declaring payments for bills that have remained unpaid beyond 30 days from its due date of payment, by the 15th of the subsequent month.
- Filing of claim within 360 days from the due date of the export bill or 540 days from expiry date of the policy cover whichever is earlier.
- Initiating recovery steps including legal action.
- Sharing of recovery.

FIGURE 15.5 Important obligations on an exporter under Standard Policy of ECGC.

Source: Export Credit Guarantee Corporation, GOI.

failure to accept the goods subject to certain conditions and risks associated with the L/C opening bank such as the insolvency of the L/C opening bank and failure of the L/C opening bank to make the payment due within a specified period normally four months from the due date. The Standard Policy also covers political risks such as the imposition of restriction by the government of the buyer's country or any government action, which may block or delay the transfer of payment made by the buyer, war, civil war and revolution or civil disturbances in the buyer's country. New import restrictions or cancellation of a valid import licence in the buyer's country, interruption or diversion of voyage outside India resulting in the payment of additional freight or insurance charges which cannot be recovered from the buyer, any other cause of loss occurring outside India not normally insured by general insurers and beyond the control of both the exporter and the buyer shall also be covered under the Standard Policy of ECGC. Figure 15.6 lists the cases which cannot be covered for claims under the Standard Policy.

2. **Small Exporter's Policy (SEP):** India has a large number of SMEs, which also export. It is estimated that 35–40 percent of India's exports come from MSMEs. In order to fulfil the requirement of these small-scale exporters, a variant of the Standard Policy has been designed by ECGC. SEP has all features of the Standard Policy, however, incorporating certain improvements in terms of cover in order to encourage small exporters to obtain and operate the policy. SEP is issued to exporters whose anticipated export turnover for the coming one year is not more than ₹5 crore. ECGC has fixed the 'maximum liability' under SEP, and it should not exceed ₹2 crore. The coverage of various risks under SEP is similar to that of the Standard Policy. The period of SEP is 12 months, and the minimum premium to be paid at the time of availing policy is ₹5,000 which shall be adjusted for the premium of the shipments. NCB in the premium rate is granted every year at the rate of 5 percent. An exporter needs to declare the shipment executed on a monthly basis to ECGC. Further, small exporters are required to submit monthly declarations of all payments remaining overdue by more than 60 days from the due date, as against 30 days in the case of exporters holding the Standard Policy. An exporter can lodge a claim in the case of non-payment, 60 days after the due date of payments. ECGC can allow the change in terms of

- Commercial disputes including quality disputes raised by the buyer, unless the exporter obtains a decree from a competent court of law in the buyer's country in his/her favour.
- Causes inherent in the nature of the goods.
- Buyer's failure to obtain necessary import or exchange authorization from authorities in his/her country.
- Insolvency or default of any agent of the exporter or the collecting bank.
- Loss or damage to goods which can be covered by general insurers.
- Failure or negligence on the part of the exporter to fulfil the terms of the export contract.

FIGURE 15.6 Cases where claims will not be considered under Standard Policy of ECGC.

Source: Export Credit Guarantee Corporation, GOI.

payment by extending the credit period if small exporters so desired or are confident of getting payment from overseas buyers with some delay. SEP is flexible to the dynamic needs of low-value merchants; for example, a small exporter may, without prior approval of ECGC, convert a D/P bill into D/A bill, provided that he/she has already obtained suitable credit limit on the buyer on D/A terms. Further, it conditioned that in cases where the value of this bill is not more than ₹3 lakh, conversion of D/P bill into D/A bill is permitted even if the credit limit on the buyer has been obtained on D/P terms only, but only one claim can be considered during the policy period on account of losses arising from such conversions. Small exporters are the most stressed and have limited knowledge and expertise in dealing with international payment realizations. Accordingly, it is allowed that a small exporter may, without the prior approval of ECGC, extend the due date of payment of a D/A bill provided that a credit limit on the buyer on D/A terms is in force at the time of such extension.

In cases where the importer has refused to take ownership of the cargo and pay at sight (D/P), a small exporter can sell the cargo to an alternate buyer without obtaining prior approval of ECGC even when the loss exceeds 25 percent of GIV. As insurance is a contract based on the utmost good faith of contracting parties, ECGC may consider the payment of claims up to an amount considered reasonable, provided that ECGC is satisfied that the exporter did his/her best under the circumstances to minimize the losses. Other conditionalities vis-à-vis SEP are same as that of the Standard Policy of ECGC.

3. **Specific Shipment Policy (SSP):** For exporters who do not have regular orders and engage into export business on an occasional basis as the nature of their business is as such that export orders are not regular, the Standard Policy or SEP is of no use. Alternatively, some of the holders of the Standard Policy are such that they have been excluded from the purview of the policy cover. The exporter can take cover under the SSP and indicate the specific risks to be covered so as to hedge his/her credit risks. The period of SSP would be valid for shipment(s) made from the date of issue of the policy and up to the last date for shipment under the relevant contract. SSP covers commercial risk, buyer risk, political risk and L/C opening bank risk. Percentage of the cover is 80 percent. SSP mandates the important obligations on the exporter.

The key highlights of the SSP are a selection of insurance cover, specific to the needs of the export transaction (Figure 15.7). For example, if the consignment is destined to Syria, a war clause should be taken; if the shipment is destined to Kenya, a civil disobedience clause is required; and if the shipment is destined to Afghanistan, a terrorism clause should be taken for such specific shipments of export order. The exporter does not have to declare all other exports if any, and it extends credit insurance cover to MTTs with prior approval by making the necessary endorsement.

4. **Service Policy:** India is fast emerging as a global services' hub with ever-growing services exports from India. The Service Policy is suitable for such service exporters who enter into contracts for the supply of services from India to their clients based abroad. Indian export firms render them services with technical or professional skills and the realization of export payments due under such service contracts are open to risks similar to those under the supply contracts. ECGC has designed a credit insurance product to facilitate protection to such exporters of services. The Service Policy of ECGC has the following variants so as to address the different needs of clients in diverse global markets:
   a. Specific Services Contract (Comprehensive Risks) Policy
   b. Specific Services Contract (Political Risks) Policy
   c. Whole-turnover Services (Comprehensive Risks) Policy
   d. Whole-turnover Services (Political Risks) Policy

   The Specific Services Policy, as its name indicates, is issued to cover a single specified contract of a service exporter. It is suitable for those service contracts which are large in value and extend over a relatively long period. It is offered as comprehensive risks and political risks products. Political Risk Policy is suitable for a country marred with political risks such as Iran, which is politically cut-off in the Middle East. Whole-turnover services policies, on the other hand, are suitable for service exporters who are rendering services to their clients on a regular and repetitive basis, for example, TCS has got 15 billion IT project to manage the pension fund of Britain's government. Incidentally, such a period of the contract is long, but the period of the delivery of specific service is relatively

- Processing fee of ₹2,000 (non-refundable) is payable.
- Upfront premium payment in full.
- Submission of monthly declaration of shipments by 15th of the subsequent month.
- Submission of payment advice slip.
- Notifying/declaring payments for bills that have remained unpaid beyond 30 days from its due date of payment, by the 15th of the subsequent month.
- Filing of claim within 360 days from the due date of the export bill or 540 days from the expiry date of the policy cover whichever is earlier.
- Initiating recovery steps including legal action.
- Sharing of recovery.

FIGURE 15.7 Import obligations on exporter under Specific Shipment Policy.

Source: Export Credit Guarantee Corporation, GOI.

short. The Whole-turnover Service Policy is issued to cover all services contracts that may be concluded by the exporter over a period of 24 months ahead. The payment settlement in services contracts is different as billing is done on landmarks achieved as per agreed formula as services are rendered, not physically delivered. The mode of payment is similar to that of merchandise trade, and the payment settlement takes place periodically based on the progress of work. ECGC expects that the exporter should secure him/her with satisfactory security in the form of the L/C or bank guarantees for assured export proceeds realization.

5. **Export Turnover Policy (ETP):** ETP is designed for the large export firms of India, which contribute more than ₹20 lakh per annum as the premium revenue to ECGC. ECGC has designed this policy so as to facilitate large turnover units with attractive premium rates and higher facilitation to complement their endeavours in India's export promotion drive. ETP is suitable for status holders' firms, which contribute large export turnover and large premium contribution to ECGC. ETP is a whole-turnover declaration-based policy wherein all export shipments are required to be covered under the credit insurance policy. The period of the policy is 12 months, and it covers all risks covered under the Standard Policy. Exclusions permitted are similar to the Standard Policy, and it includes exports made to associates and export shipments backed by the L/C. Percentage of the cover is 90 percent.
6. **Important obligations of the exporter:** ETP mandates certain obligations for an exporter. *First* is obtaining the 'valid credit limit' on overseas buyers and banks from ECGC. *Second*, exporters are required to pay a premium in four equal quarterly instalments in advance before the commencement of risks. Further, exporters are required to maintain sufficient premium deposit in advance with ECGC, based on the turnover projection at all times during the policy. *Third*, exporters should submit a monthly declaration of shipments by 15th of the subsequent month. *Fourth*, exporters should notify and declare all export bills that have remained unpaid beyond 30 days from its due date of payment. *Fifth* is the filing of a claim of any unpaid export bills within 360 days from the due date of the export bill or 540 days from the expiry date of the policy cover whichever is earlier. *Sixth*, exporters are supposed to initiate recovery steps from overseas buyers, including legal action. The last is sharing of any recovery made from importers with that of ECGC for paid claims. The highlights of the ETP are depicted in Figure 15.8.
7. **Export (Specific Buyer) Policy (BWP):** An exporter may require a specific policy for a particular buyer or set of buyers or an L/C opening bank. ECGC fulfils the credit risks associated with such cases through the specific buyer policy which provides cover for shipments made to a particular buyer or on L/C opening bank for a set of buyers. Some exporters have exports sale fairly protected by either through advance payment or established business relationship, but one or two specific buyers may be giving a tough time. The exporter needs to cover such credit risks and has to take the Exports (Specific Buyers) Policy if he/she does not hold the Standard Policy or Whole Turnover Policy. Exporters holding the Standard Policy can also avail this policy for covering shipments to individual buyers, if all shipments to such buyers have been permitted to be excluded from the purview of the Standard Policy. The period of this policy is 12 months, and risks covered are same as that of the Standard Policy. Percentage of the risk cover is 80 percent. Important obligations of an exporter under Export (Specific Buyer) Policy are listed in Figure 15.9.

The key highlights of Export (Specific Buyer) Policy are that only selective buyer can be insured. One can have the Standard Policy and simultaneously an Export (Specific Buyer) Policy for a certain importer having a tendency to default or if the importer is located in a country with volatile

- Higher percentage of cover.
- Competitive premium rate.
- NCB of 5% subject to no claim, upto a maximum of 50 percent.
- A turnover discount in the standard premium rate is offered subject to the total discount including NCB being not less than 20 percent to those exporters whose net annual premium payable exceeds ₹20 lakh.
- Additional discount in standard premium rate is offered if the actual premium exceeds beyond 10% of the projected premium.
- Discrepancy cover for L/C transactions subject to certain conditions.
- Automatic cover for resale/reshipment up to 25 percent of GIV.
- Availability of discretionary limits on the buyers on conditions.
- Cover for merchanting trade with prior approval by making necessary endorsement.

FIGURE 15.8 Highlights of Export Turnover Policy.

Source: Export Credit Guarantee Corporation, GOI.

- Processing fee of ₹2,000 (non-refundable) is payable.
- The premium is payable in four equal quarterly installments in advance before commencement of risk and sufficient premium deposit is also to be maintained in advance based on the turnover projection at all times during the policy.
- Submission of monthly declaration of shipments by 15th of the subsequent month.
- Notifying/declaring payments for bills that have remained unpaid beyond 30 days from its due date of payment, by the 15th of the subsequent month.
- Filing of claim within 360 days from the due date of the export bill or 540 days from expiry date of the policy cover whichever is earlier.
- Initiating recovery steps including legal action.
- Sharing of recovery.

FIGURE 15.9 Important obligations of an exporter under Exports (Specific Buyers) Policy.

Source: Export Credit Guarantee Corporation, GOI.

and ambiguous business environment for the business. An exporter does not have to declare all the other export shipment under Export (Specific Buyer) Policy, and the policy offers the facility of NCB of 5 percent subject to no claim, up to a maximum of 50 percent as in the case of other credit insurance products of ECGC. The exporter needs to take a separate policy for each buyer.

8. **Consignment Export Policy (Stockholding Agent):** In an era of economic globalization aimed at reaping maximum benefits from foreign trade, consignment sales has emerged as a new focal area for tapping each possible business opportunity in foreign markets. The consignment sale is an arrangement in the foreign trade in which a seller or a consignor consigns or sends or hands over his/her cargo to a buyer or consignee on the expectation of possible and emergent sale in the consignee's market. The consignment sale is executed without getting or receiving the consideration of the exported goods and trust between the consignor and consignee is the basis of EXIM transaction. The consignor is exposed to unlimited risks as the consignee or said agent may sell the cargo and does not remit the export proceeds, or cargo may not get sold.

   The consignment sale as a marketing technique is increasingly adopted by Indian exporters to have an agency agreement with independent and separate entities in foreign countries. Such business entities may be an agent, a franchisee, a licensee, a consignee and an importer who receive and hold cargo stocks ready for the sale to overseas buyers as and when orders are received, find buyers and sell to them in consideration of a commission on such sales. In order to address the credit risks associated with such unique and vulnerable transaction, ECGC has designed a separate credit insurance policy known as Consignment Export Policy, which is introduced to cover the exclusive shipments made by exporters on consignment basis to their agent. The period of the policy is 12 months. The risks covered under this policy are commercial risk on stockholding agent and/or ultimate buyers and political risk. ECGC offers very high percentage of the cover of 90 percent for EXIM transaction under Consignment Export Policy for the Standard Policy policyholder and 80 percent for others. Important obligations of an exporter under the Consignment Export Policy are illustrated in Figure 15.10.

   Highlights of the Consignment Export Policy are that the risk cover is available only for those EXIM transactions which are affected under the consignment sale. ECGC allows an extended

- Processing fee of ₹4,000 (non-refundable) is payable.
- The premium is payable on quarterly or monthly basis in advance before commencement of risks and sufficient premium deposit is also to be maintained in advance based on the turnover projection at all times during the policy.
- Obtaining credit limit on ultimate buyers beyond the discretionary limit.
- Submission of monthly declaration of shipments by 15th of the subsequent month along with statement of the stock with the agent and details of sales effected to the ultimate buyers.
- Filing of claim within 360 days from the due date of the export bill or 600 days from expiry date of the policy cover whichever is earlier.
- Initiating recovery steps including legal action.
- Sharing of recovery.

FIGURE 15.10 Important obligations of an exporter under Consignment Export Policy.

Source: Export Credit Guarantee Corporation, GOI.

period for the realization of up to 360 days. There is an automatic cover on ultimate buyers up to discretionary limits subject to buyers being in a country placed in the open cover category and not in the list of buyers on whom the corporation has adverse information referred to as Buyer Specific Approval List. The policy is unique in the sense that it offers the risk coverage even for commercial risks on sales agents. The policy also has a standard clause of offering NCB of 5 percent subject to no claim, up to a maximum of 50 percent.

15.3.2 Exposure-based Short-term Credit Insurance Products

ECGC has designed some of its credit insurance products based on the risk exposure, which is a measure of possible future loss (or losses) likely to result from export business activities. Insurance underwriters use historical data to measure the export risk exposure, which ranks the probability of different types of losses. The key variables for the export credit risk exposure are commercial and political risks of a country. ECGC continually monitors international and national events shaping the business environment of a country and updates its databases so as to guide not only Indian exporters about possible losses associated with a country but also saves national interests of India as well. The various exposure-based credit policies of ECGC are detailed below:

1. **Buyer Exposure Policy (BEP):** BEP is suitable for export firms that have a large number of export shipments to a particular buyer. The policy is framed keeping in mind the exposure limit of such buyer and works with a simplified procedure and rationalized premium. An export firm can request ECGC for the exposure limit of such a buyer, and the policy cover is issued on such exposure limit for a selected buyer. This policy offers risks coverage against commercial and political risks. Exporters have an option to exclude L/C shipment from the policy as L/C transactions are considered to be safer for the payment realization. In case the exporter wants L/C shipments to be covered, ECGC mandates that an L/C opening bank should be among top 25,000 banks as per latest Bankers Almanac. If the exporter opts for only political risks, the premium at a lesser rate is offered. The policy is for 12 months, and risks covered are similar to that of the Standard Policy of ECGC. Percentage of the risk coverage is 90 percent for the Standard Policy policyholders and 80 percent for others. Figure 15.11 mandates important obligations on the exporter for BEP.

   The key features of this policy include the protection of credit insurance up to the loss limit approved by ECGC for the selected buyer under the policy. The exporter has to pay a premium on the 'loss limit' approved on the buyer, whether the shipments are affected or not. The exporter can claim NCB of 5 percent subject to the non-claim, up to a maximum of 50 percent. ECGC has waived off the declaration procedure so as to allow the exporter to focus more on the export business. The exporter needs to take a separate policy for each buyer, and such a buyer can be insured by ECGC.
2. **IT-enabled Services Policy Single Customer (SITES):** India has emerged as a global leader for the supply of IT and IT-enabled services. India is now one of the largest suppliers of IT-enabled services in the world. India's share in global services sourcing business is around 55 percent. Indian IT exports have reached $126 billion in the financial year 2018. India's domestic market for IT is also growing and has recorded domestic revenues valuing $41 billion, thus making this industry of market size of $167 billion in 2017–2018. Realizing the innate potential of India's IT-enabled services exporters, ECGC has designed a credit insurance product for them which is known as IT-enabled Services (Single Customer) Policy. This policy can be issued for one buyer where export contracts specify for the rendering of service during a defined period

- Processing fee of ₹2,000 (non-refundable) is payable.
- Upfront premium payment in full on the loss limit.
- Obtaining prior approval for extending the due date of payment of the export bill where the total credit period of realization exceeds 180 days.
- Notifying/declaring payments for bills that have remained unpaid beyond 30 days from its due date of payment, by the 15th of the subsequent month.
- Filing of claim within 360 days from the due date of the export bill or 540 days from expiry date of the policy cover whichever is earlier.
- Initiating recovery steps including legal action.
- Sharing of recovery.

FIGURE 15.11 Important obligations on the exporter.

Source: Export Guarantee Corporation of India, GOI.

with billing on the basis of service rendered during a period say, a week, a month or a quarter. The policy is issued for the period of 12 months, and risks covered are commercial, buyer, political and L/C opening bank risk. The percentage of the cover is 80 percent only. The distinct features of any IT-enabled services contract are illustrated in Figure 15.12.

Important obligations for an exporter under IT-enabled Services Export Policy include a non-refundable payment of ₹2,000 as a processing fee, upfront premium payment in full on the 'loss limit' under the policy, monthly declaration indicating the services rendered, invoices raised and invoices paid to be submitted by the exporter by 15th of the subsequent month. Further, no

- Contract is for providing certain service during a defined period.
- Billing for the service rendered at a pre-determined interval.
- Where there is a non-payment problem, there can be certain services invoiced and accepted, certain services invoiced but not accepted and certain services rendered but yet to be invoiced.
- No requirement of physical documentation as the process is carried out through electronic media.
- Provision for correction in case of errors and omissions.
- Filing of claim within 360 days from the due date of the export bill or 600 days from expiry date of the policy cover whichever is earlier.
- The policy will be offered for contracts, which contain standard terms and conditions as per the norms and practices of the IT-enabled services export industry.
- Right to verify documents by the corporation or by an authorized agency.

FIGURE 15.12 Distinct features of the IT-enabled service contract.

Source: Export Guarantee Corporation of India, GOI.

separate overdue report will be accepted, and filing of the claim, if any, should be within 360 days from the due date of the export bill or 540 days from the expiry date of the policy cover whichever is earlier. The policy mandates the exporter to initiate the recovery steps, including legal action on non-paying importers and sharing of recovering with ECGC if any after the settlement of claim by ECGC. The key highlights of the policy are listed in Figure 15.13.

3. **Policy for MSME Sector:** ECGC has designed a policy for the MSME sector of the country, realizing their great contribution to India's exporter sector. All exporters, including traders, manufacturers and service providers, irrespective of the MSME certificate, shall be eligible for the policy subject to their export turnover up to ₹1 crore. ECGC initially introduced a policy exclusively for the MSME sector units, and subsequently, the policy has undergone some changes so as to address the exporter's specific economic realities. The policy was given a new name as Micro Exporters Policy (MEP) in 2014 by making the product more attractive with the improved cover. MEP is an exposure-based policy, which covers the following risks for MSME units in Figure 15.14.

   MEP is issued for a period of 12 months, and it requires a processing fee of ₹1,000 to be paid to ECGC by the exporter. The minimum premium mandated under the policy is ₹25,000,

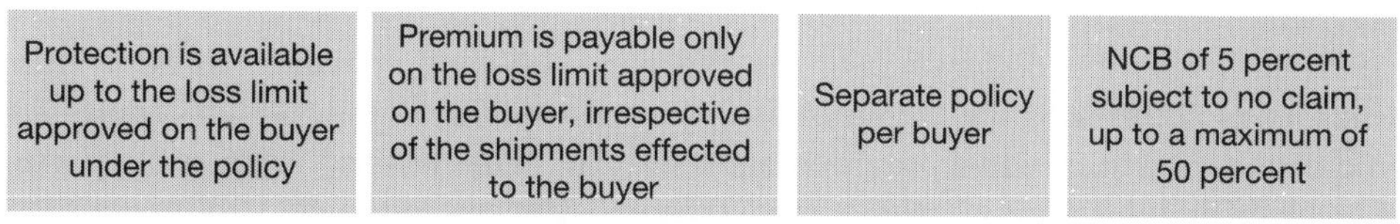

FIGURE 15.13 Key highlights of the IT-enabled service policy.

Source: Export Guarantee Corporation of India, GOI.

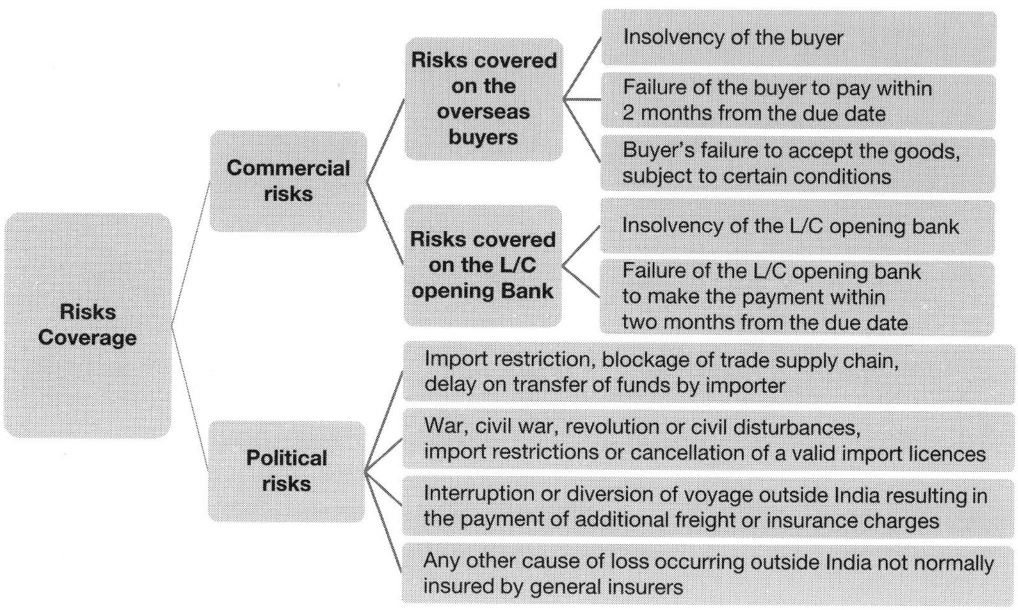

FIGURE 15.14 Risks coverage under the MEP of ECGC.

Source: Export Guarantee Corporation of India, GOI.

and the maximum loss limit is ₹15 lakh only. The policy also specifies the single loss limit of ₹5 lakh, and an exporter has to report the overdue to ECGC in case these are more than 60 days from the due date. The policy also provides a waiting period of 2 months from the due date or extended due date, and the percentage of the risk cover is 90 percent of the loss occurred.

4. **Software Project Policy (SPP):** In today's digital world, the role of a software project is ever-increasing. A software project is detailed and structured procured for the software development, which requires information gathering, business analytics, testing and maintenance and is carried out in compliance to agreed structured execution methodologies. Software projects are time bound, requiring testing of agreed quality standards and benchmarking cost practices to the best of industry standards. SPP of ECGC provides protection to such software exporters where projects are from overseas markets, and export proceeds realization has to be done in freely convertible foreign exchange. SPP of ECGC covers both on-site and off-site project development and associated software products and packages or staffing and programming services. The period of the policy is coterminous to the time of the software project. The risk coverage is the same as that of the Standard Policy. The percentage of risk coverage is 80 percent. The distinct features of SPP are shown in Figure 15.15.

   SPP mandates some obligations of the exporter such as the payment of non-refundable processing fee of ₹2,000 and the payment of upfront premium on the full 'loss limit'. The exporter would be required to submit a progress report indicating the level of completion, payment sought and received and deviations in these areas. The exporter has to specify in advance the manner in which the work in progress would be estimated. Filing of the claim is within 360 days from the due date of the export bill or 540 days from the expiry date of the policy cover whichever is earlier. The exporter is required to initiate recovery steps, including legal action against the default importer and will share any recovery with ECGC if so happen. The key highlights of SPP are listed in Figure 15.16.

- Billing for the service rendered mostly on milestones progress report.
- Exact due dates not possible.
- Where there is a non-payment problem, there can be certain services invoiced and accepted, certain services invoiced but not accepted and certain services rendered but yet to be invoiced.
- No requirement of physical documentation as the process is carried out through electronic media.
- Provision for correction in case of errors and omissions.
- No salvage in almost all the cases.
- Right to verify documents by the corporation or by an authorized agency.

FIGURE 15.15 Distinct characteristics of SPP.

Source: Export Guarantee Corporation of India, GOI.

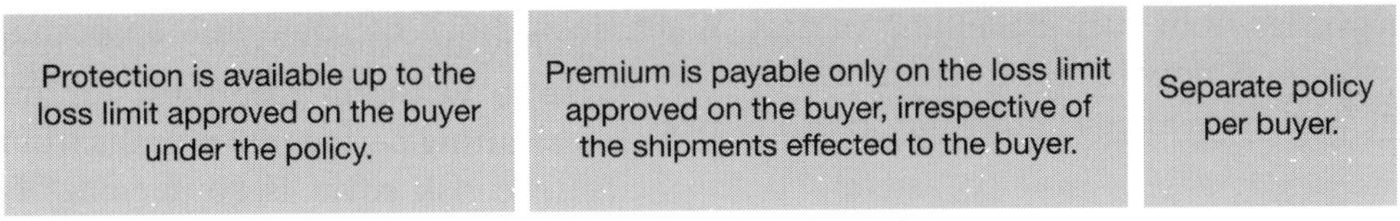

FIGURE 15.16 Highlights of SPP.

Source: Export Guarantee Corporation of India, GOI.

15.4 Basic Principles of Credit Insurance

Any insurance is a contract between an insurance company and applicant. Each contract has certain principles of conduct as contracts do not stay in vague and are implemented in the spirit of the law. A credit insurance contract comes into existence when the exporter makes an offer or proposal of a contract and ECGC accepts the proposal. A credit insurance contract should be made with free consent and a valid contract, meaning it must be made by adults and by persons of sound mind. ECGC, India's largest credit insurance company, also provides credit insurance services on four fundamental principles of insurance.

15.4.1 Utmost Good Faith

Any insurance contract is based on the utmost good faith. Hence, both the exporter and ECGC should have faith over each other as trust is the basis of any trade relationship. It is the duty of the exporter to disclose all material facts of the export transaction to ECGC, as any misdeclaration or misrepresentation may lead to the cancellation of the contract.

15.4.2 The Spread of Risk

Under the credit insurance contract, an exporter is required to declare all shipments being made except allowed exception under various kinds of policies of ECGC. ECGC has allowed certain exceptions in respect of transactions made against advance payment and/or a confirmed L/C.

15.4.3 An Exporter Is a Co-insurer

Both the parties of the contract will share the losses as per the clause of the policy; for example, an exporter has to suffer a loss of 10 percent in the Standard Policy of ECGC. ECGC normally pays 80–90 percent of the losses on account of political or commercial risks under claims. An exporter shall be a party to bear some percentage of losses so as to ensure due diligence by him/her in protecting the interest of the business at every stage.

15.4.4 Subrogation Clause

ECGC purses the cases where default or insolvency or any country risks has happened, and it has to pay the exporter under the claim procedure. ECGC acts in close coordination with its counterparts and makes recoveries from such defaulting parties. When such proceeds come into an account of the exporter, he/she is duty-bound to share it proportionately with ECGC, as insurance contracts have underlying principles of good faith and spread of risks.

15.5 Procedure for Making a Claim

An exporter may have to make a claim to ECGC in case of default or insolvency of a foreign buyer, associated country risks and insolvency of the L/C issuing bank. Under any insurance product, the policyholders can claim the risks coverage when any of the risks insured under the policy materializes. If an importer becomes insolvent, the exporter can claim the risk coverage as per the prescribed procedure and period of various polices to ECGC. ECGC also reimburses claims of additional expenses such as the loss due to diversion of vessels, additional freight paid, cargo handling and insurance charges incurred by the exporter. An exporter has to provide the proof of loss due to additional expenses in cases of interruption or diversion of voyage outside India. ECGC has provided the facility of extending the waiting period in cases where long transfer delays are experienced in some countries due to challenging political and socio-economic environment. Further, ECGC can also extend the waiting period and claims for such shipments that might be payable after the expiry of such extended period. It may happen sometimes that the importer refuses to accept the imported goods and also not pay due to quality disputes, delay in shipment and mistrust between trading parties. ECGC considers such claims after the commercial dispute between the parties is resolved and settles claims conditional to obtaining a decree in a court of law in the country of the importer. ECGC can waive off such conditions in cases where it is satisfied that the exporter has taken required steps to minimize the losses and is not at fault. In a general case, the following procedural formalities are required to be undertaken by an exporter to process the claim under credit insurance cover:

1. File the claim with ECGC.
    - Form no. 501 is for claims which are arising as the importer has refused to pay on accepted goods under the D/A or an open account method.
    - Form no. 502 is for claims wherein there is a non-acceptance of goods, or the importer refuses to accept the documents by the buyer.
    - Form no. 503 is for claims which are arising on the account of delay in transfer of funds to India.
2. A letter by the exporter stating the circumstances/particulars of the non-payment, partial payment, additional expense incurred and so on.
3. Copy of the Credit Insurance Policy availed.
4. The credit insurance claim form should be routed through the bank which is handling the export bills of an exporter for the transaction.
5. The claim must be filed within 24 months from the due date of the concerned bills, and ECGC will not entertain any request after this period.
6. The exporter should attach the following documents to support the claim:
    - Certified copy of the export order.
    - Certified copies of invoices.
    - Certified copies of bills of lading.
    - Copies of the correspondence with the buyer.

- In case of insolvency of the buyer, copy of the letter from the official receiver/liquidator admitting the claim.
- Further, in cases of protracted default by the importer, an exporter is required to submit (a) protect note, (b) original of unpaid bills, (c) advice of non-payment received from the bank and (d) copy of the plaintiff if a suit has been filed.

7. When claims are filed for the coverage of losses due to transfer delays, the exporter should submit a certified copy of the payment advice received from the collecting banker indicating the date on which the payment was made by the buyer in the local currency. ECGC verifies that there is a compliance of laid-down procedure under FEMA for the realization of export proceeds. ECGC processes credit insurance claim in Indian rupee only, and the claim proceeds are routed through the bank involved in the realization of export proceeds from abroad.

15.6 Summary

GOI established the ECGC of India Limited in the year 1957 for the purpose of strengthening and boosting the export promotion efforts by covering the risk of exporting on credit. ECGC is essentially an export promotion organization for covering the credit risk so as to increase the exports from the country, functions under the administrative control of the Ministry of Commerce and Industry, Department of Commerce and GOI. As the risk is an integral part of international trade transactions, payments for exports are always open to risks even at the best of times. Interestingly, such risks have assumed large proportions in today's globalized world due to the far-reaching political and economic changes that are sweeping every aspect of the world. An outbreak of war or civil war or political rebellion or public disturbances may block or delay the payment for goods exported, thereby putting the exporter under the dock. A coup or an insurrection may also bring the economic and political system into a halt, and an exporter may face a potential problem. Export payments have been subject to various risks even at the best of times; however, risks have become far greater in today's volatile, uncertain, complex and ambiguous times. The quanta as well as the level of risks have become far higher today due to the far-reaching political and socio-economic changes that are sweeping the world. An outbreak of war or civil war or pandemic, crippling the trade supply chain of a country, region or world economy, may block or delay the payment for goods exported. There are political risks which can be anticipated or predicted if not accurately, with wild guesstimates such as a coup or an insurrection or possibility of civil disobedience but newer waves of biological risks like the outbreak of coronavirus are beyond the comprehension of even best of scientists. Biological hazards like this is an undeclared war on mankind, hampering entire trade supply chain operations of the world economy. Economic challenges like an unfavourable balance of payment may lead a country to impose restrictions on either the import of certain goods or transfer of payments for the goods imported. In order to address such kind of credit risks, ECGC offers a variety of policies to India exporters:

1. ECIE—short-term turnover-based services
   - Shipments Comprehensive Risks (SCR) Policy
   - Small Exporters Policy (SEP)
   - SSP
   - Services policy (SRC)
   - ETP

- Exports (Specific Buyers) Policy (BWP)
- Consignment Exports Policy (Stockholding Agent; CSA)

2. ECIE—short-term exposure-based services
   - BEP
   - IT-enabled Services Policy Single Customer (SITES)
   - SMEs
   - SPP
3. ECIE—medium- and long-term services
   - Construction Works Policy (CWP)
   - Specific Policy for Supply Contract
   - SSP
   - Specific Services Policy
   - L/C confirmation cover

Any insurance is a contract between an insurance company and applicant. Each contract has certain principles of conduct as contracts do not stay in vague and are implemented in the spirit of the law. Fundamental principles of the credit insurance are utmost good faith, the spread of risk, the principle of co-insurer and subrogation clause.

CASE STUDY Application of Concepts of Credit Insurance Policies and ECGC

Mr Bala Subramanyam is the leading exporter of silk items from the historic city of Madurai. This is his family business spanning over four generations. Mr Bala buys raw silk from the domestic market, Karnataka, Telangana and Assam and also imports it from Yunnan, China. Mr Bala has got an export order for the supply of silk stoles from a buyer based at Port of Rotterdam. The following details are furnished to you by Mr Bala vis-à-vis this export order:

1. Name of the seller: Bala Silk Products Company, Madurai, India
2. Name of the buyer: Dresden Import Company, Rotterdam, Netherlands
3. Cargo description: Various silk items under HSN 50
4. Value of order: 5 million euros
5. Port of departure: Tuticorin, Tamil Nadu
6. Port of destination: Rotterdam, Netherlands
7. The final place of destination: Rotterdam, Netherlands
8. Payment mode: Time D/A 90 days
9. The currency of the invoice: Euro
10. Date of shipment: 25 June 2020

Mr Bala has suffered losses worth $1.21 million due to the non-payment or part payment by some buyer. Mr Bala has decided that he will never export unless either payment in advance or confirmed L/C or, in other cases, a system of effective credit protection is put in place. Mr Bala's total turnover was ₹125 crore in 2019.

Questions

1. He consults you to avail an ECGC policy. Guide him which policy of the ECGC is suitable and why.
2. Should Mr Bala opt for turnover-based or exposure-based policy? Explain.
3. What precautions Mr Bala needs to take as due diligence for the compliance of an ECGC policy in this order?
4. Explain to Mr Bala how he can file a claim and fulfil the allied procedure for availing the credit insurance from ECGC, if the buyer does not pay.

Review Exercises

Multiple Choice Questions

1. In which year ECGC was originally founded by GOI?
   a. 1957
   b. 1967
   c. 1955
   d. 1964
2. What was the original name of ECGC?
   a. ERIC
   b. EC&GC
   c. ECGD
   d. ECGO
3. Which of the following is the most popular policy of ECGC?
   a. Standard Policy
   b. SEP
   c. BEP
   d. IT-enabled Policy
4. In which year was ERIC rechristened as EC&GC?
   a. 1964
   b. 1957
   c. 1984
   d. 1965
5. Which of the following is not a turnover-based policy?
   a. SPP
   b. SEP
   c. SSP
   d. Services Policy
6. The turnover limit for availing SEP is
   a. Less than ₹5 crore
   b. More than ₹5 crore
   c. Less than ₹1 crore
   d. Case-to-case basis
7. In which year was EC&GC rechristened as ECGC?
   a. 1984
   b. 1964
   c. 1957
   d. 1991

8. What is the global rank of ECGC as the credit insurer in the world?
   a. 5th
   b. 9th
   c. 15th
   d. 21st
9. The claim of default/insolvency of an export transaction should be filed to ECGC within how many months from the date of default/grace period?
   a. 24 months
   b. 12 months
   c. 18 months
   d. 21 months

Critical Thinking Questions

1. Why is credit risk management considered as an important area in foreign trade? Explain the growing need for credit risk management in foreign trade.
2. What are the functions of ECGC? Elaborate.
3. Critically examine the Standard Policy of ECGC. What are its key features?
4. What are the exposure-based policies? Discuss any one scheme.
5. Write a short note on any two of the following:
   a. SSP
   b. Services Policy (SRC)
   c. ETP
   d. Exports (Specific Buyers) Policy (BWP)
6. Elaborate the principles of credit insurance and claim the procedure of credit insurance.

CHAPTER 16

Duty Drawback Claim Procedure

CHAPTER OBJECTIVES

- To discuss the concept and rationale of duty drawback.
- To explain duty neutralization schemes both pre-export and post-export in India.
- To explain the processing of drawback claims and documentary procedure therein.
- To discuss the process of fixation of brand rates and special brand rates.
- To explain the eligibility, mechanism and restrictions on the processing of drawback claims.

16.1 Introduction

Developing countries in the world economy have been using the duty neutralization schemes to enable their firms to compete in international markets, as these firms operate in a highly taxed and protected economic environment. The prime objective of duty neutralization for exporters of any country is to provide them with a platform to make their products attractive and competitive in international markets. As duty neutralization is aimed at either exemption of remission of duties or taxes on exportable products, the goods of exporters become competitive in international markets, and they are able to sell more, earn more and compete better, thus increasing the size and scale of their export operations. In compliance with the best global practices of neutralizing the incidence of taxes on exportable goods, GOI has also incorporated a dedicated chapter offering pre-export and post-export duty neutralization on exportable goods to Indian exporters. Chapter 4 of FTP 2015–2020 (Figure 16.1) prescribes the detailed policy and procedure therein for neutralization of duties and taxes in the export chain to make Indian goods more attractive and competitive in international markets. Chapter 4 of FTP 2015–2020 is

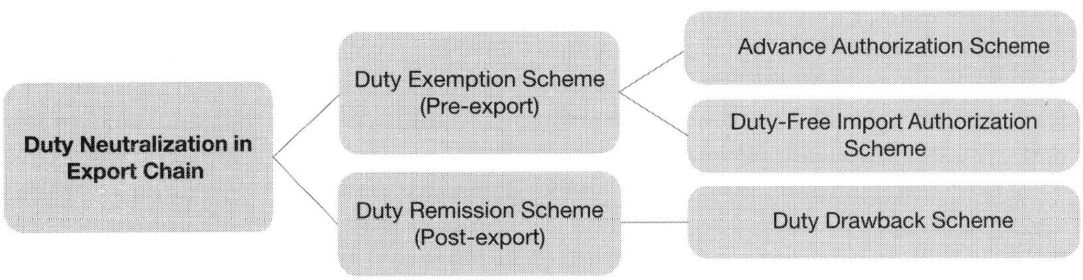

FIGURE 16.1 Duty neutralization in export chain.

Source: Adapted from Chapter 4 Foreign Trade Policy 2015–2020, Director General of Foreign Trade, GOI.

entitled as 'Duty Exemption/Remission Schemes'. Duty exemption is offered at the pre-export stage through two schemes, namely, 'Advance Authorization Scheme' and 'DFIA Scheme'. 'Duty Remission Scheme' offers post-export duty refunds of duties and taxes paid on the exportable goods, this scheme is called as 'Duty Drawback Scheme'. Another scheme entitled 'Duty Entitlement Passbook Scheme' was phased out on 30 September 2012 due to its non-compatibility with WTO rules and increasing complaints of member countries against it causing 'injury' to their exports through 'market price distortions'.

Although the taxes in developed countries are lower due to wider tax base, it is not the case in developing countries where tax rates are usually higher, especially duties on excise, customs and service tax. This makes the products of developing countries priced out in international markets; government from these countries offer their exporters the duty drawback, that is, refunds of taxes and duties paid at the input stage during manufacturing or duty paid on imported goods. The rationale behind providing such export drawbacks is based on the agreed international conventions and international regulations, like the GATT rules, which allow the use of drawbacks for least-developed and developing countries. The rules framed under WTO also justify the rationale of providing duty drawback to an exporter under special and differential treatment clauses as agreed between contracting parties at various areas of trade negotiations.

Duty drawback is the rebate given by GOI, after the export of goods, to an exporter for having paid the duty either on inputs imported after the payment of duty or procured indigenously from an excisable supplier. With the introduction of services, rules are changed to give rebate on tax chargeable for services provided during the course of manufactures of these exportable goods. Only the final exporter can claim the drawback on the material used for the manufacture of export products sourced from several suppliers. In the case of re-import of goods, the drawback can be claimed. Drawback claims can be made only for duties and taxes paid on customs paid on imported inputs plus excise duty paid on indigenous input plus services tax paid on manufactured goods and duty paid on packing material. An exporter cannot claim duty drawback on inputs imported or obtained without the payment of customs or excise duty. In the case of part payment of customs and excise duty, the rebate or refund can be claimed only on the paid part.

16.2 Duty Drawback Defined

Duty drawback is a refund of taxes and duties paid either at the time of imports of goods meant for the export in the same form or after the use or as excise, service tax along with the import duty paid on inputs to be used in exportable products. The essential element for claiming the drawback is that goods must be exported out of India, and duty must have been paid on such used inputs. In case the duty is not paid, the demand for the claim of duty drawback does not exist. Considering this, duty drawback is defined as 'a rebate given by a government on duties or taxes that were paid on imported goods that were used to create other goods or repackaged and exported again'. The Duty Drawback Scheme has been designed and developed to provide relief to exporters on the customs, central excise duties and services tax, which they have paid on the inputs used in the manufacture of an exportable product. There is a global practice of 'goods are exported; taxes are not', and accordingly, the Duty Drawback Scheme is administered in India by CBEC, Ministry of Finance, GOI. A refund of taxes is made in the favour of exporters into their nominated bank account after processing shipping bill/bill of export under claims for duty drawback, a regulatory document that acts as a proof of export. Under the Duty Drawback Scheme, an exporter is given the refunds of taxes paid on inputs of exportable goods to compensate for the burden of duty incidence of customs and central excise on basic inputs such as raw materials, components, intermediates and packing materials used at various stages of production or manufacture of exportable products. No relief of duty drawback is extended to duties suffered on capital goods, fuels and consumables used in relation to the manufacture of the export goods. It may also be noted that no relief of sales tax or octroi or any other indirect tax is given by the way of drawback. The finished stage excise duties paid on the exportable product are also not reimbursed under this scheme, and there are separate provisions for the rebate of such finished stage duties under the Central Excises and Salt Act, 1944, and Central Excise Rules, 2002. In summary, it can be said that

> The term drawback is applied to a certain amount of duties of Customs/Central excise, sometimes the whole, sometimes only a part remitted or paid by Government on the exportation of the commodities on which they were levied. To entitle goods to drawback, they must be exported to a foreign port, the object of the relief afforded by the Drawback being to enable the goods to be disposed of in the foreign market as if they had never been taxed at all. For Customs purpose drawback means the refund of duty of customs and duty of Central Excise that are chargeable on imported and indigenous materials used in the manufacture of Exported goods.[1]

It is mandatory to export the goods outside India so as to claim the refunds of such duties and taxes paid either at the time of imports of goods for re-export or having used them as inputs, raw material and components in the manufacture of goods meant for export to a place outside India.

Duty drawbacks help in reducing and eliminating the impact of duties paid by the exporter on locally sourced inputs, imported intermediates and raw materials on which either the excise or customs duty has been paid by the exporter, and such inputs, intermediates and raw materials are used in processing, producing and manufacturing the exportable products. The main motive behind such policy mechanisms by the country is to promote exports by partially or fully exempting or remitting the duty paid by exporters to provide them with the protection with anti-trade bias. Such incentives and benefits to the exporter under duty drawback systems are often justified in developing and least-developed countries as it helps them compete in the international market by neutralizing the impact of high tariffs paid on inputs, intermediates and raw materials of the exportable product, thereby increasing export competitiveness in international markets. For an emerging country like India, Duty Drawback Scheme is an important instrument to expand and diversify its foreign trade by reducing the landed prices of its exportable products in international markets as exporters can sell their goods at lower prices due to the duty neutralization through this scheme. The positive and negative aspects of the Duty Drawback Scheme are listed in Figure 16.2.

In the changing geo-economics realities under WTO, which has become a harbinger of free trade, the major question is that Is the drawback still considered a predetermined policy variable in export promotion of India? The answer to this is the harmonization of India's tax structure through GST which will reduce its anti-trade bias for both domestic and international trade and help the exporter(s) to understand better ways to neutralize the incidence of taxes in the export chain.

[1] Excerpted from CBEC (2014).

FIGURE 16.2 Positive and negative aspects of duty drawback.

16.3 Regulatory Framework for Duty Drawback

Regulatory provisions under the Customs Act, 1962, mandate two types of duty drawback: the *first* one is under Section 74 of the Customs Act, 1962, which allows the drawback (Figure 16.3) of duty paid on goods originally imported on the payment of duty and subsequently re-exported out of India. An exporter can claim back the refund of the duty paid at the time of the export by filing 'shipping bill/bill of export under the claim of the duty drawback' at the time of exports. The duty drawback is given on basic inputs such as raw materials, components, intermediates and packing materials used at various stages of production or manufacture of exportable goods. The duty drawback is never allowed for

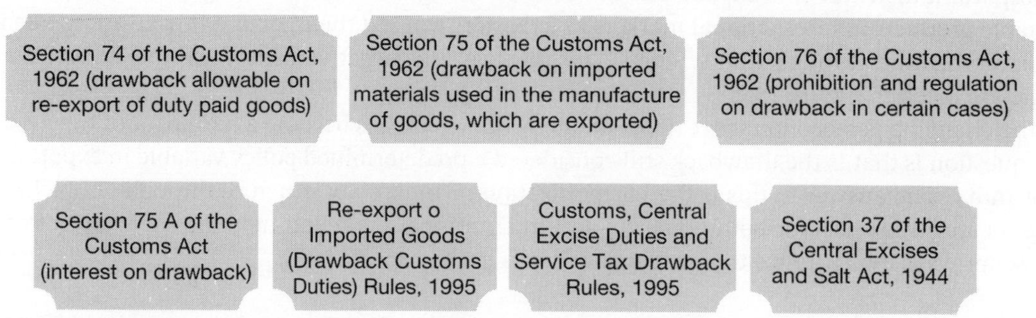

FIGURE 16.3 Regulatory framework of duty drawback in India.

Source: Author compilation of legislative references.

capital goods, fuels and consumables used in relation to the manufacture of the exportable goods. Additionally, no relief of value-added tax (sales tax) or octroi or any other direct or indirect tax imposed by the state government is given by the way of the drawback as these taxes are collected by the state government and it does not allow the refund of such taxes paid following the constitutional distribution of power between the centre and states which categorizes export and import as central under the Seventh Schedule to the Constitution of India. The finished stage of excise duties on the exportable goods is also not allowed as it is separately covered under Rules 18 and 19 of Central Excise Rules, 2002, and Central Excises and Salt Act, 1944; hence, it is separately exempted or rebated under the said rules.

There are rules governing the duty drawback procedure for such claims which are called Re-export of Imported Goods (Drawback of Customs Duties) Rules, 1995. These rules prescribe the refund of paid duty for re-export of goods without putting into use and with use. The rate of the drawback keeps on sliding 'on-period', and the maximum period allowed for the drawback is two years only. The *second* type of drawback (Figure 16.4) is processed under Section 75 of the Customs Act, 1962, and is given on manufactured goods only. This type of claim arises when goods are manufactured out of excisable material or imported material or partially excisable and partially imported material. The procedure governing the claim under Section 75 of the Customs Act is prescribed under Customs, Central Excise and Service Tax Duty Drawback Rules, 1995. For the fixation of rates under this category, there is 'directorate of drawback' which coordinates with exporters, industry associations and export promotion councils for the preparation of drawback schedule which is also known as 'all industry rates (AIRs)' and claims are processed by the respective customs house(s) and Central Excise Commissionerate.

The rates of drawback under Section 75 of the Customs Act are announced in the 'drawback schedule' which is prepared by a directorate of duty drawback every year after the budget, usually within three months from date of implementation of the budget. The rates of drawback are announced by CBEC, Department of Revenue, GOI, for various categories of goods as prescribed in ITC(HS) nomenclature. The drawback schedule is appended to Customs, Central Excise and Service Tax (Duty Drawback) Rules, 1995, for implementation and execution by various customs houses in India. The drawback schedule is also known as 'AIRs' of drawback and is worked out on the basis of broad averages of consumption of inputs, duties suffered, the quantity of wastage, FOB prices of the export products and so on by an appointed committee of CBEC. AIRs primarily aim at compensating the exporters for the average incidence of customs, central excise duties and service tax, which the exporter has suffered on the inputs and intermediate being used in his/her manufacture of exportable products.

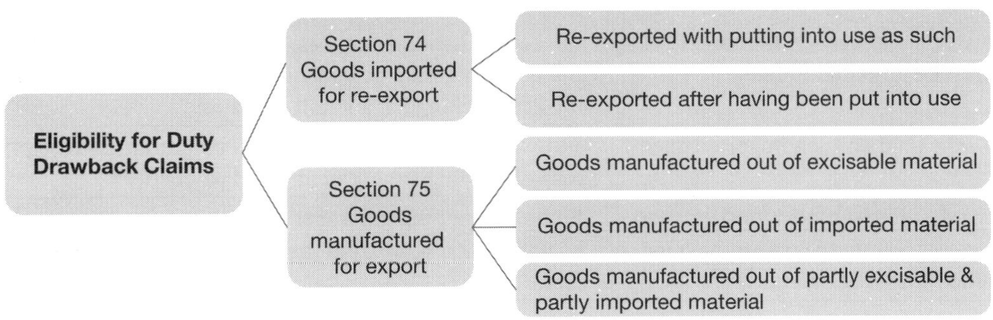

FIGURE 16.4 Eligibility for duty drawback claims.

Source: Adapted from Customs Act, 1962.

The All Industry Rates are prescribed after factoring in the Input Tax Credit of GST which is separately claimed by a business firm. Hence, the duties to be factored in fixation of All Industry Rates are primarily the customs duties suffered in the import value chain plus the incidence of excise duties which is applicable to only six industries, with the introduction of GST post 2017.

For the tariff lines for which AIRs are not declared or published, an exporter can apply for 'brand rates' within 30 days from the date of announcement of such rates by CBEC. The exporter should apply with supporting documents clearly explaining the cost sheet of his/her goods, duties suffered, allowed wastage in the production, standard inputs norms and tentative FOB value of goods, duly authenticated, verified and signed by the chartered certified engineer/certified cost and work accountant/chartered accountant to enable the committee to take the appropriate decision on time. Brand rate of duty drawback is granted in terms of Rules 6 of the Customs, Central Excise Duties and Service Tax Drawback Rules, 1995, in cases where the export product does not have any AIR or duty drawback rate. In cases where the exporter is not satisfied with AIRs and he/she feels that rates are lower than what actual duty he/she has suffered to manufacture the goods, an exporter can apply for 'special brand rates' under the Rule 7 of Customs, Central Excise Duties and Service Tax Drawback Rules, 1995. There are prescribed norms for eligibility to apply for special brand rates which is when the AIRs are less than 80 percent of the actual duties suffered in the manufacture of the export goods. Disbursal of duty drawback rates is done by the customs houses and Central Excise Commissionerates set-up all over the country.

16.4 Drawback under Section 74: Policy and Procedure

The drawback under Section 74 of the Customs Act, 1962, is processed when goods are imported and subsequently exported to a place outside India. There are two types of drawback under this category. The first is when goods are exported within three months without putting into use, and the second is when goods are used and subsequently exported. Table 16.1 lists the essential elements necessary for claiming the duty drawback along with documentary proof for an exporter.

TABLE 16.1 Essential Elements along with Documentary Evidence for Claiming Drawback under Section 74 of the Customs Act, 1962

Essential Elements	Documentary Evidence
Goods must be imported to India.	Bill of entry for home consumption, import general manifest, invoice, packing list and bill of lading.
Duty must be paid on such imported goods.	TR-6 Challan, GAR-7 Challan and bank transfer receipts in case of online banking/credit card payment.
The goods should be entered for the export within two years from the date of payment of duty on their importation.	Filing of shipping bill under the claim of duty drawback must be within two years from the date of payment of import duty.
Goods can be identified as goods imported.	The packing list as supplied by the importer at the time of import should match with packing list submitted by the exporter at the time of export.

Essential Elements	Documentary Evidence
Goods are capable of being identified as goods imported.	The prime proof is packing list, and additional proofs are certificate of inspection/certificate of export conformity, certificate of origin, certificate of insurance, bill of lading and commercial invoice.
The goods must actually be re-exported to any place outside India.	Shipping bill/bill of export with 'Let Export Order' is a prime proof along with export general manifest/exit outward order of customs.
The market price of such goods must not be less than the amount of drawback claimed.	As drawback rates slide periodically, customs check the market price of goods and match it with the commercial invoice; no claim is processed if the amount of drawback claims is higher than the market price of goods.
There must be a positive foreign exchange inflow into the country, i.e., India.	Customs checks the CIF value of imported goods from bill of entry/commercial invoice and match it with FOB value as indicated at shipping bill/commercial invoice for the export by an exporter; no claim is processed if the CIF value is higher than FOB value as it does not result in positive foreign exchange inflow into the country.
The amount of drawback should not be less than ₹50 as per Section 76 (1)(c) of the Customs Act.	Drawback rules mandate that no claim will be processed if the drawback per shipping bill is less than ₹50.

Under Section 74 of the Customs Act, 1962, two types of cases are covered. The *first* is when goods are imported and re-exported without putting into use, the amount of drawback shall be 98 percent of the duty paid by the exporter, that is, 98 percent of the actual duty paid shall be refunded by customs at the time of export which must be within three months from the date of duty payments.

In the *second* case, when the imported goods are exported after having been taken for use, the exporter can claim the drawback on such imported goods within two years from the date of the import clearance. Under such cases, the percentage of duty is refunded according to the period between the date of clearance for home consumption, that is, the date of duty payment on imported goods and the date when the goods are placed under customs control for exports, that is, filling of shipping bill/bill of export under the claim for duty drawback. The percentage of duty drawback is notified under 'Notification No. 19/65—Customs, dated 6 February 1965' as amended from time to time and the sliding rate of drawback are shown in Figure 16.5.

Drawback claims under Section 74 of the Customs Act are now being processed manually only as the customs official has to match the old set of trade documents (import documents) with that of the new set of trade documents (submitted at the time of the export), and this can happen only with manual processing of the shipping bill/bill of exports under claims for the duty drawback. In order to make a claim, an exporter has to file a shipping bill/bill of export under Section 50 of the Customs Act which is appraised under Section 51 of the Customs Act by customs officials, and if found in compliance with requisite documents, then the LEO is given by Indian customs. To supplement the details as forwarded by the exporter in the shipping bill/bill of exports, customs officials carry out the physical examination and identification of goods. Customs officials forward such appraised trade documents

Sliding Rates of Duty Drawback for Imported Goods, Re-exported after Having Been Taken for Use within 18 Months

- Drawback shall be 95 percent of duty paid if goods are re-exported within three months from the date of duty payments at the time of import
- Drawback shall be 85 percent of duty paid if goods are re-exported within six months from the date of duty payments at the time of import
- Drawback shall be 75 percent of duty paid if goods are re-exported within nine months from the date of duty payments at the time of import
- Drawback shall be 70 percent of duty paid if goods are re-exported within 12 months from the date of duty payments at the time of import
- Drawback shall be 65 percent of duty paid if goods are re-exported within 15 months from the date of duty payments at the time of import
- Drawback shall be 60 percent of duty paid if goods are re-exported within 18 months from the date of duty payments at the time of import

Sliding Rates of Duty Drawback for Imported Goods, Re-exported after Having Been Taken for Use after 18 Months but till 24 Months with Permission of Customs

- At satisfaction of chief commissioner of customs that an exporter cannot export because of reasons which are beyond his/her control (force majeure), he/she can extend maximum two permission each of three months to an exporter for re-export
- Drawback shall be 55 percent of duty paid if goods are re-exported within 21 months from the date of duty payments at the time of import
- Drawback shall be 50 percent of duty paid if goods are re-exported within 24 months from the date of duty payments at the time of import
- No drawback shall be processed, irrespective of reasons, after two years of import clearance of goods imported even if re-exported

FIGURE 16.5 Rates of duty drawback on re-export of imported goods under Section 74.

Source: Duty Drawback (Custom Duties) Rules, 1995, Central Board of Excise & Customs, Government of India.

for the disbursal subject to documentary compliance as mandated under Re-export of Imported Material (Drawback of Customs Duties) Rules, 1995. Concerned officers in the drawback division will issue either an acknowledgement of receipt of trade documents which means the claim is under process for the disbursal or a deficiency memo to an exporter, which clearly indicates the additional required documents for processing the drawback claim. The drawback claims must be disbursed within three months from the date of acknowledgement; otherwise, an exporter is entitled to interest rates as prescribed, which is 7 percent as of now unless the chief commissioner of customs may extend the period of such disbursals. An exporter has to file the documents mentioned in Figure 16.6 for processing drawback claims under Section 74 of the Customs Act, 1962.

For claiming a drawback claim on the export of goods exported as baggage under Section 74, the exporter should file the formal declaration with customs officials that he/she wishes to take the said baggage to a place outside, which he/she had brought as passenger baggage while arriving in India. Customs officials will consider the claim if the duty has been paid at the time of import, subject to other procedural compliance as discussed above in processing the claim under Section 74 for the duty drawback. Passengers claiming duty drawback of baggage cargo must furnish the shipping bill/bill of exports under the claim of duty drawback with the superintendent of customs at the airport, land customs station and maritime port and produce the import clearance documents along with the proof

Documents for Export Clearance & Drawback Processing

- Triplicate copy of the shipping bill bearing examination report recorded by the proper officer of the customs at the time of export
- Export invoice
- Packing list
- Certificate of inspection if mandated
- Certificate of insurance
- GATT declaration

Supplementary Documents to Support Claims under Section 74

- Copy of the bill of entry or any other prescribed documents against which goods were cleared for importation
- Import invoice
- Evidence of payment of the duty paid at the time of importation of goods, that is, TR-6 Challan or GAR-7 as prescribed under GOI rules
- Permission from RBI for re-exports of goods, wherever necessary
- Import packing list
- Copy of the bill of lading or airway bill or any other transport document
- Any other documents as may be specified in the deficiency memo

FIGURE 16.6 Documentation for the claim of duty drawback under Section 74.

Source: Duty Drawback (Custom Duties) Rules, 1995, Custom Act, 1962 and Custom Manual, 2018.

of duty payment. The goods are examined physically by the superintendent of customs who matches the documentary compliance, and on being satisfied with the 'identity of the goods', he/she will permit the export of baggage cargo under the claim of duty drawback. Superintendent of customs will mark necessary entries on the shipping bill/bill of export for granting the rate of the duty drawback considering the period from the date of imports to the date of exports of such baggage cargo. The duplicate copy of the declaration-cum-examination report along with the duty payment document is returned to the passenger, and the original copy is transferred to the assistant/deputy commissioner of the drawback section. In case the drawback payment is to be made to a person other than the passenger, an authority letter as included in the declaration form should be furnished by such passenger duly authenticated in presence of the superintendent of customs. The passenger claiming such drawback on baggage cargo is also required to give the receipt of drawback claim on a pre-receipted revenue stamp to the superintendent of customs. The superintendent of customs forwards these documents to the office of the assistant/deputy commissioner of customs (drawback section), which issues the cheque/bank transfer in favour of the passenger or his/her authorized agent after processing drawback claims.

In case of processing the drawback claim when goods are exported by post, an exporter can claim the duty drawback by clearly indicating, in bold letters on the outer packet of the exportable goods, 'Drawback for Export' above the name and address of the consignee/importer. An exporter should do the final packing of goods in the presence of customs officials posted at the foreign post office where such goods are transported for onward shipment for exports. An exporter should file a shipping bill/bill of exports as prescribed and deliver it to customs postal authorities along with the exportable parcel or package. An exporter must file other necessary declaration as mandated along with quadruplicate copies of the shipping bill/bill of export under the claim of duty drawback. The date of receipt of the shipping bill/bill of exports by customs postal authorities along with other prescribed forms shall be deemed to be the date of filing the drawback claim by the exporter. Customs postal officials usually acknowledge the receipt of such filled in documents, and in case documents are incomplete, they issue a deficiency memo to an exporter normally within 15 days of receipt of such documents by custom postal authorities. The exporter should comply with such deficiencies through additional and supplementary documents as demanded by customs within 30 days or earlier. The date for the resubmission of trade documents to customs postal authorities will be revised, and in compliance, customs will process the drawback claim within three months from the date of receipt of such documents from the exporter.

To claim the drawback under Section 74, an exporter must export such imported goods within two years from the date of payment of duty. Usually, claims are processed with the sliding rate of drawback up to 18 months. An exporter can seek maximum two extensions of three months each if he/she proves to the chief commissioner of customs the reasons that have prevented him/her to export and that were beyond his/her control. The time limit must be computed from the 'date of payment of duty' up to the 'date of entry of goods for export' under Section 50 of the Customs Act, 1962. The duty drawback is granted in all cases whether exported goods are appraised in normally prescribed procedure under Section 51 for export through land/sea/air or as baggage under Section 77 and as export through courier/post/E-commerce as prescribed under section 83 of the Customs Act, 1962. A claim for drawback must be filed as per the procedure mandated under Rule 5 of Re-export of Imported Goods (Drawback of Customs Duties) Rules, 1995 and a number of other public notices and circulars issued by customs houses. The time limit for filing the claim is three months from the date of 'LEO'. If there are reasons which are beyond the control of an exporter, preventing him/her from filing such claim within three months, the assistant commissioner of customs can relax the time limit by another three months.

16.5 Drawback under Section 75: Policy and Procedure

As discussed above, the drawback under Section 75 is given on goods which are manufactured in India by either using imported or excisable material as an input or using both imported and excisable material as an input in exportable goods. With the introduction of service tax in India, the scope of rules governing the drawback under Section 75 has been extended, and now, it also covers the incidence of services tax paid on manufactured goods in India with either indigenous or imported duty paid inputs and other intermediates including raw materials. Drawback rates under this category are decided in the drawback schedule, which is published by CBEC, Department of Revenue and GOI usually three months after the budget.

These are also called as AIRs and are announced for various categories of goods as classified under HS of trade nomenclature. AIRs of the drawback are fixed under Rule 3 of Customs, Central Excise Duties and Services Tax Drawback Rules, 1995, and can be amended or revised by the government under Rule 4 of the said rules. AIRs are applicable to both the manufacturer and merchant exporter and are worked out basis broad averages of consumption of inputs, duties suffered by exporters, the quantity of wastage involved in the processing, production and manufacturing of exportable products, FOB prices of the export products and so on. The essential eligibility for claiming the drawback rates is that goods must be manufactured in India. Similarly, drawback rates are not admissible in the cases mentioned in Figure 16.7, except where otherwise specifically authorized to manufacturer exporters under Section 75.

- Export of goods under discharge of Advance Authorization Scheme or Duty Free Import Authorizations Scheme issued under Duty Exemption Scheme of FTP 2015–2020.
- Manufactured partly or wholly in the bond under Section 65 of the Customs Act, 1962.
- Exported by a unit licenced under any 100% export-oriented schemes (100% EOU/EHTP/STP/agriculture/aquaculture/ etc.).
- Exported by a unit situated in a free trade zone/export processing zones.
- Manufactured and exported in terms of Rule 12 (1)(a) of the Central Excise Rules, 1944.
- Manufactured and exported in terms of Rule 13 (1)(a) of the Central Excises Rules, 1944.
- Manufactured and exported availing the facility under the import and export passbook schemes of the relevant EXIM policy.

FIGURE 16.7 Cases of inadmissibility of duty drawbacks under Section 75.

Source: Adapted from Duty Drawback (Custom Duties) Rules, 1995 and Custom Manual 2018.

The restrictions as mentioned in the above clauses are not applicable where the payment of drawback at a particular rate or amount has been specifically authorized thereunder any sub-serial number in the all industry table subject to such terms and conditions as may be specified in FTP and other notifications.

In case AIRs for any ITC code of harmonized nomenclature are not specified and available in the drawback schedule, an exporter can approach the directorate of the drawback for fixing the 'brand rates'. Brand rates of the duty drawback are fixed under Rule 6 of Customs, Central Excise and Service Tax (Duty Drawback) Rules, 1995, for a specific manufacturer exporter. Even if AIRs are specified and available in the drawback schedule for a particular and if the manufacturer observes that he/she has suffered a higher incidence of duties for manufacturing these goods, such manufacturer can apply for 'special brand rates' under Rule 7 of the said rules. For the fixation of brand rates, the manufacturer has to submit the application to the directorate of the drawback of CBEC within 30 days of the publication of the drawback schedule, which is published usually three months after the budget comes into force each year. The exporter can keep on exporting by filing the claim for the duty drawback subject to the fixation of brand rates. An exporter has to prove his/her claim for higher rates of drawback by supporting evidence such as duties suffered on inputs, value chain of inputs, specific reasons for the higher incidence of duties along with the application and other data in duplicate to the 'Directorate of the Drawback' with copies to the concerned Central Excise Commissionerates or the custom house. The brand rates are fixed by the commissioner of the directorate of the drawback on the basis of a report sent by the jurisdictional Commissionerate after the verification of data of duties suffered by the manufacturer exporter. The following are the cases when an exporter can apply for special brand rates of the duty drawback.

The rates of drawback fixed as 'AIRs' or 'brand rates' or 'special brand rates' are always a percentage of 'FOB' value of goods. If an exporter has negotiated any other INCOTERMS for sharing of responsibilities with an importer, customs will process the duty drawback claim only on the FOB value of goods. For example, if the pricing of goods is on the CIF basis, the insurance and freight bills are required to be produced to arrive at the FOB value, and it is the duty of an exporter to submit the required document, otherwise drawback directorate will deduct the 21.125 percent as the cost of freight and insurance (20% freight and 1.125% insurance) from sales contract falling under Group C and D of INCOTERMS rules. The rates are operative in terms of Section 16, read with Section 51 of the Customs Act, which defines both the applicable rates of duties for export goods and 'LEO' given by the appraiser. The AIRs of the drawback are payable subject to the restrictions and prohibitions mentioned in the General Notes of the Drawback Schedule.

With the introduction of e-commerce portal of CBEC entitled as 'ICEGATE', claims are now processed online in 95 percent of the cases. For claiming the drawback under Section 75, an exporter is required to file a 'shipping bill under the claim of duty drawback' in the prescribed format as required under Rule 13 along with the necessary declaration. The goods after the assessment are examined by the officers posted in the examination shed as required for each individual case. The examination report will indicate the nature of goods in terms of the drawback schedule for the classification and application of the correct rate. Samples may have to be drawn for testing by a lab in respect of chemicals, synthetic fabrics and so on as specified from time to time to confirm the declarations in the export documents. The triplicate copy of the drawback shipping bill which contains the examination report is the claim copy. Figure 16.8 shows the supporting documents an exporter must submit for processing the drawback claim.

The claims should be filed in the manner prescribed under Rule 13—read the public notices issued by the custom houses. The time limit for filing the claim is three months from the date of LEO. If the exporter is prevented by a sufficient cause from filing the claims within three months, then the assistant commissioner of customs can relax the time limit by three months, and the commissioner of customs can relax the time limit for a period of nine months. The claims are settled and passed by the

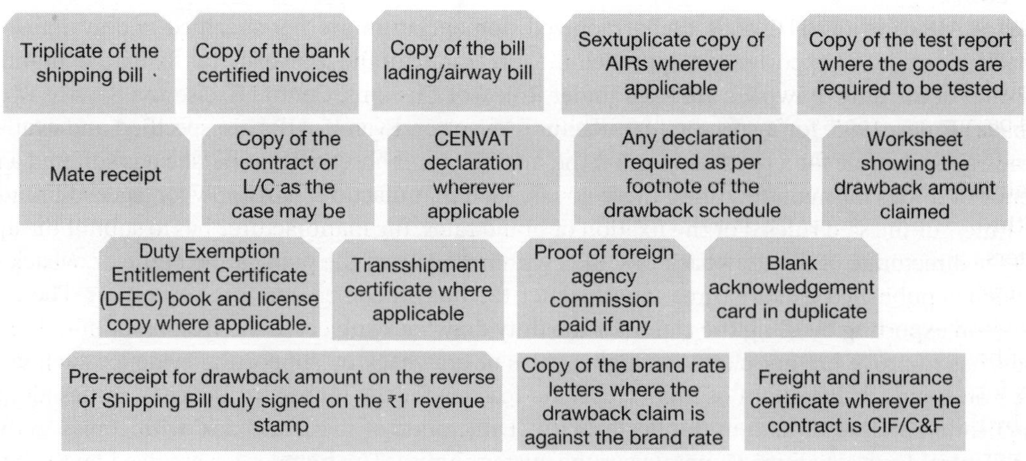

FIGURE 16.8 Supporting documents that an exporter must submit for processing of drawback claim.

Source: Duty Drawback (Custom Duties) Rules, 1995.

appraiser if the amount sanctioned is below ₹100,000, and by the assistant commissioner if the amount of drawback exceeds ₹100,000. Higher level officers may get involved if the amount of the duty drawback exceeds from the prescribed amount so as to minimize the scope of the revenue loss to the nation. After pre-audit of the duty drawback claims, funds are transferred to the core banking account of an exporter. Claims are usually processed within 30 days from the date of acknowledgement of receipt of documents failing which an exporter is entitled to interest rates at the rate of 7 percent per annum. Rule 16 of the Drawback Rules empowers the department to recover any erroneous payment of drawback without any time limit and can initiate recovery proceedings under Section 142 of the Customs Act, 1962. If the excess claim has been processed, and CBEC seeks a refund of such exceeded claim, an exporter should remit the exceeded claim within 15 days from the receipt of such communication failing which he/she will be liable to pay the interest at the rate of 18 percent to CBEC. If an exporter is not satisfied with the drawback claim, that is, if the claim amount is less than the filed amount, an exporter can file a supplementary claim in the prescribed format under Rule 15 of the Drawback Rules, 1995. The time limit for filing the supplementary claim is three months from the date of the original settlement. Figure 16.9 depicts the step-by-step mechanism of processing drawback claims under Section 75 of the Customs Act, 1962.

An exporter should be careful while filing the documents as he/she has to make it clear that whether the drawback claims should be processed along with the excise duty or he/she has already claimed the CENVAT input credit on such manufactured goods meant for exports. Hence, exporters should process the claims correctly so as to enable the EDI system to process the claim correctly and on time. If the relevant declarations are not filed along with the shipping bill, then the EDI system will not process the drawback claims; hence, exporters are advised to file the declaration along with shipping bills. After the actual export of the goods, the drawback claims will be processed through the system on the first-come, first-served basis. The steamer agents/airlines will transfer the EGM electronically to the system so that the physical export of goods is confirmed. The system will process the claims only on the receipt of EGM. The status of shipping bills and sanction of drawback claim can be ascertained from the query counter set up at the service centre. If any query has been raised or the deficiency has been noticed, the same will be shown on the terminal provided there. The exporter or his/her authorized representative may obtain a printout of the query/deficiency from the service centre if he/she so desires. The claim will come in the queue of the system as soon as the reply is entered. Shipping bills in respect of goods under the claim for the drawback against brand rates would also be processed in the same manner, except that the drawback would be sanctioned only after the original brand letter is produced to the assistant commissioner (export) and is entered in the system. The exporter should specify the S.S No 98.01 for such provisional claim. All the claims sanctioned on a particular day will be enumerated in a scroll and transferred to the nominated bank through the system. The bank will credit the drawback amount in the respective accounts of the exporters on the next day. The bank will send a fortnightly statement to the exporters of such credits made in their accounts.

For claiming drawback on goods exported by post, the exporter is required to file his/her claim at the time of booking parcel with the postal authorities in the form prescribed in the rules. The date of receipt of this form from the postal authorities by the customs authorities shall be treated as the date of filing claim by the exporter for the purpose of Section 75 A of the Customs Act. Thus, the drawback is paid to the exporter within 30 days from the date of receipt of the claim from the postal authorities. On receipt of the claim form, the intimation is to be given to the exporter. When the claim form is incomplete, a deficiency memo is issued within 15 days of its receipt from the postal authorities. The exporter can

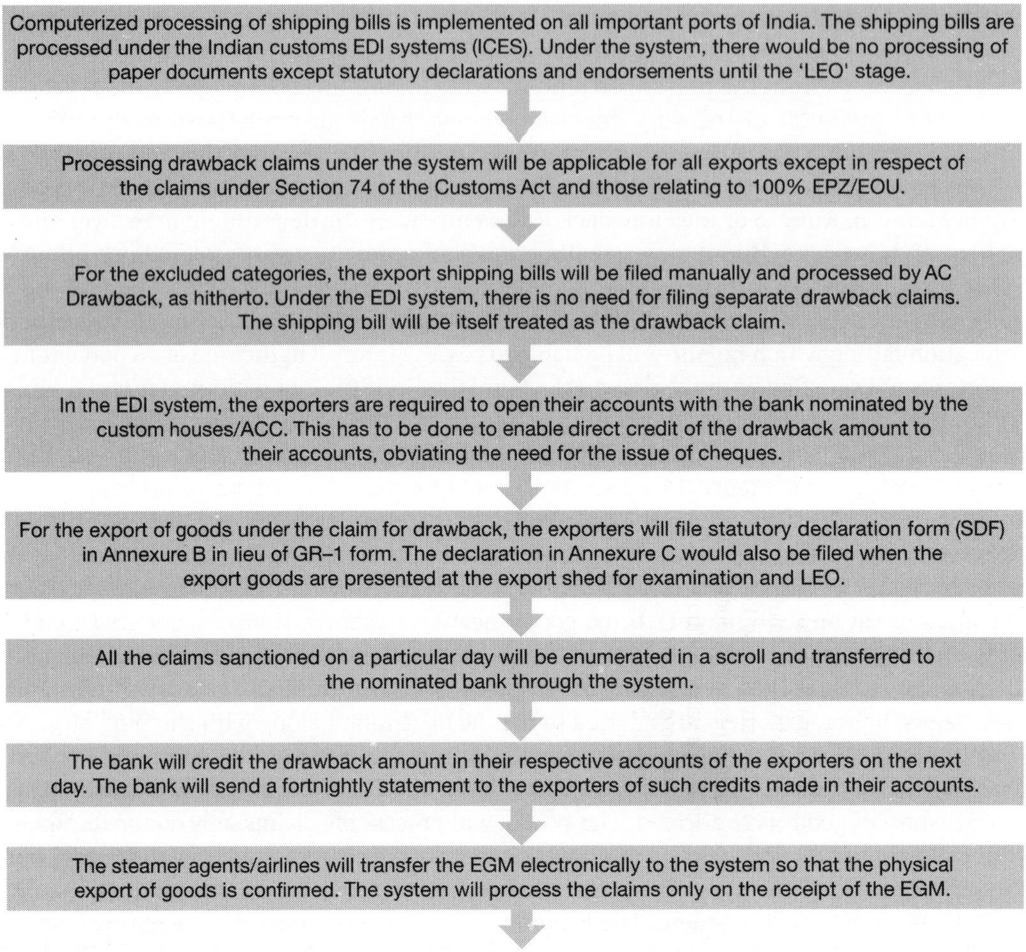

FIGURE 16.9 Step-by-step mechanism of processing drawback claims under Section 75 of Customs Act, 1962.

Source: Custom Manual, Central Board of Indirect Taxes.

resubmit this form after compliance with deficiencies within a period of 30 days. If such a claim is found to be in order, the same is acknowledged and the period of 30 days for the payment of drawback in terms of Section 75 in such cases shall commence from the date of such acknowledgement. Customs, Central Excise and Service Tax Drawback Rules, 1995, specifies the restrictions mentioned in Figure 16.10 on the grant of drawback under Section 75 on the export of manufactured goods.

16.5.1 Fixation of Brand Rates under Simplified Scheme

This scheme envisages reimbursement of customs and central excise duties suffered on inputs used in the manufacture and packing of finished export products. The brand rates are determined for specific export products exported by specific exporters.

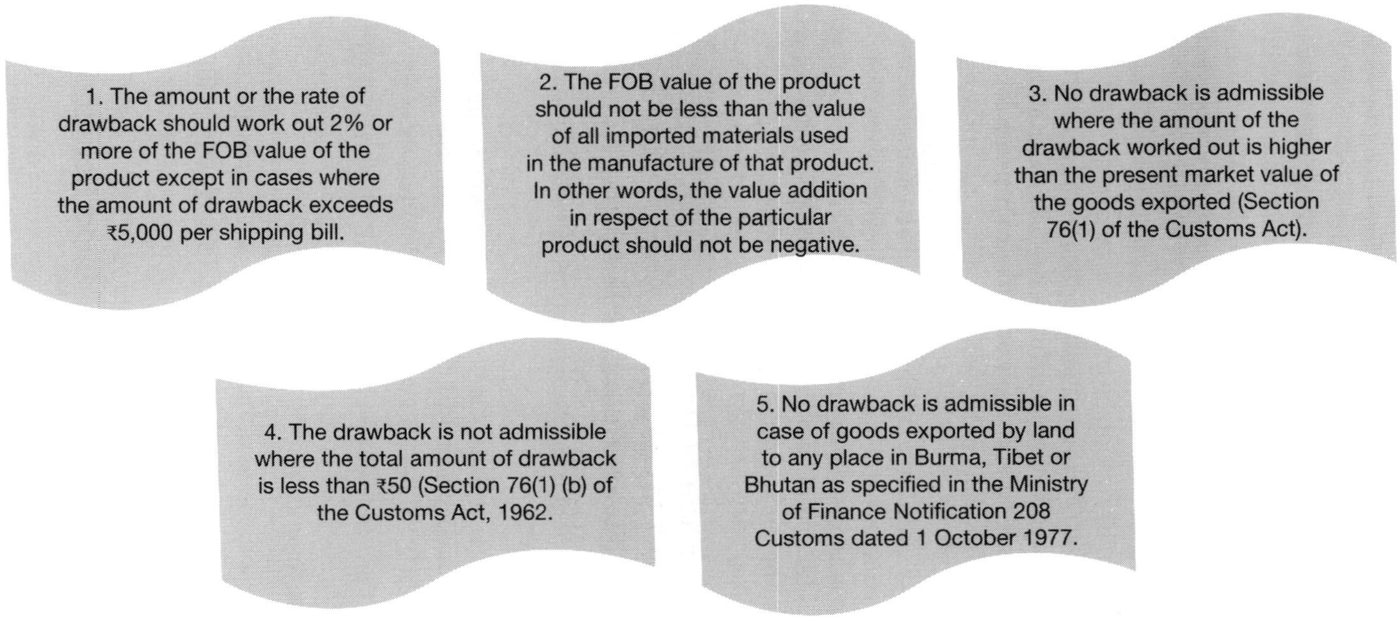

FIGURE 16.10 Cases of inadmissibility of duty drawback under Section 75 of the Customs Act, 1962.

Source: Custom Manual 2018, CBIC, GOI.

The simplified Brand Rate Fixation scheme will be available to all manufacturers—exporters who have regular production of the product for which the brand rate is being sought and who are corporate bodies having a detailed accounting system, which is normally subject to statutory audit under the company law.

Under this procedure, the manufacturer exporter, including those who have exported through the trading houses or star trading houses, has to simply file his/her brand rate application in a prescribed pro forma along with an indemnity bond. The data will have to be supported by a certificate from an independent chartered engineer, chartered accountant/cost accountant in relation to the data furnished in Statements I, II and III submitted along with the application. Taking into account the data, the directorate of drawback will fix the brand rates without insisting upon the pre-verification. The data submitted will, however, be subject to post-verification by the department, and the applicant should also take steps to assist and ensure quick post-verification. If post-verification reveals that the data furnished was incorrect in any way, then the brand rates will be suitably revised, and the applicant has to pay back any excess amount claimed. Furthermore, if the applicant fails to arrange for the post-verification of data within three months, the facility under the scheme will be withdrawn for his/her subsequent application.

The request for the extension of time limit for filing an application for the brand rate under Rules 6 and 7 of the drawback rules, the inclusion of subsequent shipments in the brand rate letter, an extension of the validity period of the brand rate letter and/or quantity enhancement can be considered with the drawback directorate under special circumstances. For details, see guidelines for the fixation of brand rates under simplified and normal procedure.

16.5.2 Application for Fixation of Drawback Rates under Rule 6 (1A) of Brand Rate or Rule 7 (1) of Special Brand Rate of Customs and Central Excise Drawback Rules, 1995 (under Normal Scheme)[2]

Statement DBK I: This is a statement of consumption norms of various inputs and should be certified by an independent chartered engineer.

Statement of DBK II: Direct imports of materials/components made by the manufacturer and foreign materials obtained locally by the manufacturer during the period commencing three months prior to the date of shipment/first shipment up to the date application for manufacture of the export product.

Statement DBK II A: Details of procurement relating to stock of imported materials as on commencement date (three months prior to the date of shipment/first shipment) based on the first-in, first-out (FIFO) principle required for the manufacture of the export product.

Statement DBK III: Materials/components of Indian origin obtained by the manufacturer during the period commencing three months period to the date of shipments/first shipment up to the date of application of the manufacture of the export product.

Statement DBK III A: Details of procurements relating to stocks of indigenous materials as on commencement date (the date three months period to the date of shipment/first shipment based on FIFO principle) required for the manufacture of the export product.

[2] http://customsmangalore.gov.in/duty-draw-back.htm (accessed on 10 May 2023).

16.6 Summary

Developing countries in the world economy have been using the duty neutralization schemes so as to enable their firms to compete in international markets as these firms operate in highly taxed and protected economic environment. The prime objective of duty neutralization for exporters of any country is to provide them a platform so as to make their products attractive and competitive in international markets. As duty neutralization is aimed at either exemption of remission of duties and taxes on exportable products, the goods of exporters become competitive in international markets and they are able to sell more, earn more and compete better, thus increasing in size and scale their export operations.

Duty drawback is the rebate given by government of India, after the exports of goods, to an exporter for having paid the duty either on inputs imported after payment of duty or procured indigenously from an excisable supplier. With introduction of services, rules are changed to give the rebate of tax chargeable for services provided during the course of manufactures of these exportable goods. Only final exporter can claim the drawback on material used for the manufacture of export products sourced from several suppliers. In case of re-import of goods, the drawback can be claimed. Drawback claims can be made only for duties and taxes paid on customs paid on imported inputs plus excise duty paid on indigenous input plus services tax paid on manufactured goods and duty paid on packing material. An exporter cannot claim duty drawback on inputs imported or obtained without payment of customs or excise duty. In case of part payment of customs and excise duty, rebate or refund can be claimed only on the paid part.

Drawback claims under Section 74 of the Customs Act are now being processed manually only as customs official has to match the old set of trade documents (import documents) with that of new set of trade documents (submitted at the time of export), and this can happen only with manual processing of shipping bill/ bill of exports under claims for duty drawback. In order to make a claim, an exporter has to file a shipping bill/bill of export under section 50 of Customs Act which is appraised under section 51 of Customs Act by customs officials and if found in compliance with requisite documents, let export order is given by Indian Customs. To supplement the details as forwarded by exporter in shipping bill/ bill of exports, customs officials carry out the physical examination and identification of goods.

Drawback under 75 is given on goods which are manufactured in India either with use of imported material or excisable material as an input or using both imported and excisable material as an input in exportable goods. With introduction of Service Tax in India, the scope of rules governing the drawback under section 75 has been extended and now it also covers the incidence of services tax paid on manufactured goods in India with either indigenous or imported duty paid inputs and other intermediate including raw material. Drawback rates under this category are decided in drawback schedule which is published by Central Board of Excise & Customs, Department of Revenue and Government of India usually 3 months after the budget.

With introduction of e-commerce portal of Central Board of Excise & Customs entitled 'ICEGATE' claims are now processed online in 95% of the cases. For claiming the drawback under section 75, an exporter is required to file a 'shipping bill under claim of duty drawback' in the prescribed format as required under Rule 13 along with the necessary declaration. The goods after assessment are examined by the officers posted in the Examination Shed as required for each individual case. The examination report will indicate the nature of goods in terms of drawback schedule for classification and application of correct rate.

APPENDIX 16.1 ► Checklist for the Duty Drawback Claim

Particulars of the Applicant:

1. Name & address of the applicant
2. Date of receipt of application in the office/section
   a. Whether application received in time
   b. If submitted late, the period of delay
3. Period of claim
4. Value of the claim
5. File no.

Documents:

1. Applied in the prescribed format as per Appendix 12 B
2. Self-certified copies of purchase invoices
3. Self-certified copy of AR-3A/supply the invoice duly endorsed by the bond officer
4. Statement of purchases made from DTA indicating invoice number, date, amount, cheque number and amount with the name of the bank.
5. Advance stamped receipt
6. Proof of purchaser being a 100% EOU
7. Payment certificates from the suppliers as per Appendix 22 A of HBP Volume I
8. Declaration for non-availing of Special Imprest Licence obtained from the suppliers
9. Original indemnity bond
10. Disclaimer certificate from suppliers if claimed by EOU/EPZ unit
11. Self-certified copy of purchase order/LOP/contract
12. Whether claim has been submitted in duplicate
13. Whether the claim is at AIR or brand rate fixed by DGFT
14. If at AIR, Sl. No. and rate of DBK
15. Whether a certificate has been produced from the local excise authorities of DTA manufacturer that they had not claimed CENVAT benefits for the period in which the supply was made (for supplies from traders, it will be presumed that CENVAT benefit has been availed)
16. Whether any drawback amount claimed is less than 1% of FOB value of the supply, and the total claim per supply is less than ₹500 (If yes, whether such claim has been deleted).
17. Amount of drawback claimed
18. Whether cut has been imposed for late submission of claim
19. Amount of drawback admissible
20. Product supplied (specification, if any)
21. Whether merchant/Mfg. supplier
22. Shipping bill of the physical export by the SEZ unit

Source: http://www.indoresez.gov.in/checklist/drawback.doc

Review Exercises

Multiple Choice Questions

1. What refers to duty drawback?
   a. Refund of input duties
   b. Refund of output duties
   c. Refund of levies and cesses
   d. Refund of inverted taxes
2. Refund of import duties on re-export of goods without any manufacturing falls under which section of the Customs Act, 1962?
   a. Section 74
   b. Section 75
   c. Section 45
   d. Section 52
3. AIRs are published by
   a. Central Board of Indirect Taxes
   b. Central Board of Direct Taxes
   c. Department of Expenditure, Ministry of Finance
   d. DGFT
4. The drawback for manufactured goods is provided under which section of the Customs Act, 1962?
   a. Section 74
   b. Section 75
   c. Section 45
   d. Section 52
5. Which of the following is not a proof of import?
   a. Bill of entry
   b. Bill of lading
   c. TR-6/GAR-7
   d. Shipping bill
6. Which of the following is not a proof of export?
   a. Bill of entry
   b. Bill of lading
   c. Electronic Bank Realization Certificate (e-BRC)
   d. Shipping bill
7. Which of the following documents denotes that these are identical goods in case of drawback claim for imported goods?
   a. Packing list
   b. Bill of lading
   c. Commercial invoice
   d. Shipping bill

8. Which of the following documents denotes the payment of duties on imported goods?
   a. Bill of entry
   b. Bill of lading
   c. TR-6/GAR-7
   d. Shipping bill
9. Which of the following is a commercial document?
   a. Bill of entry
   b. Bill of lading
   c. TR-6/GAR-7
   d. Shipping bill
10. Which of the following body processes the claim for drawback?
   a. Directorate of Drawback
   b. Directorate of Reconciliation
   c. Directorate of Revenue
   d. Directorate of Revenue Intelligence

Critical Thinking Questions

1. What is duty drawback? When is drawback given? Explain the cases when the drawback is not given.
2. What are the types of duty drawbacks? Explain the drawback of imported goods for re-export without any manufacturing.
3. Explain the process of duty drawback for manufactured goods? How are claims processed?
4. Write a short note on any two of the following:
   a. AIRs
   b. Brand rates
   c. Special brand rates
   d. Non-applicability of duty drawback

Further Reading

1. CBEC. 2014. 'Customs Manual 2014.' Available at: https://www.cbic.gov.in/resources//htdocs-cbec/deptt_offcr/cs-manual2014.pdf (accessed on 21 August 2020).

CHAPTER 17

Export Promotion Measures

CHAPTER OBJECTIVES

- To explain the importance of export promotion measures.
- To describe various export promotion measures in India.
- To explain the export incentives and duty neutralization schemes.
- To explain the export benefits and export assistance schemes for Indian exporters.
- To elucidate the refund of taxes and duties under Remission of Duties or Taxes on Export Products (RoDTEP) Scheme.

17.1 Introduction

The government, in order to promote the exports from the country, offers some export assistance and export promotion schemes so that exporters can take benefits of them improving their key weaknesses and stand up to compete in the international markets by offering quality Indian products and services. Such export promotion measures can be divided into direct and indirect assistance or programmes from the government agencies to enable Indian exporters to benchmark their products and services as per international quality and aesthetic appeal standards. Such export promotion measures may be targeted on any of these or a combination of these such as duty neutralization, export assistance, export support and export incentives granted to an exporting firm.

17.2 Export Promotion in India

After independence, the GOI accorded a very low priority to the export promotion drive, as the prime attention of the government was on focusing on the agriculture sector on which almost 75 percent of the population was dependent. Accordingly, in the First Plan, the agriculture sector was the main focus, and regarding exports, the plan had fixed up a growth rate at 5 percent, which eventually was not achieved as much of exports from India were traditional, agriculture products with least value addition and fetching low prices in the markets such as tea, jute, spices and coffee. The actual growth rate of exports during the First Five-Year Plan had been 1 percent only. The Second Five-Year Plan which focused on the large-scale industry had also neglected export promotion efforts as the economic planning itself focused on the import substitution and not on export promotion. Various efforts such as import restrictions, import substitutions, maintenance import and developmental imports were used in order to control exports. Overall, the economic policy during first two Five-Year Plans had been

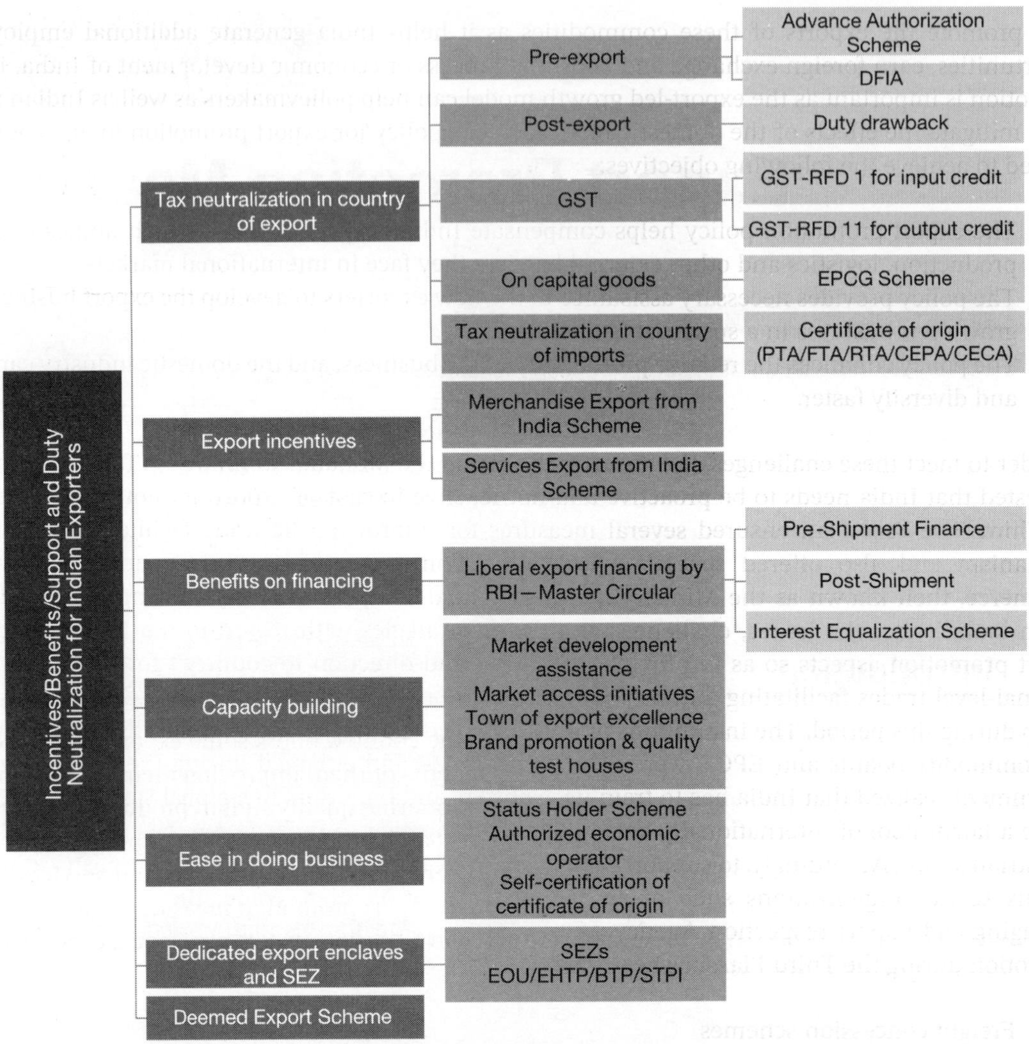

FIGURE 17.1 FTP: Incentives/benefits/support and duty neutralization for Indian exporters.

Source: Ministry of Commerce & Industry, Government of India.

haphazard and lacked the vision and direction for promoting exports from India and ultimately resulting in heavy trade account deficit and compounding problems of balance of payments due to shortages of foreign exchange in the country.

The development of external sectors, especially of exports, has an important place in the economic policy of India. The benefits of exports to a developing economy like India are many as India's domestic market size is small, and the global market provides a wide array of trade opportunities for Indian exporters. Indian exporters can leverage economies of scale in production by venturing into the export sector and exploit domestic resources to their advantage by selling in international markets. For example, India has abundant production of a number of agricultural products, such as rice, spices, fruits and vegetables, marine products and sugar, which cannot be consumed domestically but can be exported to international markets. GOI has been providing a wide array of incentives and benefits (Figure 17.1) so as to promote the exports of these commodities as it helps India generate additional employment opportunities, earn foreign exchange and boost the process of economic development of India. Export promotion is important as the export-led growth model can help policymakers as well as Indian industry to mitigate the effects of the domestic recession. The policy for export promotion in any country is devised to achieve the following objectives:

1. The export promotion policy helps compensate Indian exporters for the high-domestic cost of production, logistics and other external barriers they face in international markets.
2. The policy provides necessary assistance to the new exporters to develop the export business and grow their business in a sustainable manner.
3. The policy enhances the relative profitability of the business, and the domestic industry can grow and diversify faster.

In order to meet these challenges, the government set up the Mudaliar Committee (Table 17.1), which suggested that India needs to be proactive and not reactive in case of export promotion. Accordingly, the Third Five-Year Plan ensured several measures for improving the trade facilitating institutions mechanism and also offered several export promotion measures. An independent Ministry of Commerce, then known as the Ministry of International Trade, was created during the Third Plan, which looked after the issues, challenges and future strategies with regard to the EXIM Policy and export promotion aspects so as to provide dynamism and direction to country's foreign trade. Many national-level trades facilitating and promoting institutions, like the State Trading Corporation, were set up during this period. The institutions of specialized commodity and sector-specific bodies, such as the commodity boards and EPCs, were also strengthened and enlarged during the Third Plan. The government realized that India has to train its exporters and importers to a global standard and has to create a talent pool of internationally benchmarked manpower in order to meet its growing needs of industrialization. Accordingly, to support the export promotion efforts of the Indian industry and trade, various service organizations such as Indian Institute of Foreign Trade, the Indian Institute of Packaging and Export Inspection Agency were also set up during this plan period. The major export promotion during the Third Plan has been as follows:

1. Freight concession schemes
2. Duty drawback scheme

TABLE 17.1 Some of the Key Committees on Trade Policy and Procedure in India

S. No.	Name of Committee	Key Recommendations	Year
1.	Mudaliar Committee	Exploded the myth of import substitution and recommended the export promotion strategy	1962
2.	Alexander Committee	Simplifying the trade policy and procedure	1977–1978
3.	Tandon Committee	Export strategy for 1980s	1980
4.	Abid Hussain Committee	Trade policy and procedure	1984
5.	Murasoli Maran Committee	Policy on SEZ	2000
6.	Baba Kalyani Committee	Policy for Development of Enterprises and Services Hubs	2022

Source: Ministry of Commerce & Industry, Government of India.

3. Import replenishment schemes
4. Cash compensatory support
5. Supply of export credit at concessional rates
6. Supply of key inputs at international prices

Due to geopolitical reasons, after 1965–1966, the aid flows to India were substantially reduced by many developed nations due to reasons such as the Indo–Pak War and India's proximity to the Soviet Union. As a result, for the first time, India was made to depend significantly on its exports for acquiring foreign exchange to meet its needs of essential imports. GOI also devalued its currency so as to make Indian products cheaper in international markets, but due to some reasons, like drought condition, the economy was in shambles. The only saviour for India during that period of the rolling plan was the net positive inflow of invisibles, but that was not enough to compensate the large trade deficit which India had due to imports of food items.

Having realized and bitten by developed countries in bad times, for the first time after Independence, the export policy was given a definite shape in the Fourth Plan, which is also referred to as the golden era of India's foreign trade in post-Independence days, although not comparable to what India was during the days of Chandragupta Vikramaditya, having almost 33 percent share in global trade. To achieve the past glory of a 'golden bird', the Export Policy Resolution was passed by the parliament in 1970, which involved all sectors of the Indian economy and included all central as well as state government India's march towards export promotion efforts. The overall objectives of the economic resolution were to 'export more' and 'import more' and to eventually make India a regional hub in Asia in international trade. The result had been good as for the first time India's export was almost 93 percent of imports, and in 1972–1973, for the first time in post-Independence history, exports were more than imports. India was also successful in diversifying its trade basket from raw agricultural products to industrial products.

During the Fifth Five-Year Plan, the trade deficit increased once again due to internal disturbances and political instability. The Alexander Committee was set up to simplify the trade policy and procedure, and in 1980, the Tandon Committee was set up to devise the export strategies for the 1980s. The trade deficit further grew, and the Abid Hussain Committee was set up in 1984 to look into the matter. The Abid Hussain Committee recommended that export incentives should be widely employed as an instrument for export promotion as Indian exporters are in a disadvantageous position vis-à-vis their counterparts from both developing and developed countries due to use of such instruments in these countries for export promotion. The committee recommended that the main aim of these incentives is to increase the profitability of the export business. Accordingly, a series of export incentives were leveraged in as an instrument for export promotion; these included rebate of duties, cash compensatory support, income tax concession, interest subsidies, freight subsidy and so on. The Abid Hussain Committee underlay the importance of export incentives as an instrument of compensation to Indian exporters for the comparative disadvantages they faced in international markets. Accordingly, a multi-pronged strategy for export promotion had been evolved to achieve these goals. These included (a) an extension of the scheme for procurement of raw materials/inputs at international prices, (b) a liberal approach for making available contemporary technology to Indian exporters, (c) granting selected areas to large industries to manufacture products, which are reserved for MSMEs provided that they are export oriented, (d) full neutralization of central excise duty and (e) permission in principle to allow the use of 5–10 percent of the net foreign exchange earnings by exporters for export promotion. These incentives served a great purpose for export promotion from India.

During the Seventh Plan also, India had the trade deficit; the economy planning with regard to exports was based on hit-and-trial method rather than on fundamental changes in the policy mechanism to solve the root problems of the economy. Accordingly, in 1991, the process of economic reforms was started, and the EXIM policy was made for a period of five years. The role of all trade promotion institutions was changed from controller to facilitator and promoter, and the director general of foreign trade became the apex authority under Ministry of Commerce for devising the export promotion schemes, ensuring incentives side by side laying down the FTP under Section 5 of Foreign Trade (Development and Regulation) Act, 1992.

17.3 Promotional Measures for Boosting Exports

In the following sub-sections we will discuss some of the schemes for the export promotion and assistance under FTP of India.

17.3.1 Duty Neutralization Scheme

To neutralize the incidence of duties involved at various stages of production of exportable products, DGFT has designed two schemes, namely, 'Advance Authorization Scheme' and 'DFIA Scheme' aimed at neutralizing the incidence of customs duties. With the introduction of GST, the domestic taxes are separately dealt with under the GST refund rules. Duty exemption schemes allow duty-free imports of inputs required for export production. Advance Authorization Scheme and DFIA Scheme are pre-exports duty neutralization schemes wherein an exporter has to file for an authorization with DGFT which is issued online to Indian customs, and an exporter can import duty-free inputs to be utilized for an export consignment. Post-export duty neutralization is done through the Duty Drawback Scheme, which is separately dealt with in Chapter 16.

An advance licence is issued to allow duty-free import of inputs, wherein imported components and inputs will be physically incorporated in the export product, factoring the normal allowance for wastage that may entail in such manufacturing process. Advance Authorization Scheme also has a provision for imports of consumables and catalysts such as fuel, oil, energy and catalysts, which are consumed to obtain the export products. DGFT issues the 'advance authorization' on the basis of self-declaration as well on the basis of Standard Input Output Norms (SION). Advance authorization is issued for the following purposes:

1. Advance authorization may be issued for imports of inputs which are to be incorporated in the physical exports outside India. As SEZ is legally a territory, which is outside DTA, the authorization can be issued for the import of inputs for physical exports to SEZs. The authorization can also be issued to a merchant exporter who is linked to supporting manufacturer(s) for the import of inputs required for the export product wherein the obligation lies on merchant exporters for any compliance vis-à-vis export obligation and other terms and conditions of the authorization.
2. DGFT has also allowed the authorization for intermediates who can import goods in bulk and can supply it to other manufacturers holding an advance authorization and requiring these inputs to be used for the manufacture of goods outside India or to a deemed exporter holding an advance authorization. The terms of the condition of compliance in case of deemed exports are provided in FTP.

Similar to advance authorization, another pre-export duty-free authorization is DFIA, which is issued to allow duty-free import of inputs, fuel, oil, energy sources, catalyst and so on, which are required for the production of the export product. DFIA differs from advance authorization in many ways, and these two authorizations are aimed at meeting the requirements of varying imports of various types of exporters from various dynamic industries. DFIA shall be exempted only from payment of basic customs duty. To be eligible for DFIA, the following are the conditionalities imposed in FTP:

1. DGFT can issue DFIA to an eligible exporter 'on post-export basis' for the imports of products which are notified under SION.
2. In case the authorization is to be issued to a merchant exporter, there should be mention of name and address of supporting manufacturer of the export product on the export document, namely shipping bill/airway bill/bill of export/e-way bill.
3. An exporter should file an application to regional offices of DGFT where their jurisdiction lies and such application must be filed before the effecting export under DFIA.
4. Under DFIA, an exporter is supposed to maintain the 'minimum value addition' of 20 percent in the exportable goods. DGFT has specified the need for 'higher value addition' under advance authorization in case of certain products. Appendix 4C of FTP lists such products.

17.3.2 EPCG Scheme

EPCG enables an importer to import capital goods at zero rates of customs duty. The scheme is aimed at enhancing the export production capacity of India's exporters, thus achieving many objectives at one go. First, the exports from the country grow as a result of enhanced production along with additional employment opportunities. Second, the economic growth of the country gets a boost with additional exports, and third, there can be a lot of import substitution as the competitiveness of domestic producers enhances with such capacity building in the production. EPCG scheme mandates achievement of export obligation equivalent to six times of duty saved on the importation of such capital goods within six years from the date of issuance of the authorization. In other words, an exporter has a compulsion on the business to bring in foreign currency which is equal to 600 percent of duty saved on such importation measured in domestic currency. This is to be done within six years from availing the EPCG scheme. The goods which are manufactured by the imported machine are exported outside India. The EPCG scheme is intended for promoting exports of India, and GOI offers duty neutralization on import duties so as to lower the cost of imports. The EPCG authorization is issued by DGFT, and one should attach the following self-certified copies of the documents:

1. IEC
2. RCMC
3. PAN card
4. GST registration certificate
5. Proforma invoice
6. Brochure
7. Self-certified copy plus original of certificate of chartered accountant
8. Self-certified copy plus original of certificate of chartered engineer

17.3.3 Remission of Duties or Taxes on Export Products (RoDTEP)

In the Trade Policy Review of India, WTO has raised objections on compatibility of Merchandize Exports from India Scheme which was considered incompatible to rules of transparency and non-discrimination as member states objected that MEIS incentives to Indian exporters lead to price distortions, thus causing injury to traders of other member states. Additionally, WTO mandated for phasing out of this scheme.

Accordingly, Cabinet Committee on Economic Affairs (CCEA), Government of India approved a new scheme on 13 March 2020 known as "Remission of Duties and Taxes on Exported Products (RoDTEP)". This scheme is aimed at

1. Enhancing India's exports to international markets.
2. Making Indian exports cost competitive in international markets.
3. Creating a level playing field for Indian exporters in International market.
4. Reimbursing taxes/duties/levies at the central, state and local level since RoDTEP scheme is WTO compliant.
5. Giving a boost to employment generation in various sectors, thus refund of all levels of taxes and duties.

RoDTEP scheme is far more comprehensive than MEIS scheme. It is endeavoured that Indian exporter should not be in disadvantageous situation in a challenging time such as the outbreak of COVID-19 virus and resultant lockdown domestically as well internationally. Scheme will refund and reimburse all taxes/duties/levies at the central, state and local levels, which are currently not being refunded under any other mechanism. It will factor all taxes which are incurred by exporters from stage of sourcing of inputs, manufacture, inland transportation and finally exports. RoDTEP scheme will ensure a level playing field for Indian producers and exporters in the international market by neutralizing the domestic taxes and duties. RoDTEP is based on principle, "Goods are exported and Taxes are not". An inter-ministerial Committee will be constituted which will determine the rates and items for which the refund of taxes and duties would be provided. Similar to MEIS scheme, RoDTEP scheme will also be in the form of transferable duty credit/electronic scrip which will be issued to exporters on regulatory compliance vis-à-vis documentary proof of export, taking place out of India. Government of India has planned to incentivize Indian exporters to the tune of ₹50,0000 crore which is much higher than the current outlay under MEIS of ₹35,000 crore. DGFT will be the nodal agency for issuance, maintenance of electronic ledge, record of transfers and use. The Scheme will be digitally implemented, meaning DGFT and Icegate will be linked through EDI network for compliance. The refunds of taxes and duties under the RoDTEP scheme would be a historic step towards "zero-rating" of exports, thus supplementing the existing schemes such as Duty Drawback (Refund of Input Custom Duties) and Input GST and Output GST. Exporter's hail this scheme as it would be great step for improving the cost competitiveness of exported products in international markets and better employment opportunities in export-oriented manufacturing industries. For Indian economy to be 5 Trillion USD by 2024, India needs to increase its exports considerably by promoting various export-oriented industries and RoDTEP will a great step forward for reforming the tax neutralization of input and output taxes of all levels, central state and local so as to increase the productivity of Indian exports and contribute to the overall economy. Scheme will refund all taxes which are not refunded so far; for example, certain taxes/duties/levies are outside GST, and are not refunded for exports, such as VAT on fuel used in transportation, Mandi tax, Stamp Duty, Duty on electricity used during manufacturing, etc. These would be covered for reimbursement under the RoDTEP Scheme. The duty credit scrip under the scheme can be claimed on as a percentage of the 'Freight on Board' (FOB) value of exports. DGFT will provide electronic platform for monitoring and audit mechanism, which will be based on IT-enabled Risk Management System (RMS), so as to reduce red tape. Once the rates for an exportable product are notified under RoDTEP, the same products will be considered to be phased out from MEIS scheme. In the initial phase, rates under RoDTEP are notified for textiles and apparel sector.

17.3.4 Services Export from India Scheme (SEIS)

In order to promote services exports from India where India enjoys innate capabilities and capacities to excel in the world market and earn previous foreign exchange, DGFT has launched SEIS. It replaced the earlier similar scheme named as Served from India Scheme. The scope of the scheme has been widened, and there is greater conceptual clarity in what constitutes services exported out of India. Under SEIS, services exporters are provided duty scrip credit as an incentive over and above their actual export realization for certain categories of services subject to eligibility conditions. To be eligible for SEIS benefit, service providers of notified services, located in India, should have a minimum net free foreign exchange earnings of $15,000 in the preceding financial year. Limited liability firms/registered companies and partnership firms are eligible to avail the benefits under the SEIS. For proprietorship firm or individual service providers, the policy mandates a lower threshold limit of eligibility, which is minimum net foreign exchange earnings of $10,000 in the preceding financial year. One must be registered as an exporter or importer, that is, holding an active IEC at the time of rendering such services for which rewards are claimed. The exporter should also be registered (having RCMC) with concerned Services EPC/IT and IT-enabled EPC/Software EPC in order to be eligible for benefits under SEIS. The benefit will be dependent on the net foreign exchange earned by services exporter. The net foreign exchange earnings for SEIS is calculated as:

Net foreign exchange = Gross earnings of foreign exchange – Total expenses or payment or remittances of foreign exchange

Eligible service providers of notified services shall be entitled to duty credit scrip on the net foreign exchange earned at the rates which vary between 3 and 5 percent. Services exporters can use such duty credit scrips for the payment of import duties on procurement of services and also use such scrip for the payment of customs duty in case of default in fulfilments of the export obligation under the Advance Authorization Scheme, EPCG and so on. The conditionality of actual user condition has been waived off, and services exporters can now freely transfer duty credit scrips to other service importers, who may use it for payment of import duties for their services. DGFT has specified that duty credit scrip would be valid for a period of 18 months from the date of issue.

17.3.5 Market Access Initiative (MAI) Scheme

MAI scheme is intended to provide financial assistance for medium-term export promotion efforts with a sharp focus on a country and product. The financial assistance is available for EPCs, industry and trade associations, agencies of state governments, Indian Commercial Missions abroad and other eligible entities as may be notified from time to time. Assistance under this shall also be to export promotion organizations/trade promotion organizations/national-level institutions/research institutions/universities/laboratories exporters and so on for the enhancement of export through accessing new markets or through increasing the share in the existing markets. A whole range of activities can be funded under the MAI scheme. These include market studies, setting up of a showroom/warehouse, sales promotion campaigns, international departmental stores, publicity campaigns, participation in international trade fairs, brand promotion, registration charges for pharmaceuticals and testing charges for engineering products and so on. Each of these export promotion activities can receive financial assistance from the government ranging from 25 to 100 percent of the total cost depending upon the activity and the implementing agency. The following activities will be eligible for financial assistance under the scheme:

1. **Marketing projects abroad:** This is to support marketing projects abroad based on focus product or country approach. Under this, the following activities will be funded:
   a. Opening of showrooms and warehouses.
   b. Organizing 'trade festival of India'—a multi-sectoral event to be organized in selected centres abroad to promote 'Brand India' by showcasing our strength in services such as health (Ayurveda and yoga), the taste of India (Indian cuisine), tourism and culture besides merchandise.
   c. National-level participation in major international trade fairs and so on.
   d. Display in international departmental stores.
   e. Publication of world-class catalogues.
   f. Publicity campaign and brand promotion.
   g. Research and product development.
   h. To support recognized associations in industrial clusters for marketing abroad.
   i. Reverse visits of the prominent buyers and so on from the project-focus countries.
2. **Capacity building:** This is for the following purposes:
   a. Imparting training to Indian exporters with respect to export in general and on specific region/country basis.
   b. Upgradation/improvements in laboratories, universities and research institutions on standalone or public–private partnership basis for fulfilling SPS measures/related testing and so on including reimbursement of testing charges.
   c. Quality upgradation of the selected products for export markets (by skill upgradation using experts/designers, production process improvements, reduction in rejections, etc.).
   d. Developing common facility centres, design centres, packaging and so on.
   e. Hiring consultants in the buyer/prospective country.
3. **Support for statutory compliances:** This includes the following:
   a. Charges/expenses for compliance of statutory requirements in the buyer country including testing charges for engineering products abroad, registration charges for product registration abroad for pharmaceuticals, biotechnology and agro-chemicals clinical trials for drugs/pharmaceuticals and medical disposables, medical equipment and so on..
   b. Other commodities/product groups and the nature of compliance covered for reimbursement under the scheme shall be approved by the empowered committee on a case-to-case basis.
   c. For contesting litigation(s) in the foreign country concerning restrictions/anti-dumping duties on particular product(s) of Indian origin. The commodity/product groups, the nature

of litigation to be supported and the extent of support shall be as decided by the empowered committee on a case-to-case basis.

4. **Studies:** Studies include the following:
   a. Market studies/survey for evolving proper marketing strategies.
   b. Export potential survey of the states.
   c. Projects/studies which further clarify the objectives of the schemes.
   d. WTO studies for evolving WTO compatible strategy.
   e. All trade-related studies including Joint Study Group, FTA and so on. Like regional trade agreement (RTA) studies, only specific market studies would be undertaken, and these studies would be entrusted to reputed professional organizations.
5. **Project development:** Funds under MAI scheme can also be earmarked to generate focused projects leading to substantial improvement in the market access, and a shelf of projects in this regard shall be prepared by engaging reputed professional organizations. A special focus would be on the preparation of projects pertaining to priority sectors and sectors having substantial employment generation potential.
6. **Miscellaneous:**
   a. Developing foreign trade facilitation web portal (databases and systems for dissemination of information [electronic or otherwise to Indian exporters]).
   b. To support cottage and handicrafts units.

17.3.6 Marketing Development Assistance (MDA)

The export promotion continues to be a major thrust area for the government. In view of the prevailing macro-economic situation with emphasis on exports and to facilitate various measures being undertaken to stimulate and diversify the country's export trade, the MDA scheme is under operation through the Department of Commerce to support the below-mentioned activities:

1. Assist exporters for export promotion activities abroad.
2. Assist EPCs to undertake export promotion activities for their product(s) and commodities.
3. Assist approved organizations/trade bodies in undertaking exclusive non-recurring innovative activities connected with export promotion efforts for their members.
4. Assist focus export promotion programmes in specific regions abroad such as Focus (LAC), Focus (Africa), Focus (CIS) and Focus (ASEAN + 2) Programme.
5. Residual essential activities connected with marketing promotion efforts abroad.

The MDA scheme is intended to provide financial assistance for a range of export promotion activities implemented by EPCs, industry and trade associations on a regular basis every year. As per the revised MDA guidelines, assistance under MDA is available for exporters with annual export turnover up to ₹15 crore. These include participation in trade fairs and buyer–seller meets (BSMs) abroad or in India, export promotion seminars and so on. Further, assistance for participation in trade fairs abroad and travel grant is available to such exporters if they travel to countries in one of the six focus areas Latin America, Africa, CIS Countries, Europe, Oceania and Pacific, and ASEAN. For participation in trade fairs and so on in other areas, financial assistance without travel grant is available.

Exporting companies with an FOB value of exports of up to ₹15 crore in the preceding year will be eligible for MDA assistance for participation in trade delegations/BSMs/fairs/exhibitions abroad to explore new markets for export of their specific product(s) and commodities from India in the initial phase. This will be subject to the condition that the exporter is having a complete 12 months membership with the concerned EPC and filing of returns with concerned EPC/organization regularly. However, this condition would not apply in case of a new EPC for a period of five years from the date of its creation. Assistance would be permissible on travel expenses by air, in economy excursion class fair and/or charges of the built-up furnished stall. This would, however, be subject to an upper ceiling mentioned in Table 17.2 for each tour.

17.3.7 Towns of Export Excellence

A number of towns in specific geographical locations have emerged as dynamic industrial clusters contributing handsomely to India's exports. It is necessary to grant recognition to these industrial clusters with a view to maximizing their potential and enabling them to move higher in the value chain and tap new markets. Selected towns producing goods of ₹1,000 crore or more will be notified as Towns of Exports Excellence based on the potential for growth in exports. However, for the Towns of Export Excellence in the handloom, handicraft, agriculture and fisheries sector, the threshold limit would be ₹250 crore. Common service providers in these areas shall be entitled to the facility of the EPCG scheme. The recognized associations of units will be able to access the funds under the MAI scheme for creating focused technological services. Further, such areas will receive priority for assistance for rectifying identified critical infrastructure gaps from the Assistance to States for Development of Export Infrastructure and Allied Activities (ASIDE) scheme.

17.3.8 Brand Promotion and Quality and Test Houses

The central government aims to encourage manufacturers and exporters to attain internationally accepted standards of quality for their products. The central government will extend support and assistance to the trade and industry to launch a nation-wide programme on quality awareness and to promote the concept of total quality management. The central government will assist in the modernization and upgradation of test houses and laboratories in order to bring them at par with international standards.

TABLE 17.2 Financial Assistance to Indian Exporters under Market Development Assistance

S. No.	Area/Sector	No. of Visits	Maximum Financial Ceiling per Events
1.	Focus LAC	1	₹250,000
2.	Focus Africa (Inc. West Asia and North Africa [WANA] countries)	1	₹200,000
3.	Focus CIS	1	₹200,000
4.	Focus ASEAN + 2	1	₹200,000
5.	General areas	1	₹150,000
	Total	5	

Source: Ministry of Commerce & Industry, Government of India.

17.3.9 Trade Infrastructure for Export Scheme

The Trade Infrastructure for Export Scheme is launched to address the infrastructural inefficiencies that exist due to federal structure of India wherein the export is a central subject, and states do not have the budget to plan expenditures to develop the infrastructure which is required for exports sectors, for example, state roads, power stabilization, water effluent treatment and so on. This scheme was formally launched by the Indian commerce and industry minister on 15 March 2017. The scheme is specifically designed to address the need of Indian exporters. The emphasis is to create an infrastructure that is professionally run and sustained for the orderly and balanced growth and development of the export sector. It is provisioned that an empowered committee headed by the commerce secretary was constituted for this scheme to periodically review the progress of the projects which required and going on under the scheme. The major objectives of the scheme are to involve the state in the export promotion efforts by helping the state governments for creating an appropriate infrastructure for the development and growth of exports. The state governments shall be encouraged to participate in promoting exports from their respective states. A suitable provision has been made in the annual plan of the Department of Commerce for allocation of funds to the states on the twin criteria of gross exports and the rate of growth of exports. The states shall utilize this amount for developing infrastructure such as roads connecting production centres with the ports, setting up of ICDs and CFSs, creation of new state-level export promotion industrial parks (EPIPs)/zones, augmenting common facilities in the existing zones, equity participation in infrastructure projects, development of minor ports and jetties, assistance in setting up of common effluent treatment facilities, stabilizing power supply and any other activity as may be notified by the Department of Commerce from time to time.

The Trade Infrastructure for Export Scheme is focused on giving a fillip to setting up and upgradation of infrastructure projects with overwhelming export linkages such as border haats, land customs stations, quality testing and certification laboratories and cold chains. The scheme especially mentions that the development of trade promotion centres, dry ports, export warehousing and packaging, SEZs and ports/airports cargo terminuses and so on will help in generating an additional export capacity from India and will also bring the productivity in cutting time and cost in the export value chain of India. The scheme adds special focus to last and first-mile connectivity projects related to export logistics as these get the least attention but result in a very high cost of logistics operations. The specific purposes for which the fund allocated under the scheme can be sanctioned and utilized are given below:

1. Creation of new EPIPs (including SEZs/agri-business zone) and augmenting facilities in the existing ones.
2. Setting up of electronic and other related infrastructure in the export conclave. Equity participation in infrastructure projects including setting up of SEZs.
3. Meeting requirements of capital outlay of EPIPs/export processing zones (EPZs)/SEZs.
4. Development of complementary infrastructures such as roads connecting the production centres with the ports, setting up of ICDs and CFSs.
5. Stabilizing power supply through additional transformers and islanding of export production centres and so on.
6. Development of minor ports and jetties of a particular specification to serve the export purpose.
7. Assistance for setting up common effluent treatment facilities.
8. A project of national and regional importance.

17.3.10 Schemes for Export and Trading Houses

Merchants as well as manufacturer exporters, service providers, export-oriented units (EOUs) and units located in SEZs, AEZs, EHTPs, STPIs and BTPs shall be eligible for applying for status as star export houses. The applicant shall be categorized depending on his/her total FOB (for deemed exports) export performance during the current plus the previous three years. An eligibility criterion of the export performance for status holders is detailed in Table 17.3:

A status holder shall be eligible for the following facilities:

1. Authorization and customs clearances for both imports and exports on self-declaration basis.
2. Fixation of input–output norms on priority within 60 days.
3. Exemption from compulsory negotiation of documents through banks. Remittance/receipts, however, would be received through banking channels.
4. Hundred percent retention of foreign exchange in EEFCA subject to guidelines of RBI.
5. Enhancement in normal repatriation period from 270 to 360 days.
6. Exemption from furnishing of bank guarantee in schemes under FTP.
7. Star export house and above shall be permitted to establish export warehouses, as per Department of Revenue guidelines.

17.3.11 Authorized Economic Operator (AEO) Scheme

AEO is a trade facilitation programme which was started under the aegis of the World Customs Organization (WCO) SAFE Framework of Standards. It is aimed at securing and facilitating the foreign trade of India. The AEO programme is aimed at enhancing and strengthening the international supply chain security and facilitate the movement of traded goods across the globe. The AEO scheme addresses the issues of each stakeholder involved in the international supply chain. Under the AEO programme, a business firm engaged in international trade is approved by customs as compliant to agreed threshold standards for safe and secure supply chain including security standards which are the main concern for any country after the post 9/11 scenario. AEO-approved business firms are entitled to certain status and benefits which cut their time and cost of export–import operations. AEO is a voluntary programme aimed at securing the trade supply chain as trade benefits everybody.

TABLE 17.3 Eligibility Criteria for Export and Trading Houses

S. No.	Category Performance	Export Turnover (Million $)
1.	Export house	3
2.	Star export house	25
3.	Trading house	100
4.	Star trading house	500
5.	Premier trading house	1500

Source: Chapter 3 Foreign Trade Policy 2015–20 (policy extended till March 2023), DGFT, GOI.

The procedural mechanism under the AEO scheme enables Indian customs to enhance and streamline cargo security through close cooperation with the principle stakeholders of the international supply chain such as importers, exporters, logistics providers, custodians or terminal operators, custom brokers and warehouse operators. Under this scheme, Indian customs ask businesses to ensure the integrity of their security practices both at physical and virtual level including security of associated infrastructure and communicate and verify the security guidelines of their business partners within the supply chain. The specific benefits of the AEO scheme are listed below:

1. AEO status holder exporters/importers can fix their SION on a self-declaration basis as provided in FTP 2015–2020 in cases where SION is not notified.
2. AEO status holder will have the facility of direct port delivery of imports to ensure just-in-time inventory management by manufacturers wherein the customs clearance of imported goods can be done from the wharf of a port.
3. AEO status holder will have the facility of direct port entry for factory stuffed containers meant for exports.
4. AEO status holder will have the facility of identity cards (IDs) to be issued for their personnel for allowing entry to customs houses, CFSs and ICDs.
5. AEO status holder will have the facility of the investigation if any in a fast-tracked mode within six–nine months.
6. AEO status holder will have the facility of dispute resolution within six months.
7. It is provisioned that AEO status holder will have an e-mail notification regarding arrival/departure of a vessel carrying their consignment.
8. AEO status holder will have the facility of faster disbursal of drawback amount within 72 hours of EGM submission.
9. AEO status holder will have the facility of assessment/examination of exportable and importable cargo to be done on a priority basis.
10. AEO status holder will have the facility of faster disbursal of refund, including IGST refund and rebate for AEO status holder within 45 days of submission of complete documents.
11. AEO status holder will have the facility of automatic activation of deferred duty payment option.
12. AEO status holder will have the facility of mutual recognition agreements with other customs administrations as India has done with Hong Kong and South Korea.
13. AEO status holder will have the facility of extension of facilitation to exports in addition to imports depending on the tier of certification.
14. AEO status holder can self-certify the copies of FTA/PTA origin-related or any other certificates required for clearance would be accepted.
15. AEO status holder will have the facility of 'on-site inspection/examination'.
16. AEO status holder will have the facility of paperless declarations with no supporting documents.
17. AEO status holder will have the facility of recognition by partner government agencies and other stakeholders as part of this programme.

17.3.12 Approved Exporter System for Self-Certification of Origin

Realizing the fact that Indian exporters face considerable hurdles getting the certificate of origin, DGFT has introduced the approved exporter system for self-certification of origin. The scheme makes manufacturer exporters who are also recognized by DGFT as status holders, as eligible so as to issue and self-certify their own certificate of origin. The scheme for self-certification of a certificate of origin will be restricted to the products that are manufactured by the exporters. The scheme provisioned that such an exportable product manufactured by the exporters should be listed in the small-scale industries (SSI)/IEM/IL/LOI registration certificate. The scheme further mandates that these products must be listed in the application for recognition as an approved exporter. If these conditions are not met, such exporter shall continue to apply for certificates of origin from Export Inspection Council (EIC) or other bodies designated for the purpose.

17.4 Summary

The government, in order to promote the exports from the country, offers some export assistance and export promotion schemes so that exporters can take benefits of it improving their key weaknesses and shall stand up to compete in the international markets by offering quality Indian products and services. Development of external sectors, especially exports, has an important place in the economic policy of India. The benefits of exports to a developing economy like India are many as India's domestic market size is small, and the global market provides a wide array of trade opportunities for Indian exporters. Indian exporters can leverage economies of scale in production by venturing into the export sector and exploit domestic resources to their advantage by selling in international markets. To neutralize the incidence of duties involved at various stages of production of exportable products, DGFT has designed two schemes, namely, 'Advance Authorization Scheme' and 'DFIA scheme' aimed at neutralizing the incidence of customs duties. With the introduction of GST, the domestic taxes are separately dealt with under the GST refund rules. Duty exemption schemes allow duty-free imports of inputs required for export production. The Advance Authorization Scheme and DFIA are pre-exports duty neutralization schemes wherein an exporter has to file for an authorization with DGFT, which are issued online to Indian customs, and an exporter can import duty-free inputs to be utilized for an export consignment. The EPCG scheme enables an importer to import capital goods at zero rates of customs duty. The scheme is aimed at enhancing the export production capacity of Indian exporters. MEIS is announced for the first time in the FTP 2015–2020. The scheme aims to promote the exports of merchandised goods from India. The scope of the scheme has been widened, and there is greater conceptual clarity in what constitutes services exported out of India. Under SEIS, services exporters are provided duty scrip credit as an incentive over and above their actual export realization for certain categories of services subject to eligibility conditions. The MAI scheme is intended to provide financial assistance for medium-term export promotion efforts with a sharp focus on a country and product. In a view of the prevailing macro-economic situation with the emphasis on exports and to facilitate various measures being undertaken to stimulate and diversify the country's export trade, the MDA scheme is under operation through the Department of Commerce. The central government aims to encourage manufacturers and exporters to attain internationally accepted standards of quality for their products. Selected towns producing goods of ₹1,000 crore or more will be notified as towns of exports excellence based on the potential for growth in exports. The Trade Infrastructure for Export Scheme addresses the infrastructural inefficiencies that exist due to federal structure of India wherein the export is a central subject, and states do not have a budget to plan expenditures to develop the infrastructure, which is required for exports sectors, for example, state roads, power stabilization and water effluent treatment. This scheme was formally launched by India's commerce and industry minister on 15 March 2017. Merchants as well as manufacturer exporters, service providers, EOUs and units located in SEZs, AEZs, EHTPs, STPs and BTPs shall be eligible for applying for status as star export houses. AEO is a trade facilitation programme, which is started under the aegis of WCO SAFE Framework of Standards. It is aimed at securing and facilitating the foreign trade of India. The AEO programme is aimed at enhancing and strengthening the international supply chain security and facilitate the movement of traded goods across the globe. Realizing the fact that Indian exporters face considerable hurdles getting the certificate of origin, DGFT has introduced the approved exporter system for self-certification of origin. The scheme makes manufacturer exporters, who are also recognized by DGFT as status holders, as eligible so as to issue and self-certify their own certificate of origin. The RoDTEP scheme will refund and reimburse all taxes/duties/levies at the central, state and local level, which are currently not being refunded under any other mechanism. It will factor all taxes, which are incurred by exporters from the stage of sourcing of inputs, manufacture, inland transportation and finally exports.

CASE STUDY Application of Concepts in Exports Promotion Measures

Mr Bhosale runs an MSME unit involved in manufacturing of various hand tools falling under HSN–8201. The unit is based in Pune and exports to three regions, namely ASEAN countries, European Union and North American Free Trade Agreement (NAFTA). The tariff codes for his products are falling under HSN 8201:

His last year turnover was of ₹300 crore, and region-wise projected exports for the year 2020 are as follows:

1. ASEAN countries: ₹98 crore
2. NAFTA: ₹62 crore
3. EU countries: ₹50 crore

Mr Bhosle invoices exports orders in Indian rupees; however, realizations are in USD from ASEAN and NAFTA countries and in euro from EU countries.

Questions

1. He is seeking your advice to calculate the following exports incentives:
   a. MEIS incentive on the total turnover
   b. Duty drawback on the total turnover
   c. Interest subvention on the total turnover
   d. Tariff faced by Bhosale's export products—region wise
   e. Process of exemption of output GST (on final export produce)
   f. Process of refund of the input tax credit as Mr Bhosale has no domestic sales
   g. Listing of TBT faced by Mr Bhosale
2. He further seeks advice on rules of origin to be complied for the ASEAN region and GST benefit for the EU region.

Review Exercises

Multiple Choice Questions

1. When was EXIM Policy announced for the first-time?
   a. 1969
   b. 1952
   c. 1947
   d. 1991

2. Which of the following committees exploded the myth of import substitution and recommended the export promotion strategy?
   a. Mudaliar Committee
   b. Alexander Committee
   c. Murasoli Maran Committee
   d. Abid Hussain Committee
3. Which of the following committees recommended the export strategies for the 1980s?
   a. Tandon Committee
   b. Alexander Committee
   c. Murasoli Maran Committee
   d. Abid Hussain Committee
4. In which year did the Alexander Committee recommend for simplifying the trade policy and procedure?
   a. 1962
   b. 1977–1978
   c. 1980
   d. 1984
5. Which of the following committees recommended for setting up SEZs?
   a. Mudaliar Committee
   b. Alexander Committee
   c. Murasoli Maran Committee
   d. Abid Hussain Committee
6. Which of the following schemes facilitate the import of duty-free capital goods?
   a. EPCG
   b. Advance Authorization Scheme
   c. DFIA
   d. MEIS
7. In which of the following schemes is the duty credit scrip given to an exporter?
   a. EPCG
   b. Advance Authorization Scheme
   c. DFIA
   d. MEIA
8. Under which of the following schemes is duty-free import of inputs facilitated?
   a. EPCG
   b. Advance Authorization Scheme
   c. SEIS
   d. MEIS
9. Under which of the following schemes are services exports incentivized?
   a. EPCG
   b. Advance Authorization Scheme
   c. SEIS
   d. MEIS

10. Which of the following schemes is declared as incompatible to WTO policy norms in WTO trade policy review for India?
   a. EPCG
   b. Advance Authorization Scheme
   c. SEIS
   d. MEIS

Critical Thinking Questions

1. Critically explain the importance of export promotion measures which assess their utility for India's foreign trade.
2. Explain the various export promotion measures as provided in FTP 2015–2020.
3. What are the various incentivization schemes under FTP?
4. What are the various duty neutralization schemes in India?
5. Critically examine various export benefits and export assistance schemes for Indian exporters.
6. Critically examine the following schemes:
   a. MAI
   b. MDA
   c. Towns of export excellence
   d. Trade Infrastructure for Export Scheme
7. It is said that AEO and self-certification of certificate of origin will reduce time and costs of Indian exports. Examine.

Further Reading

1. Ministry of Commerce and Industry. 2015. 'Foreign Trade Policy.' Available at: https://howtoexport-import.com/UserFiles/Windows-Live-Writer/Foreign-Trade-Policy-of-India-2015-2020-_FB74/Foreign%20Trade%20Policy%202015-20.pdf (accessed on 23 August 2020).

CHAPTER 18

Quality Control and Pre-Shipment Inspection in Exports

CHAPTER OBJECTIVES

- To explain the concept and role of export quality control.
- To explain the different methods of export quality control.
- To discuss the various quality control measures in India.
- To explain the role of EIC in export quality control.
- To explain different ways of export cargo inspection and process therein.

18.1 Introduction

Quality of exportable goods and services has become extremely pertinent for any exporter, as one can engage, compete, sustain and manage business operations only if the firm's goods and services not only surpass the quality standards of its competitors but also excel beyond customers' expectations. The term quality refers to the defined set of attributes or specifications that a product and service should have in order to offer value to the customer for money being charged. Hence, an exporter of goods and services must first decide the quality of a product before introducing it in the international market, and this can be better done keeping in mind the national and international standards of quality as laid down by the respective national or international standard bodies. Quality specifications may vary from one country to another or from one region to another and are usually categorized as high, medium and low, depending upon how rich or poor these specifications are. In export transactions, an exporter may be governed by national, international or other negotiated specifications of quality as agreed and laid down in the export contract between the importer and exporter. Thus, the term quality should be understood in its relative sense and not in the absolute sense as it may refer to different specifications depending on negotiated terms of export contract and nature of trade. For example, the term quality has a different meaning in hotel, hospital, travelling and personal care industry where one refers 'hygiene' while suggesting quality specifications. In electronics, mechanical and electrical, one may use this term to refer to 'safety'. In travel operations, it refers to 'reliability', and in teaching, it refers to the ability of the professor to make students 'understand' the concepts easily. For a post and courier company, quality means 'speed and security of delivery' in the right hands. In a nutshell, quality refers to the compliance of established benchmarks, which are expected in the delivery of services and exchange of goods for the value of money and have been laid down by a professional regulatory body. For example, food safety standard is framed by FSSAI, standards for automobiles are framed by the Automotive Research Association of India (ARAI), and standards for computers are framed by the Bureau of Indian Standards (BIS). Some of the commonly used standards for quality control of goods and services are shown in Figure 18.1.

Marketers usually justify the price hike referring to the improved quality and measure the quality of goods and services in terms of prices they charge to their customers and clients. However, such a measurement of quality in reference to the price is not justifiable. Quality should primarily denote that the product or service is conforming to the established standard as framed by a professional body or association. In this context, the quality control for exports refers to all those steps which are focused at defining, maintaining and controlling the quality of exportable goods and services within certain pre-specified reasonable limits as agreed, negotiated and executed in an export contract. Hence, the export quality control refers to the systematic and scientific regulation of all those elements which affect the genuineness of the exportable goods and services. The quality control in export–import is, thus, the determination of quality standards, benchmark and other controlling measures that are aimed at ensuring the conformity and compliance of trade goods and services to established quality standards. The manufacturers and service providers with improved compliance to quality standards are likely to garner a higher goodwill and brand equity leverages in international markets; hence, efforts should be made not only by the respective government but also by manufacturers and service providers so as to secure the satisfactory or reasonable quality of Indian exportable goods in international markets. This helps any country to export more and effectively engage globally, thus creating viable employment opportunities and sustainable business operations in international markets. With the increase in the global competition in today's volatile and complex business environment, Indian firms in both goods and services sectors should design their business processes aimed at improving quality of goods, cutting costs and delivering value to customers so as to win their hearts and earn foreign exchange for the country.

For industrial goods • ISI marks • BIS	Non-polluting vehicle mark • Bharat stage emission standards • BIS	Purity of gold jewellery • BIS hallmark • BIS	For organically produced products • India organic • National Standards for Organic Products, 2000	Agricultural products in India • Agmark • Directorate of Marketing and Promotion
AYUSH product certification scheme • Ayush mark • Department of Ayush	Certification of silk purity in textiles • Silk mark • Silk Mark Organization of India	Least impact on ecosystem • Eco mark • BIS	ISO-9000 (series)	ISO-14000 (Series)
Hazard Analysis and Critical Control Points (HACCP) certification	WHO-Good manufacturing practice (GMP)	Software Engineering Institute (SEI) Capability Maturity Model (CMM) Level 2 & above status/certification	Fruits products in India • Fruit products order (FPO) standard • Vegetarian mark (green dot symbol) • Non-vegetarian mark (red dot symbol)	

FIGURE 18.1 List of applicable standards for various sectors of Indian Economy.

18.2 Quality Control Defined

The Oxford English Dictionary defines quality as, 'the standard of something as measured against other things of a similar kind, the degree of excellence of something'. Similarly, the Business Dictionary defines quality as, 'a measure of excellence or state of being free from defects, deficiencies and significant variations, brought about by the strict and consistent adherence to measurable and verifiable standards to achieve uniformity of output that satisfies specific customer or user requirements'. The International Organization for Standardization defines quality simply as, 'the degree to which a set of inherent characteristics fulfils requirements'. It further explains requirements as the needs or expectations, generally implied or obligatory, of interested parties such as customers, suppliers and society. In light of this, the quality control refers that the goods and services exchanged, whether in domestic or international trade, are 'conforming to certain agreed and established standards of quality'. For a manufacturer exporter, quality control refers to 'process by which an export firm previews, views and reviews the quality of all factors involved in production or rendering of services' so as to competitively engage in international marketers. Theoretically, quality control refers to all those activities of an export firm that are designed to define, maintain and control the specific quality of exportable products or services within reasonable limits or established standards that such firm offers to its varied customers in international markets. Hence, it is systematic, synchronized and well-coordinated regulation of all variables of a firm's operations that affect the goodness of the end product or service. For example, the quality of goods in international markets may be affected by poor packing even for the best of manufactured goods; thus, the quality control in international trade refers to controlling of all variables from point of manufacturer to point of consumption so as to retain the satisfied global customers. In short, it can be said that the quality control in export operations refers to steps that are aimed at not only in determining, measuring and controlling the pre-defined quality standards but also ensuring that such manufactured goods and services are traded with global customers in compliance with established standards. In order to ensure product quality in export operations, globally engaged firms always try to have the 'in-house quality control process' and ensure systematic control on all business variables for improved quality in exportable goods and services. Figure 18.2 highlights three aspects, which are always emphasized upon for improved quality in the manufacturing of goods for global markets.

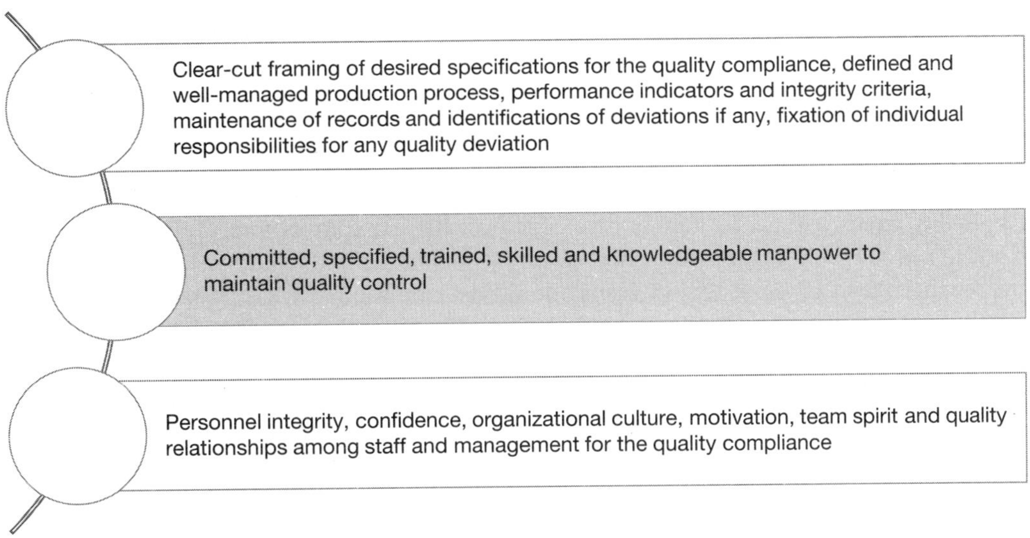

FIGURE 18.2 Framework of export quality control management.

Any export firm cannot assure the quality of goods or services meant for international markets if any of these aspects of quality management is compromised in the production process or rendering of services. Any globally engaged firm has to be extra cautious to ensure the quality control, and this can be done through pre-shipment inspection of goods so as to test export quality compliance, uncover any defects and report such deviations to the management, which has to make the decision to allow or deny the release of such cargo. In some cases, the term 'quality assurance' is also used for defining the quality compliance of exportable goods and services, which is largely aimed at improving and stabilizing the production and associated processes of the export firm. In Africa, the term 'export conformity' is used to refer to the export quality compliance which is same as export quality control in India and refers to avoiding and minimizing the variables that can lead to the defects in exportable goods and services.

18.3 Role of Quality Control in Exports

With the increasing globalization of the world economy, customers all over the world have different choices from a large number of competing export firms. The success of any firm in such globally interconnected, interdependent and competitive business environment largely depends on how far such firm has been successful to adapt and standardize its products accordingly to the accepted and established global quality standards in target markets. Winning customer's confidence in a highly competitive global market is a significant element of success for any export firm. A firm can effectively engage with global buyers only if its products and services win the customer's confidence, as well as if the firm is considered as a dependable supplier with superior quality of goods and services. Thus, the quality compliance to established benchmarks is an important element of a firm's business strategy, which helps it to win customers' minds and increase their levels of satisfaction. In order to ensure that quality compliance becomes an integral part of a firm's business operations, it is important that the firm should get the certification of its quality management system from a competent authority. The implementation of quality control in the business process helps any export firm to ensure the recognizable assurance of the quality of its goods and services to potential customers and act as an effective marketing tool to retain satisfied customers. A firm can place the quality assurance in the business process or can get the consignment-wise quality control inspection so as to assure global customers that goods and services of the firm are appropriately managed through 'established quality control system' and are certified by an independent entity. The benefits derived from the export quality control and assurance in export operations are exhibited in Figure 18.3.

In today's borderless trade regime, an exporter faces tough competition not only from the fellow exporters from his/her home country but also from other countries. Accordingly, an exporter should have an effective quality strategy to gain a competitive edge over his/her competitors. He/she should follow the endeavour to not only follow the established quality benchmarks but should also think beyond them in order to remain ahead of time. Export firms should develop a quality assurance culture among their employees, and quality control practices should be accordingly well-documented at each critical stage of the production and sales process. For any export firm to excel in quality compliance, it is important that the firm should have a clear quality policy, associated documentation for compliance and the support of its management. The exporter should ensure that goods are properly inspected at the time of export from the competent authority as desired by the buyer. Non-compliance of quality or supplying substandard goods in overseas markets brings disrepute to not only the export firm but to the country, thus associating its name as a supplier of poor-quality goods. Business firms, even in other business segments, will have

- Helps an export firm to get a competitive edge in the foreign as well as domestic markets.
- Helps in cutting operational costs as quality control systems provide sound and efficient business processes & procedures.
- Helps in minimizing the resource wastage and the time spent on reworking and repairs of exportable goods.
- The quality control provides for constant motivation for ensuring constant quality improvement and resultant satisfied customers.
- Acts as a marketing tool in boosting buyer's confidence regarding the quality of the goods.
- The quality assurance helps in winning new customers and helps the firm to improve its brand image and brand equity.
- Facilitates standardization of products and services thus a higher export compliance and resultant profits.
- A higher compliance with quality norms and standards of reduces obstacles export as well as import clearance from customs.

FIGURE 18.3 Benefits of quality management system.

problems to penetrate, expand and diversify their business in international markets. On the other side, export quality compliance helps the business improve its brand image, extend its business operations, sustainably retain existing customers and win new customers in global markets.

The exporter must realize that quality standards for any good or service are usually framed only after considering consumer's demands and associated costs and vary from country to country (Figure 18.4). These differences in quality standards from one country to another country are due to factors such as the stage of economic development, customer's willingness to pay, government's policy and awareness of citizens for health and safety. For example, the environmental standards for car manufacturers are different in India and Europe. Similarly, awareness for using economy label and customer's willingness to pay may vary between European and African countries. In India, exporters may manufacture goods conforming to varying standards; for example, when goods are manufactured for export to developed countries of Europe and North America, the manufacturer may adhere to strict quality control conformance, while the manufacturer may export goods at far lower quality standards and cost in markets such as Myanmar, Bangladesh, Uganda, Niger, Malawi and even in India. Thus, the significance of quality control in export operations should be understood in the context of factors such as consumer awareness about quality, his/her willingness to pay, import country policy and export country policy—not to allow manufacturers to manufacture low-quality goods. For example, quality compliance is an integral part of Japanese culture, and accordingly, the management and manpower of any Japanese company is highly committed towards quality products as it adds value not only to the firm's products but also to the country's image in international markets.

Realizing the fact that India's export story cannot march forward without quality complied goods and services, GOI has enacted the Export (Quality Control and Inspection) Act, 1963, which provides the necessary organizational framework, framing of quality standards and coordination among

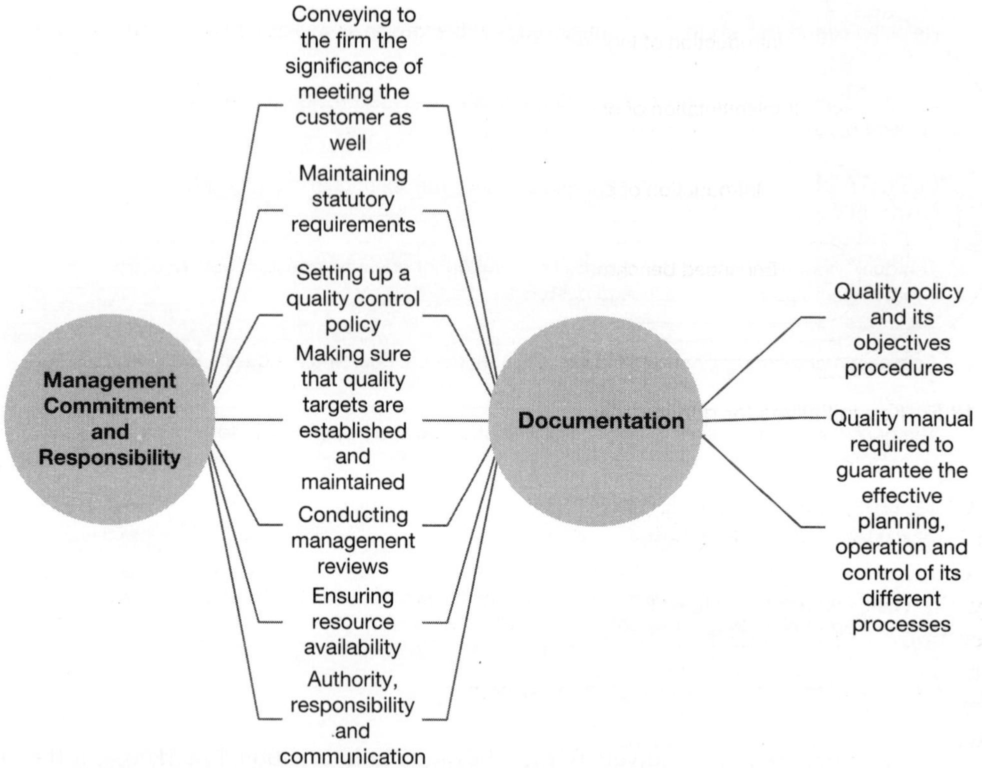

FIGURE 18.4 Framework of quality control in manufacturing operations.

Source: Adapted from ISO 9001:2015 Quality Management System, International Organization for Standardization (ISO).

different laboratories and inspection agencies to assist Indian exporters to comply with quality standards before exporting goods and services in international markets. A body created under this act is called EIC, which provides sound growth and development of India's export sector through export quality control and pre-shipment inspection services to different exporters of the country. Indian exporters, whether MSMEs or large enterprises, have to consider that they can win potential global markets for sustainable business operations only with adherence to established quality standards and benchmarks. An Indian exporter has to comply with the pre-shipment inspection if the products are notified for mandatory export compliance and may even have to get the inspection done if negotiated and agreed with the importer in the export contract. Hence, the export inspection in India may take place at the 'importer notified agency' or at 'exporter appointed agencies' depending on their mutual agreement. The global success of any enterprise depends largely on internationally accepted quality standard products only. Quality benchmarks help the exporter in making an assessment of price to be offered and material to be used. The exporter can make a better judgement of customer's requirements, price preferences and accordingly decide his/her production of the product, keeping in mind his/her margin from the exports of products and services.

In order to be globally competitive, Indian exporters must learn from Japanese and American firms, who have pioneered in fostering and implementing the quality thoughts and practices in their

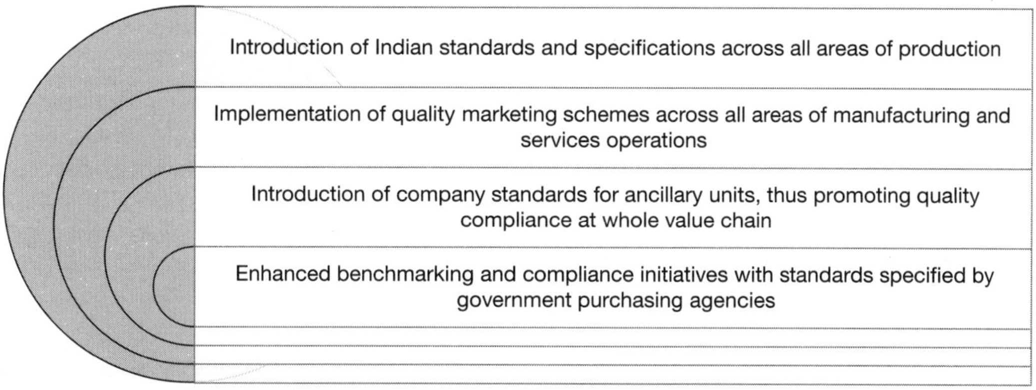

FIGURE 18.5 Key initiatives for quality improvement in India.

organizations. Japanese exporters leverage tactfully the 'Made in Japan' image assuring high-quality goods to international buyers at better prices. Japanese export firms have been successful to do so through continuous adoption of quality circles and kaizen strategies in their production process. Similarly, the US export has successfully leveraged the quality thoughts in their manufacturing and sales operations. In India, BIS has also been trying to promote quality consciousness among Indian producers and exporters. In recent years, the initiatives aimed at quality compliance both for domestic and export operations have been commendable, particularly for the small and medium enterprises, which are continuously vying international markets to sustainably continue business operations with improved quality of goods conforming to international standards. Figure 18.5 shows few such initiatives in India for quality improvement in recent years.

18.4 Methods of Quality Control

In today's globalized world, there are two types of quality control methods practiced by export firms. Both the methods of quality control, that is, 'inspection of goods' and 'statistical quality control (SQC)' have been very popular and are widely used in quality control of internationally traded cargo. Both of them are considered vital as the first method of quality control is aimed at ensuring the quality standards in export consignment and accordingly benchmarking them for the importer's help, wherein, the second method is aimed to help an exporter take all necessary steps at the production level itself. This helps an exporter to create a 'quality control chain', thus enabling an exporter to maintain internationally accepted quality standards. These methods of quality control and assurance are diagrammatically shown in Figure 18.6.

18.4.1 Inspection of Goods

The inspection of exportable cargo before the shipment has been pre-dominantly the most preferred method since the 1990s, and it is only in recent years that other alternatives, such as in-process quality control (IPQC), self-certification and implementation of recognized quality control systems, like IS 9000, have become popular. Similarly, the inspection of improved cargo has been vigorously practised

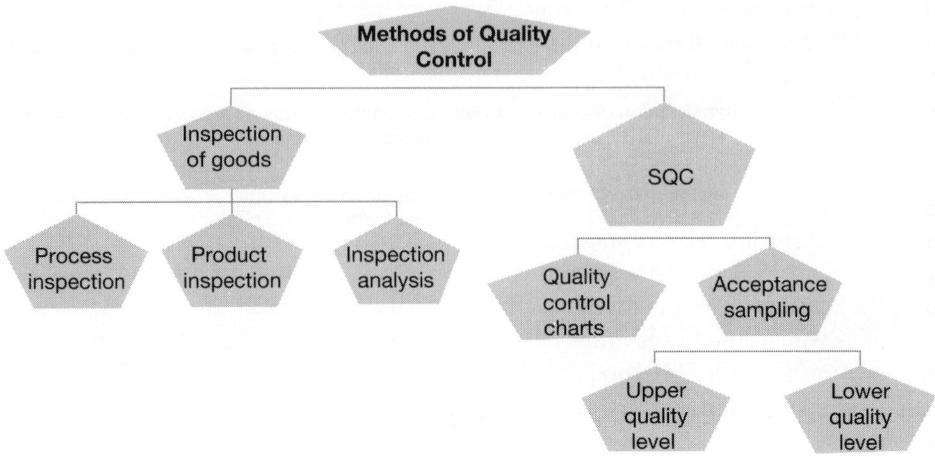

FIGURE 18.6 Methods of quality control.

Source: Export Inspection Council of India. https://www.eicindia.gov.in/WebApp1/ (accessed on 24 May 2023).

in areas such as food items, engineering goods, automobiles and medicines. The following are three ways of doing inspection of goods in both exports and imports:

1. **Process inspection:** Process inspection is one of the popular methods of quality control in manufacturing industries particularly with longer value chain as goods move from one process to another, and it is important to address the issues of quality at each level from the stage of raw material, in-process inventory to finished goods. Process inspection considers the machines and equipment as part of inspection and helps in saving the time, wastage of material and prevents process bottlenecks.
2. **Product inspection:** This method can be used only when the post-production is aimed at making the goods available in markets at zero defects and conforming to the recognized and established set of quality standards. In India, for example, the parliament has enacted a legislation known as Export (Quality Control and Pre-Shipment Inspection) Act, 1963, which statutorily mandates that the compulsory pre-shipment inspection must be done for notified exportable goods before they are exported. Similarly, legislation through a statutory body, called EIC, lays down the procedure and norms of quality control be it IPQC or self-certification scheme.
3. **Inspection analysis:** This method is aimed at eliminating all possible quality assurance mistakes as it acts on the philosophy of analysing the very process under which a particular inspection of the cargo has been completed. Hence, thoughtful and careful analysis of 'inspection results' analysis eliminates the possible areas of mistakes, promotes innovations on finds out alternative ways of quality management in the critical points in the manufacturing process.

18.4.2 Statistical Quality Control (SQC)

This method of quality control is aimed at making the right things vis-à-vis quality compliance rather than discovering and rejecting what went wrong at each stage of manufacturing operations. Hence, SQC is rightly explained as, 'a sample of quality steps be controlled in manufacturing operations are selected and are evaluated statistically so as to ensure that the established standards of quality are not only accurately maintained but are genuinely complied with'. SQC is a scientific technique aimed at the total minimization of possible deviation(s) in the quality control, compliance and assurance of exportable products and uses methods such as 'control charts' and 'acceptance sampling' to achieve the same.

1. **Quality control charts:** The control chart is a graph that is used to study how a process changes over time. Data from various stages of the production cycle of exportable cargo are plotted in time order. A control chart always has a central line for the average, an upper line for the upper control limit and a lower line for the lower control limit. This helps the export firm to understand the upper as well as the lower range of quality control. This becomes a continuous process in the manufacturing of exportable goods. Quality control lines are determined from historical data and are continuously compared by comparing the current data to these historical lines. This helps the export firm to draw conclusions about whether the process variation is consistent (in control) or unpredictable (out of control, affected by special causes of variation) and ensuring the consistent quality of export goods.
2. **Acceptance sampling:** Under the acceptance sampling method of export quality control, a sample of exportable products are checked, and the full lot is rejected if the percentage of defective exportable items is more than the predetermined limit otherwise. If the defective lot is less than the acceptable limit, the whole lot is accepted. Such percentage of defective items that is acceptable is called acceptable quality level. There are some disadvantages of the 'acceptable sampling' method as there is always a probability that an unsatisfactory exportable lot might be accepted resulting in problems that may come up when such imported consignment is checked in the importing country and rejected. Thus, acceptable sampling method has an inbuilt problem of having producers' risk his/her cargo being rejected at a stage when compensating losses may become very tough, and the exporter may lose a trusted buyer. Some exporters, however, use the method of 'lot tolerance percentage defective' in order to decide the chances of defective items. Under such circumstances, 'lot tolerance percentage defective' shall be the highest level of defects beyond which a lot will not be accepted for exports transactions. Thus, acceptance sampling may have the upper-quality level and lower-quality level to arrive at rational decisions about the quality control and assurance in export transactions.

18.5 Quality Control Measures in India

India is one of the few countries that has emphasized the importance of quality control in exports. Accordingly, Section 3 of the Export (Quality Control and Pre-Shipment Inspection) Act, 1963, mandates an important step of compulsory pre-shipment inspection of the goods that are to be exported. Under this Act, EIC was set up by GOI.

EIC has come up with a list of 1,000 exportable items/commodities organized into various groups, mandating them for a compulsory pre-shipment inspection before affecting exports. It includes food and agriculture, fishery, minerals, organic and inorganic chemicals, rubber products, refractoriness, ceramic products, pesticides, light engineering, steel products, jute products, coir and coir products, footwear and footwear products and so on. In addition to the above, GOI has come with several allied

SEI-CMM Level 5 | WHO-GMP | HACCP Certified | FSSAI

FIGURE 18.7 Quality control standards and certification in India: A snapshot.

legislation (Figure 18.7) aimed at quality improvements in exportable goods and services, and these are explained in the following sub-sections.

18.5.1 Standards of Weights and Measures (Packaged Commodities) Rules, 1977

Standards of Weights and Measures (Packaged Commodities) Rules, 1977, lays down some obligatory conditions for all commodities whether to be sold in the domestic market or export market or to be packed in a certain form having full declarations about content, quality, ingredients and precautions. The weight of the product is also given on the packing. These rules are framed, designed and operated by the Department of Weights and Measures, under the Ministry of Food and Civil Supplies.

18.5.2 Export (Quality Control and Pre-Shipment Inspection) Act, 1963

This unique Act mandates the mandatory pre-shipment inspection of around 109 goods meant for exports. The pre-shipment inspection for export cargo takes place through various export inspection agencies, working under EIC, New Delhi. Quality control and pre-shipment inspection are administered through a network of a large number of test labs/laboratories/inspection agencies located at various production centres and ports of the country.

18.5.3 Pollution Control and Eco Mark

Pollution control in the recent past has been an important subject of discussion in developed countries. Many countries in Europe have already placed 'carbon tax' on the goods, which are polluting our environment. Buyers are also very sensitive to ozone-depleting industries causing the harm to flora and fauna of the world. The exporter has to take a NOC from the Pollution Control Board. GOI has introduced an 'eco mark' label aimed at fostering customers' awareness for environment-friendly products. Similarly, 'energy star' label is aimed at promoting customer awareness about energy usage efficiency, and no product in India can be imported without conforming to these energies, eco mark and vehicular pollution marks (Figure 18.8). The key legislations governing the quality compliance for the pollution control in India is Water (Prevention and Control of Pollution) Act, 1974; Air (Prevention and Control of Pollution) Act, 1981; Hazardous Wastes (Management and Handling) Rules, 1989, and Environment (Protection) Act, 1986.

FIGURE 18.8 Eco mark label of BIS.

18.5.4 The Food Safety and Standards Authority of India (FSSAI)

Food safety is a predominant concern for any consumer, and accordingly, importers from all over the world have been asking for FBO-approved food products so as to ensure the quality compliance of goods. GOI has authorized FSSAI to issue such approval to food and eatables exporters. FSSAI was set up in 2006 under the Food Safety and Standards Act, 2006. This act consolidates various acts and orders relating to quality compliance of food-related issues under various ministries and departments under the custodianship of one body so as to ensure quality compliance and establish accountability in case of any problem. FSSAI is unique in the sense that it conducts the scientific evaluation of various food standards for articles of food. It also aims at regulating the quality control at all levels, that is, manufacture, storage, distribution, sale and import so as to ensure availability of safe and wholesome food for human consumption in India. FSSAI plays a pivotal role in food export compliance as it consolidates the functions and provisions of various central acts such as Prevention of Food Adulteration Act, 1954; Fruit Products Order, 1955; Meat Food Products Order, 1973; Vegetable Oil Products (Control) Order, 1947; Edible Oils Packaging (Regulation) Order, 1988; Solvent Extracted Oil, De-oiled Meal and Edible Flour (Control) Order, 1967; and Milk and Milk Products Order, 1992. FSSAI orders dated 21 January 2015 have made FSSAI rules applicable to food business operators. The export of goods products from India to other countries is subject to such a product, meeting the standards and specifications applicable in the importing countries. FSSAI order mandates that in such cases exportable goods can be manufactured subject to specifications/standards and food regulations of importing countries, and such products do not have to necessarily conform to Indian standards.

18.5.5 Export Homologations from ARAI

ARAI is the premier automotive R&D testing and certification organization in India which offers export homologations to automobiles exporters. ARAI works under the patronage and guidance of Technischer Überwachungsverein (TÜV) Rheinland, which is a 130-year old German multinational and one of the world's largest testing, inspection and certification agencies in the world. ARAI and TUV have joined hands to offer testing and homologation solutions to Indian and International automotive industry, especially for the operations based in India. India has emerged as a major automobiles' exporter to world markets and export compliance relating to homologations norms complying with importing country standard is prerequisite for the success in international markets. ARAI is based in Pune and provides a cutting-edge export homologation services to the Indian manufacturers in all aspects of testing and certification as per International standards such as EEC/ECE framed by United Nations Economic Commission for Europe. The certification from ARAI helps Indian exporters in smooth customs clearance in countries of import as products are manufactured conforming to safety standards of country of imports.

18.5.6 Voluntary Standards

In the globalized economic environment, voluntary standards are also becoming important. There are two organizations in India that deal with the voluntary standardization and certification systems in the food sector. These are BIS and Directorate of Marketing and Inspection (DMI). BIS looks after standardization of processed foods, while DMI is responsible for standardization of agricultural produce.

1. **Bureau of Indian Standards (BIS):** The role of BIS has become very important in quality control and assurance in India. The main functions of BIS are in two folds. *First*, BIS is responsible for the formulation and implementation of standards through promotion, voluntary requirement and third-party certification. *Second*, BIS maintains the record of most of the standards used in the processed food sector. These standards prescribed the parameters and hygienic conditions under which the product is manufactured, packed and labelled. Exporters who comply with the BIS norms obtain the Indian Standards Institution (ISI) mark which can be exhibited on the product packages. BIS has identified some of the important standards in the food sector which include food colour/additives/*vanaspati*/container for packing/milk powder and condensed milk for compulsory certification both for domestic and international trade transactions.
2. **Directorate of Marketing and Inspection (DMI):** DMI mainly frames, designs, administers and enforces the standards for agricultural products. It works under Agricultural Products (Grading and Marketing) Act, 1937. DMI prescribes the standards for agricultural and allied commodities, which are popularly known as 'agmark' standards. As the quality control under DMI is voluntary, manufacturers are willing to comply for quality norms as it gives their product an edge over their competitors in domestic as well as international markets.

18.6 EIC of India

In order to promote quality consciousness among Indian manufactures and exporters and export quality complied goods and services in international markets, GOI had enacted legislation in the parliament in 1963. The act is known as Export (Quality Control and Pre-Shipment Inspection) Act, 1963, which provides an institutional framework for the export quality control and inspection. Accordingly, EIC was set up in 1964 so as to ensure that globally accepted export quality standards and principles are not only enunciated as rules and regulations but are also communicated to Indian exporters in letter and spirit so as to promote 'Brand India' image in the international market with better, quality complied and trusted products. The export inspection is the official pre-shipment inspection and certification body in India. EIC, with a statutory mandate, has set up various export inspection agencies all over the country where personnel are trained so as to provide export quality control and inspection services to Indian EXIM

FIGURE 18.9 Various types of certification logo.

community. Various export inspection agencies ensure the quality of Indian exportable goods through export inspection certification in a systematic and scientific manner. The various initiatives of EIC are aimed at achieving excellence in quality complied Indian goods in global markets as quality complied goods are important benchmarks (Figure 18.9) for Indian exporter to not only excel in global markets but to grow, expand and diversify their business operations sustainably in long run. The network of EIC in India is pictured in Figure 18.10.

Under Export (Quality Control and Pre-Shipment Inspection) Act, 1963, GOI has powers to notify the goods for mandatory export quality control and inspection and accordingly may lay down their minimum standards of quality to be adopted for the export's certification. Quality standards can be either as laid down by EIC as per agreed global quality framework or as per importer's requirements. In addition to this, EIC also helps in setting up appropriate testing facilities along with machinery required for testing for inspection and quality control for a certain sector, for example, engineering goods, automobiles, metals and minerals. EIC has a wide network of testing and inspection labs spread all over the country, including major ports, so as to provide first-hand cargo inspection services to the Indian trade community. EIC continuously assesses and appraises the global developments in the area of quality control and compliance and accordingly guides and advises GOI on the steps to be taken to address the economic interests of Indian exporters in international markets. The following are the key functions performed by EIC and its export inspection agencies in India:

1. EIC is the apex statutory nodal agency of GOI with its functions largely aimed at ensuring the quality compliance of exportable goods as per accepted international standards through export cargo inspection and certification. EIC ensures quality compliance of Indian goods in accordance with established rules and regulations of GOI or the importer's requirements in accordance with quality rules of various countries of the world. EIC is mandated to conduct the 'consignment-wise inspection' of export shipment and help the Indian exporters to establish and lay down systems approach for 'IPQC' or 'self-certification'.
2. EIC is mandated for export compliance in other areas in addition to quality control, and these are issuing 'health certificate' for protecting flora and fauna, 'authenticity certificate' for products like basmati, thus promoting Indian exportable goods and 'phytosanitary certificate' for controlling SPS and TBT.
3. EIC is assigned as a nodal agency for issuing the 'certificate of origin' for tariff preference or neutralization under various schemes such as GSP, Global System of Trade Preferences, Bangkok Agreement, SAARC Preferential Trading Arrangement, Indo–Sri Lanka Free Trade

FIGURE 18.10 Network of EIC in India.

Source: Export Inspection Council of India.

Disclaimer: This map is not to scale. It does not depict any authentic national or international boundaries and is used for illustrative purpose only.

Agreement, health certificate for food items, pre-shipment inspection for all commodities and certificate for authenticity for basmati rice as mandated under Appendix 2B, 2C, 2D, 2E and 2F of FTP 2015–2020.

4. EIC provides the requisite testing and lab infrastructure in India and also trains the involved staff to cater to the services to exporters. The prime testing facilities of EIC offer quality compliance and certification services for physical contamination, bio-toxins, microbiological, chemical, biochemical, heavy metals, pesticide residues, additives and all other relevant parameters.

5. EIC leads in India's export quality initiatives and accordingly offers technical assistance to the industry in the installation of quality and safety management systems as practised globally, and these are HACCP, WHO-GMP and ISO-9001: 2000 version, ISO: 17025 and SEI-CMM. In recent years, EIC has taken initiatives for helping exporters lay down in-house food safety management systems and good manufacturing practices (GMPs).

In today's complex and ambiguous business environment, the proliferation of non-tariff barriers has become a potent tool to control imports, and countries, especially from the developed world, are increasingly resorting to trade restrictions by imposing the SPS and TBT. EIC of India can come forward to provide R&D assistance along with negotiation mechanism to address such challenges in international markets. EIC can also sensitize Indian exporters on the protective measures to be taken to avoid the SPS/TBT measures as used by developed countries to restrict their imports in today's volatile and uncertain times.

18.6.1 Pre-Shipment Inspection of Goods for Exports

As mandated under the Export (Quality Control and Pre-Shipment Inspection) Act, 1963, quality control of exportable goods from India can be done in four different ways: compulsory quality control and inspection, IPQC, self-certification and implementation of ISO standardization regime. Accordingly, EIC was set up under the administrative control of Ministry of Commerce and Industry, GOI, to formulate and supervise the inspection schemes. EIC executes inspection operations of exportable cargo through extensive networks of offices spread all over the country and has trained manpower for this purpose. EIC is also well-equipped with laboratories and testing facilities to carry out inspection tests and issue inspection certificates to exporters for quality control and compliance.

18.6.2 Compulsory Quality Control and Pre-Shipment Inspection

In today's complex and uncertain business environment, there are fairly a large number of export goods which are subject to compulsory quality control and pre-shipment inspection by authorized agencies of GOI. Compulsory quality control, pre-shipment inspection and certification of quality compliance of exportable goods can take place according to any of the ways discussed in the following sub-sections.

18.6.2.1 Consignment-to-Consignment Inspection

To address the larger concerns of international importers for quality compliance in certain products where GOI is receiving a large number of complaints from international buyers, EIC may notify such products (Figure 18.11) for mandatory consignment-to-consignment pre-shipment inspection. Under consignment-to-consignment basis, each exportable consignment of goods is inspected by the export inspection agency or commodity board, and on its satisfaction about the quality of these goods, it issues the certificate of inspection to the exporter. The exporter is required to submit an 'application for a certificate of inspection or intimation for inspection' well in advance to the concerned inspection agency (as prescribed in Appendix 2G of FTP 2015–2020) before the expected date of shipment of exportable goods. Mandatory inspection of such exportable cargo can be carried out either at the factory or warehouse of an exporter or at gateway ports depending on administrative convenience of the involved export inspection agency.

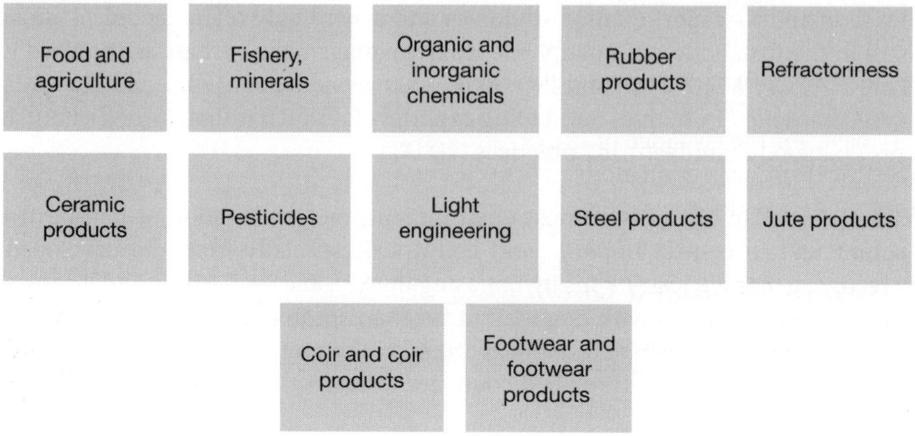

FIGURE 18.11 Commodities notified for mandatory pre-export quality control inspection.

Source: Author compilation from website of Export Council of India.

Under this system, each export consignment is subjected to detailed pre-shipment inspection by the export inspection agency which is usually done on the basis of random sample selection from one consignment. If the sample so selected is in compliance with established and recognized specifications/standards, the export inspection agency issues a 'certificate of inspection'[1] to the exporter. The inspection certificates so issued by the mandated export inspection agency carry a specific validity period within which the export consignment must be shipped to the place of destination, and this period may vary from commodities to commodities. Procedurally, an exporter must factor the suitable time period for such a certificate of inspection from export inspection agency so as to avoid shipment delays. An exporter has to attach the set of documents indicated in Figure 18.12 along with requisite fee along with the application for the certificate of inspection as prescribed in Appendix 2H of FTP 2015–2020.

On receipt of such application for the pre-shipment inspection, the concerned office of the export inspection agency or commodity board will assign an inspector for carrying out a physical examination of the goods. The assigned officer will examine such exportable cargo at exporter's factory or warehouse

FIGURE 18.12 Documents an exporter has to file along with the application for certificate of inspection.

Source: Export Inspection Council of India.

[1] Certificate of inspection is known by different names, for example, in East African countries, it is called certificate of export conformity, in Australia it is known as certificate of export compliance, in Bangladesh as certificate of quality control and in Argentina as certificate of authenticity.

on a sample basis in accordance with established and recognized standards and specifications. In case of further technical analysis, he/she can bring a random sample of goods to the laboratory or may send it for further investigation to any other approved laboratory. Based on such technical analysis of the sample drawn, such an assigned officer of EIC will prepare the field inspection report, which becomes the regulatory basis for the issuance of the certificate of inspection. An exporter will submit one such copy of the certificate of inspection along with shipping bill/bill of export to Indian customs authorities for the clearance of goods for the export.

18.6.2.2 Buyers Mandated Quality Standards and Specifications

Quality standards and specifications, especially in developed countries, are higher than Indian quality control standards or may vary from Indian standards in certain parameters of compliance. Importers or foreign buyers in such cases usually request Indian exporters to adhere to such standards and specifications of importer's country. Indian exporters have to get the cargo inspection in compliance with such enhanced or extended quality control standards to retain such global customs. Indian exporters, at the time of intimation to the nominated export inspection agency, must intimate such standards, which may or may not be in consonance with the Indian established and recognized quality control standards. Sometimes, importers may appoint an inspection agency in India which may, other than nominated by EIC of India and Indian exporters, in such cases, have to comply for the export cargo inspection from such nominated agency by foreign buyers. Exporters are advised that they should solve all these issues before the export whether they can fulfil such higher and extended quality requirement or not so as to avoid last-minute problems in export transactions.

18.6.2.3 Certified Quality Assurance Standards

Certain fast-moving consumer goods are governed by the quality at each stage of production and accordingly may be granted the status of certified quality compliance to established standards. For example, if exportable goods are manufactured in compliance with 'ISI certification' mark or 'agmark' issued by BIS or DMI, an exporter is not required to get such cargo inspected from any agency. Thus, these products do not fall under the purview of the export inspection agencies networks as such export units already have voluntary standards in place. The customs officials in India allow the export of such goods even if these goods are not accompanied by any pre-shipment inspection certificate. The list of items required mandatory certification from BIS and DMI is shown in Figure 18.13.

18.6.3 In-process Quality Control (IPQC)

There are certain products which can be manufactured in a better way if 'IPQC' measures are implemented in their manufacturing process and operations. Such products are chemicals, engineering and electrical goods, rubber and plastics goods and so on for which 'IPQC' is a better way of ensuring quality in products. Under 'IPQC', the quality inspection involves various steps to be taken by the exporter at various stages of production so as to make his/her production as 'export worthy'. Such units where the procedure of IPQC is implemented, executed and certified to this effect by export inspection agencies, the produced export goods are not required to get the pre-shipment inspection certificate from any agencies as these EOUs are following IPQC. However, for ensuring continuous compliance in quality, such EOUs are required to maintain the necessary database for IPQC for any random check by

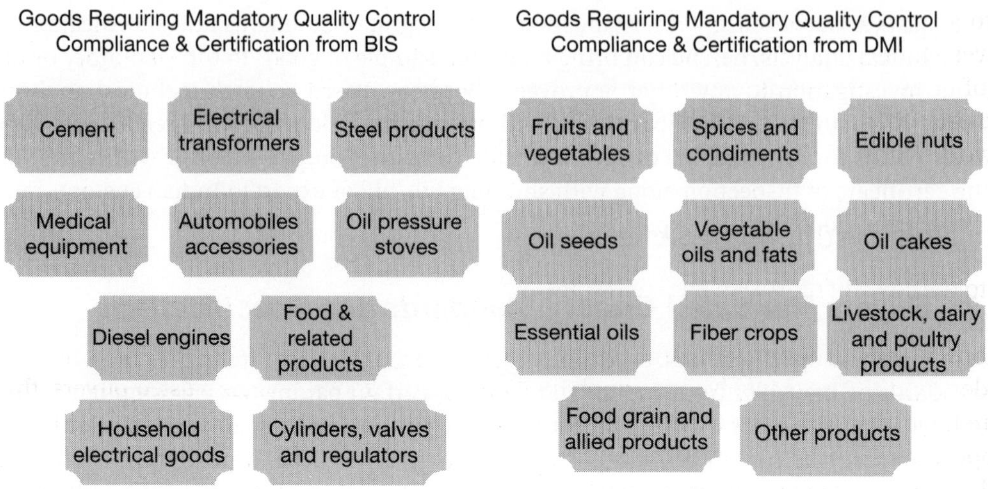

FIGURE 18.13 Items requiring mandatory certification from BIS and DMI.

Source: Bureau of Indian Standards & Directorate of Marketing & Inspection, Government of India.

export inspection officials. IPQC system focuses on the manufacturer's responsibility to ensure the quality of produced goods at all stages of production, and accordingly, he/she must systematically identify the critical stages for implementing the suitable quality measures. Export firms must also consider to lay down the quality standards at each critical level and accordingly train their staff for quality control, and the same should also be appropriately documented so as to understand the reasons for deviations if any and corrective measures can be taken. The following are critical stages where quality controls should be exercised in an IPQC system by any export firm.

In order to promote exports at lower trade costs and reduced export cycle time, such certified units are allowed to certify their export consignment for quality compliance in accordance with recognized and established standards. Such certified export units are also authorized to issue a certificate of quality compliance for other associated units as such certified units have required equipment and facilities in place for quality inspection.

For the certification of having placed the 'IPQC', any such desirous unit has to apply to the export inspection agency on the prescribed proforma along with mandated cross cheque or demand draft of fee, a copy of commercial invoice and importer's technical specification for importable cargo. EIC will appoint a panel of experts for the preliminary visit(s) wherein the panel will thoroughly investigate the quality control facilities of the unit from the stage of procurement of raw material, other key inputs to stages of production and final stage of export packing. The expert panel will submit the 'field investigation report' along with its recommendations for grant or non-grant of the certification. In case of grant of status as 'export-worthy' unit, EIC will issue an inspection certificate in triplicate with the original certificate endorsed to Indian customs authorities for taking note of such approved export-worthy unit.

18.6.4 Self-certification Scheme

Similar to the concept of 'IPQC', one–five-star export houses, as defined in Chapter 3 of FTP 2015–2020, and other large-scale manufacturers are allowed the facility of 'self-certification' for the export cargo inspection. As the exporters with large production usually produce their goods for export markets and they understand the risks involved in supplying poor-quality goods to their trusted buyers, they themselves are the best judge of the export quality standards required for a particular market for sustainable export operations. They will never manufacture anything which will spoil their international reputation and affect the brand equity of their products in the international market. Hence, EIC allows such exporters to certify the export quality of their goods by self-certification. To be eligible under Self-certification Scheme, such desirous exporters, with their status certificate or turnover certificate, should apply to the Director (Inspection and Quality Control), EIC of India, at their Delhi office. The exporter(s) must have required testing facilities and other equipment in place before applying for such facilitation from EIC. EIC will appoint a team of experts for such facilitation and based on the filed investigation report and satisfaction of proven in-house testing infrastructure, EIC will issue such facility the certificate for 'self-certification facility' for quality control and assurance for export consignments. EIC also asks the exporter to furnish an undertaking of assurance that his/her units will constantly and systematically endeavour to maintain the 'minimum quality norms' as prescribed by EIC under the Self-certification Scheme.

In today's complex and volatile business environment, self-certification is an important improvement on the long-experienced system of compulsory quality control and pre-shipment inspection scheme as it helps exporters to cut down their trade costs, cut red tape and allied documentation and reduce their export cycle times. With proliferation of various FTA/RTA, Indian companies are scaling up their operations and fast integrating into global value chain. In order to sustainably compete in such globalized set-up, the self-certification system has been introduced, which is based on the concept that an export-oriented manufacturing unit will never compromise with their established reputation and understand the responsibilities of risks involved in export of sub-standard goods, and accordingly will constantly endeavour to commit their manufacturing operations' quality assurance and compliance at each stage of production and exports. In order to qualify as a self-certification unit, it must fulfil the prescribed quality norms at various stages of production (Figure 18.14) of exportable goods.

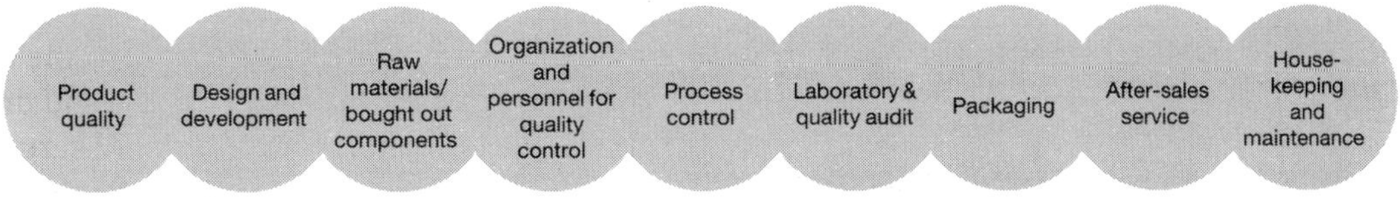

FIGURE 18.14 Stages of export quality compliance under self-certification scheme.

18.6.5 ISO 9000

The ISO 9000 series of quality standards have been evolved by the ISO, Geneva, on the basis of mutual consultations among key stakeholders. ISO 9000 series of quality control and compliance has been hugely popular, and firms, all over the world, accept these standards as the recognized and accepted benchmarks for assurance of the high quality of goods. In today's globalized trade operations, export firms tend to comply with ISO 9000 so as to project their products achieving a good quality-compliance system, thus attracting potential consumers, users, importers and associated buyers. The beauty of placing ISO 9000 standards in place guarantees the quality compliance of goods to these stakeholders as quality control under the ISO system is process-oriented following basic principles of quality management. The ISO 9000 system mandates specified procedures of quality control that an exporter has to follow in order to ensure that whatever is produced in his/her industrial premises must meet the customers' expectations and quality norms as specified by him/her. Figure 18.15 lists the underlying principles that an exporter has to follow in order to ensure quality compliance in exportable goods under the ISO 9000 series system.

As depicted above, ISO 9000 series of quality management is the process and system approach of continuous improvement largely aimed at ensuring mutually beneficial business relations, which are continuously supported by the management involvement, leadership and customer focus. The ISO 9000 system basically aims at 'quality assurance standards' and not product standards, wherein the quality management is a continuous process and is not a mere end result of the production. The focus of each involved stakeholder in production operations is on 'quality principles' and not on production, and the same is achieved not only in actions but also through the documentation at each level of the production. The implementation of key principles of ISO 9000 standards for quality control and compliance in export productions is by adhering to following steps sequentially shown in Figure 18.16.

The implementation of above ISO standards in export operations helps firms maintain an effective quality compliance system in their production and allied activities, thus demonstrating to the foreign buyer(s), importer(s) and consumers that this export firm is overtly committed to quality management at each stage of business operations and learning key lessons from any mistakes through proper

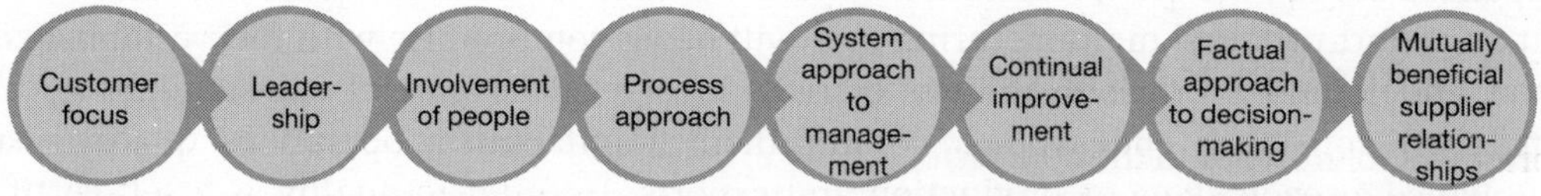

FIGURE 18.15 Key principles of ISO 9000 series system for quality control and compliance for export productions.

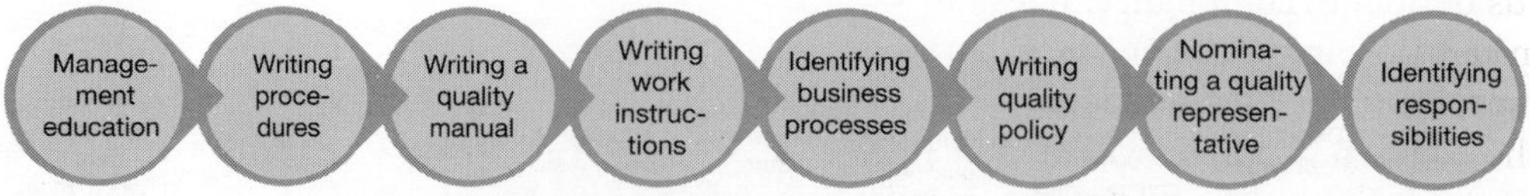

FIGURE 18.16 Implementation of ISO 9000 standards.

documentation at each stage. The ISO 9000 system of quality control and management aims at the following key objectives for excellence in export operations:

1. Achieving the importer(s), foreign buyer(s) and consumers' confidence in the products supplied by the export firm.
2. Implementing the process and system approach of continuous quality improvement at each stage of business operations, thus increasing compliance to establish and recognize quality benchmarks.
3. Implementing an integrated quality control system, thus completely eliminating the need for multiple assessments, appraisals and inspection by importers and foreign buyers in various part of the world.
4. Involving the top management including their commitment and participation to quality control initiatives and actions at any levels of business operations.
5. Benchmarking the cost–quality relationships and running operations at the level which offers the best product quality in the globally competitive business system at least possible costs.
6. Identifying unique and specific business needs of global customers and buyers and offering them what they desire and demand.

18.7 Inspection Process for Exportable Cargo

In order to get his/her cargo cleared for quality compliance under the Export (Quality Control and Inspection) Act, 1963, an exporter has to make an application in duplicate as prescribed in Box 18.1 to the concerned export inspection agency so as to carry out the pre-shipment inspection. The export agency will assign an appropriate officer for this work, and such inspection can be carried out at exporter's premises (factory or warehouse) or inspection and testing facility owned by the export agency. An exporter has to follow the processes discussed in the following sub-sections sequentially in order to get the certificate of inspection to be supplied to the importer.

18.7.1 Application for the Certificate of Inspection

An exporter has to intimate to the concerned export inspection facility in the prescribed form (Box 18.1) known as 'application for a certificate of inspection', which is a standardized pre-shipment export document.

An exporter has to attach certain documents as documentary proof along with the application for a certificate of inspection which helps the concerned officers of EIC to understand the specifications and standards of quality compliance, relevant nomenclature and other any specific issue(s) which should be taken care of (Figure 18.17). The exporter inspection agency will inspect the cargo complying it with agreed specifications and standards of quality compliance, and if the goods are in-compliance with same, the concerned officer will submit his/her report for the necessary action to EIC. An exporter must consider that he/she allows the adequate time to the export inspection agency to carry out the inspection work which can take from 4 to 7 days in India.

BOX 18.1 ► Application for Inspection of Quality Control

Exporter's name address	Invoice no. & date / Exporter's Ref.
	Buyer's order no. & date
Manufacturer's name & address Details of the manufacturer's seal, if any	To the (name & address of the inspection authority) Please inspect the consignment and issue a certificate of inspection under the Export of Dried Fish Maws (Quality Control and Inspection) Rules, 2002. A crossed cheque for ₹................................ drawn on .... is enclosed as inspection fee. Please debit our account passbook no .... enclosed. Date Signature of the exporter
Inspection required on / Weekly holiday Vessel/flight no. / Port of loading Probable date of landing / Date of sealing/flight	Address where consignment is to be inspected

Mark & no. as declared	No. & kind of packages	Description of goods	Quantity	FOB value (in ₹ or $)
		Description should include grade, size and brand.		

Technical requirements including specifications/approved samples with its characteristics as stipulated in the export contract

Other relevant information

Declarations: Certified that the goods mentioned above have been manufactured/produced to satisfy the conditions relating to quality control/inspection applicable to them under the Export .... (Quality Control and Inspection) Rules, 2002, and that the consignment conforms to the specification certified that the goods have been offered previously for inspection via intimation no. .... dated .... and the defects as pointed out earlier have been duly rectified.

Certified that no additional technical or quality requirements other than mentioned above have been stipulated by the overseas buyer. — Signature & Date

18.7.2 Deputation of Inspector and Testing

EIC deputes competent officials/staff to carry out the inspection work after the receipt of 'intimation for inspection' in the prescribed format. It is the duty of the exporter to keep the cargo ready for inspection and testing by the EIC officials and staff for which EIC usually intimates the exact day and timings to an exporter well in advance. In case of on-site cargo inspection, the exporter should arrange for facilities

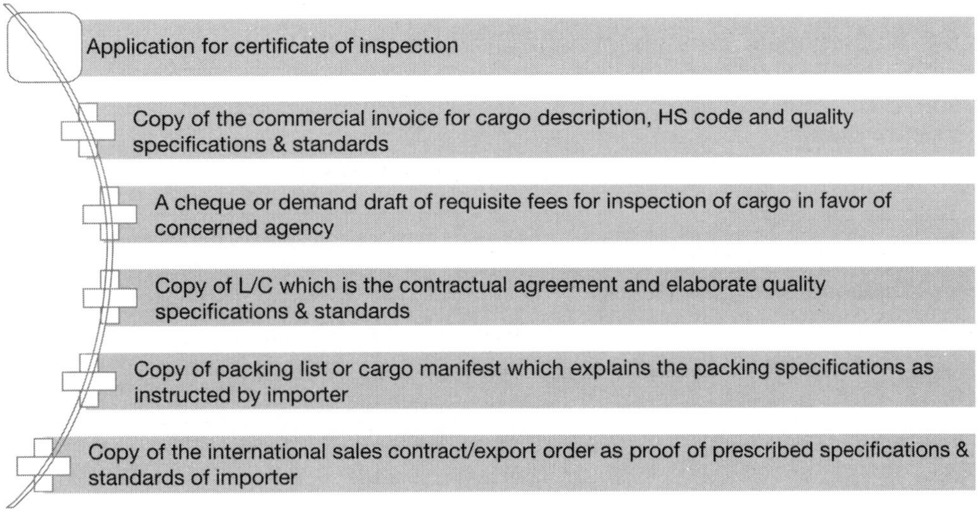

FIGURE 18.17 Documents to be submitted along with application for the certificate of inspection to EIC.

required for the testing and inspection. In case such facilities cannot be arranged on-site, the testing and inspection work can be done at any private independent laboratories.

18.7.3 Packing and Sealing of Goods

Once the EIC official, that is, the assigned inspector, is satisfied with the quality of exportable goods, he/she issues the order for packing of goods in his/her presence. After the goods are packed, the inspector marks and seals the consignment with seals and stamp of EIC declaring cargo for export. Simultaneously, the inspector prepares the report to be submitted to EIC for issuance of the certificate of inspection to an exporter.

18.7.4 Certificate of Inspection

Pre-shipment inspection for quality compliance of exportable cargo has to be done by export inspection agencies which are set up under the administrative control of EIC throughout the country. The inspector submits the field investigation report of quality compliance to EIC, and if found favourable, the deputy director of EIA starts the process for issuance of the 'certificate of inspection'. The pre-shipment inspection work is done keeping in mind the nature of products, a quality specification and standards, the importer's instructed quality norms and specifications if any. The process of the inspection may vary, as discussed above, and can be the consignment-to-consignment basis, IPQC, the Self-certification Scheme or implementation of a globally accepted quality regime like ISO quality control systems. In cases where the pre-shipment inspection is made mandatory by a particular agency as named by the importer, the export inspection has to take place essentially by the agency as intimated by the importer in agreed documents. On the submission of the above documents, the export inspection agency requires at least 4–5 days so as to conduct a quality test of the consignment of exportable goods. On its satisfaction about the exportable quality of consignment as per importer requirement/standards, it

BOX 18.2 ► Certificate for Inspection/IPQC Certificate

Exporter's name address		Invoice no. & date Buyer's order no. & date		
Manufacturer's name & address Details of the manufacturer's seal, if any Detail of seal of inspection authority, if any		Name & logo of the inspection agency		
Specification reference		Certificate no.		
Mark & nos.	No. & kind of Packages	Description of goods	Quality	FOB value (in ₹)
		Description should include grade, size and brand.		
Remarks, if any Stamp for FOB revision				

**Certification under inspection system

It is hereby declared that the consignment as per details given above has been inspected as required under the Export of .... (Quality Control and Inspection) Rules, 2002. It satisfies the conditions as applicable to it and is certified export worthy.

Date of inspection .... or

**Certification under in process quality control system

It is hereby certified, on the basis of controls carried out, that the commodities as per details given herein are in specifications prescribed under the Export of Dried Fish Maws (Quality Control and Inspection) Rules, 2002.

Seal of the Inspection Agency
Signature
Name
Designation
Date

issues the 'certificate of inspection' to the exporter in the prescribed proforma in five copies. The specimen of the certificate of inspection is given in Box 18.2.

An exporter has to submit the original copy of such inspection certificate to customs authorities along with shipping bill/bill of export at the time of export consignment clearance by Indian customs. The second copy of export inspection is to be sent to the importer along with 'shipping advice' and various other export documents. The third copy shall be retained by the exporter for any future reference. The fourth copy is to be sent to EIC at its headquarters in New Delhi, and the fifth copy shall be retained by the concerned export inspection agency for future references.

18.7.5 Issue of Rejection Note and Appeal against Rejection

In case the report as submitted by the assigned inspector/concerned official is not favourable, the deputy director of export inspection agency issues a rejection note to the exporter, thus declaring the goods not suitable for exports. The EIC rules allow an exporter to file an appeal against the 'rejection note' within 10 days from the date of the receipt of such note along with requisite fees. EIA, on receipt of such appeal, convenes a meeting of the appellate panel. The panel, if it so feels on the basis of a mutual discussion that there is a possibility of any lapse in the quality control investigation which has led to rejection report, may form a team of inspectors to examine the export consignment once again. The decision of the appellate panel is final and is binding on both the parties, the exporter and the export inspection agency.

18.8 Summary

The quality of exportable goods and services has become extremely pertinent for any exporter as one can engage, compete, sustain and manage business operations only if the firm's goods and services not only surpass the quality standards of its competitors but also excel beyond customers' expectations. The term quality refers to the defined set of attributes or specifications that products and services should have in order to offer value to the customer for money being charged. Hence, an exporter of goods and services must decide the quality of a product before introducing it in the international market, and this can be better done keeping in mind the national and international standards of quality as laid down by the respective national or international standards bodies. The success of any firm in such globally interconnected, interdependent and competitive business environment largely depends on how far such firm has been successful to adapt and standardize its products according to the accepted and established global quality standards in target markets. Winning customer's confidence in a highly competitive global market is a significant element of success for any export firm. A firm can effectively engage with global buyers only if its products and services not only win the customer's confidence, but it is also considered as a dependable supplier with superior quality of goods and services.

India is one of the few countries that has emphasized the importance of quality control in exports. Accordingly, Section 3 of the Export (Quality Control and Pre-Shipment Inspection) Act, 1963, mandates an important step of compulsory pre-shipment inspection of the goods that are to be exported. Under the Export (Quality Control and Pre-Shipment Inspection) Act, 1963, EIC was set up by GOI. In today's borderless trade regime, an exporter faces tough competition not only from the fellow exporters from his/her home country but also from other countries. Accordingly, an exporter should have an effective quality strategy to gain a competitive edge over his/her competitors. He/she should follow the endeavour not only to follow the established quality benchmarks but should think beyond them in order to remain ahead of time. Export firms should develop a quality assurance culture among their employees and quality control practices should be accordingly well documented at each critical stage of production and sales process.

In today's globalized world, there are two types of quality control methods practiced by export firms. Both the methods of quality control, that is, 'inspection of goods' and 'SQC' have been very popular and are widely used in quality control of internationally traded cargoes. Both of them are considered vital as the first method of quality control is aimed at ensuring the quality standards in export consignment and accordingly benchmarking them for the importer's help, wherein the second method is aimed to help an exporter to take all necessary steps at the production-level itself. In order to get his/her cargo cleared for quality compliance under the Export (Quality Control and Inspection) Act, 1963, an exporter has to make an application in duplicate as prescribed to the concerned export inspection agency (Box 18.1) so as to carry out the pre-shipment inspection. The export agency will assign an appropriate officer for this work, and such inspection can be carried out at exporter's premises (factory or warehouse) or inspection and testing facility owned by the export agency.

CASE STUDY Impact of COVID-19 on Global Food Supply Chain

The outbreak of COVID-19 has impacted us all. The essential fallout of this pandemic is increasing concern for public health, safety and security. Nations all over the world have already started the groundwork for enhanced public health and safety. With the globalization of the world's food supply chain, there are numerous challenges to Indian exporters, especially the one engaged in exports of fruits, vegetables, meat, fish, milk, animal fat and other products of plants and animal origin. WHO estimates that around one billion people globally become ill from the use of unsafe food each year. The problem highlights the key question that how is food managed from farm to fork in globalized food supply chain networks. In order to remain quality complied globally, Indian food exporters have to rework on pre-harvest farming techniques aimed at avoiding contamination by pesticides and other chemicals and pathogens that can be transmitted by agro-inputs and water. Further, at the post-harvest stage, these exporters should rework on how foreign materials make their way into food, hygiene storage and warehousing and cases of intentional adulteration. Logistically, Indian exporters should work with the supply chain stakeholders for safe transportation of a product (making sure temperature controls and other factors work in favour of safety), proper labelling and packaging and consumer mishandling. Beyond that Indian exporters need to factor and account for expenses to product recalls. Indian food exporters have to learn to anticipate managing potential financial losses that stem from product contamination. Consumers globally are now becoming more cognizant of current recalls, and it is high time to take steps to mitigate their risks. Regulatory bodies such as EIC and Agricultural and Processed Food Export Development Authority need to frame the regulatory framework for food producers and to raise food safety culture and awareness to reduce the impact of growing health concern on Indian food exports.

Indian exporters should avoid border rejections, recalls and investigations as they not only harm commercially but bring a bad name to the entire trade fraternity of the country. It is high time that Indian exporters meet global standards for food production and safety at each stage of the globalized food supply chain. Indian fruits and vegetable growers and animal product producers need to ensure that their farming and processing practices comply with the top recommendations for biosecurity. At the post-harvest stage, the vegetable and fruit pickers, packers and processors must also adhere to rigid standards to reduce the potential of any food contamination. Labels aimed at health safety for food products must be specific and should provide country-specific information on the allergen, pathogen and other issues. The COVID-19 pandemic has brought not only a big economic loss but also an opportunity to educate each stakeholder of food supply chain for safe food-handling procedures such as washing food (produce), cooking thoroughly, avoiding cross-contamination of utensils, cutting boards and other preparation measures and storage of foods.

India also needs to work globally on strengthening the health- and safety-related controls and regulations, which are imposed by WTO under its Agreement on the Application of Sanitary and Phytosanitary Measures in 1995. There is a need for harmonized health safety regime for protecting the interest of global consumers, instead of country-specific regulations, which have impacted Indian exports very hard. Indian food exporters are still coping with the proliferated regulatory regime due to multiple inspections, rejections and recall under the stricter standards mandated by the countries. The Export Health Certificate issued for this purpose by EIC has added products cost of Indian food exporters as they have to comply with installation of quality assurance systems in export units, consignment-wise inspection, the installation of a food safety management system and so on for ensuring food safety in their processing units.

Specific products where the Export Health Certificate has been made mandatory include fish and fishery products, dairy, honey, poultry, egg products, meat and meat products, basmati rice and black pepper. Additionally, there are some non-notified products such as coir, tea, auto parts, other additives and pre-mixtures, animal casings, crushed bones and gelatine. Further, voluntary certification is also done in case of other food and non-food products. In the changing global socio-economic order post COVID-19, the Export Health Certificate, issued by EIC, can add to the credibility of Indian food products in the global market. The certification of these products by EIC acts as an assurance of the quality and suitability of the exported item. Indian food exporters should use services of EIC for the Export Health Certificate as it is globally recognized and India's official certifier for export quality assurance and compliance. The Export Health Certificate issued by the export inspection agency of EIC increases the acceptability of the certified products in the globalized food supply chain.

Questions

1. How did Covid-19 have its impact on global food supply chain?
2. At what stage of the food chain do Indian exporters need to take precautions for food safety and compliance?
3. Why is the proliferated global regulatory regime creating problems for India's food products exporters?
4. How can Indian food exporters remain resilient and sustainable in the global food supply chain?

Review Exercises

Multiple Choice Questions

1. The headquarters of EIC is located at
   a. New Delhi
   b. Mumbai
   c. Kolkata
   d. Chennai
   e. It is virtual now
2. For quality assurance of software, which of the following standards are used?
   a. ISO 9000 series
   b. ISO 14000 series
   c. HACCP certification
   d. SEI-CMM level
   e. None of the above
3. Which of the following agencies has been set up for export quality inspection?
   a. EIC
   b. BIS
   c. Food Safety and Standard Council of India
   d. Bureau Veritas
   e. None of the above
4. Which of the following is not a standard applicable to food products?
   a. FPO standard
   b. Vegetarian mark (green dot symbol)

- **c.** Non-vegetarian mark (red dot symbol)
- **d.** FSSAI standards
- **e.** BIS standards

5. For strengthening the economic system and ensuring zero carbon footprints, which of the following labels has come?
- **a.** ISO 9000 series
- **b.** Ecolabel
- **c.** ISO 14000 series
- **d.** HACCP certification
- **e.** None of the above

6. Which of the following statements is not a benefit of the export cargo inspection?
- **a.** Helps an export firm get a competitive edge in the foreign as well as domestic markets
- **b.** Helps in cutting operational costs as quality control systems provide sound and efficient business processes and procedures
- **c.** Helps in minimizing the resource wastage and the time spent on reworking and repairs of exportable goods
- **d.** Quality control provides for constant motivation for ensuring constant quality improvement and resultant satisfied customers
- **e.** Satisfies the internal ego of the exporter

7. In which of the following years was EIC set up?
- **a.** 1964
- **b.** 2019
- **c.** 2002
- **d.** 1947
- **e.** 1978

8. Which of the following is not a type of Ecolabel?
- **a.** Energy star mark
- **b.** Eco mark
- **c.** Non-polluting vehicles
- **d.** Green dot licence
- **e.** BIS standards

9. Which of the following standard attest the purity of silk products?
- **a.** Silk mark
- **b.** Rug mark
- **c.** Smile mark
- **d.** Bug mark
- **e.** Eco mark

10. Which of the following standard will be used for assessing the purity of gold?
- **a.** ISO 9000 series
- **b.** ISO 14000 series
- **c.** HACCP certification
- **d.** BIS hallmark
- **e.** None of the above

Critical Thinking Questions

1. Discuss the concepts of quality control and assurance. Give some examples to support your answer from several industries.
2. Discuss the significance and role of quality control measures in EXIM business.
3. Explain the various methods of quality control used in EXIM business.
4. What do you mean by the SQC method of quality control? Explain the types and process used in the SQC method.
5. Explain the various methods used in quality control under the inspection of cargo methods. Give some examples to support your answer.
6. Explain the process and mechanism for availing the certificate of inspection for the export business. Which document does one have to submit to get the certificate of inspection?
7. Explain the various measures that have been taken for quality control of internationally traded goods in India.
8. Discuss the role of BIS and DMI in quality control in India.
9. Explain the role of Export (Quality Control and Pre-Shipment Inspection) Act, 1963, in the promotion of quality control measures in the export business.
10. Explain the mechanism of pre-shipment inspection for exportable goods in India.

CHAPTER 19

Dedicated Export Enclaves

CHAPTER OBJECTIVES

- To understand the concept of dedicated export enclaves.
- To understand the performance of dedicated export enclaves in India.
- To understand the procedure for bonding and operations of EOUs.
- To appraise the role of development commissioner in the administration of EOUs.

19.1 Introduction

International trade is an extension of internal trade, where domestically produced agricultural and manufactured goods and services are traded internationally, thus giving an additional boost to the economic activity and employment generation. Exports and imports of both goods and services happen between two different countries. Traditionally, it was thought that a country cannot produce everything it needs by itself; hence, it has to import from another country. That is true in the case of agricultural commodities, minerals and ores and other raw materials. With waves of technological innovations, there is a shift in the pattern of trade wherein more value-added and fast-moving consumer goods are traded, which are produced by countries in dedicated export enclaves, thus having scale advantages in production and marketing. With faster logistics operations at low costs, a country can source what it cannot produce domestically and manufacture it to fulfil the economic needs of the entire world. Nations are increasingly leveraging their economic resources to expand and diversify their exports, which acts as a catalyst for enhanced economic growth and employment generation. Nations find it advantageous to indulge in trade with other countries by exporting those commodities which they produce cheaper in exchange for what others can produce at a lower cost. The enhanced foreign trade activity can have a profound impact on the growth of an economy in terms of production, employment, technology, resource utilization and so on. In fact, the foreign trade activity has been one of the most significant determinants of economic development in a country, and countries which lag in foreign trade may have far-reaching economic consequences on their economic development. China, Taiwan, Japan, South Korea and some of the Southeast Asian economies have used foreign trade as an instrument to speed up the process of economic development. Dedicated export enclaves have played an important role in enhancing exports of these countries, and these countries have emerged as the leading suppliers of goods to world markets. India has also used STPIs to dramatically increase its software and IT exports to the world market. Figure 19.1 details the numbers of functional dedicated export enclaves along with annual exports for the period 2013–2014 to 2018–2019.

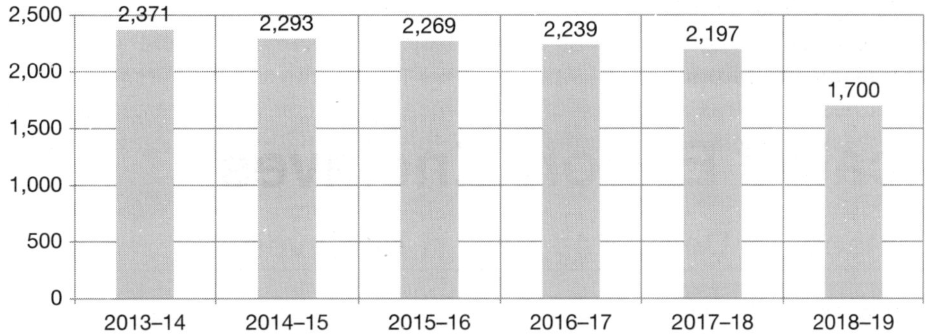

FIGURE 19.1 Number of functional EOUs in India (2013–2014 to 2018–2019).

Source: Ministry of Commerce & Industry, Government of India. https://commerce.gov.in/ (accessed on 24 May 2023).

Dedicated export enclaves in the form of the EOU Scheme were introduced in India in the year 1980. The scheme is implemented by DGFT. In order to cater to varying economic needs of different sectors of the economy, the scheme is extended in different variants, for example, for the software export, the STPI Scheme was launched which has been extremely successful in increasing services exports of India. EHTP was introduced to enhance the exports of engineering goods, and the BTPs Scheme was introduced to increase the exports of pharmaceuticals and drugs. Dedicated export enclaves are different from SEZs, which are a foreign territory located in a country where the domestic rules and regulations have limited scope. Dedicated export enclaves are within DTA and are aimed at boosting exports by creating additional production capacity. Dedicated export enclaves are a complementary scheme to the SEZs of India where SEZs are treated as a 'foreign territory' and are governed by the SEZ Act, 2005, and SEZs Rules, 2006. Dedicated export enclaves (EOU/EHTP/BTP/STPI) are regulated by Chapter 6 of the FTP and Customs Act, 1962. Hence, the scheme is for EOU/STP/EHTP/BTP and is referred to, in common parlance, as the EOU Scheme. SEZs were earlier known as the EPZ Scheme. The dedicated export scheme was introduced to attract many units due to locational restrictions. The exporters showed willingness to set up units with a long-term commitment to exports under customs bond operations provided that they had the freedom to locate them in places of their choice and given most of the benefits as provided to units set up in SEZs.

In order to address the changing geo-economic realities of the dynamic business environment, the EOU Scheme has undergone various changes, and its scope has also expanded substantially as compared to the initial scheme as enunciated in 1980. A variant has been launched known as STPI in order to create a suitable and appropriate economic system for growth and development of software services, information technology and IT-enabled services exports. Other services exports such as business consultancy, telecommunications, tour and travel, shipping and transports, medical tourism are also promoted under the scheme by ensuring dedicated outwards services from these zones. When the EOU Scheme was launched for the first time, its focus was basically for the manufacturing sector with certain minimum value addition in terms of export earnings. Presently, the units undertaking to export their entire production of goods are allowed to be set up as an EOU. These units may be engaged in the manufacture, services, development of software, repair, remaking, reconditioning, re-engineering including making of gold/silver/platinum jewellery and articles thereof; agriculture including agro-processing, aquaculture, animal husbandry, biotechnology, floriculture, horticulture, pisciculture, viticulture, poultry, sericulture and granites. The EOUs can export all products/services except prohibited items of exports in ITC (HS).

FTP 2015–2020 was released on 1 April 2015 and was supposed to remain in force up to 31 March 2020, unless otherwise specified. The policy was extended up to 31 March 2023 and a New Foreign Trade Policy 2023 came into force from 1 April 2023. The new FTP provides a framework for increasing exports of goods and services as well as generation of employment and increasing value addition in the country, integrating the 'Make in India', 'Digital India' and 'Skill India' initiatives of the government.

19.2 Concept of Dedicated Export Enclaves

For an economy like India, the exports are vital as foreign exchange earnings so made are used to finance the huge import requirements of crude oil, gas and capital goods, which are vital for the faster and comprehensive economic development of the country. Keeping this in mind, GOI has enacted the Dedicated Export Enclaves' Scheme so that dedicated export units are provided facilitative and promontory trade environment for enhanced manufacturing and services exports. The EOU Scheme is one of the export promotion schemes aimed at promoting the exports of manufactured goods from India and is in existence since 1980. The sector-specific EOU schemes are launched such as the STPI Scheme for export of software, the EHTP Park Scheme for export of electronic hardware, the BTP Scheme for export of biotechnology products. Under the 'Dedicated Export Enclave' scheme, manufacturing or service sector units are allowed to be set up with the main objective of exporting entire production of goods manufactured or services except limited sale in DTA as provided under FTP. These units help the country to export value-added items, create additional employment opportunities, promote additional economic activity, earn precious foreign exchange and above all achieve competitiveness in international trade. Figure 19.2 lists the main objectives of the EOU Scheme in India.

One has to apply to DGFT for bonding the unit under the EOU/EHTP/BTP/STPI Scheme of FTP of India and Handbook of Procedures, Volume I, and public notices/circulars issued by the Department of Commerce. Establishment of units and their performance is monitored by the jurisdictional development commissioner (DC) in accordance with the FTP provisions. Since customs bonding under Sections 9, 58 and 65 of Customs Act, 1962, is mandatory for EOUs, the scheme envisages an important role for Indian customs department. Corresponding notifications enabling duty exemption to have been issued by the Central Board of Indirect Taxes and Customs under the Customs Act, 1962, and the GST Act, 2017. Since the matter is concerning the exports and foreign exchange, there is a defined role of other agencies such as RBI, CBDT, and DGFT. Furthermore, the legislation such as the Income Tax Act, 1961; the Foreign Trade Development and Regulation Act, 1992; and the Foreign Exchange Management Act, 2000, including the notifications/circulars issued thereunder provides the regulatory framework for export and import policy of India. Specific benefits of dedicated export enclaves such as EOU/EHTP/BTP/STPI are bulleted as under:

1. EOUs are allowed to procure raw material or duty-free capital goods, either through import or through domestic sources.
2. EOUs are eligible for reimbursement of GST.
3. EOUs are eligible for reimbursement of duty paid on fuels procured from domestic oil companies.
4. EOUs are eligible for claiming input tax credit on the goods and services and refund thereof.
5. Fast-track clearance facilities.
6. Exemption from industrial licensing for the manufacture of items reserved for SSI sector.

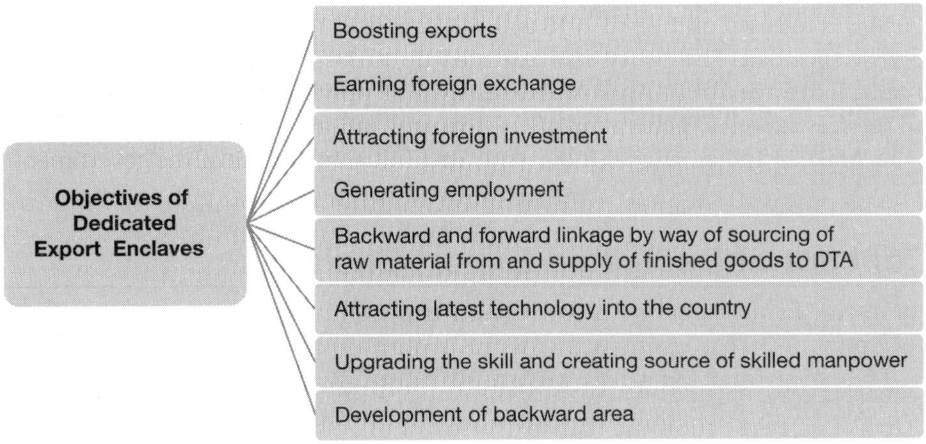

FIGURE 19.2 Objectives of dedicated export enclaves.

Source: Foreign Trade Policy 2015–2020.

19.3 Types of Dedicated Export Enclaves in India

In the following sub-sections, we will discuss the different types of dedicated export enclaves in India.

19.3.1 EOUs Scheme

The EOU was introduced by GOI in order to boost exports, increase foreign earnings and create employment in India. The EOU scheme is complementary to the schemes for Free Trade Zone, EPZ, which are much larger in area and scope of activities.

19.3.2 EHTP of India

With the rising per capita income and the growing number of middle-class families, the Indian electronics industry witnessed growth in the early years of the 21st century, in terms of both production and sales. Electronic hardware is the backbone of any growing economy, and the Indian government has encouraged the production as well as export of electronic hardware from India. EHTPs of India are being set up across the country to facilitate the growth of this resource-intensive segment. Electronic hardware is required across various industries such as telecommunications, engineering, information technology, medical electronics, industrial machinery and automation, automobile, power and solar photovoltaic, defence and aerospace, consumer electronics and appliances, and is also the largest imported item worldwide with 15 percent of global imports coming from the electronic sector. The market size of Indian electronic industry is expected to be around $400 billion, and it is the prime reason that so much thrust is given to EHTPs in India. To set up an EHTP, one needs to apply to the director, STPI, along with the project report. The application should be duly signed by a competent authority with initials on each page of the application along with the official seal of the company, and the applicant should also furnish undertaking. A fee of ₹2,500 is to be paid for the registration of the same. The EHTP Scheme is administered by the Ministry of Communications and

Information Technology through the directors of STPI across the country. DGFT frames the policy and procedure vis-à-vis export operations as EHTP are 100 percent export-oriented dedicated export enclaves. EFTP units can manufacture any item of electronic hardware for exports including hardware and software in an integrated manner. EHTP provides the required infrastructure for R&D activity, maintenance or testing and calibration services, cutting the investment by manufacturers and exporters of electronic goods.

19.3.3 STPI Scheme

In order to promote IT and IT-enabled exports from India, GOI launched the STPI Scheme, and the first STPI was set up in 1991. The operations of STPIs are governed by the Ministry of Electronics and Information Technology and the policy regime vis-à-vis exports are provided by DGFT. The STPI scheme provides a 'single-window' for starting, executing and exporting IT export services from India to world markets. STPI offers a variety of services to export-oriented firms located in STPI zones such as statutory compliance services, data communications services, incubation facilities, training and value-added services. The success of India's software and IT exports is largely attributed to various STPIs located across the country. By the end of September 2022, there were a total of 63 functional software technology parks (STPs) in India wherein more than 5000 units were registered for IT and IT-enabled operations. STPIs are contributing handsomely in terms of exports as the overall exports done by STPI registered IT/ITES units has increased from from ₹52 crore in 1992–1993 to ₹628,330 crore in 2021–2022, which is approx. 50% of the national software exports and 2.3% of India's GDP (https://stpi.in/en/about-stpi, accessed on 5 May 2023).

STPI provides a physical and virtual infrastructure so as to provide internal engineering resources, consulting, training and implementation services to various software export units located in the zone. STPI also provides services such as network design, system integration, installation, operations and maintenance of application networks and facilities in varied areas. The STPI Scheme provides various benefits to the registered units such as allowing 100 percent foreign equity participation, tax incentives, duty-free import of goods and services, duty-free indigenous procurement, DTA entitlement and deemed exports.

19.3.4 BTP of India Scheme

In order to promote and strengthen the strong ecosystem for drug and pharma research, the Department of Biotechnology has come up with the scheme of BTPs, and DGFT has notified some of them under FTP as export-oriented research, incubation and manufacturing facilities for increasing India's drug and pharma exports. BTP is a demarcated area which has laboratory space, ready-to-use facilities, pilot plant facilities, enterprise zone and all the other basic facilities. BTPs are created to assist entrepreneurs involved in research, incubation and commercialization of their life science ideas/discoveries and transform them into viable commercial ventures without risking huge investments. BTPs in India are successfully accelerating the commercialization of new technologies in the drug and pharma sector, thus nurturing the ecosystem required for maintaining emerging ventures. BTPs are also assisting new business enterprises to forge appropriate business linkages with other stakeholders of the biotechnology sector, especially with academia, intellectual property law firms and policymakers. With the help these BTPs, newer entrepreneurs are coming up to this investment-intensive sector and paving the way for more start-ups aimed at improving the life sciences and health care system. BTPs provide the required infrastructure for research and incubation at an economical rate to Indian entrepreneurs to

CASELET 19.1

Rising Profile of India's BTPs

One category of dedicated export enclaves in India includes the BTPs which are production centres for world-class pharmaceuticals and drugs, which are supplied to world markets. India's pharma and drug export is valued at $32 billion with the United States, China, the United Kingdom and Germany as the prime destinations for exports. India, in fact, has emerged as a low-cost and reliable supplier of drugs and pharma in the world. India has around 4 percent market share in the global drugs market and 2.4 percent market share for pharmaceuticals. Indian drugs and pharma products have very high demand from developing countries of Africa and Latin America, and it is continually growing, especially due to their cost-effectiveness. India has a strong ecosystem for manufacturing and export of pharmaceuticals and drugs as it is one among the world's top 12 highest-performing biotech countries, with 2 percent of the global market share. India is considered as the third largest biotech powerhouse in the Asia-Pacific region. A strong educational system coupled with robust biotech institutions and regulatory framework, the biotechnology industry in India has significantly evolved in the 21st century. The biotech sector is on the growth path with compound annual growth rate (CAGR) of 20 percent, and the Department of Biotechnology, GOI, has set up a target of $100 billion industry by 2025. BTPs shall be the backbone of any future expansion plan for India's growing domestic needs along with catering to global markets. India is a leading producer of enzymes, Hepatitis B vaccine, malaria drugs and other lifesaving drugs. The success of India's BTPs can be understood with the fact that India has the second-highest number of US Food and Drug Administration approved plants, after the United States. The key drivers for the growth and success of BTPs in India are its growing population, lifestyle changes which give rise to ailments such as stroke, cancer and diabetes, increased healthcare awareness among its people, strong educational system producing more scientists and engineers and a stable regulatory framework and increased thrust by GOI. Favourable foreign direct investments coupled with the predictable and transparent intellectual property regime have contributed to the growth of the pharma sector in India, thus contributing to the success of BTPs and enhanced pharma exports.

incubate their technology and scale up to commercial level. Kiran Mazumdar-Shaw is a success story in India, and she says her success in pharma research and business is largely credited to BTPs. DGFT provides a fair and stable policy regime for the growth and operations of BTPs (Caselet 19.1) so as to boost India's exports of pharma products in international markets.

19.4 Performance of Dedicated Export Enclaves in India

Dedicated export enclaves were a vital contributor in India's export till 2008 contributing as much as around one-fourth of India's total exports. Phasing out of certain export benefits to dedicated export enclaves has resulted in steep decline in a number of operational dedicated export enclaves in the last one decade. For example, Table 19.1 details that the export of dedicated exports enclaves was as high as ₹163,838 crore out of India's total exports of ₹655,864 crore, which is around 24.98 percent of India's total exports in the year 2007–2008, and it has declined to mere ₹36,591 crore in 2017–2018, which is mere 1.97 percent of India's total exports. This indicates that dedicated export enclaves have witnessed a downward trend over the last one decade. Although the proportion of non-functional EOUs has slowed marginally, it still constitutes around 20 percent of the total registered EOUs. Withdrawal of income tax exemption and shifting of units from dedicated export enclaves have taken away the uniqueness of the 100 percent EOU Scheme and resulted in the decline of the attractiveness of Dedicated Export Enclaves' Scheme among exporters. Unfortunately, there is no special provision in FTP to promote the unique 100 percent EOU Scheme. Similar export benefits were available to SEZs, along with an allowance for domestic sales but without any ceiling. Table 19.1 depicts the falling trends of exports from dedicated export enclaves from India.

The success of dedicated export enclave scheme depends on proper regulation, auditing and monitoring. The shift in focus of the Ministry of Commerce and Industry from the dedicated export enclaves to SEZs has not provided any facilitative internal audit mechanism to check and facilitate the functioning of EOUs. The EOU scheme has not been successful due to various reasons such as complexities that arise due to its size, lack of entrepreneurial talent, lack of promotion of the scheme and its limited share in manufacturing. The policy regulating the dedicated export enclaves has not witnessed a transformation in the changing geo-economic environment. Policy measures with specific timelines are needed to stop the downward trend of EOU growth and poor performance by utilizing the unique position of EOUs. DGFT should intervene in the process of an internal audit system wherein sector-specific internal as well as external challenges must be factored while offering the export benefits to such units. It is important to monitor the annual progress containing all relevant information on export volumes, duties forgone and DTA sales so as to assess the level of assistance and intervention required to make these units viable in changing geo-economic contexts.

For India to emerge as an export champion in the world economy, the growth and expansion of Dedicated Export Enclaves are vital as they help tap the innate talent, entrepreneurial spirit and effective utilization of the country's economic resources in exchange of freely convertible foreign currency. For India to achieve a target of $1,000 billion exports by 2020 and emerge as $5 trillion economy by 2025 and $10 trillion economy by 2030, the schemes like Dedicated Exports Enclaves can play a vital role. To make India's EOUs more focused, DGFT should address the systemic issues for their sustainable growth.

The way forward for GOI is to revise the scheme to suit the changing global environment. That means introducing new provisions to ensure proper functioning and careful monitoring, without affecting the scheme's competitiveness with other similar policies like SEZs. If these changes are not made soon, EOUs will continue to fall out of use, and the scheme will become just another ineffective trade policy.

TABLE 19.1 Share of Exports of Dedicated Export Enclaves vis-à-vis Total Exports of India

Year	Exports from EOUs	India's Total Exports	Share of EOUs Exports in India's Total Exports
2012–2013	90,180.67	1,634,318.28	5.50
2013–2014	89,642.09	1,905,011.08	4.70
2014–2015	64,321.30	1,444,720.12	4.45
2015–2016	97,493.23	1,896,378.15	5.14
2016–2017	74,771.89	1,716,365.78	4.35
2017–2018	36,591.90	1,854,167.90	1.97

Source: www.indiastat.org

19.5 Procedure for Approval of an EOU

Any firm intending to get registered as an EOU/EHTP/BTP/STPI, involving activities for either manufacturing or service sector, should submit three copies of the application in the format prescribed in Appendix 14-I-A of *Handbook of Procedures, Volume I.* This application should be submitted to the jurisdictional DC for consideration in the Unit Approval Committee (UAC). UAC under the chairmanship of DC of jurisdictional SEZs should scrutinize all such applications received for setting up of an EOU. UAC may approve or reject the application of any unit for the aforesaid purpose within a period of 15 days of the receipt of the application. All proposals which are required to have an industrial licence or for units service sector except software and IT-enabled services are to be approved by the Board of Approval (BOA). Once it is approved by BOA, a unit can place an application under the mandated form to the DC, and the approval or rejection is required to be conveyed to the unit within 45 days. The following details are required for the registration of an EOU:

1. Profile of directors/promoters/proprietors/partners
2. Name, address and experience of the directors/partners/proprietors
3. Manufacturing procedure, flow chart and description
4. Finance means/source of finance/project cost
5. Trade-in/marketing tie-up preparations
6. Estimated profit and loss account and balance sheet for five subsequent years
7. In case of transfer of DTA unit to EOU profit and loss account and balance sheet for three previous years
8. Present-day and future activity of the applicant
9. Enduring email and website of the firm/company and the digital signature of the authorized party
10. Estimated list of imported/native capital goods
11. Estimated list of imported/native raw material
12. Machinery list and raw material list that is installed or in stock if there are existing units

If a unit is approved by DC, a letter of permission (LOP), as per the format prescribed in Appendix 14-I-E of *Handbook of Procedures, Volume I*, is issued to the EOU for starting the approved manufacturing and services operations. LOP is valid for the time period of three years within which the EOU is required to commence commercial production or commencement of services. If a unit cannot start production or rendering of services within a period of three years, the validity of LOP can be further extended for another three years by DC/designated authority. A unit must start manufacturing and rendering of services within six years as any proposal for the extension of validity after six years is to be considered in the case of exceptional circumstances by the Board of Approval on a case-to-case basis. Once the unit starts the commercial production of goods and rendering services, LOP will be valid for five years from the date of commencement of such commercial production. If a unit intends to continue production and rendering of services as an EOU on the completion of five years, it should file for the extension of bonding and other allied mandatory requirements; otherwise, it can opt out of the EOU Scheme. DC is empowered to extend the approval period to those EOUs which intend to continue as an EOU, and if no information or intimation for extension of approvals is received from the unit within a period of six months of expiry of the approval period, DC should cancel the registration of such unit as an EOU unit.

19.6 Role of Development Commissioner in Administration of EOUs

The powers of DC/designated officer in administration and control of EOUs are elaborated in the list below. The jurisdiction of each DC is provided in Appendix 6J of Appendices and Aayat–Niryat Forms.

1. DC is empowered to convert a sick/closed DTA unit into EOU.
2. DC can convert the EOU to STP/EHTP/BTP and vice-versa as per the prescribed procedure under FTP.
3. DC can allow an increase in the value of capital goods in terms of Indian rupees, on account of foreign exchange rate fluctuations.
4. DC can permit capacity enhancement without any limit in the case of delicensed industries only.
5. DC can permit broadbanding for similar goods and activities mentioned in LOP or provide for backward or forward linkages to the existing line of manufacture.
6. DC can authorize a change in the name of the company or implementing agency and change from a company to another provided a new implementing agency/company undertakes to take over assets and liabilities of the existing unit.
7. DC/designated authority can permit a change of location from the place mentioned in LOP to another and/or include additional location provided that no change in other terms and conditions of approval is envisaged and that new location is within the territorial jurisdiction of DC/designated officer.
8. DC can extend the validity period of LOP beyond the initial validity period of LOP (except in the case where there is a restriction on the initial period of approval, like setting up of oil refinery projects) as per Paragraph 6.05 (a) of FTP.
9. DC can cancel LOP wherever warranted.
10. DC can permit the merger of two or more units into one unit provided those units fall within the jurisdiction of same DC/designated officer subject to the condition that activities are covered under the provision of broadbanding.
11. DC exercises powers of adjudication under Section 13 read with Section 11 of Foreign Trade (Development and Regulation) Act, 1992, in respect of EOUs as mentioned in Gazette Notification No. S.O. 194 (E) dated 6 March 2000.
12. DC can do valuation of exports declared on Software export valuation form by EOUs as per RBI AD (MA Series) Circular AP (DIR series Circular No. 9 dated 25 October 2001).
13. DC issues eligibility certificates for grant of employment visa to low-level foreign technicians to be engaged by EOUs as per the Ministry of Home Affairs Letter No. 25022/7/99-F.1 dated 20 September 1999.

19.7 Process and Procedure of Customs Bonding of an EOU

Each EOU unit is required to be bonded under the Customs Act, 1962, for two purposes. First, for the purposes of customs warehousing under Section 57 or 58 of the Customs Act, 1962, as they are entitled to import duty-free cargo to be utilized for the manufacture of the export cargo. Second, each unit is required to be registered for the 'manufacture in bond' under Section 65 of the Customs Act, 1962, and can operate under the customs bond only as per the conditions stipulated under FTP and the corresponding customs/GST exemption notifications. EOU is required to follow the procedure as prescribed in FTP and Handbook of Procedures, Volume I. For the issuance of customs private bonded warehousing licence, the application accompanied by the following information/document may be made to the jurisdictional assistant commissioner/deputy commissioner of customs:

1. A unit should submit the copy of the notification of DC, declaring the place as EOU. EOU should apply for customs bonding of location under Section 58 of the Customs Act and such application for bonding should be moved under Section 9 of the Customs Act, 1962.
2. The unit should execute the copy of LOP issued by DC along with the copy of LUT.
3. The unit should provide details of premises to be bonded including ground plan, the title of land/building in case of units engaged in aquaculture, horticulture and floriculture, granite quarrying, the physical bonding of the premises is not required; however, DC must be satisfied that the unit should comply with the established rules and regulations and manufacturing and services operations therein should not result in revenue loss to GOI.
4. The unit should provide the project report and manufacturing process to be undertaken by it after the operationalization and customs bonding.
5. The unit should provide the list of raw material, consumables, capital goods and so on, which will be used in such approved EOU.
6. The approved unit should give an undertaking that cost recovery and other charges shall be paid to the concerned authorities as mandated and agreed including merchant overtime charges. Further, EOUs having inter-linkages with the domestic economy through the procurement or sale of goods in DTA are additionally required to obtain central excise registration from the jurisdictional office of the Central Excise Department.

The operations of EOU are carried out under the 'Manufacture and Other Operations in Warehouse Regulations, 1966'. With the amendment of these regulations,[1] the requirements of customs supervision of all operations of EOU have been removed. With the objective of ensuring maximum governance to exporters and reducing red tape, the customs bonding procedure of EOUs has been liberalized by replacing physical control over EOUs by record-based controls. EOUs can decide upon their working hours, and the manufacturing is not physically supervised by DC or designated officer for this purpose.

19.8 Import/Procurement by EOUs

EOUs are not eligible for duty-free procurement of goods and services to be utilized for manufacture or rendering of exportable goods and services and shall be treated like any other operational unit of business under the GST regime beginning July 2017. GST is not exempt from any EOU unit when it sources any goods or service except the zero-rated goods and services and these units have to pay. EOU units are, however, exempt from the payment of customs duty as they manufacture under

[1] Vide Notification No. 44/98-Customs, dated 2 July 1998.

customs bond. Integrated GST is also exempted which has to be paid along with basic customs duty in case of the Advance Authorization Scheme and DFIA Scheme. The new tax regime provisioned that the exemption from the additional duties of customs, if any, under Section 3 (1), Section 3 (3) and Section 3 (5) of the Customs Tariff Act, 1975, and exemption from central excise duty will be available for goods specified under the Fourth Schedule to the Central Excise Act. Any EOU unit intending to avail the benefit of import duty exemption has to follow the procedure under the Customs (Import of Goods at Concessional Rate of Duty) Rules, 2017. Under the GST regime, there is no exemption available to the supplier when goods are supplied to an EOU unit. IGST, CGST and SGST, as applicable, will be payable by the supplier if the supplies are made from DTA to EOU. Any EOU/EHTP/BTP/STPI unit has to offset GST paid on goods received from domestic suppliers by any of the following two options:

- **Option 1:** EOU can claim 'input tax credit' of GST paid and utilize the same towards supplies made by EOU to DTA.
- **Option 2:** Any EOU can claim refund of GST paid as laid down in GST refund rules.

For ensuring effective working capital utilization, it is always advisable to go for Option 1 of offsetting the input GST for output GST when supplies are made to DTA, and Option 2 should be used only in cases when the input tax credit cannot be utilized for domestic sales.

Indian customs mandates for detailed examination of import consignments which are meant for EOUs at the port of import. Customs officers should exercise due diligence to verify the marks, numbers, gross weight and so on to classify the goods, ensure trade policy compliance and preventive action for the purpose of completion of assessment. The goods which are imported by EOU unit are examined in full at the bonded premises of the unit. For the clearance of imported goods, the EOU is required to submit following documents:

1. Into-bond bill of entry
2. Import invoice
3. Import packing list
4. Certificate of origin
5. Procurement certificate issued by the designated officer
6. Attested copy of legal undertaking
7. Attested copy of private bonded warehouse licence
8. Copy of the green card and valid LOP

The into-bond bill of entry for clearance of imported cargo of EOU is assessed at the port of import. The goods move under the cover of the into-bond bill of entry and e-way bill as mandated under the GST regime. The original copy of the bill of entry is retained at the customs station of import and three copies of the bill of entry accompany the consignment. The officer in charge of EOU records the re-warehousing and examination report on the duplicate and triplicate copies and return the duplicate copy to the assistant commissioner (bond) of customs station of import. In case of any discrepancy in goods found during the course of the examination, the same is brought to the notice of the customs station of import for the purpose of updating the original bill of entry and connected records. When the goods imported are required to be sent at the place away from the port of import, transshipment of such goods is allowed under the normal transshipment procedure. The unit is required to furnish a transit bond with the assistant commissioner in charge of the port of the import. However, in such case, a transit bond or insurance policy equivalent to the duty amount involved is required to be furnished.

19.9 Summary

The international trade is an extension of internal trade where the domestically produced agricultural, manufactured goods and services are traded internationally, thus giving an additional boost to the economic activity and employment generation. Exports and imports of both goods and services happen between two different countries. Dedicated export enclaves in the form of the EOU Scheme were introduced in India in the year 1980. The scheme is implemented by DGFT. In order to cater to varying economic needs of different sectors of the economy, the scheme is extended in different variants, for example, for the software export, the STPI Scheme was launched, which has been extremely successful in increasing services exports of India. EHTP was introduced to enhance the exports of engineering goods, and the BTP Scheme was introduced to increase the exports of drugs and pharma.

One has to apply to DGFT for bonding the unit under the EOU/EHTP/BTP/STPI Scheme of FTP of India and Handbook of Procedures, Volume I, and public notices/circulars issued by the Department of Commerce. Establishment of units and their performance is monitored by the jurisdictional DC in accordance with the FTP provisions. The export of dedicated export enclaves was as high as ₹163,838 crore out of India's total exports of ₹655,864 crore, which is around 24.98 percent of India's total exports in the year 2007–2008, and it has declined to ₹36,591 crore in 20017–2018, which is mere 1.97 percent of India's total exports. This indicates that the dedicated export enclaves have witnessed a downward trend over the last one decade.

EOUs are not eligible for duty-free procurement of goods and services to be utilized for manufacture or rendering of exportable goods and services and shall be treated like any other operational unit of business under the GST regime beginning July 2017. The new tax regime provisioned that the exemption from the additional duties of customs, if any, under Section 3 (1), Section 3 (3) and Section 3 (5) of the Customs Tariff Act, 1975, and exemption from central excise duty will be available for goods specified under the Fourth Schedule to the Central Excise Act. Any EOU intending to avail the benefit of import duty exemption has to follow the procedure under the Customs (Import of Goods at Concessional Rate of Duty) Rules, 2017. Specific benefits of dedicated export enclaves such as EOU/EHTP/BTP/STPI are as follows:

1. EOUs are allowed to procure raw material or duty-free capital goods, either through import or through domestic sources.
2. EOUs are eligible for reimbursement of GST.
3. EOUs are eligible for reimbursement of duty paid on fuels procured from domestic oil companies.
4. EOUs are eligible for claiming the input tax credit on the goods and services and refund thereof.
5. Fast track clearance facilities.
6. Exemption from industrial licensing for the manufacture of items reserved for the SSI sector.

Review Exercises

Multiple Choice Questions

1. In which year was the scheme for EOU implemented for the first time?
   - **a.** 1980
   - **b.** 1987
   - **c.** 1999
   - **d.** 2019
   - **e.** None of the above
2. EOU stands for
   - **a.** External orientation unit
   - **b.** Export orientation unit
   - **c.** Export origin unit
   - **d.** Export-oriented unit
   - **e.** None of the above
3. EHTP stands for
   - **a.** Export hardware technology park
   - **b.** Electronic handcraft technology park
   - **c.** Export handicraft technology park
   - **d.** Electronic hardware technology park
   - **e.** None of the above
4. BTP stands for
   - **a.** Biotechnology park
   - **b.** Bio-training park
   - **c.** Biotechnology place
   - **d.** Bio-training place
   - **e.** None of the above
5. STPI stands for
   - **a.** Software technology park of India
   - **b.** Soft skills training park of India
   - **c.** Soft skills technology park of India
   - **d.** Software training park of India
   - **e.** None of the above
6. The minimum investment required for EOU is
   - **a.** ₹1 crore
   - **b.** ₹2 crore
   - **c.** ₹3 crore
   - **d.** ₹4 crore
   - **e.** ₹5 crore

7. Dedicated export enclaves (EOUs) are bonded under which of the following sections of the Customs Act, 1962?
   a. Section 58 and 65
   b. Section 58 and 63
   c. Section 7 and 65
   d. Section 7 and 58
   e. None of the above
8. EOU will be exempt from which of the following tax on imports of material for manufacture?
   a. Basic duty of customs
   b. Countervailing duty
   c. Integrated GST
   d. Additional duty of customs
   e. All of the above
9. Who among the following has powers to administer the dedicated export enclaves?
   a. DC
   b. Customs commissioner
   c. Excise commissioner
   d. GST commissioner
   e. All of the above
10. What are the key challenges faced by India's dedicated export enclaves?
    a. Scale, compliance and policy support
    b. Market identification
    c. Red tape
    d. Product identification
    e. None of the above

Critical Thinking Questions

1. Critically explain the concept of dedicated export enclaves.
2. Write an essay on the performance of dedicated export enclaves in India.
3. Critically examine any two of the following:
   a. Procedure for bonding and operations of EOUs
   b. Role of DC in administration of EOUs
   c. Import/procurement by EOUs
   d. Procedure for approval of EOU
4. Critically examine the process and procedure for approval of EOU in India.
5. What are the key challenges faced by EOUs in India?

CHAPTER 20

Special Economic Zones in India

CHAPTER OBJECTIVES

- To explain the story of evolution of SEZs in India.
- To explain the present status of SEZs in India.
- To discuss the procedure involved in setting up SEZs in India.
- To discuss the incentives, exemptions and facilities available to developers and SEZ units.
- To brief the present debate on SEZs in India.

20.1 Introduction

The introduction of the SEZ scheme in India is largely based on the experiences received from similar kinds of dedicated industrial zones focusing on expanding and diversifying the exports of countries such as China, South Korea, Malaysia and Vietnam, which have leveraged SEZs as the dedicated industrial zones manufacturing goods and rendering services only for increasing the exports of respective countries. GOI, after having realized the fact that exports are vital to the country's economic success, implemented the SEZ scheme in India on 1 April 2000. Prior to that, India had introduced the concept of EPZs for promoting exports from the country. India set up port-based EPZs at Kandla, Mumbai, Cochin, Chennai, Vizag and Kolkata and land-based EPZs at Noida. There were some operational and promotional deficiencies in this scheme, and as a result, EPZs could not bring out the desired results for increasing exports from the country. In the year 2000, the Department of Commerce decided to convert the existing EPZs into SEZs, thus paving way for large industrial clusters and services zones in India, primarily for increasing the exports from the country. India has consistently been leveraging the policy (Table 20.1) of expanding SEZs at different places in the country for the purposes of tapping the innate skills of manpower and natural resources and for accumulating the foreign reserves through exports for the larger and wider development of the country.

SEZs in India played a great role in export expansion but essentially not when compared to China's SEZs, which have established China as the global factory producing products at the fraction of costs for global customers. Taking note of the success of SEZs in other countries, particularly in China, GOI realized the need to overcome the shortcomings which our EPZs have been experiencing on account of the multiplicity of controls and clearances, absence of world-class infrastructure, high transaction cost, an unstable fiscal regime and so on. GOI decided to replicate the China success story in India with model changes in its SEZ Policy, which was announced on 1 April 2000 for the purposes of promoting export, providing world-class infrastructure, reducing the transaction cost of export-oriented firms resulting in low cost of Indian products in the international market, making India a global centre of

TABLE 20.1 List of Number of Formal Approvals, Notified and Operational SEZs in India Including Approved Units Therein

1. Number of Formal approvals	408
2. Number of notified SEZs	328
3. Operational SEZs	204
4. Units approved in SEZs	4,166

Source: Ministry of Commerce & Industry, Government of India. https://commerce.gov.in/ (accessed on 24 May 2023).

manufacturing, trading and services and attracting larger foreign investments in India. In order to harmonize and standardize the policy regime governing SEZs in India, GOI has enacted the SEZs Act, 2005, and the SEZs Rules, 2006, so as to guide prospective investors, industrial houses and services providers about the transparent and promotional trade policy regime in India. As a result, SEZs in India witnessed a significant improvement in the export performance, wherein India's exports through SEZs rose from a mere $5.08 billion in the year 2005–2006 to almost $105 billion in 2020–2021. The success of India's SEZ Policy can be understood from the fact that in absolute numbers, SEZs' exports of ₹22,840 crore in 2005–2006 has increased to ₹759,524 crore in 2020–2021. Figure 20.1 depicts the increasing trend of exports from SEZs in India.

A study of state-wise distribution (Figure 20.2) of SEZs in India indicates that developers and investors of special economic zones have shown much interest in the establishment of SEZs in developed states such as Maharashtra, Andhra Pradesh, Telangana, Tamil Nadu, Karnataka and Gujarat. Although maximum formal approvals to set up SEZs have been granted to Karnataka (61), only 40 have been notified as of October 2016 wherein the formal approvals for the state of Maharashtra are 59, and 51 of

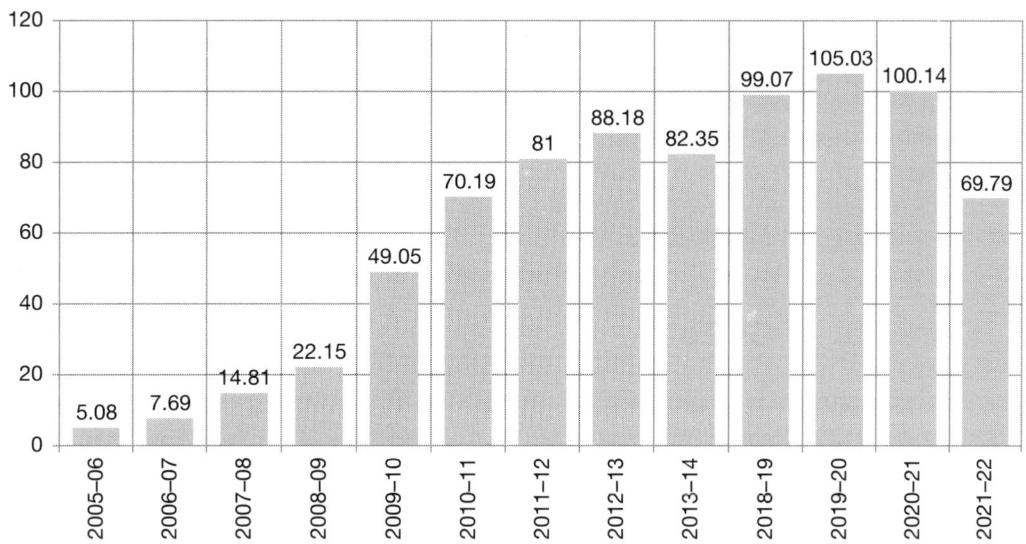

FIGURE 20.1 Trends of exports from SEZ in India (US$ billion) from 2005–06 to 2021–22.

Source: Ministry of Commerce & Industry, Government of India. https://commerce.gov.in/ (accessed on 24 May 2023).

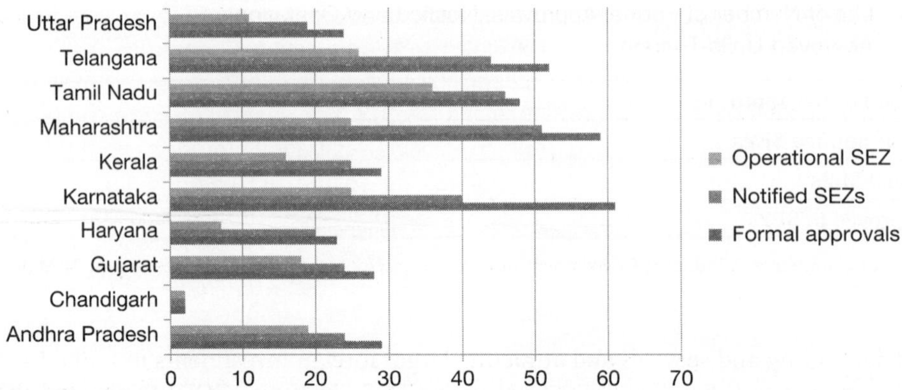

FIGURE 20.2 List of key states having major number of SEZs in India: Operational, notified and formal approvals.

Source: Ministry of Commerce & Industry, Government of India. https://commerce.gov.in/ (accessed on 24 May 2023).

them have been notified as SEZs. In terms of operational SEZs in India, Tamil Nadu has the maximum of 36, followed by Telangana having 26 and Maharashtra and Karnataka each having 25 SEZs.

In addition to export expansion, the key aim of the SEZ Policy is to encourage export-related infrastructure development through 'multi-product' and 'product-specific' SEZs. There are several product-specific SEZs approved by BOA in many states considering the factor-endowments, innate resources advantages and cost competitiveness of these states. As India has a young talent pool of engineers at a fraction of global costs, IT/ITES-centric SEZs have got a major share in the formal approvals and notified SEZs in different states of India. Other important sectors such as biotech, multi-products, engineering, pharmaceuticals/chemicals, textiles/apparel/wool and multi-services have been granted a significant number of approvals primarily in states such as Tamil Nadu, Telangana, Andhra Pradesh, Maharashtra and Karnataka. From North Indian states, Haryana and Uttar Pradesh have got a major share of product-specific SEZs. The number of formal approvals and notifications thereon for multi-product SEZs are very low due to large-scale land requirements, of over 1,000 hectares, for setting up such zones, and with land getting scarce, costly and cumbersome to procure, investors in India are focusing on product-specific SEZs. Even the notified multi-product SEZs can never take off as acquiring the land for setting up these zones is usually marred with large-scale protests from farmers, litigation and procedural red tape. The key areas of economic activities where the SEZs in India are primarily being set up are depicted in Figure 20.3.

20.2 Concept of SEZs

SEZ is a special geographical area created within the country that is treated as 'foreign territory'; hence, domestic rules and regulations governing the conduct of business are not applicable to these zones. Such zones are created with the major goal of attracting foreign investments into the country and ensuring effective utilization of the country's physical and non-physical resources in shaping the country's economic success. SEZs provide an internationally competitive and hassle-free environment (Figure 20.4) for exports. As investments in these zones are free from red tape and bureaucratic controls which otherwise are involved in DTA investments, global investors foresee a great opportunity in

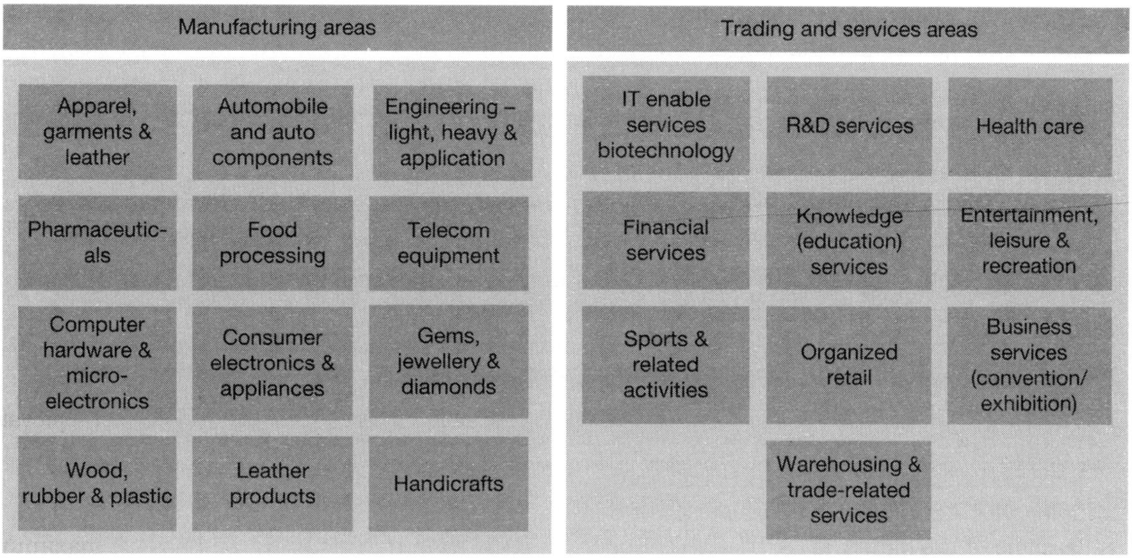

FIGURE 20.3 Key areas of economic activities in SEZs in India.

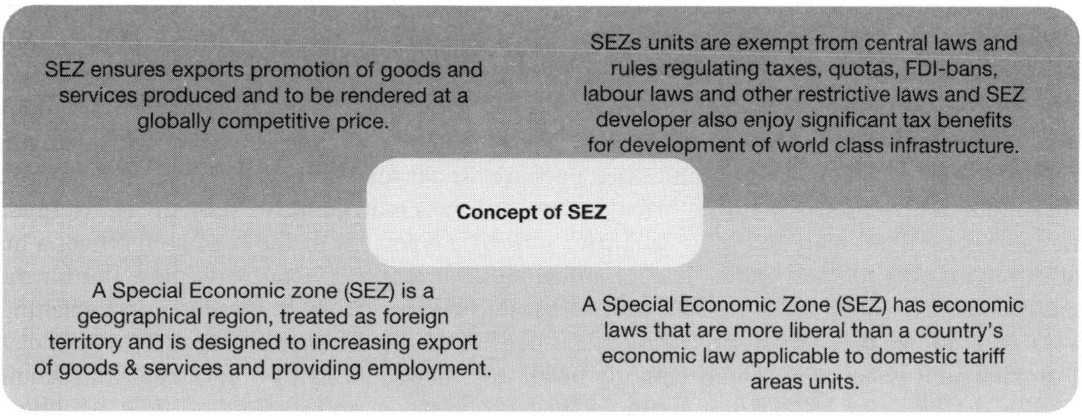

FIGURE 20.4 Concept of SEZs as per the SEZ Act, 2005.

setting up industrial clusters in SEZs. Realizing the merits and benefits offered by SEZs, the policy of SEZ was adopted by GOI in order to instill confidence among foreign investors and to ensure the 'single-window clearances' under a stable central legislation for the prospective investors, developers and units to be located in SEZ.

An umbrella and comprehensive draft SEZ Bill was prepared after extensive discussions with the various stakeholders in order to improve the country's economic growth and environment. The SEZ Act, 2005, as passed by the parliament, has ensured the clarity, stability and consistency regarding the various benefits/incentives offered by the government for promoting exports from the country, thereby generating greater economic activity and employment through the establishment of SEZs in all areas of manufacturing, services and logistical value chain. The Ministry of Commerce, GOI, planned a number of visits and interactions with various stakeholders throughout the country so as to streamline the SEZ Bill as per the industry and investor aspirations and give momentum to exports. The draft SEZ Bill got around 800 comments/suggestions from economic and trade experts, industry associations, investors, agriculture farmers and chambers of commerce. Finally, the SEZs Act, 2005, was passed by the parliament and supported by the SEZ Rules 2006, came into force on 10 February 2006, opening a new chapter in India's economic liberalization history and paving the way for drastic simplification of procedures and single-window clearances on matters relating to central as well as state governments. The main objectives of the SEZ Act are:

1. The SEZ Act was enacted to ensure that SEZ may act as a generator of additional economic activity for faster, quicker economic development of India.
2. It aims to leverage SEZ as a centre of excellence in India's efforts for the promotion of exports of goods and services and emerge as quality supplier of both.
3. The SEZ Act is enacted to ensure that simplification of procedure and cutting down the red tape will result in the promotion of investments from domestic and foreign sources, thus increasing economic activities and associated exports promotion from India.
4. The SEZ Act is enacted to create additional and incremental employment opportunities for the people of the nation.
5. The SEZ Act also aims to develop export-related physical and virtual infrastructure facilities in backward areas and help in tapping the innate resources of the nation.
6. Finally, it aims that SEZs will be a major centre of economic activity in realizing the cherished dream of Indians to make it a world-class centre of manufacturing, trading and servicing and putting it in the league of export champions of the world.

GOI has amended the SEZ Act in August 2019, thus widening the scope of entities which can set up a business in SEZs. The new definition of the 'person', as enshrined in the SEZ Act, allowed to set up his/her units in these zones includes 'trust' or 'any entity as may be notified by the central government' can set up their operation in SEZs. Unfortunately, 50 percent of the total land remains unutilized in the existing SEZs in India. The amended definition of a 'person' will allow more types of business entities to set up units in SEZs, thus increasing the number of exporting units in India. This will also help utilize the full potential of the land in SEZs and realize the dream of enhanced exports and employment generation which was the original idea behind setting up these SEZs in India. Ironically, the amended bill has not reviewed the taxes imposed on units inside SEZs, which is one of the highly debated subjects among industry captains and exporters. The amended bill also does not fine-tune the existing policy vis-à-vis state- and sector-specific policy requirement. One more area, which is neglected, to work on where India has a high import dependency is the strengthening of the existing infrastructure of SEZs and their connectivity to ports by improving both rail and road networks. India's SEZs not only are small in size but also stand nowhere in terms of infrastructure as compared to Chinese SEZs.

As a concept, SEZ is specifically delineated duty-free enclave and shall be deemed to be a foreign territory within the country for the purposes of international trade operations, duties and tariffs and foreign exchange laws. SEZ refers to the designated industrial and service zone in a country with special economic regulations that provide the preferential economic environment to units located in it and is certainly at ease and simplification from DTAs of a country. SEZ regulations are specific to the business needs of the country and contain measures that are conducive for attracting foreign direct investment. A unit located in SEZ area always receives tax incentives and exemptions or an opportunity to pay lower tariffs provided that such goods must be exported out of the country. The developer of SEZ puts all efforts to develop world-class infrastructure in SEZ so as to attract and accommodate both domestic and foreign business units in the SEZ area. The role of state government in the SEZ legislation gets enhanced as it was decided that the land will often be provided for SEZ purposes by the state governments at concessional rates and both the developer and the operating units are entitled to get tax exemption up to 15 years subject to the condition that they are export-oriented and net foreign-exchange earners. Red tape and Inspector Raj were cut short as the provisions in the SEZ Act ensured single-window clearance mechanism for the units located in the zone. Figure 20.5 illustrates the various stages of evolution of the concept of SEZs in India.

Historically, it is recorded that the first-ever known SEZ was set up in Puerto Rico in 1947, and learning from its experiences, countries such as Ireland and Taiwan followed the steps to set up SEZ for their economic development. Most extensive and successful use of SEZ as an engine of economic growth and expansion and diversification of foreign trade is done by China, which has set up a series of SEZs in the country since 1980. GOI adopted the SEZ policies in the year 2000, thus replacing the existing EPZs by making necessary changes in the EXIM Policy of the country. However, a harmonized and standardized special economic regime came into the country with the enactment of the SEZ Act in the year 2000 followed by the SEZ Rules, 2006. The SEZ Act was umbrella legislation aimed at providing the establishment, development and management of SEZs for promoting exports and generating additional economic activities, employment and infrastructure development of the country including attracting hassle-free foreign investments in the key economic activities. The SEZ Act and Rules provide drastic simplification of procedures and single-window clearance on matters relating to central as well as state governments, thus paving the way for creating the engines of exports in important sectors of the Indian economy. The salient features of the SEZ Act, 2005, are highlighted here:

1. The developer and SEZ units are exempted from payment of customs duty, excise duty, etc., on the import as well as domestic procurement of goods for the development, operation and maintenance of SEZs and the units therein.
2. SEZ units are exempted from 100 percent payment of income tax for five years, 50 percent for the next five years and 50 percent of ploughing back of profits for five years thereafter.

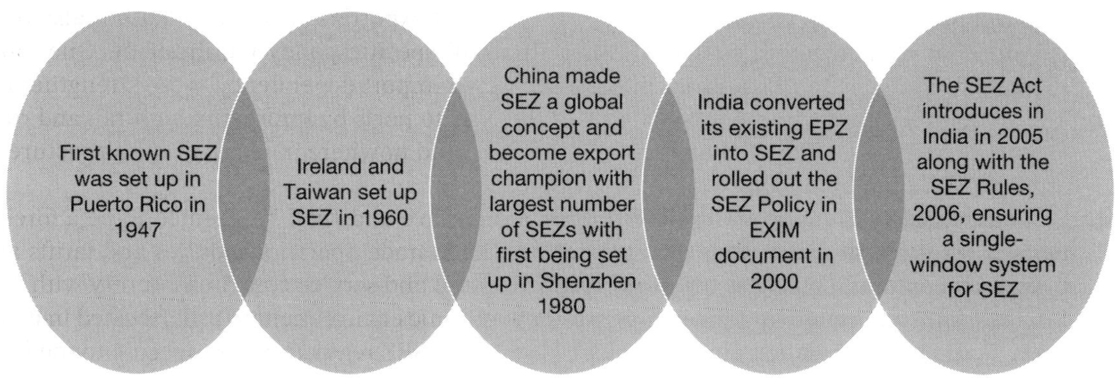

FIGURE 20.5 The evolution of concept of SEZ in India.

Source: Ministry of Commerce & Industry (2005).

3. SEZ units are also exempted from the payment of capital gains on transfer of an undertaking from an urban area to SEZ.
4. Developers of such zones are exempted from payment of 100 percent income tax for a block of 10 years in 15 years to be chosen in the initial 5 years.
5. Developers and co-developers shall be exempted from the payment of dividend distribution tax.
6. There is a 100 percent income tax exemption for five years and 50 percent for the next five years for offshore banking units located in SEZs.
7. A provision for setting up of an International Financial Services Centre in SEZ has been proposed with the same incentives and facilities as available to offshore banking units.
8. A developer of SEZ and SEZ units shall be exempted from the payment of minimum alternate tax.
9. A developer of the zone as well as SEZ units shall be exempted from the payment of CST on inter-state purchase of goods.
10. In order to provide greater administrative, financial and functional autonomy to these zones, the SEZ Act has provisioned for the constitution of an SEZ authority for each SEZ developed by the company and PSU.
11. There is a provision for the establishment of designated courts and a single enforcement agency to ensure speedy trial and investigation of offences committed in SEZs.
12. The central government encourages state governments to liberalize state laws and delegate their powers to DCs of SEZs to facilitate single-window clearance so that more investment may flow to their states, and they may emerge as a centre of economic activity and employment generation.

The countries where SEZ has been very successful in export promotion and the country's external economic engagements are China (with great success), the United Arab Emirates, Malaysia, India, Jordan, Poland, Kazakhstan, Philippines, Russia and to some extent North Korea. By the mid of the year 2016, there were over 4,000 special investment zones in the world. Countries such as China, the United Arab Emirates and Malaysia have emerged in the global trade map in a very short span of time due to SEZ because of the following reasons:

1. SEZ has emerged as focal points for promoting foreign investments anywhere they are set up with right planning and promotion.
2. A World Bank report indicates that SEZ has attracted almost over 20 percent of foreign direct investment into the top 10 countries in the period 2005–2014.
3. The share of SEZ units in the total exports of the country is almost 25 percent of the country's exports to overseas markets. Same is true in the case of India, where the exports from SEZ were around $82 billion in the total exports of around $300 billion in the year 2013–2014.
4. SEZ has served as testing grounds for reforms in economic, trade, industrial and foreign exchange policies for the countries where they are set up and has acted as a catalyst for reforming the overall economic and business regime of countries.
5. SEZ has helped in improving the competitiveness of the local and indigenous industry, job creation, local skill upgradation and technology absorption as the overall economic environment of the country gets a boost from foreign direct investment (FDI), international business and management practices and norms.

20.3 Procedural Formalities for Setting Up SEZs

For setting up an SEZ (Figure 20.8) in India, one has to fill up the application in 'Form A' as prescribed along with the name, address and status of the promoter. One should also provide the necessary details in the form of a project report clearly indicating details such as the proposed SEZ's location, the details of infrastructure that already exists, details of the infrastructure that will be established and the total area of the proposed SEZ along with the application form. The developer of an SEZ has to submit the project report proposing the financing mode and the project's viability along with the application form including the details of proposed investments. He/she should also make it clear whether the proposed SEZ would be a 'multi-product' or 'product-specific' and details of the foreign equity if any. The developer should submit all these details in the application as prescribed in 'Form A' along with the project report for setting up an SEZ Unit to the chief secretary of the state. The developer should submit at least 15 copies of the application, indicating name and address of the applicant, status of the promoter along with a project report covering the particulars, as shown in Figure 20.6, may be submitted to the chief secretary of the state.

A state government is the key nodal agency for getting the approval for SEZ as clearance related to land, electricity, public utilities and constructions are provided by the state government in India. After the review of such application, the state government forwards the application to the Department of Commerce, GOI, along with observations if any. The key observations from any state government include issues such as environmental clearances, electricity, water, construction permits, power generation, transmission and power distribution inside the SEZ. Additionally, the state government has to give its observations for exemption of state-specific taxes such as sales tax, turnover tax and mandi tax on the goods that are supplied from the area of domestic tariff to the units in the SEZ. The state government should also clearly provide its observations and commitments regarding declaring the units located in the SEZ as a public utility service, thus paving way for the 'single point clearance system' and 'minimum inspection' for the compliances to be ensured by the state government such as the Shop Act and the Minimum Wages Act. Figure 20.7 illustrates who can set up SEZs in India.

- Location of the proposed zone with details of existing infrastructure, and that is recommended to develop in the proposed zone
- Areas of SEZ, its distance from the nearest sea port/airport/rail/road depot (ICD/CFS) and so on in compliance with the established rules
- Financial details, including investment proposed, mode of financing and viability of the project in compliance with the established procedure
- Total foreign investment including details of foreign investors and terms and condition on repatriation of dividends and so on, if any
- The business focus of zone, whether it will allow only product- or service-specific industries or will be a multi-product zone

FIGURE 20.6 Prerequisites for setting up of SEZs in India.

Source: SEZ Act 2005 and SEZ Rules 2006.

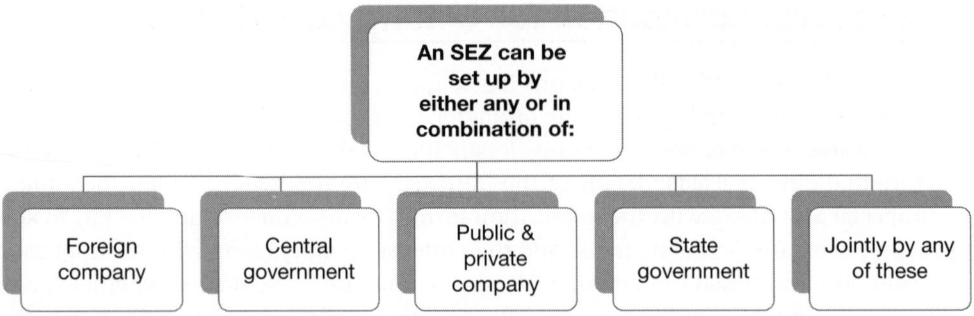

FIGURE 20.7 Who can set up an SEZ.

Source: SEZ Act, 2005, SEZ Rules 2006 of Ministry of Law & Justice, GOI.

The SEZ Act, 2005, is unique in the sense that it also envisages a key role for the state governments in export promotion and creation of related infrastructure, hence involving the state government as an active partner in the export promotion drive. The application for setting up SEZs will be processed in a single-window clearance mechanism through a 19-member inter-ministerial SEZ BOA. The applications which are duly recommended by the respective state governments/union territories administration shall be considered by BOA periodically on consensus for setting up the SEZ. In India, SEZs can be set up by the state government or its various agencies or any public, private, joint sector and even foreign companies can set up SEZs in India (Table 20.2). The application that is forwarded by the state government to the Department of Commerce for approval and notification of SEZ incorporates the state government's commitments as discussed above, and then it will be considered by the Department of Commerce's inter-ministerial committee. If BOA accepts the proposal, a permission letter is issued to the developer (applicant) for setting up the proposed SEZ, and in case of refusal, it will issue the refusal note to the developer of the SEZ and also inform the state government. Any individual, co-operative society, company or partnership firm can file an application for setting up an SEZ. The application is to be made in Form A to the concerned state government and BOA in the Department of Commerce, GOI. However, the application would be considered by the BOA only when the state government recommendation is received. The step-by-step approval procedure for setting up the SEZ is summarized in Table 20.2.

Once the BOA gives formal approval, and the concerned DC gives an inspection report certifying the contiguity and vacancy of the area, the same is notified as SEZ.

20.3.1 Key Considerations in SEZ Approvals

BOA under the Department of Commerce has to approve and reject a proposal for setting up SEZ as per criteria laid down under the SEZ Act, 2005, and SEZ Rules, 2006, read in conjunction with observations of the respective state governments where such an SEZ is to be located. Accordingly, the key considerations for members of BOA while taking such a decision for setting up an SEZ are listed in Figure 20.8.

1. The SEZ Act and Rules thereunder prescribe the minimum size of SEZ for different types of categories (Table 20.3), for example, multi-product, product-specific, location-specific and sector-specific

TABLE 20.2 Approval Procedure of Setting up SEZ in India

Stage 1: Form-A	**First step:** Proposal by the person intending to set up SEZ to the concerned state government	Proposal may also be made directly to the board after the approval by the board; the person will require to obtain state government concurrence within a period of six months.
	Second step: The state government forwards the proposal along with its recommendations to the board	Within 45 days, the state government to ensure that requirements of minimum land area, and that exemption of taxes at state level, delegation of powers to DC as recommended are made available to the developer & units.
	Third step: Approval or refusal by the board	The board may approve proposal with or without modification or reject proposal. In practice, the board accords in-principal approval pending land acquisition in Form B-1
Stage 2: Form-B	Issuance of letter of approval by the GOI	Within 30 days of receipt of BOA recommendation, the letter of approval will incorporate any additional conditions imposed by the board in its recommendation. The letter of approval's validity is for three years, during which time the developer shall take the effective steps to implement the approved proposal.

Source: SEZ Act, 2005, SEZ Rules 2006 of Ministry of Law & Justice, GOI.

SEZ in a port or airport

- SEZ in a port or airport means SEZ in an existing port or airport for SEZ.

Free trading & warehousing zones

- Free trading and warehousing is a special category of SEZ with a focus on trading and warehousing. The objective of such a zone is to create a trade-related infrastructure to facilitate import and export and import of goods and services with freedom to carry out trade transactions in free currency.
- In a stand-alone free trading and warehousing zone, at least 50% of the area shall be earmarked for developing processing area, free trading and warehousing may also be set up as a part of SEZ for multi-product.

SEZ for multi-product

- SEZ for multi-product means SEZ where units may be set up for the manufacture of two or more goods in a sector or goods falling in two or more sectors or for trading and warehousing or the rendering of two or more services in a sector or rendering of services falling in two or more sector.

SEZ for sector-specific

- SEZ for specific sector means SEZ meant exclusively for one or more products in a sector or one or more services in a sector.

FIGURE 20.8 Types of SEZs in India.

Source: SEZ Act, 2005, SEZ Rules 2006 of Ministry of Law & Justice, GOI.

TABLE 20.3 Minimum Area Requirement for Various Categories of SEZs in India

Type	For States Other Than Special Category States/Union Territories		Areas for Special Category States/Union Territories	
	Minimum Total Area Requirement	Processing Area Requirement (%)	Minimum Total Area Requirement	Processing Area Requirement (%)
Multi-product specific	1,000 Hectares	35	200 hectares	35
Single product or single service specific	100 hectares	50	100 hectares	35
Location specific (port/airport)	100 hectares	50	50 hectares	50
Electronic hardware and software or IT-enabled services	10 hectares with a minimum built up area of 1 lakh sq. metre	50	10 hectares with a minimum built up area of 1 lakh sq. metre	50
Gems & jewellery	10 hectares with a minimum built-up area of 50,000 sq. metre	50	10 hectares with a minimum built-up area of 50,000 sq. metre	50
Biotech/non-conventional energy including solar energy equipment/cells	10 hectares and a minimum built-up area of 1 lakh sq. metre for IT	50	10 hectares and a minimum built-up area of 1 lakh sq. metre for IT	50
Free trade warehousing zone	40 hectares a minimum built-up area of 1 lakh sq. metre	50	40 hectares and a minimum built-up area of 1 lakh sq. metre	50

Source: SEZ Act, 2005, SEZ Rules 2006 of Ministry of Law & Justice, GOI.

SEZ. A multi-product SEZ cannot be less than 1,000 hectares; however, this limit would not apply to the existing EPZs, which are converted into SEZs in the year 2000. In order to address the challenges of acquiring land, especially in small states and union territories, this limit is prescribed as 200 hectares only. Similarly, the minimum area requirement for SEZ for a single-product or service is 100 hectares with no exemption for small states. There is a minimum area requirement of 10 hectares only if an SEZ is to be set up in sectors such as electronics, IT, gems and jewellery and the biotech sector, and the limit is same even for small states/union territories of India. For location-specific SEZs, the minimum area requirement is 100 hectares, and for small states/union territories, it is a mere 50 hectares. For setting up free trade and warehousing zones, it is mandated that there has to be a minimum area requirement of 40 hectares. Table 20.3 lists the minimum required area, a specific requirement for the build-up area and the percentage of processing and non-processing area for setting up SEZs in India.

2. Table 20.3 depicts that each SEZ must have processing areas and non-processing areas. The developer is required to ensure that at least 50 percent area of the SEZ shall be used for processing purposes like developing industrial area for setting up such units. The processing area is that area in an SEZ where units can be located for the manufacture of goods or rendering of services. The processing area shall have specified entry and exit points and be fully secured by taking such measures approved by the board. The land or built-up area or free trade warehousing zone shall be given on lease only to entrepreneurs holding a valid letter of approval for not less than five years, and the lease rights would cease to exist on the expiry or cancellation of the letter of approval. The non-processing area is intended to provide support facilities to the SEZ processing area activities. No vacant land in the non-processing area shall be leased for businesses and social purposes, such as educational institutions, hospitals, hotels, recreation and entertainment facilities, residential and business complexes, to any person except a co-developer approved by the board. The developer or co-developer may lease the completed infrastructure along with the vacant land. The infrastructure for business or social purpose in the SEZ as approved by the board shall be entitled to exemptions, concessions and drawbacks.
3. In addition to the compliance to the SEZ Act and Rules, the developer of SEZ and units located in the SEZ area are supposed to abide by the local laws, rules, regulations or by-laws with regard to the local area planning, sewerage and disposal system, pollution-control mechanism and the like. They are also required to comply with industrial and labour laws and such other laws, rules and regulations as may be locally applicable to other units for ensuring better administration and management of the area. Hence, the SEZ developer is required to make adequate arrangements to fulfil all the requirements of laws, rules and procedures applicable to such SEZs.
4. The developer of the zone will allow only those units which are approved under the SEZ schemes for setting up their units in the SEZ area.

20.3.2 Mechanism and Approval for Setting Up Units in the SEZ Area

For setting up a manufacturing, trading or service units in an SEZ, three copies of project proposal in the prescribed format need to be submitted to the DC of an SEZ. Unit approval committee of the SEZ will consider the following points while extending the permission for the same:

1. Residence proof in respect of individual/partnership firms of all directors/partners (passport/ration card/driving licence/voter identity card or any other proof to the satisfaction of DC).
2. Income tax return of all the promoters for the last three years.
3. Experience of the promoters.
4. Marketing tie-ups.
5. In the case of EOUs, the inspection of the project site by an officer.
6. A report from other DCs as to whether any case under SEZ/EOU schemes in regard to diversion of goods and so on is pending.

If necessary, the above may be verified through a personal interview with the promoters of the project. In the event of the promoter being a well-established entity, the procedure of personal interview may be dispensed with. The unit approval committee shall meet on Monday every week. In case of the absence of DC, the meeting will be held by the next senior officer in the zone. The unit shall intimate the problems being faced by them in advance. In the meetings, apart from the promoters, the other concerned agency with which difficulties are being faced by the unit may also be called. All approvals are given by the unit approval committee headed by the DC. The clearance from the Department of Industrial Policy and Promotion/BOA, wherever required, will be obtained by the DC before the LOI is issued to such a unit for the commencement of business operations. Each approved unit has certain obligations, and it must fulfil those obligations in order to qualify as the SEZ units. These obligations are:

1. The SEZ unit has to be the positive net foreign exchange earner as per the formula prescribed in the SEZ Rules. It must execute a legal undertaking to the DC, at the time of issuance of the LOI to this effect.
2. The approved SEZ unit has to provide periodic reports to the DC and zone customs as mandated under the SEZ Rules.
3. The approved unit is required to execute a bond with the zone customs for its operation in the SEZ area.
4. Any company set up with foreign direct investment has to be incorporated under the Indian Companies Act, 2013, with the registrar of companies for undertaking the business operations in India.

20.4 Administrative and Institutional Set-Up of SEZ

The functioning of the SEZs is administered in a way that there shall be a hassle-free regulatory environment with minimum scope for red tape and bureaucratic controls. The regulatory functioning of SEZ is governed by a three-tier administrative set-up which mainly comprises BOA, approval committee and DC. BOA is the apex body and is headed by the secretary of the Department of Commerce. The approval committee at the zone level deals with the approval of units in the SEZs and other related issues. Each zone is headed by the DC, who is an ex-officio chairperson of the approval committee. To assist and support these three main heads of functioning, a 'proper officer' of customs is deputed to look after the day-to-day functioning with regard to customs administration. Once an SEZ has been approved by BOA, and the central government has notified the area as SEZ, units can be set up in the SEZ. All the proposals for setting up the units in SEZ are approved at the zone level by the 'approval committee' consisting of the DC, the customs authorities and representatives of the state government. All post-approval clearances including a grant of the importer–exporter code number, change in the name of the company or implementing agency, broadbanding diversification and so on are given at the zone level by DC. The performances of the SEZ units are periodically monitored by the approval committee, and units are liable for penal action under the provisions of the SEZ Act and Rules thereunder and the Foreign Trade (Development and Regulation) Act. The one who develops the zone is called the 'developer' and may be supported by a 'co-developer' so as to fulfil the financing and administrative requirements of the zone. The developer is the lead person of the company which has the responsibility for the development of the SEZ, and sometimes, there can also be a co-developer as the size of the SEZ may be very big, or the developer wants to include a co-developer so as to use his/her specialized knowledge in the development of the SEZ or to meet the financing requirement. The developer is responsible for planning the overall development of the SEZ, preparing future development plans, demarcating and developing the proposed SEZ site, allocating and transferring plots buildings to approve SEZ units, regulating the erection of the building in accordance with the

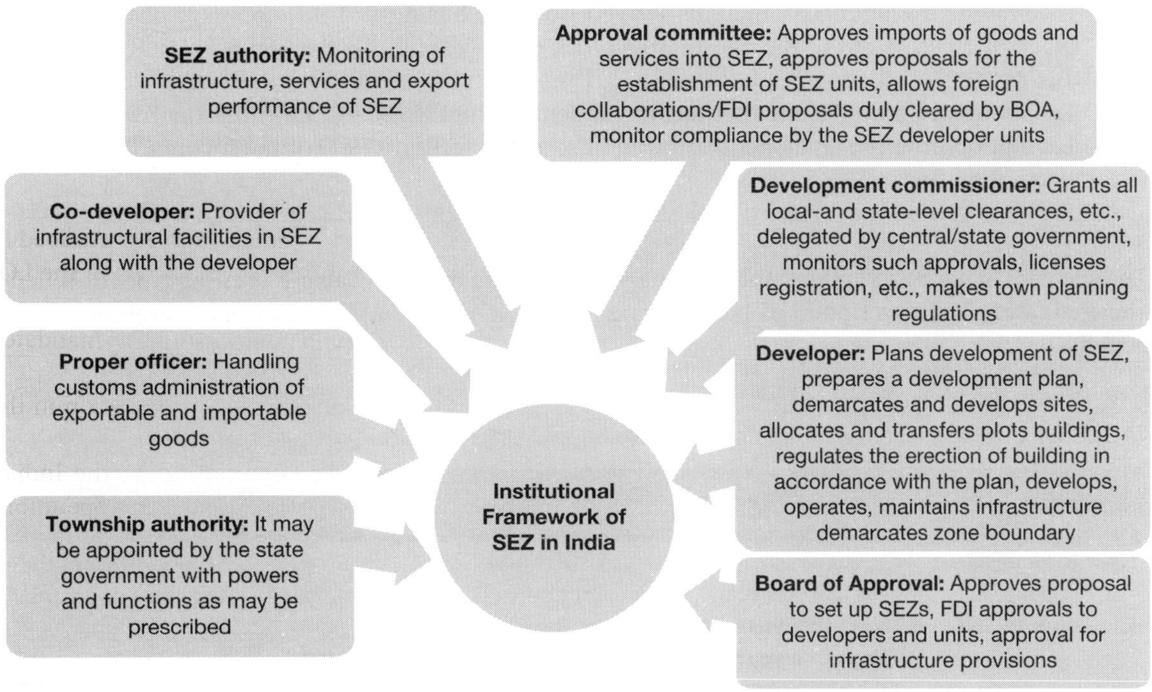

FIGURE 20.9 Overview of institutional framework of SEZ in India.

Source: SEZ Act, 2005, SEZ Rules 2006 of Ministry of Law & Justice, GOI.

approved plan of the SEZ and finally maintaining the infrastructure for effective functioning of the zone. If there is a co-developer, he/she will assist the developer in providing suitable and systematic infrastructural facilities in the zone. Figure 20.9 depicts the key functions of each of the constituents in the administration and functioning of the SEZ.

The other important institutional agencies which facilitate the working and functioning of SEZs are the township authority, which may be appointed by the state government to look after the local and command area development and ensure that the township may have full-fledged facilities and services as prescribed under the rules. The SEZ authority monitors the overall performance of the SEZ vis-à-vis export performance and infrastructural improvement in the area.

20.5 Incentives and Facilities to the SEZs

The SEZ Act, 2005, and the SEZ Rule, 2006, provide a very attractive regulatory regime for the establishment, development and management of SEZs so as to use them as an engine for the economic growth and export promotion. The SEZ Rules are historic in the sense that they provide drastic simplification of procedures and single window clearance on matters relating to the central as well as state governments to an SEZ developer. The following benefits and incentives are available to the SEZ developer/co-developer:

1. Exemption from customs/excise duties for the development of SEZs for authorized operations approved by BOA.

2. Income-tax exemption on income derived from the business of development of the SEZ in a block of 10 years out of the chosen in a block of 15 years under Section 80-IAB of the Income Tax Act.
3. Exemption from minimum alternate tax under Section 115JB of the Income Tax Act.
4. Exemption from the dividend distribution tax under Section 115-O of the Income Tax Act.
5. Exemption from CST.
6. Exemption from the service tax (Section 7 and 26 and the Second Schedule of the SEZ Act).

The specifics of such exemptions, incentives and benefits are tabled in Table 20.4 citing types of benefits and the nature and description of benefits and legislative provision regulating such exemptions and benefits.

TABLE 20.4 Fiscal Incentives/Benefits to Developer and Units in SEZs

S. No.	Types of Benefits	Nature and Description of Benefits	Legislative Provision
1.	Income tax holiday (for units in SEZ)	1. For first five years: 100 percent of the eligible profits or gains 2. **Next five years:** 50 percent of the eligible profits or gains 3. **Next five years:** 50 percent of the eligible profits or gains subject to creation or specified reserve.	Section 10AA of the Income Tax Act, 1962
2.	Income tax holiday to developer	Deduction of 100 percent of profits derived from developing a SEZ for a period of 10 consecutive assessment years out of the first 15 years from the year in which the SEZ is notified by the central government	Section 80-IAB of the Income Tax Act, 1962
3.	Minimum alternate tax	Exemption from the provisions of minimum alternate tax for the developer as well as SEZ unit.	115JB of the Income Tax Act, 1962
4.	Service tax	Exemption from the service tax under Chapter 6 of the Finance Act, 1994, on taxable services provided to a developer or unit to carry on authorized operation in SEZ	Under the CENVAT Rules, 2004
5.	Provisions regarding capital gains	Exemption from capital gains or transfer or specified assets in consequence to shifting of industrial undertaking from urban or other areas to SEZ subject to certain conditions.	Under the Income Tax Act, 1962
6.	Custom duty relief	Exemption from customs duties for development of SEZ for authorized operation approved by BOA	Under the Customs Act, 1962
7.	Excise duty	Exemption from any duty or excise, under the Central Excise Act, 1944, or the Central Excise Tariff Act, 1985, or any other law for the time being in force, on goods brought from DTA to SEZ or unit, to carry on the authorized operations by the developer or entrepreneur.	The Central Excise Act, 1944, & the Central Excise Tariff Act, 1985
8.	Dividend distribution tax	Exemption from dividend distribution tax declared or paid after 1 April 2005 by an enterprise engaged in developing or developing and operating or developing, operating and maintaining a SEZ.	Section 115-O of the Income Tax Act, 1962

S. No.	Types of Benefits	Nature and Description of Benefits	Legislative Provision
9.	Securities transaction tax	Exemption from the securities transaction tax leviable under Section 98 of the Finance (No.2) Act, 2004, in case the taxable securities transactions are entered into by a non-resident through the international finance service.	Under the Income Tax Act, 1962
10.	Import duty	Duty-free Import domestic procurement of goods for development, operation and maintenance of SEZ units	Under the Customs Act, 1962
11.	Central sales tax	Exemption from Central Sales Tax/VAT on sale or purchase or goods.	Under CST

Source: SEZ Act, 2005, SEZ Rules 2006 of Ministry of Law & Justice, GOI.

In addition to the exemptions and benefits, as shown in Table 20.4, the units located in SEZ are offered the following other benefits and exemptions aimed at attracting foreign investments into these zones and making them attractive to potential business units as business centres for providing services, trading and manufacturing activities. These are:

1. SEZ units are entitled to duty-free import/domestic procurement of goods for the development, operation and maintenance of SEZ units.
2. SEZ units are entitled to be exempted 100 percent from the payment of income tax exemption on export income for SEZ units under Section 10AA of the Income Tax Act for the first five years, 50 percent for next five years thereafter and 50 percent of the ploughed back of profit for the next five years.
3. SEZ units are entitled to exemption from minimum alternate tax under Section 115JB of the Income Tax Act.
4. SEZ units are entitled to external commercial borrowing up to $500 million in a year without any maturity restriction through recognized banking channels.
5. SEZ units are entitled to exemption from CST.
6. SEZ units are entitled to exemption from the service tax.
7. SEZ units are entitled to single-window clearance for the central and state-level approvals.
8. SEZ units are entitled to exemption from the state value-added tax and other levies as extended by the respective state governments.

20.6 Present Debate on SEZ

India has emerged as the rare exception in the global economy which has remained largely untouched from the economic challenges that the world economy faced post the sub-prime and Euro-zone crisis. It has consistently registered a respectable economic growth and has strong economic indicators almost on all fronts, and thus, it is seen as a potentially very attractive destination for investments. With the introduction of programmes such as 'Make in India', 'Skill India' and 'Digital India', Indian economy is poised to witness a quantum transformation from mere importers of goods to the manufacturer of both goods and services. Business firms, both domestic and foreign, see a great business opportunity in the Indian economy and are keen to set up SEZs as they wish to make India a base for manufacturing, trading and services due to cost advantages and an attractive market. The SEZ Act and Rules have paved the way for simplification in procedural hurdles and is a red-carpet to global investors to invest in India. However, there is a debate going on as to what all our SEZ Policy has achieved in the last 10 years as India has not been able to match the expectations of investors in comparison with Chinese, Taiwanese and South Korean firms. Some of the major areas of debate among policymakers, academia and public are as follows:

1. **Revenue loss to the state:** Policymakers including RBI have cautioned on revenue implications from duty and taxes foregone from the mushrooming of SEZs across the country. RBI is very critical of the policy of SEZs and has raised questions on the sustainability of the revenue inflow to the state, which may cause severe mismanagement of public finances. Although it is expected that SEZs would boost investment and economic growth in the nation, these could also aggravate the uneven pattern of development by pulling out resources from the less-developed areas to more prosperous or coastal areas. It is evident that developers, especially in the case of the manufacturing sector, prefer to locate their SEZs in coastal areas only due to logistics cost advantages. The Ministry of Finance is worried that the development of SEZs and the duty and taxes so forgone would result in unjustified revenue loss to the exchequer due to the direct tax drain; it is only expected that it will be around 0.5–0.7 percent of the GDP. RBI has also echoed the concern and cautioned the government about such heavy revenue losses. It further emphasizes that such benefits/incentives may be justified if the SEZ units can ensure forward and backward linkages with the domestic economy, thereby catalysing greater competitiveness of the whole economy rather than only zones.
2. **Uneven economic development:** The success of SEZs in regional economic development largely depends on how smartly the state can play its role in the promotion of commercial activities from such zones as the role of the state government is vital in the development of these zones. It has been seen in India that different state governments differ in economic orientation and models of development as some state governments focus more on social development and inclusion while others wish to emerge as a champion of industrialization. For example, two Indian states, namely Gujarat and West Bengal, have a different story with regard to the development of SEZs. Where Gujarat has been a leader in starting the operations from such zones, West Bengal has been consistently in turmoil with political problems leading to the inertia in the developer's mindset such as the Salim Group (chemicals), TCS (IT). In fact, many approved SEZs have been shelved out by the developer as they do not see any economic dividend in a politically divided state like West Bengal; for example, Infosys (IT and IT-enabled services) has refused to start operation due to the unfavourable business climate.
3. **Misuse of agriculture land:** There were also allegations that a large portion of agriculture land was being converted into SEZs. This statement, however, holds no ground as the total proposed area for SEZs is about 75,000 hectares, only 0.000625 percent of India's total area under cultivation. Similarly, the land is usurped for developing SEZs where the only non-processing area is developed and sold, and subsequently, the area is de-notified as a non-SEZ area where the purpose of acquiring the land of poor peasants in the name of public development stands defeated as only a handful of developers, in connivance with corrupt politicians, make money and run away.

4. **Tax benefits supersede exports as the prime objective:** Most of the developers of SEZs are filing an application for the establishment of the SEZ to avail the tax benefits offered to the developer. SEZ units are also locating their business operations to SEZ areas from existing areas as the SEZ Act and Rules allow 100 percent exemption from corporate income tax for the first 5 years, 50 percent exemption for the next 5 years and for the final 5 years, 50 percent of the profits ploughed back will be exempted from the tax to units and an exemption for 10 years in the block of 15 years to the developer. Another factor which has driven the companies for filing so many applications is the fact that existing income tax exemptions to EOUs such as STPI/BTP are supposed to be discontinued by DGFT in the due course.
5. **Absence of scale advantages:** India is densely populated with a large concentration of population in agricultural areas. As a result, acquiring a large tract of land for developing such zones is a big problem. Chinese SEZs have become an engine of economic growth as they are very big in size and help create scale-related advantages, which is not the case of Indian SEZs. Most of the SEZs being planned in India are very small in size and scale of operations. The SEZ Act and Rules thereunder allow the minimum area for the SEZ area to be 1,000 hectares (3.9 square miles) for multi-product zones, 100 hectares for product-specific zones and just 10 hectares for IT, gems and jewellery and biotechnology zones (subject to minimum built-up area norms) that is very small when compared with other countries' standards.
6. **Labour law challenges:** The new SEZ law is unlikely to address the critical issue of labour flexibility. A restrictive labour law environment has posed innumerable hurdles to the development of the Indian manufacturing sector. Although GOI has abolished many irrelevant labour laws and has come up with a standardized code, it is a challenge to operate as labour laws in India are administered by state governments, known to have corrupt bureaucracy.
7. **Private sector not involved in infrastructure development:** One of the objectives behind the SEZ Policy is that it helps develop export-related dedicated infrastructure, thus improving the quality of services to exporters and making them competitive in the international market. In fact, private investment is not flowing into the development of these facilities, and most of the infrastructure facilities for SEZs tend to be with public investments. Moreover, the private sector is keen on developing only service-based SEZs where the investment is low, and they make money by overcharging to units located in the non-processing area, thus making huge profits. The private sector has not shown interest in the development of multi-product large-sized SEZs, which can transform the economic landscape of the country.
8. **Poor execution of SEZ model:** Some policymakers are of opinion that the SEZ Policy is not properly implemented in India, and as a result, only existing units are relocating their business operations to the SEZ area, which results in the revenue loss to the government without any incremental exports, economic activity and employment generation. More so, the existing SEZ Policy does not seem to be in tune with Indian SMEs, which contribute almost 40 percent of India's foreign trade. The present SEZ Policy has failed to create bigger inroads into small- and medium-scale manufacturing and trading. Efforts should be made to make the existing SEZs Policy particularly helpful for small- and medium-scale entities, which cannot afford to set up captive infrastructure facilities, but can certainly emerge as competitors in cost and scale of operations due to their specialization in the horizontal production line and can successfully attract foreign capital and technology in their specialized areas of activity. Moreover, India has to make its SEZ Policy such that it promote and encourage India's manufacturing exports in international markets so that India can also stand up at par with China as a low-cost supplier of goods to the world.

SEZs can become a more dynamic and potent medium for expanding and diversifying India's foreign trade if some of the corrective steps are taken by the government. India is already implementing the scheme for coastal economic zones, which will be created in coastal states as it cuts significant logistics cost of the export-oriented industry. Existing SEZs located in the coastal areas should be a part of any future industrial strategy as it will synergize the country's efforts in promoting faster exports. Additionally, another GOI project named as the Sagarmala project, which aims to promote a port-led development strategy, should factor on improving connectivity and other infrastructural issues of existing SEZs. Proper infrastructural inter-linkages of coastal economic zones, SEZs, DTAs and Sagarmala project will create a win-win situation for the country. The removal of minimum alternate tax as imposed on entities will improve their profitability and will make SEZs an attractive destination for investment and manufacturing. The present SEZ Policy also needs to factor the 'low-cost housing' and other basic amenities required for workers who work there.

In conclusion, it can be said that even after all these challenges, India should continue its policy of SEZs so as to take benefit of advantages such as availability of large and skilled workforce, intrinsic comparative advantage in several industries, a strong policy framework, availability of complementing and supporting ancillary industry, ensuring backward and forward linkages to the domestic industry, emerging export-oriented entrepreneurship and catering to the needs of vast local markets. It is expected that through SEZs, India can combine these factors into powerful alchemy to attract the best technology and large inflows of foreign investment, and if domestic regulation is strengthened further including looking at prevalent rigid labour laws, supportive bureaucracy, cutting down red tape, improving overall infrastructure and so on, SEZs will automatically become a panacea for all economic problems and diseases. The differences of opinions will always be there on the incentives, benefits and facilities to SEZs, but it shall not hamper India's march towards emerging as a global hub for manufacturing, trading and services and cherishing our past glory of export champions by 2020 by garnering 5 percent share in world trade.

CASELET 20.1

DESH Bill: Can It Be a Game Changer?

To give a renewed boost to India's external engagements, the Ministry of Commerce and Industry has stepped up efforts by signing new FTAs/comprehensive partnership agreements and is now revamping the SEZ law of India. The reasons for such revamping of SEZ law are both external and internal, as various disruptive events around the world such as US–China trade wars, COVID-19 pandemic and Russia–Ukraine war are accelerating global shifts in supply chains. New global alliances are coming up; resultantly, shifting industries from China to elsewhere and India under such scenario is vying for opportune investment-intensive manufacturing capabilities in the crucial sectors of India economy. On a policy front, there is a pressure from the WTO to eliminate all export-related incentives, benefits and subsidies which are there in the existing SEZ law. Internally, there is a view that it is high time to extend an enabling and attractive environment to Indian industries to scale up production, renew their export promotion efforts, embrace an ecosystem of research and innovation to leverage Indian talent to innovate, ensure ease of doing business and overcome the other operational challenges in the hitherto SEZ Act.

New Law is Need of The Hour

The Ministry of Commerce and Industry is consulting all associated stakeholders, especially the developers and units located in the existing SEZs, academia and prospective investors to overcome the shortcomings of existing SEZ Act while introducing the Development of Enterprise and Service Hubs (DESH) Bill in the monsoon session of Parliament. The reforms proposed under DESH bills are to broad-base the objectives of DESH business units on criteria such as growth, employment generation, research and innovation, contribution to environment sustainability, etc. and is not limited to mere earning of net positive foreign exchange as under the existing SEZ law, a feature disputed under WTO legal framework. The DESH bill proposed specific policy support to both manufacturing and services sector units to bring it close to actual requirements of unit operators. Ensuring streamlined processing of applications for grant of approval, notification, de-notification, fiscal incentives, non-fiscal benefits, tax exemptions, and transitory provisions, DESH bill proposes to create a dynamic and robust structure of governance and compliances, thus ensuring ease of doing business. The digital and transparent governance under strengthened 'Single-Window' is the key feature of DESH bill. Furthermore, the DESH bill intends to synergize India's overall policy regime, that is, supplementing and simultaneously complementing the existing flagship schemes introduced by Government of India, that is, Production Linked Incentives, Assemble in India, GATI-Shakti, MOOWR, Dedicated Export Enclaves (EOU/BTP/STPIs), Start-up India and Digital India.

Ambiguity Needs to Be Cleared

In the realm, although the draft is a step forward but there are concerns of industry, for instance, the definition of 'export' under proposed Section 2(m) needs to bring clarity on supplies made as 'deemed export' to EOU units, embassies, UN and other notified multilateral organizations and against Advance Authorisation and Export Promotion Capital Goods Scheme. The draft bill can further incorporate the provisions on treatment of supplies made from various kinds of industrial clusters and parks, for instance Textile Park, Apparel Park, Pharma Park, Agri-Park, Lace Park, etc. This will bring in greater synergy in the overall developmental efforts of various ministries and departments. The notable concern of the industry is that of Section 47(1, d) which, although lucidly, provides for exemption from payment of taxes, duties or cess under all enactments specified in the 4th Schedule of the said Act. A closer look of 4th Schedule of the said Act shows omission of Income Tax Act, hence the exemption extended to DESH units of Income Tax @15% as proposed under Section 115BAB shall continue to be governed and regulated by Income Tax Act, 1961. This will expose the new units to the risks associated with withdrawals of tax relief or even tax rate changes which will not be under the consultation, purview and review of the DESH bill. Furthermore, Section 115BAB which provisions that 'no deduction on account of depreciation in respect of such machinery or plant has been allowed or is allowable under the provisions of this Act in computing the total income of any person for any period prior to the date of the installation of machinery or plant by the person' will be retrograding step for new investments to percolate into such zones from country like China under 'China-plus-One' strategy. This should further be read with Manufacture & Other Operations in Warehouse Regulations (MOOWR) which also stipulate similar provisions on treatment of depreciation, hence the industry is of the view it as another policy document without additional and motivating fiscal and non-fiscal benefits to attract investments to transform the export ecosystem of India. The DESH bill should further incorporate rule-based but transparent provisions on transitory provisions for units willing to switch-over from SEZ units to DESH units. One of the major compliance issues for India's export industry is that of Foreign Exchange Management Act, and how units located in DESH area will be facilitated under Single-Window including the facilitative powers of

Development Commissioners, is missing in the circulated draft. The enabling provisions of documentary compliance of creating logistics channels between zones, zones and DTA area, zones & dedicated export enclaves/MOOWR units, and zones and exit and entry gateway ports will add in, ensuring ease to industry to transact from such zones.

Time to Rise The Occasion

India has missed many opportunities of emerging as export champion, but now as the time and circumstances are opportune, it is the time to offer an enabling and facilitative policy regime particularly to foreign investors to invest, scale-up and leverage India as a centre of global manufacturing, trading and services. DESH bill is a needed policy intervention to scale-up, scope-up, start-up, and to stand-up among export champions of the world, commensurate with India's growing stature globally. Let us hope, DESH bill to be a game-changer!

Questions

1. What are the key reasons for revamping the SEZ law of India?
2. Based on the learnings in the chapter, elaborate why SEZ has not emerged as the engine for economic growth and employment in India.
3. What kinds of changes are proposed in SEZ law to be replaced with Development of Enterprise and Services Hubs as proposed by the Ministry of Commerce and Industry?
4. What are your views on promoting India's exports?

20.7 Summary

The introduction of the SEZ scheme in India is largely based on the experiences received from similar kinds of dedicated industrial zones focusing on expanding and diversifying the exports of countries such as China, South Korea, Malaysia and Vietnam, which have leveraged SEZs as the dedicated industrial zones manufacturing goods and rendering services only for increasing the exports of respective countries. SEZ is a special geographical area created within the country that is treated as a 'foreign territory'; hence, domestic rules and regulations governing the conduct of business are not applicable to these zones. Such zones are created with the major goal of attracting foreign investments into the country and ensuring effective utilization of the country's physical and non-physical resources in shaping the country's economic success. For setting up SEZs in India, one has to fill up the application in 'Form A' as prescribed along with the name, address and status of the promoter. One should also provide the necessary details in the form of a project report clearly indicating details such as the proposed SEZ's location, the details of infrastructure that already exists, details of infrastructure that will be established and the total area of the proposed SEZ along with the application form. After the review of such application, the state government forwards the application to the Department of Commerce, GOI, along with observations if any. The key observations from any state government include issues such as environmental clearances, electricity, water, construction permits, power generation, transmission and power distribution inside the SEZ. The applications which are duly recommended by the respective state governments/union territories administration shall be considered by BOA periodically on consensus for setting up the SEZ. If BOA accepts the proposal, a permission letter is issued to the developer (applicant) for setting up the proposed SEZ, and in case of refusal, it will issue the refusal note to the developer of SEZ and also inform the state government. Many benefits and incentives are available to the SEZ developer/co-developer.

The functioning of SEZs is administered in a way that there shall be a hassle-free regulatory environment with minimum scope for red tape and bureaucratic controls. The regulatory functioning of SEZ is governed by a three-tier administrative set-up, which mainly comprises BOA, an approval committee and a DC. BOA is the apex body and is headed by the secretary of the Department of Commerce. The approval committee at the zone level deals with the approval of units in the SEZs and other related issues. Each zone is headed by the DC, who is an ex officio chairperson of the approval committee. Business firms, both domestic and foreign, see a great business opportunity in the India economic story and are keen to set up SEZs as they wish to make India a base for manufacturing, trading and services due to cost advantages and an attractive market. The SEZ Act and Rules have paved the way for simplification in procedural hurdles and are keen as the red-carpet to global investors to come and invest in India.

Review Exercises

Multiple Choice Questions

1. When was the policy on SEZs introduced in India?
   a. 2001
   b. 2002
   c. 2000
   d. 2005
   e. None of the above
2. In which of the following years was the SEZ Act enacted?
   a. 2005
   b. 2006
   c. 2007
   d. 2000
   e. None of the above
3. Which of the following is the first known country of having set up the first SEZ in the world?
   a. Puerto Rico
   b. China
   c. Taiwan
   d. Ireland
   e. None of the above
4. What is the minimum land requirement for setting up the 'multi-products' SEZ in India?
   a. 100 hectares
   b. 10 hectares
   c. 40 hectares
   d. 1,000 hectares
   e. None of the above

5. Which of the following countries has effectively leveraged the SEZ as an engine of economic growth, employment generation and transforming the economy from developing to advanced?
   a. India
   b. China
   c. Taiwan
   d. Japan
   e. South Korea
6. What is the minimum land requirement for setting up the product-specific SEZ in India?
   a. 100 hectares
   b. 10 hectares
   c. 40 hectares
   d. 1,000 hectares
   e. None of the above
7. The key incentives for SEZ units include which of the following?
   a. Exemption from CST
   b. Exemption from service tax
   c. Single-window clearance for central- and state-level approvals
   d. Exemption from state value-added tax and other levies
   e. All of the above
8. Which of the following benefits are not entitled to the developer of a SEZ as per the SEZ Act and Rules?
   a. Exemption from minimum alternate tax
   b. Exemption from dividend distribution tax
   c. Exemption from CST
   d. Exemption from service tax
   e. Exemption from payment of income tax, wealth tax and gift tax
9. In which of the following sector are the maximum number of SEZs being set up in India?
   a. IT
   b. Biotech and pharmaceuticals
   c. Steel and aluminium
   d. Mobile and computers hardware
   e. None of the above
10. Which of the following states of India has the maximum number of operational SEZs?
   a. Andhra Pradesh
   b. Telangana
   c. Maharashtra
   d. Karnataka
   e. Tamil Nadu

Critical Thinking Questions

1. What is an SEZ? Write an essay on the development of SEZs in India.
2. Examine the roles of the developer, state government, BOA and DC in setting up an SEZ in India.

3. What are the exemptions and benefits offered to an SEZ developer and SEZ units under the SEZ Act, 2005, and the SEZ Rules, 2006?
4. Explain with diagram the administrative and institutional mechanism for setting up an SEZ in India.
5. Critically examine the framework of the procedure for setting up an SEZ in India.
6. Write an essay on the present debate of SEZs in India.

Further Readings

1. Ministry of Commerce and Industry. 2005. *Annual Report 2005–2006*. Available at: https://commerce.gov.in/publications/ar2005_06.pdf (accessed on 19 August 2020).
2. Ministry of Law and Justice. 2005. 'The Special Economic Zones Act, 2005'. Available at: https://lcommerce.gov.in/writereaddata/aboutus/actspdfs/SEZ%20Act,%202005.pdf (accessed on 19 August 2020).

CHAPTER 21

Legal Framework of Customs Law

CHAPTER OBJECTIVES

- To understand the historical perspectives in the evolution of Indian customs law.
- To explain the role of the Customs Act, 1962, and the Customs Tariff Act, 1975.
- To understand the various duties which are imposed under customs law.
- To explain the online system of export and import cargo clearance under the ICEGATE system.

21.1 Introduction

The collection of revenue has been an important activity for efficient administration of the state from ancient times, and customs duties are one of the oldest forms of taxation in India. The customs duties are as old as the history of international trade itself. The customs duty is a tax which is collected by the nation state on goods imported into or exported out of the territorial boundaries of the country. Customs duties contribute a significant part of the revenue to all the countries throughout the globe, including India, where they contribute almost 8 percent of the total tax collection of the country. Customs duties in India are applicable to exports as well as imports depending on the case for which the applicable rates are determined by the Department of Revenue, Ministry of Commerce. The procedure for application is published in schedules of the export and import of the Customs Tariff Act, 1975. For assessing whether the duty will be applicable or not, it is essential to find out the taxable event of import and export from India as per the law. The export duties are virtually non-existent in India and are applied sometimes in order to control the export of a particular item from India by making it expensive. Some of the prime reasons for imposing the duty on the export are to mop up excess profitability in the international price of goods in case the domestic prices of the commodity are lower. On the contrary, import duties are prevalent on a large scale, particularly in developing economies, as they are used not only to collect revenue but also to provide protection to the domestic industry. India has come a way in decreasing customs duties from a peak of 350 percent in the 1980s to 7.5 percent in 2020. Customs duties are far lower in India on some products such as lifesaving drugs and essential nutritional products such as pulses and edible oil. Figure 21.1 illustrates the value of imports and net import duties collections.

Being a sovereign nation, the authority for tax collection in India is vested in Article 265 of the Constitution of India, which lays down that 'no tax shall be levied or collected except by the authority of law'. In case of customs duty, such authority is vested with the Central Board of Indirect Taxes and Customs, which draws its power for the levy and collection of customs duties from the Customs Act, 1962. The legislation relating to the Customs Act has been enacted by the parliament by the exercise of the

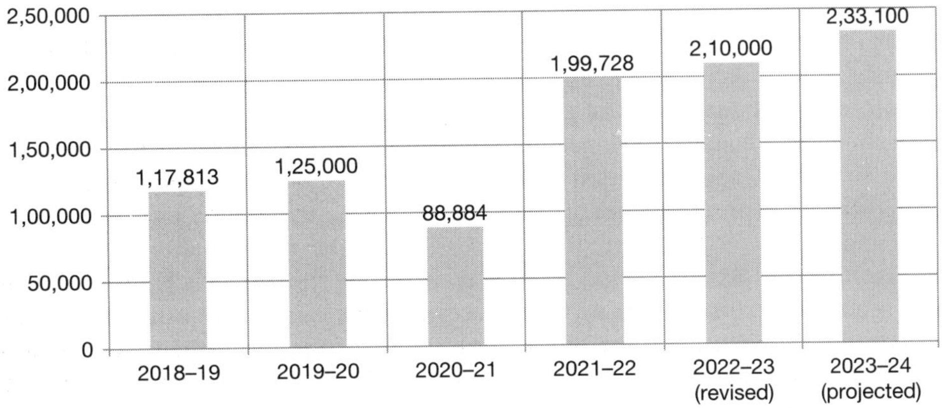

FIGURE 21.1 Net import duties (₹ crore).

Source: India Budget. https://www.indiabudget.gov.in/budget2021-22/index.php (accessed on 10 May 2023).

exclusive power vested in it under Article 246, Entry 83 of list-I of the Seventh Schedule of the Indian Constitution.

21.2 Historical Overview of Customs in India

Customs duty is sometimes also referred to as the 'external excise tax', as it includes an export duty or an import duty on the cargo traded across national boundaries. The origin of customs duty is as old as human history itself as 'customary levies' by the trading societies in the Indus Valley Civilization have been common in ancient times. Even in recorded history, we have the evidence of the prevalence of customs duty as a source of revenue to the state—the *Kautiliyam Arthashastram* (circa 321–300 BC), briefed that the highest revenue officer of the time was called the Samaharta (collector-general), and he was assigned the responsibility to arrange the revenue collection for the state from seven types of places. This was largely done to ensure that the state shall play an important role in being a welfare state. Accordingly, in the Mauryan Kingdom, the levy or tax on trade was collected from both the land routes and sea routes so that the state can undertake developmental activities in providing better services to the public. *Chungi* was the common tax to be imposed on the goods moving from one state to another during the Mughal Empire (1526–1707) in India. During the British Empire in India, the customs duty was an important source of revenue for the state, and as recorded in history, the customs duty in 1839–1840 was almost ₹4,103,298, hence contributing around 5 percent share in the total public revenue. The customs duty was once abolished during the British Empire in 1788 by Lord Cornwallis, but it was reintroduced again in 1801.

The present system of the customs administration came into the Indian subcontinent at the beginning of the 20th century as the process of consolidation of the customs law, regulation and administration began in 1878 after Queen Victoria acceded to the throne. The customs administration in India has been designed on the pattern of the British system by enacting the Sea Customs Act ensuring legal authority for the levy and collection of customs duty in India. The customs administration, in the beginning, was in the hands of the respective provincial government till 1924, but it was brought under the control of the federal government by establishing a Central Board of Revenue under the Central Board of Revenue Act of 1924, thereby ensuring all power for the levy of customs duty to the federal government. The Land Customs Act was also enacted in 1924 in order to enable the central government to enforce the control on the movement of goods and passengers by land routes and frontiers from the Indian subcontinent to adjoining territories and vice versa. This was done as Britishers have already consolidated their political administration in India, and they want to ensure proper revenue generation system by imposing taxes on the transit of cargo from one country to another in the Indian subcontinent. In Independent India, efforts were made to consolidate the customs administration, and accordingly, the Indian Customs Act, 1962, was enacted by repealing the previous Customs Act and putting the system of sea customs, inland bonded warehouses customs, land customs into one act only instead of three acts during the British empire. For determination of the tariff, the Customs Tariff Act was enacted in 1975 by repealing the Tariff Act, 1934. Figure 21.2 lists the major events shaping the custom administration in India.

In Independent India, the customs duty along with GST (excise duty on few products) is one of the most important sources of revenue to the state contributing as much as 25 percent of the total central government revenue in 2020.

- The development of modern customs administration in India began in 1786, when the Britishers formed the first Board of Revenue in Calcutta.
- In 1808, a new Board of Trade was established on the expansion of territorial boundaries of British empire In India.
- Customs Duties Act was enacted in 1859 after the British had consolidated their administration on India after the first war of Independence paving the way for uniform duties on all provincial territories of India rather than the provincial import duties.
- The applicable rate of duty was reduced from 10% (1859) to 7.5% in 1864.
- The Sea Customs Act was passed by the government in 1888.
- The Warehousing of Bonded Goods Act was passed in 1896.
- The Land Customs Act was passed in 1924.
- Air customs having been covered under the India Aircrafts Act of 1934.
- After Independence, the Sea Customs Act and other allied enactments were repealed by a consolidating and amending legislation entitled the Customs Act, 1962.
- The share of collections from customs duties are declining in total tax collections in India as the rates of duties are lowered as per WTO commitment and various PTAs/FTAs being signed.

FIGURE 21.2 Major events shaping the modern customs administration in India.

Source: Central Board of Indirect Taxes & Customs.

21.3 Meaning of Customs Duty

The customs duty is a kind of indirect tax which is collected by the central government on the import and export of goods from India. It has also been referred to as consumption tax in the true economic sense. The customs duty imposed by the government with regard to imported goods is known as the import duty, and the duties which are realized in the export of goods are known as the export duty. Hence, it can be said that the customs duty is the kind of tariff which is imposed on export and import of goods, and the list for such a tariff is provided by the Department of Revenue, GOI, every year based on ITC (HS) classification as the leviable rate or amount of the customs duty may vary from commodity to commodity. Being an indirect tax, the incidence of the customs duty is actually borne by the end consumer of the goods and not by the importer or the exporter who pay for such duty while exporting or importing. Figure 21.3 illustrates the kinds of duties imposed in India.

21.4 Scope and Coverage of Customs Law

There are several acts, rules and regulations (see Table 21.1) which prescribe the conduct of the customs law in India. Two major acts have been discussed here—the Customs Act, 1962, and the Customs Tariff Act, 1975.

21.4.1 The Customs Act, 1962

The Customs Act, 1962, is one of the basic acts governing the levy and collection of customs duty in India. The Act details the various provisions regarding the procedure and process of imposition of the customs duty on imports and exports of goods and merchandise including the baggage of people coming into and going out of India. This act details the procedure regarding the functions of officers of customs; appointment of customs ports/airports/warehousing stations; prohibitions on importation and exportation of goods; detection of illegally imported goods and prevention of the disposal thereof; prevention or detection of illegal export of goods; power to exempt from the provisions of, levy of and exemption from customs duties, indicating the amount of duty in the price of goods, advance rulings, provisions relating to conveyances carrying imported or exported goods; clearances of imported goods and export goods, goods in transit; warehousing; duty drawback; special provisions

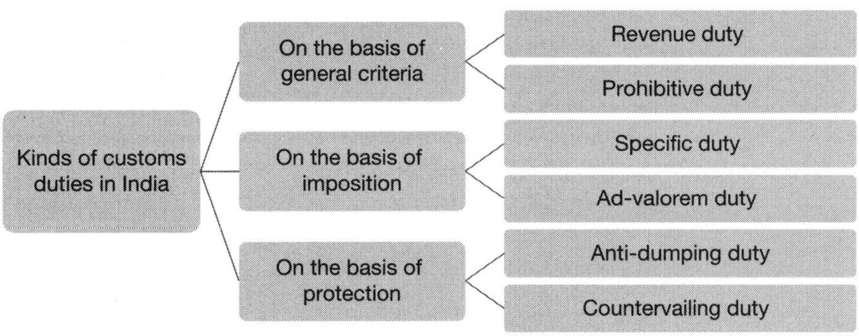

FIGURE 21.3 Kinds of customs duties in India.

TABLE 21.1 Acts, Rules, Regulations for the Customs Administration in India

Legislations Regulating Customs Procedure	Regulations under the Custom Act	Rules under the Customs Act
1. Customs Act, 1962 **2.** Customs Tariff Act, 1975 **3.** Central GST Act, 2017 **4.** State GST Act, 2017 **5.** Integrated GST Act, 2017 **6.** Foreign Trade (Development and Regulation) Act, 1992 **7.** Foreign Trade (Regulation) Rules, 1993 **8.** Foreign Trade (Exemption from Application of Rules in Certain Cases) Order, 1993 **9.** Central Excise Tariff Act, 1985 **10.** Central Excise Act, 1944	**1.** Customs (Provisional Duty Assessment) Regulations, 1963 **2.** Unclear Goods (Bill of Entry) Regulations, 1972 **3.** Imported Packages (Opening) Regulations, 1963 **4.** Shipping Bill for Aircraft Spares Ex-bond Regulations, 1975 **5.** Imported Stores (Retention on Board) Regulations, 1963 **6.** Bill of Coastal Goods (Form) Regulations, 1976 **7.** Warehoused Goods (Removal) Regulations, 1963 **8.** Import Report (Form) Regulations, 1976 **9.** Transportation of Goods (Through Foreign Territory) Regulations, 1965 **10.** Export Report (Form) Regulations, 1976 **11.** Bonded Aircraft Stores (Procedure) Regulations, 1965 **12.** Import Manifest (Aircraft) Regulations, 1976 **13.** Manufacture and other Operations in Warehouse Regulations, 1966 **14.** Export Manifest (Aircraft) Regulations, 1976 **15.** Passenger's Baggage (Levy of Fees) Regulations, 1966 **16.** Export Manifest (Vessels) Regulations, 1976 **17.** Baggage (Transit to Customs Stations) Regulations, 1967 **18.** Boat Notes Regulations, 1976 **19.** Levy of Fees (Customs Documents) Regulations, 1970 **20.** Bill of Entry (Forms) Regulations, 1976 **21.** Import Manifest (Vessels) Regulations, 1971	**1.** Foreign Privileged Persons (Regulation of Customs Privileges) Rules, 1957 **2.** Denaturing of Spirit Rules, 1972 **3.** Customs (Attachments of Property of Defaulters for Recovery of Government Dues) Rules, 1995 **4.** Accessories (Condition) Rules, 1963 **5.** Specified Goods (Prevention of Illegal Export) Rules, 1969 **6.** Re-Export of Imported Goods (Drawback of Customs Duties) Rules, 1995 **7.** Notice of Short-Export Rules, 1963 **8.** Customs Tariff (Identification, Assessment and Collection of Countervailing Duty on Subsidized Articles and for Determination of Injury) Rules, 1995 **9.** Customs and Central Excise Duties Drawback Rules, 1995 **10.** Customs Tariff (Identification, Assessment and Collection of Anti-Dumping Duty on Dumped Articles and for Determination of Injury) Rules, 1995 **11.** Customs Valuation (Determination of Price of Imported Goods) Rules, 1988 **12.** Notified Goods (Prevention of Illegal Import) Rules, 1969 **13.** Customs Tariff (Determination of Origin of Goods under the Bangkok Agreement) Rules, 1976 **14.** Customs (Settlement of Cases) Rules, 1999 **15.** Customs (Import of Goods at Concessional Rate of Duty for Manufacture of Excisable Goods) Rules, 1996

Legislations Regulating Customs Procedure	Regulations under the Custom Act	Rules under the Customs Act
	22. Customs House Agents Licensing Regulations, 1984	**16.** Customs (Publication of Names) Rules, 1975
	23. ATA Carnet (Form of Bill of Entry & Shipping Bill) Regulations, 1990	**17.** Rules of Determination of Origin of Goods under the Agreement on South Asian Free Trade Area
	24. Customs Refund Application (Form) Regulations, 1995	**18.** Customs Tariff (Identification and Assessment of Safeguard Duty) Rules, 1997
	25. Import of Gold and Silver by Passengers (Form of Bill of Entry) Regulations, 1994	**19.** Baggage Rules, 1998 Customs Tariff (Determination of Origin of Other Preferential Areas) Rules, 1977
	26. Goods Imported (Conditions of Transhipment) Regulations, 1995	**20.** Customs Tariff (Determination of Origin of Goods under the Free Trade Agreement between the Democratic Socialistic Republic of Sri Lanka and the Republic of India) Rules, 2000
	27. Shipping Bill and Bill of Export (Form) Regulations, 1991	
	28. Customs (Fees for Rendering Services by Customs Officers) Regulations, 1998	
	29. Bill of Entry (Electronic Declaration) Regulations, 1995	
	30. Project Imports Regulations, 1986	
	31. Courier Imports and Exports (Clearance) Regulations, 1998	

Source: Central Board of Indirect Taxes & Custom.

relating to SEZs; special provisions regarding baggage goods imported or exported; provisions relating to coastal goods and vessels carrying coastal goods; searches seizure and arrest; confiscation of goods and conveyances and imposition of penalties; settlement of cases, appeals and revision, offences and prosecutions; miscellaneous provisions regulating the customs duty collection in India. The main objective of the Customs Act, 1962, is to prevent the illegal imports and exports of goods from and into India. The Customs Act extends to the whole of India.

21.4.2 The Customs Tariff Act, 1975

The customs duty is imposed on goods which are imported into India or exported from India at the specified rates under the Customs Tariff Act, 1975. This act comprises two schedules: Schedule I which gives classification and rate of duties to be imposed on goods imported and Schedule II which gives classification and rates of duties to be imposed on the exports. The schedules of the act had been replaced in 1986 as India has decided to follow the ITC (HS) system replacing the Standard International Trade Classification. A Customs Tariff Act is a federally enacted act under entry number 82 of List-I (Union List) to Schedule VII. Further Section 12 of the Customs Act details that duties of customs which shall be levied at such rates as may be specified under the Customs Tariff Act, 1975, or any other law for the time being in force, on goods imported into or exported from India.

Goods become liable to duty if there is import into and export from India. The customs duty is one of the most important sources of revenue to the national exchequer and the main objectives for levy of customs duty are as follows:

1. Raising the revenue for the national exchequer, which can be fruitfully used for developmental purposes.
2. Regulating and controlling the imports of foreign goods into India, thereby ensuing order in the market.
3. Conserving foreign exchange and regulating the supply of essential and needy goods into domestic market.
4. Providing protection to the domestic industry by restricting and prohibiting the import of selected goods through imposition of high duty, import licensing, quota system and outright import ban and enabling the domestic industry to stand up against foreign competition.

21.4.3 The Tariff Schedules

There are two tariff schedules—Schedule I describes the import duties and Schedule II prescribes the export duties. There are only 50 products on which export duties are imposed. Import duties are far more comprehensive and are prescribed in tariff lines of 98 + 1 chapters of the Custom Tariff Nomenclature. Such duty can be imposed on both import and export duties; however, the revenue contributed by export duties is nominal as it is imposed only to stabilize internal market condition and control the supply of such goods in the market. Recently, GOI has imposed export duty on steel as the prices of steel in the domestic market were rising very fast, and the government has imposed duty on steel so as to make it expensive and uncompetitive in the international market. The customs duty on the export of coffee at the rate of $1,200 per metric ton has been another important case of the export duty in the recent past. Basic structures of the duties which are imposed under the central excise Tariff Act, 1975, are as follows:

1. **Basic customs duty:** All goods which are imported into India are chargeable with the basic customs duty under the Customs Act, 1962. The applicable rates of the basic customs duty are given in the First Schedule of the Customs Tariff Act, 1975, as amended from time to time under the finance acts. The basic customs duty can be fixed on the basis of an ad valorem rate or on a specific rate basis. The ad valorem duty is applied when the rates of commodity are not subject to sudden changes as such duty paid varies with the prices of products. On the other hand, the specific duty is easy to assess and is applicable where the goods are tough to measure and quantify. The present applicable rate of basic customs duty as per the Union Budget 2008–2009 is 8 percent only as the basic customs duty can be reduced or exempted by the central government on any goods.
2. **IGST in lieu of additional duty of customs:** Additional duties of custom are also known as countervailing duties/IGST levy. The additional duty of customs or countervailing duty is a customs duty which is imposed on goods which have received government subsidies in the originating or exporting country. As there is a global convention of not to impose taxes on exportable goods, the exporter of any country is in an advantageous position vis-à-vis the domestic manufacturer who has to pay GST. In order to normalize this anomaly, GOI imposes countervailing duties which are equivalent to rates of GST in India and are collected as IGST, meaning it is the interim tax and shall be set off by the importer on subsequent stages of import sales. The

importing country in order to reduce the impact of such subsidies and low cost of products, flooding into the domestic market, may impose such duty for the protection of the domestic industry and neutralize the impact of subsidies. For customs purposes, it is treated in the same way as anti-dumping duty. It is possible to have both anti-dumping duty and countervailing duty on the same product. This countervailing duty is leviable as additional duty on goods imported into the country and the rate structure of this duty is equal to GST on like articles produced in India. The base of this additional duty is the CIF value of imports plus the duty levied earlier. If the rate of this duty is on the ad valorem basis, the value for this purpose will be the total of the value of the imported article and the customs duty on it.

3. **Social welfare surcharge:** The social welfare surcharge on imported goods has been imposed, and it shall be levied and collected on the basic duty of customs. The legal framework for the imposition of the social welfare surcharge is enshrined in the First Schedule to the Customs Tariff Act, 1975, and the event for imposition shall be on goods being imported into India. The social welfare surcharge replaces the erstwhile cesses such as the primary and secondary education cess and the Krishi Kalyan Cess. The social welfare surcharge is imposed to fulfil the commitment of the government to provide and finance education, health and social security. The rate of the surcharge is 10 percent and shall be collected on the aggregate of duties, taxes and cesses which are levied and collected by the central government in the Ministry of Finance (Department of Revenue) under Section 12 of the Customs Act, 1962. The social welfare surcharge will not be collected on the following duties:
   a. The safeguard duty referred to in Sections 8B and 8C of the Customs Tariff Act.
   b. The countervailing duty referred to in Section 9 of the Customs Tariff Act.
   c. The anti-dumping duty referred to in Section 9A of the Customs Tariff Act.
   d. The social welfare surcharge on imported goods levied under Sub-section (1).

21.5 Commonly Used Terms in Customs

One needs to understand certain terms used in customs clearance in India in order to understand the process and procedure involved for clearance of both exportable and imported cargo. In the following sub-sections we cover the details of such terms.

21.5.1 ITC (HS) 2017

With the change in the international economic environment during the Uruguay round of trade negotiations paving way for globalization of the world economy, the trade practices also started getting streamlined and standardized. Accordingly, nations including India subscribe to ITC (HS) as it has been evolved by WCO based in Brussels. ITS (HS) is used for the purpose of assessment of the customs duty on products as each product has an identification code under this system. ITC (HS) trade codes are divided into two schedules. Schedule I details about the rules and guidelines regarding the import policies whereas Schedule II details regarding the rules and regulation related to export policies as prescribed by DGFT under the Ministry of Commerce. Schedule I of the ITC (HS) code is divided into 21 sections, and each section is further divided into chapters. The total number of chapters in Schedule I are 98. The chapters are further divided into sub-headings under which different HS codes are mentioned. Schedule II of the ITC (HS) code contains 97 chapters giving all the details about the guidelines related to the export policies. An example of the Import Policy (Schedule I) is illustrated in Table 21.2.

The introduction of ITC (HS) code in the 1990s in the classification of more than 8,000 products internationally has largely replaced the previously used Standard International Trade Classification; however, Standard International Trade Classification remains in the use for statistical purposes. ITC (HS) 2017 has around 11,738 tariff lines at 8-digit level in India. In drawing up the national tariff, the revenue departments often specify the rate of customs and GST with reference to the HS code of the

TABLE 21.2 An Example of ITC (HS) Classification of Products

EXIM Code	Item Description	With Effect from	Policy	Condition Relating to the Policy	Note
0208: Other meat and edible meat offal, fresh, chilled or frozen					
0208 10 00	Rabbits or hares		Free		
0208 20 00	Frogs' legs		Restricted		
0208 30 00	Primates		Free	Import of parts and products of wild animal as defined under Wildlife (Protection) Act, 1972 is prohibited.	
0208 40 00	Whales, dolphins and porpoises (mammals of the order cetaceans), of manatees and dugongs (mammals of the order Sirenia)		Free	Import of parts and products of wild animal as defined under Wildlife (Protection) Act, 1972 is prohibited.	
0208 50 00	Reptiles (including snakes and turtles)		Free	Import of parts and products of wild animal as defined under Wildlife (Protection) Act, 1972 is prohibited	
0208 90	Other:				
0208 90 10	Wild animals	1 March 1999	Prohibited	Not permitted to be imported	
0208 90 90	Other		Free	Import of parts and products of wild animal as defined under Wildlife (Protection) Act, 1972 is prohibited	
0209 00 00	Pig fat, free of lean meat and poultry fat, not rendered or otherwise extracted, fresh, chilled, frozen, salted, in brine, dried or smoked		Prohibited	Not permitted to be imported	

Source: ITC (HS), Director General of Foreign Trade.

product. In some countries and customs unions, 6-digit HS codes are locally extended to 8 digits. In India, the 8-digit code is used as on today, but India has committed at WTO to use 10-digit codes as agreed among contracting parties in 2017. Negotiations are already at WTO among trading parties on 12-digit codes for classification of some tariff lines. Some countries including the European Union have already been using 10 digits for further tariff discrimination.

21.5.2 Taxable Event

Goods are subject to the import duty or export duty when there is 'import into India', or 'export from India'. The Customs Act defines the following taxable events:

1. 'Import', as defined in Section 2 (23), means 'bringing into India from a place outside India'.
2. 'Export', as defined in Section 2 (18), means 'taking out of India to a place outside India'.
3. 'India' is defined in Section 2(27) to include the territorial waters of India.
4. Article 1 of the Constitution of India defines 'India' as the union of states. The General Clauses Act defines India to mean all territories for the time being which comprise territorial boundaries (including sea areas) India.

21.5.3 Territorial Water of India

Territorial waters as defined by the UN Convention on the Law of Sea and subsequently incorporated as an Act in India, namely the Territorial Waters, Continental Shelf, Exclusive Economic Zones and Maritime Zones Act, 1976, mean that the portion of the sea that is adjacent to the shores of India will be known as the territorial waters of India. As per Section 3 of this Act, the territorial waters of India are extended up to 12 nautical miles (22 km) from the baseline at the coast of India and will include any gulf, harbour, creek or tidal river. Before this Act, as per international conventions, the territorial waters of India were only up to 6 nautical miles from the baseline, but they have been extended up to 12 nautical miles (1 NM, 1.852 km) in 1967. The maritime claims of India are tabled in Table 21.3.

It is important to have clarity regarding the territorial waters of India as it determines the chargeability of the customs duty because when goods enter into India's territorial water, they become taxable.

21.5.4 Indian Customs Water

The Customs Act, 1962, defines, 'Indian customs waters means the waters extending into the sea up to the limit of the contiguous zone of India under Section 5 of the Territorial Waters, Continental Shelf,

TABLE 21.3 Maritime Claims of India

S. No.	Maritime Claims	Distance in Nautical Miles (NM)
1.	Territorial sea	12 NM (22 km)
2.	Contiguous zone	24 NM (44 km)
3.	Exclusive economic zone	200 NM (371 km)
4.	Continental shelf	200 NM or to the edges of the continental margin

Source: CIA (2018).

Exclusive Economic Zone and other Maritime Zones Act, 1976, and includes any bay, gulf, harbour, creek or tidal river.'[1] The contiguous zone of India is extended up to another 12 nautical miles from the territorial waters of India. Hence, the Indian custom water is up to 24 nautical miles. The sale on high seas as allowed under FTP 2015–2020 can take place beyond the Indian customs water as the goods entry into Indian customs water makes it a taxable event. The knowledge of Indian customs waters is essential as certain provisions of the Customs Act, which empower the customs officers to take actions in Indian customs water include:

1. Under Section 100 of the Indian Customs Act, 1962, lies the power to search suspected persons entering or leaving India provided that the proper officer has reason to believe that any person to whom this section applies has withheld about this person, any goods liable to confiscation or any documents relating thereto, he/she may search that person who has landed from or is about to board or is on board with any vessel within the Indian customs waters.
2. Under Section 104 of the Indian Customs Act lies the power to arrest. Hence an officer of customs empowered in this behalf by the general or special order of the commissioner of customs has reason to believe that any person in India or within the Indian customs waters has committed an offence punishable under Section 132 or Section 133 or Section 135 or Section 135A or Section 136, he/she may arrest such person and shall, as soon as may be, inform him/her of the grounds for such arrest.
3. Under Section 106 of the Customs Act, 1962, lies the power to stop and search the conveyances if the proper officer has a reason to believe that any aircraft, vehicle or animal in India or any vessel in India or within the Indian customs waters has been, is being or is about to be used in the smuggling of any goods or in the carriage of any goods which have been smuggled, he/she may at any time stop any such vehicle, animal or vessel or in the case of an aircraft, compel it to land.

21.5.5 Customs Authority

The customs is an authority or agency in a country which has been made responsible for collecting and safeguarding customs duties and for controlling the flow of goods including animals, personal effects and hazardous items in and out of a country. The Central Board of Indirect Tax and Customs as created under the Ministry of Finance has the customs authority in India. It has the authority to issue public notices, framing customs, GST and excise rules with inputs from the Department of Revenue and collecting the duties in India.

21.5.6 Red and Green Channels

The customs clearance for passengers travelling or coming to India is through two channel systems, which have been adopted almost internationally in all airports and are as follows:

1. Green channel for the passengers who do not have any dutiable goods.
2. Red channel for the passengers who have dutiable goods.

[1] Section 2 (28) of the Customs Act, 1962.

In addition to this,

1. All the passengers arriving in India are required to file the correct declaration of their baggage in the form as prescribed by authorities.
2. The passengers entering through the green channel are required to deposit the customs portion of the disembarkation card to the customs authorities at the gate while leaving the airport terminal.
3. The declaration of foreign exchange/currency has to be made before the customs officers in the cases where the value of foreign currency notes exceeds $5,000 or equivalent and further where the aggregate value of foreign exchange including currency exceeds $10,000 or equivalent.

If passengers do not follow these guidelines as specified by authorities while walking through the green channel with dutiable/prohibited goods, they are subject to prosecution/penalty and confiscation of goods as the case may be.

21.6 Online System of Customs Clearance under ICEGATE

A famed and historic step in the trade facilitation and transaction cost reduction in Indian foreign trade as the Ministry of Commerce and Finance has decided and envisaged a plan to electronically exchange the trade documents at all ports/airports/ICDs/CFS/land customs stations with agencies involved in the trade such as the financing bank, RBI, DGFT, custodians of imports and exports goods and other regulatory agencies. At the beginning of 1991, the government made its objective clear that the export promotion is vital to India's growth, and accordingly, steps were made to facilitate the exporting community with a slew of initiatives for better trade facilitation. The National Informatics Centre and Central Board of Indirect Taxes and Customs in December 1992 had decided to run the pilot phase of the EDI system of EXIM clearance of customs at a number of customs houses throughout the country. On the success of the pilot phase, a more detailed execution study at the Delhi Custom House in April 1994 was planned and executed through the Indian Customs EDI System (ICES). In March 1996, it was decided that ICES gateway will be extended to 20 other customs locations. Today, the ICES gateway is successfully commissioned at 157 locations in the country covering all the major ports, airports, ICDs and land customs stations. The Central Board of Indirect Taxes and Customs has initiated several steps to create awareness for the acceptance and use of ICES gateway at the user level, thus paving way for smooth change from the traditional method of clearance of customs documents to electronic clearance of export and import consignments. ICES gateway has been of immense help in ensuring transparency and accountability by reducing the arbitrariness and uncertainty in the processing of documents. There is an automated random allocation of electronic declarations to the appraising officer. A declaration, once registered with the system, is handled on a first-come, first-serve basis. At the time of the declaration, the validation features ensure that only valid data is accepted by the system and invalid data is rejected at the service centre. The system provides for management of parameters such as exchange rates, drawback rates and rates of duty on the basis of directories which are updated by the systems manager, thereby eliminating errors previously encountered in the manual processing of documents. A concept of 'green channel' has been introduced, which provides a waiver of examination by customs on the basis of importers profile. The only interface between customs and trade is at the time of collection of goods.

This project entitled as ICES gateway (Figure 21.4), the all-India computerization of custom houses in India, has started accepting the EXIM documents and exchange of information electronically in the centralized/structured formats with other organizations involved in the foreign trade value chain. With the introduction of the EDI system in Indian customs, the trade documents would move from one organization to another organization in the electronic form, and the same will be when the documents moved within the organization from one desk of customs officer to another, thereby paving the way for paperless trade, time and cost reduction, transparency, accountability, and above all trade facilitation so as to reduce transaction and logistical cost of Indian foreign trade, which is one among the highest in the world at 12 percent of GDP. Hence, ICES initiated a new era of trade facilitation and transaction cost reduction in the country by ensuring:

1. Paperless trade
2. Trade facilitation rather than control

21.6.1 Benefits of ICEGATE/EDI System

ICEGATE offers numerous benefits to the Indian trade community, and the same are elaborated below:

1. Traders save cost as the improved customs clearance and inspection procedures have become faster ensuring more certain and ultimately less costly international trade transactions.
2. Computerization of customs procedures has made the international traders' job very easy, as the cost of doing business has got reduced significantly in the EDI system. There is time

The pilot project was launched in the year 1994-95 at Delhi Customs House.

ICES were made operational for exports processing at Inland Container Depot, Tughlakabad in August, 1997; Sahar Air Customs, Mumbai in November, 1997; Jawaharlal Nehru Port Trust, New Mumbai in November, 1997; Chennai Air Customs in December, 1997.

ICES were extended to Bangalore Air Customs in February 1998, and Container Freight Station, Patparganj in March 1998.

As on today ICES is operational at 24 locations throughout the country.

More modules on Transshipment, Warehouse, Reexamination and Bonds, etc.; have been designed and Risk Management System is under trial under pilot phase. On its successful completion it will be extended throughout the country.

157 Customs Stations are extending paperless services to Indian trade communities which are available 24×7.

Under AEO Scheme, facility of Direct Port Delivery (DPD) and Direct Port Export (DPE) is provided to Indian importers and exporters.

FIGURE 21.4 EDI of customs: The journey so far.

Source: Central Board of Indirect Taxes & Customs.

and cost savings to the traders as preparing, handling, storing and delivering the customs documentation.

3. EDI has facilitated significant improvements in communications, access to information and transparency in customs processes resulting in the increased certainty and fairness.
4. The EDI system can also provide information regarding the good compliance track record of exporter and importer resulting in faster clearance and less intrusive verification techniques.
5. Importers know the number of duties and taxes as a result of the clear and consistent rules. More efficient clearance will produce time and cost savings and provide the certainty required to exploit modern business practices such as 'just-in-time' inventory.
6. Exporters benefited from having similar customs rules and procedures applicable across the international market, thus increasing market access opportunities while reducing costs and complexity.
7. Customs brokers have the opportunity to refocus their services from dealing with forms and complexity to using their expertise and knowledge to bring a new range of professional services to clients operating in an expanding and evolving trade market.
8. Carriers benefit from faster service, lower costs and the ability to use their equipment to its utmost capacity rather than having it delayed at customs.

21.6.2 Process of Flow of Exports under EDI

The process of the documentary flow for exports (Table 21.4) under the ICEGATE is explained below:

1. The exporters/CHAs are required to submit duly a shipping bill under a claim of duty drawbacks for the export of goods online at ICEGATE commissioner of customs. The shipping bill should be accompanied with required copies of the commercial invoice and packing list.
2. The service centre staff enters the data into the system and generates a 'checklist' to be verified by the exporter/CHA for correctness on verification if the data is found to be correctly recorded. The exporter/CHA will sign the checklist and return it to the service centre, signalling the final submission. Then, the service centre will generate the shipping bill number, which will be

TABLE 21.4 Elements of Two Main Module Used in EDI

Main Modules of ICES/Import			
Bonds	Service centre	Licence	Appraising
Baggage	Audit	Systems manager	MIS
Cash	Ex-bond	Examination	DEEC/100% EOU
E-Sanchit	Import General Manifest (IGM)	Assistant commissioner	Transshipment

Main Modules of ICES/Export		
Service centre	Examination	Duty drawback
Assistant commissioner	Additional commissioner	Preventive officer
Licence	Export General Manifest	Systems manager
MIS	E-Sanchit	

Source: Central Board of Indirect Taxes & Customs.

recorded manually on the top right of the checklist and returned to the exporter/CHA, thus completing the registration of the document. The service centre will also generate three copies of the TR-6 Challan for payment of cess wherever the cess element is involved.

3. The following types of shipping bill will be put to the assistant commissioner queue for clearance:
   a. Duty-free shipping bill—FOB value over ₹10 lakh
   b. DEEC shipping bill—FOB value over ₹1 lakh
   c. Drawback shipping bill—drawback over ₹1 lakh
   d. Free trade samples—FOB value over ₹1 lakh

   Having completed the process of clearance of the export documents from the assistant commissioner, these export documents will be put in goods registration in order to ensure the examination of the cargo.
4. All other shipping bills which are below the value as aforesaid mentioned in point 3 are straightaway put under examination in the goods registration queue and such export documents do not require any prior assessment of documents.
5. The exporter/CHA is required to present the cargo for examination to authorities within two days from the date of registration of the document at the service centre.
6. The exporter/CHA has to submit duly filled in data sheet explaining about shipping bill number, vessel number, freight and insurance charges, the total number of packages, types of packages (boxes, cartons, bags, etc.,), numbers marked on the packages, gross weight (in kgs), net weight (in kg), date of receipt of full consignment, container particulars, name of the sealing agency, whether factory stuffed or not and so on to the systems examination officer who will register the entry of goods in the system.
7. At this stage, the system randomly picks up certain shipping bills for examination to be carried out and the rest of the shipping bills are subjected to inspection by authorities for the description of cargo through marks, labels and numbers.
8. With the directions so generated by the EDI system, the shipping bill will be moved to the appraising officer's screen, who will verify whether the data available in the system and as shown in physical documents are similar and correct or not.
9. The appraising officer will mark the shipping bill to various examiners who are working under his/her control with necessary directions regarding the examination to be carried out.
10. The examiners will carry out the examination of the cargo and accordingly will enter the examination report in the EDI system.
11. The shipping bill will once again move back to the appraising officer's system screen for the LEO seal. In case of the cessable shipping bills, the appraising officer will verify the examination report as submitted by examiners after the physical examination of the cargo, duty payable on cargo and so on and grant the LEO seal to the export documents.
12. After LEO is given by the appraising officer, the system will generate two copies of the shipping bill. The appraising officer will obtain the signatures of the examiner and exporter/CHA in the designated places besides signing himself/herself on the documents.
13. Under EDI, the FEMA compliance is done in electronic mode; accordingly the FEMA Form SDF is merged with S/B and the system itself transmits the data to RBI-Export Data Processing and Monitoring System (EDPMS) system, and there is no need to physically submit the documents to banks by exporter anymore.

14. The shipping bill will then move electronically to the preventive section where preventive officers will supervise the stuffing of cargo into containers and stuffing report will be recorded in the system.
15. The container will be loaded into the vessel by obtaining the goods-received stamp from the chief officer/master of vessel exporters on the copy (hard copy) of the shipping bill.
16. On verification of the goods received stamp, the preventive officer will record sailing report in the EDI system.
17. The shipping bill will then move into the shipping agent's queue for filing of EGM.
18. After the EGM is recorded in the system, the drawback claims are put in drawback processing queue. DEEC bills will be put in the DEEC superintendent's queue for log-in details and other shipping bills will form part of the history database.
19. Drawback and DEEC shipping bills after completing the respective formalities will join the other shipping bills in the history database, thus completing the cycle of the shipping document.

21.6.3 EDI Procedure for Export of Goods under the Claim for Drawback

The EDI procedure for export of goods under the claim for drawback is given below:

1. The present system under EDI can process all duty drawback claims for exports, except in respect of duty drawback claims under Section 74 of the Customs Act, 1962, which are with regard to use of importable material used in export consignments, exports made in the name of the third party and the exports relating to EPZs/100 percent EOUs.
2. Every exporter is required to open an account with the authorized bank with the customs (restriction has been relaxed as the majority of banks in India are now IT-enabled) at designated places, so that the respective customs house can directly credit the amount of duty drawback into their accounts. Hence, the exporter should give the account numbers and the details of the bank through which the export proceeds are proposed to be realized.
3. For exports under a claim of duty drawback, the exporters will file a declaration as prescribed by the Central Board of Indirect Taxes and Customs. The declaration by the exporter will also be filed when the export goods are presented at the shed for the examination. The exporters/CHAs are essentially required to give all relevant declarations in the prescribed format otherwise, the service system will not process the duty drawback claims (Figure 21.5).
4. The exporter can file two or more duty drawback claims together, and there is no need to file separate drawback claims for each consignment of exports. The only condition is that the exporter will file the claims only after the actual export of the goods and all such duty drawback claims will automatically be processed through the system on first-come, first-serve basis.
5. In case of any query being raised or any deficiency memo being issued by the appraising officer (drawback) or by the assistant commissioner (drawback), the same should be printed at the EDI Service Centre, and the reply should be filed at the earliest through the service centre.
6. All the claims which have been processed and sanctioned by the duty drawback directorate on a particular day will be enumerated in a system scroll and will be transferred to the concerned bank at the customs house through the service system only. The bank usually credits the drawback amount in favour of exporters in their accounts on the next day. The bank sends a fortnightly statement to the exporters of such credits being made in their accounts.

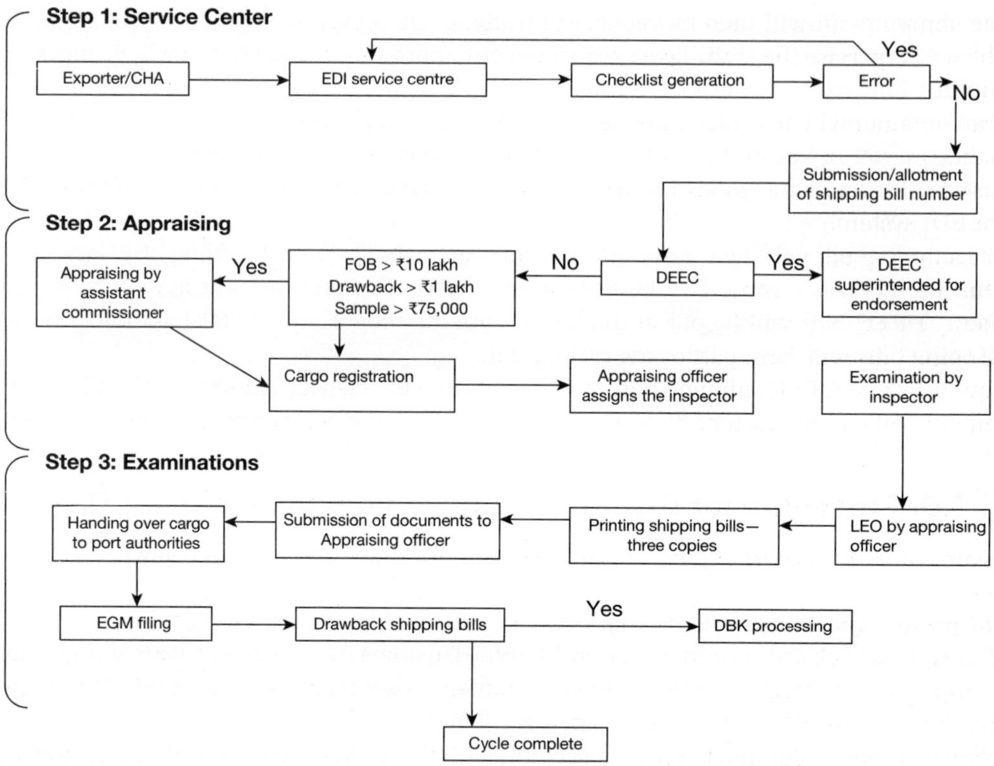

FIGURE 21.5 Processing of shipping bill in export transaction under the EDI system.

Source: Central Board of Indirect Taxes & Customs.

21.6.4 EDI Procedure for Export of Goods under DEEC, EOU, EPCG Scheme:

The procedure for export of goods under DEEC, zero percent EOU and the EPCG Scheme will be similar to the one which is adopted for white/drawback shipping bills with exception in the followings points:

1. All the exporters under the procedure for export of goods under DEEC, EOU and the EPCG Scheme are required to get registered their import–export codes with EDI. The FEMA compliance vis-à-vis the exchange control document is now done in EDI mode; accordingly, ICEGATE has been synced with the RBI-EDPMS system and data vis-à-vis exports is shared electronically.
2. In case of DEEC shipping bills, exporters are required to file the declaration as prescribed by the Central Board of Indirect Taxes and Customs at the time of goods arrival.
3. In case of export of goods under the EPCG Scheme, green shipping bills, that is, shipping bills with drawback claims details should be filed.
4. In the case of 100 percent EOU, the examination report of exportable cargo should be filed in the proforma as prescribed vide P.N.17/2000.

5. The exporters are required to get registered their DEEC licences at the customs houses from where the actual exports are being made and the appraiser in charge of DEEC cell will verify the shipping bills in the licence from the computer as per the procedure prescribed by the Central Board of Indirect Taxes and Customs.
6. In the case of 100 percent EOU Scheme, the exporters can get the exportable cargo examined by GST Custom's officials at the premises of his factory or warehouse even prior to filing the shipping bill.
7. The examination report shall be made available in the form as prescribed for examination report for factory-sealed packages/containers of units working under 100 percent EOU Scheme by the Central Board of Indirect Taxes and Customs and duly signed and stamped by the examining officer and the supervising officer at the factory.
8. All the exporters who are intending to file their shipping bills under the EPCG Scheme are first required to get registered their EPCG licence with the export section.
9. This EPCG registration with the export section is similar to the DEEC registration. It is mandatory for an exporter to mention the registration number while filing the data entries in such shipping bills.
10. All the EPCG shipping bills would be processed on by the appraiser (EPCG cell) on the system screen itself and also by the assistant commissioner/deputy commissioner (exports).
11. Having filed the EGM by the shipping company, such a shipping bill is put to the appraiser queue for logging/printing of ledger.

21.6.5 Filling of IGM in EDI

The procedure for the filing of IGM in EDI is as follows:

1. In order to get an approval for allowing the entry of the ship (vessel) to the port, the official of the shipping company has to contact the preventive officer at the central berth (at the designated docks of port trust) and request them for granting 'entry inwards' to the vessel. The official of the shipping company should make sure before making the application for grant of entry inwards that the person in charge of the vessel has made payment of the lighthouse dues if any.
2. The shipping company has to give a detailed report of all the cargo on board the ship in a report known as 'IGM' which must be filed within 24 hours after arrival of the vessel to the proper officer at the designated port. The IT revolution in LPG&M era has made the importer's job easy as IGM can be electronically filed in the computer at the EDI service centre. The importer can also file IGM in advance, that is, before the arrival of the ship.
3. The preventive officer at the central berth will retrieve the IGM in the system at the terminal at the central berth by entering the IGM number, update the database by entering the arrival date, amount of lighthouse dues paid, challan number, date and grant entry inwards for the ship.
4. In case of advance filed IGMs by the shipping company, the relevant bill of entry will be automatically regularized by the service system after entry inwards is granted as and when the ship arrives at the designated port.
5. In case the shipping company wishes to request for any amendments in the IGMs which are submitted in the EDI system, the same can be done by giving a written application to the assistant commissioner/deputy commissioner who are in charge of the appraising and assessing the duty payable at the concerned customs house. After the acceptance of the amendment by assistant commissioner/deputy commissioner, the document should be presented to the data entry operator and IGM amendment section of the concerned customs house.

21.6.6 Journey of the Import Documents

The journey of the import documents is as follows:

1. For getting his/her import consignment cleared, the importer or his/her representative or CHA have to submit the duly filled in the declaration form for filing a bill of entry to the commissioner of customs at the EDI service centre in order to initiate the process of clearance of imported cargo. The process flow of Import Clearance under EDI is depicted in Figure 21.6.
2. On having received the information for the customs clearance of importable cargo, the service centre will put the details regarding commodities, process of valuation and so on in the service system and generate the checklist for the importer or his/her representative or CHA verification of the same. On verification of the details and having satisfied that they are correct and in sync with the one fed by the importer or his/her CHA in the system, the importer can sign the checklist and give it back to the service centre for final submission. The service centre, on receipt of the same, will generate the number for the bill of entry, and the bill of entry will be put into appraisal and custom assessment queue.
3. Having generated the number for the bill of entry, the system will also allocate trade documents to different appraising and assessing groups based on the declaration as having been submitted by the importer.
4. The appraising officer then can access the available information on his/her system and can start the process of evaluation of duty payable if any on first-come, first-serve basis.
5. The appraisal and assessment of importable cargo are done onscreen through the available information in the bill of entry by the appraising officer. The appraising officer usually does not do any physical verification of documents himself/herself at this stage, but if he/she has doubt,

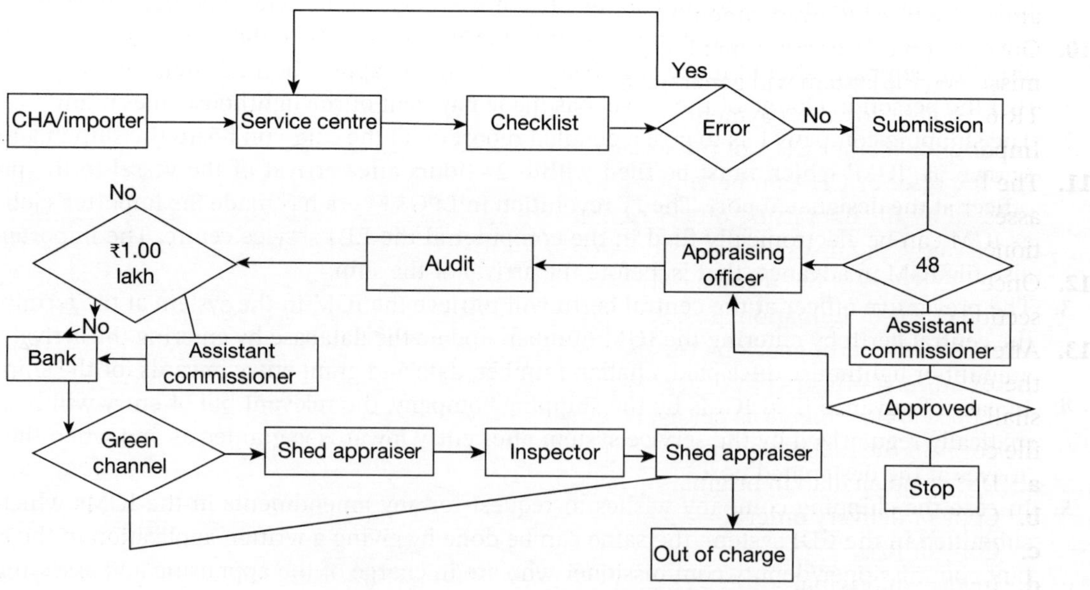

FIGURE 21.6 General process of flow of processing of bill of entry in the EDI form.

Source: Central Board of Indirect Taxes & Customs.

then he/she will give directions to the examining staff in the form of an open order. If the appraising officer has any doubt regarding classification and valuation of cargo and needs to see some vital documents and information in order to extend the notification benefit or accept the classification and valuation in the importer's declaration, he/she can raise the query memo to the importer/CHA.

6. The importer or his/her CHA can find the location and status of his/her bill of entry by looking at the status display counter at the service centre or from the customs house office. If the status of importable cargo indicates the 'query raised', then he/she or his/her CHA needs to rush to the service centre and collect the query memo as issued by the appraising officer in order to know the exact details of reasons and any additional information demanded. The importer or his/her CHA is required to give the detailed reply on the issued raised and any additional information demanded by the appraising officer on notifications and so on at the service centre reply counter. If any documents are to be physically presented to satisfy the appraising officer query or objection, the same may be physically presented before the appraising group.

7. After appraisal and assessment by the appraising officer, the bill or entry will be marked to the internal audit appraising officer who will verify the correctness of the assessment.

8. After an internal audit, the bill of entries which have values more than ₹1 lakh will be marked to assistant commissioner/deputy commissioner (group) for the assessment of payable duty. All the other bills of entry will be marked to the bank for payment of duty.

9. In case the importer or his/her CHA wishes to have some amendment in the bill of entry which they have filed for consignment clearance, the same should first get approval from the assistant commissioner/deputy commissioner (group), and then, it has to be submitted to the service centre. The amendment so entered in the service system will then automatically come on the screen of the appraiser who may accept or reject the amendment. The amendment thereupon is put to the assistant commissioner/deputy commissioner group screen who will finally decide the amendment. After every amendment of a bill of entry, it is put for reassessment.

10. Once the process of assessment of duty payable is over by the appraising officer or assistant commissioner, the system will generate one (customs) copy of the bill of entry and three copies of the TR-6 challan for the payment of customs duty. The documents will be handed over to the Importer or his/her CHA at the service centre for the same purpose.

11. The importer or CHA on behalf of him/her will have to pay the customs duty which has been assessed by the appraising officer or assistant commissioner in the bank, which is usually stationed in the premises of the custom house by a demand draft or cash.

12. Once the payment of customs duty is over, the bill of entry will move to the goods registration section in the examination area.

13. After registration of goods by the examining officer, the bill of entry will move to the screen of the examining officer (physical examination). Along with the bill of entry, the importer/CHA shall present documents as per list below, and the documents should preferably be arranged in a file cover in the following order.

   a. Duty paid challan in original
   b. Copy of delivery order
   c. Copy of B/L
   d. Invoice in original
   e. Packing list in original
   f. Certificate of origin in original

- **g.** Exemption certificate in original, if the notification so requires
- **h.** Copy of the bond or undertaking executed, if any
- **i.** GATT declaration duly signed by the importer
- **j.** Technical literature, catalogue and so on
- **k.** Copy of the request for green channel clearance, if any
- **l.** Clearance of ADC or any other agency/authority, where required
- **m.** Any other documents required

14. The examiner will then examine the cargo as per directions given by the appraising officer/assistant commissioner (assessment) and enters the examination report in the system.

15. The bill of entry will then move to the appraising officer (examination) screen for 'out of charge permission'. On the verification of the examination report given by the examiner, the appraising officer (examination) will grant 'out of charge order' on the screen.

16. Once 'the out of charge' is declared by the appraising officer (examination), the system generates two copies of the bill of entry (importer, bankers), three copies of out-of-charge order (customs, importer and custodians) and one copy of the examination report.

17. The appraising officer (examination) will retain the customs copy of the bill of entry, the customs copy of out-of-charge order, examination order and all original documents, namely invoice, P/L and so on.

18. The importer will then approach custodian for delivery of the goods by using the out-of-charge order (custodian copy) granted by the customs.

21.7 Summary

The collection of revenue has been an important activity for the efficient administration of the state from ancient times, and customs duties are one of the oldest forms of taxation in India. The customs duties are as old as the history of international trade itself. The customs duty is a tax which is collected by the nation state on goods imported into or exported out of the territorial boundaries of the country. Being a sovereign nation, the authority for tax collection in India is vested in Article 265 of the Constitution of India which lays down that 'no tax shall be levied or collected except by authority of law'. In the case of customs duty, such authority is vested with the Central Board of Indirect Taxes and Customs, which draws its power for the levy and collection of customs duties from the Customs Act, 1962. The present system of customs administration came into the Indian subcontinent at the beginning of the 20th century as the process of consolidation of the customs law, regulation and administration began in 1878 after Queen Victoria acceded the throne. The customs administration in India was designed on the pattern of the British system by enacting the Sea Customs Act ensuring legal authority for the levy and collection of customs duty in India. In Independent India, efforts are made to consolidate the customs administration, and accordingly, the Indian Customs Act, 1962, was enacted by repealing previous customs acts and putting the system of sea customs, inland bonded warehouses customs, land customs into one Act only instead of three Acts during the British empire. For the determination of tariff, the Customs Tariff Act was enacted in 1975 by repealing the Tariff Act, 1934. There are two tariff schedules, the Schedule I describes the import duties, and the Schedule II prescribes the export duties. There are only 50 products on which export duties are imposed. Import duties are far comprehensive and are prescribed in tariff lines of 98 + 1 chapters of Custom Tariff Nomenclature. The social welfare surcharge on imported goods has been imposed, and it shall be levied and collected on the basic duty of customs. A famed and historic step in the trade facilitation and transaction cost reduction in Indian foreign trade as the Ministry of Commerce and Finance has decided and envisaged a plan to electronically exchange the trade documents at all ports/airports/ICDs/CFS/land customs stations with agencies involved in the trade such as financing bank, RBI, DGFT, custodians of imports and exports goods and other regulatory agencies.

Review Exercises

Multiple Choice Questions

1. Which of the following legislations was enacted for collection of customs duties in India for the first time?
   - **a.** Sea Customs Act, 1888
   - **b.** Land Customs Act, 1924
   - **c.** Air Customs Act, 1934
   - **d.** Customs Act, 1962
2. Which of the following legislations provides powers to the Central Board of Indirect Taxes and Customs for the collection of customs duties?
   - **a.** Indian Customs Tariff Act, 1975
   - **b.** Customs Act, 1962
   - **c.** Goods and Services Act, 2017
   - **d.** Customs (Bonding of Goods) Rules, 1896
3. Which of the following legislations empowers the Central Board of Indirect Taxes and Customs for defining the rates of customs duties in India?
   - **a.** Indian Customs Tariff Act, 1975
   - **b.** Customs Act, 1962
   - **c.** Goods and Services Act, 2017
   - **d.** Customs (Bonding of Goods) Rules, 1896
4. How many customs stations in India are EDI-enabled, thus clearing goods electronically for exports and imports?
   - **a.** 157
   - **b.** 24
   - **c.** 202
   - **d.** 321
5. Which of the following documents does one have to file to clear import cargo?
   - **a.** Bill of entry
   - **b.** Bill of lading
   - **c.** Bill of exports
   - **d.** Bill of invoice
6. Territorial waters of India are up to how many nautical miles?
   - **a.** 12
   - **b.** 24
   - **c.** 200
   - **d.** 212

7. EDI portal of Indian custom is known as
   a. ICEGATE
   b. MAINGATE
   c. CUSTOMGATE
   d. DUTYGATE
8. Which of the following documents should be filed by an exporter for claiming the duty drawback?
   a. Shipping bill under claim of duty drawback
   b. Shipping bill for dutiable goods
   c. Shipping bill for duty-free goods
   d. Shipping bill for ATA Carnet
9. Which of the following bodies is responsible for the collection of customs duties in India?
   a. Central Board of Indirect Taxes and Customs
   b. Central Board of Direct Taxes
   c. Indian Revenue Authority
   d. Central Revenue Collection Authority
10. E-Sanchit is the latest module added to the EDI platform and is aimed at
    a. Depository of documents
    b. Depository of tax collection
    c. Depository of duty receipts
    d. Record of revenue receipts

Critical Thinking Questions

1. Critically examine the historical perspectives of the evolution of Indian customs law.
2. Write a short note on any two of the following:
   a. Taxable event
   b. Contagious zone of India
   c. ITC (HS)
   d. Social welfare surcharge
3. Critically examine the role of the Customs Act, 1962, and the Customs Tariff Act, 1975.
4. What are various duties imposed in India for the assessment of imported cargo?
5. Explain step by step the online system of export and import cargo clearance under the ICEGATE system?

Further Reading

1. CIA. 2018. *The World Fact Book*. Available at: https://www.cia.gov/library/publications/the-world-factbook/geos/print_in.html (accessed on 25 August 2020).

Index